The 1980s

The 1980s

A Critical and Transitional Decade

Edited by Kimberly R. Moffitt and
Duncan A. Campbell

LEXINGTON BOOKS
A division of
ROWMAN & LITTLEFIELD PUBLISHERS, INC.
Lanham • Boulder • New York • Toronto • Plymouth, UK

Published by Lexington Books
A division of Rowman & Littlefield Publishers, Inc.
A wholly owned subsidiary of The Rowman & Littlefield Publishing Group, Inc.
4501 Forbes Boulevard, Suite 200, Lanham, Maryland 20706
www.lexingtonbooks.com

Estover Road, Plymouth PL6 7PY, United Kingdom

British Library Cataloguing in Publication Information Available

Library of Congress Cataloging-in-Publication Data
The 1980s : a critical and transitional decade / edited by Kimberly R. Moffitt and Duncan
A. Campbell.
    p. cm.
Includes bibliographical references and index.
ISBN 978-0-7391-4313-1 (cloth : alk. paper) — ISBN 978-0-7391-4314-8 (pbk. : alk.
paper)
1. United States—History—1969- 2. United States—Politics and government—1981-
1989. 3. United States—Social conditions—1980- 4. United States—Foreign
relations—1981-1989. 5. Popular culture—United States—History—20th century. 6.
Reagan, Ronald I. Moffitt, Kimberly R. II. Campbell, Duncan A., 1968-
    E876.A145 2011
    973.927—dc22   2010043809

∞™ The paper used in this publication meets the minimum requirements of American
National Standard for Information Sciences—Permanence of Paper for Printed Library
Materials, ANSI/NISO Z39.48-1992.

Printed in the United States of America

Contents

Acknowledgments

This exciting volume is the result of a friendly, yet ongoing debate between colleagues about the significance of the 60s and 80s to American culture. It does not appear that the debate has been settled, but an amenable compromise has brought us to a place in which we both acknowledge and affirm the contributions of the 1980s to much of what we understand about American culture today.

With great appreciation we must thank Lenore Lautigar for her support, encouragement, and diligence as our editor on this project. Her quick responses, extensive emails, and knowledge of the production process cannot be overstated. It made all the difference between a volume and a *great* volume! And a huge thank you to our colleagues in American Studies at the University of Maryland Baltimore County (UMBC), especially Warren Belasco and Pat McDermott, who offered consistent feedback and advice at every level of the writing and production process. Thanks, too, go out to each and every one of our dedicated contributors for their original and insightful chapters on the many aspects of this remarkable decade.

I, Kimberly, would also like to thank my two friends and colleagues, Heather Harris and Suzuko Morikawa, for planting the seed for this book project while driving across town in Chicago one cold November day listening (and singing in unison) to the great hits of the 80s on WILV 100.3 FM. To my co-editor, Duncan, I can only say "well done!" You have been a great colleague who I have had the pleasure to work beside, learn from, and share with! Finally, I extend much gratitude to my family and friends who support my many interests and endure even more the conversations, parties, and proclamations about how great the 80s were as a decade.

I, Duncan, likewise thank my co-editor, Kimberly, with whom it has been a great pleasure and privilege to work, both on this volume and in the department as a whole. It is only right to acknowledge that had it not been for her inspiration and dedication, this project would never have seen the light of day. I am also very grateful to my family and friends for their input and advice, but in particular my wife, Bobbie Jo, for her unfailing support, patience and love.

Revisiting the 1980s has been almost as exhilarating as it was living through them. In some ways more so, as one gains not only the advantages of hindsight lacking at the time, but also the recognition that so many of that decade's most significant events and issues are still being played out in the present.

Introduction

The 1980s as a Decade

Kimberly R. Moffitt and Duncan A. Campbell

Let it be said at once that there are obvious dangers in describing or categorizing decades in the manner that we do identifiable events or movements such as, say, "the Enlightenment" or "Civil Rights." In the first place, such phenomena rarely fit any chronology as convenient as a decade. Second, they have for the most part clearly identifiable and agreed-upon attributes which ten-year periods virtually never do. While there certainly are expressions that describe the mood and activity of particular historical moments, such as "Zeitgeist" or "spirit of the age," none perfectly coincide with the ten-year period the decade.

The problem is compounded by the fact that much is lost by identifying particular events and movements with specific decades. Thus, much of what took place in the United States between 1920 and 1929 does not suit the sobriquet the "Roaring Twenties." Equally many of the movements and events associated with the "Swinging Sixties" predated 1960 and, in several cases, actually occurred after 1969.

Nonetheless, ever since French commentators christened the 1890s the *Fin de siècle*, there has been a tendency to affix to decades or, at least, certain decades, labels which supposedly sum up their inherent characteristics. Some, such as the "Roaring Twenties" (or the "Golden Twenties" as it was called in Europe), mentioned above, are on the face of it, obviously so named. Some, like the 1960s, remain hotly contested political and intellectual territories. Still others remain unfairly labeled, such as the 1930s, named a "low dishonest decade" by W. H. Auden who was decrying the appeasement (and isolationist) policies in the face of fascist aggression. Yet if the 1930s was the decade of Benito Mussolini, Adolf Hitler, Francisco Franco and Neville Chamberlain it was also the decade of Franklin Roosevelt and the New Deal.[1]

One such awkward ten-year period is the so-called "decade of greed" or, the

1980s. Although recent scholarship has demonstrated little or no difficulty in describing decades such as the 1920s, 1960s or 1970s as critical periods of so-cial/political/cultural upheaval development the same has not been generally true of the 1980s. Insofar as the trends and events of the 1980s have been exam-ined, they have not been done so within the context of a decade. Indeed, the only reputation the 1980s as a decade seems to enjoy is that of playing the role of conservative foil to the 1960s and 1970s.[2]

Yet if the period from 1980 until 1989 was marked by the election of Ronald Reagan to the presidency signaling a profound change in U.S. political culture, this is only a part of the story. The 1980s were also marked by one of the three internationally recognized watershed years of the twentieth century, 1989 (the other two are 1918 and 1945). The 1980s proved to be the beginning of the end for both the Union of Soviet Socialist Republics and the Apartheid regime in South Africa. This undeniably marked the birth of a new geopolitical era, one famously dubbed by political scientist Francis Fukuyama as "The End of His-tory." The fatwa issued by the Ayatollah Khomeini against Salman Rushdie, in 1989, however, foreshadowed a different future than Fukuyama had predicted. Similarly, that same year, the Chinese government's brutal crackdown on the demonstrators in Beijing's Tiananmen Square also suggested that history might yet have a few more chapters left to go.[3]

The decade certainly had its share of grim markers, from the Iran-Iraq war, to the French and U.S. marines' barracks bombing in Beirut, to the Soviet shoot-ing down of South Korean flight 007, the explosion of Pan Am Flight 103 over Lockerbie, Scotland, the Montreal massacre, to the invasions of Grenada and Panama, the assassinations of Indira Gandhi and Olaf Palme, as well as the Challenger, Bhopal, Chernobyl and Exxon Valdez disasters to say nothing of the AIDS crisis. At the same time, events such as Live Aid, the "We Are the World" concert, Hands across America, the formation of the Rainbow Coalition, the anti-Apartheid struggle, not to mention the massive anti-nuclear weapons dem-onstrations, all pointed to an unquenched idealism on the part of millions to fight for a better world.[4]

Now that we are more than twenty years since the end of the 1980s, we have the opportunity to examine the decade in perspective, and are in a position to question the glib assertion that the 1980s were a mere conservative foil to the 1960s. Each chapter in this volume explores the events, individuals, and institu-tions that shaped the 1980s within the context of the period as both a critical and transitional decade. We refer to this as a critical and transitional decade because the 1980s, in many respects, marked the end of the era (1945-1989), and the beginning of another (1989 to the present).

Without a doubt, the world in 1979 was very different to that of 1989. The long period of economic growth and accompanying affluence that had taken place not only in the United States, but in much of the West as a whole since the conclusion of the Second World War, had apparently come to an end. The new term used to describe the combination of inflation (the rising cost of goods and services) and stagnant wages was "stagflation." This process had begun with the OPEC oil embargo from 1973-1974, resulting in a stock market crash generally regarded as being the first since the Great Depression to have a persistent economic effect. Prior to that, the Bretton Woods system, established in 1946, of international monetary management collapsed in 1971.Under the Bretton Woods system, world trade had increased by an unprecedented annual rate of 7%. This system was effectively supported by the U.S. dollar as an international currency and the strength of the American economy. The last, however, was no longer as strong as it once was due in part to a combination of factors not least of which was the disastrous war in Vietnam. The peak post-war year for the American economy, relative to the rest of the world, had been 1968 when U.S. industrial production was more than one-third of the global total. Thereafter, the U.S.'s relative economic decline weakened the dollar and undermined Bretton Woods. When President Richard Nixon cut the link between gold and the dollar in 1973, national currencies were essentially cut adrift.[5]

If economic circumstances were problematic, the same was true in the arena of international relations. Although President Jimmy Carter had negotiated the Camp David Accords, ending hostilities between Israel and Egypt in 1979, within two years, the Egyptian president Muhammad Anwar Sadat had been assassinated, and elsewhere, events deteriorated. In 1979, the Shah of Iran—an ally of the United States—was overthrown and his government replaced by Islamic fundamentalists headed by the Ayatollah Khomeini. In a world supposedly divided between two superpowers and their allies, and more crudely, by two ideologies, capitalism and communism, the Iranian revolution's proposition "neither East nor West, but Islam is best," baffled foreign policy experts and political scientists alike. While this political upheaval helped cause the second oil crisis of the decade, more alarming was the Iran hostage crisis, where fifty-three Americans were held by Iranian militants for 444 days, beginning in 1979. A failed rescue attempt by the United States that same year helped secure the militants' position. In that same year, the Soviet Union invaded Afghanistan, raising alarm at the possibility that the USSR was extending its reach towards the oilfields of the Persian Gulf. Not only that but by the end of the 1970s, as a result of a massive naval build-up, the first genuine Soviet air-craft carriers appeared; it was the first time the United States had faced a naval force this powerful since Imperial Japan's in the Second World War. Increasing numbers of individuals believed—not entirely without reason—that the outcome of the Cold War was now moving in the favor of the Soviet Union.[6]

In other areas, too, the promises of the 1960s seemed to be on the wane. For example, the independence of African states starting in the 1950s and continuing into the 1970s had been heralded as a new beginning for the former colonized nations (especially at the Bandung Conference in 1955). Yet the replacement in many cases of elected African heads of state and government by men such as Idi

Amin, Jean-Bédel Bokassa and Mobutu Sese Seko, not to mention accompanying coups, natural disasters, and in too many cases, economic decline, appeared to betray that promise. Further, two African nations were, to all intents and purposes, colonial regimes, namely Rhodesia and the Republic of South Africa—the latter infamous for its policy of apartheid or racial segregation. The situation was not a lot healthier in South America, where democracy was either non-existent or on the retreat, most famously in Chile in 1973. In Asia, meantime, Pol Pot's Khmer Rouge regime embarked upon a policy of genocide from 1976-1979 that would cost 2.5 million Cambodians their lives.[7]

If the problems of the United States at home were of a considerably smaller order, it was nonetheless present and palpable. President Carter, assuming office in 1977, inherited an office still reeling from the aftershock of Nixon's disgrace and resignation in 1974, and served a nation still sharply divided by the political upheavals of the 1960s including, especially, the war in Vietnam. Added to these problems, an apparently deteriorating situation abroad, rising crime rates, and an economic downturn placed the Carter administration in a very difficult situation. Fairly or unfairly, he was perceived as being incapable of solving both the domestic or foreign crises that sprang up (even though many were the result of events that occurred before he took office) nor did his so-called "Crisis of Confidence Speech" (often referred to as the "Malaise" speech, even though the President never used the term) in July 1979 recover for him any lost ground.[8]

The situation did not look a lot better for many of the United States' allies, either. In Britain, for example, the years 1978-1979 were marked by the so-called "Winter of Discontent" in which the country was hit by widespread strikes and other industrial action. In dealing with these problems, the current Labour Government, led by Prime Minister James "Sunny Jim" Callaghan appeared to be as out of its depth as Carter's administration. The British economy, meantime, suffered from a decade of relative economic decline in comparison with its neighbors, which had earned the nation the title "the sick man of Europe"—a title formerly belonging to the Ottoman Empire. Yet the sick man of Europe was simply one of the worst cases, because all the major economies, including that of France and (then) West Germany suffered slower growth, rising inflation, and higher rates of unemployment. This was exclusive of increased political violence including the activities of West Germany's Baader-Meinhoff, Italy's Red Brigades, and the Irish Republican Army. To claim, as some conservative historians have done, that the syndrome of unemployment, economic upheaval, political instability, and aggression abroad gave the Seventies the air of chronic insecurity so characteristic of the Thirties is to exaggerate. What is true is that much of the idealism and optimism, naïve or otherwise, to say nothing of the healthy economic growth that marked the post-war world was, by 1979, looking increasingly like a bad joke.[9]

In hindsight, there was always going to be some sort of reaction to all of the

above, both in North America and in Europe. As it happened, at the level of
national politics, there was a shift to the political right starting in Britain in 1979
with the election of Margaret Thatcher as Prime Minister, followed by Ronald
Reagan as President of the United States in 1980, Helmut Kohl as West German
Chancellor in 1982, Yasuhiro Nakasone as Prime Minister of Japan in 1982 and
finally Brian Mulroney as Prime Minister of Canada in 1984. Thus, by the mid-
1980s, five of the G-7 nations–or what was in effect, the economic leadership of
the developed world–had elected at least nominal right-wing political leaders
(and in some cases, entire governments). Although these individuals and the
parties and the nations they represented differed in decidedly significant ways,
they were nonetheless in general broad agreement on the need for greater trade
liberalization, the dismantling of trade barriers and greater free-market economic
practices. Both goods and capital, therefore, were allowed to freely travel across
national boundaries (accompanied by, as an example of the law of unforeseen
consequences, increased mass migrations of people) while at the same time,
government intervention in the domestic economies would be reduced. They
were also united in their belief that a tougher stance towards the Soviet Union
and its allies needed to be taken. Finally, they were all seen to be inclined
towards a more nationalist, not internationalist, world view, with the partial
exception of Kohl who, despite ultimately overseeing the unification of the two
Germanys, effectively sublimated German nationalism into "European"
nationalism.

How much and how far this effectively international shift to the political
right and the reaction to it altered the course of world history remains the topic
of much debate. What cannot be denied is that a shift took place, both within the
western democracies and elsewhere. Despite a major recession from 1981-1982,
in terms of economics, inflation was brought under control and if unemployment
levels only slowly declined (after having first gone up) they did nonetheless
trend downwards. Likewise, if the levels of economic growth seen in the United
States, West Germany and the United Kingdom did not match that of the 1960s,
they were nonetheless an improvement over the previous decade. More
importantly, however, these gains proved durable. Thus, the Wall Street crash
on "Black Monday," October 19, 1987, when the Dow Jones Industrial Average
lost 22.6% of its total value, despite being almost twice the 12.9% loss in 1929,
did not herald a return of a Great Depression, but merely a recession from which
most of the advanced economies had emerged by the early 1990s.[10]

Internationally, meantime, the Soviet Union's new General Secretary,
Mikhail Gorbachev, worked towards a position of détente and arms limitation
agreements with the United States and its NATO allies. He also pursued policies
of political and economic reform within the Soviet Union, including most
famously *perestroika* (increased economic liberalism) and *Glasnost* (increased
political liberalism). He also made it clear that the Soviet Union would no longer
interfere in the domestic affairs of Warsaw Pact members and withdrew Soviet

forces from Afghanistan. The result in Eastern Europe was the overthrow of the existing communist regimes (almost all of them peacefully, with the notable exception of Romania). Despite the problems such as the (peaceful) separation of the Czech and Slovak republics and violent break-up of Yugoslavia, most eastern European nations established themselves as democracies. East Germany was similarly peacefully absorbed into the Federal Republic of Germany.

In fact the spread of democracy appeared to be an outstanding global phenomenon of the 1980s. In 1982, following their defeat in the Falklands War, Argentina's military Junta, led by General Leopoldo Galtieri, was overthrown and civilian, democratic rule restored in that nation. In 1985, Brazil had made the transition to civilian rule and by 1990 even Chile's Augusto Pinochet had stepped down. A similar process took place in Asia with South Korea, Taiwan, and the Philippines all becoming democracies by the end of the decade. Africa, meantime, was not far behind. Majority rule came to Rhodesia, renamed Zimbabwe in 1980. By the end of the decade, South Africa's last President under the Apartheid system, F. W. De Klerk, reversed the ban on anti-apartheid activity and released activist Nelson Mandela from prison after twenty-seven years. Four years later, Mandela became the first South African president elected by universal suffrage.

At this stage one must sound a note of caution. Certainly the spread of democracy did not begin in the 1980s. Besides the independence of India in 1948, Greece, Spain and Portugal all made the transition from military to civilian rule in the 1970s. Similarly, there were still outstanding failures, places where the move to democracy was halted in its tracks, whether we are speaking of Cuba, Burma, the Congo or most significantly, the People's Republic of China. Many of the new democracies remain fragile and there is no guarantee that, as has recently been the case in Zimbabwe, the gains made cannot be reversed or undermined. Why these trends took place remains the subject of intense political and scholarly debate. That noted, for anyone in 1979 to say that democracy was the way of the future, would have stood out as a very rash soothsayer indeed. By 1989, what was formerly a wild prediction was now virtually common wisdom. The world was a very different place.[11]

Politics and economics, however, are merely part of the picture and due attention must be paid to an important, closely related, third subject: culture. No one can seriously claim that the 1980s were in any meaningful sense culturally barren. Many of the decade's events and concerns were reflected in the arts whether as regards to Oliver Stone's *Wall Street* (1987) or Tom Wolfe's *The Bonfire of the Vanities* (1987). In terms of the novel, the 1980s was a particularly strong decade which witnessed the first publication of numerous acknowledged modern classics such as Margaret Atwood's *The Handmaid's Tale* (1985), Don DeLillo's *White Noise* (1985), Cormac McCarthy's *Blood Meridian* (1986), Toni Morrison's *Beloved* (1987) and Salman Rushdie's *The Satanic Verses* (1988). Morrison's novel won the Pulitzer Prize that year and the author would go on to collect the Nobel Prize for Literature in 1993. Although often derided as the decade of the mindless blockbuster, the age of movies such as the last two installments of the *Star Wars* trilogy (1980 and 1983), *ET: The Extra-terrestrial* (1982), *The Terminator* (1984), *Aliens* (1986), *Top Gun* (1986) and *Die Hard* (1988), the 1980s were marked by other, more significant, films including Ridley Scott's *Blade Runner* (1982), Lawrence Kasdan's *The Big Chill* (1983), David Lean's *A Passage to India* (1984), Randa Haines's *Children of a Lesser God* (1986), David Lynch's *Blue Velvet* (1986), Richard Attenborough's *Gandhi* (1986), Stanley Kubrick's *Full Metal Jacket* (1987), Adrian Lyne's *Fatal Attraction* (1987), Spike Lee's *Do the Right Thing* (1989) and Edward Zwick's *Glory* (1989). There is scarcely a genre or a topic that some film of the 1980s did not at least attempt to táckle and many did so successfully.[12]

The appearance of MTV proved to be one of the most significant influences on popular music since the album/LP and very quickly spread worldwide. To list the musical performers who became global phenomena thanks to MTV would require an introduction all to itself but three of the most notable included Michael Jackson, Prince and Madonna. Jackson, a former child music star whose career dated back to the 1960s, through his 1982 album *Thriller* (which remains the best-selling album of all time) in many respects virtually invented the musical video and made MTV's success possible. Prince, whose career like that of Jackson's predated the 1980s, was another such pioneer whose song, "Darling Nikki" from the album *Purple Rain* (1984), led to the creation of the Parents Music Resource Center. This organization, whose most prominent founder was Tipper Gore, managed to persuade the music industry to label products that might contain material unsuitable for minors—a labeling system that exists to this day. Finally, Madonna, with her second album *Like a Virgin* (1984) shrewdly combined both visual and musical performance to become the most successful female recording artist in history. As with Prince, what notoriety she attracted, helped rather than hindered her success and, by the mid-1980s these three performers, thanks in large part to the new music medium, MTV, were genuine international pop icons.

Another sign of an increasing globalized culture was the international television audience—estimated to be some 750 million people—who watched the heir to the throne of England, Prince Charles marry Lady Diana Spencer on July 29, 1981. The year before, television viewers the world over, from London to Tokyo to Johannesburg, asked "who shot J.R.?" The question was in response to the attempted murder of television character J.R. Ewing, the chief villain on *Dallas*. It was the shot heard around the world.[13]

Probably more influential than *Dallas*, however, was Steven Bochco's *Hill Street Blues* which collected 98 Emmy Award nominations during its six-year run (1981-1987). The show's multifaceted, intertwined story lines which focused on the conflicts between the working and private lives of the characters marked a shift towards greater levels of complexity and nuance in television drama. This seminal program would go on to influence shows as diverse as *St. Elsewhere*, *NYPD Blue* and *E.R.* Bochco would continue to develop the techniques first used in *Hill Street Blues* in other popular dramas of the decade such as *L.A. Law*.

Yet the success of these shows was to be dwarfed by two other television phenomena. September 20, 1984 marked the first airing of *The Cosby Show*, the most popular television program of the 1980s. The show almost single-handedly revived the sitcom genre and paved the way for a new generation of television programs with predominantly African-American casts (and Bill Cosby, by resurrecting the concept of standup comedians making the transition to sitcom, was the trailblazer of such later hits as *Seinfeld* and *Everybody Loves Raymond*). As significant as *The Cosby Show* was, perhaps even more influential was the *Oprah Winfrey Show* which first broadcast locally in 1984 and then nationally in 1986. At the time of writing, the *Oprah Winfrey Show* is the longest-running daytime television talk show and remains a significant popular cultural event—it enjoys a large overseas audience as well—caused no doubt in part by Winfrey's consistent reinvention of her program's format and style.

The transformation of the media continued by the arrival of Ted Turner's Cable News Network in 1980 and by the appearance of the fourth network, the Fox Broadcasting company in 1986. CNN was the first twenty-four hours news network and had a transformative effect on news coverage. Rupert Murdoch's Fox, meantime, introduced a series of new and influential programs, including most famously, *The Simpsons* which began as a series of sketches on the *Tracey Ullman Show* in 1987 and became a self-contained half-hour show in 1989. To date, the show remains the longest-running comedy in television history. The 1980s is also the decade of the first infomercial.

Scandal was not in short supply in the 1980s either, the most famous of which took place in the financial world. So, Ivan Boesky, the arbitrageur who had formerly made the front cover of *Time* magazine, was indicted for insider trading in 1986 and informed against junk bond king Michael Milken, indicted in 1989. Both men served prison terms. In professional sports, meantime, Cincinnati Reds player, Pete Rose, was banned for life from playing (and managing) when it was discovered that he had been gambling on baseball games in 1989. In the 1987 presidential election, the putative Democratic Party frontrunner, Gary Hart, found his political aspirations dashed when compromising photographs emerged of him and a young lady, Donna Rice, on the Senator's appropriately named yacht, *Monkey Business*. Compromising photographs also dented the career of Vanessa Williams who, in 1983, became the first African-American woman to be crowned Miss America. Williams was pressured into resigning the title when nude pictures of her surfaced. Despite this, Williams resolutely recovered from the incident, going on to enjoy a successful career as an actress and Grammy-winning singer.

If resolution to the conflict in Vietnam was not reached in the 1980s, it was at least the beginning of a degree of reconciliation regarding the conflict. Although the last U.S. soldiers had withdrawn by 1973 and the government of South Vietnam had fallen in 1975, it was not until 1980 that Congress authorized three acres for the site of a memorial. It took two years, and a tense-filled debate about the monument's design (chosen by competition) and its prospective creator, before the memorial wall—designed by Maya Lin—inscribed with the names of the fallen was completed (sculptor Frederick Hart's statue "The Three Soldiers" was added in 1984). When it came to the divisive legacy of the Vietnam War in the 1980s, Americans at least agreed on the subject of properly memorializing their dead.

The 1980s were also significant in laying the groundwork for the technological transformation of society. Our "wired" present-day reality was prepared by the arrival of the personal computer in the early 1980s and Microsoft, founded in 1975 by the then-unknown Bill Gates, rose to dominate the home computer operating system with MS-DOS shortly thereafter. The World Wide Web was invented in 1989. Indeed, the 1980s were, technologically speaking, a goldmine. It was the decade of the first practical cell phones, private satellite dishes, camcorders, compact discs, the first artificial heart transplant, and the space shuttle.

Aerobics, granola bars, Lean Cuisine, all began in the 1980s, as did Prozac and post-it notes. It was the decade of the "Yuppies" (as in young, urban professionals) as well as the first Sundance Film Festival. At the same time, this supposedly conservative decade gave us the first female Supreme Court Justice, Sandra Day O'Connor, the first woman vice-presidential running mate for either major party, Geraldine Ferraro as well as the first Martin Luther King Jr., Day. In short, the legacy of the cultural, political, social, and technological transformation of the United States and the world during this critical and transitional decade remains with us to this day.

This volume cannot be all-inclusive and is also not intended to be a chronicle of the 1980s with respect to the United States or the rest of the world. Further, given space constraints, this work is also unapologetically American-centered in its approach. That noted, however, this work contains five essays on the 1980s which examine events outside the boundaries of the United States. The purpose of our text is not to simply highlight the significant phenomena of the period, but rather demonstrate how so many apparently disparate events, including those outside of the United States, were, in fact, closely inter-related and products of their age. This holistic analysis of the decade focuses on major turning points, developments in literature, art, entertainment, politics, and social experimentation. The work is unapologetically interdisciplinary in nature in an effort to capture the decade from perspectives beyond only one. What it does is explore the 1980s as a phenomenon exhibiting its significance in the American landscape.

Understanding the 1980s: The Chapters of the Volume

Certainly the fortieth president of the United States looms large over any discussion of the 1980s. Personifying in many key respects the political shift to the right, not just in America but in the west as a whole and the consequences both domestically and internationally, Reagan remains a controversial and, at times, ambiguous, figure. Jeffery Cook explores the man himself in "Ronald W. Reagan: Redefining the Presidency." One aspect of Reagan's political legacy is explored in Ivan Greenberg's "Reagan Revives FBI Spying" and the administration's response to political dissent. Scott Merriman in "The 'Real' Right Turn: The Reagan Supreme Court," looks at the President's appointments to the Supreme Court and their mixed legacy. Robert Weiss, meantime, examines the curious conflux/confluence between private enterprise and the punitive criminal justice policies that marked the 1980s in his "Privatizing the Leviathan State: A 'Reaganomic' Legacy." Reaganomics and what it meant for organized labor is the central theme of Jana Lipman's "'Airlines? Lousy Unions.' Airline Workers in the Era of Deregulation and Hostile Takeover."

The politics of the 1980s were said to herald a turn to the right, but the American political system has two main parties and what the Democratic Party got up to in the face of a popular Republican president is the theme of Tom Schaller's "Triumph of The 'Gipper' and the Democratic Party Malaise in the 1980s." Among the President's and the Republicans' strongest supporters were the Christian right and they are the focus of Andrew Murphy's "The Christian Right's Traditionalist Jeremiad: Piety and Politics in the Age of Reagan." This, in turn, was tied directly into the many points of contention of the culture wars that marked the 1980s political debate, as Jessie Swigger demonstrates in "New Right, New History, Common Ground: Populism and the Past." The curious combination of marketing and militarism that played out its part in the Cold War, meantime, is the subject of Demian Ryder's "An Army of One in 1:18 Scale: The Profit and Patriotism in G.I. Joe," while Michael Dwyer describes the vagaries of cultural nostalgia and popular culture in "'Fixing' the Fifties: Alex P. Keaton and Marty McFly."

The political sphere, however, was only one part of the 1980s and social issues too, took center stage. One of the most significant events of the 1980s was the AIDS crisis. Its effect on Broadway Theater is the subject of Virginia Anderson's "How Broadway Has Cared: The AIDS Epidemic and the Great White Way." Art and its purpose is a perennial topic, but the debate took a new twist in the 1980s especially with the work of Robert Mapplethorpe, one of the issues examined by Philip Glahn in his "Counterpublic Art and Social Practice." Although the 1980s is traditionally assumed to be the decade of a reaction against feminism, as famously postulated by Susan Faludi in her *Backlash: The Undeclared War Against American Women* (1991), Caryn Neumann paints a more complex and nuanced picture in her study of the increased recognition of acquaintance sexual assault in her "Date Rape and Sexual Politics." The question of sexual assault was also at the heart of the child molestation cases of the decade, the ultimate results of which would be the increased supervision of children to the point of virtual incarceration in the home. How this all came about is discussed in N'Jai-An Patters' "A Culture in Panic: Day Care Abuse Scandals and the Vulnerability of Children." Heather Harris' "What's Class Got to Do with It?: Facets of Tracy Chapman through Song," meanwhile examines the artist as social critic and icon.[14]

The 1980s were an outstanding decade for globalization as the policies of governments and expansion of political and economic liberalization increasingly meant that the trends of the decade were increasingly replicated across national boundaries. Suzuko Morikawa explores the impact MTV had upon Japan in her "Reading MTV: Proliferation of United States Culture in the Age of Globalization." The international campaign against Apartheid is the subject of Paul Pressley's "The United States and Apartheid." Events in China, meantime, demonstrated that contrary to what is so often claimed, economic liberalization does not necessarily lead to political liberalization—the central theme of Jim Schnell's "The Opening of China and the Evolution of China-U.S. Cross-Cultural Understanding." Despite the gradual spread of democracy, the 1980s were, in many respects, a grim decade for much of Latin America, which found domestic differences and difficulties exacerbated by Superpower interference, particularly on the part of the United States. This is the topic of Kristin Sorensen's "U.S. Foreign Policy in Latin America on Film: The Case of *Salvador*." The paradigm-shifting international event of the 1980s, however, was the fall of the Berlin Wall and this is the central topic of Kirk Tyvela's "Cold War Crucible: The Berlin Wall and American Exceptionalism."

The decade was also a breakthrough period for African-American athletes, musicians and actors on the international stage, whether we are speaking of musical performer Michael Jackson or basketball superstar Michael Jordan or standup comedian turned actor Eddie Murphy, all of whom are the subject of Reynaldo Anderson, et al.'s "Fear of a Black Planet: Michael Jackson, Eddie Murphy, Michael Jordan and The Globalization of Black Masculinity." As noted above, the 1980s were not an artistically barren decade and how American authors interpreted the era is the subject of Alan Bilton's "Matter and Mammon: Fiction in the Age of Reagan." MTV often stood (and stands) accused of being nothing more than extended advertisements, the destruction of popular music through its crass consumerist format. By emphasizing a deadening conformity in terms of appearance and imagery, MTV robs popular music of its potentially challenging nature, whether socially or politically. One challenge to MTV came in the form of college radio, the subject of David Uskovich's "Alternative for Alternative's Sake: Progressive College Radio's Programming Struggles." Another musical breakthrough from outside the mainstream which took place in the 1980s was Hip Hop as James Braxton Peterson discusses in "'Life in

Marvelous Times': Commemorative Narratives of the Golden Era in Hip Hop Culture," Music and the movies were two of the most important mediums of popular culture in the 1980s and Steve McVeigh examines the mythology promoted by the latter in his "'Do We Get to Win this Time?' Movies, Mythology, and Political Culture in Reagan Country."

As noted above this work cannot be the final word on the 1980s as a critical and transitional decade. It essentially can only serve as a starting point in the long overdue re-evaluation of the decade and how the events and personalities thereof helped determine the political and social contours of the world we now inhabit. Yet, as George Elliot observed in *Middlemarch*, every limit is a beginning as well as an ending. The editors of this volume can only hope that this work will achieve its aspiration to be the former.

Notes

1. The term *fin de siècle* is not precisely analogous to a decade since the term was meant to mark the end of the nineteenth century. Nor was this the first time a decade was given a name—in nineteenth-century Britain the 1840s were referred to as the "Hungry Forties." Yet the *fin de siècle* was viewed as a global phenomenon and thus seems more applicable. The line "a low dishonest decade" is derived from Auden's poem "September 1, 1939." This was the date Great Britain declared war on Nazi Germany.

2. There are not a great many studies emphasizing the 1980s as a critical and transitional decade. Insofar as the events, arts, and popular culture of the 1980s have been examined, they have been done so under other rubrics, such as foreign relations, fiction, biographies, and the impact of gender, music, or economics. Three useful texts are: G.T. Sewell, ed., *The Eighties: A reader* (New York: Perseus Books, 1997); J.D. Torr, ed., *The 1980s (America's decade)* (Farmington Hills, MI: Greenhaven Press, 2000); and G. Thompson, *American culture in the 1980s* (Edinburgh, UK: Edinburgh University Press, 2007).

3. In 2009, *Time* Magazine published one of its special commemorative editions "1989: The Year That Defined Today's World," featuring a story on each of these events and many more. Of especial interest is "A Good Year: The Underrated Memory of a Profound Time" by Martin Ivens who puts forward a persuasive argument that the late 1980s was of far more global significance than the late 1960s. Francis Fukuyama's end of history thesis positing that the conclusion of the Cold War proved that there was no other viable political competitor to liberal, capitalist, free-market democracy was first published as "The End of History?" in *The National Interest*, 16 Summer 1989, pp. 3-18. Fukuyama expanded upon this article in *The End of History and the Last Man* (London: Hamish Hamilton, 1992). Often viewed as an American declaration of triumph following the collapse of the Soviet Union (although Fukuyama denies this) the work has had its share of critics. Perhaps the most famous of these is Samuel Huntington's *The Clash of Civilizations and the Remaking of World Order* (New York: Simon and Schuster, 1996) which was written at least partially in response to Fukuyama's work.

4. Works listed in this introduction's endnotes are restricted to topics not specifically

discussed by the chapters in this collection. Thus, no mention of works on Apartheid is listed here, because Paul Pressley directly addresses that subject in his chapter. The Falklands war is intelligently discussed in Max Hastings and Simon Jenkins, *The Battle for the Falklands* (New York: Norton, 1984). On the Beirut bombing see, Rick Hampson, "25 Years Later, Bombing in Beirut Still Resonates," *USA Today*, October 16. 2008, p.1. On KAL 007, see Marilyn Young and Michael Launer, *Flights of Fancy, Flight of Doom: KAL 007 and Soviet-American Rhetoric* (Lanham, MD: University Press of America, 1988). The issue of Pam Am 103 is still ongoing, most recently with the government of the United Kingdom's decision to release one of the convicted bombers. The Montreal Massacre, occurred when a gunman, Marc Lépine, murdered twenty-eight people, all but four of whom were women, before shooting himself, at the École Polytechnique in Montreal, Canada in 1989. The person or persons responsible for Swedish Prime Minister Olof Palme's 1986 assassination remain unknown. Indira Gandhi was murdered by Sikh separatists in 1984. The environmental disasters and the U.S. response to them are considered by Matthew Kahn, 'Environmental Disasters as Risk Regulation Catalysts? The Role of Bhopal, Chernobyl, Exxon Valdez, Love Canal, and Three Mile Island in Shaping U.S. Environmental Law," *Journal of Risk and Uncertainty*, 35 (2007) pp. 17-43.

5. See, A. Van Dormael, *Bretton Woods: Birth of a Monetary System* (London: Macmillan, 1978) and Harold James, *International Monetary Cooperation Since Bretton Woods* (New York: Oxford University Press, 1996). See, also, Alan S. Blinder, *Economic Policy and the Great Stagflation* (New York: Academic Press, 1979); Paul Johnson and William Thompson, eds., *Rhythms in Politics and Economics* (New York: Praeger, 1985) and David Yergin, *The Prize: The Epic Quest for Oil, Money and Power* (New York: Simon and Schuster, 1993).

6. There is no shortage of books on the Carter presidency, but an interesting one is John Dumbrell, *The Carter Presidency: A Re-Evaluation*, (Manchester, UK: Manchester University Press, 1995). See, also, Fink, Gary M. and Hugh Davis Graham, eds., *The Carter Presidency: Policy Choices in the Post-New Deal Era*, (Lawrence: University Press of Kansas, 1998) and David Harris, *The Crisis: the President, the Prophet, and the Shah—1979 and the Coming of Militant Islam*, (London: Little, Brown, 2004). A contemporary discussion of Soviet military capabilities is Robert Legvold, "The Nature of Soviet Power," *Foreign Affairs*, 56, 1977, pp. 49-71.

7. A good starting point on Africa is Basil Davidson's *Modern Africa: A Social and Political History*, 3rd ed. (London: Longman, 1994). A contemporary view of Bandung is George McTurnan Kahin, *The Asian-African Conference, Bandung, Indonesia* (New York: Ithaca, Cornell University Press, 1956). A modern recounting is See Seng Tan and Amitav Acharya, *Bandung Revisited: The Legacy of the 1955 Asian-African Conference for International Order* (Singapore: National University of Singapore Press, 2008). Chile and Cambodia are covered in Julio Faundez, *Marxism and Democracy in Chile: From 1932 to the fall of Allende* (New Haven: Yale University Press, 1988) and Ben Kiernan, *The Pol Pot Regime: Race, Power, and Genocide in Cambodia under the Khmer Rouge, 1975–79* (New Haven: Yale University Press, 1996).

8. An intriguing re-examination of Carter's speech is Kevin Mattson, *"What the Heck are You up to, Mr. President?:" Jimmy Carter, America's "malaise," and the Speech that Should have Changed the Country* (New York: Bloomsbury, 2009).

9. For a reconsideration of Britain in the 1970s, see, Andy Beckett, *When the Lights Went Out: Britain in the Seventies* (London: Faber and Faber, 2009). On the subject of

Europe during this era, readers can do worse than consult Tony Judt's *Post-War: A History of Europe Since 1945* (New York: Penguin, 2005), especially xiv-xvii. The comparison of the 1970s to the 1930s is made by Paul Johnson in his *Modern Times: A History of the World From the 1920s to the Year 2000* (London: Phoenix, 1999), 685.

10. See, Jeremy Black, *Britain since the Seventies: Politics and Society in the Consumer Age* (London: Reaktion Books, 2004) and *Europe Since the Seventies* (London: Reaktion, 2009), by the same author. See, also, Judt, *Post-War*, xviii-xxii. There is a wealth of material on Britain's "Iron lady," but a reasonably balanced study is John Campbell, *Margaret Thatcher* (London; Jonathan Cape, 2000). See, also, Subroto Roy and John Clarke, eds., *Margaret Thatcher's Revolution: How it Happened and What it Meant* (London: Continuum, 2006). Thatcher speaks for herself in Margaret Thatcher, *The Downing Street Years* (London: Harper Collins,.1995). Another broad useful study is John O'Sullivan, *The President, the Pope and the Prime Minister: Three Who Changed the World* (Washington, D.C.: Regnery, 2006).

11. An interesting recent re-evaluation of the end of the Soviet Union and the "end of history" thesis is Azar Gat, *Why Democracy Won in the 20th Century and How it is Still Imperiled* (Lanham, MD: Rowman and Littlefield, 2009).

12. For an introduction to movies of the 1980s, see William Palmer, *Films of the Eighties: A Social History* (Carbondale: Southern Illinois University Press, 1993).

13. For all things relating to *Dallas* see, Barbara Curran, *Dallas: The Complete Story of the World's Favorite Prime-Time Soap* (Nashville: Cumberland House, 2005).

14. Susan Faludi, *Backlash: The Undeclared War Against American Women* (New York: Crown, 1991).

PART 1:

"Freedom and Security Go Together": Reagan's Influence During the 80s

Chapter 1

Ronald W. Reagan: Redefining the Presidency

Jeffery B. Cook

By the end of the 1970s the United States appeared to be in a serious decline. Socially, economically, and internationally America appeared to be rudderless and in full retreat. A clear manifestation of the country's weakened state appeared when Iranian militants stormed the United States Embassy in Tehran, Iran where they captured and held fifty-two Americans hostage for 444 days.[1] The Soviet Union took advantage of the distraction in Tehran, invading Afghanistan, surrounding the capital city of Kabul, and assassinating the country's prime minister. Pundits and talking heads alike argued that the office of the presidency was too complicated for one man to handle, and issued a clarion call for reform and the establishment of a stronger and more relevant presidency.[2] However, at this point of weakness, the country stood at a transitional phase, preparing for one of its greatest rebounds in history. The transition started within the ranks of the Republican Party, culminating in the nomination of Ronald W. Reagan for president in 1980. Reagan's victory in the general election proved to be a defining moment in American presidential history when an ordinary man transformed the political landscape in a manner that could only be rivaled by the presidency of Franklin Roosevelt.[3] Reagan's decisions to challenge the Soviet Union and to jump-start the American economy through across-the-board tax cuts were heavily criticized by the intelligentsia and Congressional Democrats, but they resurrected the economy, brought an end to the Cold War, and revitalized the presidency.

The defeat of Republican Senator Barry Goldwater by President Lyndon B. Johnson in the 1964 presidential election had left the Republican Party shaken and in complete disarray. The entire election process revealed deep divisions within the Republican Party between the established East-Coast country-club wing of the party as represented by Nelson Rockefeller, and the conservative wing that had been responsible for Goldwater's nomination. Prior to the election the intraparty conflict had spilled over into a very public feud, with Rockefeller referring to conservatives as the "radical right" and the "lunatic fringe." Rockefeller managed to garner considerable support from urban America by asserting that Goldwater's failure to denounce the "radical right" was a disservice to the conservative movement.[4] The conflict within the Republican ranks received extensive news coverage, and the charges of extremism were amplified by the media and the Johnson administration. Johnson, of course won a lopsided victory, securing a 16 million vote advantage in the popular vote, and Democrats secured thirty-eight seats in the House and two in the Senate. On paper it was a complete disaster for the Republican Party. But it turned out to be the high-water mark for Lyndon B. Johnson and the liberal movement.

While radicals and revolutionaries captured the national spotlight in the 1960s, conservatives worked behind the scenes spreading and sharing some of the guiding ideas of the conservative movement. Over the course of the next sixteen years, American conservatives managed to build an effective grassroots political movement. They worked diligently to challenge liberals and won elections on the state and local levels. Success on the state and local levels, however, was not mirrored by any significant success in the national arena. Republican presidential candidates avoided many of the hot-button issues and failed to embrace and articulate many of the movement's defining principles, notably individual freedom and a limited federal government. Conservatives were thus forced to swallow hard and vote for moderates Richard Nixon (1968, 1972) and Gerald Ford (1976), who tried to steer a murky middle course. In this context, Ronald Wilson Reagan emerged onto the national scene to champion conservative politics and lead a beleaguered country from the malaise of mismanagement.[5]

Ronald Wilson Reagan was a lifelong Democrat who had voted for Franklin Roosevelt four times. Reagan admired Roosevelt's leadership style and ability to connect with the American people, and he embraced the New Deal's central aim, preserving the American middle class. This conservative purpose enabled Reagan to overlook Roosevelt's move away from the Jeffersonian principle of limited government. But he came to realize that post–New Deal liberalism was not as limited, believing as it did that an all-knowing centralized government could eradicate all of the country's social evils through the passage of some new government program. Reagan drew a clear distinction between the social insurance mentality of the New Deal and the social engineering approach that formed the cornerstone of Great Society liberalism.[6] For Reagan, the Great Society came to symbolize all that had gone wrong with America, notably the dramatic move away from its constitutional moorings and the Jeffersonian principle of limited government toward the establishment of the administrative state. The disillusioned Reagan believed that the Democratic Party had a vested interest in fostering the continued expansion of the administrative state, and he thought the party was naïve about the dangers of Communism. As a result, he formally joined the GOP in 1962.[7]

Reagan embraced a number of very important core principles of conservatism. He rejected socialism and communism, dismissing the Marxist maxim "From each according to his ability; to each according to his need." Reagan rejected not only the basic premise of communism, but also the heavy-handed approach of Stalin and others who imposed the communist state upon its people. Reagan favored individualism, private ownership of property, and free enterprise, leaning toward the variety articulated by Milton Friedman and the Chicago School of economics. He opposed government intervention in enterprise through regulations and trying to steer the economy along an acceptable path in order to determine both winners and losers. Most importantly, Reagan had considerable respect for those organizations and institutions that had the most influence on daily life, notably the family, the church, and the public schools, and for the values and traditions that had served the people of the country. Reagan did not think of himself as a radical conservative, but he came to believe that the federal government was robbing the American people of their hard-earned money and their individual freedom. Consistent with the teachings of Jefferson, he believed that it was time to return America to those values and traditions that made her the most prosperous country in the world.

In October 1964, Ronald Reagan was selected to give a prerecorded speech to a nationally televised audience trumpeting the candidacy of the Republican nominee Senator Barry Goldwater.[8] The speech, later known as "A Time for Choosing," echoed many of the themes and ideas Reagan had perfected while serving as a spokesman for General Electric. It called for a reduction in federal spending, eliminating some of the more useless government programs, and returning power to the local level. Reagan's polish, calm demeanor, and stage presence worked to his advantage. But near the end of the address, he grew animated when he told the studio audience and the millions of Americans watching on national television, "You and I have a rendezvous with destiny. We can preserve for our children this, the last best hope of a man on earth or we will sentence them to take the first step into a thousand years of darkness."[9] Reagan's address not only electrified the conservative base, as shown by the ensuing phone calls to the GOP and the increase in Republican campaign contributions, but represented the opening volley of the American conservative revolution. Goldwater was defeated in the election, but Reagan had drawn the conservative spirit to the party. This New Deal Republican who was heavily influenced by the teachings of Jefferson pointed the way out of the political abyss, though the journey that followed would be fraught with setbacks.[10]

The "Time for Choosing" speech provided Reagan with national exposure and impressed several business leaders in California, who saw Reagan as the man who could effectively challenge two-term governor Pat Brown in the 1966 gubernatorial race. Brown was a man of the political left, a firm believer in the government's ability to solve every problem confronting humanity. He had trounced Richard Nixon for the governorship in 1962.[11] Intent on ending Brown's tenure as governor, forty-one wealthy Californian businessmen formed the "Friends of Ronald Reagan" to sponsor Reagan's candidacy. These men represented thousands of self-made business leaders who felt constrained by post–New Deal liberalism, restricted and frustrated by government regulations, and punished by confiscatory tax policies. Moreover, the rhetoric of the political left was anti-business, making many ambitious businessmen feel like targets rather than contributors to their country's economic growth. As a collective body, the small-business community represented a powerful voting bloc, one that could effectively steer the course of the campaign. When Reagan announced his intention to run for governor in January 1966, Pat Brown salivated over the possibility of bringing down another marquee Republican.

From the start of the campaign, Reagan was marginalized by the political opposition, denounced as a washed-up B-movie actor or "the crown prince of the far right."[12] Many of his critics contended that Reagan lacked the sophistication and necessary experience to manage the largest economy in the country. Some of the partisan attacks were quite shrill, pushing the standard of decency to new lows. In one Democratic campaign advertisement, for example, Governor Brown told a black student: "I am running against an actor. And you know it was an actor that shot Lincoln, don't you."[13] But Reagan ignored the personal attacks, using his charm to convince voters that he was a competent "citizen-politician" who just happened to be a former actor. Brown set himself up for a disappointment by grossly underestimating his challenger: Reagan won by a stunning one million votes.[14]

As the elected governor of California—the most populous state in the Union, with the world's seventh largest economy, Reagan established himself as a cautious, able administrator, and a man who could work with the Democratic-controlled legislature.[15] He defended America's involvement in Vietnam, battled the radical student movement, and pressed for a tough welfare reform bill that reduced the case load by 300,000 during a three-year period, imposed a hiring freeze, and cut agency budgets. He demonstrated his self-confidence by vetoing 900 pieces of legislation.[16]

He also continued to speak out on national issues. At speeches on college campuses, he was ridiculed and treated badly on a routine basis. In 1967 he participated in a one-on-one debate with Robert F. Kennedy on a CBS television special "Town Meeting of the World." CBS linked the governor in Sacramento and Kennedy in New York with eighteen college students in London.Most of the forum focused on Vietnam, and as 15 million American viewers watched on their television sets, the self-absorbed students basked in the opportunity to attack two men who represented a country they found reprehensible.[17] Kennedy was clearly sympathetic to their views, and he failed to conceal this sentiment. Governor Reagan, on the other hand, stood his ground, delivering crisp, cogent answers; it was clear he had adequately prepared for the forum. In the end, the debate demonstrated that Reagan was no political lightweight, and very well informed on Vietnam. A reporter for *Newsweek* opined that "it was the political rookie" Reagan who had left "the old campaigner blinking when the session ended."[18] The American public agreed with this assessment, and thousands of cards and letters poured into the governor's office applauding his defense of the United States. Kennedy directed his aides to never put him on the same stage with "that son of a bitch again." Frustrated at being out-performed by a political neophyte on national television, Kennedy screamed: "Who the fuck got me into this?"[19]

Predictably, Reagan's success on the national stage was mirrored by success at the ballot box. The people of California voted in 1970 by a majority to return Reagan to Sacramento for a second term as governor. Throughout the decade, Reagan reaffirmed his commitment to limited government and free enterprise, and, most importantly, his steadfast opposition to Communism. Reagan's vocal denunciations of the Soviet Union came at a time when both Democrats and many Republicans had chosen to refrain from making any sort of public criticisms. Reagan, on the other hand, adamantly rejected containment because this flawed policy as devised by George Kennan merely confined the Soviet Union to its postwar borders and left the people of Eastern Europe enslaved to the Kremlin. Reagan had no interest in simply containing the Soviet Union—he wanted to defeat the Red Menace and free the people who were held hostage by the tragedy of the Cold War. Reagan's hopes and intentions were quite clear to those in the Kremlin. Russian commentator Yhuri Zhukov, writing in *Pravda,* observed: "The resurrected political dinosaur proposes a...policy of rolling back communism." Most astonishingly, Zhukov noted that, Reagan "promises the restoration of the old system" in the countries of Eastern Europe. As the political scientist and Reagan biographer Paul Kengor points out: "Clearly the Kremlin understood the stakes."[20]

Since total victory over the Soviet Union was Reagan's stated goal, détente, or the easing of tensions, was reprehensible to him. Détente had started under Nixon and continued through the Ford and Carter years; it was promoted through treaties and trade. However, the easing of tensions between the two superpowers meant nothing to the millions of people living under Soviet rule. Détente prolonged and sustained the Soviet Union, perpetuating the totalitarian existence of its people and Soviet control, thereby contributing to the deaths of those people who dared to resist the iron grip of the Kremlin. Détente also established a moral equivalency between the United States and the Soviet Union, and asserted that both countries had mutual self-interests. To Reagan, the people in Eastern Europe who had been overrun by the Red Armies during the Second World War remained in something of a time warp, still occupied and denied the basic human freedoms, their governments dependent on Moscow.[21]

In 1976, for the second time in his political career, Reagan sought the Republican nomination for the presidency. Eight years earlier he had made a half-hearted attempt to take the nomination away from Richard Nixon, and had almost derailed Nixon's bid.[22] In 1976, incumbent President Gerald Ford was damaged politically by his pardoning of Richard Nixon following the Watergate scandal, and extremely vulnerable to a challenge from the conservative wing of the Republican Party.[23] Reagan also benefitted from changes in political rules that increased the number of primaries; in addition, the delegates were no longer selected by party bosses in smoke-filled hotel rooms, but directly by the voters in open primaries. Reagan in the flesh had charisma that the stumbling Ford could not even hope to muster and an edge in his ability to appeal to the average Republican voter. Reagan criticized Ford for allowing America's military to become second rate, and for embracing a policy of surrender on American possessions, notably the Panama Canal Zone. Reagan also attacked Ford for appointing liberals like Nelson Rockefeller to his administration, and he ridiculed Ford's management of the economy, calling for a balanced budget and accusing Ford of recklessly engaging in wasteful deficit spending.[24] Reagan very narrowly lost the nomination by 117 delegates, causing many of his closest advisors and contemporary observers to conclude that he had performed his last curtain call.[25] However, Reagan had a better sense of his own destiny: "Whether it is this job or whether it is early training from long ago just now coming clear. I find myself believing very deeply that God has a plan for each of us. Some with little faith and less testing seem to miss it in their mission, or perhaps we fail to see the imprint on the lives of others. But bearing what we cannot change, going on with what God has given us, confident there is a destiny, somehow seems to bring a reward we couldn't exchange for any others. It takes a lot of fire and heat to make a piece of steel."[26]

Ford limped away from the bruising Republican primary to take on the Democratic newcomer and former Georgia governor James (Jimmy) Earl Carter in the general election. Carter the outsider and a virtual unknown was carefully packaged and sold to the American public. He had a twenty-point lead in the polls over President Ford when the incumbent began his fight to win the Republican nomination.[27] Carter was able to build a campaign infrastructure from scratch and to determine what the American public wanted in a presidential candidate.[28] In spite of his charm and smile, Carter played hardball, trying to draw connections between Nixon's character and Ford, but his mud-slinging did not work as well as hoped. By October 1976, the Carter camp was hemorrhaging support, losing about half a point in the public opinion polls per day. By the middle of the month, Ford had closed the gap in the South, making the race a virtual dead heat. A writer for the *National Review* asserted that the election was now between a crippled hare and a stumbling tortoise. It wasn't until the presidential debates, when Ford gaffed by claiming that Eastern Europe was not dominated by the Soviet Union, that the bleeding stopped. On Election Day,

Carter managed to defeat Ford by fewer than 2 million popular votes, and both houses of Congress went Democratic as well.[29]

Jimmy Carter's election was largely the result of the public's hangover from the long drawn-out conflict in Vietnam, the Watergate affair, and President Ford's pardoning of Nixon for his part in the scandal. Americans looked upon inside-the-Beltway, professional politicians with some disdain. Carter had effectively campaigned as an outsider who would work on behalf of the people rather than the political establishment. The fact that Carter was a southerner, and a self-proclaimed "born again Christian," helped craft an image of a conservative, moral man untarnished by the dark underside of American politics. After the election, Carter's honeymoon period lasted about six months, with Carter riding high in the public opinion polls. He came across as likable and down-to-earth. But could he govern the United States?, many observers asked. During the course of the first year, Carter floundered and appeared inept.Journalist Victor Lasky wrote bluntly: "Rarely in the history of the Republic has there been an occupant of the Oval Office who demonstrated so quickly an inability to conduct even the simplest affairs of the state. He is perceived both at home and abroad as a politician of limited and uncertain talents, a well-meaning man whose power derives far more from the office lucked into than the qualities of personal leadership he has been able to exert."[30] Lasky's assessment comports with British Prime Minister Margaret Thatcher's. Carter's first meeting with Thatcher was a disaster. Thatcher lectured Carter on foreign policy and found him "ill-suited for the presidency, agonizing over big decisions and too concerned with detail. In leading a great nation decency and assiduousness are not enough."[31] Carter functioned best in campaign mode, relying on an active bureaucracy to conduct the day-to-day affairs of governance. However, the illusion of leadership evaporated like dew after the noon-day sun whenever a crisis surfaced.[32]

Carter presided over the worst economic downturn since the Great Depression. He failed to develop a clear blueprint for combating inflation and boosting an economy that stopped growing in 1978. In addition, instability in the Middle East with the overthrow of the Shah of Iran interrupted the world's oil supply, driving the cost at the pumps to record highs. The gasoline lines were a complete surprise, and Carter reacted by trying to develop a national energy plan to break American dependence on Middle Eastern oil. But in spite of a Democratic majority in both houses, Carter failed to work well with the professional politicians who ran the halls of Congress, and his energy policy fell flat. The failure was sufficient evidence to an anxious public that the president was clearly over his head. To make matters worse, when the Soviet Union deployed its SS-20 intermediate-range missiles without warning NATO, and expanded its influence into Afghanistan, Central America, and the Middle East, Carter appeared weak and ineffectual. With the president's standing in the public opinion polls sinking, militants in Iran stormed the American embassy in November 1979, taking fifty-two Americans hostage. Six weeks later, the Soviet Union invoked the

Brezhnev Doctrine and invaded Afghanistan.[33] Carter missed all of the early warning signs, and in an interview on New Year's Eve he stated: "This action of the Soviets has made a more dramatic change in my own opinion of what the Soviets' ultimate goals are than anything they've done" while "I've been in office." To many, Carter's views were both naive and dangerous. Reagan thought Carter's evaluation of the Soviet Union "would be laughable if it was not so tragic." In separate correspondence Governor Reagan asserted: "It is frightening to hear a man in the office of the presidency has just discovered that the Soviets can't be trusted, that they lied to him."[34] Carter complained that a crisis of confidence had seeped into the body politic, and blamed the American people for their problems. The American people responded in November 1980 by voting him out of office.

It was obvious to most people that the Cold War had expanded to the far reaches of the globe, and with troubles mounting at home and abroad the stage had been set for Ronald Reagan's return to the national scene. After sixteen years of building a formidable grassroots organization, conservatives had defeated the party's East Coast wing and nominated Governor Reagan for the presidency. In order to unify the party, Reagan had proposed the formation of a Dream Team with Gerald Ford serving as his vice presidential candidate, but Ford had wanted to serve as a co-president, sharing power with Reagan. Reagan had balked at this arrangement and selected George H. W. Bush as his running mate.[35] Reagan had campaigned against Carter on the themes that had become a hallmark of the Reagan arsenal: he called for a reduction in the size and scope of the federal government and a revitalized military, and repudiated the failed policy of détente. Reagan was prepared to forcefully challenge the Soviet Union and defeat the Red Menace once and for all. He emphatically rejected Carter's creed of failure, and was optimistic that the country was not in a permanent decline.[36]

The 1980 election results were heavily influenced by the power of Reagan's ideas and his clear vision for the country. He saw America as a global power committed to preserving freedom and a great "City on the Hill" that held out the hope of liberty. Reagan was not thinking in utopian terms nor expressing a delusional call for the establishment of the perfect world.[37] But he was envisioning a world free of Soviet Communism. Presidential historian Robert Dallek points out: "Reagan's success was in knowing where he wanted to lead the country and understanding how to convince the country to follow him."[38] He was, in fact, one of the greatest visionary leaders in American presidential history, and his persuasive powers and dedication to clear themes reaped rewards for not only himself but the conservative movement, the Republican Party, and the country as a whole.

On November 4, 1980, Reagan handed President Jimmy Carter and the Democratic Party one of the worst defeats in American political history. Reagan secured 489 electoral votes to 49 for Carter, who managed to win only six states.

The popular vote was 44 million for Reagan to Carter's 35 million, with third-party candidate John Anderson, an Illinois congressman who had opposed Reagan's nomination, siphoning votes from the victor. Carter made history that evening, however, by becoming the first incumbent president to be defeated at the polls since Herbert Hoover in 1932.[39] Reagan went on to become one of the great vote winners in American politics. He not only dispatched Carter in 1980, but trounced Carter's hapless vice president, Walter Mondale, in 1984. Though Mondale had the benefit of running with the first woman vice presidential candidate, New York Representative Geraldine Ferraro, Reagan demolished the Democratic ticket. His forty-nine-state landslide was so complete that, had the contest been a street fight, someone would have mercifully intervened and stopped it.[40]

Reagan's success coincided with the emergence of a number of conservative pro-family interest groups that objected to the cultural excesses of the sixties. Reagan and the conservative revolution brought such organizations as Concerned Women for America, Campus Crusade for Christ, Young Americans for Freedom, and Phyllis Schafly's Eagle Forum to the forefront of American politics. Christian evangelicals like the Rev. Jerry Falwell and his Moral Majority encouraged other evangelicals to become actively engaged in politics, and the Moral Majority supported legislation that concerned the traditional family.[41] Considerable intellectual gravitas was provided by a large community of thinkers called neo-conservatives. These neo-conservatives were liberals who had been "mugged by reality," according to Irving Kristol, and included disillusioned supporters of Lyndon Johnson's Great Society who were outraged by the anti-Americanism that had become an element of modern liberalism; they were also anticommunist.[42] The Republican Party had clearly been transformed from the party of "big business" to the party of ordinary taxpayers and religious believers, with its base in the South and the Midwest.

Reagan's inauguration in January 1981 sounded a hopeful note to many Americans. It seemed as if the country's malaise was lifting. When Reagan announced to the American public that the fifty-two American hostages in Tehran had finally been released, the nation celebrated. The *New York Times'* above-the-fold headline declared, "Minutes Later, 52 U.S. Hostages in Iran Fly to Freedom After 444 Day Ordeal." Within weeks of his inauguration, Reagan zeroed in on the Soviet threat and assembled a group of Pentagon policy wonks to formulate a "defense guidance" that aimed to "reverse the geographic expansion of Soviet control and military presence throughout the world" and "encourage long-term political and military changes within the Soviet empire."[43] The new administration was clearly preparing to alter the political landscape permanently, but there were many challenges ahead.

Once in office it was clear that Reagan's leadership and managerial style differed from those of many of his predecessors. Reagan established the objectives for his administration and the direction he wanted to pursue, but he did not get involved in all of the details of every policy, nor did he directly supervise the operations of the executive branch. In his autobiography, he asserted: "I don't believe a chief executive should supervise every detail of what goes on in his organization. The chief executive should set broad policy goals and ground rules, tell people what he or she wants them to do, then let them do it; he should make himself (or herself) available, so that the members of his team can come to him if there is a problem. If there is, you can work on it together and if necessary, fine tune the policies."[44] He left much of the supervisory role to his staff, notably Jim Baker, Donald Regan, Bill Clark, Richard Allen, and Edwin Meese, which afforded him the room to engage in strategic thinking. Yet some scholars assert that Reagan's dedication to delegation and lack of oversight brought on one of the worst disasters in his presidency, the Iran-Contra scandal.[45]

While the president was clearly the strategic thinker and did not care to micromanage his staff, he was concerned about the image of the presidency. Over the course of the 1960s and 1970s the office had lost some of its glamour and the American people had lost respect for it. Of course, Johnson's "crisis of credibility" over Vietnam, Nixon's misdeeds, and the bumbling Gerald Ford who was lampooned by Chevy Chase on the comedy show *Saturday Night Live* all contributed to the public's negative view. Reagan cared a great deal about the image of the presidency and the message he was conveying to the media and the American people. Reagan was always "on" when on camera and conscious of the significance of television in modern political life, and he tried to restore some dignity to the office through effective use of the medium. The actor in chief worked best with a script, and nearly every aspect of his public life was carefully scripted, from where he placed his feet during an appearance to the speeches he delivered. The scripting of nearly every action would have been stifling to most people, but the former actor used this system very effectively. Reagan put it this way to former staffer Dinesh D'Souza: "The camera will always unmask the actor standing before it but only an actor who truly believes his lines can produce a convincing performance before the lens."[46]

Even a near tragedy presented some opportunities for revealing the character of the man to the American public and for improving the image of the presidency. On March 30, 1981, after Reagan delivered a speech to a group of union officials at the Washington Hilton, John Hinckley Jr., a twenty-five-year-old drifter, attempted to draw attention from the Hollywood actress Jodie Foster by firing six shots at the president.[47] Reagan's press secretary, James Brady, crumpled to the ground with a bullet to his head. The policeman Thomas Delahanty and the Secret Service Agent Timothy McCarthy were also wounded. Agent Jerry Parr threw the seventy-year-old president into the limousine, while other agents and police rushed Hinckley and seized his weapon. The president did not realize he had been hit, so Parr requested permission to inspect Reagan more closely. During this intimate pat down, President Reagan began coughing up blood, so the limousine rushed to George Washington University Hospital, where doctors located a bullet less than one inch from the president's heart. After surgery, Reagan was in good spirits and joked with family, doctors, and staff. When his wife, Nancy, visited him, the president recycled Jack Dempsey's response after being drubbed by Gene Tunney: "Honey, I forgot to duck." Prior to being wheeled into the operating room, Reagan had said to the doctors, "Please tell me you are all Republicans," and in the recovery room the joker in chief told the nurses: "All in all, I'd rather be in Philadelphia." Reagan's endearing humor and rather quick recovery contributed to a surge in his popularity. Although many of the scenes from the hospital were quite touching, they were carefully scripted for their maximum impact on the opinion polls.[48]

After his near assassination, President Reagan believed that he was destined to defeat communism once and for all. However, national security and victory in the Cold War were connected to restoration of the American economy, as a strong national infrastructure was needed to wage an effective campaign against the Soviets. Reviving an American economy that displayed signs of atrophy was going to be a challenge. When the new administration took office the economy was in dreadful shape. In the late 1970s, unemployment had run around seven to eight percent, and prime interest rates had reached a record 21.5 percent. In addition, the economy was plagued by a new phenomenon, stagflation, which combined slow economic growth and inflation. In fact, during one month in 1980, inflation measured 18 percent, which was devastating to people living on fixed incomes. The high inflation rate was very similar to a tax in that people will modify their behavior in order to avoid spending their money; thus society does not derive any benefits. For example, people will avoid carrying cash, which makes it difficult to purchase any items on impulse or use the money for entertainment. Consequently, businesses will not have disposable income on hand to deal with emergencies, and when a crisis arises credit is used to cover the expenses.[49]

The new president argued that the country's economic woes had been created by government regulation, heavy taxation, and runaway government spending. Moving first on inflation, the Reagan administration pursued a path that had been followed by the Carter administration, reducing inflation through the careful restraint of the money supply by the Federal Reserve Board. Under Fed Chairmen Paul Volcker and Allen Greenspan, inflation was brought under control, and it ceased to be an issue throughout much of Reagan's time in office. This was no small achievement since inflation had contributed to the demise of at least two previous administrations. The Reagan administration also continued the Carter policy of deregulation, but accelerated the pace by deregulating trucking, airlines, telecommunications, banking, and oil. The enormous Federal Register was sliced in half by the end of the first term, but the Carter recession lingered. The grip was finally broken through nonconventional means.[50]

The cornerstone of the Reagan economic recovery was not Keynesian orthodoxy, but sustained economic growth through the reduction of personal in-

come taxes.[51] Reagan was a firm believer in "supply side economics" and insisted that by cutting taxes and reducing regulations the federal government
could provide greater incentives to the providers of goods and services.[52] The
basic premise behind the sweeping tax reduction was based on the writings of
George Gilder, the author of *Wealth and Poverty*, and those of other noted economists, including Nobel Laureate Milton Friedman and Arthur Laffer, who argued that tax cuts would leave more money available for investment and that the
accompanying economic surge would propel the economy out of the depression.[53] This idea was articulated in 1974 when Laffer, an associate professor at
the University of Chicago demonstrated to some of his friends on a napkin that
tax rates beyond a certain level were counterproductive because the wealthy
looked to tax shelters rather than more productive investment ventures.[54]

In July 1981, Congress passed the largest single tax reduction in American
history, calling for a 25 percent phased reduction over a three-year period. This
reduction and subsequent tax cuts sliced the upper-income marginal tax rates
from a stifling 70 percent to 28 percent by the time the Gipper left office in January 1989. These reductions were accompanied by a simplified tax system in
1986, and together with the package of deregulatory actions they provided a
major jolt to business. By 1983 the economy was in full recovery and the growth
continued well into the 1990s.[55] The successes of the Reagan tax policies were
implicitly endorsed by his successors, although President Bill Clinton was far
more of a supply-sider than Reagan's Republican successor, George Herbert
Walker Bush.

Some politicians and historians defend Keynesian orthodoxy by asserting
that the benefits of the tax cuts were unproven or that they were responsible for
the runaway deficits of the 1980s. On the first point, history should be the guide.
Both the Coolidge and Kennedy administrations rejected conventional wisdom
embraced largely by the intellectual community and successfully lowered marginal tax rates as an engine for economic growth.[56] The second argument is easily dismissed through an examination of the federal government's tax receipts,
spending, and deficits during Reagan's tenure. Arthur Laffer and the supply-
siders were correct, as a steady stream of revenue poured into the federal coffers
after the Tax Reform bill was pushed through Congress. There were budget
deficits on Reagan's watch, but part of the responsibility lay in the struggle between the executive and legislative branches of government. The president frequently requested reductions in domestic spending, but Congress controlled the
purse strings and demonstrated a willingness to shortchange military spending
for the sake of domestic politics. Reagan watched the people's representatives
spending like drunken sailors, and began demanding the line-item veto, which
would have given the president the authority to control spending by vetoing specific lines of the federal budget.[57]

In the meantime, Moscow was paying close attention to the president during
the first months of his term, and Reagan's smashing of the Professional Air

Traffic Controllers Organization (PATCO) had foreign policy implications. In August 1981, the 12,000-member air traffic controllers union had threatened a national strike if their demands for a 100 percent salary increase and a reduction of their workweek were not accepted. The president found himself in a tough situation since PATCO was the one labor organization that had supported his bid for the presidency in 1980. The union leadership assumed that Reagan would concede or attempt to craft an amicable solution in order to circumvent a lengthy strike. However, as governor, Reagan had squashed two public-sector strikes, including one by the State Water Resources Department, whose workers were threatened with termination if they did not return to work. On July 29, 1981, the air traffic controllers violated their "no strike oath" and walked out. Right before 11 a.m., an agitated president emerged in the Rose Garden to address the Washington press corps. His actions were not motivated by any anti-labor sentiment. The great communicator simply asserted that public sector strikes would not be tolerated: "I must tell those who fail to report for duty this morning they are in violation of the law, and if they do not report for work within 48 hours, they have forfeited their jobs, and will be terminated." Inside the administration, cabinet members had advised the president to warn the union beforehand and not draw such an uncompromising line in the sand. But Reagan stuck by his guns, and the administration terminated the air traffic controllers, imposed millions of dollars in fines, and started legal proceedings with the Federal Labor Relations Authority to have the union decertified. For the Soviets, who were keenly watching the entire process, the message was clear: America was under new leadership and this man keeps his word.[58]

As president, Reagan operated from the clear conviction that the totalitarian Soviet state was an evil empire, and he was not afraid to confront it. He created the Reagan Doctrine as a low-cost way of assisting anti-communist forces in Africa and Central America, and supported the mujahedeen in Afghanistan in their battle to defeat the Soviet Union. In 1983 the president dispatched forces to Grenada to overthrow a Marxist regime, and three years later he ordered the bombing of Libya in retaliation for a terrorist attack on a Berlin disco frequented by American military personnel. When the Solidarity Movement emerged in Poland, Reagan hoped to create a crack in the iron curtain by secretly working with the pope to assist the Polish labor movement while breaking Moscow's grip on the people of Poland.[59]

In retrospect it is clear that the administration viewed the entire global state of affairs through a Cold War lens, which makes the events that played out in Lebanon even more incomprehensible. In 1982, after Yasser Arafat's Palestinian Liberation Organization (PLO) attempted to assassinate the Israeli ambassador to Great Britain, the Israeli Prime Minister Menachem Begin ordered bombing attacks on PLO-held installations inside Lebanon. When the PLO retaliated with rocket strikes on northern Israel towns, the Israeli Army invaded Lebanon to track down and eliminate members of the PLO. To restore order, the United

States joined a peacekeeping force that was dispatched to Beirut to buttress Christian troops and counter the Soviet-backed Serbian forces. Muslim militants, however, viewed the Americans not as peacekeepers dispatched to restore stability and protect human life, but as allies of Israel. On April 18, 1983, a truck packed with over a thousand pounds of explosives plowed into the United States Embassy in Beirut, Lebanon, killing over sixty people. Seventeen Americans were among the casualties, including eight employees of the CIA; two were chief Middle East analyst Robert Ames and station chief Kenneth Haas. The administration asserted that the attack was perpetrated by Iranian- and Syrian-backed Hezbollah, so intelligence operatives landed in Beirut to gather intelligence, but no significant military measures followed. Then, on October 23, six months later, a suicide bomber drove a truck packing a 1,500-pound bomb into the U.S. Marine barracks at Beirut International Airport. This time 241 United States Marines were killed, and over 100 were severely wounded. Intelligence identified those responsible for the attack, and the president deployed the marines to ships off the coast of Lebanon. With one phone call, President Reagan could have ordered his national defense team to work out an operation and strike the militants with impunity. The blood of 241 U.S. Marines gave him the moral authority to order an attack. But he did not retaliate, and the U.S. withdrawal most likely was seen as a sign of timidity by the terrorists.[60] Reagan's feckless response communicated that terrorists could attack American installations and kill American citizens without facing a retaliatory strike. The U.S. missteps in Lebanon encouraged militants throughout the Middle East, and terrorist attacks continued until September 11, 2001.[61]

The Reagan administration's repudiation of détente and active assistance to those resisting communism should have been no surprise to anyone who was familiar with Reagan's career, as the Soviet leadership certainly was. In a radio address before being elected president, Reagan had lampooned the policy of détente: "Isn't that what a farmer has with a turkey—until Thanksgiving Day?"[62] Détente had been a failure in his mind, and America's lack of resolve had enabled the Soviets to shift the balance of power in their direction. Now, with the American economy percolating, Reagan began to push the Soviets toward bankruptcy. He cut American trade and credits to the Soviets which had been advanced in the 1940s as a way to contain communism and keep it from spreading. By the 1980s, there was sufficient evidence that distributing America's wealth did not deter communist expansion, so American trade and credit to the Soviets was cut and the exportation of advanced technology was prohibited. At the same time, overall defense spending was more than doubled, increasing from $134 billion during the final year of the Carter administration to $282 billion during Reagan's seventh year in office.[63] Reagan pledged to rebuild the navy to a fleet of 600, construct MX missiles (nicknamed the peacekeepers), and deploy 572 Pershing II missiles among America's Western European allies. The administration also moved forward with a number of technologically advanced weapons that reduced the need for combat troops on the ground, while developing the Tomahawk cruise missile and the Patriot anti-missile missile, both of which were used during the first Gulf War.[64]

One of the major results of the increased military spending was restoration of the strategic nuclear balance. For nearly a decade Russia had been outspending the United States by 50 percent on missiles. The arms race, however, became incredibly expensive when President Reagan unveiled the Strategic Defense Imitative (SDI), or "Star Wars" as it was ridiculed by a chorus of liberal critics, many of whom deemed the idea pure science fiction. The president understood that the Soviet Union could launch a missile attack on the United States or one of her allies at any moment, and that aside from tracking the incoming missile there was nothing the United States could do to stop the warhead from striking its target. The policy of Mutual Assured Destruction (MAD) had dominated the thinking of strategists in the 1970s, and Reagan and Secretary of Defense Robert McFarlane rejected the entire notion because it placed the United States and the Communist bloc countries on the same moral and technical level. Reagan hoped to transcend America's weakness in defense, and called on the scientific community to develop a defense shield that could intercept incoming missiles.[65] On March 23, 1983, the president challenged the scientific community to develop an effective defensive shield against an intercontinental missile attack that "could make nuclear weapons obsolete."[66] The mainstream media and their allies in the Democratic Party attacked Reagan's plan and dismissed the entire notion out of hand. Former Secretary of Defense Robert McNamara referred to the plan as "pie in the sky." Strobe Talbot, writing for *Time* magazine, opined that it "sounds more like an arcade video game." Massachusetts Senator Ted Kennedy, his eyes fixed on a run for the presidency in 1984, blasted the president for his "misleading Red Scare tactics and reckless Star Wars schemes." The liberal *New York Times* called SDI a "pipedream," and other mainstream media continued to refer to SDI as Star Wars after the popular science-fiction movie. The Soviet Union reacted with similar hysteria. General Secretary Andropov called SDI "insane" and a clear attempt to "disarm the Soviet Union."[67]

In his book *Special Providence*, Walter Mead, a preeminent foreign policy expert, examined the debate over SDI within the context of American foreign policy traditions since the founding of the Republic.[68] The Jeffersonian school, according to Mead, was opposed to SDI because it was not seen as cost-effective. It was a "Maginot Line in the sky," one that would cost billions to develop and upgrade in order to stay ahead of enemy countermeasures. The Wilsonians, on the other hand, objected to SDI because of their deeply entrenched opposition to the arms race and weapons development. They also feared that a workable defense shield might enable the United States to disengage from the rest of the world and return to its isolationist tradition.[69] Mead's analysis is accurate in identifying those in Congress who opposed SDI on principle, but there were also partisans, who were willing to embrace extreme measures to defeat SDI, undermine and embarrass the president, and score political points.

In the aftermath of Watergate, the pendulum of political power had swung from the executive office toward the legislative branch. Intoxicated by power, members of Congress had worked to consolidate and expand their influence, converting the federal government into "a huge amorphous blob, like a creature out of science fiction."[70] President Reagan's success, public popularity, ideological advocacy of limited government, and opposition to governmental expansion made him a natural firewall against congressional power. SDI simply became a rallying point for partisans in much the same way that Vietnam had the previous decade. It was not surprising that Senator Edward "Teddy" Kennedy, an advocate of post–New Deal liberalism and a true believer in big government, was one of the president's harshest critics. In May 1983, according to a highly sensitive KGB document, Kennedy instructed John Tunney, a close personal friend and a former California senator, to transmit a message to the Soviet leader Yuri Andropov. Kennedy proposed forming a working alliance with Andropov to thwart Reagan's foreign policy plans and forestall his reelection.

According to this document, Kennedy was very concerned about the state of Soviet-American relations, which he believed was due to Reagan's policies rather than the actions of Andropov. The senator asserted that the president's popularity and stubbornness made policy modifications unlikely, but that the clock could be turned back if Reagan were defeated at the polls in 1984. "The only real threats to Reagan are problems of war and peace and Soviet-American relations. These issues," Kennedy said, would "without a doubt become the most important of the election campaign." Kennedy therefore proposed meeting Andropov in Moscow in order to "arm Soviet officials with explanations regarding problems of nuclear disarmament, so they [would] be better prepared and more convincing." The senator also suggested a charm offensive, a coordinated and systematic attempt to humanize Andropov and lower-level Soviet officials through the use of the American media. Kennedy suggested a one-on-one interview with Barbara Walters or Walter Cronkite so the Soviets could "appeal directly to the American people about the peaceful intentions of the USSR, with their own arguments about maintaining a true balance of power." Kennedy's willingness to collaborate with the Soviets may not have been a new development, but it was planned for his political benefit.[71]

Reagan, on the other hand, believed that it was immoral. He also believed that the president had a constitutional imperative to protect the American people.[72] When Reagan delivered his SDI speech, he did not indulge in hyperbole, nor make any references to "laser beams" or "space weapons." In fact, in his diaries Reagan stated: "I made no optimistic forecasts—said it might take 20 years. Or more, but we have to do it."[73] To keep the Soviets nervous, a fake test was conducted and the results proclaimed very successful.[74] By October 1986 it was clear to the president that SDI had the potential to end the Cold War. The

"Soviets if faced with an arms race would have to negotiate—they can't squeeze their people any more to try & stay even with us," Reagan reasoned.[75]

Soviet officials realized the United States held a decisive lead in technology and thought that America's scientific community could indeed develop the missile system. Moreover, the Soviets viewed Reagan as more anti-Soviet than any of his predecessors. The Soviets essentially took the bait, dedicating considerable financial resources to espionage and attempting to shape public opinion through support of the anti-nuclear movement.[76] It was clear to the Reagan administration that the Soviets took SDI quite seriously, which bolstered Reagan's belief that the project was viable.

The president continued the U.S. arms buildup and remained committed to SDI while negotiating with the Soviet government. In November 1985, Reagan met with Mikhail Gorbachev, the charming Soviet leader, in Geneva. Their first meeting was somewhat awkward at points, but both parties agreed that the Soviets and the Americans must work together.[77] Their next meeting took place in Reykjavik, Iceland, in 1986, where they came very close to reaching a formal agreement on the reduction of certain nuclear weapons. One of the major sticking points was Reagan's devotion to SDI, which the Soviets argued would destabilize the balance of power. But Reagan continued to hold fast, and Gorbachev came to recognize that the Soviet economy was in a virtual meltdown and that there was a need to direct all finances to meet the country's pressing domestic problems. After nine months of negotiations, Gorbachev met with the president again in Washington, D.C., on December 9, 1987, and signed a treaty to eliminate intermediate-range missiles (i.e., those with ranges of 300 to 3,000 miles). This was the first time in history that an entire class of nuclear weapons had been eliminated through direct negotiations, and it opened the door to subsequent talks and further reductions.[78] In addition, the Soviet Union began a phased withdrawal from Afghanistan and eased its controls on Eastern Europe. Within a year, much to the surprise of U.S. think tanks and Soviet studies departments at universities, the "evil empire" was collapsing. By 1991 the Soviet empire had been relegated to the ash heap of history. Reagan had envisioned a world without Soviet communism, and that dream had finally arrived.

In spite of Reagan's pledge to the American people to curb the size of the federal government, the president found dismantling a well-entrenched bureaucracy to be a formidable challenge. He was forced to adapt to the realities of American politics and focus on a handful of his long-term goals.[79] But Reagan managed to peel away layers of federal regulations and return the Republican party to a political party of ideas. He also tried to eliminate some of America's social ills by reshaping the United States Supreme Court. Reagan wanted to rein in the power of the Court and its influence on American society and culture, and the appointment of judges was the best mechanism for checking the power of the judiciary. Generally, many of Reagan's predecessors had appointed judges as a reward for service to their party, not because of any established commitment to a set of constitutional ideas. For example, Harry Truman appointed cronies to the bench, while Jimmy Carter placed considerable emphasis on making minority appointments. Other presidents like Franklin Roosevelt made appointments with certain ends in mind, but these appointments rarely achieved the desired result. Reagan, on the other hand, was most concerned about the candidate's judicial philosophy, leaning toward those candidates who were constitutionalists. The Reagan approach was designed to eliminate cronyism and the practice of selecting a candidate because of his view on a specific political issue; it was based more on the candidate's understanding of the role of the Court and its constitutional limits.[80] Reagan employed this approach in appointing both Sandra Day O'Conner and Antonin Scalia.

Yet Reagan's approach to the judicial process was a bit of a mixed bag. Reagan and his advisors found that making appointments on the basis of philosophy was no guarantee that once appointed to the highest court the judge would remain true to his or her expressed convictions. Moreover, selecting candidates on the basis of their qualifications and views of the Court and the constitution, although laudatory in principle, became the focal point of partisan conflict, most notably when liberal Democrats in the Senate Judiciary Committee unleashed a vicious attack on judicial scholar and longtime professor of law Robert H. Bork in 1987.[81]

All in all, however, Reagan's appointments at various levels of the judiciary had a profound impact on the American judicial system. And his attempt to return the court system to its constitutional moorings was a way to curb the judicial activism and gradually purge the culture of the sixties radicalism that outraged the president's conservative supporters.[82]

Reagan's successor, George Herbert Walker Bush, followed the Reagan administration's pattern when it came to Supreme Court nominees, but he was quite listless in fulfilling other judicial appointments. In fact, the Senate Judiciary Committee managed to detain a number of Bush appointments, leaving his successor, Bill Clinton, the opportunity to fill the vacant slots.

As one of the few two-term presidents of the twentieth century, Ronald Reagan left an incredible legacy. He demonstrated that the office of the presidency was still relevant, reshaped the contours of American politics, and made conservatism respectable. What's more, his contagious optimism rescued the country from its feelings of malaise and despair, and his commitment to across-the-board tax cuts allowed the American people to take the risks that are necessary in a free-market economy. He also broke the back of inflation and ushered in twenty years of economic growth. Those were no small achievements.

Many of Reagan's detractors claim the 1980s was the decade of greed and selfish materialism. But the improved economy that became the norm after 1983 brought financial rewards to more than those in the upper-income group. By 1989 unemployment had dipped to 5.3 percent and inflation had declined to 4.7 percent. Further, during the 1980s charitable giving grew at a much faster pace than in the previous decades. In real dollars, charitable contributions jumped upward from $77.5 billion in 1980 to $121 billion by the end the 1980s.[83] In addition, many of the devices produced by the high-tech revolution that started in the 1970s were not commercialized until the 1980s. It is clear that the elimination of some of the more onerous regulations and the lowering of inflation and taxation provided an economic and political climate conducive to the high-tech revolution, which became the backbone of the economy of the 1990s.

These accomplishments aside, Reagan worked against partisan obstructionists and with close personal advisors to bring an end to the forty-five-year struggle against the Soviet Union.[84] John Lewis Gaddis, the dean of the Cold War historians, contends that Reagan "was as skilled a politician as the nation had seen for many years, and one of its sharpest grand strategists ever."[85] Reagan developed an interlocking strategy that rejected détente and mutual co-existence on moral grounds and challenged the Soviet Union militarily, economically, and diplomatically. His instincts about the condition of the Soviet state proved correct, and SDI provided an effective defense of the United States and her allies from the moment Reagan and Robert McFarlane conceived the idea. Soviet generals and high-ranking officials within the Kremlin believed SDI was workable and that they could not compete with it, and the evil empire collapsed. In 1992, Soviet foreign policy expert Vladimir Lukhim exclaimed: "SDI accelerated our catastrophe by at least five years."[86]

Yet Reagan never boasted or took any individual credit for freeing millions of people from Soviet rule. Perhaps the closest he came was in 1997, while debilitated by Alzheimer's. Reagan was walking through Armand Hammer Park near his California home when he was approached by Yakob Ravin and his grandson. Ravin cheered and thanked the president "for everything you did for the Jewish people, for Soviet people, to destroy the Communist empire." Though somewhat confused and unaware, Reagan responded simply: "Yes, that is my job."[87] It most certainly was.

Notes

1. See, for example, David Farber, *Taken Hostage: The Iran Hostage Crisis and America's First Encounter with Radical Islam* (Princeton: Princeton University Press, 2005); Mark Bowden, *Guest of the Ayatollah: The Iran Hostage Crisis: The First Battle in America's War with Militant Islam* (New York: Grover Press, 2006); and James H. Kyle, *The Guts to Try: The Untold Story of the Iran Hostage Rescue Mission by the On-Scene Desert Commander* (New York: Ballantine Books, 1995).

2. Joseph Kraft, "The Post-Imperial Presidency," *New York Times,* November 2, 1980, http://www.proquest.com/ (accessed December 18, 2009).

3. See, for example, Peter Robinson, *How Ronald Reagan Changed My Life* (New York: Regan Books, 2003), 125; Dinesh D'Souza, *Ronald Reagan: How an Ordinary Man Became an Extraordinary Leader* (New York: Touchstone, 1999); an ·

Hayward, *Greatness: Reagan, Churchill and the Making of Extraordinary Leaders* (New York: Three Rivers Press, 2005), 62. America's leaders tend to emerge from the ranks of the ordinary: one can quickly cite Lincoln, Truman, Nixon, Carter, Reagan, and Clinton as examples.

4. Tom Wicker, "Rockefeller Attack On Rightists Gets Support in Capital: Others Mentioned Little Optimism," *New York Times,* July 16, 1963, http://www.proquest.com.e zproxy.umuc.edu/ (accessed October 24, 2009); and Steven F. Hayward, *The Age of Reagan: The Fall of the Old Liberal Order, 1964-1980* (New York: Three Rivers Press, 2001), 50.

5. The best of the many books on President Reagan are Lou Cannon, *President Reagan: The Role of a Lifetime* (New York: Public Affairs, 1991); D'Souza, *Reagan;* Michael A. Deaver, *A Different Drummer: My Thirty Years with Ronald Reagan* (New York: Harper Collins, 2001); and Peggy Noonan, *When Character Was King: A Story of Ronald Reagan* (New York: Penguin Books, 2002). For a less sympathetic study, see Laurence J. Barrett, *Gambling with History: Ronald Reagan in the White House* (New York: Doubleday and Company, 1983).

6. Ronald Reagan, *An American Life: The Autobiography* (New York: Simon and Schuster, 1990), 119. For a thorough discussion of the distinction between the social insurance mentality and the social engineering approach, see the first five chapters of Hayward, *Age of Reagan.*

7. D'Souza, *Ronald Reagan*, 57-62; and Reagan, *An American Life*, 135-36. Reagan claimed that "the first crack in my staunch liberalism appeared in the last year and a half of my military career." See Ronald Reagan and Richard Hubler, *Where's the Rest of Me? The Ronald Reagan Story* (New York: Duell, Sloan and Pearce, 1965), 123. However, after the war Reagan joined the liberal Americans for Democratic Action and campaigned for Harry S. Truman and for the liberal incumbent Helen G. Douglas against Richard Nixon for a seat in the United States Senate. Reagan would vote for Eisenhower and campaign for Richard Nixon in 1960, but the party officials thought it would be very persuasive for Reagan, a registered Democrat, to campaign for the Republican Nixon. In 1959, Nixon asserted that he was "greatly encouraged by the apparent trend on the part of the American people to question the tax and tax, spend and spend...elect and elect philosophy. Speeches such as yours [Reagan's] should do much to cause some solid thinking about the inherent dangers in this philosophy with the final result being a nationwide demand for reform." See Stephen E. Ambrose, *Nixon: The Education of a Politician, 1913-1962* (New York: A Touchstone Book, 1987), 541.

8. For more on Goldwater, see Lee Edwards, *Goldwater: The Man that Made a Revolution* (Washington, DC: Regnery, 1995).

9. Craig Shirley, *Rendezvous with Destiny: Ronald Reagan and the Campaign that Changed the World* (Wilmington: Intercollegiate Studies Institute, 2009), 8.

10. Paul Kengor, *The Crusader: Ronald Reagan and the Fall of Communism* (New York: Regan, 2006), 28; Reagan, *An American Life*, 138-145; Noonan, *Character*, 85-89; and Deaver, *Drummer*, 51.

11. Deaver, *Drummer*, 18-19; Cannon, *President Reagan*, 26; and Stephen Ambrose, *Nixon*, 650-674.

12. Kengor, *Crusader*, 32; and D'Souza, *Reagan*, 63.

13. Gil Troy, *The Reagan Revolution: A Very Short Introduction* (New York: Oxford University Press, 2009), 15.

14. Cannon, *President Reagan*, 26-27.

15. Reagan acknowledged in 1980 "that the most enduring lesson of his governorship for his presidency was the realization that he could work successfully with the legislature." See Cannon, *President Reagan*, 90.

16. Troy, *Reagan Revolution*, 16-17; and D'Souza, *Reagan*, 68.

17. James Piereson argues that the "New Left" was anti-American and that this clearly delineates its movement from earlier liberal manifestations. See James Piereson, *Camelot and the Cultural Revolution: How the Assassination of John F. Kennedy Shattered American Liberalism* (New York: Encounter Books, 2007).

18. Hayward, *Age of Reagan*, 167-170; and Kengor, *Crusader*, 33.

19. Kengor, *Crusader*, 35.

20. Kengor, *Crusader*, 43. The Soviets saw Reagan as a real threat so they conducted an investigation. But "apart from confirming Reagan's reputation as a Cold War Warrior," it seems nothing damaging was uncovered except "alleged evidence of his weak intellectual capabilities." See Christopher Andrew and Vasili Mitrokhin, *The Sword and the Shield: The Mitrokhin Archive and the Secrete History of the KGB* (New York: Basic Books, 1999), 242.

21. Kengor, *Crusader*, 43-44.

22. Hayward, *Greatness*, 88. The crafty Nixon quickly outmaneuvered Reagan, making a series of deals with Southern Republicans, notably Strom Thurmond of South Carolina, in order to chip away at Reagan's base and secure the nomination. Walter Edgar, *South Carolina: A History* (Columbia: University of South Carolina Press, 1998), 561.

23. Active measures against Reagan had begun during his unsuccessful bid for the Republican nomination in 1976. Moscow understood that "Reagan was far more anti-Soviet than either the incumbent president, Gerald Ford, or the Democratic contender, Jimmy Carter." See Andrew and Mitrokhin, *Sword and the Shield*, 242.

24. Hayward, *Age of Reagan*, 455-482.

25. Hayward, *Age of Reagan*, 483-484; Hayward, *Greatness*, 43; Deaver, *Drummer*, 47.

26. Reagan to Mrs. Van Voohis, in Skinner, Anderson, and Anderson, eds., *Reagan: A Life in Letters* (New York: Free Press, 2001), 277-78.

27. Ford's popularity dropped quickly after issuing a blanket pardon to Richard Nixon. See, for example, Thomas J. Whalen, *A Higher Purpose: Profiles in Presidential Courage* (Chicago: Ivan R. Dee, 2007), 205-229.

28. Christopher Matthews, *Hard Ball* (New York: Summit, 1988), 60. Nathan Miller contends that Jimmy Carter "was as close as the American people have ever come to picking a name out of the phone book and giving him a job." See Miller, *Star Spangled Men: America's Ten Worst Presidents* (New York: Touchstone, 1998), 25.

29. Steven Hayward, *The Real Jimmy Carter: How Our Worst Ex-President Undermines American Foreign Policy, Coddles Dictators, and Created the Party of Clinton and Kerry* (Washington, DC: Regnery, 2004), 82-83; Martin Plissner, *The Control Room: How Television Calls the Shots in Presidential Elections* (New York: Touchstone, 1999), 139.

30. Victor Lasky, *Jimmy Carter: The Man and the Myth* (New York: Marek Publishing, 1979), 11.

31. Margaret Thatcher, *The Downing Street Years* (New York: Harper Collins, 1993), 69.

32. The permanent campaigner has now become more common in the television age. See Joe Klein, *Politics Lost: How American Democracy Was Trivialized by People Who Think You're Stupid* (New York: Doubleday, 2006), 38-44.

33. John Lewis Gaddis, *The Cold War: A New History* (New York: The Penguin Press, 2005), 202; Troy, *Reagan Revolution*, 46; Hayward, *The Real Jimmy Carter*, 161-166; Geoffrey Hosking, *The First Socialist Society: A History of the Soviet Union from Within* (Cambridge: Harvard University Press, 1992), 453-455.

34. Kengor, *Crusader*, 58.

35. Hayward, *Greatness*, 93; and Hayward, *Age of Reagan*, 661-672.

36. Reagan was clearly upbeat and was inspired by the political success of Great Britain's conservative Prime Minister Margaret Thatcher. Thatcher was "Reagan's John the Baptist," elected in 1979, eighteen months before Reagan's inauguration, and like her American counterpart she was dedicated to dismantling the welfare state, slashing the budget, cutting taxes, and privatizing portions of the economy. See Paul Johnson, *Modern Times: The World From the Twenties to the Nineties* (New York: Harper Perennial, 1992), 749. Another very helpful work is Nicholas Wapshott, *Ronald Reagan and Margaret Thatcher: A Political Marriage* (New York: Sentinel, 2008).

37. Paul Johnson, *A History of the American People* (New York: Harper Collins, 1997), 919.

38. Robert Dallek, *Hail to the Chief: The Making and Unmaking of American Presidents* (New York: Oxford University Press, 1996), 35.

39. See Matthew Dallek, *The Right Movement: Ronald Reagan's First Victory and the Decisive Turning Point in American Politics* (New York: Free Press, 2000); and Shirley, *Rendezvous with Destiny*.

40. Johnson, *History of the American People*, 918; and Andrew and Mitrokhin, *Sword and the Shield*, 243.

41. Pundits, academics and the intellectual community did not understand why Christian evangelicals refused to support President Carter, a self-professed "born-again Christian," and threw their weight behind the once-divorced Governor Ronald Reagan.

42. Troy, *Reagan Revolution*, 38.

43. Kengor, *Crusader*, 74-75.

44. Reagan, *An American Life*, 161.

45. Hayward, *Greatness*, 38. Martin Anderson in *Revolution: The Reagan Legacy* (New York: Harcourt Brace, 1988) makes a similar argument. However, while Reagan was directly involved in the selling of arms to the Iranians to secure the release of American hostages, transmitting the money generated by the arms sales to the Nicaraguan contras did not involve delegation. Reagan did not grant Colonel Oliver North or John Poindexter the authority to provide money from the arms sales to the contras. Even the independent counsel Lawrence Walsh argues that there is no evidence to support the assertion that Reagan orchestrated or even knew about the transfer of funds. See Lawrence Walsh, *Firewall: The Iran-Contra Conspiracy and the Cover Up* (New York: Norton, 1997).

46. D'Souza, *Reagan*, 45. In *The Quest for the Presidency 1984* (New York: Bantam Books, 1984), Peter Goldman, Tony Fuller, et al. asserted that the president's "command of the medium was instructive and sure; no one since John Kennedy had played the role of president nearly so well" (29). Bruce Buchanan in *The Citizen's Presidency: Standards of Choice and Judgment* (Washington, DC: Congressional Quarterly Press, 1987), 166, writes that Reagan was able to "win the confidence and support of the electorate.

And he could do it better than anybody else on the scene. This fact made experience and expertise secondary."

47. Two of Reagan's cabinet members, Al Haig and Caspar Weinberger, thought the gunman was acting on behalf of the Soviets who desired to deal with Reagan's more moderate vice president, George Herbert Walker Bush. See Michael Beschloss, *Presidential Courage: Brave Leaders and How They Changed America, 1789-1989* (New York: Simon and Schuster, 2007), 284.

48. Deaver, *Drummer*, 127-142; D'Souza, *Reagan*, 206-207; Cannon, *President Reagan*, 90-91, Johnson, *History of the American People*, 921; Paul Kengor, *God and Ronald Reagan: A Spiritual Life* (New York: Regan Books, 2004), 183-186; Robert Reinhold, "A Bullet Is Removed From Reagan's Lung In Emergency Surgery," *New York Times*, March 31, 1981, http://www.proquest.com.ezproxy.umuc.edu/ (accessed November 30, 2009).

49. See, for example, Arthur Laffer, Stephen Moore, and Peter J. Tanous, *The End of Prosperity: How Higher Taxes Will Doom the Economy If We Let it Happen* (New York: Threshold Books, 2008), 1-83. David Hackett Fischer argues that falling or stable inflation causes an improvement in the moral fiber and the moral character of nations. See Fischer, *The Great Wave: Price Revolution and the Rhythm of History* (New York: Oxford University Press, 1999).

50. Kengor, *Crusader*, 80.

51. John Maynard Keynes in *We Can Conquer Unemployment* advocated government spending to fuel the economy, and his *General Theory of Employment, Interest, and Money* established the doctrine that justified higher government spending.

52. In a nutshell, supply-side tax theory asserts that economic recessions are not a problem of demand, but rather a problem of production. For those interested in supply-side economics, refer to Richard B. McKenzie, *What Went Right in the 1980s* (San Francisco: San Francisco Pacific Research Institute, 1994); Paul Craig Roberts, *The Supply-Side Revolution* (Cambridge: Harvard University Press, 1984); John W. Sloan, *The Reagan Effect: Economics and Presidential Leadership* (Lawrence: University Press of Kansas, 1999); Martin Anderson, *Revolution: The Reagan Legacy* (New York: Harcourt Brace, 1988); and Robert Bartley, *The Seven Fat Years* (New York: Free Press, 1982).

53. Larry Schweikart, *The Entrepreneurial Adventure: A History of Business in the United States* (Fort Worth, TX: Harcourt Brace, 2000), 338-340 and 542-546.

54. See Laffer, *End of Prosperity*.

55. Johnson, *History of American People*, 923.

56. See Burton W. Folsom, Jr., *The Myth of the Robber Barons: A New Look at the Rise of Big Business in America* (Herndon, Virginia: Young Americas Foundation, 1991), 103-120; and Robert F. Dallek, *An Unfinished Life: John F. Kennedy, 1917-1963* (New York: Little, Brown and Company, 2003), 583-589.

57. Kengor, *Crusader*, 80.

58. D'Souza, *Reagan*, 230-231; Rudolph W. Giuliani, *Leadership* (New York: Hyperion, 2002), 245-250; and Hayward, *Greatness*, 132-136.

59. John Yoo, *Crisis and Command: A History of Executive Power From George Washington to George W. Bush* (New York: Kaplan Publishing, 2009), 354; Carl Bernstein, "The Holy Alliance: Ronald Reagan and John Paul II," *Time*, February 24, 1992, 28-35; Peter Schweitzer, *Victory: The Reagan Administration's Secret Strategy That Hastened the Collapse of the Soviet Union* (New York: Atlantic Monthly Press, 1994).

For an excellent biography of the pope, see George Weigel, *Witness to Hope: The Biography of Pope John Paul II, 1920-2005* (New York: Harper, 2005).

60. Paul Pillar, *Terrorism and U.S. Foreign Policy* (Washington, DC: Brookings Institution Press, 2001), 20; Louis J. Freeh, *My FBI: Bringing Down the Mafia, Investigating Bill Clinton, and Fighting the War on Terror* (New York: St. Martin's Press, 2005), 303; and Bevin Alexander, *How America Got It Right: The U.S. March to Military and Political Supremacy* (New York: Crown Forum, 2005), 201-202.

61. Libya would be the one notable exception here. After Libyan-supported terrorists planted bombs in the airports at Rome and Vienna in December 1985, the United States unleashed thunderous air and naval attacks on Libya in April 1986. During the same month Libyan-sponsored terrorists attacked a West German discotheque that was frequented by American military personnel. The administration took the gloves off and launched a massive attack on Libya, killing forty people and destroying the family quarters of Libyan dictator Muammar al-Qaddafi. The heavy-handed response kept Qaddafi quiet and reduced the number of militant attacks for about a year.

62. Gaddis, *Cold War*, 217.

63. Fred C. Ikle, "The World is Our Oyster: Meeting the Soviet Military Challenge," in *The Fall of the Berlin Wall: Reassessing the Causes and Consequences of the End of the Cold War*, ed. Peter Schweizer (Stanford: Hoover University Press, 2000), 61.

64. Kengor, *Crusader*, 82.

65. For the origins of SDI, see Robert McFarlane, *Special Trust* (New York: Cadell & Davies, 1994), 227-235.

66. D'Souza, *Reagan*, 175.

67. D'Souza, *Reagan,* 176.

68. Mead identifies four schools of thought: the Hamiltonians, the Jeffersonians, the Jacksonians, and the Wilsonians. See Walter Russell Mead, *Special Providence: American Foreign Policy and How It Changed the World* (New York: Alfred A. Knopf, 2001). Mead, however, downplays the influence of America's first grand strategist, John Quincy Adams.

69. Mead, *Special Providence*, 300-304.

70. Forrest McDonald, *The American Presidency: An Intellectual History* (Lawrence: University Press of Kansas, 1994), 340.

71. See Kengor, *Crusader*, 205-210; and Herbert Romerstein, "Ted Kennedy: Collaborationist," *Human Events*, December 8, 2003. Andrew and Mitrokhin in *Sword and the Shield* 211, 240-41, and 291, state that the KGB targeted Kennedy and an "inner circle" of well-connected powerbrokers in order to gain information. One Democratic activist became an important source of information for the KGB after being "recruited during a visit to Russia by the Second Chief Directorate." This agent "had a wide circle of influential contacts in the Democratic party," including "Governor Jerry Brown, Senator Eugene McCarthy, Senator Edward Kennedy, Senator Abraham Ribicoff, J. William Fulbright, and Congressman John Conyers, Jr. During the 1976 presidential election the agent was able to provide inside information from within the Carter camp and a profile of Carter himself."

72. Some pundits and political opponents advanced the ridiculous notion that Reagan got the idea for SDI from one of the B movies he played in during the 1950s. There is not an iota of evidence to support this assertion. See, for example, D'Souza, *Reagan*, 173; and McFarlane, *Special Trust*.

73. Ronald Reagan, *Reagan Diaries,* ed. Douglas Brinkley (New York: HarperCollins, 2007), 140.

74. Tim Wiener, "Lies and Rigged Star Wars Test Fooled the Kremlin and Congress," *New York Times,* August 18, 1993.

75. Reagan, *Reagan Diaries,* 444.

76. Andrew and Mitrokhin, *Sword and the Shield,* 242-243.

77. Hayward, *Greatness,* 154.

78. Hayward, *Greatness,* 145.

79. This thought parallels Robert Dallek's assessment of Reagan as well. See Dallek, *Hail to the Chief,* 55.

80. McDonald, *American Presidency,* 304-305.

81. Liberal Democrats on the Senate Judiciary Committee launched a vicious attack on Bork in 1987 and on Clarence Thomas in 1991. Bork was rejected, but Thomas (nominated by Bush) ultimately made it through the judicial process.

82. Gil Troy in *Reagan Revolution, 121* wrote that "Bush's nomination of this ideologue [Clarence Thomas] reflected an attempt to extend Ronald Reagan's judicial revolution, perhaps the most effective flank in Reagan's multidimensional onslaught against the Great Society."

83. McKenzie, *What Went Right in the 1980s.* 57-73.

84. It was common among those men who did not make decisions on the basis of polling data or focus groups, notably Abraham Lincoln, Harry S. Truman, and Ronald W. Reagan, to go against their advisors.

85. Gaddis, *Cold War,* 217. The myth that Reagan was a dunce was an image that was crafted and honed by his political enemies, but it gained considerable support in the media and academia to become an accepted truth.

86. McFarlane, *Special Trust,* 23. This observation comports with the public comments expressed by former Soviet president Mikhail Gorbachev at Princeton University in 1993. See, for example, "SDI, Chernobyl Helped End Cold War, Conference Told," *Washington Post,* February 27, 1993, A17.

87. Lawrence Altman, "Reagan's Twilight-A Special Report," *New York Times,* October 5, 1997.

Chapter 2

Reagan Revives FBI Spying

Ivan Greenberg

After the "reform" of the Federal Bureau of Investigation (FBI) in the mid-1970s, Ronald Reagan instructed the Bureau to resume aggressive domestic spying once he became President. The revival of "political policing" did not come as a surprise: During the 1980 presidential campaign, Reagan criticized Jimmy Carter for restraining the FBI and promised to increase domestic spying if elected.[1] Using the Freedom of Information Act (FOIA), I obtained nearly a dozen FBI spy files to reconstruct little known material on government surveillance during the 1980s. Under the rubric of fighting "terrorism," the FBI targeted a broad range of peaceful groups: Critics of U.S. policy in Central America, the anti-nuclear and peace movement, environmental activists, gay and lesbian groups, animal rights activists, and black elected officials. As in prior years, records were kept on people who merely attended a meeting of a suspect group. Informers were deployed to find out from the inside about plans for protest, in addition to the use of phone taps, mail covers, and break-ins. By equating domestic dissent with terrorism, instead of using the broader investigative category of "subversion" employed for decades by FBI Director J. Edgar Hoover, Reagan not only falsely associated violence with lawful protest but foreshadowed the development of a "terror scare" in U.S. politics.[2] The FBI opened thousands of investigations to identify and contain as many forms of dissent as possible. Freedom of political expression came under attack as Reagan unleashed the repressive apparatus of the state on his critics.

In 1981 and 1982, the new Senate Subcommittee on Security and Terrorism, chaired by conservative Republican Jeremiah Denton of Alabama, held 27 separate hearings and helped develop the terror framework Reagan relied on to develop security policy. Denton argued two related points: Soviet KGB agents backed many of the President's domestic political opponents and the nation faced a formidable terrorist threat. The domestic roots of the threat were tied to the Soviets' active sponsorship of terror worldwide. The born-again Christian

Denton, who had been a prisoner of war in North Vietnam for seven years, hoped to smear liberal-left Americans as not only pro-Soviet but also pro-terrorist. He said, "When I speak of a threat, I do not just mean that an organization is, or is about to be, engaged in violent criminal activity. I believe many share the view that the support groups that produce propaganda, disinformation, or 'legal assistance' may be even more dangerous than those who actually throw the bombs." A key political objective was to expand the definition of terrorism to include nonviolent activity. Denton named the National Lawyers Guild, *Mother Jones* magazine, and the Institute for Policy Studies as examples of U.S groups which aided the Soviet terror conspiracy.[3]

Civil liberties groups worried that Denton and his allies in government would revive Cold War witch hunts. As Aryeh Neier wrote in the March 1982 edition of the *Bulletin of Atomic Scientists*, "Denton has suggested that some persons and organizations that have sought controls on the activities of the intelligence agencies, ostensibly on civil liberty grounds, are actually motivated by an interest in aiding a Soviet plot to bring down the West by terrorism. This has aroused concern in some quarters that the anti-terrorist campaign of [Alexander] Haig, Denton and company will be the vehicle for the rebirth of McCarthyism."[4] Victor Navasky, editor of the *Nation* magazine, echoed this view, as did Kathy Engel, director of the Fund for Open Information and Accountability, who stated bluntly, "Terrorism becomes an excuse, then, for developing a repressive mechanism to be used against those who oppose administration policies . . . Terrorism is the new bugaboo."[5]

The domestic ramifications of the Reagan Administration's fight against international communism included spying on critics of the Cold War. In a major effort, the FBI targeted Americans sympathetic toward socialists in Central America, monitoring and disrupting their political activity. For example, the FBI investigated the Committee in Solidarity with the People of El Salvador (CISPES) for five years subjecting more than 2,300 people and 1,200 groups to surveillance merely for their political views. Intelligence analysts ignored their own reports to charge that CISPES was violent-prone. Why did the situation in El Salvador command so much attention? According to CIA Director Bill Casey, "El Salvador was symbolically the most important place in the world. If the U.S. could not handle a threat in its backyard, Reagan's credibility would be at risk in the rest of the world."[6]

The CISPES probe involved all 56 FBI field offices with photo and visual surveillance of demonstrations in 22 cities; undercover agents attended CISPES meetings in five cities; informants inside CISPES (six cities); trash exams (six cities); the examination of bank records (six cities); the study of telephone records (four cities); FBI interviews of people visiting Central America (six cities); as well as the frequent use of records of activists' driver's licenses, credit reports, and employment earnings.[7] The FBI reverted to 1950s Cold War constructs, seeing in the group a secret program hidden from most members, as well as the group's use of "front groups." Jinsoo Kim of the Center for Constitutional Rights noted: "So, when a field office reported that a local CISPES chapter pursued only such projects as teach-ins, slide shows, and pickets, the headquarters would remind the field office of the covert program . . . Any organization which ever worked with CISPES, signed a petition, co-sponsored a demonstration or event, or had a single overlapping member, might be a front, and as any legal activity might be a cover for the covert program, there was no limit to the depth or breadth of the investigation."[8]

Secret FBI memos on CISPES show the policing of free speech. For example, the New Orleans field office wrote to the Dallas office, "It is imperative at this time to formulate some plan of attack against CISPES and specifically against individuals [text deleted] who defiantly display their contempt of the U.S. Government by making speeches and propagandizing their cause. . . ." The FBI reported in detail on lawful, peaceful protest. The Director wrote, "The following information was obtained from the assets of several of our field offices. The information pertains to the peace march scheduled for Nov. 12, 1983, in Washington, DC, and other major cities in the United States. The Chicago CISPES chapter plans to be well represented at the march . . . Over sixty organizations have signed on to make the march the largest ever on Central America." A June 15, 1984, memo to the Director noted Chicago CISPES had about 250 members. The memo said, "To date, the Chicago FBI has no direct indication that CG [Chicago] CISPES is influenced by a foreign power." The memo lists two items as its "objective of investigation." First, they wanted to identify the leadership of the group. Second, "The group's bank records are of utmost interest to the Chicago FBI and will be the target of future investigation to determine the group's money flow." About six informers were working the case and "the Chicago Office of the FBI has obtained the toll records for the CG CISPES office telephone . . ."[9] The widening net of surveillance on anyone merely associated with a CISPES event is evident in an Atlanta field office memo. "Observation of the Little Five Points Community Center, the evening of February 23, 1985, determined that there were only about a dozen vehicles in the parking lot and that a dance program was scheduled at the facility that evening. On February 23, 1985, the following license plates were observed on vehicles parked at the Little Five Points Community Center . . . [Forty-one numbers follow.]"[10] The total FBI file on CISPES is approximately 142,500 pages with material from various field offices.[11]

A Senate committee later faulted FBI conduct by pointing to a "serious failure in FBI management, resulting in the investigation of domestic political activities that should not have come under governmental scrutiny."[12] FBI leader Oliver "Buck" Revell, who finally shut down the CISPES investigation in 1985, writes in his memoir that he "was surprised to find an investigation that had spread all over the country and taken on a life of its own . . . This is exactly the kind of domestic security investigation that had gotten the Bureau into trouble before—an investigation that could appear politically motivated, as the country was then at odds with itself over Central American policy. If the FBI was discovered running a poorly focused investigation of political activists, it could well incite uniformed outrage."[13]

In addition to CISPES, other groups that opposed U.S. policy in Central America were put under surveillance. FBI Headquarters holds a 37-page file on Witness for Peace, a religious-based group started in 1983 that sponsored more than 4,000 visits to Nicaragua by members to serve as a "shield of love" in the event of a U.S. invasion. Activists from many of the nation's peace and anti-war organizations participated in its work, including members of the American Friends Service Committee, the Fellowship of Reconciliation, and the Women's International League for Peace and Freedom. FBI and U.S. Customs harassed many of the Americans traveling to Nicaragua by "interrogating them in detail about their trips and professional lives, and searching, seizing and photocopying their address books, diaries, research materials and other written materials." The FBI acknowledged conducting about one hundred interviews in 1985, and several hundred over the next four years. Some travelers were investigated at their homes and jobs and subjected to tax audits.[14]

The FBI file described Witness for Peace as nonviolent and refers to its legal activity, so why were they under investigation? On Dec. 31, 1984, a memo offered this description of Witness for Peace activity in Vermont and New Hampshire. "The group," the FBI wrote, "is attempting to get pledges for people to commit themselves to either non-violent civil disobedience or other types of lawful protests. . ." An Albany, NY, memo quotes at length a Witness leaflet that urges nonviolence. According to FBI intelligence, "Non-violence training is being made available for all those who have not previously received it. All who wish to take part in civil disobedience are requested to take this day-long introduction to the philosophy of nonviolence. Those participating in legal demonstrations are also urged to receive this training." The memo lists 23 political organizations that support Witness for Peace actions. The Bureau discusses the possibility of "civil unrest," which resulted in alerting the Secret Service to their activity.[15]

FBI Headquarters holds a 41-page file on the Pledge of Resistance, a group that also opposed U.S. war against Nicaragua. Formed in 1983 by religious peace activists who feared the recent U.S. invasion of Grenada was a prelude to an invasion of Nicaragua, the Pledge circulated a petition for people to sign that in the event of a U.S. attack they would "go immediately to Nicaragua to stand unarmed as a loving barrier in the path of any attempted invasion" or, alternatively, stage protests at U.S. Congressional offices. The Pledge worked with the seven regional offices of Witness for Peace and established a national office at the National Council of Churches in New York. By 1986, more than 80,000 Americans signed the Pledge with support across the nation–Florida, Virginia, North Carolina, Texas, Colorado, Wisconsin, Massachusetts, New Jersey, California, and New York. More than three hundred local Pledge groups formed to hold nonviolent training sessions and several thousand Pledge members were arrested during street protests during the late 1980s.[16]

The terrorist bogeyman again reared its head. A FBI report on a Pledge demonstration in Chicago was titled, "Nicaraguan Terrorist Matters: International Terrorism–Nicaragua."[17] No FBI memos indicate the Pledge endorsed violence or participated in criminal activity. There are no specific references to overseas or international connections. The Bureau describes protests in several cities and the names of people arrested by city police were forwarded to FBI Headquarters.[18] People who engage in civil disobedience may become the subject of new investigations, as the Bureau searches to contain and neutralize leading activists. In San Diego, the FBI described the routine surveillance of legitimate protest.

> Approximately 75 individuals demonstrated outside the San Diego federal building during the noon hour to protest U.S. support of the soldiers of the El Salvadoran government. Approximately 40 demonstrators then entered the federal building and demonstrated at Congressman Bill Lowery's 41st. District office located in Suite 6-S-15 of the Federal building. Spokeperson(s) for the demonstrators engaged in dialogue with the Congressman's assistant. Demonstrators milled around the reception area and in the hall next to the congressman's office.[19]

The FBI tracked the early development of an antiwar movement. A Boston memo discussed activism in several cities. "526 persons were arrested for trespass after notice [in Boston]. The number arrested in Springfield, Massachusetts, was 136 persons; Pittsfield, Massachusetts, was 16; Williamstown, Massachusetts, and Greenfield, Massachusetts, reported two arrests. No injuries to demonstrators or police personnel were reported in any of the four above-mentioned towns."[20] In Louisville, Kentucky, a small protest of 100 people prompted an FBI memo to Headquarters regarding "domestic terrorism" and "information relating to actual or threatened civil disorders."[21]

In an ominous sign, the federal government developed a top-secret emergency plan to construct ten military detention centers within the United States to house domestic opponents of a war against Nicaragua. The National Security Council and the Federal Emergency Management Agency (FEMA) developed this plan, which became known as "Rex 84," and in preparation for its implementation an index of FBI dossiers on 12,000 Americans was forwarded to FEMA headquarters.[22] The Rex 84 plan recalled the era of J. Edgar Hoover, when the Bureau maintained since 1939 a Security Index list of Americans to be put into detention camps in the event of a "national emergency," such as a hot war with the Soviet Union. This list at its height included 26,000 names. Although Congress repealed the Emergency Detention Act in 1971, its revival in a new form demonstrated that political detention plans remained an integral part of security planning.[23]

Spying on the Nuclear Freeze Movement

The FBI refused to view peace organizing as an authentic response to the threat of war, which seemed greater under Reagan, who deployed more missiles in Europe, claimed that a nuclear war was winnable, and refused to renounce the policy of first use of nuclear weapons. Surveillance of the anti-nuclear peace movement, centered on the Nuclear Freeze, publicly was acknowledged when

Reagan mistakenly linked the Freeze movement to the Soviets. The Freeze gained a mass following, with an estimated 10 million adherents, of which about one million participated in multiple protest events in any given year. Freeze groups were started in more than 40 cities and Freeze resolutions were adopted by the electorates of eight states. Close to 200 Congressman backed the Kennedy-Hatfield Freeze resolution in 1982, reflecting the mainstreaming of the movement. Its ready embrace of electoral politics–a Freeze Voter PAC was established in 1983—illustrates that the Freeze incorporated itself comfortably within the liberal wing of the Democratic Party.[24]

We know the FBI infiltrated the Physicians for Social Responsibility chapter in San Francisco, an organization of doctors who spoke about the medical horrors related to a nuclear war. Freeze supporters sometimes were added to the FBI's terrorism files. For example, in 1982 ABC-TV aired a fictional movie, *The Day After*, about the outbreak of nuclear war. More than 100 million Americans watched this realistic account of the devastating destruction that would follow a nuclear exchange. A group of prominent scientists took out a full-page advertisement in *The New York Times* urging the public to write to them about their response to the movie, and to support the Freeze with donations. The advertisement bore a post office box address and FBI headquarters directed agents to put a mail cover on the box to record the names of all people who responded.[25] In a separate case, FBI agents went undercover in the Freeze campaign in Orlando, Florida, for at least seven months. One of the agents donated money to win the allegiance of local activists.[26] When the Washington, D.C, office of the Committee for a Sane Nuclear Policy (SANE) was broken into in 1986, some suspected the FBI.[27]

In 1983, the FBI's investigation of the Freeze movement received a public airing when the House Intelligence Committee declassified an FBI report titled, "Soviet Active Measures Relating to the U.S. Peace Movement." The report concluded, "Based on information available to us, we do not believe the Soviets have achieved a dominant role in the U.S. peace and nuclear freeze movement, or that they directly control or manipulate the movement." Although this finding undermined Reagan's claims, the Freeze still aroused Bureau suspicions. A major portion of the report focused on an anti-nuclear demonstration in New York's Central Park in June 1982 in which close to 1 million people gathered. The FBI infiltrated the planning of the rally and again harking back to 1950s Cold War thinking warned that members of the Communist Party USA had a major hand in organizing through one of its front groups, the U.S. Peace Council. "Soviet-controlled organizations participated at the highest levels of the June 12 Committee" that planned the Central Park rally, the FBI said, and during meetings the American Communists "actively campaigned to direct the focus of the demonstration exclusively against U.S. weapons systems."[28] Of course, U.S. peace activists would focus their attention on U.S. nuclear policy: They live in the United States, not the Soviet Union. Despite this report, the FBI was not finished investigating Freeze groups. The FBI believed KGB agents were "attempting to develop contacts with religious figures in the United States" and were collecting information on American peace activists to determine if any of them might be "vulnerable to [KGB] recruitment operations."[29] FBI infiltration of peace groups remained a priority as long as large numbers of Americans protested the arms race in defiance of the government.

The full scope of FBI activity against the anti-nuclear movement is largely unknown because many of the groups disbanded without filing requests for their FBI files. I made FOIA requests on several older peace groups, which the FBI investigated under Hoover (SANE and the War Resisters League) and was told by Headquarters that these groups were not investigated under Reagan. In addition to the FBI, other police agencies also investigated the Freeze. For example, we know the Connecticut state police infiltrated several organizations and when a Hartford newspaper exposed this spying, the head of the State Police Criminal Intelligence Division commented, "I know people don't like it, but if you go to a demonstration, you're probably waiving [your] right to privacy."[30] In northern California, Navy intelligence planted informers inside the Livermore Action Group (LAG), an anti-nuclear civil disobedience organization. In 1982-1983, LAG organized about a dozen blockades outside the Lawrence Livermore weapons laboratory, as well as at army bases, in which almost 3,800 protestors were arrested. An informer spied from inside the group throughout most of this period, preparing monthly reports that were passed on to the FBI. For example, in January 1983, the informer attended a planning session of 50 protest organizers and recorded plans for demonstrations. In February, he reported that activists "were ecstatic at the total number of protestors that participated" at an action at the Concord Naval Weapons Station in San Francisco. Before the protest, the informer provided logistical information, and he promised that "the forthcoming meeting regarding the spring-summer demonstration will be monitored and intelligence will be appropriately disseminated." In March, he wrote: "During a conversation with one prospective demonstrator, source was advised that although the march is being organized as a peaceful demonstration, the group is encouraging civil disobedience such as laying in the street."[31]

FBI agent Jack Ryan protested the designation of anti-nuclear groups as terrorist, which resulted in his termination from the Bureau. Ryan worked on these investigations until he wrote a memo in 1987 to his superior in Springfield, Illinois, indicating his opposition to U.S. nuclear policy and the investigation of peace groups for terrorism. Ryan believed the Bureau was "using this investigation not as a means of developing a case to be prosecuted but as an end in itself, a way of intimidating. And I know well how intimidating it can be to be investigated by the FBI." Ryan focused on the Plowshares, a group that engaged in civil disobedience. "I do not see the activities committed by the 'Plowshares' group to be in any way acts of violence . . . To my understanding, the term 'plowshares' is drawn from the Biblical edict: 'they shall beat their swords into plowshares,' and most pointedly refers to neutralizing military violence. The actions of Jean Gump et al. [a local Plowshares group] are obvious violations of Destruction of Government Property statutes and I would have no problem investigating such matters but I do not believe any of their actions in this case constitute acts of violence bringing them under the scope of Domestic Security Guidelines . . ."[32]

During the 1980s, Plowshares engaged in about 30 break-ins of army or navy missile sites. Protestors symbolically hammered on the heads of the missiles and poured their blood on to them. In their view, they were beginning the process of disarmament. As radical pacifists, they embraced religion and their acts were accompanied by prayer or other ceremonies. They made no effort to conceal their activity, waiting for police to arrive and they peacefully submitted to arrest. In their view, they became anti-war political prisoners. About 100 people were arrested in these symbolic actions.[33] When I requested the FBI file on the Plowshares, Headquarters tried to conceal their records and sent me only 8 pages.

What is the place of civil disobedience within the American notion of the "rule of law"? People who take to the streets to engage in civil disobedience expect to get arrested and to face the legal penalties imposed on them. They are working within the rule of law.[34] The peace movements of the 1980s embraced *nonviolent* direct action. Whether the issue was Central American policy or the nuclear arms race, groups of committed activists practiced mass civil disobedience to advance the movement and build nonviolent communities. Many of these groups engaged in elaborate training to keep protests peaceful and developed strategies to avoid violent confrontations with the police. They engaged in political action through affinity groups, practiced decision-making by consensus, and shared an ideology that combined feminism, ecology, and grassroots democracy.[35]

The full extent of FBI surveillance on the environmental movement is difficult to determine with precision. In 1982, the assistant Secretary of Agriculture claimed socialists and communists led the Audubon Society and the Sierra Club.[36] Were these charges based on FBI investigations? When I filed FOIA requests on these two groups, Headquarters reported "no records" on the Audubon Society. The Sierra Club FBI file is 107 pages with the last dated material from 1973.[37] However, we do know that the Bureau actively targeted the militant wing of the environmental movement, including Greenpeace USA and Earth First!

When progressive journalist Chip Berlet went undercover to a private security conference in 1991, he heard that Navy intelligence designated Greenpeace a terrorist threat. There is other evidence. Gerry Leape, the Oceans Campaign Coordinator for Greenpeace, recalled: "I worked for a member of Congress until 1989. In 1991, that Congressman called me to tell me that a constituent of his had been denied a security clearance because he said that he was a supporter of Greenpeace and that, at least at that time, Greenpeace was still listed by the FBI as a terrorist organization."[38] In 2000, the Headquarters file on Greenpeace USA supposedly totaled 135 pages. The Bureau describes the type of protest activity organized by the group. "Actions have been taken by Greenpeace in opposition to U.S. offshore drilling, and to nuclear submarines coming into port; in opposition to Spanish whaling; and against Japanese and Soviet fishing and whaling violations." An effort by the Bureau to broaden its investigation to other groups, based on association with Greenpeace, failed. "FBIHQ records do not reveal any information concerning connections of Greenpeace with other organizations."[39] Another memo noted, "On July 10, 1987, Greenpeace, an aggressive pro-ecology organization, launched a campaign called the 'nuclear free seas campaign' to protest the nuclear powered ships, military vessels and submarines that carry nuclear weapons. The campaign is particularly aimed at the American, British and French navies. The planning for the campaign originated at Greenpeace headquarters, 2007 R Street, N.W., Washington, D.C."[40] The file also notes that when activists were arrested, their names were forwarded to FBI headquarters. According to one memo: "Greenpeace had entered the Japanese Consulate in Chicago on Nov. 19, 1981 to protest the killing of whales by Japanese fisherman. Police subsequently arrested the following group members for disorderly conduct after they refused to leave the premises: [text redacted]." The FBI kept press clippings on the group, which claimed 250,000 U.S. members.[41]

Spying on African-American Elected Officials

During the 1980s, many black Americans wondered if the FBI had ceased their long history of racial policing. Should it come as a surprise that the Bureau, working with local police, targeted a wide range of black elected officials? According to the United Nations Commission on Human Rights, "A number of black elected officials were placed under surveillance, their phones tapped, subjected to investigations, spied on by cameras for corruption or embezzlement and juries hearing cases involving some of them were manipulated."[42] This FBI effort tried to police the emergence of mainstream black leadership in the post-civil rights era. In 1964, approximately 280 black elected officials served nationwide, a low number. But by the late 1980s, the figure grew to more than 5,000.[43] The FBI resisted this progress by starting dubious investigations of eight black Congressman (Ronald V. Dellums, Floyd Flake, Harold Ford, Mervyn Dymally, John Conyers, Charles Rangel, William Clay, and William Gray); seven black mayors (Andrew Young, Maynard Jackson, Tom Bradley, Coleman Young, David Dinkins, Harold Washington, and Marion Barry); and several other black leaders (Julian Bond, Clarence Mitchell III, and Alcee Hastings). Only Marion Barry was found guilty of a crime and questions remain about entrapment. In the case of Alcee Hastings, the FBI's attempt to remove him from the federal bench included partly falsifying evidence and making false and distorted statements before a legal panel. The Justice Department concluded that the FBI also "may have provided misleading testimony about the results of forensic tests [used] in the impeachment proceedings."[44] Hastings later was elected to the U.S. House of Representatives.

In two other ways, the FBI fought black activism. During the Congressional debate about establishing a national holiday for the Rev. Martin Luther King, Jr., the FBI secretly gave derogatory King material to members of Congress to urge them to vote against the holiday.[45] Race also came into play in the hunt for terrorists on the issue of South African apartheid. The FBI monitored some critics who advocated divestment–getting U.S. companies and the U.S. government to pull out of all business dealings in South Africa as a way to punish the white regime. Hundreds of people were arrested in peaceful civil disobedience, including several members of Congress. Terrorism? The FBI never found any, but the fact that U.S. activists expressed support for Nelson Mandela's African National Congress (ANC)–a terrorist group according to Reagan's government–was enough to justify guilt by association investigations. We know that in Albany, N.Y., in 1981 the FBI and police infiltrated the Coalition Against Apartheid and Racism. On the day of a major rally, agents broke into the home of one of the group's leaders based on an informer's erroneous report that the group stockpiled weapons. The FBI confiscated files, papers, and an address book, while detaining two of the leaders on bogus charges.[46] In New York City, nine members of the May 19 Communist Organization were arrested for trespassing during an anti-apartheid protest outside the South African Airways ticket office and the Bureau characterized this protest as a "terrorist incident" because the May 19 organization was a radical group already under investigation.[47]

In general, peaceful street protests can activate surveillance. In 1983, the Georgia Committee Against the Death Penalty held a vigil at the state capitol. Two FBI agents were among the protestors, dressed in plainclothes and wearing a green ribbon, the emblem of the protestors. One of the agents carried a video camera and filmed the demonstration for their files.[48] In 1985, the All People's Congress planned a demonstration in Washington during Reagan's Second Inaugural ceremony. Although the Buffalo FBI office informed Washington ahead of time that the group had "no propensity for violence," the FBI's Revell personally rejected this assessment and ordered surveillance of the protestors.[49] In 1991, protestors gathered outside a Manhattan court building during the murder trial of El Sayyid A. Nossair, accused of assassinating Rabbi Meir Kahane of the Jewish Defense League (JDL). As angry Jews and Muslims faced off, the FBI stood by filming the protestors, taking notes on each one of them. At the time, the FBI had a large on-going investigation of the JDL. The Muslim supporters of Nossair were not yet under FBI investigation, but their mere presence on the street exercising their First Amendment rights prompted one.[50]

In a variety of other contexts, the FBI spied on Americans fighting for their civil rights. The watchful eye of the state applied the terrorist label to a social service and educational group, the Gay Men's Health Crisis in New York, as well as the Coalition for Lesbian and Gay Rights and Senior Action in a Gay Environment. The protest group ACT-UP (AIDS Coalition to Unleash Power) also became a target. Founded in 1987, ACT-UP sponsored civil disobedience and vociferously criticized the Reagan Administration's lack of attention to the AIDS health crisis. The FBI investigated ACT-UP as a terrorist group because they claimed the group might throw HIV infected blood during protests. At least 16 field offices were involved in the probe, including the use of informers and undercover agents at meetings. In 1995, the FBI released a small portion of their file (22 pages taken from 451 documents on the group).[51] In an interview, James

Wentzy, one of their leaders, told me: "By the early '90s people in ACT UP were starting to get paranoid (and perhaps not without cause) about 'Who was an informer'. . .Until the voice of reason was adopted saying, 'Look, we don't care who is or isn't an informer. Our work is open and public and is not about the FBI but rather fighting AIDS and the bureaucrats who continue to foster the AIDS crisis.' To my knowledge, no ACT UP member was 'knowingly' interviewed by the FBI. No doubt, however, members of the FBI were at general open-to-the public meetings."[52]

Another context for surveillance involves animal rights and the FBI used guilt by association. Since one radical group, the Animal Liberation Front (ALF), engaged in property vandalism, other non-violent groups were put under surveillance. The FBI investigated People for the Ethical Treatment of Animals (PETA), the largest animal rights group in the nation, looking for ties to the ALF. One FBI memo noted, the head of PETA "declined to be interviewed by the FBI in connection with a bomb threat investigation being conducted in 1985, wherein another international group called the Animal Liberation Front (ALF) was the primary suspect."[53] A memo from the Charlotte, North Carolina, FBI office has the subject heading, "People for the Ethical Treatment of Animals (PETA) and Animal Liberation Front (ALF); Domestic Security" and discusses PETA demonstrations against corporations that use animals in research testing. "U.S. Surgical [corporation] has apparently been the target of a PETA demonstration and action. U.S. Surgical currently has a $1.5 million grant relationship with Duke University research and development, Durham, North Carolina. [text redacted] recently learned that Jeanie Rausch, executive director of PETA, has stated that her organization has a disgruntled employee source at the Duke research and development center and that PETA plans to discredit Duke University due to its relationship with U.S. Surgical. [text redacted] would contact the Duke University Department of Public Safety and make them aware of the above information."[54]

In preparations for the 1984 Democratic Party convention in San Francisco, the local police and FBI conducted a massive spying program on more than 100 Bay Area political groups, including the ACLU, gay groups, and labor unions.[55] In another case, when musician Willie Nelson, actor Robin Williams and several other entertainers gave a benefit concert in 1987 to raise funds for the legal defense of Leonard Peltier, the Los Angeles FBI office sought retribution. They sent agents to local radio stations requesting they cease to play Nelson's music.[56]

Reading habits became suspect under the Library Awareness Program. Conducted from 1982 to 1988, the FBI visited both private and public libraries in ten states to enlist librarians to spy on patrons. The FBI wanted information on readers who accessed public government documents about scientific and technological issues. During Congressional hearings, Representative Don Edwards (D-CA) articulated the fundamental problem with such monitoring: "The FBI should recognize that libraries and books and reading are special. In our nation libraries are sacred institutions that should be protected and nurtured. Going into libraries and asking librarians to report on suspicious users has ominous implications for freedom of speech and privacy." When library groups and individual librarians protested the surveillance program, these critics were subjected to investigation to see if they were collaborating with Soviet agents. At least 266 FBI background checks were conducted in 1989, according to Herbert Forestel, who wrote a critical book on the FBI program and was one of those under investigation.[57]

At a Brooklyn Public Library, an agent told a librarian to "look out for suspicious-looking people who wanted to overthrow the government." She should write down the books they read and call the Bureau. At a public library in Fort Lauderdale, Florida, an agent told the librarian, "We know for a fact that there are agitators in this area who are using the library for information." At three university libraries (Pennsylvania State University, the University of Wisconsin at Madison and the University of Michigan) the FBI had specific targets in mind, asking librarians to track the reading habits of Russian scholars. On at least 30 occasions the FBI tried to recruit librarians as paid informants.[58] The legacy of distrust between librarians and the FBI was evident in later years, as one librarian wrote in the *American Libraries* magazine. "Most online catalogs don't retain histories of patron use because once upon a time (about ten years ago) the FBI was leaning hard on libraries to release that information to them. . . That is why so many states have patron confidentiality laws. One rule of thumb is if it can be subpoenaed, it needs to be destroyed."[59]

Surveillance of Right-Wing Groups

Although a right-wing ideologue, Reagan turned the FBI's attention to a variety of small white supremacist groups with ties to violent crimes, including bank robberies and the assassination of Jewish radio personality Alan Berg. For the federal government, an ideology of radical "whiteness" posed a threat only when it became associated with violence and revolution. In 1985, 52 agents worked full-time investigating Aryan Nations, Christian Identity and neo-Nazi groups. One informer claimed there were "dozens" of undercover operatives inside Aryan Nations. The surveillance reached into prison, where from 1982 to 1989 the FBI investigated a California gang known as the Aryan Brotherhood.[60] Overall, more than 100 white supremacists were indicted for crimes between 1980 and 1989, effectively decimating the leadership of many of these groups. The FBI arrested Richard Butler, head of the Aryan Nations, for sedition after advocating in a speech the violent overthrow of the government. Robert J. Mathews, the founder of the Order, engaged in several crimes, became a fugitive, and died in a shootout with the FBI. His group emerged in 1983 as the most violent of all the right-wing organizations in response to the fatal police shooting of right-wing leader Gordon Kahl of the Sheriff's Posse Comitatus. Members of the Christian Identity movement interpreted Kahl's death as extreme government repression that justified violence on their part.[61]

The FBI opened an investigation of the neo-Nazi National Alliance in 1984.

At least six field offices monitored Alliance activities. They focused surveillance on William Pierce, a guru figure on the extreme right. Putting him under surveillance proved useful as a way to keep a watch on others. The legal basis of the investigation was advocacy of violence. The Alliance continued to speak about the need for racial conflict as a prelude to some vague notion of a white power revolution. The FBI focused on the fictional *The Turner Diaries*, describing the book as "a guide and 'bible' for members." The group's headquarters in Mill Point, West Virginia, came under heavy surveillance, as did Alliance activities in at least 11 other cities. While many Alliance members owned guns, the FBI was unable to pin any illegal weapons charges on them. Nonetheless, several FBI memos contain the following warning: "All individuals in this investigation should be considered armed and dangerous with unlimited ammunition and weapons, and appropriate caution should be exercised during any phase of investigation. Additionally, be advised of possible threats by [text redacted] members toward FBI personnel." The Alliance file includes membership lists, photographs, license plate numbers, phone numbers, correspondence, financial records, and political pamphlets. On one occasion a FBI agent in Mill Point followed an Alliance member to a local garbage dump and retrieved a large cache of internal group documents.[62]

The FBI file on the loosely organized Sheriff's Posse Comitatus, based in the rural mid-West, totals 2,147 pages with records between 1980 and 1986. Founded in 1969 by Henry Beach, the group believed the nation's founders wanted to establish a Christian Republic and that no legitimate law enforcement authority existed above the county sheriff. They advocated abolishing the tax system and voiced strong anti-Semitic and anti-black views. The FBI identified all of its chapters, gathered information about the group's finances, and recruited informers from within. The Director outlined at least seven aspects to the investigation in a memo to the Minneapolis field office.

Identification of all chapters; (2) Identification of all leaders and violence prone members; (3) Specific actions taken by members of the SPC which would justify continuation of the DS/T [Domestic Security/Terrorism] matter; (4) Information regarding finances; (5) Reports of informants and/or identification of individuals who may be targeted as informants against the SPC; (6) Results of contacts with local law enforcement officials; (7) Threat assessments of the various chapters based on the above information.[63]

When white supremacist Louis Beam, promoter of the idea of a "leaderless resistance," organized a weeklong gathering at Hayden Lake, Idaho, in July 1984, about 100 people attended, a virtual who's-who of the extreme right. About 60 of these people are mentioned in declassified FBI files, of whom eight subsequently were convicted for various crimes.[64]

By the end of the decade, a Senate Intelligence Committee report stated that spying on peaceful protests had become a "fairly routine practice." The U.S. House Subcommittee on Civil and Constitutional Rights found that the Reagan

Administration used FBI undercover operatives as a standard practice.[65] Funding for the FBI almost tripled during the 1980s, rising from $621 million to about $1.7 billion.[66] The FBI's long history of preserving the secrecy of their records remained in tact. When the Government Accounting Office (GAO) issued the first report ever to examine the FBI's program to counter international terrorism, the FBI refused to give the GAO full access to its files so it was unable to determine the extent of FBI violations or misconduct. The GAO found a large number of investigations for the period 1982 to 1988–approximately 19,500 separate investigations and any single investigation can include one or many people. About 60 percent focused on immigrants or immigrant groups living in the U.S with a large amount of attention to Arab-American organizations critical of U.S. support for Israel.[67]

Conclusion

In 1978, civil liberties attorney and author Frank Donner asked in *The Nation* magazine, "Has the FBI really changed?"[68] Reagan's policies answered that question negatively. After a brief effort to end political policing under Ford and Carter, the government embraced it once again without much consideration for civil liberties. As the Cold War raged, the FBI continued to believe that the Soviet Union was spreading its influence through groups tied to the American Communist Party. They conducted surveillance and disruption against subjects who challenged U.S. policy. Despite vocal anti-statist rhetoric for domestic policy, represented in such slogans as "government is the problem" and "get government off our backs," the Reagan Administration increased the political power of the federal government to fight social movements.

Reagan ushered in a major change by deliberately linking domestic dissent to terrorism. This labeling proved to be lasting, adopted by his post-Cold War successors who gradually replaced the top-down fear of communism with the fear of terrorism. By stigmatizing many forms of lawful protest, the American state advanced ultra-conservative political goals. The significance of this change should not be underestimated. In popular political culture, the terrorist came to be viewed as the horrible Other, who "becomes the paradigm of inhuman bestiality, the quintessential prescribed or tabooed figure our time." [69] The "terror" in terrorism implies fear, fright, horror, panic, and the breakdown of all norms. Political leaders speak of "the unspeakable act of terrorism." Its perpetrators are wild and savage; they transgress everything and favor systematic disorder. If the government used the more neutral term "political violence," the threat would not loom as so significant a social phenomena or require such dramatic departures from democratic traditions to respond to it.

Official repression is the logical outcome of such labeling. Government violations of civil liberties become necessary to fight and contain this monster. The designation of political dissidents as dangerous outsiders is part of a scapegoating process and reminds others to "stay in line."[70] The construction of enemies is needed for elites to maintain social control. Robert S. Robins and Jerold M. Post write: "Because enemies are necessary for self definition, it is necessary to have enemies in our midst . . . An important aspect of the development of group identity is symbols of difference shared by the other–symbols on which to project hatred."[71]

As the Administration came to a close, academic and popular writers began to note the emergence of an American "surveillance society." The increased role for FBI spying endangered the privacy of individuals, as did new surveillance technologies utilized by both government and the private sector. In the digital information age, these powerful entities increased recordkeeping on Americans by building computer databases on a wide range of activity. They also deployed electronic "eyes" or monitoring in public places and at the workplace. In 1987, the Congressional Office of Technology Assessment issued a report, "'The Electronic Supervisor," at the request of Don Edwards. Edwards told the *New York Times*, "'We are becoming a surveillance society.'"[72] Writing in 1988, sociologist Gary T. Marx claimed the U.S. was heading toward a society in which "the line between the public and private is obliterated; we are under constant observation, everything goes on a permanent record, and much of what we say, do, and even feel may be known and recorded by others we do not know. Data from widely separated geographical areas, organizations, and time periods can be merged and analyzed easily."[73] Most of the new surveillance was done without popular knowledge or approval and this "transparency" is not democratic: As ordinary people's lives are opened up for scrutiny, the same cannot be said for elites. While the authoritarian potential of the new surveillance may not directly affect most citizens within democratic societies, its impact would be felt disproportionately by political dissidents, minorities, and the poor.[74] Moreover, computerized informational systems increasingly became available to the FBI for political intelligence objectives.

Under Reagan dozens of major government databases gathered information on such matters as citizen finances; passport and voter registration; social security benefits and unemployment insurance; and many other forms of governmental assistance. In a major new development, the federal government began to conduct "computer matching" to merge data within separate databases often for punitive purposes. For example, Reagan ordered the Internal Revenue Service (IRS) to use its computerized records to help the Selective Service identify youth who failed to register for the military draft. Such punitive record matching was not entirely new. During the late 1960s and early 1970s, government joined FBI files and IRS files to conduct politically motivated tax audits. But Reagan's initiatives accelerated the trend toward informational social control. By the mid-1990s, the federal government relied on computer matching in hundreds of programs.[75]

In later years, private industry constructed vast computerized databases on Americans and shared this information with the intelligence community. For example, after 9/11 the Florida company, Seisint used their vast data—they hold some 20 billion records on Americans—to tag certain people as having a "High

Terrorist Factor." Seisint gave the FBI a list of 120,000 names it believed posed a risk to public safety.[76] The roots of this development again date to the 1980s with the innovation of digital credit and banking records based on the development of the ATM machine and "smart card" technology. Private companies had began to engage in "data mining" by merging all these records and selling information in the marketplace. By 1990, a survey of U. S. agencies identified six which sourced data from the private sector, including the computer credit records on over 100 million Americans.[77]

From a civil liberty perspective, mass data surveillance rivaled any threat depicted in George Orwell's seminal novel *1984*, although Orwell could not imagine such informational systems of control writing from the vantage point of the late 1940s. The full formation of the American surveillance society was evident by the year 2000. As Reg Whitaker observed in *The End of Privacy*, "The technical scope of surveillance today and in the immediate future has far surpassed the capacities of the totalitarian states of the immediate past."[78] While the level of violence did not compare to these states, the ability to conduct mass surveillance in a myriad of forms was unparallel in human history developing in the absence of effective privacy and data protection laws.

The end of the Cold War did not reduce the level of FBI spying. There was no "peace dividend." Both Presidents Bill Clinton and George W. Bush built on Reagan-era security policy to demonize dissent under the banner of national security. Clinton expanded FBI power after the 1995 Oklahoma City bombing carried out by Timothy McVeigh and Bush responded to the 9/11 attacks by initiating a long War on Terrorism. The enhanced power to investigate political activity deliberately sought to silence outspoken voices for social justice. While the free speech of Americans is protected under the Constitution, the Bureau nonetheless found reasons to spy on thousands of innocent individuals. All Presidents struggle to balance the relationship between national security and constitutional rights, but Reagan heavily tipped the scales away from protections for freedom of political expression.

Notes

My thanks to Michael Ravnitzky, Dolores Greenberg, and Nancy C. Carnevale for their comments on an earlier version of this chapter.

1. Rhodri Jeffrey-Jones, *The FBI: A History* (New Haven: Yale University Press, 2007), 202-203.
2. As late as 1980, the Carter Administration defended the end of political policing. The Attorney General Guidelines for the FBI, known as the Levi Guidelines, were issued by President Ford before he left office and were considered to be effective. As Carter's Attorney General Benjamin R. Civiletti testified, "I believe the experience of the last three years with the Levi Guidelines has been highly encouraging. It has demonstrated

that guidelines can be drawn which are well understood by Bureau personnel and by the public and which can be filed and reviewed by the appropriate congressional committees." FBI Director William H. Webster noted in a speech, "From two important standpoints, these Guidelines have been effective. Since their introduction four years ago, there has not been a single successful tort claim against any special Agent of the FBI for violation of a citizen's constitutionally protected rights. This record is matched by a steady decline in terrorist bombings." (Statement of Benjamin R. Civiletti, U.S. House of Representatives, "FBI Charter Bill Hearings," 1979-1980, 4; William H. Webster speech before the Atlanta Bar Association, Oct. 17, 1980, Clarence M. Kelley FBI File.) The legal basis for the unleashing of the FBI was put in place in 1981 with Executive Order 12333 and in 1983 with the imposition of Attorney General William French Smith's Guidelines for the FBI, which replaced the Levi Guidelines. Reagan empowered the Bureau to start investigations of political activity based on a low standard, which included "advocating violence." In 1984, a federal appeals court in a 6 to 1 ruling upheld the Smith Guidelines. (Geoffrey R. Stone, "The Reagan Administration, the First Amendment, and FBI Domestic Security Investigations," in *Freedom At Risk: Secrecy, Censorship, and Repression in the 1980s,* ed., Richard O. Curry (Philadelphia: Temple University Press, 1988), 276-283; Eve Pell, *The Big Chill: How the Reagan Administration, Corporate America, and Religious Conservatives are Subverting Free Speech and the Public's Right to Know* (Boston: Beacon Press, 1984), 190-194; "FBI Spying Is Permitted," *Washington Post,* Aug. 11, 1984.

3. The Subcommittee's staff counsel, Samuel T. Francis, worked as a policy analyst for the conservative Heritage Foundation and recommended the Reagan administration vastly increase surveillance of dissent. Pell, *The Big Chill,* 191; Stone, "The Reagan Administration, the First Amendment, and FBI Domestic Security Investigations," 277; Chip Berlet and Matthew N. Lyons, *Right-Wing Populism in America: Too Close for Comfort* (New York: Guilford Press, 2000), 224-225.

4. "Aryeh Neier Reviews," *Bulletin of Atomic Scientists,* March 1982, 31-32.

5. Victor Navasky, "The New Boys on Terrorism," *San Francisco Chronicle,* Feb. 14, 1981; Pell, *The Big Chill,* 191.

6. Quoted in Bob Woodward, *Veil: The Secret Wars of the CIA 1981-1987* (New York: Simon & Schuster, 1987), 38-39.

7. Philip B. Heymann, *Terrorism and America: A Commonsense Strategy for a Democratic America* (Cambridge: MIT Press, 1998), 148; Interview with Frank Varelli, Fund for Open Information and Accountability, n.d.; "FBI Broke into Group's Office, Informant Tells Subcommittee," *Chicago Tribune,* Feb. 22, 1987. See also Ross Gelbspan, *Break-ins, Death Threats and the FBI: The Covert War Against the Central America Movement* (Boston: South End Press, 1991); Diarmuid Jeffreys, *The Bureau: Inside the Modern FBI* (New York: Houghton Mifflin, 1995), 253-254.

8. Jinsoo Kim, "Government Surveillance and Erosion of the Fourth Amendment: The CISPES Investigation," paper presented at "Ending the Cold War at Home" conference, American Civil Liberties Union, 1991.

9. Jeffreys, *The Bureau,* 253-254; SAC Chicago to Director, June 15, 1984, "Committee in Solidarity with the People of El Salvador (CISPES)," National Archives FBI file.

10. Jeffreys, *The Bureau,* 253-254.

11. FBI memo, "Transfer of Records to the National Archives and Records Administration (NARA)," Feb. 22 1991, National Archives FBI file. See also James X. Dempsey

and David Cole, *Terrorism and the Constitution: Sacrificing Civil Liberties in the Name of National Security* (New York: The New Press, 1992), 29-30.

12. Quoted in Whitfield Diffie and Susan Landau, *Privacy on the Line: The Politics of Wiretapping and Encryption* (Cambridge: MIT Press, 1998), 147-148.

13. Oliver "Buck" Revell and Dwight Williams, *A G-Man's Journal: A Legendary Career Inside the FBI* (New York: Pocket Books, 1998), 293.

14. Christian Smith, *Resisting Reagan: The U.S. Central America Peace Movement* (Chicago: University of Chicago Press, 1996), 76-80, 282-285.

15. Boston FBI report, "Pledge of Resistance Network, Vermont-New Hampshire, Witness for Peace," Dec. 31, 1984; SAC Albany to Director, March 5, 1985. Witness for Peace FBI file.

16. Smith, *Resisting Reagan*, 60, 78, 81-86.

17. Gelbspan, *Break-ins, Death Threats and the FBI*, 16.

18. SAC Chicago to Director, Feb. 24, 1986; SAC Boston to Director, June 25, 1985; SAC Indianapolis to Director, May 14, 1985. Pledge of Resistance FBI file.

19. SAC San Diego to Director, June 13, 1985. Pledge of Resistance FBI file.

20. SAC Boston to Director, May 9, 1985. Pledge of Resistance FBI file.

21. SAC Louisville to Director, June 13, 1985. Pledge of Resistance FBI file.

22. Smith, *Resisting Reagan*, 285, 290, 310-311. The FBI also investigated the group Quest for Peace, which provided humanitarian aid to Nicaragua. Richard O. Curry, "Introduction," in *Freedom at Risk*, ed. Curry, 19-20.

23. Athan G. Theoharis, *Spying on Americans Political Surveillance from Hoover to the Huston Plan* (Philadelphia: Temple University Press, 1978), 46, 56.

24. John Lofland, *Polite Protestors: The American Peace Movement of the 1980s* (Syracuse: Syracuse University Press, 1993), 139, 254-255.

25. Gelbspan, *Break-ins, Death Threats and the FBI*, 90.

26. Nat Hentoff, "Someone to Watch Over Us," *Washington Post*, June 19, 1984.

27. David Cortright email to Ivan Greenberg, Aug. 23, 1999. Cortright was executive director of SANE in the 1980s. He remembers that right-wing groups tried to portray the Freeze movement as communist-led, and linked him to this alleged conspiracy. Yet, he does not recall FBI surveillance of the Freeze. "I'm not aware of any evidence or files on FBI surveillance on the freeze movement. Such evidence probably exists, but we never thought to check into it. Government surveillance is not something that came up in our conversations and planning. We always operated very openly, so there was probably no need for FBI [secret] spying. They could have learned everything they wanted to know by coming to meetings or reading our newsletter and reports . . . There was probably extensive surveillance of the various international delegations that we organized, including the early trips to the USSR, and the later delegation to Geneva for the Reagan-Gorbachev summit."

28. "Soviet Role in Nuclear Freeze Limited, FBI Says," *Washington Post*, March 26, 1983; "Reagan Again Says Soviet Union Influences anti-Nuclear Groups," *Washington Post*, Dec. 11, 1982.

29. "Soviet Role in Nuclear Freeze Limited, FBI Says"; Pell, *The Big Chill*, 190-199.

30. Hentoff, "Someone to Watch Over Us."

31. Brian Glick, *War at Home: Covert Action Against U.S. Activists and What We Can Do About It* (Boston: South End Press, 1989), 1-2; Jack Anderson, "Navy Infiltrates Group Opposing Nuclear Arms," *Washington Post*, Jan. 28, 1984; Barbara Epstein, *Po-*

litical Protest and Cultural Revolution: Nonviolent Direct Action in the 1970s and 1980s (Berkeley: University of California Press), 130-131.

32. Ryan also wrote: "I personally find certain actions and positions presently being taken by our government, in particular relating to Central America, as violent, illegal and immoral. While I do not condone the use of illegal actions by anyone to oppose this position of our government, I realize such acts are often effective and have a longstanding tradition in our country's history, i.e., the Boston Tea Party, Civil Rights marches in the South, etc. and are especially effective because the perpetrators are usually willing to face the consequences of their illegal acts." "An FBI Dissenter," by Jack Ryan, Political Research Associates, 1994, 1; "Firing of Pacifist FBI Agent Upheld," *Chicago Tribune*, Jan 23, 1991.

33. Fred A. Wilcox, *Uncommon Martyrs: The Berrigans, the Catholic Left, and the Plowshares Movement* (Reading: Addison-Wesley, 1991), 205-231; Lofland, *Polite Protestors*, 35, 152.

34. Catherine Valcke, "Civil Disobedience and the Rule of Law–A Lockean Insight," in *The Rule of Law*, ed., Ian Shapiro (New York: New York University Press, 1994), 45-59.

35. This is the conclusion of Epstein, *Political Protest and Cultural Revolution*; Lofland, *Polite Protestors*; and Smith, *Resisting Reagan*. Hoover's surveillance of the peace movement is discussed in Robbie Lieberman, *The Strangest Dream: Communism, Anticommunism and the Peace Movement, 1945-1963* (Syracuse: Syracuse University Press, 2000).

36. Herbert Mitgang, *Dangerous Dossiers: Exposing the Secret War Against America's Greatest Authors* (New York: Donald I. Fine Books, 1988), 293.

37. Most of the Sierra Club file focuses on a lawsuit, *Environmental Defense Fund, Inc., et al. v. Environmental Protection Agency and William D. Ruckelshaus.*

38. Meghan Houlihan email to Ivan Greenberg, Oct. 18, 1999.

39. FBI Director to Legal Attache, Paris, Oct. 18, 1985. Greenpeace FBI file.

40. Acting Director to Washington field office, Sept. 24, 1987. Greenpeace FBI file.

41. Anchorage office to Director, July 23, 1983. Greenpeace FBI file.

42. "Special Rapporteur's Mission Report to USA," United Nations Commission on Human Rights, Jan. 16, 1995, 14. www1.umn.edu/humanrts/commission/country51/78add1.htm (accessed Sept 14, 2009).

43. Michael Parenti, *Land of Idols: Political Mythology in America* (New York: St. Martin's Press, 1994), 140.

44. David J. Langum, *William M. Kunstler: The Most Hated Lawyer in America* (New York: New York University Press, 1999), 265-266. On the Marion Barry case, see Clarence Lusane, *Pipe Dream Blues: Racism and the War on Drugs* (Boston: South End Press, 1991): 142, 165-167, 186-191.

45. Kenneth O'Reilly, *Hoover and the UnAmericans: The FBI, HUAC, and the Red Menace* (Philadelphia: Temple University Press, 1983), 217.

46. Glick, *War at Home*, 2.

47. Ward Churchill and Jim Vander Wall, *The COINTELPRO Papers: Documents from the FBI's Secret Wars Against Dissent in the United States* (Boston: South End Press, 1990), 310.

48. Hentoff, "Someone to Watch Over Us."

49. Stanford J. Ungar, "The FBI on Defensive Again," *New York Times*, March 15, 1988.

50. "N.Y. Bomb Probe Seeks Clues From '91 Trial," *Washington Post*, March 21, 1993.

51. Dempsey and Cole, *Terrorism and the Constitution,* 52-53; "AIDS Groups Aware of FBI Spies," *Associated Press*, May 15, 1995.

52. James Wentzy email to Ivan Greenberg, Sept. 2, 1999.

53. FBI Director to Legat Paris, Nov. 27, 1990. PETA FBI file

54. SAC Charlotte to FBI Director, Aug. 2, 1992. PETA FBI file.

55. Dempsey and Cole, *Terrorism and the Constitution*, 85.

56. Ward Churchill and Jim Vander Wall, *Agents of Repression The FBI's Secret Wars Against the Black Panther Party and the American Indian Movement* (Boston: South End Press, 1988), 379.

57. Herbert N. Forestel, *Surveillance in the Stacks: The FBI's Library Awareness Program* (New York: Greenwood Press, 1991), 4-5, 14, 30, 112-115

58. Natalie Robins, *Alien Ink: The FBI's War on Freedom of Expression* (New York: William Morrow, 1992), 380-389.

59. Karen G. Schneider, "So They Won't Hate To Wait: Time Control for Workstations," *American Libraries*, Dec. 1998, 2.

60. "The FBI on Defensive Again" Thomas Martinez, *Brotherhood of Murder* (New York: McGraw Hill, 1988), 213. The FBI file on the Aryan Brotherhood is 141 pages.

61. Brent L. Smith, *Terrorism in America: Pipe Bombs and Pipe Dreams* (New York: State University of New York Press, 1994), 13-14, 19, 25-26; Kevin J. Flynn, *The Silent Brotherhood: Inside America's Racist Underground* (New York: Free Press, 1989): 87-89; Morris Dees, *Gathering Storm: America's Militia Threat* (New York: HarperCollins, 1996), 43.

62. FBI memo, Cincinnati office, June 3, 1985; FBI memo, Pittsburgh office, Sept. 10, 1987; FBI memo, Washington office, Sept. 22, 1987. National Alliance FBI file.

63. Director to Minneapolis field office, Nov. 21, 1983. Sheriff's Posse Comitatus FBI File.

64. Daniel Levitas, *The Terrorist Next Door: The Militia Movement and the Radical Right* (New York: Macmillan, 2002), 294.

65. Dempsey and Cole, *Terrorism and the Constitution*, 55; Churchill and Vander Wall, *Agents of Repression*, 376-378.

66. Athan G. Theoharis, ed., *The FBI: A Comprehensive Guide* (New York: Oryx Press, 1999), 5.

67. "Report Cites F.B.I.'s Following of Terrorist Suspects," *New York Times*, Oct. 9, 1990.

68. Frank J. Donner, "The Terrorist as Scapegoat," *Nation*, May 20, 1978. Donner authored two early books on domestic spying, *The Age of Surveillance: The Aims and Methods of America's Political Intelligence System* (New York: Random House, 1980) and *Protectors of Privilege: Red Squads and Police Repression in Urban America* (Berkeley: University of California Press, 1990).

69. Joseba Zuliaka and William A. Douglas, *Terror and Taboo: The Foibles, Fables, and Face of Terrorism* (New York: Routledge, 1996), 6, 29, 149-150, 158-160, 189. See also Edward Herman and Gerry O'Sullivan, *The "Terrorism" Industry: The Experts and Institutions That Shape Our View of Terror* (New York: Pantheon Books, 1989); and Corey Robin, *Fear: The History of a Political Idea* (Oxford: Oxford University Press, 2004).

70. Gary T. Marx, "External Efforts to Damage or Facilitate Social Movements: Some

Patterns, Explanations, and Complications," in *The Dynamics of Social Movements*, Mayer N. Zald and John David McCarthy, eds., (Cambridge: Winthrop Publishers, 1979), 117.

71. Robert S. Robbins and Jerold M. Post, *Political Paranoia: The Psychopolitics of Hatred* (New Haven: Yale University Press, 1997), 91-92.

72. "Report Says Computers Spy On 7 Million Workers in U.S.," *New York Times*, Sept. 28, 1987.

73. Gary T. Marx, *Undercover: Police Surveillance in America* (Berkeley: University of California Press, 1988), 221.

74. David Lyon, *The Electronic Eye: The Rise of a Surveillance Society* (Minneapolis: University of Minnesota Press, 1994), 88. See also William G. Staples, *The Culture of Surveillance: Discipline and Social Control in the United States* (New York: St. Martin's Press, 1998).

75. David H. Flaherty, *Protecting Privacy in Surveillance Societies* (Chapel Hill: University of North Carolina Press, 1989), 344-355; Christian Parenti, *The Soft Cage: Surveillance in America, From Slavery to the War on Terrorism* (New York: Basic Books, 2004), 165-67; William G. Staples, "Surveillance and Social Control In Postmodern Life," in *Punishment and Social Control,* Thomas G. Bloomberg and Stanley Cohen, eds., (New York: Walterde Gruyter, 2003), 191; John A. Andrew III, *Power to Destroy: the Political Uses of the IRS from Kennedy to Nixon* (Chicago: Ivan R. Dee, 2002); Roger Clarke, "Computer Matching by Government Agencies: The Failure of Cost/Benefit Analysis as a Control Mechanism," *Information Infrastructure and Policy,* 4 (March 1995), 29-65.

76. Under President George W. Bush, financial institutions also were compelled to report any suspicious activity to the special U.S. Treasury Department agency termed Fin-Cen. By 2003, about 300,000 suspicious activity reports were shared with the FBI, which literally "interrogated the data." In 2008, FinCen shared more than 1.2 million reports with the Bureau. Robert O'Horrow, Jr., *No Place to Hide* (New York: The Free Press, 2005), 98-102, 260, 262, 266; "Reclaiming Patriotism: A Call to Reconsider the Patriot Act," American Civil Liberties Union, March 2009, 13.

77. Parenti, *The Soft Cage*, 96-100, 106; *Computers and Privacy: How the Government Obtains, Verifies, Uses and Protects Personal Data*, United States General Accounting Office, Aug 1990, 30.

78. Reg Whitaker, *The End of Privacy: How Total Surveillance is Becoming a Reality* (New York: New Press, 2000), 4. Whitaker, unlike most writers on the surveillance society, also sees possibilities for resistance and progressive networking. See also Daniel J. Solove, *The Digital Person: Technology and Privacy in the Information Age* (New York: New York University Press, 2004) and Gary T. Marx, "Electric Eye in the Sky: Some Reflections on the New Surveillance and Popular Culture," in *Computers, Surveillance and Privacy,* David Lyon and Elia Zureik, eds., (Minneapolis: University of Minnesota Press, 1996), 193-236.

Chapter 3

The "Real" Right Turn:
The Reagan Supreme Court

Scott A. Merriman

With the election of Ronald Reagan to the White House, the U.S. government developed an increasingly conservative face in the 1980s. At the public level, some of this attitude represented conservative backlash against perceived erosion of moral standards throughout the 1970s. Things like the gay and lesbian revolution, increased feminism, the rising crime rate, and the rising divorce rate were lumped together by the religious right and trotted out as proving the increased need for Christianity. Conservative religious groups like the Moral Majority backed Reagan's bid for the White House, and his election brought growing legislative acceptance of their viewpoints. Over the course of his eight years in office, Reagan sought to bring conservative change to the nation at a number of levels.

In the legal sphere, Reagan sought to change the make-up of the Supreme Court to correct the perceived mistakes made by "liberal" courts of the 1950s, 1960s, and 1970s. Similar to what Richard Nixon had done a decade before, Reagan and other conservatives blamed the judicial branch for a rise in crime because of decisions granting defendants the right to counsel and mandating the reading of the *Miranda* v. *Arizona* (1966) warning to anyone placed under arrest. They painted the Supreme Court as activist, suggesting it had overreached its goals and started legislating, rather than simply interpreting the Constitution. In particular, Reagan hoped to appoint conservative justices who would overturn the controversial *Roe* v. *Wade* (1973) decision. He also promised to appoint a female Supreme Court justice, and did so in the person of Sandra Day O'Connor. Ultimately, his appointees and the decisions they made and influenced both reflected and intensified the conservative trend of the 1980s, but did not lead the successful counter-revolution he wanted. As the Chief Justiceship changed hands in the mid-1980s, the court might be best examined as the Reagan Supreme Court, rather than as the Burger Court or the Rehnquist Court.[1]

The left-leaning Warren Court, which had existed from 1954 to 1969, received much of the focus of the Reagan Court's attempted right turn. Chief Justice Earl Warren[2] was probably best known for his opinion in *Brown* v. *Board of Education* (1954) and other civil rights rulings, but most mainstream conservatives did not directly attack him for those rulings. The Warren Court also ordered the redrawing of state legislative districts, holding that each vote had to be equal in state elections. Although this provoked a lot of controversy at the time, it also brought relatively little effort to reverse it fifteen years later in the Reagan Administration.[3] Instead, Reagan and his advisors, many affiliated with the religious right, criticized decisions that eventually led to public school busing in the 1970s and 1980s.

Criminal justice and prayer in the public schools were other areas that caused conservatives to become irate. Many critics argued that Warren and his colleagues were too soft on crime, as the court had extended the right of counsel to indigent defendants in 1963 and had required that police officers read defendants their rights in the famous Miranda case of 1966.[4] Conservatives considered such judgments to be detrimental to society because they limited the scope of power previously enjoyed by law enforcement officials. The Warren Court's decision in *Engel* v. *Vitale* in 1963, which banned mandatory prayers at the start of each school day, evoked even more conservative ire. In this case, the justices' ruling was perceived as an attack upon American morality. While the Warren Court had also prohibited Bible readings the year before, the prayer ruling seemed to attract much more attention over time.[5]

In 1969, the Burger Court succeeded the Warren Court, and continued into the Reagan years. This court was generally more acceptable to the right, particularly as its chief justice had been appointed by the conservative president Richard Nixon. However, the court did issue the *Roe* v. *Wade* decision, which legalized abortions in the first trimester all across the country and produced probably the most outcry of any case since *Brown* v. *Board*. However, unlike *Brown* v. *Board*, the controversy surrounding *Roe* v. *Wade* persisted for decades across the entire nation. Reversing *Roe* became one of the Reagan administration's two main goals, with the other being, as noted, to make the court more conservative.[6]

Appointing a female justice was a campaign promise that President Reagan fulfilled when he appointed Sandra Day O'Connor as the first female justice on the Supreme Court. He also appointed the conservative Antonin Scalia to the court in 1986, when he elevated William H. Rehnquist to be Chief Justice. O'Connor was usually conservative, but she became a strong centrist force on the court. The court did move towards the right, making O'Connor in the center, but O'Connor also was more of a centrist force than those who appointed her would have liked. Reagan was probably more pleased with his choice of Antonin Scalia who was a very reliable conservative, and with his elevation of Rehnquist, who led a generally more conservative court.

Near the end of his presidency, in 1988, Reagan also appointed another person believed to be a conservative, Anthony Kennedy. But Kennedy, like O'Connor, became widely viewed as more a moderate than a strong conservative. The two together thwarted the goals of some conservative politicians, especially in the area of abortion. Both Kennedy and O'Connor were westerners (O'Connor from Arizona and Kennedy from California) and agreed generally that Roe should be upheld. However, Kennedy more believed in a grand theory of liberty, which allowed Roe to stand while O'Connor more focused on the facts and stare decisis, or letting past decisions stand, as reasons to uphold Roe. [7]

Reagan's choices of nominees developed from a variety of needs, though he always sought to place more conservative justices on the bench. His first nominee, Sandra Day O'Connor, was based in Reagan's electioneering. In his 1980 campaign, in order to appear somewhat progressive, he promised to nominate the first woman to the Supreme Court, and O'Connor was a safe choice. She had been active in Republican politics in Arizona and had not rocked the boat there. Additionally, her legal background was impeccable. She had finished Stanford Law School in two years instead of the usual three, and then worked in the state attorney general's office, as a state legislator, and then as a state judge, the position she held at the time of her nomination. O'Connor replaced Potter Stewart, a moderate, so Reagan hoped she would move the court to the right. In Reagan's recollection, O'Connor had admitted that she found abortion "repugnant," while O'Connor claimed that she had not stated her opinion on the issue. The latter view is the more respected one judicially, as justices are not supposed to decide cases before hearing them, while most presidents want to pick justices who agree with them ideologically. With O'Connor's gender, few could safely oppose her, and she had no votes cast against her nomination.[8]

Reagan's next choices, to elevate Rehnquist to Chief Justice upon Burger's retirement and appoint Scalia to replace him as Associate Justice, were mostly controversial due to Rehnquist's background. Rehnquist was the only safe conservative nominee for Reagan in 1986, if he wanted to elevate a current justice. O'Connor had only been on the court a few years and was not as conservative as Rehnquist, and the other justices of the time were all either moderates or liberals. However, Rehnquist was attacked because he had authored a memo supporting segregation in 1952 and 1953, when he served as a law clerk to Robert H. Jackson of the US Supreme Court. In that memo, Rehnquist contended that *Plessy* v. *Ferguson*, which had created the idea of "separate but equal," had been rightly decided. Rehnquist argued in 1971, when he was initially considered as an associate justice, and again in 1986, that he was simply summarizing Justice Jackson's views, not stating his own. Jackson's friends disagreed. Jackson himself was dead by this time, and the evidence of other Justices on the court at the time as to Jackson's initial views on *Brown*, and on whether *Plessy* should be

upheld in 1952, is unclear. Thirty-three senators voted against Rehnquist's nomination, which was significantly more than the number who opposed his successor, John Roberts, in 2005. However, with sixty five supporting, Rehnquist was
still easily approved.[9]

The person nominated to fill Rehnquist's Associate Justice seat, Antonin Scalia, was easily confirmed, with no one voting against his nomination. This was
due, in large part, to how much controversy accompanied the Rehnquist nomination. Scalia's appointment, however, was even more important than that of
Rehnquist, as Scalia effectively replaced Burger on the court and was the one
most responsible for moving the court to the right. His appointment shows that
appointments of regimes in power need to be constant in their opposition, rather
than varied, as failing to oppose Scalia has allowed him to move the court
rightward in his near quarter century on the bench. In defense of those opposed
to Scalia, though, there was no "smoking gun," or, more relevantly, no *Brown*
memo in Scalia's past, as best has been determined, and so some may have
thought that the opposition was irrelevant as even Rehnquist, with his authorship
of the Brown memo, was still handily confirmed. Thus, Scalia and O'Connor
both won easy confirmation and may have lulled Reagan somewhat into a mistake with his next nomination in 1987.[10]

In the summer of 1987, Lewis Powell resigned. Powell was a moderate and so
his replacement was seen as more important than Scalia's appointment the year
before. Many Democrats were also beginning to tire of the Reagan revolution
and so were looking for a chance to challenge him. Reagan ignored these warning signs, though, and nominated someone with impeccable conservative credentials, Robert H. Bork. Bork had served in the Nixon administration, proving
his loyalty by following Nixon's famous 1973 order to fire the special prosecutor who was looking into the Watergate investigation after his two superiors in
the Justice Department resigned rather than obey the President's edict. This was
the infamous "Saturday Night Massacre." In addition to this service, Bork had
been a professor at the Yale Law School and a judge on the United States Court
of Appeals for the District of Columbia Circuit for 5 years.[11]

While on the Court of Appeals, Bork continued building his conservative reputation, and in an opinion announced his disagreement with the Supreme Court's
announced right to privacy. That right, in turn, had been the underpinning of *Roe
v. Wade*, and so this brought him to the attention of the Reagan Administration
and others. Previously, while a professor at Yale, Bork had argued for giving
more control to the government, particularly in areas where legislation might
infringe upon individual liberties. He also argued that judges (and Supreme
Court justices) needed to employ judicial restraint and thus to refrain from striking down laws unless they were clearly and strongly at variance with the Constitution. Between his ideas about increased governmental authority, judicial restraint and privacy, and his deference to Richard Nixon during the Watergate
Crisis, Bork demonstrated to many that he was a strong conservative who would

increase government power and vote to overturn *Roe*. All of this resonated with the Reagan Administration.

Reagan, in turn, tried to sell Bork as a moderate, but opposition groups quickly emerged. Bork did not help his nomination when he argued with the Senate committee overseeing his nomination and when he confrontationally tried to defend his views on *Roe* v. *Wade* and his opposition to a general right to privacy. Besides drawing criticism from Democrats, his behavior was considered pedantic, and his speeches were perceived as lectures to the Congressional leaders charged with approving or denying his appointment. Bork's behavior in front of the committee is still viewed by many as a textbook way of how NOT to handle oneself in such a situation. His nomination failed with a vote of 58 against and 42 in favor.[12] Before Reagan's nomination of Bork, the president to have a Supreme Court nominee rejected was Richard Nixon when both G. Harrold Carswell (1969) and Clement Haynsworth (1970) were rejected.

Reagan followed that selection with Douglas Ginsburg. Ginsburg's nomination was marked by controversy of a different sort. He had admitted previously that he had smoked marijuana during his studies at the University of Chicago Law School and while teaching at Harvard. Ginsburg's use, particularly the fact that it was over several years (including a period while he was a professor), seemed to disqualify him. In fact, such a practice might not have been enough to force his withdrawal if he had been the first candidate, but after the experience with Bork, some seemed to sense blood in the water. The rising opposition and Reagan's pronounced stance against drugs, including Nancy Reagan's authorship of the "Just Say No" (to drugs) campaign, together forced his withdrawal.[13]

Reagan's third choice was Anthony Kennedy, who had served on the Ninth Circuit Court of Appeals since 1975, and who was generally viewed as a moderate. Kennedy had a favorable view towards privacy and gave individual liberty more worth than Bork had done, and so was more of a centrist. These views, along with his lukewarm support of Roe, had led the Reagan administration to not consider him before now. However, by the third choice, Reagan wanted someone who would be sure to be confirmed, and Kennedy was, by a vote of 97 to 0.[14]

Thus, O'Connor and Scalia's appointments changed both the ideological temperament and the makeup of the court, as he appointed the first woman and the first Italian American. Kennedy's appointment did not mark any drastic change in the court that much, but it did allow Reagan, with his three appointees and one promotion, to collectively have a significant impact upon the court.[15]

The Reagan Court decided cases in six significant areas: education, the separation of church and state, state power, discrimination, criminal rights, and abortion. While not all of these decisions showed a rightward move, the general trend was towards a more conservative perspective than what was seen under the 1970s Burger Court, and definitely the trend was towards a more conservative situation than what occurred under the 1950s and 1960s Warren Court. There was not, however, the rightward swerve or u-turn that Reagan and his conservative backers wanted.

The two main Supreme Court decisions relating to state aid to education and the separation of church and state accelerated the already right-leaning decisions made by the Burger Court in the 1970s. *Muller* v. *Allen* (1983) and *Aguilar* v. *Felton* (1985) both dealt with what level of state aid to religious education was allowable. Federal aid to education had been standard since the 1960s, and the Department of Education had been created in 1980 without much constitutional question, as, by the 1980s this governmental prerogative was generally accepted.[16] However, questions remained about whether religious institutions or classes imparting religious content could be eligible for this aid.

The general test used for religious aid throughout the 1980s was the *Lemon* test, named for the case of *Lemon* v. *Kurtzman* (1971). The Lemon test had three parts: "first, the statute must have a secular legislative purpose; second, its principal or primary effect must be one that neither advances nor inhibits religion; finally, the statute must not foster 'an excessive government entanglement with religion.'"[17] By retaining the test, the court demonstrated something of a moderate attitude. A total rightward shift would have eliminated the test and given the government total power in this area. The whole idea of the wall of separation between church and state was considered fairly liberal. Therefore, although conservatives typically wanted less government interference in state and individual activities, they wanted the government to be able to act more freely with regards to religion. Several specific decisions generally continued the policies of the early Burger Court, but allowed a rightward turn.

In the 1982 case of *Mueller* v. *Allen*, the program at issue was a Minnesota state tax deduction for educational expenses. Monies could be spent on either public or private schools, and private schools included both religious and non-religious schools. Thus, money spent on religious education would qualify for tax relief. Not all expenses were allowed, but tuition was, along with transportation and textbooks. Because public education was and is tuition free, most public school parents would not spend enough to qualify for the deduction, or, if they did, they would not receive enough of a refund to make the hassle of claiming the expense worthwhile. Private school parents, in contrast, would frequently qualify for the deduction and would receive enough to make the paperwork worthwhile. The court had to decide whether a program of tax deductions that mostly benefited those who spent money on private religious schools was a violation of the separation of church and state.

The court turned to the *Lemon* test outlined above. Justice Rehnquist wrote the opinion. He held that the secular purpose was one of advancing education by helping to remove a burden on those paying for it, and held that the main effect of the bill was not to advance religion, as the bill applied to all who paid such expenses. The court's majority gave wide latitude to those who wrote the tax code and refused to disallow a tax deduction based on who used the program.

The third prong of the *Lemon* test, that of entanglement, only touched on the program slightly. Deductions for religious textbooks were not allowed, meaning state officials would have to be able to tell which textbooks were religious and which were not to allow individuals' deductions. The vote was close, with four justices dissenting because they felt the program should be cancelled because its main benefit was for those using religious schools. This overall decision continued the Court's conservative trend, and reflected the increased influence of conservative groups throughout the nation. It was the first time that a tax benefit that mostly helped out those paying for religious school was allowed. An earlier program, in a different state, of tax credits available only to those who had children in non-public schools had been struck down in 1973.[18]

The next major case where the Reagan court demonstrated its position in relationship to religion and the public schools was *Aguilar* v. *Felton* (1985). There the court dealt with New York City providing teachers to come to religious schools and help disadvantaged students, similar to how the state sent around teachers to help out similar students in public schools. The teachers were only allowed to help out with non-religious subjects. The courts again turned to the *Lemon* test, in an opinion written by Justice Brennan. However, in this case, the five to four vote struck down the program.

The opinion did not deny a secular purpose or a main benefit for the students, but focused instead on the issue of entanglement. As the teachers were not supposed to assist in any religious subject, there needed to be considerable monitoring which in turn created an entanglement in and of itself. Additionally, one justice noted the possibility for religious strife due to the program and argued that the First Amendment aimed to prevent such strife. This decision did not end remedial education for parochial school children, but largely just moved it off of school grounds.[19] Here, though the court demonstrated slightly more moderate leanings than in the earlier case, the justices Reagan either had appointed or would promote supported the conservative perspective. Associate Justices Rehnquist and O'Connor both dissented (along with Chief Justice Burger and Justice White), arguing that there had been no complaints and that it was actually the court imposed monitoring that created the entanglement, meaning the programs were unconstitutional due to the courts' requirements, not their own designs.

Thus, conservatives, who generally favored religious schools, won a key victory in the area of aid to religious schools early in the Reagan years when tax credits for educational expenses, including religious school expenses, were permitted. However conservatives lost the battle to keep publicly funded aides for disabled students on parochial school grounds. The court maintained the *Lemon test*, and the vote was close in both cases.

Beyond the question of religion's relationship with school funding, larger issues surrounding church-state separation arose during the years of the Reagan Court. The court did not directly roll back the decisions of previous courts, even though some decisions eventually resulted in a lowering of the wall of separa-tion between church and state and an increased involvement of the government in the area of religion. In these cases, the social and political pull exerted by the religious right began to move into the legal sphere.

Just before Reagan came into office, the Supreme Court considered a case that had been moving through the legal system for some time. Several Kentucky families objected to a state law mandating the Ten Commandments be posted in public schools. Although the state used private funds to pay for the posted signs, the families objected that their presence in the schools violated the separation of church and state and that the law represented excessive entanglement of gov-ernment and religion. The court did not even hear arguments on this case, *Stone* v. *Graham* (1980), but five justices issued a per curium ruling, holding that there was no secular purpose for the law. A per curium decision is one authored by all of the agreeing justices jointly rather than by any one justice. The state had claimed that the commandments were the "fundamental legal code" behind the US common law, but the court held that the effect of their posting was undoub-tedly religious and so was not allowed. There were four dissenters, including Rehnquist, but the law was struck down. It would be 2005 before the Supreme Court allowed some public displays of the Ten Commandments to be allowed (while disallowing others), directly lowering the wall of separation between church and state, and these would not be in schools.[20] This is an area where the *Lemon* test caused the court to resist the conservative pull exerted by society. Indeed, the *Lemon* test would consistently draw the court towards moderation when it was applied.

Another direct challenge to the church-state divide came in the 1984 case of *Wallace* v. *Jaffree*. There, Alabama had passed a law requiring a moment of silence at the start of each school day. A number of different purposes were stated for this moment, but the one most questioned was "for meditation or vo-luntary prayer." The Supreme Court, in a 6-3 decision, struck down the statute. Justice Stevens wrote the decision, stating the law's effect was an endorsement of religion. The more important opinion, though, was probably O'Connor's con-currence. Here, she let it be known that, although appointed by a right-wing president, her decisions would be based in constitutional law and legal prece-dence, rather than excessive influence from her political supporters. O'Connor concurred in the judgment only, meaning that she agreed with the result, but not the reasoning. She held that the question was not one of the law's effect, but whether or not the law endorsed religion. This law she held did. She went on to note that the court, in her view, did not ban a moment of silence, which could be used for voluntary silent prayer, but just did not allow the legislature to state that the purpose of the moment was prayer. In the 1990s, just such a statute, allowing a moment of silence without giving any reason for that moment, came in front of the Eleventh Circuit Court of Appeals and was allowed based on the reasoning set forth in O'Connor's 1984 concurrence.[21]

Additionally, the content of public school science classrooms came under conservative fire. Fundamentalists and those who believed in the literal, word for word truth of the Bible, opposed evolution, as that scientific idea argued for an earth that was billions of years old and suggested that one type of animal could change into another. The literalists, on the other hand, held that the earth was 6,000 (or so) years old and that God had created all species at the same time, as noted in the Book of Genesis in the Bible. Thus, it is no surprise that fundamentalists have been trying to pass legislation altering the teaching of evolution for the last hundred years or so. In the 1920s total bans on the teaching of evolution were passed in a few states, but they faced public ridicule after the Scopes Trial in 1925. It took, however, some forty years before the Supreme Court ruled that such bans were illegal religious statements, as the state was endorsing one religion with its supporting of the fundamentalist view.

Not to be deterred, fundamentalists started supporting research into "scientific" support for a 6,000 year old earth. Believing themselves to find some, they grouped this research under the umbrella term of "creation science" and argued that this should be given equal classroom time with evolution, if either was taught at all. Those favoring creation science seemed to understand that straightforward bans on the teaching of evolution or straightforward requirements to teach creation science would not work. Louisiana passed a bill requiring equal teaching, if either was taught, in 1982, and the bill was immediately challenged, coming in front of the Supreme Court in *Edwards* v. *Aguillard* (1987).[22]

By this time, two of Reagan's three nominees had been seated, and the conservative Rehnquist had been promoted to chief justice. However, again legal precedent and the *Lemon* test held sway. The court, in an opinion by Brennan held that there was no secular purpose for the bill. It held that creation science took a religious stand and requiring its teaching was, in turn, religious. Justice Scalia dissented here, holding that those who had religious motives were not automatically wrong, and he stated that the key test was one of whether the legislation's goal was to advance religion. Scalia did not believe that this was the goal here, trusting the legislature when it stated that the goal was the advancement of academic freedom, and so would have allowed the law to be sustained. However, only Chief Justice Rehnquist agreed with this view, and so it did not carry the day.[23] O'Connor voted with the majority. Clearly, political and social forces only had a limited impact on Supreme Court decisions.

Challenges to the separation of church and state outside of schools included a public holiday display. In a 1989 case, *County of Allegheny* v. *ACLU*, the Supreme Court had to decide the relative constitutional merits of a nativity scene placed by itself near a county courthouse and a menorah placed near a Christmas tree near that same courthouse. Now one might not think that it was relevant what was near a nativity scene or a menorah, but the court held, in a close decision, that it was. The court allowed the menorah as it was part of a larger holiday display that did not advance a specific religion, but did not allow the nativity scene, holding that its location, off by itself, presented a religious message. This was relatively in keeping with previous decisions and so the wall of separation between church and state that was recognized by the Warren Court (and the previous Vinson Court) was not lowered by this case.[24] By this time, all three of Reagan's nominees had been seated, and O'Connor and Kennedy were both becoming recognized as moderates, rather than right wing conservatives. This decision generally maintained the relatively strict guidelines preventing government from endorsing religion.

However, other cases in the 1980s addressed how much the government could restrict one's right to express religion. These cases were harder to classify in relationship to political and social leanings. At issue was not whether a state entity promoted religion, but the circumstances under which individuals could express their own religion. The government has generally used a compelling interest test in these cases, holding that the government must have a compelling interest to restrict any First Amendment freedom, which, of course, includes the freedom of religion.

In California, Los Angeles airport commissioners had adopted a regulation banning all First Amendment activities in the airport. Their goal was to eliminate the various people that asked for donations. However, the ban was, obviously, very broad, covering religious proselytizers and people doing surveys and it technically even banned people talking. The overall policy was challenged and came in front of the court in 1987 in the case *Airport Commissioners* v. *Jews for Jesus*. This case placed differing conservative goals against one another, as general conservative attitudes suggested that the wall separating church and state was a liberal construction, but also argued that individual freedom of religion was enshrined in the constitution.

The court held that the regulation was far too broad and that total bans were almost never allowed, particularly when they could not be safely constitutionally narrowed. Regulations, some justices hinted, might have been constitutional, but not total bans. Thus, the court supported the rights of constitutional minorities, those who wanted free speech, and religious groups. It maintained the wall of separation between church and state and supported individual religious expression. The overall effect was to impose a federal limit on a state's government power.[25]

Concerning the area of religion, most conservatives have favored allowing governmental programs to support religion and have desired a rollback of the Warren Court decisions banning school prayer and emphasizing a separation of church and state. The 1980s court, however, generally did not move in the conservative direction to any great extent, although it did set the grounds for a later decision allowing moments of silence as long as they were not expressly created for allowing prayer. In general, this shows that societal and political forces may only have a slow impact on the Court, as its members are appointed for life and typically serve through several presidential administrations.

Besides religion and education, the Supreme Court also considered cases dealing with governmental power. Conservatives do not generally favor allowing a strong government. They believed that state and federal governments had grown too big and had undertaken a number of unconstitutional actions. The conservatives wanted support from the Supreme Court that would have narrowed government's role. However, Supreme Court decisions in the 1980s only minimally decreased that power.

In 1983, the Court examined the constitutionality of some Congressional acts. Congress had stated that Immigration and Naturalization Services (INS) could be prevented from deporting an individual if doing so would have created "extreme hardship" for the deportee. A person had to gain support from only the House of Representatives or the Senate to veto the deportation and be allowed to remain in the country based on the "extreme hardship" standard. The Constitution does not directly state anything about immigration policy, though it does specify that Congress can set it. It also states that *presidential* vetoes can only be overridden by a 2/3 majority in *both* houses. The question for the court, then, was whether this meant that the Constitution intended all vetoes to pass through both houses.

In *INS* v. *Chadha* (1983), the Court issued its ruling. Noting that the intent of having both houses was to maintain a balance of power, the court ruled that a one-house veto of any sort was unconstitutional.[26] This directly rolled back Congress' power and was somewhat of a victory for the conservatives. However, not that much legislation had a direct one-house legislative veto, and so its practical power was somewhat limited and other legislative actions have taken its place.

Later in the decade, the Court voted to maintain a strong government when conservatives wanted action to protect President Reagan and his actions. Conservatives objected to the presence of an independent counsel appointed by the executive branch to investigate itself. In *Morrison* v. *Olson* (1988) the court then had to determine whether such independent counsel was constitutionally allowable. The case asked to whom the executive branch was answerable. Independent counsels tried to investigate the executive branch without resorting to an impeachment trial. However, conservatives argued that the only check on presidential power was impeachment, and that the counsel was not an acceptable presence under the Constitution. The reality was that President Reagan was facing an investigation by Special Counsel, and conservatives wanted to protect him from any such scrutiny. There was no Congressional push for impeachment, and the real issue was whether the President could be investigated when his actions did not draw negative attention rising to the level of impeachment from Congress.

However, the Supreme Court held that the independent counsel was still a part of the executive branch, and so was still inside of the constitutional framework. Thus, the counsel was allowed to continue and this did not roll back any of the power of the federal government, and really kept federal power where it was, rebutting those who wanted the 1980s court to reduce federal power and definitely rebuking those who wanted a less limited executive.[27]

Other Supreme Court decisions applied to the relationship between Federal law, the Constitution, and various state laws. One of the longest reaching (in terms of years) of these decisions came in 1985. The application of labor laws to municipalities was relatively late in coming. Although businesses had been forced to follow such laws since the 1940s, it was 1985 before state governments were required to obey the federal standards. Conservatives argued that, in particular, the Fair Labor Standards Act (FLSA), which created wage and hour controls, impaired states' and localities' ability to function. They felt that applying this and other, similar laws to municipalities infringed upon federalism. In the 1970s, the Supreme Court had actually supported the conservative position, declaring that traditional state functions were protected under the 10th Amendment against such federal government regulation.

In 1985, the court returned to the issue in the case of *Garcia* v. *San Antonio Metro Transit Authority* (SAMTA). Essentially, SAMTA claimed to be exempt from federal minimum wage and overtime requirements, but an employee, Garcia, argued he should be eligible for the overtime pay provided by the FLSA. The court sided with Garcia, holding that the FLSA could be applied to state governments and that the legislative representation that cities and localities effectively had in the federal Congress were sufficient protection against infringement of their rights. Dissenters argued that the Supreme Court needed to respect federalism and the original Constitution and so should strike down this application (but not strike down the whole FLSA – in this case it was the reach of the statute, not the overall statute, that caused a complaint).[28] Here federal power was not decreased at all, and, as a matter of fact, the 1980s court increased federal power as compared to the 1970s court.

Earlier in the decade the Court had ruled on an unusual case, upholding increased government power in Hawaii's use of eminent domain. In Hawaii, most of the land not owned by the government was owned by fewer than 100 people, and the state government decided that this was an unacceptable situation. To remedy it, the state adopted a law based in the concept of eminent domain. They seized private land (paying the previous owners for it) and then redistributed it to other private individuals. Eminent domain had traditionally been used to justify actions such as seizing land to build a highway, rather than what was done here. One of the former landowners petitioned the courts, and the Supreme Court upheld this act, in *Hawaii Housing Authority* v. *Midkiff* (1984) as they held that the redistribution of the land benefited the public and so fulfilled the eminent domain provisions. This, obviously, expanded the powers of the government.[29] The case has had bearing on future decisions involving eminent domain, as several municipalities or states have sought to seize private land and redistribute it to land developers, arguing that the development would benefit the public good.[30]

On the whole in the decade, the level of governmental power remained largely at the same level, which was disappointing to some conservatives. Indeed, government power actually increased in the Hawaii case and in the case dealing with the Fair Labor Standards Act. It remained unchanged by the ruling that the executive branch could still be investigated by an independent counsel. Although government power decreased in the INS case, the situation was unique and unlikely to impact a wider range of legislative decisions.

In the area of education, there was a minimal rollback of the decisions of the Burger and Warren courts. In religion, there was also only a minimal rollback, although preparations were made for future such moves, and in the area of governmental power, the level of power was largely kept the same. Thus, in the first three areas to be examined, the decisions of the 1970s court and before were largely continued and the Reagan era court did not take the significant right turn conservatives had hoped for.

In other areas, however, the Supreme Court demonstrated a distinctly conservative shift in the 1980s. Rulings throughout the decade struck down equal rights legislation, reduced defendants' rights in criminal justice cases, and limited access to abortion. These rulings resulted in decreased government controls and a reversal of earlier Supreme Court positions.

Affirmative action laws have come under fire from conservatives, as they are perceived as special rights available only to some and thus actually creating situations of inequality. Conservatives achieved a significant victory in this area at the end of the decade, after Reagan had left office. In the case of *Richmond v. Croson* (1989) the Supreme Court struck down an affirmative action system crafted by the city of Richmond, Virginia. The wide-reaching plan guaranteed a certain percentage of government contracts would be awarded to minorities. However, the Supreme Court stated that the law was not narrowly tailored enough, holding that the list of minorities was a catch all list, rather than only including those who had been specifically found to have suffered past discrimination. The decision set up a situation where governments had to find specific past discrimination and target affirmative action to remedy that unfairness, rather than just adopting affirmative action plans for groups who had suffered from bias in general. This case led to decreased government ability to help disadvantaged groups.[31]

The court also addressed the issue of gender discrimination in several cases. One case in which conservative goals were thwarted dealt directly with a similar plan to Richmond's. A California county's transportation system had no women who were road dispatchers in one division, in spite of having many women employees. To remedy this, the county promoted one woman over an equally qualified man who interviewed somewhat better. The Supreme Court, in *Johnson* v. *Transportation Agency* (1987), upheld this system as there was no quota system in place, the county was certified as an affirmative action employer, there was evidence of discrimination, gender was only one of the factors considered, and the county did not create a barrier to the advancement of men.[32]

Similarly, the court upheld a state statute requiring a private organization to end gender bias. The Jaycees had a long-standing practice of excluding women from becoming full members and justified it under the freedom of association clause of the First Amendment. A state law banned such gender based policies and the Jaycees fought against the legislation in court. The Supreme Court weighed the organization's right to freedom of expressive association against the state's interest in ending discrimination and also investigated how much that freedom of association would be burdened by admitting women to full membership. (It should be noted that the Jaycees already admitted women, but not as full members). The Court, in *Roberts* v. *US Jaycees* (1984), held that the statute should be upheld as the freedom of expressive association was not damaged, particularly as the admission of women in general was not forced (it was only their entrance into full membership that was forced).[33]

However another gender discrimination case was decided along more lines less favorable to women, and thus somewhat more conservative lines. An all women's state college in Mississippi denied admission to a man who wanted to study nursing. The Supreme Court, in *Mississippi University for Women* v. *Hogan* (1982), had to consider whether this discrimination violated the equal protection clause of the Constitution and held that it did, causing the school to become coeducational. Thus, narrowly tailored programs were allowed, but overall bans, particularly for state schools, were more questionable.[34]

One of the most significant discrimination cases coming out of the decade was 1986's *Bowers* v. *Hardwick*. The decision, which allowed state laws criminalizing homosexual sodomy, would ultimately be overturned by a 2005 Supreme Court case. The Georgia sodomy law under challenge in 1986 was seldom used but carried a 20 year potential prison sentence. The Supreme Court upheld the law, holding that there was no fundamental right to engage in homosexual sodomy. This was a clear conservative victory, as, although it generally increased government power, it supported claims by the religious right that homosexuality was immoral. Gay and lesbian rights activists would spend the next 19 years waiting for the ruling to be reversed.[35]

The case validated the power of the government to criminalize homosexual conduct. It additionally needs to be read within the context of general events in the 1980s, including the AIDS crisis, as many conservatives blamed this disease on homosexuals and homosexual behavior, and so supported laws such as this one. During oral arguments in the Bowers case, counsel supporting the law paraded a list of horrible behaviors that would occur, including AIDS, if this law was to be struck down. This case and the AIDS epidemic motivated gay activists to fight harder even while the conservative revival in the 1980s made their accomplishments more difficult. The mobilization of the federal government to fight AIDS in the late 1980s and beyond, and the eventual overturning of Bowers in 2005 show how court victories (as Bowers was for conservatives) are not permanent and how in fact such decisions, along with the huge increase in the AIDS disease, sparked a rebirth of gay activism and political mobilization.[36]

The Supreme Court thus moved to the right in this area as it restricted the ability of the government to craft solutions which aimed to eliminate racism and tacitly supported discrimination against homosexuals, decisions which found favor with conservatives in the area of the government's handling of race, sex and gender issues. The only decisions by the Supreme Court which were opposed by conservatives were the ones that forced the Jaycees to admit women as full members and that allowed a California county to adopt an affirmative action plan.

Conservative goals were advanced significantly in the area of the criminal courts in the 1980s. Two Supreme Court decisions significantly decreased the rights of the accused. Conservatives had wanted those accused of crimes to have fewer legal protections as they felt that many of these just allowed the guilty to go free. Liberals, in turn, argued that these protections were necessary to prevent innocent people from being sent to prison.

The *New York* v. *Quarles* case in 1984 dealt with the famous Miranda warning given to people after they are arrested. At this time, it had been required for 20 years. The issue here was whether the warning was required when the safety of the public was at risk. The court held that if the public was endangered, a person could be taken into custody without giving the warning, creating a "public safety" exception.[37]

The second case, *United States* v. *Leon* (1984), dealt with the exclusionary rule which has been developed under the Fourth Amendment. That amendment requires that warrants be obtained before evidence is seized, and the exclusionary rule holds that evidence must be excluded from the courtroom if illegally seized. In this case, evidence seized under a faulty warrant came into question. Police seized evidence under a warrant that they believed was valid (but really wasn't), and then wanted to use that evidence. The court here held that the evidence could be used, as excluding it would not deter police from violating the Fourth Amendment (as here the police thought that they were following the rules), but the exclusion would only harm society. This created the so-called "good faith" exception to the exclusionary rule. Thus, in both here and in *Quarles*, the conservatives' aims were achieved and the court took somewhat of a rightward turn. These decisions also limited the rulings of the previous courts thus somewhat achieving that goal of the conservatives as well.[38] It did not wholly achieve their aims, though, as the Miranda warning was still in force, the exclusionary rule still applied, and people were still guaranteed counsel under *Gideon*. The limitations were mostly near the edges.

Finally, and most controversially, the Supreme Court continued to rule in abortion rights cases. Conservatives in general wanted, throughout the 1970s and 1980s, to overturn *Roe* v. *Wade*, or, that failing, heavily limit the decision. This goal was a prime focus of Reagan's judicial appointments, and one of the reasons he only put Justice Kennedy's name forward with great reluctance. The limiting was much more successful than the overturning, as O'Connor turned out to be as much of a moderate as Kennedy on this issue, and only Scalia proved to be a hard line conservative.

The first opportunity for the Supreme Court to weigh in on the issue of abortion was *Harris* v. *McRae* (1980). There the Supreme Court considered whether or not the federal government could refuse to fund abortions. It held, by a 5-4 vote, that such a refusal was constitutional. The court ruled that just because something was legal and medically necessary did not mean that Medicaid, the government's program for the poor, had to fund it.[39] This limited *Roe* in that poor women now had to find other means of funding even legally obtained abortions.

The second opportunity for the Supreme Court was *City of Akron v. Akron Center for Reproductive Health* (1983). There the court had to decide whether requiring a 24 hour waiting period and counseling violated the principle of *Roe*. Six justices held that it did, although this number was down from the seven who had voted for Roe 11 years earlier. The court struck down the regulation, as *Roe* had held that during the first trimester the only allowed regulations were those which promoted the health of the woman. This particular waiting period applied throughout the pregnancy, and thus was not permissible. Other regulations, including forcing women to have abortions in hospitals, and preventing them in any other facility, however safe, were also held to be impermissible. Thus, the court did not promote conservative goals here, as the decision on the first regulation allowed for quick access to abortion and limited opportunities for abortion opponents to access women seeking abortions, and the decision on the second regulation essentially legalized the creation of abortion clinics.[40]

A third case in the area of abortion was *Thornburgh* v. *American College of Obstetricians and Gynecologists* (1986). Here again, the court here upheld *Roe* v. *Wade*, but only five justices voted for the opinion. Later that year, Justice Scalia joined the court, and conservatives hoped to overturn *Roe* the next time the issue came in front of the court.[41]

The most important case in the 1980s on abortion was *Webster* v. *Reproductive Health Services* in 1989. Here, although *Roe* was not overturned, it was significantly limited. Missouri was allowed to pass a law forbidding the use of state funds in abortions or in encouraging abortions. The only exception was where a woman's life was in danger. This obviously led to a limit on *Roe* as now, only those who had independent funding could have abortions, and people had to research abortions without the help of state funded documents. The more important impact, though, was in the language that the court used in allowing the redens," it could restrict access to abortions, which presented heavy limitations to the *Roe* decision.[42]

Even though the Reagan Administration and conservatives desired a significant rightward turn in the 1980s and a repudiation of many of the Warren Court (and even some of the Burger Court) decisions, this did not happen for the most part. Perhaps one of the most significant features of the Supreme Court in this era was its resilience against political pulls. Although the court did make some significant decisions supporting conservative goals, it also showed that a body appointed for life can make decisions without simply kowtowing to political backers, and this independence was part of the framer's intent for the court. In the areas of education and the separation of church and state, there was very little reversal of earlier decisions, even though there was somewhat of a rightward turn. In the areas of how much power the state had and what power the state had to fight discrimination, there was somewhat of a rollback, particularly in the area of affirmative action. It was only in the areas of abortion, the rights of minorities, including homosexuals, and the rights of the accused that there was any substantial reversals of previous trends, and a movement to the right, and even there the conservatives were largely unhappy as the basic constitutional provisions of the Warren Court, including Miranda and the right to counsel, survived on the whole and *Roe* v. *Wade* was not overturned, in spite of three appointments by Ronald Reagan who had vowed to appoint justices who would overturn *Roe*. Thus, there was a rightward turn in the 1980s, but it was more of a significant slice than a hard pull, and the court shows how, at least in the 1980s, that it is not always a sure thing to accomplish one's goal of remaking a court.

Notes

1. Supreme Courts are often labeled after the Chief Justice and Warren Burger was the Chief Justice through 1986 and William Rehnquist was Chief Justice from 1986 through the end of the decade. Rehnquist also provided some views of how the Court should function in his *The Supreme Court* (New York: Vintage, 2002).

2. Earl Warren was Chief Justice from 1954 through 1969 and he presided over a court that heard many landmark cases, including those on the 1964 Civil Rights Act, as well as the ones noted above. See, among others, Bernard Schwartz, *Super Chief: Earl Warren and His Supreme Court: A Judicial Biography* (New York: New York University Press, 1983).

3. James MacGregor Burns, *Packing the Court: The Rise of Judicial Power and the Coming Crisis of the Supreme Court* (New York: Penguin Press, 2009), especially 211-216, 218-232; Jeffrey Toobin, *The Nine: Inside the Secret World Of the Supreme Court* (New York: Doubleday, 2007); Thomas M. Keck, *The Most Activist Supreme Court in*

History: The Road to Modern Judicial Conservatism (Chicago: University of Chicago Press, 2004), 97-100; Frank B. Cross, Thomas A. Smith and Antonio Tomarchio, "The Reagan Revolution in the Network of Law," *Emory Law Journal* 57 (2008): 1227-1257.

4. See Keck, 94, 110-111.

5. Bruce J. Dierenfield, *The Battle over School Prayer: How Engel V. Vitale Changed America* (Lawrence: University Press of Kansas, 2007); Keck, 97-102. See also, generally, Scott A. Merriman, *Religion and the Law in America: An Encyclopedia of Personal Belief and Public Policy* (Santa Barbara, CA: ABC-CLIO, 2007).

6. Mark Tushnet, *A Court Divided: The Rehnquist Court and the Future of Conservatism* (New York: W.W. Norton, 2005), 30-38 and generally. See also N.E.H. Hull and Peter Charles Hoffer, *Roe v. Wade: The Abortion Rights Controversy in American History* (Lawrence: University Press of Kansas, 2001); David J. Garrow, *Liberty and Sexuality: The Right to Privacy and the Making of Roe v. Wade* (New York: MacMillan Publishing, 1994); Howard Ball, *The Supreme Court in the Intimate Lives of Americans: Birth, Sex, Marriage, Childrearing, and Death* (New York: New York University Press, 2005); Leslie J. Reagan, *When Abortion Was a Crime: Women, Medicine, and Law in the United States, 1867-1973* (Berkeley: University of California Press, 1997); and Elisabeth Albrecht Cawthon, *Medicine on Trial: A Handbook with Cases, Laws, and Documents* (Santa Barbara, CA: ABC-CLIO, 2004).

7. Richard A. Brisbin, *Justice Antonin Scalia and the Conservative Revival* (Baltimore, MD: Johns Hopkins University Press, 1997); Lisa K. Parshall, "Embracing the Living Constitution: Anthony M. Kennedy's Move Away From a Conservative Methodology of Constitutional Interpretation," *North Carolina Central Law Review*, 30 (2007): 25-74; Stephen A. Newman, "Political Advocacy on the Supreme Court: The Damaging Rhetoric of Antonin Scalia," *New York Law School Law Review*, 51 (2006/2007): 908-926; For a general study of Kennedy's views on liberty, see Helen J. Knowles, *The Tie Goes to Freedom: Justice Anthony M. Kennedy on Liberty* (Lanham, MD: Rowman and Littlefield, 2009); See specifically Knowles, 9, 29, 163-165 and 161-194 generally, for Kennedy's views on abortion and for his similarities with O'Connor; Frank J. Colucci, *Justice Kennedy's Jurisprudence: The Full and Necessary Meaning of Liberty* (Lawrence: University Press of Kansas, 2009), especially 9-37, 38-74; Tushnet, 34-35. See also the books cited in the previous footnote.

8. "Transcript of GOP debate at Reagan Library," January 30, 2008. http://edition.cnn .com/2008/POLITICS/01/30/GOPdebate.transcript (accessed February 11, 2010); Ronald Reagan, *The Reagan Diaries* (New York: Harper Collins, 2007), 53, See also pages 50, 54 and 70 in Reagan; Joan Biskupic, *Sandra Day O'Connor: How the First Woman on the Supreme Court Became its Most Influential Justice* (New York: ECCO, 2005), 74-88 and generally; L.A. Powe, Jr., "Conversations about Sandra Day O'Connor: Judges Struck by Lightning: Some Observations on the Politics of Recent Supreme Court Appointments," *Arizona State Law Journal* 39 (2007), 875-894; See also Sandra Day

O'Connor, *The Majesty of the Law: Reflections of a Supreme Court Justice* (New York: Random House, 2003); Burns, 211-213, Merriman, 381-383.

9. John W. Dean, *The Rehnquist Choice: The Untold Story of the Nixon Appointment that Redefined the Supreme Court* (New York: Free Press, 2001), especially 265-284; Burns, 213.

10. Brisbin, 59-62; Burns, 213-214; Nina Totenberg, "Essays on the Supreme Court Appointment Process: The Confirmation Process and The Public: To Know or Not to Know," *Harvard Law Review*, 101 (1988): 1213-1229.

11. Burns, 213-214; Kenneth B. Noble, "New Views Emerge Of Bork's Role in Watergate Dismissals," *New York Times*, July 26, 1987, 123; Totenberg cited previously; Robert Bork at the "Judges of the United States," produced by the Federal Judicial Center, available at http://www.fjc.gov/servlet/tGetInfo?jid=216m (accessed August 4, 2009); Ethan Bronner's *Battle for Justice: How the Bork Nomination Shook America* (New York: W.W. Norton, 1989), especially 209-276.

12. Burns, 213-214; Tushnet, 173-174, 333-338, 340-41.

13. Burns, 215-216; Joseph L. Rauh, Jr., "Nomination and Confirmation of Supreme Court Justices: Some Personal Observations," *Maine Law Review*, 45 (1993): 7-17.

14. Jan Crawford Greenburg, *Supreme Conflict: The Inside Story of the Struggle for Control of the United States Supreme Court* (New York: Penguin Books, 2007), 53-60; Collucci, 9-13 and generally; Rauh and Totenberg cited above; and Burns, 217.

15. "Antonin Scalia," NNDB, http://www.nndb.com/people/895/000023826/ (accessed February 11, 2010); "Religion of the Supreme Court," Adherents.com, http://www.adherents.com/adh_sc.html (accessed February 11, 2010); Antonin Scalia, *A Matter of Interpretation: Federal Courts and the Law* ed. Amy Gutman. (Princeton: Princeton University Press, 1997); Antonin Scalia, *Scalia Dissents: Writings of the Supreme Court's Wittiest, Most Outspoken Justice* (Washington, DC: Regnery Publishing, 2004); James B. Staab, *The Political Thought of Justice Antonin Scalia: A Hamiltonian on the Supreme Court* (Lanham, MD: Rowman & Littlefield, 2005); David A. Schultz and Christopher E. Smith, *The Jurisprudential Vision of Justice Antonin Scalia* (Lanham, MD: Rowman and Littlefield, 1996); Burns, 211-216; see Brisbin, *Justice Antonin Scalia and the Conservative Revival*, in general, especially, 1-11, 325-349.

16. "About ED— Ed. Gov," Department of Education, http://www.ed.gov/about/land ing.jhtml?src=gu (accessed February 12, 2010); See, among others, *Helvering* v. *Davis* 301 U.S. 619 (1937).

17. *Lemon* v. *Kurtzman*, 403 US 602, 612-613 (1971); see generally Christopher L. Eisgruber and Lawrence G. Sager, *Religious Freedom and the Constitution* (Cambridge, MA: Harvard University Press, 2007); Mary C. Segers and Ted G. Jelen, *A Wall of Separation?: Debating the Public Role of Religion* (Lanham, MD: Rowman & Littlefield Publishers, 1998); Douglas Laycock, "Why the Supreme Court Changed Its Mind About Government Aid to Religious Institutions: It's a Lot More than Just Republican Appointments," *Brigham Young Law Review*, no. 2, 2008: 275-294; Frank S. Ravitch,

"Rights and the Religion Clauses," *Duke Journal of Constitutional Law & Public Policy* 3 (2009): 91-109; Stephen M. Feldman, "Divided We Fall: Religion, Politics, and the Lemon Entanglements Prong," *First Amendment Law Review* 7 (2009): 253-306; Kedrick N. Whitmore, "Shifting Toward Balance, Not Conservatism: The Court's Interpretation of the Lemon Test's Legislative Intent Prong and Reaction from The Electorate," *Journal of Race, Religion, Gender and Class* 7 (2007), 437-458.

18. Mark Strasser, "Repudiating Everson: On Buses, Books, And Teaching Articles of Faith," *Mississippi Law Journal* 78 (2009): 567-636, especially 605-612; Mueller v. Allen at http://supreme.justia.com/us/463/388/case.html (accessed February 12, 2010).

19. Strasser, 611-612; Merriman, 118-120; Aguilar v. Felton at http://supreme.justia.com/us/473/402/case.html (accessed February 12, 2010); Neal E. Devins, ed. *Public Values, Private Schools* (London: Falmer Press, 1989); Stephen V. Monsma, *Church-State Relations in Crisis: Debating Neutrality* (Lanham, MD: Rowman & Littlefield, 2002).

20. Edith Brown Clement, "Public Displays Of Affection . . . For God: Religious Monuments After Mccreary And Van Orden," *Harvard Journal of Law and Public Policy* 32 (2009): 231-260; Merriman, 479-480; Stone v. Graham at http://supreme.justia.com/us/449/39/case.html (accessed February 12, 2010).

21 Dierenfield, *The Battle over School Prayer*, 187-211; Linda D. Lam, "Silence of the Lambs: Are States Attempting to Establish Religion in Public Schools?," *Vanderbilt Law Review* 56 (2003): 911-937; Debbie Kaminer, "Bringing Organized Prayer in Through the Back Door: How Moment-of-Silence Legislation for the Public Schools Violates the Establishment Clause," *Stanford Law and Policy Review* 13 (2002): 267-322; Merriman, 509-510; Wallace v. Jaffree at http://supreme.justia.com/us/472/38/case.html (accessed February 12, 2010).

22. Edward J. Larson, *Summer for the Gods: The Scopes Trial and America's Continuing Debate over Science and Religion* (New York: Basic Books, 1997); Randy Moore, *Evolution in the Classroom: A Reference Guide* (Santa Barbara, CA: ABC-CLIO, 2002); Merriman, 23-28, 209-212, 462-466.

23. Edward J. Larson, *Trial and Error: The American Controversy over Creation and Evolution* (Oxford: Oxford University Press, 2003); Brisbin, 215-216; Merriman, 23-28, 209-212; Staab, 198-199, 200, 208, 224; Schultz and Smith, 105-122, esp. 115; Edwards v. Aguillard at http://supreme.justia.com/us/482/578/case.html (accessed February 12, 2010).

24. Colucci, 14-16; Knowles, 91-93; James M. Lewis and Michael L. Vild, "A Controversial Twist of Lemon: The Endorsement Test As The New Establishment Clause Standard," *Notre Dame Law Review* 65 (1990): 671-698; County of Allegheny v. ACLU at http://supreme.justia.com/us/492/573/case.html (accessed February 12, 2010).

25. Merriman, 120-121; Airport Comm'rs v. Jews for Jesus at http://supreme.justia.com/us/482/569/case.html (accessed February 12, 2010).

26. Barbara Hinkson Craig, *Chadha: The Story of an Epic Constitutional Struggle* (New York: Oxford University Press, 1988), 188-233, vii-ix; Bernard Schwartz. *The*

Ascent of Pragmatism: The Burger Court in Action (Reading, MA: Addison-Wesley, 1990), 76-81; Darren A. Wheeler, "Actor Preference And The Implementation Of INS V. Chadha," *BYU Journal of Public Law* 23 (2008) 83-117; INS v. Chadha at http://supreme.justia.com/us/462/919/case.html (accessed February 12, 2010). See also generally Tinsley E. Yarbrough. *The Burger Court: Justices, Rulings, and Legacy* (Santa Barbara, CA: ABC-CLIO, 2000), in addition to the general treatment in Bernard Schwartz's book cited previously in this footnote.

27. Brisbin, 97-102, 120, 122; Morrison v. Olson at http://supreme.justia.com/us/48 7/654/case.html (accessed February 12, 2010); Keck, 193-194; See also Mark Tushnet. *I Dissent: Great Opposing Opinions in Landmark Supreme Court Cases* (Boston: Beacon Press, 2008); Katy J. Harriger, "The Law: The President and the Independent Counsel: Reflections on Prosecutors, Presidential Prerogatives, and Political Power," *Presidential Studies Quarterly* 31 (2001): 338-348; and Katy J. Harriger, *The Special Prosecutor in American Politics*, 2nd ed. (Lawrence: University Press of Kansas, 2000).

28. Bernard Schwartz, "National League Of Cities Again–R.I.P. Or A Ghost That Still Walks?," *Fordham Law Review* 54 (1985): 141-166; Keck, 110, 149, 190-192, 235, 242; Garcia v. San Antonio Transit Auth at http://supreme.justia.com/us/469/528/case.html (accessed February 12, 2010).

29. Richard Epstein, *Takings: Private Property and the Power of Eminent Domain* (Cambridge, MA: Harvard University Press, 1985), 161-162; Hawaii Housing Auth. v. Midkiff at http://supreme.justia.com/us/467/229/case.html (accessed February 12, 2010); See also Steven Greenhut, *Abuse of Power: How the Government Misuses Eminent Domain* (Santa Ana, CA: Seven Locks Press, 2004), 103-106; See generally Richard Epstein, *Supreme Neglect: How to Revive Constitutional Protection For Private Property* (Oxford: Oxford University Press, 2008); Robert Paul Malloy, *Private Property, Community Development, and Eminent Domain* (Burlington, VT: Ashgate, 2008).

30. Kelo v. City of New London at http://supreme.justia.com/us/545/04-108/case.html (accessed February 12, 2010).

31. George R. La Noue, "The Impact Of Croson On Equal Protection Law And Policy," *Albany Law Review* 61 (1997): 1-41, especially 1-7; Alexandra Natapoff, "Race And Remedy In A Multicultural Society: Note: Trouble in Paradise: Equal Protection and the Dilemma of Interminority Group Conflict," *Stanford Law Review* 47 (1995): 1059-1096; Colucci, 109, 126-132, 161; Brisbin, 152-157; Knowles, 137-138; City of Richmond v. J. A. Croson Co at http://supreme.justia.com/us/488/469/index.html (accessed February 12, 2010).

32. Nicolaus Mills, ed. *Debating Affirmative Action: Race, Gender, Ethnicity, and the Politics of Inclusion* (New York: Delta Trade Paperbacks, 1994), 100-103; M. Ali Raza, A. Janell Anderson, and Harry Glynn Custred, Jr., *The Ups and Downs of Affirmative Action Preferences* (Westport, CT: Praeger, 1999), 35-36; Brisbin, 166-168; Johnson v. Transportation Agency at http://supreme.justia.com/us/480/616/index.html (accessed February 13, 2010).

33. Robert J. Bresler, *Freedom of Association: Rights and Liberties under the Law* (Santa Barbara, CA: ABC-CLIO, 2004), 62-72, 205-211; James E. Leahy, *The First Amendment, 1791-1991: Two Hundred Years of Freedom* (Jefferson, NC: McFarland, 1991), 250-251; Roberts v. United States Jaycees at http://supreme.justia.com/us/468/609 /index.html (accessed February 13, 2010).

34. Phillippa Strum, *Women in the Barracks: The VMI Case and Equal Rights.* (Lawrence: University Press of Kansas, 2004), 172-181; Christina M. Calce, ed. "Tenth Annual Review Of Gender And Sexuality Law: Education Law Chapter: Single-Sex Education," *Georgetown Journal of Gender and the Law,* 10 (2009): 573-597; Tracy Eubanks Dawe, "Casenote: Equal Opportunity at VMI," *Southern Illinois University Law Journal,* 22 (1998): 443-466; Mississippi Univ. for Women v. Hogan at http://supreme.justia.com/us/458/718/ (accessed February 13, 2010).

35. Lisa K. Parshall, "Redefining Due Process Analysis: Justice Anthony M. Kennedy And The Concept Of Emergent Rights," *Albany Law Review* 69 (2005): 237-298; Ryan Goodman, "Beyond the Enforcement Principle: Sodomy Laws, Social Norms, and Social Panoptics," *California Law Review* 89 (2001): 643-740; John P. Safranek and Stephen J. Safranek, "Can Homosexual Equal Protection Claims Withstand The Implications Of Bowers V. Hardwick?," *Catholic University Law Review* 50 (2001): 703-729; Edward Stein, "Privacy Rights In A Post Lawrence World: Responses To Lawrence V. Texas: Introducing Lawrence V. Texas: Some Background And A Glimpse Of The Future," *Cardozo Women's Law Journal* 10 (2004): 263-288; David A.J. Richards, *The Case for Gay Rights: From Bowers to Lawrence and Beyond* (Lawrence: University Press of Kansas, 2005); Daniel Pinello, *Gay Rights and American Law* (New York: Cambridge University Press, 2003); Lee Walzer, *Gay Rights On Trial: A Handbook with Cases, Laws, and Documents* (Indianapolis, IN: Hackett Publishing Company, 2004); Colucci, 21-28; Knowles 94-98, 114-121, 187; Bowers v. Hardwick at http://supreme.justia.com/u s/478/186/ (accessed February 13, 2010).

36. Peter Irons, *The Courage of Their Convictions: Sixteen Americans Who Fought Their Way to the Supreme Court* (New York: Penguin, 1990), 379-407; Randy Shilts, *And the Band Played On: Politics, People, and the AIDS Epidemic* (New York: St. Martin's Griffin, 2007); John-Manuel Andriote, *Victory Deferred: How AIDS Changed Gay Life in America* (Chicago: The University of Chicago Press, 1999); Larry Kramer, *Reports from the Holocaust: the Story of an AIDS Activist* (New York: St. Martin's Press, 1994). See previous footnote for articles on *Lawrence and Garner* v. *Texas* (the 2005 case that overturned Bowers).

37. Rolando V. del Carmen, *Criminal Procedure: Law and Practice* (Pacific Grove, CA: Brooks/Cole, 1991), 64-65. 165-167; John F. Decker, *Revolution to the Right: Criminal Procedure Jurisprudence During the Burger-Rehnquist Court Era* (New York: Garland, 1992), 26; New York v. Quarles at http://supreme.justia.com/us/467/649/index.h tml (accessed February 13, 2010); William F. Jung, "Not Dead Yet: The Enduring Miranda Rule 25 Years After the Supreme Court's October Term 1984," *St. Louis University Public Law Review* 28 (2009): 447-458; See also generally Akhil Reed Amar, *The Constitution and Criminal Procedure: First Principles* (New Haven, CT: Yale University

Press, 1997) and Donald A. Dripps, *About Guilt and Innocence: The Origins, Development, and Future of Constitutional Criminal Procedure* (Westport, CT: Praeger, 2003).

38. del Carmen, *Criminal Procedure*, 298-299, 317-318; Decker, *Revolution to the Right*, 26; United States v. Leon at http://supreme.justia.com/us/468/897/index.html (accessed February 13, 2010); See also generally Amar, *The Constitution and Criminal Procedure* and Donald A. Dripps, *About Guilt and Innocence,* both cited in the previous footnote.

39. Frances Olsen, "The Supreme Court, 1988 Term: Comment: Unraveling Compromise," *Harvard Law Review* 103 (1989): 105-135; Janet Benshoof, "Commentary: The Chastity Act: Government Manipulation Of Abortion Information And The First Amendment," *Harvard Law Review* 101 (1988): 1916-1937; Harris v. McRae at http://www.oyez.org/cases/1970-1979/1979/1979_79_1268 (accessed February 13, 2010).

40. Claudia Pap Mangel, "Legal Abortion: The Impending Obsolescence Of The Trimester Framework," *American Journal Of Law And Medicine* 14 (1988): 69-108; Jessica Bertuglia, "Preserving the Right to Choose: A Minor's Right to Confidential Reproductive Health Care," *Women's Rights Law Reporter* 23 (2001): 63-77; Akron v. Akron Center for Reproductive Health at http://caselaw.lp.findlaw.com/scripts/getcase.pl?navby=CASE&court=US&vol=462&page=416 (accessed February 13, 2010).

41. David A. J. Richards, "Constitutional Legitimacy And Constitutional Privacy," *New York University Law Review* 61 (1986): 800-862; Rebecca Dresser, "Conflicting Interests in Reproductive Autonomy and Their Impact on New Technologies: The State's Interest: The Implications of Gonzales v. Carhart and Other Recent Cases: From Double Standard to Double Bind: Informed Choice in Abortion Law," *George Washington Law Review* 76 (2008): 1599-1622; Keck, 162-163; Thornburgh v. Amer. Coll. of Obstetricians at http://supreme.justia.com/us/476/747/index.html (accessed February 13, 2010).

42. David K. Koehler, "Justice Souter's 'Keep-What-You-Want-and-Throw-Away-the-Rest' Interpretation of Stare Decisis," *Buffalo Law Review* 42 (1994): 859-892; Kimberly Sharron Dunn, "The Prize And The Price Of Individual Agency: Another Perspective On Abortion And Liberal Government," *Duke Law Journal* 81 (1990): 81-117; Dawn Johnsen, "Webster V. Reproductive Health Services: From Driving To Drugs: Governmental Regulation Of Pregnant Women's Lives After Webster," *University of Pennsylvania Law Review* 138 (1989): 179-215; Colucci, 38-49 and 38-74 generally; Hull and Hoffer, 225-229; Brisbin, 277-78, Knowles, 161-165, 174-194; Burns, 216; Thornburgh v. Amer. Coll. of Obstetricians at http://supreme.justia.com/us/476/747/ (accessed February 13, 2010); See, generally: Ball, *The Supreme Court in the Intimate Lives of Americans* and Garrow, *Liberty and Sexuality.*

Chapter 4

Privatizing the Leviathan State: A "Reaganomic" Legacy

Robert P. Weiss

"Man is not free unless government is limited."
"One way to make sure crime doesn't pay would be to let the government run it."
                                        –Ronald Reagan

The 1980s was a watershed decade in the racial and class history of US criminal justice, repudiating 20 years of political and social activism that expanded civil liberties and due process and fostered liberal and "critical" criminology movements stressing prisoner rights, decarceration, decriminalization, and socioeconomic "root causes" of criminal behavior. The election of Ronald Reagan in 1980 reflected an abrupt change in the political mood of the nation attending the capitalist crisis of the 1970s. The new president promptly launched a reactionary agenda that moved public policy sharply rightward – diminishing legal rights, enhancing the authority of police and prosecutors, and creating an enormous penal state targeting young black and Latino offenders.[1] Reagan's "war on drugs" was the principal rationale for expanding state repressive apparatuses.[2] Declaring in 1986 his campaign against illegal drugs a "national security" objective, Reagan's drug interdiction program called for greater militarization of crime control domestically, expansion of the military and law enforcement presence at US borders, and Pentagon and CIA involvement in Latin American government drug interdiction and eradication programs. The first presidential administration to wed neoconservative and neoliberal ideologies to public policy in a systematic and substantial way, the Reagan administration provided a strong foundation for integrating national security into criminal justice (today, under the counter-terrorism rationale).[3] The national security rationale for militarizing crime control – with its war metaphor and preemptive approach – moved criminal justice farther away from its domain concerns under welfare liberalism, which had stressed community control in policing, and correctionalism[4] in punishment. Community relations, due process, root causes, and redemption are not in the arsenal of warfare.

At the same time as neoconservative politicians were busy enhancing state repressive apparatuses to combat internal and foreign enemies, they were promising a smaller, leaner, less intrusive and more efficient government. This contradiction seemed even more pronounced given the dismal fiscal condition of government at all levels during this deeply recessionary period. To pay for all the new prisons, States made drastic cuts in public education, health care, and welfare. Beyond that, middle class voters resisted public financing (especially through bond issues) of the infrastructure to fully implement the "get tough" approach they so applauded at election time. The magic solution to this neocon policy dilemma was *privatization*: The Reagan administration vigorously enlisted private corporations and venture capitalists into their project to expand state coercive power, establishing the institutional groundwork for the current "security-industrial complex"[5] of private security, prison, and military companies that together wield considerable political influence. Expanding state repressive apparatuses while "downsizing" government through privatization is the enduring Reaganomic solution to drug wars and fiscal crises.[6] The purpose of this chapter is to provide a political-economic context with which to understand the intensification of criminal justice militarization and privatization during the 1980s, and the alliances it established between military, police, commercial organizations, and the political sector in the creation of a globalized institutional security complex that has "deformed"[7] our democracy to this day.

The Political Economy of Privatized Repression

The political setting for the New Right's repressive agenda was shaped largely by the economic and social crises of the late 1970s and the national anxiety they generated. Declining corporate profits, "stagflation," the OPEC oil crisis, deindustrialization and labor unrest were accompanied by what appeared to be an alarming rise in the crime rate.[8] The Moral Majority and other reactionary social movements blamed deterioration in the nation's wellbeing on the permissiveness and welfarism of the 1960s. The moral panic generated by the "crime wave" provided the occasion for the Reagan administration to shift the focus of repressive legislation and criminal prosecution away from crimes of the powerful, where they had been under the Jimmy Carter administration's pursuit of white-collar and corporate criminals,[9] to crimes of the powerless. David Garland[10] aptly conveyed the moral essence of shifting surveillance and control from Wall Street inside-traders and corporate chieftains to "street criminals": ". . . conservative calls for tighter order and control ought to have clashed head on with the policies of deregulation and market freedom that were, at precisely the same time, releasing individuals and companies from the grip of social regulation and

moral restraint." Conservative Republicans might have touted small government, the new federalism, and individual responsibility when it came to social
welfare but, in the realm of criminal justice, Reagan presided over the creation
of a nasty state leviathan.

In what critics[11] see as a brazen yet clever Republican strategy to deflect attention from the structural causes of the nation's economic decline, White House
strategists were able to redirect much of the growing resentment and anxiety of
downwardly mobile white working class men and women ("Reagan Democrats") from the managerial class and its political minions to its poorest victims,
whom they branded "welfare queens" and "underclass." Never mind that Republicans were conducting a vigorous assault on organized labor and effecting a
dramatic redistribution of wealth through big tax breaks for the rich and deregulation of the corporate sector. Intensifying Richard Nixon's "war on crime,"
Reagan fostered a "penal politics"[12] targeting members of the vastly expanding
"surplus population,"[13] social detritus of neoliberal economic policies of the 70s
and 1980s economic restructuring that led to the elimination of millions of man-
ufacturing jobs. Young blacks and Latinos, the core of the new "dangerous
classes,"[14] were made scapegoats for economic decline in the face of global
competition. Rising drug abuse and increasing violence provided the policy focus.

After nearly two decades of broad public toleration of recreational drug use
among white middle-class youth, public sentiment abruptly reversed in the early
1980s. With media attention focused on young black drug violators, the Reagan
administration had a perfect political occasion to effect a "sudden and violent
transition"[15] in drug policy. Declaring a new "war on drugs" in a 1982 Rose
Garden speech, Reagan soon embarked on a packing frenzy of draconian judges
to all levels of the federal bench. Fate enabled him to make crucial Supreme
Court appointments: Sandra Day O'Connor in 1981, Antonin Scalia in 1986,
William Rehnquist as Chief Justice in 1986 and, in 1988, Anthony M. Kennedy
as Associate Justice. The conservative Court quickly diminished the rights of
suspects and greatly enhanced the power of prosecutors. Going after the much-
maligned exclusionary rule, their rulings made it easier for police to base search
warrants on anonymous tips (*Illinois v. Gates* 1983), and use defective search
warrants executed in "good faith" (*United States v. Leon* 1984). 1982 Congressional anti-crime legislation expanded the Organized Crime Drug Enforcement
Task Force Program (OCDETF), and in 1986 federal courts – perhaps influenced by all the mid-1980s media coverage of "crack heads" and "crack babies"
– upheld the draconian 1984 Federal Bail Reform Act that created mandatory
drug sentences.

Elite universities and "think tanks" were quick to advance the neoconservative
movement. A number of prominent "public intellectuals" served as handmaidens
of reactionary public policy, providing the academic clothing for the political
sector's voracious penal monster. Academics like Princeton's John J. DiIuluo,

Jr. helped inform conservative members of Congress in their creation of a hard-line, law-and-order legislative agenda by painting the specter of an urban land-scape of morally impoverished "super-predators" wreaking havoc on middle class America. Subscribing to a neoliberal model of human motivation, and re-suscitating long discarded theories of criminal behavior, neoconservatives pro-moted a rational (and hedonistic) model of human conduct that emphasized in-dividual responsibility and called for a vengeful penality. Some – Wilson and Herrnstein,[16] for example – added to the moral perspective a biological one, much like the "born criminal" variety popular in the late 19th century. Not sur-prisingly, the 1980s sounded the final blow to rehabilitation as a guiding philos-ophy of punishment and ushered in deterrence and incapacitation as exclusive penal goals. Andrew von Hirsh, James Q. Wilson, Ernest von den Haag and William Bennett were among the leading neocon "public intellectuals" widely covered by the mass media. Among the most influential articles were Kelling and Wilson's 1982 *The Atlantic Monthly* piece, "Broken Windows,"[17] which advocated zero-tolerance policing, and Wilson's 1983 *Atlantic Monthly* article, "Thinking About Crime,"[18] which promoted the efficacy of deterrence. And federal research money flowed to this line of reasoning. Throughout the 1980s, National Institute of Justice research funding was awarded almost exclusively to pragmatic crime control research with "practical" applications. Many liberals joined the "nothing works" critique of rehabilitation programs and, not to be left out of the dialogue or totally ignored in policy circles, a Left Realism or "realist criminology" contingent of critical criminologists, mostly British, argued that the Left had tended to romanticize criminals and failed to take a practical inter-est in common crimes that victimized the working class. They advocated "smart" policing, prevention, and victim restitution schemes over the idealism and relativism of "abstentionist" criminology popular in the 70s.[19]

On the legislative front, federal sentencing guidelines shifted sentencing dis-cretion from judges to prosecutors in a series of astonishing laws. Part of the Comprehensive Crime Control Act of 1984, the Sentencing Reform Act of 1984 (P.L. No. 98-473, 98 Stat. 1987) established a Sentencing Commission to craft mandatory minimum sentences, so-called "truth-in-sentencing," that effectively ended parole at the federal level. Other Congressional legislation encouraged state and local police to pursue narcotics cases in federal court so as to benefit local authorities from asset forfeiture. The 1986 Anti-Drug Abuse Act (P.L. 99-570) shifted criminal justice procedure profoundly by establishing most of the era's drug-related mandatory minimum sentencing and drug conspiracy penal-ties.[20] The Omnibus Anti-Drug Abuse Act of 1988 created a cabinet-level "drug czar" to further militarize the drug war by coordinating law enforcement, mili-tary, and intelligence agencies under the Office of National Drug Control Policy. This law also established a federal death penalty for "drug kingpins," and created a mandatory minimum of five years for simple possession of more than five grams of crack cocaine, opening an inequitable prison sluice for hundreds of thousands more young black offenders. Then, the Reagan administration set the drug nets wider, encouraging school and workplace drug testing – today a ubiquitous and widely accepted form of surveillance and control. To help enforce this hard line, the Reagan administration encouraged greater militarization of domestic policing, building on a process begun by the Nixon administration.

In their pursuit of drug war enemies, States deployed the National Guard in marijuana search and seizure missions and even dispatched troops to patrol ghetto neighborhoods, developed paramilitary SWAT teams with federal training, then sent them on thousands of deployments annually. Much of this military involvement in law enforcement had been banned under the Posse Comitatus Act of 1878. But, beginning in 1981, Congress authorized various amendments, beginning with the Defense Authorization Act of 1982 permitting the use of Department of Defense assets, including equipment, intelligence, and training facilities, to assist civilian drug enforcement agencies. The Defense Drug Interdiction Assistance Act of 1986 followed, and by the end of the decade surplus military armories filled with battlefield equipment–including armored personnel vehicles, grenade launchers, helicopters–were opened to civilian police departments to rummage through. Under the leadership of Vice President George H. W. Bush and Attorney General Edwin Meese III, the National Narcotics Border Interdiction System in 1986 launched Operation Alliance, which coordinated joint operations of over a dozen local, state, and federal agencies, the Defense Department, and the National Guard on border interdiction efforts. The Defense Authorization Act of 1989 continued this expansion and formalization of military involvement in drug law enforcement.

A Prison Crunch and a Fiscal Crisis: Free Enterprise to the Rescue

Zero–tolerance, the modern victims' rights movement, and aggressive street patrols focused on black neighborhoods (such as Washington, D.C.'s 1987 Operation Clean Sweep), combined with increased sentence lengths and restricted parole, promptly flooded prisons and jails. The federal system became especially strained.[21] The "imprisonment binge"[22] forced States to undertake huge prison-building programs, mostly to accommodate the dramatic increase in blacks and Latinos sentenced for drug possession or sale. Before the end of the decade, and first time outside of the Deep South, African-Americans became a majority entering prison – most as casualties of the drug war. By 1990, over 60% of narcotics convictions were African-Americans,[23] largely for mere possession. Women's incarceration also increased significantly. The number of women incarcerated in US prisons increased more than six-fold from 1980 to 1993.[24] In California, incarceration for drug related crimes went from 4 per 100,000 in 1980, to 46 per 100,000 by 1990 (the rate would climb to 54 by 1998).[25] To help make this Great Incarceration more efficient and cost-effective, the Reagan administration borrowed from Great Britain's privatization and deregulation initiatives, launched by Prime Minister Margaret Thatcher's government in 1979.

A central tenet of the "The Reagan Revolution" was free market superiority, and one of its policy centerpieces was the expansion of the private sector into the delivery of government services. Free-market advocates argued that profit-seeking organizations could perform public services more efficiently and cost effectively than could governmental agencies. In privatizing criminal justice services, this market ideology struck deep into the heart of the state. Critics asked, "shouldn't the powers to punish or police be exclusively governmental functions?" Punishment, especially, would seem to be an inherently governmental function, an issue of sovereignty, and thus a function that cannot be delegated. Neoliberal pundits at "think tanks" like the Reason Foundation argued to the contrary, that: "many public services, including justice, are not inherently public goods."[26] Aside from the validity of this theory of the state, the unspoken reality was that, with deterrence and incapacitation – or, simply, warehousing – as primary penal objectives, and cost-efficiency a cardinal value, *any entity* could be contracted to perform the service on behalf of the state. So, notwithstanding those advocates of privatization who argued that contractors could deliver improved treatment or avoid "red tape" in constructing facilities faster to alleviate overcrowding, among other operational advantages, *cost savings became the decisive factor*. Governments had the additional fiscal benefit, in the unlikely event that demand slackens, of flexibility in discontinuing service when contracts expire, alleviating themselves of civil service employee tenure and the traditionally generous health care and retirement packages negotiated by civil service unions. Driven on the demand side by fear (seemingly infinite in the 1980s), and with growing concentration on the supply side, the security industry was poised for astonishing market growth and profitability.

Deregulation and privatization advanced the New Right's anti-union agenda as well, especially in the public sector. Early opportunity came at the Immigration and Naturalization Service (INS), which was faced with detention facility overcrowding from the hundreds of thousands of Central Americans fleeing civil war, repression, and economic dislocation (products of U.S.-exported neoliberal economics and proxy wars against socialists and left-wing revolutionaries). In 1983, Corrections Corporation of America (CCA), the first and now the largest private prison corporation, was awarded a contract to operate a 350-bed illegal alien detention facility in Houston. More federal prisons were outsourced in the 1980s, marking the birth of what is today an enormous, hellish, and very profitable "illegal alien" privately-operated detention archipelago in the Southwestern region of the United States.[27] Reagan's privatization initiative gained more momentum with the Grace Commission Report of 1984, whose recommendations promised to reduce federal employment and tax expenditures significantly through privatization. The 1987 President's Commission on Privatization identified numerous targets and priorities for private contracting. With Washington

setting the privatization tone, individual States were quick to pursue prison outsourcing – especially in the South where anti-union traditions were strong.

Corporate Penology

The private for-profit sector had well-established markets in prison technologies
and auxiliary services before the Reagan era. These included security systems;
data processing; various medical, educational and food services; general operational supplies, and a few prison industries. During the 1980s, the penal profit-
seekers added services at the soft end of criminal justice, including electronic
monitoring[28] and residential treatment facilities. Soon, though, companies offered full-blown high security prisons. Fiscally strapped local and state governments arranged prison deals through "lease-purchase" agreements of detention
facilities, funded out of regular appropriations rather than bond measures to
avoid taxpayer resistance. Or, they could finance prison construction through
Wall Street firms, including E.F. Hutton, Lehman Brothers, and Shearson Leh-
man/American Express. Private companies also offered to finance, build and
operate private prisons, jails, and other detention facilities for adults and juve-
niles as package deals. Companies also provided medical and mental health care
and drug treatment programs. In fact, the whole justice continuum, from court to
probation and parole services to maximum-security confinement and even ex-
ecution, entered the marketplace during the decade of the 1980s.[29]

Making a business profit from prisoners is an old idea reappearing, resurrected
from the era of the convict lease and contract prison industrial system of the
nineteenth century.[30] CCA, the twentieth century reincarnation of commercial
imprisonment, began as a cocktail party brainstorm of Tennessee real estate and
insurance investor, Thomas Beasley. As former Chairman of the Tennessee Republican Party, Beasley was well connected to the State's political power bro-
kers, enabling him to get a business foothold in the state with a 500-bed county
workhouse in Hamilton County and a juvenile facility in Memphis. In 1985,
CCA made a brash (for the time) bid for a 99-year lease of the State's entire
prison population. Before the end of the decade, CCA became the largest prison
company, taking over a federal treatment facility, two INS detention facilities,
and a large minimum-security prison in Texas. Today, CCA employs 17,000
"correctional professionals" to oversee 64 correctional facilities and detention
centers housing 75,000 inmates.

Making its appearance in 1984, Wackenhut Corrections Corporation, a GEO
subsidiary of Wackenhut Security, operated as the second largest prison operator
in the 1980s. After several years of scandals alleging abuse of inmates in Texas,
Florida, New Mexico and Louisiana during the 1980s, and after several States
stripped them of contracts during the 1990s for abuse, neglect, and rape of inmates, Wackenhut divested itself of its GEO prison unit in 1999. In a rather
convoluted ownership history, in 2000 they merged with a Copenhagen conglo-

merate, Group 4/Falck, and then in 2003 they split from Group 4, after which GEO's Board of Directors approved a name change from Wackenhut to the GEO Group, Inc. Today, they manage 61 facilities totaling approximately 60,000 beds worldwide. Their web page boasts of "a wide range of diversified services including the design, construction and financing of state and federal prisons, immigration and detention centers, medical and residential treatment centers and other special needs institutions." In addition to the US, they have penal facilities in Canada, South Africa, and the UK. Privatization and denationalization policies spread globally in the 1980s, adopted in Italy, France, Australia, South Africa and, as part of neoliberal structural adjustment, to Latin America. Even China introduced private security operations.[31]

For-profit prison industry in the US dates back to the contract system of the Auburn model prisons, and flourished in various forms through the late 1800s and into the early twentieth century. After a 20-year decline and replacement with the "state-use" system, the death knell came to private prison industries with the Depression-era federal legislation banning the interstate commerce of prison-made goods (Hawes-Cooper Act of 1929 and the Ashurst-Summers Act of 1935). Prison industrial enterprises were revived during the Carter administration, with the creation in 1979 of the Prison Industry Enhancement (PIE) Certification Program, exempting State and local certified corrections departments from legal restrictions on the sale of prisoner-made goods sold in interstate commerce. The idea was to provide employment opportunities for prisoners that approximated real-world conditions, and the program, under the name Free Venture, became a policy darling during the Reagan administration. Its importance to conservatives was epitomized by a 1981 speech and a 1985 article by Chief Justice Warren Burger[32] advocating the transformation of prisons into "factories with fences." This gave the program more legitimacy. The PIE program was expanded from seven to 20 states in 1984, and by 1989 there were 69 prison-based industries selling on the open market – a 150 percent increase over the number of enterprises operating in 1984. While never reaching the potential of a national private prison industrial system, by 1998 there were 20,000 prisoners producing $600 million in sales, a small but not trivial economic impact.[33] Nevertheless, the prison industrial revival has been criticized as an anti-union initiative using neo-slave labor.[34]

Private Security

"While private prisons and convict labor represent a modest example of privatization, security firms forged an indispensable niche for themselves as the class and racial divide widened in the 1980s and downtown businesses sought to put a moat around their free-enterprise zones," observes Tony Platt.[35] The 1980s were boom years for private policing, both as "low security" of the rent-a-cop and alarm system variety, and high-end security, such as corporate espionage and government surveillance subcontracting. Like prison privatization during the decade, the security industry *grew fast*, *concentrated*, and *globalized*. The out-of-control financial speculation of the savings-and-loan industry helped fuel the proliferation of shopping malls and gated communities, creating what Shearing and Stenning[36] refer to as, "mass private property," a security bonanza. The security industry saw further concentration during the 1980s, with the US market dominated by three firms: the pioneer, Pinkerton, followed by Burns, and then Wackenhut.[37] Total private security employment grew from 1.05 million in 1980, to 1.6 million by 1993. The industry expanded rapidly abroad, as well. According to Jones and Newburn,[38] the UK security market, "dominated by five firms, with Group 4 the leader," experienced "rapid growth. . .during the second half of the 1980s." UK neoliberalism widened the class divide, raising crime fears, despite defensive architecture and gated communities.[39] Latin America [40] and France[41] were among other nations to see a dramatic increase and market concentration of private security services.[42] At the "high security" end of the market, corporate espionage, labor espionage (an old service revitalized to abet the decade's assault on labor unions), and foreign security operations thrived. Private firms also grew with the expansion of the global arms industry in the 1980s.

By commodifying security and control apparatuses, and making efficiency and profit making chief values, the Reagan administration fostered a disciplinary system guided by a technocratic ethos. The notion that private sector entities can be agents of the justice system denies the value of public service as a profession of governance. As Frankfurt School critical theorists Max Horkheimer and Theodor Adorno observed,[43] a "technological rationale is the rationale of domination." The privatization of prisons increases the objectification of prisoners, who are typically guarded by a low-paid, unskilled, nonunion service industry proletariat, often recruited from the same class stratum as inmates, and sometimes not far removed in general norms of conduct. Socioeconomic background, coupled with the ambiguous source of authority (a problem of legitimacy), means that guards are more likely to rely on *personal* authority of the worst kind, physical force, to control their charges, as has been the case with private security guards used to patrol homeless shelters. In private policing, the norms of efficiency and client allegiance trump the public values of due process and participatory decision-making. The deleterious effects of privatization on workplace democratization is a concern of legal scholar, David A. Sklansky:[44]

Police privatization threatens the unfinished project of democratizing the internal operations of police departments—especially if private security firms do not just take over some work previously performed by public law enforcement agencies, but actually transform public policing by making it more about management and less about governance. In a recent, illuminating study of a large Canadian security firm, George Rigakos found a workplace marked by extraordinary efforts at monitoring, controlling, and disciplining employees, and by levels of alienation and cynicism remarkable even in comparison with what we have come to expect from public law enforcement officers. There is no reason to think other security firms would look strikingly different in these regards.

Foreign Policy Militarization and Privatization

"Mercenaries were a common sight on Cold War battlefields," observes Ken Silverstein,[45] with British and French commandos fighting in the Belgian Congo, Morocco, and Rhodesia, while American soldiers of fortune fought leftist rebels in El Salvador, Guatemala, and Bosnia. Private military contracting did not begin in the 1980s, but it got a considerable boost and organizational development under the Reagan Doctrine and the war on drugs. Under Reagan, the drug war became a "new US national security doctrine,"[46] and a replacement ideology for the Cold War that was fast winding down and losing its "fear" potential. The Reagan administration went after weaker nations with a vengeance, taking a hard line on socialist and communist governments in the Third World, like tiny Grenada, which the US invaded in 1983 to oust the left-wing government of Maurice Bishop. Throughout Central America, the US provided overt and covert financial and military support for various counter-revolutionary groups and soldiers of fortune. While Dick Cheney and his sidekick, George W. Bush, "perfected the art of contracting-out key functions of government," Paul R. Verkuil[47] observes, outsourcing was "nurtured through several prior administrations, including Clinton and Bush I. It was the Reagan administration, however, that seems to have grasped most fully what privatization of policymaking was all about. Indeed, the Iran-Contra Affair provides a virtual textbook in how to establish a private foreign and military policy shop." He argues that Iran-Contra was a preview of the secrecy and unaccountability of Iraq War private contracting. [48]

Reagan nurtured larger contract security businesses as well, as with the creation in 1983 of Civilian Military Assistance, an Alabama group that funneled military aid to the contras and were assigned missions inside Nicaragua with Miskito Indian troops.[49] The "State Department's use of private security firms such as DynCorp or Blackwater (now Xe) ... goes back to the aftermath of the bombing of the U.S. Embassy in Beirut in 1983," observes David Isenberg.[50] This was a start, and bigger players followed quickly. In 1985, the Army's Logistics Civil Augmentation Program (LOGCAP) was established as the major federal contracting process. Contractors materialized quickly from among the former ranks of the federal executive. Among LOGCAP's first customers was Noel Koch, who oversaw terrorism policy for the Pentagon in the early Reagan administration. Upon retirement in 1986, he established TranSecur as a "private intelligence organization."[51] In 1987, retired Army General Vernon Lewis founded Military Professional Resources, Inc. (MPRI), based in Alexandria, Virginia, which established military training contracts for the Pentagon and served as a clearinghouse for retired army personnel, an old-boy network[52] to this day.

Privatizing researchers Verkuil, Silverstein and P.W. Singer[53] warn that our nation's sovereignty is being outsourced to powerful security and privatized military corporations, with MPRI serving as an example. The company's slick web page boasts, "integrated, multi-disciplinary 'whole of government' solutions to the challenges of national defense, law enforcement, rule of law, international development, public health, climate change, institutional and governmental capacity building and security sector reform."[54] CorpWatch reports[55] that MPRI, employing over 4,000 operatives in 40 countries, provides services "in the National Security and Homeland Security sectors, international governments and agencies, state and local governments, and major corporations." MPRI is today part of a larger conglomerate, L-3 Communications, which hires a dozen lobbyists, including former Senate Majority Leader, Tom Daschle and his wife. L-3, one of the US Governments top ten contractors, is listed on the New York Stock Exchange, was formed by Lehman Brothers and acquired business units of Lockheed and Martin Marietta. This security behemoth provides intelligence for the Pentagon and Joint Chiefs of Staff, among other "Command, Control and Communications, Intelligence, Surveillance and Reconnaissance' services. L-3 is only one among dozens of large private intelligence, military and security companies doing business for multinational corporations and the US and foreign governments, many with no-bid contracts. Congress recently detailed "massive" use of private contractors in Iraq, over 310 since 2003,[56] on whose services for that war alone the US taxpayer spent over $100 billion. What is on the horizon with the Obama administration? Will we regain lost sovereignty?

A Bright Future for Awful Legacies?

The "Greed Decade" – which brought, among other extravagances and outrageousness, the savings-and-loan scandal, inside traders Ivan Boesky and Mike Milken, and hundred-million dollar executive bonuses – also bequeathed a gargantuan repressive apparatus aimed at the domestic and foreign losers – surplus populations – of the "new economic order" of unfettered capitalism. The neoliberal economics that celebrated over-consumption for the winners, subjected the losers to an unforgiving disciplinary society. And the criminal justice maw did not ensnare just the "social junk" segment of the surplus population; it was aimed also at "social dynamite."[57] On the home front of the Reagan Doctrine, a growing number of anti-imperialist groups gained the attention of the FBI, which then zeroed in on the Committee in Solidarity with the People of El Salvador (CISPES), labeling them a domestic "terrorist" group. Under Reagan, the FBI was "unleashed" from much of its 1970s Post-Watergate reform constraints, freed (or forced) to engage in extensive domestic surveillance of U.S. citizens and groups opposed to the administration's policies in Central America .[58]

Despite fears expressed by privatization advocates about the Obama administration – "Outlook Bleak for Competitive Sourcing Under Obama Administration, Democratic Congress," warns an industry report[59] – the future appears bright for profit-seekers in the security industry. Democrats and Republicans alike are locked into the security-industrial complex, which has been a bipartisan venture all along. There are plenty of neoliberals, neocons, and military-industrial advocates in the Democratic Party willing to neglect government oversight of private military contractors. The security industry has come to full-blown maturity with the wars in Iraq and Afghanistan,[60] providing intelligence, fighters, interrogators, and prisons. Under the Obama administration, "outside contractors now make up approximately half our fighting forces in the two countries."[61] The new Commander in Chief has increased the number of private security contractors working for the Defense Department in Iraq by 23 percent, and he has increased their presence in Afghanistan by 29 percent, for a total of 250,000 security contractors.[62] Even the controversial Blackwater remains a player in Middle Eastern security, with contractors filling the void left by the withdrawal of US troops from Iraq until it was thrown out of the country in February of 2010.

On the domestic front, State governments "are swimming in red ink and realizing the effects of the recession will be felt long after the economy recovers," said Leonard Gilroy, editor of the report and director of government reform at Reason Foundation: "Interest in privatization is sky-high and rightly so. Now more than ever, policymakers need to study their priorities, re-examine what are really core government functions, and then tap the private sector's expertise in all of the areas where they can save taxpayer money and improve the delivery of services."[63] Gilroy points hopefully to Arizona, where officials announced in October 2009 that the State would soon seek bids for the prison complexes housing its entire prison population, nearly 40,000 – a privatization effort officials hope will save the State $100 million.[64] Already, private companies confine 30 percent of the State's prisoners, and Alaska and Hawaii's prisoners have been housed in Arizona's CCA prisons. No wonder that Macquarie Research, in a security analyst's report for the GEO Group (formerly part of Wackenhut's private prison division), predicts "their shares will increase in value by 39 percent in the coming year," outperforming the rest of the stock market.[65]

On the federal level, immigration prisons are the hottest profit markets. Initially, detention prisons were financed privately and built on speculation. But, GEO and CCA are now promoting speculative public-private or "joint venture" projects with impoverished rural communities, with the prospect of getting rich sharing federal per diem money. Counties and municipalities throughout the Southwest have incurred huge bond debt in enterprises that are "publicly owned by local governments, privately operated by corporations, publicly financed by tax-exempt bonds, and located in depressed communities. Because they rely on project revenue instead of tax revenue, these prisons do not need voter approval."[66] Giant private prison companies have perfected a socialistic type of capitalism, shifting all of the financial risk to local taxpayers while pocketing most of the profit.

The Reagan Revolution: Ironies and Contradictions

The Reagan Revolution defined itself by the core values of liberty, competition, public policy for the "little guy," small government, anti-regulation, and security and freedom from fear and danger. Yet, because the Reagan administration helped transform security into a commodity – a matter of supply and demand, subject to the market forces of capitalism – the antithesis of Reagan Revolutionary values resulted. Aside from the issue of whether privatization saves taxpayers money,[67] the entire private security industry – police, prisons, military – is largely held unaccountable and threatens democratic processes globally. The secrecy and unaccountability of privatized repressive apparatuses make them less responsive to the will of the electorate through government oversight.[68] Private police are not constrained by constitutional criminal procedure or by effective State regulation. Private prison operators are notorious in their failure to protect human rights, and failed State Department oversight of security contractors in Iraq, for example, contributed to the 2007 Monsour Square massacre involving Blackwater Worldwide, which tried to hush criticism of the episode with $1 million in bribes to Iraqi officials.[69]

The security-industrial complex makes us unnecessarily fearful, more willing to surrender our civil liberties for protection. As oligopolistic enterprises, the big security and prison firms must sell themselves to investors in order to continue raising sufficient capital for the expansion of market share. GEO, CCA, Securitas, Blackwater and DynCorp are constantly marketing themselves, promoting fear and searching for political influence to get federal contracts, which is a staple of their businesses. Collective *insecurity* is the profit driver, making political fear an economic enterprise in its own right.[70] Private contractors have certainly been given an assist by other components of the security-industrial complex. Over the past 30 years, the media and politicians deftly conjured up and transformed the bogeymen necessary to warrant huge tax outlays for defense: from the "evil empire" of the Cold War, to Willie Horton of George H. W. Bush's drug war, and then to the "evil axis" of George W. Bush's war on terror. The growing surveillance of schools, workplaces, and the Internet have profited the "surveillance-industrial complex" [71] enormously, creating fear not only of "terrorists" and criminal predators, but of the elites who spy on us in the name of protection.[72] Meanwhile, the poor and working class lack genuine security. Privatization of force promotes inequality in government services and weakens public sector policing. "You can see the public police becoming like the public health system," said Thomas M. Seamon, a former deputy police commissioner for Philadelphia who is president of Hallcrest Systems Inc., a leading security consultant. "It's basically, the government provides a certain base level. If you want more than that, you pay for it yourself."[73]

Hopeful signs are emerging that some of the Reagan-era legacy can be undone, or at least mitigated. On the regulation front, corporate providers may not be able to conceal their operations behind the business mantle, as the *Annual Privatization Report 2009*[74] suggests in its warning about a recent Tennessee State court ruling that CCA, "as an equivalent of a public agency," must comply with open records laws. *The Report* views this and similar federal rulings as attacks on "the ability of the private sector to protect proprietary information." And the *Report* warns of more controls in the offing: On May 15, 2009, Representative Sheila Jackson-Lee (R-TX) introduced H.R. 2450—the Private Prison Information Act—that would subject all prisons holding federal inmates to Freedom of Information Act (FOIA) requests and make them report all the same information as publicly operated federal facilities. Regulation is important, but the size of the beast must be reduced.

The most important hopeful indication of change seems to be coming from our nation's approach to drug legislation. New York has finally modified its draconian Rockefeller era penalties, and a recent Gallup poll found 44 percent of Americans favor full legalization of marijuana.[75] Certainly, more citizens have come to realize that the nation no longer can afford the repressive leviathan, privatized or not, and also pay for higher education and health care and roads.[76] After decades of seeing States shift billions of dollars annually from higher education to prison systems, college students and their parents are beginning to understand that funding the prison-industrial complex is a zero-sum game, made at the expense of higher education. In his 2010 State of the State Speech, California Governor Arnold Schwarzenegger spoke to this new sentiment: "priorities have become out of whack. . . . 30 years ago, 10% of the general fund went to higher education and 3% went to prisons. Today, almost 11% goes to prisons and only 7.5% goes to higher education." He announced a plan to save money by privatizing prisons and linking the funding of universities and correctional facilities. [77] Anxious and angry over soaring tuition costs, families have an opportunity to help restrain the prison-industrial complex—to stymie the leviathan after its 30 years of unfettered growth that has strangled social welfare expenditures and stunted democracy.

Notes

1. U.S. Bureau of Justice Statistics, "Correctional Surveys: Adult correctional populations, 1980-2007." 2009 Washington, D.C.: U.S. Government Printing Office. http://www.ojp.usdoj.gov/bjs/glance/tables/corr2tab.htm (accessed January 22, 2010).

2. As a concept developed by Louis Althusser, repressive state apparatuses, or RSAs, include courts, police, prisons and military, and are used to maintain order and reproduce

capitalist relations of production and curtail working-class action. To be contrasted with ideological state apparatuses (ISAs), which include churches, education, media and family, that transmit dominant values of the state. See: Louis Althusser, "Ideology and Ideological State Apparatuses (Notes towards an Investigation)," in *Mapping Ideology*, ed. Slavoj Zizek (London: Verso, 1995), 36-59.

3. "The counter-terrorism framework incorporates and combines elements of criminal justice and national security.... Pre-crime counter-terrorism can be traced through a number of interlinking historical trajectories including the wars on crime and drugs, criminalization and, more fundamentally, in colonial strategies of domination, control and repression." Jude McCulloch and Sharon Pickering. "Pre-Crime and Counter-Terrorism: Imagining Future Crime in the 'War on Terror'," *British Journal of Criminology* 49, no. 5 (2009): 628.

4. David Garland, *The Culture of Control* (Chicago: University of Chicago Press, 2001), 168-69.

5. Robert P. Weiss, "From Cowboy-Detectives to Soldiers of Fortune: The Recrudescence of Primitive Accumulation Security and Its Contradictions On the New Frontiers of Capitalist Expansion," *Social Justice*, 34, Nos. 3-4 (2007-08): 1-19; Conor O'Reilly and Graham Ellison. "'Eye Spy Private High' Reconceptualising High Policing Theory," *British Journal of Criminology* 46 (2006): 641-660.

6. By neoliberal accounting, privatizing criminal justice and military operations turns tax expenditures into a source of business profits. As James O'Connor, in his *Fiscal Crisis of the State* (New York: St. Martin's Press, 1973, 7; 150-53) observed, privatization turns *social expenses of production* – services required to maintain social harmony (many of which used to be assumed by corporations as welfare capitalism or the Pinkertons) – into *social investments* that increase the rate of profit.

7. Jonathan Simon, *Governing Through Crime* (Oxford: Oxford University Press, 2007).

8. The crime rate rose sharply in the late 1960s and early 1970s, but between 1980 and 1993 most FBI Index crimes declined and violent crime stabilized, while incarceration (especially black) skyrocketed. See: "US Crime Rates, 1960-2004," http://www.scribd.com/doc/13609654/United-States-Crime-Rates-1960 (accessed January 22, 2010); U.S. Bureau of Justice Statistics. 2004. "Crime in the US, 1960-2004." Washington, D.C.: U.S. Government Printing Office; Department of Justice, Federal Bureau of Investigation, "Crime in the United States, 1986-2005." http://www.fbi.gov/ucr/05cius/data/table_01.html (accessed January 23, 2010).

9. Albeit, this can be overstated. As Tony Poveda observes, "in the process of operationalizing white-collar crime, the Justice Department transformed the traditional (Sutherland) definition ... so that targeted offenders are not limited to the economic and political elite, but instead are drawn from all social classes." See: Tony Poveda, *The FBI in Transition: Lawlessness and Reform* (Pacific Grove, CA: Brooks/Cole, 1990), 136.

10. Garland, *The Culture*, 99.

11. Bruce Western, *Punishment and Inequality in America* (New York: Russell Sage Foundation, 2006), 4-5; Christian Parenti, *Lockdown America* (New York: Verso, 2008), 55, 168.

12. Garland, *The Culture*, 13.

13. The concept, "relative surplus populations," comes from Karl Marx in Chapter 25, *Das Kapital*, and refers to temporarily unemployed or irregularly employed as a result of periodic changes in the industrial cycle (structural unemployment).

14. Diana R. Gordon, *Return of the Dangerous Classes: Drug Prohibition and Policy Politics* (NY: W.W. Norton, 1994).

15. Philip Jenkins, *Moral Panic* (New Haven, Conn.: Yale University Press, 1998), 224.

16. James Q. Wilson and Richard J. Herrnstein, *Crime and Human Nature* (New York: Simon and Schuster, 1985).

17. George L. Kelling and James Q. Wilson. "Broken Windows: The police and neighborhood safety," *The Atlantic Monthly*, March 1982.

18. James Q. Wilson. "Thinking About Crime," *The Atlantic Monthly*, 252, No. 3 (September 1983): 72-88.

19. John Lea and Jock Young, *What Is To Be Done About Law and Order — Crisis in the Eighties* (Harmondsworth: Penguin, 1984); John Lea, "Left Realism: A Defense," *Contemporary Crises* 11 (1987): 357-70; Roger Matthews, "Taking realist criminology seriously," *Crime, Law and Social Change* 11, no. 94 (December 1987): 371-401.

20. Sentencing mandates included five and ten year minimums for drug distribution or importation of any "mixture or substance" containing a "detectable amount" of prohibited drugs commonly used today.

21. From 1980-93, State incarceration rates nearly tripled, according to J. Ziedenberg and V. Schiraldi, "The Punishing Decade: Prison and Jail Estimates at the Millennium," *The Justice Policy Institute* (Washington DC, 1999), 1. And the total prison population increased by nearly 620,000 (*Bureau of Justice Statistics Bulletin*. June1994. "Prisoners in 1993"). NCJ-147036 Washington, D.C.: U.S. Government Printing Office http://www.ojp.usdoj.gov/bjs/pub/ascii/pi93.txt

22. John Irwin and James Austin, *It's About Time: America's Imprisonment Binge* (Belmont, California: Wadsworth, 1996).

23. *Sourcebook of Criminal Justice Statistics, 1991.* http://bjs.ojp.usdoj.gov/index.cfm?ty=pbdetail&iid=1423 (accessed January 23, 2010).

24. *Bureau of Justice Statistics Bulletin, June 1994*, "Prisoners in 1993" (NCJ-147036 Washington, D.C.: U.S. Government Printing Office) http://www.ojp.usdoj.gov/bjs/pub/ascii/pi93.txt (accessed January 23, 2010).

25. California Department of Corrections and Rehabilitation, "Incarceration Rates for Drug Related Crimes, 1970-2005," http://ag.ca.gov/cjsc/glance/cht17.php (accessed January 23, 2010).

26. Philip Fixler, Jr. and Robert W. Poole, Jr., "Can Police Services Be Privatized?" *The ANNALS of the American Academy of Political and Social Science*, 498, 1 (1988): 108-118; E.S. Savas, *Privatizing the Public Sector* (Chatham, N.J.: Chatham House Publishers, 1982).

27. Tom Barry, "A Death in Texas: Profits, poverty, and immigration converge," *Boston Review* 34, No. 6 (November/December 2009): 7-15.

28. Craig Paterson, "Commercial Crime Control and the Electronic Monitoring of Offenders in England and Wales," *Social Justice*, 34, Nos. 3-4 (2007-08): 98-110.

29. G.W. Bowman, S. Hakim, and P. Seidenstat, *Privatizing the United States Justice System* (Jefferson, NC: McFarland & Company, 1992).

30. Robert P. Weiss, "The Reappearance of 'The Ideal Factory': The Entrepreneur and

Social Control in the Contemporary Prison," in *Transcarceration: Essays in the Sociology of Social Control*, ed. John Lowmam, Robert J. Menzies and T.S. Palys (Aldershot: Gower Publishing Company, 1987), 272-90; R. P. Weiss, "Private Prisons and The State," in *Privatizing Criminal Justice*, ed. Roger Matthews (London: Sage Publications, 1989), 24-51; Matthew J. Mancini, *One Dies, Get Another: Convict Leasing in the American South, 1866-1928* (Columbia, SC: University of South Carolina Press, 1996).

31. "The contemporary era of private security began with the establishment of the Chinese Shekou Private Security Firm on December 18, in 1984. In 1986, Premier Li Peng publicly encouraged the development of private security firms." Susan Trevaskes, "The Private/Public Security Nexus in China," *Social Justice*, 34, Nos. 3-4 (2007-08): 40.

32. Warren E. Burger, "Prison Industries: Turning Warehouses into Factories with Fences," *Public Administration Review*, (Nov. 1985): 754-57.

33. Robert P. Weiss, "'Repatriating' Low-Wage Work: The Political Economy of Prison Labor Reprivatization in the Postindustrial United States," *Criminology* 39, 2 (May 2001): 253-91.

34. Gordon Lafer, "Captive Labor: America's Prisoners as Corporate Workforce," *The American Prospect* 46 (September/October 1999): 66-70.

35. Anthony M. Platt, "Social Insecurity: The Transformation of American Criminal Justice, 1965-2000," *Working Papers in Local Governance and Democracy* 3 (2000): 1.

36. C. Shearing and P. Stenning, "Private Security: Implications for Social Control," *Social Problems* 30, no. 5 (1983): 493-506.

37. And concentration has continued: Securitas, a Stockholm, Sweden conglomerate acquired Pinkerton in 1999, and then bought Burns Security in 2001. In 2003, these and several other American security companies were merged into a new company, Securitas Security Services USA. These acquisitions made Securitas one of the largest security companies in the world.

38. Trevor Jones and Tim Newburn, *Private Security and Public Policing* (Oxford: Oxford University Press, 1998), 60.

39. "As crime rates multiplied during the 1980s, so did the sale of commercial security equipment and private security services such as guards and patrols. In 1988 the total amount of money spent on security by the public was estimated to be £1,600 million, which dwarfed the government's Home Office expenditure of about £15 million on crime prevention." *Crime Prevention Information & News*, "A chronology of British developments and key publications in urban security and crime prevention during the last two decades," University of the West of England, Bristol, 2004. http://environment.uwe.ac.uk/commsafe/ukcron.asp (accessed 3 January 2010).

40. Mark Ungar, "The Privatization of Citizen Security in Latin America: From Elite Guards to Neighborhood Vigilantes," *Social Justice*, 34, Nos. 3-4 (2007-08):20-37.

41. Frédéric Ocqueteau, "Legitimation of the private security sector in France," *European Journal on Criminal Policy and Research*, Volume 1, no. 4 (December 1993): 108-122.

42. Jeffrey T. Kessler, "Converged A-Comin'?" *Security Industry Annual Report 2006*. Prepared by Sandra Jones & Company, for Lehman Brothers, In-House Report, 2006.

43. Max Horkheimer and Theodor W. Adorno, *Dialectic of Enlightenment* (New York: Herder and Herder, 1972), 121.

44. David A. Sklansky, "Private Police and Democracy," 43 *Am. Crim. L. Rev.* 89 (2006), 101; 103.

45. Ken Silverstein, *Private Warriors* (New York: Verso, 2000).

46. Walrtraud Queiser Morales, "The war on drugs: a new US national security doctrine," *Third World Quarterly*, 11, 3 (July 1989): 147-169.

47. Paul R. Verkuil, *Outsourcing Sovereignty* (New York: Cambridge University Press. 2007), 9-10.

48. Dave Whyte, "Crimes of Neo-Liberal Rule in Occupied Iraq," *British Journal of Criminology* 47, no. 2 (2007): 117–195.

49. Ken Silverstein, *Private Warriors* (New York: Verso, 2000), 157-58.

50. David Isenberg, "Dogs of War: WPPS World," Washington (*UPI*), Sep 19, 2008.

51. "NC4, Inc., the leader in Situational Readiness solutions for incident monitoring, crisis management, and secure collaboration, announced today its agreement to acquire TranSecur, the nation's oldest continually operated provider of global security information and industry-leader in travel risk management," *PRNewswire*, El Segundo, Calif. (September, 18, 2009).

52. Silverstein, *Private*, 170.

53. Peter W. Singer, *Corporate Warriors: The Rise of the Privatized Military Industry* (Ithaca, NY: Cornell University Press, 2004).

54. http://www.mpri.com/esite/ (accessed 28 February 2010).

55. Tim Shorrock, *Spies for Hire: The Secret World of Intelligence Outsourcing* (New York: Simon & Schuster, 2008).

56. James Glanz, "Report on Iraq Security Lists 310 Contractors," *New York Times*, October 28, 2008, 1(A).

57. Steven Spitzer, "Toward a Marxian theory of deviance," *Social Problems*, 22 (June 1975): 638-651.

58. "It is important to realize that the FBI, at least initially, resisted the Reagan administration's definition of the threat posed by domestic terrorism." Tony Poveda, *The FBI in Transition: Lawlessness and Reform* (Pacific Grove, CA: Brooks/Cole, 1990), 127.

59. Leonard C. Gilroy, ed., *Annual Privatization Report 2009* (Los Angeles, CA: The Reason Foundation), 1; 124-26.

60. Vincenzo Ruggiero, "Privatizing International Conflict: War as Corporate Crime," *Social Justice* 34, 3-4 (2007-08): 132-145; Dave Whyte, *"Market Patriotism and the War on Terror,"* *Social Justice* 34, 3-4 (2007-08): 111-131.

61. Michael Winship, "The Privatization of 'Obama's War'," *truthout*/Perspective (June 6, 2009), http://www.truthout.org/060609A (accessed January 26, 2010).

62. Jeremy Scahill, *Blackwater: The Rise of the World's Most Powerful Mercenary Army*. New York: Nation Books, 2007; J. Scahill, "Obama Will Not 'Rule Out' Private Security Contractors in Iraq," *The Nation.com*, 2008 http://www.infowars.com/obama-will-not-rule-out-private-security-contractors-in-iraq/ (accessed January 28, 2010); J. Scahill, "Obama Has 250,000 'Contractors' in Iraq and Afghan Wars, Increases Number of Mercenaries," *Truthout*, 2009, Rebel Reports, http://www.truthout.org/060309B (accessed January 28, 2010).

63. Gilroy, ed., *Annual Privatization*, 124.

64. Jennifer Steinhauer, "Arizona May Put All State Prisons In Private Hands," *The New York Times*, October 24, 2009, A1.

65. Bryant Urstadt, "Locking In Our Profits: Private prisons as a gold-plated investment opportunity," Annotation, *Harper's Magazine* (December 2009), 74-75.

66. Tom Barry, "A Death in Texas: Profits, poverty, and immigration converge." *Bos-

ton Review, 34, no. 6 (November/December) 2009, 7-15.

67. Prison privatization produces almost no savings, according to a Department of Justice study. Bureau of Justice Assistance, "Emerging Issues on Privatized Prisons," February 2001, http://www.ncjrs.gov/pdfiles1/bja/181249.pdf (accessed January 5, 2009).

68. In a strange alliance, conservatives, libertarians and business groups, including the U. S. Chamber of Commerce, have joined liberals in calling for a halt to "overcriminalization." In an interview at the Heritage Foundation, former Reagan administration attorney generals, Edwin Meese III and Dick Thornburgh, bemoaned an "out-of-control criminal justice system." See: Adam Liptak, "Right and Left Join Forces on Criminal Justice," *New York Times*, November 23, 2009, 1(A).

69. Mark Mazzetti and James Risen, "Blackwater Said to Pursue Bribes to Iraq After 17 Died," *New York Times*, November 11, 2009, 1(A).

70. Corey Robin, *Fear: The History of a Political Idea*. Oxford: Oxford University Press, 2004, 230.

71. Jay Stanley, "The Surveillance-Industrial Complex: How the American Government Is Conscripting Businesses and Individuals in the Construction of a Surveillance Society." *2004 Report*. New York: ACLU.

72. Robin, *Fear*, 162.

73. Amy Goldstein, "Some Question the Granting of Police Power to Security Firms," *Washington Post*, October 31, 2008, 1(A).

74. Gilroy, *Privatization*, 126.

75. Karl Vick, "Support for legalizing marijuana grows rapidly around U.S. Approval for medical use expands alongside criticism of prohibition," *Washington Post*, November 23, 2009, 1(A); John Hoeffel, "Bid to legalize marijuana in California takes key step," *Los Angeles Times*, January 29, 2010. http://www.latimes.com/news/local/la-me-marijuana-initiative29-2010jan29,0,6132946.story (accessed February 18, 2010).

76. Nicholas Riccardi, "Cash-strapped states revise laws to get inmates out," *latimes.com*, 2009, http://www.latimes.com/news/nationworld/nation/la-na-prison-release5-2009sep05,0,5705309.story (accessed September 5, 2009).

77. Shane Goldmacher and Larry Gordon, "Governor's call for giving colleges priority over prisons faces hard political tests," *latimes.com* 2010, latimes.com/news/local/la-me-education-prison7-2010jan07,0,3859928.story (accessed January 7, 2010).

Chapter 5

"Airlines? Lousy unions."
Airline Workers in the Era of
Deregulation and Hostile Takeovers

Jana K. Lipman

"Airlines? Lousy unions."
–Gordon Gekko, *Wall Street 1987*

In 1987, Michael Douglas won an Academy Award for his portrayal of Gordon Gekko, the quintessential corporate raider in Oliver Stone's *Wall Street*. The film was a critical and box office hit. Gekko's reptilian name and his "Greed . . . is good" speech became symbols of the 1980s corporate culture. As a cultural text, part-critique, part-paean, *Wall Street* represented the greed, the excesses, the big hair, and big expense accounts of the 1980s bull market. However, beneath the flashy veneer and stylish shots of the New York City skyline is a less-talked-about plot of airline finances and trade unions.[1] In this cinematic portrait of the 1980s, the plot hinged on Gekko leveraging Blue Star Airlines with the cooperation of the mechanics, flight attendants, and pilots' unions. In order to squeeze the maximum profits from the deal, Gekko intended to betray the unions and dismantle the airline piecemeal. In a final twist, the unions pledged themselves to a rival "white knight" who promised to protect their union jobs and the company's integrity, albeit at 20 percent wage concessions. Given the film's supposed moral critique of Wall Street, it portrayed Gekko as a dominant and seductive figure, represented corporate raiders as potentially benevolent, and assumed union members' wage concessions to be a necessary element of any deal.[2]

Wall Street's economic battlefield was the airline industry and its unions. The film reflected the contemporary moment of the mid-eighties with the Professional Air Traffic Control Organization's (PATCO's) devastating defeat, Continental Airlines machinists' strike in 1983, United Airlines pilots' strike in 1985,

TWA flight attendants' strike in 1986, and it anticipated Eastern Airlines' 1989 union-management showdown. Airline labor confrontations provide a way to investigate the 1980s economy, its corporate culture, and the implications of abstract finance schemes on working people. Nationally, airline strikes were the most visible labor conflicts of the decade.[3] These strikes occurred during an era when unions were under siege, and the national labor movement debated tactics and strategies in a hostile political climate.[4] Yet while most industries saw a decline in the number of strikes and work stoppages, the militancy of airline unions increased during the 1980s.[5]

Airline worker activism was one consequence of the 1978 Airline Deregulation Act, Congress' first major stab at deregulation. Deregulation advocates gained traction in the 1970s, and they were successful beyond their wildest expectations.[6] By the end of the 1980s, the government had deregulated, and thus fundamentally restructured, the airline, trucking, utilities, telecommunications, and banking industries. Up until 1978, the Civil Aeronautics Board (CAB) had monitored the commercial airline industry by selectively certifying new carriers, administering subsidies, setting fare structures, and mandating service to small communities.[7] By the mid-1970s, critics on both the left and the right denounced the CAB and lobbied hard for airline deregulation. Through the language of consumer rights, Ralph Nader argued that the CAB had been "captured" by the industry and doled out favorable routes and fares, rather than best serving passengers. In contrast, academic economists and think tanks, such as the Brookings Institute and the American Enterprise Institute for Public Policy, articulated faith in unfettered markets and argued that regulation cost U.S. businesses billions of dollars a year, resulting in expensive market inefficiencies.[8] Thus, with bipartisan support, albeit for often conflicting reasons, the Republican Ford Administration set deregulation into motion, and Democrats like Ted Kennedy and Jimmy Carter shepherded it through Congress.[9] In 1978, CAB chair Alfred Kahn dismantled the agency and removed the federal government's regulatory authority in all areas except safety. Under deregulation, new airlines could enter the market as long as they passed the FAA's safety regulations, which opened the industry to competitive pricing and upstart airlines.

Deregulation fundamentally restructured the industry and the government's relationship to the airlines. It opened the door to new airlines, ushered in the hub-spoke system with individual airlines dominating regional "hubs," and threatened airlines that could not adapt quickly. With airline giants floundering and unsure in a volatile industry, some airlines expanded at breakneck speed, others targeted weak competitors for hostile takeovers, and many incurred high debt loads.[10] The industry had numerous casualties, and major carriers such as Braniff Airlines, PanAm, and Eastern all went bankrupt in the 1980s.

In this turbulent new environment, ticket prices fell, but in the process, management sacrificed workers and wages. Numerous non-union carriers, like New York Air, Peoples Express, and Frontier Airlines, entered the industry and pushed labor costs down in the name of competition. Corporate raiders looked to slash labor costs as the fastest way to compete in the new market. Real wages for pilots, flight attendants, and mechanics declined due to deregulation, and wage discrepancies within the industry skyrocketed. Far from a benign government policy, deregulation put airline employees' jobs at risk and sparked a battle between management and labor over wage cuts, take backs, rule negotiations, stock options, bankruptcy, and employee control. With consumer prices lauded as the ideal, airline workers suffered the most under deregulation.[11]

In this era defined by government deregulation and the glamorization of corporate raiders and Wall Street kingpins, airline employees fought for their jobs, wages, and security. Through the process, airlines became one of the fiercest, most visible, and potentially most disruptive arenas for labor confrontation during the 1980s. The resulting conflicts demystify the 1980s corporate culture and reveal the effects of government deregulation, industrial restructuring, and corporate raiding on airline employees and their work.

The failed 1981 PATCO strike marked the nadir of the labor movement's political power and consolidated Ronald Reagan's anti-labor credentials and administrative policies. On August 3, 1981, close to 13,000 air traffic controllers, led by Robert Poli, went on strike after more than a year of contentious bargaining with the Federal Aviation Administration (FAA). Within four hours, Reagan publicly threatened the controllers that they had forty-eight hours to return to work, or they have "forfeited their jobs and will be terminated."[12] In short, they would be fired. Reagan dramatically redefined the expectations of labor conflicts, when he unapologetically fired and later blacklisted 11,345 workers. Several months later, the Federal Labor Relations Authority (FLRA) ruled PATCO had broken the law and decertified PATCO's rights as a union.[13] These unprecedented steps shocked labor leaders. Victor Gotbaum, the head of New York City's public employee union, surmised, "Not even Eisenhower or Richard Nixon did that [fired public employees]."[14] Reagan's dramatic actions set the tone for the eighties and normalized employers' abilities to fire striking workers and hire permanent replacements.[15] The PATCO strike framed the 1980s labor battles. It resonated throughout the decade's airline strikes and allowed the major airlines to cut their losses and consolidate their strength in the face of deregulation.

PATCO's labor negotiations intensified after unsatisfactory bargaining in 1978 in which the FAA insisted that an air traffic controller's work was "no more stressful than that of a bus driver."[16] Promising greater militancy, Robert Poli replaced PATCO's president John Leyden in 1978 and mobilized PATCO members in a showdown against the FAA. Laying the groundwork from 1978-1981, Poli coordinated a network of organizers, dubbed "choirboys," accumulated a strike fund, and systematized a national organizational structure. The internal organization and PATCO workers' love for the daredevil job led to a tightly oiled union, ready to strike, but without alliances in the airline industry or the labor movement.[17]

PATCO's strength was in its internal organization that allowed thousands of members to act collectively across the nation.[18] It also gained support from international air traffic controllers, and for a short time the Canadian and Portuguese controllers offered the most substantial alliances and refused to track U.S. planes through their national airspace. Although these acts of solidarity were short-lived, they called attention to the international dimension of air travel and the possibility of a global grounding. Notably, PATCO's strike occurred while the Solidarity movement in Poland was strong and in the public eye. With Reagan supporting striking government workers in Poland, many activists remarked on the U.S. government's hypocrisy and failure to grant U.S. public employees' full trade union rights.[19]

As the gatekeepers of safe skies, PATCO controllers believed their labor was indispensable and trusted their expertise would guarantee a victory. PATCO intended to sway public opinion by pointing to the safety risks inherent in novice controllers and understaffed towers. Editorial cartoons in the mainstream media and headlines such as "Fear of Flying," and "How Safe Are Our Airways?" reflected the public's anxiety and the potential for disaster.[20] However, the government repeatedly declared that the system was safe, and the controllers lost a potential pillar of support when the Air Line Pilots Association (ALPA) publicly affirmed that the system was running smoothly with replacement workers. Even though PATCO consistently maintained that the FAA was under-reporting and intentionally whitewashing "near misses," the FAA's ability to prevent a major accident in the strike's first few weeks stole the safety issue away from PATCO.[21]

Unknown to the PATCO organizers, the FAA along with the major airline carriers decided to space flights more evenly throughout the day (rather than pack flights in at peak times), so fewer controllers were in fact needed. Both left wing economists, like Richard Hurd, and establishment business periodicals, like *Fortune* magazine, commented that the PATCO strike enabled the FAA to surreptitiously re-regulate the industry.[22] Weeks before the strike date, the FAA had turned to the major airline carriers and asked for their cooperation in creating a strike contingency plan. In addition, the FAA relied on almost a thousand military controllers to man the towers. With the aid of military controllers and the airline industry, the government devised a way to provide air traffic control with a reduced workforce. In essence, the PATCO controllers underestimated their ability to be replaced. Dennis Reardon, a PATCO negotiator, admitted that PATCO organizers were ignorant of the FAA's contingency plans: "We would have considered it in making a final decision . . . we're not interested in jumping off a cliff and onto a sword."[23]

The FAA's strike plan provided a new degree of regulation in the market and limited the number of flights per day. This offset the spiral of cut-rate competition and overextended flight routes spawned by deregulation. Frederick Thayer, a professor at the University of Pittsburgh, argued that the PATCO strike allowed airlines to collectively drop empty flights which had been losing money under deregulation without charges of monopoly or conspiracy: "The controllers' strike did for the airlines what they could not do for themselves."[24] Conservative academics commented that "re-regulation" through the PATCO strike hurt new, non-union carriers and benefited established airlines.[25] Few journalists or politicians commented on the FAA's use of military controllers; however, the use of the armed forces as scabs also enabled the strikebreaking plan to succeed. Thus, the state mobilized corporate interests and its military authority in order to crush PATCO.

The Reagan administration made sure that PATCO not only lost the strike, but that the union was devastated. The government rehired only a few dozen of the striking controllers. Although technically allowed to work for other federal agencies, the government blackballed many, while some strikers were even sent to jail.[26] Unlike commercial airline workers, air traffic controllers were public employees, fighting the government rather than private corporations, and public employees did not have the right to strike. Federal employees, including air traffic controllers, took loyalty oaths, which had their roots in the McCarthy era's loyalty-security programs.[27] Drew Lewis, Reagan's Secretary of Transportation, reiterated, "These people signed an oath to support the Constitution of the United States and not to strike against the federal government...the very system of law that we've developed over the last 200 years is in jeopardy."[28] Reagan's stand against public employees paved the way for private companies to dismantle unions and cast a pale on the labor movement throughout the decade.

The PATCO debacle was a crisis for the labor movement. The AFL-CIO leadership resented PATCO's bullheaded strike, which it called without considering national strategy. The president of the United Auto Workers (UAW), Douglas Fraser, publicly chastised the union, "PATCO should have talked to the other unions."[29] William Winpisinger, the chair of the International Association of Machinists (IAM) suggested a machinists' sympathy strike, but the AFL-CIO leadership decided the public would not have supported mass illegal strikes in favor of PATCO.[30] The AFL-CIO refused to call sympathy strikes, union boycotts of the airlines, the expulsion of ALPA from the AFL-CIO, or a national one-day action to support PATCO.[31] Labor activists like Kim Moody and Jerry Brenner believed the AFL-CIO's slow and tepid support for PATCO only served to emphasize the labor movement's impotence and concessionary politics. In retrospect, the labor movement's failure to mobilize and protect PATCO jobs established a precedent that was to be repeated in the private sector throughout the decade.

Paired together, deregulation and PATCO demonstrated the government's new approach to airlines as profit making corporations, rather than as public utilities in need of stringent government supervision. For workers in the airline industry, PATCO stood as a tangible and unforgettable reminder of the risk of striking. Still, throughout the 1980s, airline employees began to strike with unusual regularity because of the wage and benefit cuts sparked by deregulation.

The 1980s marked an era of economic extremes, and the corporate culture glorified raiders and junk bond kings with Michael Milken and Donald Trump

achieving superstar status.[32] Leveraged buyouts, junk bonds, and economic ma-
nipulations made airlines high stakes investments, and Frank Lorenzo and Carl
Icahn entered the prestigious, but financially unstable airline industry. Airline
deregulation encouraged the proliferation of small airlines, and Lorenzo's Texas
International launched the first major non-union carrier, New York Air. Although most start-up, non-union carriers were financial failures, their cut-rate
operations weakened unions and depressed wages.[33] Workers' narratives are
often absent from the 1980s corporate culture, but they were directly affected by
corporate raiders and business deals on Wall Street. In this new economic calcu-
lus, airline employees struggled to redefine their roles in the industry and ensure
their jobs.

Deregulation allowed airlines to reevaluate labor costs. As 1982 CAB Chairman Dan McKinnon asked, "What is the value of an airline captain or a copilot
or a flight crew member, or even other employees that work for the airline on
the ground, if somebody is going to do the job and just as good a job for less
money?"[34] With this philosophy and governmental mandate, airline CEOs had
the green light to cut wages and fight their unions. Airline operational costs such
as fuel and airport slots were largely fixed, and therefore, in a deregulated market, labor costs were often the first cut. For example, in 1978 labor accounted
for 42 percent of the industry's annual expenditures, but by the end of the 1980s,
it was only 34 percent of airlines' total costs.[35] In addition, deregulation
spawned dozens of mergers, restructured the airlines' route structures, and resulted in lost jobs.

The government's absence from the airline industry had material consequences for airline employees. Prior to deregulation, workers were protected by
government regulated Labor Protection Plans (LPPs), which guaranteed workers' jobs and seniority rights during mergers. Deregulation ended this practice.
For example, Frank O'Connell, the vice-president of the flight attendants'
Transport Workers Union (TWU) testified before Congress about Eastern Airlines acquisition of Braniff's South American routes. When Eastern took over
Braniff's routes, it did not hire a single Braniff flight attendant from the United
States. Instead, it only retained the South American flight attendants at far lower
wages. As a result, 8,500 Braniff employees were laid off because of the merger.[36] In a desperate attempt to corner the market before the industry re-
consolidated, airline executives disregarded and disrespected long-term employees. As the President of the Association of Flight Attendants argued:

> I think that what has happened in the airline industry as a result of deregulation is a
> magnified game of Pac-Man, where we have all of the airlines out there gobbling up
> one another's routes. Without labor protective provisions, what you are asking the
> airline employees to do is to go and gobble up one another's work.[37]

Moreover, airline unions were notoriously divided along craft lines, which undermined sustained collective action. This weak legal position alongside fragmented unionism placed workers at a significant disadvantage vis-à-vis corpo-

rate moguls and Wall Street tycoons.

Frank Lorenzo became the most visible 1980s airline raider. One union leader declared him the "number one union buster in this country," as he systematically sought to consolidate a giant commercial air fleet without a union.[38] A Harvard business graduate who supported himself through school as a teamster truck driver for Coca Cola, Lorenzo's Texas Air Corporation raided Continental Airlines and presided over a hostile takeover in 1981. Through this maneuver, Texas Air controlled both the non-union New York Air and the unionized Continental. Lorenzo engaged in a practice called "double breasting," which enabled him to siphon off Continental's assets to New York Air, pay New York Air employees cut-rate wages (e.g., sometimes only a quarter of union pilots' salaries), and demand huge concessions from Continental employees, in effect, egging them on to strike.[39] Between 1981 and 1983, Lorenzo gained $100 million worth of concessions from pilots. In the summer of 1983, the mechanics, flight attendants, and pilots were all negotiating contracts without coordinating with each other. When Continental announced its intentions to subcontract union jobs and cut mechanics' wages by as much as $3 an hour, the IAM voted to strike.[40] From August until September, the pilots and flight attendants conspicuously disrespected IAM picket lines, and Continental remained in the air. However, in mid-September, Lorenzo requested $60 million more in concessions from Continental's pilots and $40 million from its flight attendants.[41] Then, rather than bargain with the unions in good faith, Lorenzo filed for Chapter 11 bankruptcy, fired 12,000 employees, and hired back 4,000 at lower, non-union wages. Pilots' salaries plunged from $73,000 to $43,000, and flight attendants' salaries dropped from $28,000 to $15,000.[42]

This manipulation of Chapter 11 was unprecedented and systematically dismantled Continental's unions.[43] Shocked at Lorenzo's blatant disregard of their negotiated contracts, the pilots and flight attendants joined the IAM strike. However, by initially dividing the unions and then aggressively hiring new pilots, Lorenzo outflanked the workers and succeeded in restructuring Continental into a non-union carrier. The unions attempted to fight back with legal strategies and lawsuits. They argued that Continental had not been financially insolvent and bankruptcy had been a ploy to break its unions. Despite these efforts, the Supreme Court ruled in favor of Lorenzo. The unions' initial fragmentation and Lorenzo's brinkmanship tactics divided their interests and then demolished their jobs.

Cognizant of the industry's shaky finances and propensity to cut wages, unions at other airlines fought for greater financial transparency and a seat in the boardroom. The 1983 contract between Eastern Airlines and its employees epitomized the convergence of union negotiations and the corporate world. The company led by former astronaut, Frank Borman, had financial difficulties throughout the 1970s and suffered from an ill-timed buying spree of Airbus aircraft.[44] The IAM, led by Charles Bryan, insisted that the unions needed greater access to the company's finances, and he positioned himself as a stormy adversary against Borman. In 1983, outside auditors estimated that unless Eastern restructured and cut costs, it would lose $367 million in 1984 and possibly go bankrupt.[45] After the audit, IAM, ALPA, and the TWU agreed to a compromise where employees accepted wage concessions in return for stock holdings in the company for a two-year period. The pilots agreed to a 22 percent pay cut, and all other workers agreed to 18 percent cuts. In return, the unions would control 12 million shares (25 percent) of Eastern's stock.[46] The unions also gained seats on Eastern's board of directors and access to Eastern's financial reports, so they could evaluate its profits and expenses. This agreement made the Board of Directors jumpy, and many believed Borman had sold out to the unions.[47] Hardcore unionists were also skeptical of accepting the unions' business veneer, but given the grim economic outlook, the members voted for the plan: "Our leadership and advisors agree that the company has an immediate financial problem with the banks. This is the best solution they can come up with. I'll stand by Charlie [Bryan] on this one. He hasn't misled us yet."[48]

Unfortunately for the union members, when it came time to turn the clock back and reinstate wages in 1985, Borman unilaterally refused to "snap back" wages to their original levels. When Eastern demanded even more cuts, changes in work rules, and the institution of two-tier pay scales, the pilots, machinists, and flight attendants felt betrayed. As the ALPA leader, Larry Schulte said, it amounted to a "rape of the wages and working conditions" at Eastern.[49] Asking for heavy concessions and threatening bankruptcy, Eastern hoped the unions would cave in to its demands. When the unions refused, the Eastern board of directors sold the company to labor's nemesis at Continental, Frank Lorenzo.[50] Eastern's unions' failed attempt at boardroom politics and faith in stock options symbolized the unions' narrow bargaining position and the omnipresent role of high stakes Wall Street competition within the airline industry.

Airline workers, particularly the pilots and flight attendants, were notoriously fragmented. The power differential between the pilots and the flight attendants underscored class tensions and gender discrimination within the labor rank and file. As a result, the mid-1980s witnessed several single craft strikes, including the United Airlines pilots in 1985 and the TWA flight attendants in 1986, which highlighted the divisions within the industry even as the structural changes affected all employees.

Of all the airline employees, ALPA's pilots were distinct for being conservative, highly skilled, and most likely to identify with management. Pilots had unionized before World War II when they were largely an elite group of Navy veterans trained by the military before transferring into the commercial air industry.[51] Composed almost exclusively of white men with high salaries, ALPA often viewed itself more as a professional association than as a labor union. As Webster Todd Jr., the former chairman of the National Traffic Safety Board said, "It was more like the American Medical Association than the Steelworkers."[52] ALPA pilots pointedly had not backed the PATCO strike and were known for crossing IAM picket lines, but now, with threats to their salaries, benefits, and prestige, they began questioning their affinity with management. When deregulation led to new companies, non-union pilots, and harsh pay cuts, ALPA pilots began identifying more with labor. Lorenzo's bankruptcy tactics and the failed IAM and ALPA strikes at Continental clearly demonstrated the pitfalls of single union strikes and the industry's lack of solidarity. One ALPA official explained, "The Continental situation more than anything else taught the pilots' union some religion. The pilots' union decided it was better to start honoring other unions' picket lines, at least for a while, or the unions weren't going to get anywhere."[53] This new resolve intensified the pressure on airlines, because pilots, unlike mechanics and flight attendants, were not easily replaceable. In these labor disputes, pilots also capitalized on their prestigious image and the public's trust in their service. For example, in media reports, pilots always appeared in their full uniforms, complete with pilot's cap and union picket. These symbols of pilots' professionalism invoked their trusted position and intended to lend legitimacy to their protest. Through their uniforms pilots intentionally distinguished themselves from the IAM or other blue-collar unionists. By the mid-1980s, pilots balanced this line between elite professionals and labor militants.

In 1985, United pilots proved that they could ground an airline and demand union victories even in a hostile labor environment. Withholding their labor, pilots demonstrated their specialized skills and their ability to puncture an airline's valuable public image by casting doubts on its safety standards. United's management wanted to instill a two-tier wage scale, under which newly hired pilots would advance on a lower pay scale for twenty years. Charles Craypo, a labor analyst explained that this created a divided labor force, violating the principle of equal work for equal pay.[54] Not only did a two-tier wage scale jeopardize job security and undermine professional respect, but ALPA argued that safety would be endangered. Joseph Leroy, a 727 captain, said, "The cockpit depends on mutual respect and trust. We cannot afford that kind of trouble."[55] ALPA developed an in-depth educational program and communication network to reach its members, and it successfully mobilized veteran pilots to fight pay cuts for new hires.[56] Five thousand pilots went on strike against United for more than four weeks. Although United threatened to fire the pilots, it was unable to find qualified replacements fast enough, and its customers simply turned to other airlines. Rapidly losing money, United negotiated with ALPA and compromised on a two-tier pay scale, which would merge into a single scale after five, rather than twenty, years of employment.[57] In a decade of few successful strikes, the pilots' strike was remarkable for its relative success and for its mobilization of generally conservative, strike-averse pilots.

In stark contrast, flight attendants, the vast majority of whom were women, found themselves in a weaker bargaining position. Flight attendants had been organizing since the 1940s, but the airlines remained a male dominated industry with its almost exclusively male pilot corps, mechanics, and corporate executives. In the 1960s and 1970s, flight attendants faced sex discrimination, compulsory retirement policies for married women, and airline advertising campaigns that commodified their sexuality.[58] Although they gained victories throughout the era and job security for married and pregnant women, unlike pilots, flight attendants were more easily replaced. Despite the fact that flight attendants worked at an altitude of 30,000 feet, their work was analogous to other low skill service jobs. As airlines sought to reduce costs, veteran flight attendants railed against the company's attempts to replace them with rookie attendants at far lower wages. In a bitter contract fight, Pan Am trained hundreds of new recruits as possible strike breakers/permanent replacements and then offered stark new B-scale salaries and early retirement plans for older workers. A union negotiator for the flight attendants believed, "You have a lot of 40-year-old gals who have come to depend on the job who are terrified the company wants to replace them with cute 18-year-olds," and the union literature mocked, "Nineteen, pretty, single, and cheap."[59] Pan Am's flight attendants' union pushed gender equity as its central message, but in the end it did not have the alliances or strength to strike. The final contract codified a B-scale starting pay that dropped flight attendants salaries from $1235 to $784 a month and cut overtime pay, vacations, and pensions. The Independent Union of Flight Attendants concluded, "The contract is just awful . . . many of us really think that this is a piece of garbage."[60]

In 1986, the flight attendants at TWA did go on strike, but despite their militancy and cohesiveness, they could not close the airline or inflict economic damage. Leading up to contract negotiations, TWA chairman Carl Icahn demanded a 20 percent wage cut from all his employees. The IAM fought for and won a 15 percent cut, and Vicki Frankovich, the president of the Independent Federation of Flight Attendants (IFFA), believed her workers should be offered a similar deal. Gender was a key component, and Icahn dismissed the flight attendants' economic concerns and explicitly privileged the majority male IAM. Frankovich reported that:

> Icahn has stated that we are not breadwinners and therefore can give more [concessions] than employees who have to support a family...Does Icahn believe that he can take more from flight attendants than from machinists because we are a predominantly female workforce? Does he believe we are not prepared to fight?[61]

Rejecting the proposed 17 percent wage cuts and increase in flight hours, six thousand flight attendants went on strike. Within days, TWA hired thousands of replacement workers and kept the airline flying. These immediate actions broke the strike. The IFFA filed a sex discrimination complaint with the EEOC, but many flight attendants eventually crossed the picket lines and of those who held out, few were rehired.[62] Icahn effectively broke the flight attendants' union and demonstrated the vulnerability of the airlines' low paid, female employees.

The question of solidarity was acute. ALPA categorically refused to respect the IFFA's picket lines, and IAM chair, William Winpisinger, blamed Frankovich for poor strategy and a lack of solidarity with other unions. Frankovich had failed to ensure AFL-CIO support or alliances with IAM or ALPA, and the media criticized her for unrealistic expectations and unsavvy bargaining. She also publicly insisted that flight attendants were "not blue collar workers," further undercutting her ability to build alliances.[63] Without the IAM or ALPA's support or industry wide action, the flight attendants did not have the ability to financially harm the airline. In fact, TWA welcomed the strike as a way to jettison highly paid veteran attendants and hire new ones for less.

Under siege by a brutal industry restructuring, without political allies or government support, and often at the mercy of corporate raiders, airline employees adopted a range of strategies, from entering novel corporate power-sharing agreements to conducting old-fashioned strikes. This five-year trajectory mirrored the turbulence of the airline industry. Through mergers and hostile takeovers, corporate raiders plundered airlines for their most valuable assets with little regard for their workers. The corporations whittled away union contracts, enforced two-tier pay scales, and wage-cuts were the norm.

However, unlike other industries where unions disappeared, airline unions dug in their heels, insisted on their continued relevance and specialized skills, and occasionally won. Airline strikes also happened on a national stage, and mainstream magazines and daily papers covered the strikes with an intensity absent in other industries. Affecting public transportation on a continental scale, if unions could ground an airline, they could generate a national and public response. These mid-eighties strikes created a mixed legacy, and in 1989 Frank Lorenzo, Charlie Bryan, leveraged buyouts, bankruptcy court, and worker solidarity would all reappear in a final showdown between Eastern Airlines and its unions.

The highly visible and widely reported 1989 Eastern Airlines strike consciously invoked PATCO's legacy.[64] The Eastern Airlines strike also effectively marked deregulation's ten-year anniversary. Long-term airline labor activist and analyst, Paul J. Baicich, blamed labor-management's rock bottom relations on deregulation and quoted an airline executive's sentiment that deregulation was "the greatest anti-labor bill ever passed."[65] By the time Eastern's mechanics, pilots, and flight attendants went on strike, the major airlines had largely consolidated and readjusted to deregulation's new rules. Select industry giants had captured key airport gates and through the lucrative hub and spoke networks, they directed passengers from smaller cities into an urban hub. American, United, and Delta effectively cordoned off most of the country, routinized one-stop flights, and essentially created an oligopoly with each major carrier dominating a single region. Although Eastern Airlines carried profitable east coast flights, it had weaker hubs, a history of poor investment, high debt burden, and hostile labor relations. When Eastern's unions went on strike against deep wage cuts and Frank Lorenzo's blatantly anti-worker management style, the national labor movement mobilized behind them.[66] The AFL-CIO hoped that a union win at Eastern would be a watershed moment and break Reagan's anti-labor legacy

with national consequences. However, as the strike dragged on the labor movement's internal weaknesses and the government's continued pro-business bias
provided a muddied endgame far from a clear-cut labor victory.

When Frank Lorenzo bought Eastern Airlines in 1986, he acquired a hemorrhaging company and labor-management discord, which added to his already
anti-union politics. When Lorenzo's holding company, Texas Air, bought the
airline, he announced a 29 percent labor cut and demanded that the IAM members concede $265 million in pay and benefits.[67] From across the political spec-
trum, from the *Wall Street Journal* to *Labor Notes*, the media agreed that Lorenzo was dumping Eastern's assets, demonstrating paper losses, and thereby
forcing labor concessions. A former Lorenzo supporter, Ferrell Kupersmith explained, "If one were creating junk, this [Texas Air] would be at the bottom of
the barrel. We have a pro-business bias, but the system here is being abused."[68]
The unions accused Eastern of "double breasting" which enabled Lorenzo to
"carve up Eastern to benefit non-union Continental."[69] The most egregious case
was when Lorenzo "sold" Eastern Airlines profitable reservation system to Texas Air for a $100 million junk bond, when it had been valued at over $200 million, and then charged Eastern a fee to use the system.[70] The unions believed
Lorenzo deliberately rearranged Eastern's accounts in order to demand deep
wage cuts.

After the string of labor losses in the 1980s, IAM, TWU, and ALPA embarked
on a new round of negotiations. Outflanked by business for more than a decade,
unions realized that even in prolonged strikes, corporations often had the capital
power to come out ahead. It was clear after a string of brutal labor losses
throughout the eighties (e.g., PATCO, Phelps Dodge, and Hormel), that a strike
alone could and would be crushed. As a result, the airline unions first launched a
corporate campaign, filed lawsuits, and lobbied politicians to generate public
support for their cause. Airlines, because of the possibility for extreme acci-
dents, relied on a good public image and a belief in a calm, well-managed company with safety being the ultimate concern. Airlines were therefore vulnerable
to corporate campaigns, and in this case, the unions sought to demonize Lorenzo
and damage the reputation of Eastern's safety record.[71] They petitioned the FAA
to investigate Eastern's safety record, invoking the public's fear of flying and
questioning Eastern's concern for public safety. The corporate campaign's
second flank was to deliberately target Lorenzo in the press; labor hoped that the
general public would be outraged rather than awed by his excesses. Bryan repeatedly reiterated to the press, "This is a Frank Lorenzo strike," and it was a
battle of "the purest case of evil vs. good."[72] The unions also initiated lawsuits
and lobbied legislators to beat Eastern in the courts and on the political stage.

In March 1989, with labor hostilities at a breaking point, ALPA, TWU, and
IAM petitioned the federal government to intervene and order a 60-day mediation period as allowed by the Railway Labor Act (RLA), which governed the
airlines.[73] The RLA encouraged mediation, discouraged strikes, and authorized
direct government intervention because of the transportation industry's importance to public service and the national economy. The IAM threatened second-

ary boycotts on the railroads, in order to create an "emergency" and force government intervention.[74] The Bush Administration threatened that if other unions (i.e., railroads, buses, or other airlines) tried to exercise their secondary boycott rights, he would support new legislation stripping the RLA of those protections.[75] The unions supported federal intervention, because they believed the National Mediation Board (NMB) would rule in their favor; however, President Bush refused to enter the dispute. Bush's Transportation Secretary, Samuel Skinner, reiterated, "The Administration believes in free market principles…We do not believe that government should be in the business of drafting the economic terms of labor agreements."[76] By failing to order both sides to negotiate before the NMB, President Bush took an active stance in favor of Eastern Airlines. The government's pro-corporate position dismissed the RLA's intentionally drawn-out bargaining procedures and forced the unions into a corner.

Eastern's IAM went on strike in 1989, and ALPA and TWU soon joined their picket lines for the first concerted attempt at union solidarity in the airline industry. Because ALPA believed Lorenzo was stripping the company for profit, 98 percent of its members supported the strike.[77] With ALPA respecting the IAM picket lines, it created a momentum and optimism for the labor movement.[78] ALPA even published a full-page ad in *USA Today* against Texas Air, and one pilot wrote an editorial in *Newsweek*, asserting, "We chose to join our mechanics and flight attendants in a sympathy strike we hoped would force someone to look at the situation and realize that capitalism can run amok."[79]

The strike also became a symbolic action against Wall Street culture and high stake junk bonds. *The New Republic* characterized Eastern Airlines as symbolic of the quintessential "greed and reckless manipulation, of sham financial transactions" of the Reagan years.[80] The AFL-CIO also established the "Fairness at Eastern" strike fund, lobbied government officials, and sponsored local rallies to broaden national support for the strike.[81] The unions hoped that the glamour would wear off the junk bond kings, and they intended to rally support for workers hurt by corporate excesses and gamesmanship. Broderick concluded, "We join the thousands across our country today who have been caught in restructurings, leveraged buyouts, bankruptcies, sell-offs, and mountains of debt."[82] However, despite this solidarity and stand against unrestrained capital, inequities remained on the picket line; ALPA provided its members with $2400/month strike benefits, while IAM strikers received $400/month, and TWU flight attendants went without a strike fund.[83]

Throughout the strike, Lorenzo struggled to put Eastern flights in the air, escape liquidation, and court a new owner to save the financially collapsing airline. Lorenzo filed for Chapter 11 five days after the strike began. According to *Labor Notes*, Lorenzo operated at a $350 million annual loss, owed $300 million to European creditors, and $700 million in junk bonds.[84] During this time, the unions tried to woo other buyers, namely Carl Icahn, Donald Trump, and former baseball commissioner, Peter Ueberroth, or buy the airline themselves with Chicago options trader, Joseph Ritchie. However, their own shaky funding structure meant that huge concessions would be necessary under almost any agreement, thus forcing wages down even further.[85] Essentially, the unions were not wealthy enough to compete with Donald Trump or Peter Ueberroth, and in the process they lowered the bar to the point where they suggested concessions even deeper than Lorenzo's initial offers. In a cycle of bad business deals, the unions did not have the power to save the airline.[86] After a year of back and forth bargaining, Eastern collapsed under increasing pressure in bankruptcy court, and Lorenzo cashed out with $30 million when he sold his investments to Scandinavian Airlines System.[87] Four months later, Eastern Airlines closed for good.

While the unions succeeded in demonstrating their power, the company's ultimate demise presented a mixed victory at best. At the outset of the strike, national union leaders heralded the strike as a turning point for labor. William Olwell, the vice president of the Food and Commercial Workers union remarked, "This strike is a good one," and Greg Tarpinian, the Director of the Labor Research Association, believed, "The strike probably has been the most successful labor action of the decade..."[88] With a clear-cut villain in Lorenzo, the labor movement had hoped to rally the public against the corporate raiders who had devalued workers' jobs and tried to crush their unions. Still, even with the airline unions' newfound solidarity, Eastern Airlines continued to fly, and rather than new contracts, the airline collapsed. Without widespread national boycotts or direct government intervention, the unions could not force Lorenzo or Texas Air to the table. Texas Air's multiple assets and Lorenzo's own protected capital meant that the company could sacrifice Eastern.

Even at the end when Eastern closed, some workers took satisfaction in the company's demise. Although in some ways, workers struck themselves out of a job, they also worked together against a corporation that had given every sign of dismantling the union carrier for the better half of the decade. For example, Ernie Mailhot, a ramp worker, member of the IAM, and writer for *The Militant*, a New York socialist paper, reported that one worker said, "I wouldn't have missed this for the world," and another said, "I'm very happy this day came. It's been a long twenty-two months but fighting is the only way. If others follow our example, we'll have strong unions."[89] Other labor activists were less sanguine. Paul J. Baicich, argued that Eastern lost its opportunity to be the post-PATCO example. He believed that the AFL-CIO's reluctance to sponsor secondary boycotts or capitalize on public sympathy, ultimately limited Eastern's possibility to rejuvenate the labor movement. Still, he believed the strike demonstrated the power of solidarity, inter-craft cooperation, and remained an important line in the sand for airline CEOs.[90] Kim Moody responded even more harshly that the strike only re-emphasized the AFL-CIO's ineffective and impotent strategies: "PATCO was not redeemed so much as repeated." He also lamented the union's attempts to enter the corporate raider boardrooms and compete for a "white knight." Moody argued that these ultimate business unionist tactics were out of the hands of the rank-and-file members and epitomized the corporatization of the unions. Finally, he lambasted the unions for sexism, which failed to compensate striking flight attendants, while ALPA and IAM members all received healthy strike benefits and compensation.[91] In short, Reagan's ghost remained, and labor would need to rebuild yet again.

Deregulation challenged the U.S. airline industry's ability to navigate its dual role as a competitive private industry and a public utility. Airlines continued to both deliver a service to the public and create millions of dollars of corporate capital. In the 1980s, deregulation did not erase the state's interest in the industry. The government's defense of private enterprise ostensibly allowed the free market to rule; however, as Duane E. Woerth, the Vice-President of ALPA, argued succinctly, "The single biggest myth that must be exposed is that because the domestic airline industry was deregulated in 1978, U.S. government policies since that time have had a benign or neutral effect on the airline industry. Nothing could be more naïve or further from the truth."[92] Years of legislation and precedent had cemented the government's ability to intervene in the airline industry. At one extreme, Reagan's use of military air traffic controllers revealed the state's ability to use military expertise to override labor and public employees. On the opposite end, Bush's decision against intervention in the Eastern airlines strike demonstrated how government inaction could have a decidedly pro-business bias.

Airline executives and union leaders both appealed to fliers as consumers with considerable power in airline strikes. The government heralded deregulation as a boon to consumers. Passengers might complain about poor service, late flights, and delays, but many travelers had more flight options. Union members, from PATCO to Eastern's pilots, hoped to sway public opinion by emphasizing safety concerns and invoking the risks of flying without responsible workers. But rather than focusing on underpaid and overworked airline employees, the media story was generally more sympathetic to consumers and "harried travelers" who were inconvenienced by the strikes.[93] The airline industry and the government framed the unions' interests as being counter to the general public's interests in lower fares and smoother flying. As such, the press tended to highlight individuals who faced poor service during a strike, such as a passenger who paid $3500 for a first class trip to Paris, but was served only cold cuts during the flight attendants' strike.[94] In another example, the *Wall Street Journal* reported that governors from western states were "among the victims" of the United pilot strike, because they were unable to attend a conference in Hawaii.[95] Classifying the passengers, particularly high-powered politicians, as victims reveals how the mainstream media valued consumers over workers and defined their interests as antithetical. Thomas Petzinger, a writer for the *Wall Street Journal*, countered that passengers' interest in well-managed airlines included safety and good labor relations as well as a cheap ticket.[96]

Despite, or perhaps because, of the industry restructuring, airline unions adapted to the political and economic realities of the industry as the decade progressed. Peter Cappelli, a professor at the Wharton School of Management, surmised that the airline industry was perhaps the only division where unions gained strength during the 1980s.[97] Despite this growing militancy and solidarity, striking pilots still declared, "I'm not a big union man but..." or "I'm a typical mainstream American who dislikes unions."[98] This accepted commonsense epitomized the labor movement's 1980s image problem, and a political climate that disparaged unionism. In high-profile interviews and essays, these pilots felt a need to separate their cause from the "unions," even as they struck and marched on picket lines. This sense of unease and recognition of labor's poor status in the media complicated the upsurge in union pride. At the same time, the 1980s forced the separate craft unions to acknowledge their common interests for the first time, even when political and economic forces remained adamantly opposed to union labor. Eastern Airlines failed to be the turning point for the labor movement union leaders had hoped it would be, but it was critical for the airline industry. Airline workers recognized their jobs were at risk, mobilized, and demanded that corporations account for their workers. Although their successes were limited, the industry remained highly unionized.

As the 1990s progressed, airline unions remained powerful as the political climate changed. The Clinton Administration reversed the Bush Administration's deliberate aloofness and actively intervened to prevent airline strikes. In 1993, American Airlines flight attendants went on strike over Thanksgiving and disrupted American's service to a far greater extent than had been anticipated. After five days, Clinton used his executive influence and American Airlines agreed to resolve the dispute through arbitration. Clinton again used his authority to avert a pilots' strike at American Airlines in 1997. While labor leaders might have been too optimistic when they claimed the flight attendants' strike and Clinton's actions were "the rebirth of the labor movement," it did reveal the government's power to take a stand for labor.[99] Clinton's pro-labor position demonstrated the government's ongoing influence in labor-management disputes and the potential value of state support.

Given economists' rosy promises of free trade, Reagan's anti-union stands, and the glamorous Wall Street raiders, the airline industry offers a compelling window onto the intersection of corporate finance, government power, and workers' rights throughout the 1980s. Therefore it seems more than mere coincidence that *Wall Street's* Gordon Gekko manipulated an airline deal and tried to break its unions in the decade's iconic film. From PATCO to the Eastern Airlines' strike, airline unions suffered losses and developed new techniques to contend with deregulation, leveraged buyouts, and the government's studied disinterest. Pilots, machinists, and flight attendants became more militant and fought to save their unions even as they accepted wage concessions and two-tier pay scales. Caught in a rapidly changing industry, a hostile political environment, and a weak labor movement, airline unions managed to remain relevant, which in the 1980s was a victory in and of itself.

Notes

1. For example, in a 1987 review, film critic Roger Ebert did not comment on the airlines or the role of trade unions in the film. Roger Ebert, *Chicago Sun Times*, December 11, 1987.

2. Not surprisingly, labor activist Kim Moody critiques the film's labor-management politics: "In *Wall Street*, the movie, there are good raiders and bad. The unions stop the evil Lorenzo-style raider from breaking up Blue Star Airlines by threatening direct action. But they willingly grant concessions to a benevolent British raider who promises to turn the ailing airline around. In real life, corporate takeovers do not involve the sentimental salvation of troubled companies." Kim Moody "Confrontations Spread Throughout Industry," *Labor Notes* March 1988, 15.

3. Under "strikes" in the *New York Times Index*, only coal and railroad strikes came close to the airlines in the overall mention of "strikes" between 1981 and 1991. While this is admittedly an imperfect barometer and fails to include job actions that were not characterized as strikes, it does indicate the extensive media coverage of airline labor disputes. For an analysis of twentieth century labor history through the *New York Times* and *London Times* Indices see Beverly J. Silver, Giovanni Arrighi, and Melvyn Dubofsky, eds., "Labor Unrest in the World-Economy, 1870-1990," *Review of the Fernand Braudel Center* 18, no. 1, winter 1995.

4. Kim Moody, *An Injury to All: The Decline of American Unionism* (New York: Verso, 1988); After years of attrition, union density dropped in the nonagricultural workforce from 32.5% in 1953 to 17.5% in 1986, and the total number of union members fell from 22.2 million in 1975 to 17 million in 1986 (Moody 4).

5. For decline in overall strike figures, see U.S. Department of Labor, "Work Stoppages involving 1,000 workers or more, 1947-2000," http://www.bls.gov/news.release/hist ory/wkstp_02092001.txt (Accessed November 15, 2009); Laurie Schoder, "Flying the Unfriendly Skies: The Effect of Airline Deregulation on Labor Relations," *Transportation Law Journal* 22 (1994): 132.

6. Martha Derthick and Paul J. Quirk, *The Politics of Deregulation* (Washington DC: The Brookings Institution, 1985), 238-58.

7. John R. Meyer, Clinton V. Oster, Ivor P. Morgan, Benjamin A. Berman, and Diana L. Strassmann eds., *Airline Deregulation: The Early Experience* (Boston: Auburn House Publishing Company, 1981), 1-38.

8. Derthick and Quirk, *Politics of Deregulation*, 35-39; Robert Kuttner, *Everything for Sale: The Virtues and Limits of Markets* (New York: Alfred A. Knopf, 1997), 231-236.

9. Paul MacAvoy and John W. Snow, eds. *Regulation of Passenger Fares and Competition Among the Airlines: Ford Administration Papers on Regulatory Reform* (Washington DC: American Enterprise Institute for Public Policy and Research, 1977); Thomas Petzinger, Jr., *Hard Landing: The Epic Contest for Power and Profits that Plunged the Airlines into Chaos* (New York: Random House, 1995), 77-94; and Derthick and Quirk, *Politics of Deregulation*, 51-56.

10. Petzinger, *Hard Landing*, 95-151. For additional works on airline deregulation, see MacAvoy and Snow, eds. *Regulation of Passenger Fares and Competition Among the Airlines*; Meyer, et al., *Airline Deregulation: The Early Experience*; Kuttner, *Everything for Sale,* 255-70; Steven Morrison and Clifford Winston, *The Economic Effects on Airline Deregulation* (Washington DC: The Brookings Institution, 1986); George Williams,

The Airline Industry and the Impact of Deregulation (Ashgate: Ashgate Publishing Limited, 1993); Katherine Van Wezel Stone, "Labor Relations on the Airlines: The Railway Labor Act in the Era of Deregulation," *Stanford Law Review*, 42 (July 1990): 1540-41; and Isaac Cohen, "Political Climate and Two Airline Strikes: Century Air in 1932 and Continental Airlines in 1983-5," *Industrial Labor Relations Review*, (January 1990), 314.

11. The legacy of airline deregulation remains hotly contested. For supporters of deregulation, see Steven Morrison and Clifford Winston, "The Remaining Role for Government Policy in the Deregulated Airline Industry," in *Deregulation of Network Industries: What's Next?* eds. Sam Peltzman and Clifford Winston (Washington DC: AEI-Brookings Joint Center for Regulatory Studies, 2000), 1-40. They conclude, "If the public is to enjoy the full benefits of airline deregulation, airports and air traffic control may need to be privatized" (4). In a rebuttal against deregulation, see Paul Stephen Dempsey and Andrew R. Goetz, *Airline Deregulation and Laissez-Faire Mythology* (Westport, CT: Quorum Books, 1992). In contrast, they argue, "We crawled out from under rocks to write this book because the story needs to be told: the Emperor has no clothes. Deregulation is a failure" (xvi).

12. Moody, *An Injury to All*, 140-1.

13. Arthur B. Shostak and David Skocik, eds. *The Air Controllers' Controversy: Lessons from the PATCO Strike* (New York: Human Sciences Press, 1986), 126-132.

14. John S. DeMott, "Labor's Unhappy Birthday," *Time*, November 16, 1981, 124-5.

15. "Traffic Snarl" *New Republic*, August 22-29, 1981, 6.

16. "Traffic Snarl" *New Republic*, 70.

17. Richard Hurd, "A Retrospective on the PATCO Strategy," in *The Air Controllers' Controversy: Lessons from the PATCO Strike*, eds. Arthur Shostak and David Skocik, 210.

18. Hurd, "A Retrospective on the PATCO Strategy."

19. Letter to the Editor, *Newsweek*, August 31, 1981, 6, George S. Burson Jr. wrote, "It is interesting that when Polish Government workers strike, they are striking a blow for freedom, but when American Government workers strike, they are unpatriotic lawbreakers." In an interview with Moe Biller, President of the American Postal Workers Union, Biller said, "Don't we all admire the Solidarity trade-union movement in Poland for essentially doing the same thing as the air traffic controllers – striking against their own government?" *US News and World Reports*, August 24, 1981, 18.

20. "Fear of Flying," *Time*, August 31, 1981, 19; David Nagy, "How Safe Are Our Airways?" *U.S. News and World Reports*, August 24, 1981, 14-21.

21. Shostak and Skocik, *Air Controllers' Controversy* 184-5.

22. Richard W. Hurd, "How PATCO Was Led Into a Trap," *The Nation*, December 26, 1981, 696-8; Hurd, "A Retrospective on the PATCO Strategy," 206-14; Richard Hurd and Jill Kriesky, "Communications 'The Rise and Demise of PATCO' Reconstructed," *Industrial and Labor Relations Review* (October 1986), 115-121; Edward Meadows, "The FAA Keeps Them Flying," *Fortune*, December 28, 1981, 48-52.

23. Richard Hurd, "How PATCO was Led into a Trap."

24. Frederick Thayer, "Strike Means Friendly Skies for Airlines," *Atlantic Monthly*, December 1981, 14-9.

25. Herbert R. Northrup, "The New Employee-Relations Climate in Airlines," *Industrial and Labor Relations Review* (January 1983): 167-181.

26. "Two Get 90 Days for 1981 Walkout: Former PATCO Strikers Jailed in Texas," *Labor Notes,* May 26, 1993, 1; Dan La Botz, "PATCO – Lest We Forget: Labor Notes Interviews Jailed Air Traffic Controller," *Labor Notes,* August 23, 1983, 7. The government indicted seventy-seven controllers for striking against the government, a federal felony. Six cases went to trial, and four controllers served 90-day sentences for their participation in the strike.

27. Ellen Schrecker, *Many are the Crimes: McCarthyism in America* (Boston: Little, Brown, and Company, 1998), 271.

28. "Should the U.S. Grant Amnesty to Air Controllers?" *U.S. News and World Reports,* August 24, 1981, 19.

29. "Four Ways to Botch a Strike," *U.S. News and World Reports,* August 24, 1981,14-15.

30. Shostak and Skocik *Air Controllers' Controversy,* 106-7.

31. "AFL-CIO Convention Sidesteps Strong Support for PATCO," *Labor Notes,* November 23, 1981; Jerry Brenner, "Defense of PATCO Must Go Beyond Tactics" *Labor Notes,* January 21, 1982, 13.

32. Carol B. Swanson, "The Turn in Takeovers: A Study in Public Appeasement and Unstoppable Capitalism," *Georgia Law Review* (Summer 1996), 968.

33. Dempsey and Goetz, *Airline Deregulation and Laissez-Faire Mythology,* xiv; Northrup, "The New Employee Relations Climate in Airlines."

34. Senate Subcommittee, *Airline Merger Related Labor Protection,* 10.

35. Peter Cappelli, "Introduction," *Airline Labor Relations in the Global Era: The New Frontier,* ed. Pater Cappelli, (Ithaca, NY: Cornell University Press, 1995), 1-10.

36. Senate Subcommittee on Aviation of the Committee on Commerce, Science, and Transportation, *Airline Merger Related Labor Protection,* 97th Congress, 2d Session, September 24, 1982, 100-101.

37. Senate Subcommittee on Aviation, *Airline Merger Related Labor Protection,* 90-91. As a result of union activism and the feminist movement, many female flight attendants rejected the term "stewardess" and embraced the more professional sounding "flight attendant" by the late 1970s. Kathleen Barry, *Femininity in Flight: A History of Flight Attendants* (Durham, NC: Duke University Press, 2007), 205-209.

38. Dempsey and Goetz, *Airline Deregulation and Laissez-Faire Mythology,* 24-32.

39. Isaac Cohen, "Political Climate and Two Airline Strikes," 308-322.

40. Jane Slaughter, "Machinists Picket Pilots for Scabbing on Continental Airlines Strike," *Labor Notes,* August 23, 1983, 1.

41. Isaac Cohen, "Political Climate and Two Airline Strikes," 314-5.

42. Roy Rowan, "An Airline Boss Attacks Sky-High Wages," *Fortune,* January 9, 1984, 66-73.

43. Athanassios Papaioannou, "The Duty to Bargain and Rejection of Collective Agreements Under Section 1113 by a Bankrupt Airline: Trying to Reconcile RLA with Bankruptcy Code," *Transportation Law Journal* 18 (1990): 219-253; Francis Garb, "'Share the Pain, Share the Gain': Airline Bankruptcies and the Railway Labor Act," *Transportation Law Journal* 24 (1996): 1-23.

44. Dempsey and Goetz, *Airline Deregulation and Laissez-Faire Mythology,* 110.

45. Joseph Blasi and James Gasaway, "The Great Experiment: Labor-Management Cooperation at Eastern Airlines," *Airline Labor Relations in the Global Era: The New Frontier,* ed. Peter Cappelli (Ithaca: Cornell University Press, 1995), 184-200.

46. Paul J. Baicich, "Airline Unions Grant Concessions at Eastern in Exchange for Company Stock," *Labor Notes*, December 20, 1983, 6.

47. Blasi and Gasaway, "The Great Experiment," 192-193.

48. Baicich, "Airline Unions Grant Concessions."

49. Paul J. Baicich, " 'Worker Participation' Doesn't End Eastern's Concession Demands," *Labor Notes*, January 1986, 1.

50. Paul J. Baicich, "Machinists Reject Concessions at Eastern: Airline to be Sold to Lorenzo," *Labor Notes*, April 1986, 3.

51. George E. Hopkins, *The Airline Pilots: A Study in Elite Unionization* (Cambridge: Harvard University Press, 1971); Kenneth Labich, "America's Most Arrogant Union," *Fortune*, November 10, 1986.

52. Leonard M. Apcar, "Militant Fliers: Pilots' Bitter Strike Against Continental Changed their Union," *Wall Street Journal*, March 17, 1988, 1.

53. William M. Carley, "Pan Am Reaches Back-to-Work Accord with Pilots; Mechanics Remain on Strike," *Wall Street Journal*, March 2, 1985, 2.

54. "Two-Tier Pay Sparks a Strike" *U.S. News and World Report*, May 27, 1985.

55. Barbara Rudolph, "United Pilots Walk the Line," *Time*, March 27, 1985, 59; "United Strike's Impact on Rivals and Passengers," *U.S. News and World Reports*, June 10, 1985, 100.

56. Leonard M. Apcar, "Pilots Union Against United Air Signals New National Strike Strategy," *Wall Street Journal*, May 22, 1985, 16.

57. Roger Neal, "The $13,000 Pilot," *Forbes*, June 17, 1985, 48.

58. The most recent and comprehensive study of female flight attendants and labor activism is: Barry, *Femininity in Flight*. Also see, Georgia Panter Nielsen, *From Sky Girl to Flight Attendant: Women and the Making of a Union* (Ithaca: Cornell University Press, 1982).

59. William M. Carley, "Pan Am Takes an Even Harder Line Against Possible Strike by Attendants," *Wall Street Journal* March 27, 1985, 6.

60. William M. Carley, "Pan Am Union of Attendants Agrees to Pact," *Wall Street Journal*, April 2, 1985, 15.

61. Phill Kwik, "TWA Flight Attendants Form 'Solidarity Network'" *Labor Notes*, April 1986, 2.

62. Kim Moody, "Failure of Solidarity Leaves TWA Flight Attendants on the Street," *Labor Notes*, July 1986, 5; William M. Carley, "Flight Attendants Unions Are Losing Strength," *Wall Street Journal*, April 8, 1986, 6.

63. Carolyn Friday and David Pauley, "A Fatal Flight Takes Its Toll: TWA Workers Finally Grapple with Harsh Reality," *Newsweek*, September 8, 1986, 38-40.

64. David Shribman, "Classic Struggle: Strike at Eastern Tests Ability of Big Labor to Re-Establish Itself," *Wall Street Journal*, March 6, 1989, 1 and 4.

65. Paul J. Baicich, "The Myth of Deregulation," *Labor Notes*, November 1988, 3.

66. David J. Walsh, *On Different Planes: An Organizational Analysis of Cooperation and Conflict Among Airline Unions* (Ithaca: Cornell University Industrial and Labor Relations Press, 1994), 147-156.

67. Kim Moody, "Confrontations Spread Throughout Industry," *Labor Notes*, March 1988, 3.

68. Paul J. Baicich, "The Myth of Deregulation."

69. Paul J. Baicich, "What a Choice: Lorenzo, Trump, or Icahn!" *Labor Notes*, No-

vember 1988, 3.

70. Henry Fairlie, "Air Sickness," *New Republic*, June 5, 1989, 14-18.

71. Bob Cohen, "Labor's New Arsenal," *Newsweek*, May 23, 1986, 48; Paul Jarley and Cheryl Maranto, "Union Corporate Campaigns: An Assessment," *Industrial and Labor Relations Review* (July 1990): 505-524.

72. Janice Castro, "Eastern Goes Bust," *Time*, March 20, 1989, 52-3; John Schwartz, "A Boss They Love to Hate," *Newsweek*, March 20, 1989, 20-4.

73. In 1936, Congress expanded the RLA to include the airline industry. The RLA predates the 1935 National Labor Relations Act (NLRA).

74. Kim Moody, "Eastern Machinists Draw the Line on Union-Busting," *Labor Notes*, April 1989, 1 .

75. Janice Castro, "Going for Broke at Eastern," *Time*, March 13, 1989, 42.

76. House Subcommittee on Aviation, Committee on Public Works and Transportation, *Eastern Airlines Labor disputes Emergency Board*, March 7, 1989, 10-11.

77. Castro, "Eastern Goes Bust"; Moody, "Eastern Machinists Draw the Line."

78. Albert R. Karr, "Uncharacteristic Solidarity Keeps Pilots from Crossing Picket Lines," *Wall Street Journal*, March 6, 1989, A4.

79. Fairlie, "Air Sickness"; Pat Broderick, "A Fed-Up Pilot Speaks Out," *Newsweek*, April 23, 1990. 8.

80. Fairlie, "Air Sickness."

81. Walsh, *On Different Planes*, 148.

82. Broderick, "A Fed-Up Pilot Speaks Out."

83. Joe De Cordoba, "Eastern Air's Striking Pilots Stand Firm Despite Disappointment Over Failed Deal," *Wall Street Journal*, April 17, 1989, A4.

84. Moody, "Eastern Machinists Draw the Line."

85. Kim Moody, "Eastern Strike Headed for a Showdown: Will Union-Backed Buyout Mean Bigger Concessions?" *Labor Notes*, July 1989, 5.

86. Kim Moody, "Eastern Pilots Pick New, More Militant Leader; Bankruptcy Court Gives Lorenzo More Time," *Labor Notes*, October 1989, 15.

87. Kim Moody, "Lorenzo Takes Off with $30 million," *Labor Notes*, September 1990, 3.

88. David Shribman, "Classic Struggle: Strike at Eastern Tests Ability of Big Labor to Re-Establish Itself," *Wall Street Journal*, March 6, 1989, 1; Letter to the Editor, Greg Tarpinian, *Wall Street Journal*, March 28, 1989, A19.

89. Ernie Mailhot, Judy Stranahan, and Jack Barnes, *The Eastern Airlines Strike: Accomplishments of the Rank-and-File Machinists and Gains for the Labor Movement* (New York: Pathfinder, 1991).

90. Paul J. Baicich, "What's Happened to the Eastern Airlines Strike?" *Labor Notes*, January 1990, 11.

91. Kim Moody, "The Eastern Strike: A Missed Opportunity," *Labor Notes*, February 1990, 10.

92. Duane E. Woerth, "International Aviation," *Airline Labor Relations in the Global Era: The New Frontier*, ed. Pater Cappelli (Ithaca, NY: Cornell University Press, 1995), 42-3.

93. Harlan Byrne, "United Airlines, Pilots Union Agree to Hold Talks with Mediators in Strike," *Wall Street Journal*, May 20, 1985, 2.

94. William M. Carley, "Flight Attendants Unions Are Losing Strength," *Wall Street*

Journal, April 8, 1986, 6.

95. *Wall Street Journal Index,* 1771; Article published, 18 June 1985, 33.

96. Petzinger *Hard Landing,* 422-425. It is notable that as low-cost carriers continued to proliferate, Southwest, the industry's model, operated with a union and made a profit.

97. Cappelli, *Airline Labor Relations in the Global Era,* 1-10.

98. Harlan Byrne, "United Air and Pilots Agree to Hold Talks with U.S. Mediators," *Wall Street Journal,* May 20, 1985, 2; Broderick, "A Fed-Up Pilot Speaks Out."

99. "Thanksgiving 'Gift' to Fliers Ruffles Some CEO Feathers," *Wall Street Journal,* November 24, 1993: A3, A5.

PART 2:

"Yeah, Well, History's Gonna Change": Understanding the 80s Beyond Reagan

Chapter 6

Triumph of "The Gipper" and the Democratic Party Malaise in the 1980s

Thomas F. Schaller

Introduction

The 1988 election is rarely mentioned as one of the significant contests in recent presidential history. But with the benefit of two decades' hindsight, the results that year were loaded with portent. Republican Vice President George H.W. Bush won 54 percent of the national popular vote, beating Democratic nominee Michael Dukakis in all but nine states. Bush's win was the third consecutive victory for the Republicans—the only time in the 60 years since 1948 either party has accomplished that feat, and the first time in 80 years since the GOP had won three presidential contests in a row. Although Democrats retained control of both houses of Congress in 1988, as they had for most of the previous four decades, little did they realize that their congressional dominance would soon come to an end as well.

In many ways, the Democrats reached bottom in 1988. Matters would get worse for the party in the opening years of the twenty-first century, of course, when more conservative elements within the Republican Party, led by Bush's son George W., established a firm grip on national and state politics. But by the end of the 1980s, signs of the Democratic Party's coming fate were plain to see. The 1988 election was the beginning of the end, if only for one reason: many Democrats were blithely puttering along with little to no recognition of what was headed their way, and what they ought to do about it—indeed, *whether* anything needed to be done at all.

Through a mix of complacency, false confidence, a misreading of the political tea leaves, and outright blunders, the Democrats during the 1980s compounded and exacerbated a set of underlying problems facing their party. In this chapter, I investigate the causes and consequences of the party's political problems during a decade that signaled the end of the Democrats' New Deal majority.

Thomas F. Schaller

The New Deal Anchor

In many mid-century American households, pictures of Franklin Roosevelt were displayed as prominently above their living room mantles as portraits of Jesus Christ. Partisan identity was strong and readily socialized into children. New Deal Democratic rule was familiar and comfortable.

The New Deal also had bipartisan reach and appeal. Riding the coattails of their popular presidential nominee, Dwight D. Eisenhower, Republicans captured both chambers of Congress in the 1952 election—the first time they controlled the House and Senate since before the start of the New Deal. But Eisenhower's presidency ultimately reinforced rather than rebuked New Deal principles. The Democrats quickly recovered from their congressional losses, recapturing control of both chambers in the 1954 midterm cycle. From that point until Ronald Reagan's groundswell election helped turn the Senate over to the GOP in 1980, the Democrats essentially owned Congress. To put their congressional dominance on the eve of that 1980 election into perspective, consider that for any American at that time still under 47—that is, those who were 21 years old or younger in 1954—the Democrats had controlled both chambers of Congress for their entire voting age-eligible lifetime. Likewise, during the 48 years of their voting-age lives, any American in 1980 who was 69 years old or younger could recall only those two years of Republican rule at the start of Ike's presidency.

As familiar as Democratic rule on Capitol Hill was to voters, it was equally taken for granted by Democratic elites in Congress. Though the size of their majorities had shrunk a bit by the late 1970s from their New Deal and Great Society peaks, Democrats were comfortably ensconced in power, particularly on the House side of the Capitol. They maintained power throughout Richard Nixon's and Gerald Ford's combined eight years in the White House. And in 1986, aided by political tailwinds from the Iran-Contra Scandal, Democrats recaptured the Senate by knocking off many of those same Republican freshmen Reagan helped sweep into office six years earlier. Given this veritable hegemony from 1930s through the end of the 1980s, Democratic congressional leaders could reasonably conclude that America had resolved itself to their legislative fiefdom.

But two trends, always bubbling just beneath the surface, should have given pause to the Democratic leadership during the 1980s.

The first was a general, rising trend toward incumbent security. Well chronicled by a platoon of political scientists starting with David Mayhew's pathbreaking work, the decline in so-called "marginal" seats—resulting from strategic gerrymandering and rising use of the congressional franking and other privileges—insulated members of Congress from both parties against demographic or partisan undercurrents.[1] Because Democrats were in power during the postwar period when this incumbent effect began to take hold, they were the initial beneficiaries of this newfound electoral buffer. However, if majority control could be wrested away, electoral security would quickly turn into a bulwark to power, rather than a buffer.

The second trend, about which the Democrats were more aware, even a bit nervous, was the partisan revolt occurring in the South. Starting as a whisper during the 1948 presidential bid of Strom Thurmond, building to a rumble by George Wallace's 1968 candidacy, and emerging as a full-throated roar by the time Reagan ran in 1980, calls from beleaguered southerners to shake off their century-long commitment to the Democratic Party were hard for Washington Democrats to ignore. As veteran yellow dog Democrats began to lose at the polls, retire or die, their seats were quickly snapped up by a new generation of Republicans led by the likes of Howard Baker, Jesse Helms, Trent Lott and Newt Gingrich.

What was especially discouraging for Democrats about the state of the two parties by the end of the decade was that a ticket featuring California's Reagan and Connecticut-raised Bush could harvest so many southern electoral votes and soon after native southerner Jimmy Carter dominated the region in 1976. Throughout the New Deal, the Democrats maintained firm one-party control over the South by resisting early attempts to desegregate the region and its political and social institutions. By the 1980s, however, the Democrats were forced to either retain this historical posture or make good on promises made by its more progressive southern leaders, most notably President Lyndon Johnson, during the tumultuous civil rights era. After the turmoil of the 1960s and 1970s settled, the Democrats found themselves on the horns of a coalitional dilemma, and the Republicans were all too happy to capitalize. "Several underlying factors have helped the Republicans secure enormous votes from southern whites in the post-Great Society era," wrote southern politics experts and brothers Earl and Merle Black in a post-1998 analysis. "The list begins—but hardly ends—with the parties' contrasting positions on civil rights and race relations. Traditional southern one-party politics was premised in part on the notion that the Democratic Party was the white South's instrument in national politics for maintaining racial segregation. When the Democratic Party shifted to a pro-civil rights position in response to the civil rights movement of the early 1960s, southern Democratic politicians correctly expected the party to lose support among white conservatives."[2]

By the end of the 1980s, the Democratic Party found itself astride a chasm, with one foot on each side of the divide. Its right foot was planted firmly and confidently in the past and the glories that attended political dominance associated with Roosevelt, Truman, Kennedy and Johnson; its left foot was cautiously affixed to the new, less firm terrain of a post-New Deal and, suddenly, post-Great Society political environment. As the chasm widened, and despite the resistance to leaving the surefooted comfort of their past dominance, there was no choice but to step forward into the uncertain future.

That process would not happen overnight. Instead, the 1980s began a quarter-century period of internal struggle that would not begin to resolve itself until at least the late stages of the George W. Bush era. For almost five decades, the ideas and promise of the New Deal served as an anchor for Democrats: providing stability throughout political storms, mooring them to a set of political principles and safeguarding political victories. But as the political tides changed, that anchor eventually became a liability, preventing their partisan boat from staying afloat as it clung too close to a shoreline that was steadily moving further and further out toward sea.

Blinded by Reagan

Any account of the partisan environment during the 1980s must begin with the most notable political figure of the decade: Ronald Reagan. The Washington arrival of the former actor and California governor had a powerfully rejuvenating effect on his party. Reagan's emergence also had a crippling effect on the Democrats, in ways both obvious and ironic.

The first and most obvious effect of Reagan's 1980 presidential win was to dispel the very idea that the post-Watergate national Republican Party was in shambles and utterly unredeemable. Just a few years before Reagan captured the White House, with Richard Nixon's resignation still fresh in the minds of American voters, the Democrats seemed indomitable. The Democrats had elected a huge class of post-war generation members of Congress in the Watergate election of 1974; two years later former Georgia Democratic Governor Jimmy Carter recaptured the White House. The Republican National Committee literally went dark in the middle of the 1970s, shuttering its door for lack of donations to pay its bills. What's more, the map of Carter's winning electoral coalition—he carried almost all the states east of the Mississippi River and almost none west of it—bore a strong geographic resemblance to those that had elected Democratic presidents for two generations, from Franklin Roosevelt to Harry Truman to Lyndon Johnson. For Democrats, happy days were here again.

Reagan's convincing win, coming despite the millions of votes he lost to moderate Republican John Anderson's third-party candidacy, shattered the notion that Democrats had one foot firmly planted on the neck of a helpless and beleaguered GOP. Winning states that had not voted Republican for decades— no less on an anti-tax and anti-government platform that challenged the core principles of New Deal identity—Reagan administered a hard dose of political reality to national Democrats from coast to coast. The Republicans flipped enough seats in the Senate in 1980 to gain a majority in that chamber for the first time in nearly three decades.

Few of Reagan's ideas were new: Anti-tax, anti-regulation and anti-communist sentiments had been bubbling up with conservative circles and had infused the language of national Republicans going back to at least the days of Senator Robert Taft. "While many Americans had been sympathetic to Barry Goldwater's conservative message, they found the messenger frightening and too extreme for the nation's highest office . . . For all of the nation's inherent conservatism, of which Taft spoke, modern conservatives were generally associated with naysaying, contrarianism, and opposition to even the most meager effort to assist Americans in need," writes presidential speechwriting expert Michael Cohen. "Reagan smoothed the rough edges of conservatism."[3] Reagan literally embodied the hopes and ideas of long-disheartened conservatives who had been searching for a savior figure.

Reagan's win also had the ancillary, if ironic benefit for Republicans of instilling a certain false confidence among Democrats. Reagan was a telegenic former actor, master of the well-timed political anecdote: He was the "Gipper," the "Great Communicator." The power of Reagan's persona made it all too easy to chalk up the presidential defeats of Democrats Jimmy Carter and Walter Mondale to temporary circumstances occasioned by the rise of a once-in-a-generation politician with a unique rhetorical skill set who happened to win office during a time of high inflation and high interest rates, and at a moment following shortly on the heels of both the Soviet invasion of Afghanistan and the unnerving Iranian revolution. Reagan, it might easily have been surmised, was little more than a passing American fancy—a fad as certain to fade as fast as the one-gloved pop star who was then filling concert arenas from coast to coast. Had Speaker Tip O'Neill and his fellow Democrats instead been out-charmed by a less talented Washington insider—had they lost forty-nine states to another Nixon, as they had in 1972, but a defeat from which they nevertheless quickly recovered—instead of losing forty-nine states again in 1984 as they did to Reagan, perhaps more Democrats would have recognized the true magnitude of their party's problems, or at least acknowledged them sooner.

Indeed, by 1988, Reagan's demonstration of the power of political celebrity was fostering Democratic notions of responding in kind. The presumed answer to Reagan was New York Gov. Mario Cuomo, a smooth operator and smoother orator from the same Empire State that produced the party's last empire-builder. With Jack Kennedy having already broken the glass ceiling for Catholic contenders, Cuomo was the darling choice of many party leaders who had pinned the hopes for revival on finding the Democrats' own larger-than-life figure. (Gary Hart briefly emerged as a similar figure in 1984.) Of the party's unsettled and uncertain mood at the outset of the 1988 presidential cycle, *Newsweek's* Peter Goldman and Tom Mathews wrote:

> The remedy most commonly sought was Mr.—or perhaps, in the new order of things, Ms.—Right, that mythic lost godchild of FDR who would somehow return the party to its old glory. It was a rescue fantasy, of course, a search as dogged and as vain as the quest for the Holy Grail in Arthurian legend. Its failure was all but foreordained, starting as it did from the premise that anyone actually running must be Mr. or Mrs. Wrong. Yet the Democrats had been obsessed with the dream at least since the death and transfiguration of Jack Kennedy a generation ago. They were waiting for the redeemer and, in his absence, choosing sides among men of lesser clay. The result had been a series of debilitating fights for the nomination and for the dubious further honor of losing in November.[4]

In short, Democrats grappling with a raft of identity and ideological problems were looking for a savior rather than solutions.

The 1986 tax reform was a perfect example of how much Reagan had altered the political and partisan landscape in the five years since taking office. The reform package brokered by the president, Senate Majority Leader Howard Baker of Tennessee and Speaker O'Neill included significant reduction in corporate tax rates in exchange for elimination of a host of preferences in the tax code for various industries. "[T]he 1986 measure clearly extended the Reagan revolution's policy agenda. Democrats played a large, indeed decisive, role in this extension," political scientist Walter Dean Burham wrote at the end of the decade. "In this, as in the entire posture of the 1988 Dukakis presidential campaign, the party's leadership reflected the kind of politics of defeat and marginalization that have classically affected victims of earlier realignments . . . The presidential out-party's problems of defining itself and projecting a credible alternative to the many who have not notably benefitted from the new order have thus been deeply intensified."[5] Prior to Reagan, major policy debates were largely intramural battles fought among liberal and conservative Democrats on Capitol Hill. Reagan's eight-year presidential reign forced congressional Democrats into a new and awkward choice between being obstructionist or letting themselves to be co-opted by the White House's agenda.

Democrats were not completely oblivious to their mounting political problems during the decade. After the 1984 results, many fretted about the possibility of a conservative realignment in the making, argues Kenneth Baer in *Reinventing Democrats*, his analysis of the rise of the centrist movement within the Democratic Party led by Bill Clinton, Al Gore and other key "New Democrat" pioneers who formed the Democratic Leadership Council in the middle of the decade in response to the surging Republican threat. Yet, writes Baer:

> Other analysts were almost optimistic about the Democratic prospects. They pointed to the fact that Democrats were still very successful at the subpresidential level, and to the way that 1984 represented a continuation of postwar second-term reelection landslides. Even William Galston, Mondale's issue director and an intellectual founding father of the New Democrats, pointed out that "in the special circumstances of 1984, a Democratic ticket headed by Jesus with Moses in the second spot would have gotten about 45 percent of the vote against Reagan and Bush." The recession that generated victories in 1982 had disappeared. Times were too good, and the incumbent Reagan was too popular for anyone to defeat him. In this view, there was no realignment under way and no crisis that merited the wholesale rethinking of Democratic ideology and strategy.[6]

In sum, the Reagan era provided strong, but mixed partisan signals. Were the Democrats' problems systematic and internal? Or were they merely suffering a temporary paralysis caused by a frustratingly popular political figure whose inevitable departure would return them to their glory days?

When a less dynamic, less charismatic Washington insider recovered in 1988 from a 17-point summertime deficit to comfortably defeat Democratic nominee Michael Dukakis, the Democrats had their answer. Although no sitting president had won the White House since 1836, George H. W. Bush did just that, and the former Central Intelligence Agency director and Republican National Committee chairman won with a national popular vote share and margin unmatched by any presidential candidate since. In stark contrast to the actor-turned-governor with the folksy, western cowboy image, this was George Bush the patrician Connecticut blue-blood, the master of the malapropism, and the second-fiddle White House "wimp" of the Reagan era.

For Democrats, losing to the "Gipper" was one thing. Losing to "Poppy" was quite another.

A Coalition Behind the Times Yet Ahead of Its Moment

Franklin Delano Roosevelt's New Deal reconfigured American electoral politics for two generations. Working-class white ethnics and key voting non-white voting blocks forged a dominant alliance. The Democrats' big tent also included room for Jews, blacks, white ethnics and, of course, organized labor. FDR and Harry Truman were, for the most part, able to negotiate the conflicting interests of various identity groups without allowing these internecine battles among the Democratic Party's competing elements to destroy the party from within. For example, during World War II Roosevelt deftly balanced the competing demands from white and black union leaders seeking for their laborers a fair share of wartime industrial jobs and contracts.

More to the point, this image of the Democratic Party as an assemblage of aggrieved identity groups had not yet to become an external liability that strategic opponents could exploit for political and electoral gain. But as Rick Perlstein demonstrates in *Before the Storm: Barry Goldwater and the Unmaking of the American Consensus*, his study of the rise of post-war conservatism in the United States, these submerged conflicts eventually became susceptible to the political attacks and divide-and-conquer strategies of conservatives and Republican opponents. As Perlstein chronicles, in the span of just one presidential cycle— from Lyndon Johnson's Great Society-affirming Atlantic City nomination and landslide election in 1964, to the riot-filled Chicago convention and Hubert Humphrey's 1968 loss to Nixon in a three-way conspicuously clouded by segregationist candidate George Wallace—an internally harmonious and victorious Democratic coalition devolved into an outwardly divisive and chaotic party of self-destruction and defeat.[7]

By the 1980s, these internal conflicts had relocated from the violent streets to the cozier confines on back-room intraparty negotiations. Changes of venue, however, could not eliminate the core tensions. Most notably, the rise of the Rev. Jesse Jackson as the first truly viable African American presidential contender in the Democratic Party brought these internal tensions into high relief.

Jackson's presence in particular created tensions within the Democratic coalition between blacks and both Jews and labor. In 1984, explains Adolph Reed, Jackson's presidential bid created a whole subset of problems for the establishment campaign of former vice president Walter Mondale. "Practically from the first, Jackson defined the labor movement as antagonistic," writes Reed. "[D]uring the campaign Jackson adopted the rhetoric, propagated by [fellow Democratic contenders Gary] Hart, [John] Glenn, and the Republicans, that castigated the AFL-CIO as a nefarious 'special interest' bent on hijacking the party and unfairly exercising its allegedly great and unaccountable power in pursuit of its own narrow gain. He consistently pitted black aspirations against labor's, contraposing the two groups as competitors for priority in the party's distributive queue." Similar tensions existed between Jews and blacks, with Jackson's candidacy reviving long-held suspicions that Jews had allied with the more-numerous blacks within the Democratic Party to tear down institutional bulwarks created by white Protestants to the greater benefit of Jews than blacks.[8]

Although some key constituencies remained loyal, working-class white union members gravitated to Reagan to form the backbone of the so-called "Reagan Democrats." Despite Mondale's selection of New York congresswoman Geraldine Ferraro to be his vice presidential running mate—an act of identity politics of the first (or at least second) order—many female voters similarly defected to the Republicans during the 1980s. In fact, Reagan and Bush won the two-party share of the female vote in all three presidential victories during the decade, something no Republican, including Bush during his failed 1992 re-election bid, has achieved since. "By 1984, the Democratic Party struggled to mobilize an electorate no longer attuned to the New Deal legacy," writes political historian Michael Schaller, summarizing the party's electoral problems. "Many party activists and members defined themselves by 'identity politics,' meaning they thought and acted first as gay Democrats, environmental Democrats, or feminist Democrats, lacking any unifying direction. Looked at from the outside, the Democratic Party seemed like Humpty Dumpty—after the fall."[9] With nearly 60 percent of the national popular vote, Reagan crushed Mondale, who lost every state but his home Minnesota.

The situation was not much improved four years later. Hyper-sensitive to his depiction as a candidate beholden to the identity groups within his party, especially Jackson and his African American backers, ethnically Greek presidential nominee Michael Dukakis tried to deftly distance himself from certain elements within his party. In *All By Myself*, Christine Black and Thomas Oliphant's account of the 1988 election, the authors describe the general "neglect" of black voters by a Dukakis campaign seeking to recapture so-called "Reagan Democrats" by deflecting GOP accusations that the Massachusetts governor was just another race liberal anchored to 1960s identity politics. "Until the very end of the campaign, the governor did not reach out to black communities in America, didn't campaign in them early enough in the day for his appearances to make the network news shows, didn't emphasize his very real commitment to justice, didn't utter the words 'I need your help,' and didn't visibly target significant campaign resources," they write. "The Dukakis campaign's focus on the Democrats who had supported Ronald Reagan in the 1980s was not misplaced, but it never required slighting black Democrats to be effective; a great many black Americans got the message loud and clear."[10]

Barack Obama's 2008 victory was the triumph of a long dreamed-about Democratic coalition, conceived during the Lyndon Johnson-led 1960s, yet still in a transitional stage during the 1980s. Constructed as it was on backs of the so-called "Obama surge" voters—younger, first-time, college educated, and non-white voters—Obama's winning coalition was precisely the sort Democrats long hoped to assemble. Prior to Obama's arrival, the latent but unrealized growth of minority populations prevented Democrats from being able to free themselves from a dependence on white male votes. Fellow political scientist Phil Klinkner and I argue that three pathbreaking legislative acts signed by LBJ within in a very short time—the Civil Rights Act, the Immigration and Nationality Act, and the Higher Education Act—would inevitably empower the very groups of voters who fueled Obama's rise. But the political-electoral effects of these landmark legislative acts took decades to be felt.

In summary, prior to 1968, and against the background of overt racial violence and more subtle forms of sexism that offended Middle American sensibilities, Democrats during the Kennedy-Johnson era were still capable of supporting civil rights and racial equality without paying the full electoral price of the party's new marriage to the politics of identity. By 2008, the Democrats' dependence on white voters, and particularly southern white men, had shrunk to the point where the penalties for identity-style politics were no longer fatal. Indeed, more than a few political observers concluded that Obama's race was, on balance, an advantage rather than a liability. White voters and men preferred LBJ by solid margins in 1964, carrying him to victory. But John McCain's majority support from white voters and men was insufficient to beat Obama in 2008 which, not coincidentally, was the first presidential election in which non-whites accounted for one-quarter of all votes cast and white men accounted for less than one-third of the electorate. It was also a year in which record shares of unmarried, pro-choice and pro-gay rights voters cast ballots. In short, whatever electoral penalty the Democratic Party once paid for its association with minority and identity politics voters could now be duly counterbalanced by the electoral clout of those same voters.

Running in the elections more or less at the midpoint of the four-decade window between 1964 and 2008, Mondale and Dukakis thus found themselves in a temporal trap: They arrived on the political scene at a time after the Democratic Party's post-Great Society identity politics has been exposed as an electoral anchor, yet too soon to be buoyed by the demographic changes of the ensuing two decades. They were inheritors of a policy and political legacy that had grown stale to wide and disgruntled swaths of the white American electorate, and at the same time their candidacies came too early to benefit from the electoral upside of their party's connections to that legacy.

Conclusion

As the 1980s opened, American politics was at the cusp of a new partisan era. Although there were ample earlier warning signs of the changes the decade wrought looming ahead—George Wallace's segregationist presidential bid in 1968, California's property tax revolt, the Iranian hostage crisis, Republican Vice President Spiro Agnew's dismissal of the media as "nattering nabobs of negativism"—the power of these political undercurrents and their eventual impact on two-party competition in America would not be fully realized until Ronald Reagan and his Republican cohorts had figured out ways to capitalize politically.

As Thomas and Mary Edsall explain in their book, *Chain Reaction*, the disparate strands of post-war conservatism—resistance to racial preferences; demands for lower taxes and less regulation; virulent animosity to communism; ardent defense of patriotism—came together during the pivotal decade of the 1980s. The Democrats, once unchallenged in its role as the party that championed both middle-class economic priorities and values had ceded that role to the Republican Party, which used the culture wars, tax fights, racial unrest and fears about Soviet aggression to fashion a new "conservative populism" that, under Ronald Reagan's stewardship, reconfigured American party politics in lasting and irreversible ways.[11]

By decade's end, so much had changed. Many voters and even politicians spurned the Democratic Party for its lost ability to properly represent them. Older voters still nursing psychological scars of the Great Depression were replaced by their children and grandchildren with no such connections to the coalition Franklin Roosevelt assembled in the 1930s. "The term *liberalism* became vague and could refer to a variety of viewpoints, and the Democrats no longer had a single unifying message on which all members of the party could agree," writes Gerard Brandt, in his study of Reagan's clash with congressional Democrats during the decade."[12]

The Democrats' hegemony had slowly and perhaps inevitably but collapsed. This was their lost decade. The seeds of its demolition had been sown well before the decade opened and before Ronald Reagan captured the White House, of course. And congressional Republicans would have to wait a few more years before their moment of great triumph arrived in 1994. For partisan politics in the second half of the twentieth century, the 1980s will be remembered as the turning point decade, and one for which the effects are still being felt a generation later.

Notes

1. David Mayhew, *Congress: The Electoral Connection* (New Haven: Yale University Press, 1975).

2. Earl Black and Merle Black, "The 1988 Presidential Election and the Future of Southern Politics," in *The 1988 Presidential Election in the South: Continuity Amidst Change in Southern Party Politics,* ed. Laurence W. Moreland et al. (Santa Barbara, CA: Praeger, 1991), 256.

3. Michael A. Cohen, *Live from the Campaign Trail* (New York: Walker & Company, 2008), 372-373.

4. Peter Goldman and Tom Mathews, *The Quest for the Presidency 1988* (New York: Simon & Schuster, 1989), 45-46.

5. Walter Dean Burham, "The Reagan Heritage, in *The Election of 1988: Reports and Interpretations,* ed. Gerald Pomper (London: Chatham House, 1989), 23.

6. Kenneth S. Baer, *Reinventing Democrats: The Politics of Liberalism from Reagan to Clinton* (Lawrence, KS: University Press of Kansas, 2000), 54-55.

7. Rick Perlstein, *Before the Storm: Barry Goldwater and the Unmaking of the American Consensus* (New York: Hill & Wang, 2001).

8. Adolph L. Reed, Jr., *The Jesse Jackson Phenomenon* (New Haven: Yale University Press, 1986). See chapters 6 and 7 as well as page 85 to review specific quote used.

9. Michael Schaller, *Right Turn: American Life in the Reagan-Bush Era* (Oxford: Oxford University Press, 2007), 40. (The author is of no relation).

10. Christine M. Black and Thomas Oliphant, *All By Myself* (New York: Globe Pequot Press, 1989), 318-319.

11. Thomas Byrne Edsall and Mary D. Edsall, *Chain Reaction: The Impact of Race, Rights, and Taxes on American Politics* (New York: W.W. Norton and Company, 1992).

12. Karl Gerard Brandt, *Ronald Reagan and the House Democrats: Gridlock, Partisanship, and the Fiscal Crisis* (Columbia, MO: University of Missouri Press, 2009), 7.

Chapter 7

The Christian Right's Traditionalist Jeremiad: Piety and Politics in the Age of Reagan

Andrew R. Murphy

For many scholars of American religion and politics, the 1980s was the decade of the Christian Right: the public profile of such figures as Jerry Falwell and Pat Robertson, to name just two, played an important role in the coalition that brought Ronald Reagan to the presidency in 1980 and maintained him there in a resounding 1984 reelection victory.[1] Reagan gave strong (if primarily rhetorical) support to Christian Right positions on school prayer, limited government, abortion, and national defense – even publishing an antiabortion pamphlet while in the White House – and white evangelicals formed one of his most loyal constituencies, supporting his domestic agenda as well as the American arms build-up and Reagan's opposition to "godless" Soviet communism and leftist governments in Central America. Christian Right leaders also took aim at a welfare state that they saw as not only discouraging the work ethic but also threatening the independence of religious institutions, as became evident when the IRS attempted to revoke Bob Jones University's tax-exempt status during the Carter administration. Indeed, the 1988 Republican primaries saw Pat Robertson himself enter as a candidate, placing second in the Iowa caucuses and parlaying his electoral support into the Christian Coalition, which kept the Christian Right's agenda on the national scene during the Clinton years.

There was always, of course, more to the religio-political landscape than white Republican-leaning evangelicals, and it must be pointed out that the same year that witnessed Robertson's run for the presidency also saw the Reverend Jesse Jackson capture nearly 7 million votes in the Democratic primaries and briefly emerge as the front-runner for the Democratic nomination.[2] In addition, a nascent religious Left emerged during these years, energized by support for a nuclear freeze and opposition to U.S. policy in Central America and the Reagan administration's cuts in antipoverty funding. The United States Council of Catholic Bishops issued their controversial pastoral letter *The Challenge of Peace*, which criticized the nuclear arms buildup and sought to articulate an alternative to the bellicose rhetoric of the Reagan administration, in 1983.[3]

But this Religious Left was a largely reactive movement, responding to and seeking to counter the better-funded, better-organized, and more media-savvy representatives of the Christian Right. Accordingly, this chapter will focus on the political narrative that powered the Christian Right's political emergence during the late 1970s and into the 1980s, probing its main features and exploring its cultural resonances down to our own day. Indeed, such an account is important to have before us as we look back on the 1980s as well as for more contemporary reasons, since the cultural conservatism that the Christian Right championed increasingly predominates within the Republican Party of our own day. More specifically, I frame the Christian Right return to political involvement during the 1980s as an example of the power of traditionalist political narratives—in this case, the American jeremiad tradition, with its rhetoric of sin, repentance, renewal, and national chosenness—to mobilize those unified by a deep concern for the moral health of the nation and a deep dissatisfaction with the moral status of post-1960s America, as the most recent example of a recurrent phenomenon in American public life.

The Christian Right Re-enters American Politics

Although the emergence of the Christian Right in the 1970s and 1980s took many Americans by surprise, the values and concerns that white evangelicals brought with them into the political arena were hardly unprecedented. Indeed, evangelical energies had fired some of the most important social movements in American history, from the revivals of the eighteenth and nineteenth centuries to abolitionism and women's suffrage. In the wake of the Scopes trial, however, many American fundamentalists withdrew from political involvement. The result was a growing network of fundamentalist educational institutions, radio ministries (and, later, televangelist ministries), and publishing enterprises, a veritable parallel universe of religious organizations and institutions that needed only the right combination of ministerial exhortation and political opportunity to be reactivated. While never entirely separated from politics—the rise and prominence of Billy Graham provides just one example of American fundamentalism's ongoing concern with the nation's spiritual health and the need for spiritual revival – conservative Protestantism played a diminished role in mainstream American politics during much of this time.[4]

The rise of the Christian Right must be understood, then, against this backdrop, and against the increasingly tumultuous and countercultural activism of the 1960s and as part of an emerging conservative movement (both religious and secular) that emerged in opposition to it. Rick Perlstein has skillfully laid out this often-overlooked aspect of the 1960s and early 1970s: all was not antiwar protests, free love, sexual revolution, and Woodstock during those years. The nation also saw the seeds of what would later become the Christian Right and the resurgent conservatism of the 1980s. Such conservative luminaries as Karl Rove, Antonin Scalia, George W. Bush, and Pat Buchanan, flit across the pages of Perlstein's *Nixonland*: Buchanan, who would become one of the nation's most vociferous defenders of "traditional, Judeo-Christian values" (running for president himself three times on a platform of cultural conservatism and Judeo-Christian values), began his career as an assistant to Nixon. In the Nixon White House, Buchanan was charged with preparing the chief executive's daily news summary, and in doing so he made sure to highlight issues of culture and politics, and the threat he saw to traditional moral teachings from the forces of the counterculture. In *Nixonland*, Perlstein also guides the reader through the tangled thicket of state-level movements supporting school prayer – and opposing abortion, sex education, and homosexuality – that needed only the skillful rallying-cry of Jerry Falwell and the Moral Majority to become a major force in national politics during the 1980s.[5]

The cast of characters mentioned above shows that an adequate understanding of the term "Christian Right" ought not to limit itself to fundamentalists and evangelicals, but to encompass a broader political understanding of the coalition's appeal to Roman Catholics, orthodox Jews, and even religiously ambivalent citizens who were nonetheless increasingly worried about the decline of traditional moral teachings at home and an increasingly tenuous American profile around the world in the wake of Vietnam. Leaders of the Christian Right narrated their reentry into American politics as a defensive maneuver brought on by a sense of siege, as conservative Americans experienced a host of social and political changes as direct threats to their communities' ability to live according to the values they held dear. Jerry Falwell said that

> The invasion of humanism into the public school system began to alarm us back in the sixties. Then the *Roe v. Wade* Supreme Court decision of 1973 . . . shook me up . . . [I]t became very apparent that the federal government was going in the wrong direction and if allowed would be harassing non-public schools....So step by step we became convinced we must get involved if we're going to continue what we're doing inside the church building.[6]

Falwell's collaborator Ed Dobson cited a growing pornography industry, movements for gay rights and the Equal Rights Amendment, the breakdown of the traditional family, removal of prayer from the nation's public schools, and *Roe v. Wade* as examples of the "forces of secularism" in American culture during the 1960s and 1970s.[7] Many other figures in the Christian Right movement, similarly, told the story of their reentry into the political world in terms that emphasized its defensive nature.[8]

In moving that reentry forward, in crystallizing the lament over the nation's jettisoning of its traditional moral and spiritual foundations, probably no figure played a more central role than Jerry Falwell, described by Susan Friend Harding as "a fundamentalist ventriloquizing evangelicalism."[9] Falwell built bridges between these two powerful faith communities, delivering countless sermons over the course of the 1970s and articulating a narrative of national spiritual decline that possessed broad appeal across the spectrum of conservative Protestantism. The formation of the Moral Majority in 1979 gave Falwell the institutional platform to further his attempts at building coalitions with like-minded Roman Catholics (who were nonetheless suspicious of his anti-Catholic theology) and even with more secular "cultural conservatives" worried about social permissiveness and declining respect for traditional sources of authority. These efforts, like the wary and tenuous Christian Right relationships with Mormons, met with mixed success in the near term; although many Catholics expressed sympathy for Christian Right policy positions, they generally hesitated to actually join Christian Right organizations, given the traditional anti-Catholicism of fundamentalist, and to a lesser degree evangelical, Protestants over the course of American history. Over the course of the 1980s and 1990s, Christian Right organizations continued their efforts at outreach to Catholics, which culminated in the 1994 release of *Evangelicals and Catholics Together*, an ecumenical document that sidestepped thorny theological issues and spoke of the necessity of a common witness against an encroaching culture of secularism.[10]

Falwell also worked closely with traditional American conservatives who had historically been more concerned with the threat of communism or the growth of the federal government, but who shared a broad opposition to the legacy of the 1960s and 1970s.[11] Given the rhythms of American politics, a backlash against the 1960s was bound to happen sooner or later – or, rather, the conservative movements nurtured in opposition to the 1960s were bound to gain the ascendancy at some point – and when it did, the Christian Right's political narrative was ready to fill the void for Americans looking for a way to articulate their dissatisfaction with the direction that the nation was headed.

The Christian Right Jeremiad

Scholars have long recognized the centrality of the jeremiad to the American experience, in the nation's literature as well as its social, religious, and political traditions. More than thirty years ago, Sacvan Bercovitch laid out the ways in which the prophetic critiques and self-understandings of early New England Puritans – their conception of themselves as a people set apart, their views of covenantal relationships as indicating a heightened bond amongst themselves and between their communities and God, their parallel status with the early Israelites, their concern about flagging spiritual energies and the potential for divine punishment of ungodly behavior – as key to a developing sense of American mission and a trope that continues down through the nineteenth century.[12] Scholars since Bercovitch have refined and extended his formulation, carrying the analysis down to the present day and rethinking some of Bercovitch's initial formulations based on a broader reading of the historical record.[13]

The term itself – "jeremiad" – evokes the Hebrew prophetic tradition, not only Jeremiah but also the long line of critics who, driven by a sense of crisis and a deep anxiety about their community's health, interpreted Israel's history as a story of decline from covenantal faithfulness and continually called the community to repentance and recommitment to its foundational values.[14] Jeremiah provided a rationale for the misfortunes that the community was currently experiencing (it had abandoned the covenant sworn at Sinai), reminded it of its covenant and its responsibility to God, and, perhaps most importantly, held out the hope of restoration: "Return, O faithless children, I will heal your faithlessness."[15]

As a genre, as a species of political rhetoric, then, jeremiads generally contain several elements. First, they lament problems that signal decline vis-a-vis the past. Second, they identify a point in the past in which the harmful idea or practice responsible for decline first made its appearance, and trace out the injurious consequences from its earliest inception to the present day. And finally, they call for reform, repentance, or renewal: recommending a specific course of action (or a specific political agenda) to reverse contemporary decline and reclaim the original promise of communal life.

The jeremiad played an important role in the emerging self-understandings of many of the early settlements, and fueled the idea of the American Revolution as the American Israel rising against its oppressors.[16] It remained strong throughout the early nineteenth century and into the Civil War, where notions of national mission and national sin framed the destruction and carnage of that conflict.[17] And fears of moral and spiritual decline continued into the twentieth century, as fundamentalists lamented the rise of Darwinian ideas and the continuing movement of the American mainstream away from orthodox Christian ideals.

The Christian Right's jeremiad, its narrative of spiritual decline and divine judgment, is fairly straightforward. American society, as the 1970s wound down and the 1980s approached, found itself awash in sin and the fruits of sin: abortion, sexual promiscuity, crime, divorce, media violence, dishonesty, disrespect for elders and traditional authorities, and a rising incidence of teen pregnancy and births outside wedlock. Such indicators were symptoms of a deeper malady in the nation's soul: it had forsaken the spiritual principles on which it was founded and had embraced an ideology of secularism (often referred to as "secular humanism") and a political philosophy of big-government welfare-state liberalism, each of which (and both of which, together) were hostile to the traditional Christian or Judeo-Christian tint of an earlier American era. The vision for a redeemed American future, accordingly, involved recapturing, to the degree possible given changed circumstances, the traditionalist foundation upon which the nation had been founded, and regaining God's promise for the American nation, the promise of blessings that would attend continued faithfulness to God's ways in the world.

The Sins of the Present

Perhaps the most significant transformation that had taken place in America during the 1960s and 1970s had to do with changing notions of human sexuality and appropriate sexual behavior. Such changes spanned a range of hot-button political issues – abortion, homosexuality and the growing movement for gay rights, the increasing prevalence (and acceptance) of pre- and extramarital sexual activity, pornography, feminism, divorce and remarriage, contention over gender roles within the family, and the Equal Rights Amendment. Such issues were hardly new in American history,[18] but they gained a new currency in the minds of religious conservatives in the wake of the 1960s. Abortion became a Christian Right rallying cry, and Carl Henry argued that "it is not America at her best when we chart the massacre of a million unborn citizens a year..."[19] The rise (and rising tolerance) of homosexuality, especially in the wake of the Stonewall riots of 1969, was similarly highlighted as both a sin and a symptom of a far deeper spiritual malady: "We would not be having the present moral crisis regarding the homosexual movement if men and women accepted their proper roles as designed by God," wrote Falwell in his 1980 book *Listen America!*. Homosexuality, on this account, is "a symptom of a sin-sick society."[20] Not surprisingly, the early reactions to the AIDs epidemic viewed the virus in the context of society's departure from traditional sexual standards and as a punishment for deviant sexual behavior.[21]

But there was always far more to the Christian Right's appeal than an obsession with sex and sexual propriety. A broader set of concerns about the marginalization of traditional religion in American public life drove the movement and fed into support for voluntary school prayer, as well as denunciations of mainstream media for peddling filth and violence and for its negative portrayals of people of faith. The nation's courts often came in for criticism along these lines as well: Christian Right spokespeople rarely failed to connect the removal of prayer from the nation's public schools in the 1962 Supreme Court *Schempp* decision with the later tumultuous events of that decade; and more generally, *Schempp* represented just one example of a growing hostility to traditional religion among the nation's elites.[22]

But it wasn't just *Schempp* and issues of religion that attracted the ire of Christian Right Jeremiahs. A much broader transformation in the notion of privacy had emerged during the 1960s and 1970s, a transformation that found its culmination in the 1973 *Roe v. Wade* decision, which brought together issues of sexuality and privacy in explosive new ways. Given the intimate nature of sexual behavior, and the way that notions of proper sexual conduct grow out of larger moral systems and views of human nature, these decisions displayed a new understanding of privacy and its connection with individual liberty and autonomy. In *Griswold v. Connecticut* (1965), the Court had invalidated a Connecticut law that prohibited the use of "any drug, medicinal article or instrument for the purpose of preventing conception" by referring to a "right to marital privacy."[23]   Seven years later, in *Eisenstadt v. Baird* (1972), the Court had extended *Griswold*'s protections to unmarried citizens, again referring to privacy rights: "If the right of privacy means anything, it is the right of the individual, married or single, to be free from unwarranted governmental intrusion into matters so fundamentally affecting a person as the decision whether to bear or beget a child."[24]   Finally, and perhaps most controversially, we find Justice Blackmun's majority opinion in *Roe*, that "[t]his right of privacy...is broad enough to encompass a woman's decision whether or not to terminate her pregnancy."[25] The equation of a right to privacy – nowhere explicitly spelled out in the constitutional text – with a right to end a pregnancy struck Christian Right leaders as nothing short of state-sanctioned murder.

More generally, the Christian Right's lament about the decline of religion in the public square and the growth of new understandings of liberty, privacy, and autonomy was part of a broader critique, often drawing on Tocqueville's analysis of nineteenth-century America, about the importance of civil society, state and local government, and intermediate institutions as engines of American vitality and civic virtue. The ability of these institutions to play a vital role in fostering American public life was threatened by a growing federal government and the centralization that went along with it. And, not coincidentally, the federal government had already proven willing, during the Carter administration, to use its taxing ability to threaten religious institutions that did not toe a secularist line.

Along with these domestic issues, the Christian Right narrative stressed the omnipresent threat to American values posed by Soviet and Chinese Communism. More generally, the blows to American prestige in the wake of Vietnam – including the Iranian hostage situation and the Soviet invasion of Afghanistan – only illustrated how far the nation had fallen and how inept its political leadership seemed to have become, unable to stand firm against the forces of godlessness around the world.[26]

The Glories of the Past

As mentioned above, the jeremiad is a narrative; that is, far from a mere dispassionate or abstract criticism of current states of affairs, Jeremiahs offer a story of how and when a blessed society went horribly wrong. Thus intricately related to the account of what is wrong is always a reference to the way that previous generations got things right. The Christian Right jeremiad is no exception, and in their retrospective casting for an American Golden Age, its spokespersons offered two possible candidates for past glory, historical eras from which to critique post-1960s relativism: the colonial and founding eras on the one hand, and the 1950s on the other.

Christian Right accounts often traced the roots of American religiosity back to the earliest colonial settlements, referring to Jamestown, the Mayflower Compact, the deeply religious roots of the Massachusetts Bay and Pennsylvania colonies, and the church-driven foundings of American universities. The American experience was not the product of secular humanists or cultural relativists, they argued, but of deeply committed believers who risked much to make the perilous ocean crossing and erect godly societies in the American wilderness. Although it is true that many of the nation's founders were hardly orthodox Christians – indeed, whether Jefferson believed in basic Christian doctrine at all has continued to animate scholarly dispute – Christian Right thinkers claim the founders as moral exemplars who consistently linked Judeo-Christian piety and American national identity, and understood religion as essential to the maintenance of virtue in the citizenry. Along the same lines, such critics tend to differentiate the American Revolution from the French one; the former was friendly to, indeed fired by, religion, and the American founders were "united by a common belief in the importance of religion as an aid and a friend to the Constitutional order [and] spoke with one voice about the importance of religion in civic life."[27] Such an attachment to public religion obtained regardless of the degree of belief or nonbelief in any given founding figure.

Given this importance of religion in the nation's early history, it should not be surprising, said Christian Right Jeremiahs, that even though disestablishment was instituted as constitutional policy after 1789, a general culture of religiosity, more particularly of Protestant religiosity, remained central to the nation's public life well into the twentieth century. But one need not reach hundreds of years into the past to find a time period worth emulating: if the 1960s instituted a break with these founding understandings of religious authority and American public life, then one need only look to the other side of that great cultural divide, to American culture even into the 1950s, for examples of a balanced relationship between church and state. As Phillip Hammond put it,

> It was the prevalent, established religion of the 1920-1960 period that was assaulted by the social revolution arising in the 1960s, and continuing today....[W]hat was being assaulted was the assumption that church involvement...was a good thing because it signified conventionality and fundamental attachment to core American values.[28]

The 1950s, then, represent a decade that still maintained some contact with the moral and religious spirit of previous American eras. Pat Robertson later looked back on his own upbringing and recalled that "there was a time not long ago that the Christian view of sexuality prevailed....I can remember clearly the college days after World War II...Even the wildest fraternity crowd did not condone adultery."[29] The 1960s brought with them the drug culture, rock and roll, the sexual revolution, and a general countercultural trend that shook the cultural foundations of American life. And to Robertson and others in the Christian Right, these countercultural trends represent more than just an adjustment of attitudes to social realities: they represent the tip of a much broader iceberg of social transformation that jettisoned the founders' views on the subject of church and state. (Hence, the defensive justification by Christian Right thinkers about their entry into American politics in the years leading up to the 1980s: they were forced into politics by an expanding federal government and an increasingly hostile set of American elites: Supreme Court justices, media with liberal bias, and so on.) Pat Robertson placed the 1960s into a much larger historical perspective, emphasizing the radical break that those years signified from a religiously-ordered era prior to that decade to a relativistic and humanistic period after:

> Until modern times, the foundations of law rested on the Judeo-Christian concept of right and wrong and the foundational concept of Original sin - that humans are capable of wrongdoing by nature. It was the belief of traditional law that without suitable social and moral restraints and a strong legal code, society would inevitably degenerate into chaos and anarchy. Modern secular sociology, however, shuns such biblical teachings in favor of an evolutionary hypothesis based on the ideas of Darwin, Freud, Einstein, and others. This view, often called "secular humanism," takes the view that man has evolved from the slime and that with time and ever greater freedoms, mankind will ascend to the stars. These ideas, which are contrary to the Word of God, have led directly to the bitter conflict and social chaos of our day, and furthermore, they have somber implications for the future health of the justice system in this country.

> The legacy of the 1960s is still with us today. The free-love, anti-war, psychedelic 1960s proclaimed not only the right of dissent but the right to protest against and defame the most sacred institutions of the nation....Free love, the rise of pagan cults, and the New Age movement have all thrived in this atmosphere of defiance. And what may prove to be the greatest holocaust in history – the abortion movement – is one of its most sinister expressions.[30]

Looking to the Future

But again, as noted above, the jeremiad never stops at a lament and backward looking criticism: part and parcel of the critique it offers is a call to renewal and repentance for national sins, and to a commitment to a reformed national future. During the 1980s, the Christian Right political platform, as indicated in the public pronouncements and legislative efforts of the Moral Majority and like-minded organizations, involved the move to outlaw abortion, ban homosexual rights, and defeat the Equal Rights Amendment; to return voluntary prayer to the nation's public schools; to outlaw or restrict pornography and violent or sexually explicit images in the media; to shrink the size of the federal government, as well as its reach into the religious lives of Americans and the tax burden imposed upon them; to rearm the nation against Soviet Communism; and to enact school choice programs, so that evangelical parents could educate their children in accord with their own values.

The main features of the Christian Right's vision for a reformed future followed rather directly from the way that it lamented the past, and the particular elements of the past that it laments. Recall, for example, that issues of sexuality and proper sexual expression were key to the power of the Christian Right jere-miad during these years. Sexuality in contemporary America, Falwell claimed, had become disordered as a result of the 1960s emphasis on immediate gratifica-tion. Thus a goal for a reformed future would involve a return to earlier stan-dards of sexual modesty, traditional gender roles, and a public endorsement of heterosexual marriage as the socially preferred outlet for sexual expression. "We have to teach [boys and girls] how to date. We have to teach them how to love one another rightly. We have to teach them how to marry and how to raise children again. The whole country has forgotten that...."[31]

Much of the erosion of traditional standards of sexual behavior, of course, had been aided and abetted by an increasingly secular-minded court system, and especially by a Supreme Court that had removed prayer from school classrooms and nationalized abortion. The call for judges who would "interpret the consti-tution as written" and not invent new rights – that is, who would endorse some version of an originalist jurisprudence – became a siren song for the Christian Right effort to reform the nation back into its own pre-1960s image. The politi-cal furor over President Reagan's nomination of Judge Robert Bork to the Su-preme Court set the stage for an increasingly acrimonious, politicized, and con-tentious nominating process well into the twenty-first century.

In addition to these questions of sexuality and judicial philosophy the Chris-tian Right called for a host of related measures to shore up the moral foundations of the American nation, and to enable it to defend itself against enemies abroad. A strong supporter of the Reagan arms buildup and its moves against Soviet influence in Eastern Europe as well as leftist rebels in Central America, the Christian Right also proved a strong supporter of Israel in its conflict with the Palestinians. Biblical rhetoric about the historical alliance between American Christians and the Jewish state mingled with apocalyptic and eschatological musings about the importance of Israel in hastening Christ's return.

Ralph Reed, who became director of the Christian Coalition after Pat Robert-son left that post, summed up the movement's vision for a reformed American future just a few years after the 1980s had drawn to a close:

> America would look much as it did for most of the first two centuries of its exis-tence, before the social dislocation caused by Vietnam, the sexual revolution, Wa-tergate, and the explosion of the welfare state. Our nation would once again be as-cendant, self-confident, proud, and morally strong. Government would be strong, the citizenry virtuous, and mediating institutions such as churches and voluntary organi-zations would carry out many of the functions currently relegated to the bureaucra-cy.[32]

The Sacred Story

The jeremiad in America has always had more to it, though, than a mere litany of decline and a call for renewal. A sacred story – America, and later the United States, as a land richly blessed by God, specially marked out for a unique role in the hastening of God's purposes on earth – has played a central role in the self-understanding of American elites since the Puritans landed at Massachusetts Bay in 1630. The Christian Right was fired by an evangelical commitment to this sort of theological American exceptionalism, and indeed, as mentioned above, the religious character of the early American experience made the nation's decline all the more lamentable. Commenting on the fact that only twenty-five years separated Columbus's voyage to the New World from the beginning of the Reformation in Europe, Vern McLellan reflected that "[i]t was as if God had preserved a great 'Island in the Sea' as a place of refuge for persecuted believers from continental Europe."[33] Pat Robertson saw the colonists' victory in the Revolution as nothing short of (literally) miraculous, and many Christian Right leaders saw the revolutionary experience and the early national period as examples of a political enterprise undertaken in covenant with God. The American rise to power, on such a view, was facilitated by God's favor as expressed toward this "Christian nation" and, as such, depended on the continued willingness of Americans to honor those religious values and principles.[34]

The 1980s and Beyond

The traditionalist agenda articulated by the Christian Right did not always lead to concrete policy successes: Indeed, many scholars have pointed out that for all its publicity and bluster the Christian Right achieved a paucity of concrete policy victories during the 1980s.[35] Another way of putting this would be to say that the jeremiad that proved so successful in *mobilizing* Americans into politics during the 1980s proved rather less able to effect measurable policy successes and to follow up on the original promise of that mobilization.

Even so, one would have been hasty to dismiss the Christian Right's cultural influence – its reaction against the sexual revolution and the countercultural influences of the 1960s, its commitment to traditionalist understandings of morality – due to its lack of specific policy successes. Indeed, traditionalists were not without occasions for celebration during the 1980s. One such occasion came with the Supreme Court's 1986 decision in *Bowers v. Hardwick*. Relying on the notion of privacy that the Court had laid out in such cases as *Griswold*, *Eisenstadt*, and *Roe* (mentioned briefly above), the Georgia Court of Appeals for the Eleventh Circuit had ruled that homosexual activity was a "private and intimate association" beyond the realm of state regulation under the Ninth Amendment and the Due Process Clause of the Fourteenth Amendment.[36] Against the backdrop of the increasingly robust defense of the right of privacy as it related to sexual behavior, and the growing push to extend such privacy rights to homosexual conduct, *Bowers* presented the Court with an opportunity to extend such privacy rights to homosexual conduct. But the Supreme Court overturned the Georgia Court's ruling, and made clear that the important expansions of the right to privacy notwithstanding – the succession of cases from the 1960s and 70s including *Griswold* through *Roe* – it would not extend these notions of privacy to homosexual activity. In order to be considered a "fundamental right" and thus qualify for the heightened protection sought by Hardwick, wrote Justice White, homosexual activity would have to have been "deeply rooted in this nation's history and tradition" or "implicit in the concept of ordered liberty."[37] He concluded that "It is obvious to us that neither of these formulations would extend a fundamental right to homosexuals to engage in acts of consensual sodomy," even if the law outlawing such behavior was based on the majority's notions of morality and were likely driven by religious belief:[38]

> The law...is constantly based on notions of morality, and if all laws representing essentially moral choices are to be invalidated under the Due Process Clause, the courts will be very busy indeed.[39]

Chief Justice Burger's brief concurrence in *Bowers* provides a more detailed discussion of the specific moral visions at work, and the power of traditionalist and religious language when dealing with questions of sex. Burger's concurrence supplements the majority opinion's evidence with the additional fact that "condemnation of those practices is firmly rooted in Judeo-Christian moral and ethical standards...under Roman law...and during the English Reformation."[40] The English common law prohibition of sodomy entered the American legal tradition during colonial times, and a declaration of sodomy as a fundamental right would cast aside "millennia of moral teaching."[41] It was the willingness of the American political system to cast aside such moral teachings that had animated the Christian Right's entry into American politics during the 1970s and 1980s in the first place.

And yet the seeds of its own reversal were contained in the *Bowers* decision; the line of reasoning that Justice Blackmun laid out in his dissent laid the foundation for the Court's overturning of *Bowers* less than twenty years later in *Lawrence v. Texas* (2005). In his dissent, Blackmun identified a concern for public decency as the core justification offered by the State of Georgia for its antisodomy legislation. Yet any such notions of decency ultimately involve moral, often religious, notions based on longstanding animus toward homosexuality, and thus must be constitutionally suspect. He noted that the state's invocation of Leviticus, Romans, Aquinas, and medieval sources fails to establish a legitimate justification for such legislation:

> That certain, but by no means all, religious groups condemn the behavior at issue gives the State no license to impose their judgments on the entire citizenry. The legitimacy of sexual legislation depends instead on whether the State can advance some justification for its law beyond its conformity to religious doctrine....A State can no more punish private behavior because of religious intolerance than it can punish such behavior because of racial animus....Private biases may be outside the reach of the law, but the law cannot, directly or indirectly, give them effect.[42]

This notion of a thread connecting the 1980s and the first decade of the twenty-first century – from *Bowers* to *Lawrence* – leads to a second point to note about the Christian Right in the 1980s: the cultural conservatism of the 1980s, though perhaps falling short in terms of concrete successes in the policy realm, survived and even thrived during the two Clinton terms, using such cultural hot-button issues as gays in the military and Clinton's affair with Monica Lewinsky to keep the faithful attentive and ready to mobilize. As Ralph Reed wrote in 1994, looking back at critics who cheered the demise of the Moral Majority in 1989,

> What these critics did not realize was that even as they danced on the grave of the Moral Majority, a new pro-family movement was rising, phoenix-like, from the ashes....Falwell...had passed the torch to a new generation of leadership who launched new organizations and redirected the pro-family impulse in a more permanent, grassroots direction.[43]

Reed's leadership of the Christian Coalition, which grew to fill the vacuum left by the disbanding of the Moral Majority and to capitalize on the database that Pat Robertson amassed during his 1988 run for the presidency, helped keep the Christian Right vital during the Clinton years, and provided a bridge to the presidency of George W. Bush, where evangelical voices again gained an audience at the highest levels. Far from a blip on the 1980s political scene, the Christian Right reflected larger trends and dynamics in the American social landscape: as Ronald E. Hopson and Donald R. Smith put it, "The place of the Christian Right on the American scene is best measured by the extent to which their ideas and meanings are absorbed within the larger culture and begin to define the 'mainstream'."[44] By that standard, I would suggest, what began in the 1970s and 1980s, as a reaction against the upheavals of the 1960s, continues alive and well into the twenty-first century.

Conclusion

I have argued elsewhere, and at greater length, that the Christian Right's traditionalist jeremiad constructs a past that serves as a limiting or constraining condition, a sort of empirical checklist that critics hold up to the present in order to assess the propriety of certain features of contemporary life: family structure, gender roles, sexual behavior, and religious piety. In other words, the past is presented as a model for the future, and the political goal of such narratives is largely to retain as much similarity between past and present practices as is possible.[45] The claims of Christian right thinkers *not* to want to "return to the past" ring a bit hollow given their well-established yearning for the social conditions of pre-1960s America: in Ralph Reed's words quoted above, an America that looks "much as it did for most of the first two centuries of its existence...."[46]

James Davison Hunter and James Morone have each argued that cultural conflict between Americans with competing moral orientations has generated some of the nation's most significant political movements. And yet none of these movements have existed in a vacuum: the mobilization efforts essential to creating a political movement like the Christian Right (including the crafting of a compelling political narrative) inevitably call forth counternarrative and countermovements. Take, for instance, the Christian Right's celebration of the traditional family and what has come to be known as "family values." The traditional family stood in for a number of other traditionalist notions about sexual behavior and authority in the home and the political realm, and worries about its resilience during the 1980s and beyond betray larger anxieties about masculinity, femininity, and sexual orientation. Yet Stephanie Coontz argues, in response, that the traditional family so celebrated by the Christian Right turns out upon closer examination to be a fiction that never existed, "an ahistorical amalgam of structure, values, and behaviors that never coexisted in the same time and place."[47] In Coontz's telling of the story of the American family, the postwar traditional family was *itself* the outlier, shaped by specific historical factors. But importantly, Coontz does not simply present data to refute the Christian Right's valorization of traditional family structures, but proposes a competing narrative, by arguing that in some ways today's families are even *more* connected than those of bygone eras.

These political struggles, between those espousing a traditionalist view and those emphasizing the complexity and multiplicity of the American past, characterized much of the religio-political landscape during the 1980s. The Christian Right offered just the latest iteration of a longstanding trope in the American experience: the jeremiadic lament over contemporary decline, the search for a Golden Age of virtuous ancestors, and the call to renewal and repentance, to reclaim the communal blessing that God had placed on this land at its inception. Such language cemented the close connection between piety and politics in early New England, fired the imaginations of both sides during the American Civil War, and continues to animate political debate in our own time. There seems no reason to expect that it will cease to do so anytime soon.

Notes

1. See, e.g., Clyde Wilcox and Carin Larsen, *Onward Christian Soldiers? The Christian Right in American Politics*, 3rd ed. (Boulder: Westview Press, 2006).

2. Allen D. Hertzke, *Echoes of Discontent: Jesse Jackson, Pat Robertson, and the Resurgence of Populism* (Washington, DC: Congressional Quarterly Press, 1993).

3. National Conference of Catholic Bishops, *The Challenge of Peace: God's Promise and our Response*, 19 May 1983, online at *www.usccb.org/sdwp/international/TheChallengeofPeace.pdf*.

4. Nancy T. Ammerman, "North American Protestant Fundamentalism," in *Fundamentalisms Observed*, ed. Martin E. Marty and R. Scott Appleby (Chicago: University of Chicago Press, 1991); Steven P. Miller, *Billy Graham and the Rise of the Republican South* (Philadelphia: University of Pennsylvania Press, 2009).

5. Rick Perlstein, *Nixonland* (New York: Scribner, 2008).

6. Falwell, ed., with Ed Dobson and Ed Hinson, *The Fundamentalist Phenomenon: The Resurgence of Conservative Christianity* (Garden City, NY: Doubleday, 1981), 144.

7. Dobson, "The Bible, Politics, and Democracy," in *The Bible, Politics, and Democracy*, ed. Richard John Neuhaus (Grand Rapids, MI: Eerdmans, 1987), 3.

8. Carl F. Henry, *Twilight of a Great Civilization: The Drift Toward Neo-paganism* (Westchester, IL: Crossway Books, 1988), 172; Joel Carpenter, *Revive Us Again: The Reawakening of American Fundamentalism* (New York: Oxford University Press, 1997).

9. Harding, *The Book of Jerry Falwell: Fundamentalist Language and Politics* (Princeton: Princeton University Press, 2000), 272.

10. See Mary Bendyna, John C. Green, Mark J. Rozell and Clyde Wilcox, "Catholics and the Christian Right: A View from Four States," *Journal of the Society for the Scientific Study of Religion* 39: 3 (2000): 321-332; Merlin B. Brinkerhoff, Jeffrey C. Jacob, and Marlene M. Mackie, "Mormonism and the Moral Majority Make Strange Bedfellows?: An Exploratory Critique," *Review of Religious Research*, 28 (1987); 236-251; and *Evangelicals & Catholics Together: The Christian Mission in the Third Millennium, First Things* 43 (May 1994), 15-22.

11. Irving Louis Kristol, *Reflections of a Neoconservative: Looking Back, Looking Ahead* (New York: Basic Books, 1983).

12. Bercovitch, *The American Jeremiad* (Madison: University of Wisconsin Press, 1978); see also Ernest Tuveson, *Redeemer Nation: The Idea of America's Millennial Role* (Chicago: University of Chicago Press, 1968).

13. Andrew R. Murphy, *Prodigal Nation: Moral Decline and Divine Punishment From New England to 9-11* (New York: Oxford University Press, 2008); Richard T. Hughes, *Myths America Lives By* (Urbana: University of Illinois Press, 2003).

14. Walter Bruegemann, *Old Testament Theology: The Theology of the Book of Jeremiah* (Cambridge: Cambridge University Press, 2007), 67, 79. See also my "New Israel in New England: The American Jeremiad and the Hebrew Scriptures," *Hebraic Political Studies* 4, no. 2 (Spring 2009): 128-156.

15. Jeremiah 3:22.

16. See the collected *Political Sermons of the Founding Era*, ed. Ellis Sandoz (Indianapolis: Liberty Fund, 1998), and *God's New Israel: Religious Interpretations of American Destiny*, ed. Conrad Cherry (Chapel Hill: University of North Carolina Press, 1998).

17. Harry S. Stout, *Upon the Altar of the Nation: A Moral History of the Civil War* (New York: Vintage, 2006).

18. See James Morone, *Hellfire Nation: The Politics of Sin in American History* (New Haven and London: Yale University Press, 2003).

19. Henry, *Twilight of a Great Civilization*, 40.

20. Falwell, *Listen, America!* (Garden City, NY: Doubleday, 1980), 181, 183.

21. See David Carter, *Stonewall: The Riots that Sparked the Gay Revolution* (New York: St. Martin's, 2004); and Randy Shilts, *And the Band Played On: Politics, People, and the AIDS Epidemic* (New York: St. Martin's, 1987).

22. See *Abington v. Schempp*, 374 U. S. 203 (1963); Falwell, *Listen, America!*, 205; Dobson, "The Bible, Politics, and Democracy," 3-4; Richard John Neuhaus, *The Naked Public Square: Religion and Democracy in America* (Grand Rapids: Eerdmans, 1984); Charles Colson, *Kingdoms in Conflict* (Grand Rapids: Zondervan/William Morrow, 1987).

23. *Griswold v. Connecticut*, 381 U.S. 479 (1965).

24. *Eisenstadt v. Baird*, 405 U.S. 438 (1972), 453.

25. *Roe v. Wade*, 410 U.S. 113 (1973), 153.

26. Wilcox and Larsen, *Onward Christian Soldiers?*, 34-36; Philip Jenkins, *Decade of Nightmares: The End of the Sixties and the Making of Eighties America* (New York: Oxford University Press, 2006), 84-85.

27. William J. Bennett, "Religious Belief and the Constitutional Order," in *Piety and Politics: Evangelicals and Fundamentalists Confront the World*, ed. Richard John Neuhaus and Michael Cromartie (Washington, DC: Ethics and Public Policy Center, 1987), 366. See also, more generally, Pat Robertson, *America's Dates With Destiny* (Nashville, TN: Thomas Nelson, 1986); and Vern McLellan, *Christians in the Political Arena: Positive Strategies for Concerned Twentieth-Century Patriots* (Charlotte, NC: Associates Press, 1985).

28. Hammond, *Religion and Personal Autonomy: The Third Disestablishment in America* (Columbia: University of South Carolina Press, 1992), 135.

29. Robertson, *The Ten Offenses* (Nashville, TN: Integrity, 2004), 149.

30. Robertson, *The Turning Tide: The Fall of Liberalism and the Rise of Common Sense* (Dallas: Word Publishing, 1993), 112-113.

31. Falwell, *America Can Be Saved!*, 118.

32. Reed, *Politically Incorrect: The Emerging Faith Factor in American Politics* (Dallas: Word Publishing, 1994), 36-37.

33. McLellan, *Christians in the Political Arena*, 103-104.

34. Robertson, *The Ten Offenses*, ch. 1.

35. See Michael D'Antonio, *Fall From Grace: The Failed Crusade of the Christian Right* (New Brunswick, NJ: Rutgers University Press, 1992); and Steve Bruce, *The Rise and Fall of the New Christian Right* (Oxford: Clarendon Press, 1988).

36. *Bowers* at 189. *Bowers* upheld the constitutionality of state antisodomy legislation.

37. *Bowers* at 191-2.

38. *Bowers* at 192.

39. *Bowers* at 195.

40. *Bowers* at 196.

41. *Bowers* at 197. Interestingly, fourteen years before the ruling in *Bowers*, Burger had been the lone dissenter in *Eisenstadt*.

42. *Bowers* at 212.

43. Reed, *Politically Incorrect*, 192.

44. Ronald E. Hopson and Donald R. Smith, "Changing Fortunes: An Analysis of Christian Right Ascendance Within American Political Discourse," *Journal for the Scientific Study of Religion* 38 (1999), 10.

45. See my "Longing, Nostalgia, and Golden Age Politics: The American Jeremiad and the Power of the Past," *Perspectives on Politics* 7: 1 (2009), 125-141; and more generally, my *Prodigal Nation*.

46. Reed, *Politically Incorrect*, 36. See also: "This is a Christian nation" (Falwell, *America Can Be Saved!*, 23); "[T]he changes of the last half-century have had disastrous consequences for the nation" (Robertson, *The Turning Tide*, 168).

47. Coontz, *The Way We Never Were: American Families and the Nostalgia Trap* (New York: Basic, 1992), 9.

Chapter 8

New Right, New History, Common Ground: Populism and the Past

Jessie Swigger

The 1980s were pivotal in altering the relationship between the public and the past. The implementation of new history at historic sites was directly followed by the ascendency of the New Right and heated debates about the role that public history does and should play in American life. How the rhetoric of populism—which shares much with both the New Right and new history—is implemented at outdoor history museums speaks to its inability to achieve many of the New Left goals in which new history is rooted.

Populism has long played an important role in shaping American politics. For most historians, populism found full political expression in the Farmer's Alliance of 1872 and the People's Party in 1892, but its definition broadened as politicians with divergent beliefs employed its basic language. Alan Brinkley explains that unlike populists of the 1890s, who were engaged in an "active effort to construct an alternative to the emerging, centralized, corporate economy," populists of the 1930s, like Huey Long and Father Charles Coughlin, proposed solutions that relied upon the federal government. Following the 1930s, a wide array of politicians and social movements used the rhetoric of populism to articulate their goals demonstrating populism's shift from political platform to political language. Recently, for example, both President Barack Obama and anti-tax Tea Party reformers have defined their goals as populist.[1] Michael Kazin writes that the "most basic and telling definition of populism" is that it is a language "whose speakers conceive of ordinary people as a noble assemblage not bounded narrowly by class, view their elite opponents as self-serving and undemocratic, and seek to mobilize the former against the latter."[2]

↓ populism → work for the people

Image for
populism

Essentially, then, populism is a rhetorical tool used to express the divide between elites and the people, and the question of who counts as what depends on
the politician. What links the spectrum of populists is not only language but also
images. While the movements of the 1890s and the 1980s shared little in terms
of their platforms and proposed solutions, their rhetoric conjured nostalgic depictions of the small town, comprised of middle-class homes, successful local
businesses, and independently owned farms.[3]

Throughout the 1980s, public historians implemented interpretive programs
that drew on new history, which aimed to complicate celebratory representations
of America's past, including wholly positive depictions of the small town. By
the early 1990s, the Smithsonian Institute adopted this approach. In 1991, "The
West as America: Reinterpreting Images of the Frontier 1820-1920" asked
viewers to consider visual representations of the frontier in the context of cut-
throat entrepreneurialism, city boosterism, and the federal government's policies
concerning Native Americans. While comment books showed that visitors responded to the wall-texts with mixed reactions,[4] opponents published articles in
the *Washington Post, Time, The Boston Globe*, the *New Republic*, and the *Times
Literary Supplement*.[5] At the exhibit opening, historian Daniel Boorstein wrote
in the comment book that the Smithsonian had created a "perverse, historically
inaccurate, destructive exhibit." Senator Ted Stevens from Alaska said that the
exhibit bred "division within our country." [6]

The reaction to "The West as America," however, paled in comparison to the
grassroots opposition to the planned "Enola Gay" exhibit. Veterans and politicians organized when they learned that curators planned to place the plane that
dropped the atomic bomb on Hiroshima, effectively ending World War II, in a
series of contexts. Exhibit panels would include information about the number
of Japanese civilians killed, the number of those who died due to radiation poi-
soning, historians' debates about whether dropping the bomb was necessary to
end the war, and a discussion about the legacy of the atomic bomb. In 1995,
after two years of negotiating with veterans and politicians, the Smithsonian
scrapped the original script and Director Martin Harwit resigned. Conservative
politicians pointed to the proposed "Enola Gay" exhibit and "The West as
America" as evidence that public historians were disconnected from their audiences.[7] Historians held a referendum on the profession. Were historians isolated from the rest of America? If so, how could they bridge the gap between
themselves and their lay audiences?[8]

By 1991, many public historians trained in new history were in positions of
significant power, and had long been at work changing the historic landscape.
For example, in 1977, the president of Colonial Williamsburg, Carlisle Humel-
sine, hired Cary Carson, a history Ph.D. from Harvard University, to revise the
site's interpretive program with the new history approach in mind.[9] Similarly,
Harold Skramstad, who held a Ph.D. in American Civilization from George
Washington University, was appointed president of the Henry Ford Museum and

Greenfield Village in 1981.[10] Both led their staffs in the creation of new curricula and interpretive programs for their respective museums, two of the most popular in the United States, and both added bottom up histories by the end of the decade. They were not alone. Across the country numerous efforts to add new histories to historic landscapes meant that by the end of the 1980s, millions of visitors encountered new history at historic sites, museums, and National Parks. Why, then, were so many Americans appalled by the exhibitions at the Smithsonian Institute?

A contemplation of the nation's changing representation of the past in arenas outside of the Smithsonian provides some answers. The proliferation of historic commercial districts and outdoor history museums depicting small towns participated in creating visual texts that grounded the American past in a populist rhetoric. Consequently, even at places like Colonial Williamsburg and Henry Ford's Greenfield Village, where academics trained in new history added explicit narratives that challenged patriotic understandings of the past, their approaches were ultimately undermined by the cultural image of the small town and the narrative frameworks its landscape encouraged interpreters to use, ones tied to the language of populism.

The Small Town Landscape

One landscape directly linked to populist language is that of the small town. Politicians and manufacturers debated the virtues of the small town landscape as early as the 19th century when considering whether the United States should expand its domestic industrial economy.[11] By the early twentieth century, industrialism expanded urban landscapes and cultures, but discussions about the competing virtues of city and country continued. Works like Booth Tarkington's *The Gentleman from Indiana* (1900), Zona Gale's *Friendship Village* (1908), and Meredith Nicholson's *A Hoosier Chronicle* (1912) depicted the small town as bastion of virtue, community, and participatory democracy, while other writers led a revolt from the village. Floyd Dell, Sherwood Anderson, and perhaps most famously, Sinclair Lewis, pointed to what Frederick Lewis Allen called the parochialism of the "Main Street state of mind" exemplary of America's cultural, intellectual, and political shortcomings.[12]

By 1920, when more Americans called cities home, small towns seemed on their way out as workable community models. Industrialization moved jobs into metro-areas. Farmers who remained were largely tenants or share-croppers. Almost half of all farms in the South and Mid-West were operated by non-owners at the beginning of the Great Depression. Indeed, Henry Ford opened Greenfield Village in 1929, in part to preserve the small town way of life—even if it was a fictional one—on the landscape. Americans continued to move to cities and metro-areas during the Great Depression and World War II. And in the post-war period small towns and specifically central commercial districts were challenged by the development of superstores and suburban malls.

But the small town enjoyed a cultural comeback during the 1980s. In the film *Footloose* (1984) actor Kevin Bacon played high school student Ren McCormack. McCormack reluctantly moves with his mother from Chicago to the small town of Beaumont where he finds there is a local ban on dancing. MCormack convinces Reverend Moore (John Lithgow), a powerful, compassionate, but misguided minister to change the town council's policy. With the help of Ariel Moore (Lori Singer), the Reverend's daughter, McCormack organizes a dance, and in the film's final scene, Beaumont's reticent teens become exuberant, expressive, and culturally enlightened through dance.[13] One year later Garrison Keillor's *Lake Wobegon Days* (1985) was published. The stories were based on his popular radio show, *A Prairie Home Companion*, and document the lives of residents in a fictional Minnesota small town where "all the women are strong, all the men are good looking, and all the children are above average."[14] Keillor depicted Lake Wobegoners as idiosyncratic, but ultimately kind and intelligent people; his book was a national best-seller. But filmmakers and novelists were not the only ones to use the small town as a tool. For Ronald Reagan, the small town linked him to his constituency, particularly when framed in populist rhetoric.

"It's Morning Again in America"

Ronald Reagan's presidential campaign slogan for re-election in 1984, "It's Morning Again in America," was articulated visually through a series of political ads. In one, a soothing male narrator listed Reagan's purported accomplishments during his first term:

> It's morning again in America. Today, more people will go to work than ever before in our country's history, with interest rates and inflation down more people are buying new homes and our new families can have confidence in the future. America today is prouder and stronger, and better.

Viewers saw eight clips of Americans at work and play. In soft focus a small fishing boat pulls out of a harbor, people walk across a busy city street in conservative business attire, a cowboy herds cattle; a station wagon arrives at a large, white, two-story home; in an outdoor setting, a young woman in a white wedding dress embraces her grandmother as her new husband and family surround her; an older white man raises the American flag at his home; a young white man raised yet another American flag at his small business; and two children of uncertain ethnic heritage gaze up at what we can assume is a third American flag. The commercial closes with a final fourth American flag waving in the wind as the narrator asks: "Why would we want to return to where we were less than four short years ago?"

The clips included in the commercial are indicative of Reagan's unabashed appeal to patriotism; clearly, Reagan's first term resulted in more Americans saluting the flag. They are also, however, exemplary of what Lisa McGirr called Reagan's and the New Right's "populist conservatism."[15] In his 1965 campaign for governor of California, Reagan appealed to suburban California's interest in "limiting the use of the state for purposes of more equitable economic distribution." He supported a "reliance on private enterprise, a return to local control, and a simultaneous reinforcement of state power as enforcer of law and order and moral traditionalism."[16] Other New Righters adopted a similar approach, rejecting federal intervention in almost every arena but the personal. The images in Reagan's 1984 advertisement embody these beliefs. Americans, as represented in the ad, are successful entrepreneurs, home owners, and members of nuclear heterosexual families constructed by participating in the religious ritual of marriage.

These images also send messages about a specific view of America's past. It is morning *again* in America; the nation has returned to its appropriate social, economic, and cultural order. The ad suggests that just "four short years ago," America's small business owners and traditionally constructed families were under assault by the unpatriotic and amoral. Reagan's ad critiques the immediate history of the 1960s and 1970s, while simultaneously embracing values associated with a mythical and nostalgic past. Reagan and neoconservatives did not reject the technological advances that increased the array of weaponry available to wage the Cold War, or the culture of consumption that shaped the post-war era.[17] The past that Reaganites sought to return to was rooted in a specific vision of community, as evidenced by Reagan's campaign advertisement which, on the whole, celebrated iconographic images associated with small towns.

Reagan's political coup was his ability to convince white working class voters that the Democratic Party, which used to fight for the "working families of America," was now fighting for "special interests."[18] Reagan artfully linked treatment of the American past to politics when he accused Walter Mondale of erroneously depicting America's history as a series of failures rather than successes. Mondale wasn't just Reagan's opponent; he was also an opponent of America's heritage and traditions. In June of 1984, Reagan's advisor Richard Darman wrote a memorandum to campaign re-election staff in which he said: "Paint RR as the personification of all that is right with or heroized by America. Leave Mondale in a position where an attack on Reagan is tantamount to an attack on America's idealized image of itself—where a vote against Reagan is in some subliminal sense, a vote against mythic 'America.'"[19] Reagan won re-election in a landslide victory.

Why, though, did so many Americans find Reagan's rhetoric appealing? One explanation is that Reagan's version of the past resonated with a variety of other historical experiences on the landscape, ones solidified through the preservation of small commercial districts.[20] The small town and its commercial district's use of mixed space and distinct architecture visually separated it from the suburban mall. During the late 1970s and throughout the 1980s, preservationists used this difference to market adaptive re-use to struggling independent business owners. Preservationists explained that downtown business owners could compete with the mall by marketing a unique shopping experience, one steeped in nostalgia for the past.

The Preservation Movement and the Populist Landscape

The 1980s witnessed growth in the preservation movement. Two tax acts initiated small business owners' interest in preservation. The first was the Tax Reform Act of 1976, which "removed incentive for demolition of older buildings and provided five-year rapid writeoff for certified rehabilitation of historic buildings."[21] During the bicentennial, entrepreneurs sought to capitalize on the nostalgia and patriotism engendered by the nation's birthday. Adaptive-reuse offered financial incentives to business, long an opponent of preservation initiatives. The 1978 Revenue Act went further, establishing investment tax credits for those who rehabilitated historic buildings.[22]

The National Trust also formed the National Main Street Center (NMSC) in 1980 to facilitate the preservation of small commercial districts. The NMSC provided guidance to local and city governments interested in revamping their commercial districts with the goal of competing with suburban malls and shopping centers.[23] The 1981 Economic Recovery Tax Act assisted Main Street proponents by offering a 25 percent tax incentive for the rehabilitation of historic buildings.[24] Despite the 1986 Tax Reform Act, which cut back on incentives to restore historic buildings, in 1994, the Main Street Center claimed that their efforts resulted in the restoration of 60,000 buildings and the creation of over 174,000 jobs.[25] Today, the NMSC claims over 220,000 communities as participants.[26]

Preservationists' success and growth during the 1980s was accompanied by an embrace of business, long defined as an enemy of the movement. By focusing on the restoration of historic buildings and on the economic needs of the present, the NMSC and others solidified a populist image of the Main Street landscape in part by recasting small business owners not as elites opposed to preservation, but as important allies oppressed by superstores and malls. They also began to use nostalgia not only as a political rallying tool, but also as a product. Small town business owners could compete with the impersonal and bland visual experience of mall shopping by selling positive cultural memories of small-town life defined by community, traditional values, and the economic dream of the self-made entrepreneur. Throughout the 1980s, restoration and rehabilitation of historic buildings was encouraged by local and state funding, and received the support of business interests. It is this form of public history with which many Americans interacted. Public historians trained in new history contended not only with the consensus histories long celebrated at their institutions, but with nostalgic and mythical pasts preserved on the everyday landscape. New historians' own tendency to use populist language to create connections between audiences and the histories of the poor and enslaved would limit their efforts to challenge visitors.

New History and Public History

In his introduction to *The New American History* (1990), Eric Foner announced that in the "course of the past twenty years, American history has been remade." New histories were defined by their "emphasis on the experience of ordinary Americans," their use of "quantification and cultural analysis" and their focus beyond conventional studies of political and intellectual history.[27] Academics who found employment at public history sites often worked to add this information to the interpretive programs or exhibits for which they were responsible. At outdoor history museums and historic house museums, new history's impact was most clearly evidenced by the increasing inclusion and representation of African American history. Perhaps one of the most well documented of these efforts took place at Colonial Williamsburg.

Colonial Williamsburg opened in 1929. The plan to turn Williamsburg, VA into a heritage tourist destination was initiated by Reverend W.A.R. Goodwin, a former resident vision for Williamsburg, and sponsored by John D. Rockefeller Jr. Rockefeller's restoration was guided by architectural historians. But the interpretation at the site was led by various patriotic impulses, from anti-fascism to the Cold War. During World War II and through the 1950s, the site's educational mission was grounded in celebrating the "American faith."[28]

New social historians were hired at Colonial Williamsburg as early as the late 1960s, and by the early 1980s, many of their programs were in place. Restoration of the site focused on implementing a broader approach to African American history and, as Anders Greenspan explains, escaping its "pristine presentation of the past."[29] Restorers used whitewash instead of paint to create a more realistic cover on the surfaces of buildings, laundries, and stables.[30] Rex Ellis spearheaded the implementation of the Black History Program and initiated the "Other Half Tour," which discussed the lives of the black men and women who accounted for over half of Williamsburg's population in the late eighteenth century.[31] And there was a new emphasis on representing the lives of the white working class. In 1978, Zora Martin Felton criticized the site's missing histories of the town's black residences. When she returned in 1984, she found that Williamsburg had implemented a living-history project in which black and white actors used first-person narration to represent enslavement.[32] The actors were so convincing, in fact, that one visitor left the site and reported to local authorities that blacks were being held captive at Colonial Williamsburg.[33] The problem was mediated by ensuring that the interpreters introduced their performances, and followed it by answering questions and providing visitors with historical context.[34]

In 1990, anthropologists William Handler and Eric Gable argued that the site's implementation of new social history was impeded by internal politics that created a social hierarchy separating administrators from frontline employees, essentially replicating some of the class divisions that existed in Colonial Williamsburg. Interpretively, they argued, social history failed on the ground because in their depictions of enslavement, the stories told downplayed the "hierarchical relationship (white over black) of the two groups in favor of a type of benign multiculturalism in which group differences are all similar and therefore unthreatening…it minimizes a critique of social class in favor of a celebration of individual success."[35] In essence, Handler and Gable identified the populist rhetoric at Colonial Williamsburg. The enslaved and the colonialists are both persecuted by ambiguous elites. For slaves, the elites are their enslavers, but this identity is complicated by the fact that the Europeans are also being oppressed by policies enacted from across the Atlantic. The complex political, social, and cultural systems that are not made immediately palpable by places and material objects consequently remain invisible. Another popular outdoor history museum that added new histories to its landscape during the 1980s was Greenfield Village.

Greenfield Village: A Case Study

Biographer Steven Watts explains that Henry Ford's belief in "civic obligation; the Protestant work ethic, with its insistence on the moral value of labor; and the values of market 'producerism,' which claimed that the ownership of property and the production of useful goods bestowed social dignity and economic independence on the citizen," mark his politics as populist.[36] Ford translated his values into a visual rhetoric when he constructed an outdoor history museum modeled after the small town landscape and populated it with famous and not so famous farmers, merchants, inventors, and educators. Although Greenfield Village is often mentioned in histories of historic preservation, history museums, and biographies of Henry Ford, scholars are more likely to comment on its unique place on the landscape of public and popular history.[37] The Village's idiosyncratic representation of the past, and its association with one of the most controversial figures of the twentieth century, mark it, in the minds of many scholars, as a distinctive and atypical historic site that reflects little in the way of broader trends and issues in the representation of America's past. But like Colonial Williamsburg, the site is popular, telling us much about the desires of patrons when it comes to consuming the past.

The site is also relevant because of its location in the Detroit metro-area, a landscape that reflects how the urban model was rejected by whites. Beginning in the 1940s, the white middle class moved out of the city of Detroit and into suburban communities where they used racial covenants, intimidation, and violence to keep the black community segregated.[38] One of these was Dearborn, just a short drive from the enormous Rouge Factory, where Ford cars were manufactured, where Ford lived in his Fairlane mansion, and where he opted to construct his outdoor museum. Greenfield Village's depiction of a rural, pre-industrial past whose primary historical narratives herald the invention of the light-bulb and the automobile, then, is particularly fascinating given its location in a community made by white flight. The populist conservatism that defined the New Right is embodied by the landscape of Dearborn and, until new historians arrived, in many ways defined the Village grounds, too.

Ford christened his representation of the past "Greenfield Village," in honor of the small township where he met and courted his wife Clara. The title foreshadowed the personal nostalgia that motivated Ford's construction, and served as a constant source of consternation for later administrators and staff. When it opened to the public in 1934, Greenfield Village consisted of both real and replicated buildings from the mid to late-nineteenth century that Ford collected or commissioned to be built. A reconstruction of Menlo Park laboratory celebrated his mentor Thomas Edison. It also set the principal theme for the site: America's success could be traced to the free market and the Protestant work ethic. Ford's outdoor museum placed the common man, the inventive spirit, and middle-class domesticity at the center of America's history. Along with Edison's Menlo Park, patrons could explore the birthplaces of self-made men such as the Wright brothers' home and cycle shop, Noah Webster's home, and (of course) Henry Ford's childhood farmhouse. Henry Ford was so pleased with his creation that he spent most of his free time in the Village until his death in 1947.[39]

The Village's popularity increased shortly after it opened. During 1950, 500,000 people toured Greenfield Village, and by 1968, 1.3 million people passed through the site's gates, peaking at over 1.6 million in 1976. In 1977, however, the Henry Ford Museum and Greenfield Village reported a decrease in attendance. Three years later, administrators tried to use the Republican National Convention as a public relations platform in part by re-narrating the Detroit metro-area as a friendly tourist destination rather than a landscape marked by racial conflict and economic decline, but attendance rates continued to slump.[40]

The administration shifted its public relations campaign by appointing Harold K. Skramstad president. It was hoped that Skramstad, a 39-year old Ph.D. who served as director of the Chicago Historical Society and held management positions at the Smithsonian, could improve the Henry Ford's image as a museum.[41] When Skramstad arrived, he faced two primary problems. The first was a decrease in yearly attendance rates and subsequently, revenue. The second, which Skramstad saw as related to the first, was an identity crisis. For decades, administrators struggled to find ways of locating the Village in the broader scheme of museums. For Skramstad, the solution was to commit to the idea that the site's first and foremost purpose was to serve the public as an educational institution.

Skramstad's first initiative was the organization of a Curriculum Committee charged with defining the site's historical resources and considering alternative methods of interpretation. After learning that 85 percent of the museum and Village's collections dated from 1800-1950, Skramstad and his team determined that the Village's new interpretive program would focus on the Industrial Revolution, broadly defined. Skramstad's goal was to offer a complex view of how technology altered daily life, one that separated it from value judgments. He explained to a reporter that, "We're not telling people to have a particular attitude pro or con technology, but that technology and the change it wrought are part of the world. And to think about that, in a historical way."[42] Skramstad believed that the methods and practices of living history could make palpable the relationship between daily life and technology and social relationships. "Displaying furniture and decoration, the things of daily life is important," Skramstad said, "but our challenge is to have people in those houses carrying on the chores of daily life, so the visitor understands the complex social and economic system."[43] His idealistic goals for the Village were tempered, however, with pragmatism. Skramstad recognized that many visitors used the Village for leisure: "it's a tranquil, safe, park-like setting where they can have a nice walk."[44] To challenge the leisure experience, Skramstad took steps to remind people of the "grim realities" of the past through details. The Village staff would "leave the horse manure on the road a while...dump ashes out beside the house when we reactivate our machine shop," and "point out how people constantly got mangled in the machinery." "People were sick and in pain much of their lives," Skramstad said, "so it was a different existence in many ways, but the life of the mind, the soul, was much the same."[45] Although he recognized that the site would inevitably be viewed by many patrons as a theme park, he sought to make that theme more historically significant than those explored at strictly commercial institutions.

The 1981 Curriculum Committee supported Skramstad's view that the site was plagued by an identity problem. The Village staff, they wrote, was characterized by a "lack of agreement among the staff and in the public mind as to what the Edison Institute is all about."[46] For some, the committee recognized, the Village was clearly "History as Nostalgia."[47] In fact, this approach was "explicit in marketing the Henry Ford Museum and Greenfield Village as 'the good old days.'"[48] They concluded that a new curriculum should not "deny the nostalgic impulse," but should "take that emotional reaction and build upon it an understanding of historical truth as much as it can be known."[49] They encouraged others to embrace Skramstad's vision of the Village collections as an architectural document of the "shift from a pre-industrial to an industrial society."[50]

The "new" curriculum offered a series of very different understandings of history. Included in the list were "History as Inquiry," "History as Meaning," and "Modernization." To achieve these goals, they recommended remapping the Village into thematic areas; developing the Henry Ford Birthplace into a living history farmstead and instituting changes to existing interpretive scripts. The Curriculum Committee clearly viewed its report as bold, innovative, and controversial. In the closing paragraph, members wrote that they were aware the report might disappoint some and "outrage others."[51] Its members were optimistic about the potential to distinguish the Village from other museums while adding to its prestige among other museums as well as among academics.

In 1982 the Village was re-mapped. The "Village Green" and "Commercial Area" were renamed "Community Area," and the "Early Industrial Area" was renamed "Trades and Manufactures." The new titles reflected the staff's efforts to create a paradigm shift. They encouraged patrons to consider the ways in which small town businesses, religious institutions, and the government operated collectively. In 1984, the Village received a $1 million grant from the National Endowment for the Humanities.[52] Skramstad said that the funds would be used for restoration and aimed at upgrading buildings based on "historical research done on them," to "bring them into a higher state of historical conformity."[53] In 1984, the Michigan Council for the Humanities provided funds for the recreation of a 1912 Tent Chautauqua.[54] By applying for and winning grants from institutions that supported scholarly work, Skramstad and his administration worked to not only add more educational programming, but also to improve its credibility in the public history and educational professions.

One year later, the Village added the most significant piece of architecture since Ford's death. In 1982 Raymond Firestone decided that the family's summer homestead, built in 1828 by Harvey Firestone's great-grandfather, was in need of preservation.[55] Raymond Firestone looked to the Firestone Foundation and Greenfield Village for assistance. The Firestones and Fords had a longstanding personal and business relationship. Harvey Firestone, Henry Ford, Thomas Edison, and author John Burroughs often visited the Firestone farm in Columbiana, Ohio during the 1920s. The Firestone Company provided the first 2,000 sets of tires for Ford's Model-T, and in the 1980s continued to be the largest supplier of tires to Ford Motor Company.[56] Consequently, the movement of the family farm to the Village seemed natural. The Firestone Foundation provided $2 million to disassemble, move, rebuild, and maintain the home, and the Village offered an historic setting to which to relocate the site.[57]

On the day of the dedication in 1985, fifty relatives representing four generations of the Firestone family stood alongside former President Gerald Ford and William Clay Ford.[58] For Raymond Firestone, the farm clearly represented his father's humble beginnings. For Skramstad, however, the farm was an opportunity to create a living historical farm, perceived as one of the most effective and cutting-edge interpretive techniques for outdoor history museums. Staff working at the Firestone farm would dress in period clothing, although they would speak from a present perspective, care for the animals on-site, and prepare daily meals from the adjacent garden. Skramstad felt that buildings would provoke visitors, encouraging them to consider everyday life on a working farm. Despite Skramstad's progressive goals, visually, the Firestone farm and the living history interpreters who worked there did not overtly challenge positive portrayals of small town life.

The farm pays homage to self-made manhood, the yeoman farmer, and the nuclear family. Because of its distance from the remainder of the Village, it seems to be a self-contained economic unit. The home is brick, and quite large, and it implicitly links the nuclear family and middle-class material culture to Harvey Firestone's success. The interpreters who work the farm demonstrate the importance of collective action on the farm, but in material terms, there is little to demonstrate how the family is connected to larger political, social, and economic processes (Fig 8.1).

If the Firestone farm marked the most significant architectural addition, adding a discussion of enslavement to the Susquehanna plantation was the most dramatic alteration to the site's interpretative program. The Susquehanna home had depicted the colonial past by representing the lifestyle of a planter living in Maryland during the mid-seventeenth century since Henry Ford had moved the building to the Village in 1942. During the 1980s, researchers found that the Susquehanna home had actually been owned by tobacco planter and slave owner Henry Carroll.[59] Upon this discovery, staff closed the building, completed their research, and developed a new interpretive manual.[60]

When the Susquehanna reopened to the public in 1988, Nancy Diem, public relations manager at the time, admitted that the new exhibit focused primarily on the life of former plantation owner, Henry Carroll, rather than on slavery. Instead of placing enslavement at the center, "reminders" of human bondage, such as a bedroll in the kitchen appeared throughout the house.[61] Guide talks noted that the home, fairly modest in size, and limited furnishings, reflected Carroll's obsession with using his income to build his human capital, rather than add to his other material possessions. Cousins told reporter Roger Chesley that, "We tried to make the point that this system of slavery kind of perverted the way people lived because they became so obsessed with value in human beings and in land."[62] Interpreters such as Lydia Senton wore 1860s style dress and used third person interpretation as they pointed out, for example, that the enslaved built the home and that the owner's "comfort" depended on "human labor."[63]

How did visitors encounter these new representations of the past on the Village landscape? Unlike "The West as America" exhibit and the planned "Enola Gay," there were no protests at Greenfield Village. A steady stream of visitors continued to populate its grounds. Reception is difficult to assess and determine without statistical data. Unfortunately, there is none available on these early visitor encounters with the Firestone Farm and the Susquehanna Plantation. An analysis of responses to the Village's addition of more strident efforts to portray African American life at the Village in 1991, however, is suggestive of how audiences consumed the past at the site during the mid to late 1980s and explicates the role that its small town landscape and the language of populism play in shaping audience encounters with the past.

In 1991, eight years of historical research culminated with the opening of the site's two Hermitage slave houses and the Mattox house during a three day weekend celebration of the signing of the Emancipation Proclamation. Ford moved two brick slave houses to the Village from Savannah, Georgia, in 1941. Staff occasionally used the cabins in tandem with their discussion of the Abraham Lincoln County Courthouse, but they were largely excluded from the general tour. The Curriculum Committee was assigned the task of broadening the interpretive scope of each building. Drawing on archeological research, interpreters and staff used the cabins to tell a national and local story about enslavement. In one slave house, a running tape presented readings from the slave narratives of Elizabeth Keckley, Jacob Stroyer, Frederick Douglass, Charles Equiano, and Henry Box Brown. And panels describing the lives of each were placed on the interior.[64]

In the adjacent cabin, docents used third-person interpretation, or played a tape to tell the story of Henry McAlpin's rice plantation and what everyday life was like for the approximately 200 enslaved peoples living there. The interior was furnished with a cot, several gourds, some tools, and a gun, and interpretation was conducted by a docent or through a running tape. Interpreters were encouraged to draw visitors' attention to the unique qualities of the McAlpin Plantation; the brick slave cabins were anomalous and McAlpin was one of few planters to employ the task system. Finally, interpreters discussed how the enslaved retained many African traditions as evidenced in African American religion and music.[65]

The Mattox house was also opened to the public in 1991. Ford bought the Mattox house in 1943 in Ways, Georgia from Andrew and Charlotte Mattox, who made their living as tenant farmers. Skramstad and his staff created a new interpretive manual that drew on oral histories with family members and friends, such as Charles Heoles, who knew the Mattox family. African American interpreters dressed in 1930s period costume used third person interpretation to explain that the Mattox house told the "story of a particular family...within the general setting of African-American rural life between the two world wars."[66] Docents were asked to "populate visitors' imaginations with stories of specific people who had owned their land and home, earned their living through resourcefulness, sustained important family relationships, maintained a sense of dignity and propriety, valued religion and education, and preserved and expressed their culture, while simultaneously struggling to triumph over racism and poverty."[67] To achieve these goals, interpreters and the tape drew on the furnishings of the home and its surroundings, which included a small field with growing crops. Interpreters were asked to discuss the important role that Andrew and Charlotte Mattox played in their community, and the hardships they endured before Ford's purchase of the home.

Almost immediately following their opening, Skramstad established three teams to evaluate the visitor experience at the slave houses and the Mattox house. The first team was comprised of internal staff and included the original exhibit design team, representatives from the School and Community Programs Department, and staff members from Program Development.[68] The second consisted of interpreters who had worked at each building. The third group included Detroit-area teachers participating in the 1991 Summer Institute on "African and African-American Heritage."[69]

Interpreters who worked at each building noted some of the most common comments made by visitors. In the furnished slave house interpreters said that when the tape was used, several visitors commented that "slaves didn't have it so bad," or that "many poor whites didn't live this good."[70] Another interpreter explained that "Most visitors accept all furnishings" as historically accurate with the exception of "the bed and gun."[71] Interpreters identified some of the most popular questions asked by visitors as: "was this owner more kind, gentler than others?" "Did they really have a gun?" and, "How many people lived in the house?"[72] The number one question that children asked was where the enslaved children slept.[73] Almost all of the interpreters interviewed mentioned that visitors were "surprised," that the cabins were the only double walled cabins in the U.S. [74] In a series of questions about visitor responses to the unfurnished cabin, interpreters noted that many visitors just walked through to get to the furnished building and others said that visitors did not ask many questions about that building.[75] Respondents from the Summer Institute on "African and African-American Heritage," offered comments similar to those noted by interpreters. Teachers feared that students would assume that most enslaved peoples lived in brick slave quarters. For example, one educator expressed her concern that patrons might leave the exhibit thinking that "slavery was not so terribly bad after all."[76] Interpreters could intervene and challenge visitors who asked these questions, but for many interpreters and educators the African American Family Life and Culture was inadequate because it failed to effectively communicate the emotional trauma and political injustice of human bondage. For visitors, the representation of enslavement might have been dismissed because the material conditions weren't stark enough.

Each of these responses reflects the way in which visitors, comprised almost entirely of white Americans, sought to fit their encounter with the cabins into their own preconceived notions about enslavement, whether that meant that the furnished Hermitage slave house was too "nice" or not nice enough. While Skramstad and his staff hoped that white visitors would find commonalities between their interior lives and those of the enslaved, they focused primarily on identifying the ways in which the *material* conditions of enslavement were either similar to or different from their understandings and definitions of extreme poverty.

In the Mattox House visitors made strong connections between their own or their family's material history and the past depicted. For example, one interpreter said that older visitors often made comments like, "I know about the newspaper on walls. I lived in a house like this."[77] Other comments centered on patrons' personal memories associated with the material objects in the home. Interpreters noted that many visitors said things like:

> My mother had a trunk like that.
> We played checkers with bottle caps.
> This furniture reminds me of the furniture that my family had.[78]

White patrons may have left the Mattox House, however, forgetting about the vast differences between whites' and African Americans' legal rights and social and cultural status during the Jim Crow era.

Patrons who did not identify with the Mattox family due to similar experiences with poverty, reacted by challenging its veracity or attempting to fit it into the site's longstanding narrative of self-made manhood. The most frequently asked question listed by interpreters was: "Did they really have newspaper on the wall?" And the second was: "What was Mr. Mattox famous for?" Again, visitors sought to impose familiar understandings of the American past onto unfamiliar terrain.[79]

Why were the new history interpretive plans at Greenfield Village limited? Skramstad and his team followed the tenets of new history by conducting historical research and they addressed the stories of people long ignored by consensus versions of the past. Visitors, however, responded to these shifting encounters by fitting them into popular memories of the people they commemorated, or into well-established narratives about self-made manhood and American heroism. In part, the new history narratives could not compete with the Village landscape. In general, the Village pays homage to traditionally defined notions of American success. These are Americans who, to use Horatio Alger's phrase, made millions through pluck and luck. Their humble beginnings ensure that they retain a populist identity. The familiar figures at the Village are male, white and inherently tied to ideas about being "self made." Henry Ford may have been wealthy, but on the Village landscape it is his humble beginnings that are depicted and celebrated. There is a system depicted on the landscape. But through the Post Office, the General Store, the Church, the Village Green, and the machine shops, the Village privileges local organizations over larger, federally funded ones. There is an implied collective at the Village, but one bound by a set of populist conservative values rooted in property ownership, entrepreneurialism, and the nuclear family.

When new history was added to public history, staff focused on creating empathy between visitors and unfamiliar historical subjects. To connect white visitors to the pasts of black Americans, public historians pointed to the material challenges of everyday life. The focus on internal emotional experiences and external living conditions, however, often precluded a discussion of systemic power relationships. Visitors saw their own struggles in the Mattox family's efforts to make ends meet and put food on the table, but not that Amos Mattox could not sit at the same lunch counter or drink from the same water fountain as whites.

New History and the Problem of Populism

Throughout the 1990s, museums implemented daring and experimental forms of new history. For example, in 1994, Colonial Williamsburg directly challenged audiences to empathize with enslavement by reenacting a slave auction. Initially opposed by the NAACP, the performance was ultimately described as a striking and important portrayal of the realities of enslavement.[80] At the Village, though Skramstad left Greenfield Village in 1992, and the site recast itself as a "History Attraction" soon afterwards, staff continued to build on their interpretations of African American history. In 2006, Emancipation Weekend was a popular special event and included a celebration of black history and culture through performances by gospel choirs, and actors playing famous historical figures such as Sojourner Truth. The museum continues to expand its interpretation of African American life. Still, questions remain concerning the efficacy of new history.

Public historians face challenges that encourage them to veer toward more populist narratives. Visitation is guided by a variety of factors; the visitor may be at the museum for leisure, for education, or for nostalgia. Public historians cannot grade visitors for their retention or analysis of historical information. They are particularly tasked with maintaining their often paying audience's interest. One way to grasp a visitor's attention is to use the language of populism. Common or famous, men and women become are cast as heroes and heroines, "just like you and me" facing various challenges. It is useful to remind visitors of the common ground between individuals, but to achieve new history goals this must be a point of departure, not arrival. This is particularly relevant for public historians operating in the context of small town landscapes, which are historically and culturally linked to versions of populism that pit individuals against vaguely defined elites.

Populism is seductive, but because celebratory depictions of the small town have long been used by political conservatives, to express their values and goals, new historians operating in this setting dilute their message when they frame the past in populist language. The image of the small town is flexible, fitting easily into a variety of political paradigms; the interpretation, then, must work not only to add new historical information, but also to tackle the visitor's perception of small towns. Public historians trained in new history aspire to use material culture and interpretation as a means of creating an intellectual confrontation, to expose the System, and through that exposure, to encourage participatory democracy in the present. New historians must dramatically part from populist narratives in their interpretation of small town landscapes if they are to move beyond empathy, beyond "us versus them," to an understanding of the tentacles of economic, social, and cultural power.

Notes

1. For example, Alessandra Stanley, "A Populist Promise to Press on with Goals," *The New York Times*, January 28, 2010, http://www.lexisnexis.com, describes President Barack Obama's State of the Union address as an attempt to remind voters that he is a populist and remains committed to the concerns of "ordinary Americans." Carl Hulse, "Both Parties Seek Ways to Channel Populist Ire," *The New York Times*, January 21, 2010, http://www.lexisnexis.com, explains how Tea Party activists are using "populist anger" to move their concerns into mainstream politics.

2. Michael Kazin, *The Populist Persuasion*, (Ithaca: Cornell University Press, 1995), 1.

3. For a discussion of how the New Right drew on visions of community that emphasized entrepreneurialism, the suburb, and the church in its rhetoric, see Lisa McGirr, *Suburban Warriors: the Origins of the New American Right*, (Princeton: Princeton University Press, 2001), 192.

4. "Showdown at 'The West as America' Exhibition," *American Art*, 5, no. 3 (Summer 1991): 2-11. According to the Smithsonian's review to the first volume of comments "Of approximately 735 comments 509 were specifically positive about some aspect of the show. One hundred and ninety-nine people singled out the wall texts for praise, while 177 felt negatively about them. An additional 136 people wrote about other comments or other issues."

5. Mary Panzer, "Panning 'The West as America': or, Why One Exhibition Did Not Strike Gold," *Radical History Review*, 52 (1992): 105-113.

6. Eric Gibson, "Putting Politics on View at Smithsonian," *Washington Times*, June 6, 1991, 1(E).

7. Edward T. Linenthal, "Anatomy of a Controversy," in *History Wars: the Enola Gay and Other Battles for the American Past*, eds. Edward T. Linenthal and Tom Engelhardt (New York: Owl, 1996), 9-62.

8. Further analysis of the Enola Gay by David Thelen, Richard H. Kohn, Martin Harwit, Martin J. Sherwin, Edward T. Linenthal, Neil Harris, Thomas A. Woods, John Rumm, Gerald Zahavi, Rinjiro Sodei, and John W. Dower, appeared in the *Journal of American History* 82 (December 1995): 1029-1144. A special edition of the *Journal of Social History* 29 (1995: supplement) included articles on historians, conservative impulses, and social history. Authors include Peter N. Stems, Richard Jensen, Gary B. Nash, Jan Lewis, Barry W. Bienstock, Jurgen Kocka, John K. Walton, Joe E. Trotter, Judith P. Zinsser, Roy Rosenzweig, George Reid Andrews, and Louise A. Tilly. Public historians David Thelen and Roy Rosenzweig responded to these debates by studying how Ameri-

cans used the past through a survey in *Presence of the Past: Popular Uses of History in American Life* (Chicago: Illinois University Press, 1996).

9. Anders Greenspan, *Creating Colonial Williamsburg*, (Washington D.C.: Smithsonian Institution, 2002), 148.

10. James S. Wamsley, "Harold K. Skramstad, Jr.," Box 63, Accession #235, Edison Institute Records, Benson Ford Research Center, The Henry Ford, 3.

11. John Kasson, *Civilizing the Machine: Technology and Republican Values in America 1776-1900*, (New York: Hill & Wang, 1976), 20. Kasson explains that in the early nineteenth century, advocates of American manufactures had to first "remove the stigma" created by the industrialization of England, that their cause worked against the ideology of republicanism.

12. Frederick Lewis Allen, *Only Yesterday: An Informal History of the 1920s*, (New York: Harper and Row, 1931), 198.

13. *Footloose*, dir. Herbert Ross, Paramount Pictures, 1984.

14. Garrison Keillor, *Lake Wobegon Days*, (New York: Penguin Books, 1985) and *A Prairie Home Companion*, American Public Media, http:www.prairiehome.org

15. Lisa McGirr, *Suburban Warriors: the Origins of the New American Right*, (Princeton: Princeton University Press, 2001), 192.

16. McGirr, *Suburban Warriors*, 192.

17. Ibid., 261.

18. Mike Wallace, "Ronald Reagan and the Politics of History," in *Mickey Mouse History and Other Essays on American Memory*, (Philadelphia: Temple University Press, 1996), 265.

19. Paul D. Erickson, *Reagan Speaks: The Making of an American Myth* (New York: NYU Press, 1985), 100.

20. Erickson, *Reagan Speaks*, 264-265. For Wallace, the answer is found in the conscious or unconscious embrace of a historical narrative that justified one's economic, social, or cultural privilege. Wallace contends that Reagan also appealed to many Americans' "collective celluloid unconscious." Unlike history, Hollywood's version of the past was laden with American myths that provided a clear roadmap for the future.

21. Erickson, *Reagan Speaks*, 58.

22. Ibid., 58.

23. Ibid., 173-177.

24. Ibid., 58.

25. Ibid., 58 and 174.

26. "Reinvestment Statistics: The Main Street Program's Economic Success," http://www.preservationnation.org/main-street/about-main-street/reinvestment-statistics.html.

27. Eric Foner, ed., *The New American History: Revised and Expanded Edition*, (Philadelphia: Temple University Press, 1997), ix.

28. Greenspan, *Creating Colonial Williamsburg*, 1-15.

29. Ibid., 154.

30. Ibid., 154.

31. Ibid., 154.

32. Ibid., 229.

33. Ibid., 229.

34. Ibid., 229.

35. Richard Handler and Eric Gable, *The New History in an Old Museum*, (Durham: Duke University Press, 1994), 116.

36. Steven Watts, *The People's Tycoon: Henry Ford and the American Century* (New York: Alfred A Knopf, 2005), 62.

37. The following scholars have written most extensively and critically about Greenfield Village. Charles B. Hosmer, *Preservation Comes of Age: From Williamsburg to the National Trust 1926-1949* (Charlottesville: Published for the Preservation Press, National Trust for Historic Preservation in the United States by the University Press of Virginia, 1981). Hosmer includes a lengthy discussion of Greenfield Village's construction in his chapter entitled "Outdoor Museums," 74-132. Michael Wallace studies Greenfield Village in two essays. "Visiting the Past: History Museums in the United States," in *Mickey Mouse History and Other Essays on American Memory* (Philadelphia: Temple University Press), 4-32 and "Reflections on the History of Historic Preservation," in Susan Porter Benson, Stephen Brier, and Roy Rosenzweig eds., *Presenting the Past: Essays on History and the Public* (Philadelphia: Temple University Press, 1986). In both of these essays, Wallace identifies the site as emblematic of Ford's nostalgia for a union-less workforce. This project accepts Wallace's assertion, but argues that the site functions beyond Ford in varying ways. Patricia West also writes briefly about the site in *Domesticating History: The Political Origins of America's House Museums* (Washington D.C.: Smithsonian Institution Press, 1999). Diane Barthel similarly mentions Greenfield Village in her book *Historic Preservation: Collective Memory and Historical Identity* (New Brunswick, N.J.: Rutgers University Press, 1996). Finally, Warren Leon and Margaret Piatt place Greenfield Village in the larger context of living-history museums in "Living-History Museums," in Warren Leon and Roy Rosenzweig, eds., *History Museums in the United States: a Critical Assessment*, (Urbana: University of Illinois, 1989), 64-97.

38. Thomas Sugrue has written most extensively about Detroit's racial politics and subsequent urban crisis in *The Origins of the Urban Crisis: Race and Inequality in Postwar Detroit*, (Princeton: Princeton University Press, 1996).

39. Geoffrey C. Upward, *A Home for Our Heritage: The Building and Growth of Greenfield Village and Henry Ford Museum, 1929-1979* (Dearborn, MI: The Henry Ford Museum Press, 1979), 76.

40. See Upward, 76 for 1934 visitor statistics and 124 for 1950 statistics. Attendance rates after 1968 come from Denise Thal, "The Henry Ford Museum and Greenfield Village Attendance: 1950-2006," e-mail to author, December 5, 2007.

41. Wamsley, "Harold K. Skramstad, Jr.," 3.

42. Ibid., 6.

43. Ibid., 7.

44. Ibid., 8.

45. Ibid., 8.

46. "Curriculum Committee Report, 1981," Box 1, Accession #88, Edison Institute Records, Benson Ford Research Center, The Henry Ford, 3.

47. Ibid., 19.

48. Ibid., 19.

49. Ibid., 20.

50. Ibid., 20-24.

51. Ibid., 64.

52. Roddy Ray, "Museum, Village Get a $1 Million Challenge," *The Detroit Free Press*, December 17, 1984, http://www.newsbank.com. Museum and Village staff mem-

bers were challenged to raise $3 million in new or increased support over the course of three years and the government would match those funds with $1 million.

53. Ray, "Museum, Village Get a $1 Million Challenge."

54. John Guinn, "Greenfield Village Recreates the Era of Tent Chautauquas," *The Detroit Free Press*, May 6, 1984, http://www.newsbank.com.

55. Maryanne George, "Firestone Family Farm Joins Greenfield Village," *The Detroit Free Press*, June 30, 1985, http://www.newsbank.com.

56. Maryanne George, "Firestone Family Farm Joins Greenfield Village."

57. Ibid.

58. Ibid.

59. Ibid.

60. Ibid.

61. Ibid.

62. Ibid.

63. Ibid.

64. "Evaluating the Interpretive Program Presented at Hermitage Slave Houses and Mattox House: Comments from Members of the Transition Team," Accession #186, Edison Institute Records, Benson Ford Research Center, The Henry Ford, 7.

65. "Evaluating the Interpretive Program," 7.

66. Ibid., 11.

67. Ibid., 11.

68. Ibid., 1.

69. Ibid., 1.

70. Ibid., 110.

71. Ibid., 111.

72. Ibid., 117.

73. Ibid., 118.

74. Ibid., 106.

75. Ibid., 107-108.

76. Ibid., 108.

77. Ibid., 125.

78. Ibid., 127.

79. Ibid., 134.

80. "Tears and Protest at Mock Slave Auction," *New York Times*, Oct 10, 1994, sec. A16.

Chapter 9

An Army of One in 1:18 Scale: The Profit of Patriotism in G.I. Joe

Demian Ryder

Before G.I. Joe, boys did not play with dolls. Manufacturers did not challenge this assumption until 1964, when Hasbro revealed the world's first "action figure." G.I. Joe links World War II slang for the American infantry to a present day household word for patriotism. Since its inception, the product has existed as a multimedia artifact with a triumvirate market presence in physical goods, print publication, and film/television. The unique legal and political realities of the 1980s fueled successful brand dynamism. This popular construct now provides a unique mythological lens for examining the mainstream consciousness of the transition in the perceived meaning of military power from the 20th century Cold War to the 21st century War on Terrorism.

A Soldier 12" Tall: The History of the Original G.I. Joe Toy

As seen by 1960s industry, boys' play did not involve what can be described as medium-scale role-playing. Boys who "played soldier" did so at one of two extremes: weaponry scaled to their own size (such as the venerable pop gun) or miniaturized into representation rather than character (the rigid plastic 'army men' sold in sack assortments). When girls 'played house,' they frequently treat Barbie or other medium-scale dolls as individual dramatic characters. This kind of material culture has significance: "The things which people interact are not simply tools for survival, or making survival easier and more comfortable. Things embody goals, make skills manifest, and shape the identities of their users."[1] The ability to project life and personality into a character supports the ability of the child to create both a private refuge world fashioned from their imagination as well as a practical laboratory for experimenting with new ideas and rehearsing social behaviors. Styles of play considered perfectly acceptable for boys by the 1980s were hard-fought innovations in the business of toys two decades earlier.

From a marketing perspective, the toy has a further appeal: selling a doll creates demand for its clothing and accessories, what Barbie's business and creative mother, Ruth Handler, described as the "razor/razor blade principle."[2] This strategy succeeded; "in the first two years of the doll, Mattel's revenues doubled."[3] In 1963, designer Larry Reiner hit upon the concept of using this modular product design in an articulated, medium-scale soldier toy for the male market. His boss rejected the idea, saying "Boys will never play with dolls!"[4]

The Hassenfeld brothers were Polish Jews who immigrated to the United States in 1903, with neither capital nor the English language. They built a business in Providence whose success is the sort of true 'rags to riches' underlying the 'American Dream' (literally, as business historian G. Wayne Miller points out, with a start in textile remnants). Their first factory went up in 1922, but the enterprise had nothing to do with toys until eighteen years later, when early forays into toys included "junior air raid warden kits."[5] Patriotic defense of America, one of the most basic themes in G.I. Joe, may therefore be traced in its manufacturer's product aesthetics for over sixty years.

Still, Hasbro employees reacted doubtfully to Reiner's concept: "I didn't want my son to play with a doll!" Asked in 2009 what reversed this opinion for him, product engineer Sam Speers replied (speaking of the prototype): "when he was put into uniform."[6] Another designer drew his appreciation from his own experience "as a dogface in World War II." Artist Janet Downing provided the transformative language: "I then suggested that we refer to the toy soldier as a G.I. Joe."[7] The decision went to Merril Hassenfeld, who understood the broad range of success and failure in tackling risky ideas in children's entertainment. His division's success and relative independence had been achieved by the staggering popularity of 1951's Mr. Potato Head—and nearly obliterated in a $5 million loss from 1963's recall of Flubber.[8] Hassenfeld, the son of an immigrant, chose to gamble on the success of the patriotic American toy.

"Give a boy an Army Field Manual, and his fanciful imagination will carve reality out of thin air!" So states the narration on Hasbro's 1964 presentation to potential retailers for "G. I. Joe: America's Movable Fighting-Man." The figures advertised were nearly a foot tall, with "twenty-one movable parts" (compared to five for Barbie and Ken). The series boasted four parallel subtypes of accessories and uniforms for each of the four major branches of the U.S. Armed Forces. The company claimed that these were all "regulation gear... scaled to size."[9] These range from as violent as machine-guns, to as basic as tents, to as formal as dress colors. Designers of the line have said that friendly relationships with National Guard armories in Rhode Island and Massachusetts allowed them access for modeling purposes (they had arms and gear sitting around in the offices, a situation almost unimaginable in the post-9/11 environment—one team member recalls using a machine-gun as a footrest until the post recalled it for inspection). The military offered "very good support from the beginning."[10]

The multimedia roots of the G.I. Joe brand date to this presentation, promising: "...to promote this revolutionary concept, Hasbro will use the most strategic advertising campaign ever put behind a toy," including television spots, comic book and magazine space, and colorful retail packaging.[11] This plan of multimedia marketing attack presaged the technique used for the brand in the 1980s. The video presented the sale of G.I. Joe as a militant mission, and the mission succeeded. 1964 saw sellout retail action of $5.3 million and brought the toy division $895 thousand in profit, revitalizing Hasbro's market.[12] The utility of patriotism and military aesthetics as signature aspects of the brand form the first of several themes that would become G.I. Joe's foundation in the 1980s. 1965 saw the emergence of a second such theme: diversity in the American Armed Forces. In an era of racial tension, Hasbro declared its side with the first African American G.I. Joe figure. G.I. Joe became international a year into his service, selling in England and later in Japan.[13] Merril Hassenfeld teased President Lyndon Johnson, who was speaking of his need for additional manpower in Vietnam, with a note that said "*I* have more men in uniform than *you* do!" Figures published in patent litigation indicate the scale: "over 60,000 television commercials" had been part of greater than $4 million in advertising, achieving better than 7 million items sold. By 1967-68 the company claimed over 400 thousand members in its collectors' club and over $100 million grossed on the line.[14]

Seeking evolution in what had become the company's flagship product led to the third theme in the brand: an appeal to intelligence. Deluxe "Action Soldier of the World" sets in 1966 appeared with "Counter Intelligence Manuals" providing historical, biographical information about the various international infantry characters (an important ancestor to a vital aspect of the 1980s line). Bright children were also courted with a new sort of national hero: the G.I. Joe Action Astronaut featured a spacesuit carefully modeled on one loaned by NASA (who also provided spaceflight crew recordings, used to make a three-minute record included with the toy). Library of Congress blueprints allowed the design of a new G.I. Joe vehicle: John Glenn's *Friendship 7*. The brand reached another futuristic milestone in 1967 with the introduction of the G.I. Nurse, or G.I. Jane. This first female "action figure" had practical medical accessories and the same sort of positioning ability as G.I. Joe.[15] Literally, the G.I. Nurse can stand on her own two feet, a task beyond any Barbie.

Twenty-six million dollars in 1973 sales represented the high-water mark of classic G.I. Joe.[16] By 1978, with Hasbro suffering financial losses for the first time in its public-trading history, the line became a business casualty.[17] Antiwar sentiment did not cause the end; the brand's original continuous run outlasted the Vietnam conflict by three years. By the time it departed, however, it had evolved considerably beyond the initial shape of "America's Movable Fighting Man," becoming an international "Adventure Team." The lessons learned along the journey may be traced in four themes (patriotism, diversity, intelligence, and multimedia) which would prove instrumental in G.I. Joe's 1980s recreation.

Marching Again at 3 3/4" Tall: The 80s Transformation

Stephen Hassenfeld assumed the chief executive officer role in 1980, a milestone achievement for a man who had loved the toy business on a deeply personal level since visiting his father's factory as a child in the mid-1940s. Stephen's brother Alan started the decade off with the largest licensing deal in Hasbro history: $2 million at a time when company profits overall were only $5 million.[18] This cash contribution came from arranging G.I. Joe/Action Man for the overseas markets, powerfully documenting the ongoing potential for the brand—but Stephen was not to be swayed by a proposed return to classic 20th century military imagery. The perceived public view of national conflicts was negative; moreover, lacking a major "hook" like the Star Wars franchise, the ability of an old-model war toy to "get noticed" seemed limited.

Still, as marketer Bob Prupis noted in February 1980, American patriotism was a theme that retained its energy, as shown by the famous "Miracle on Ice." Prupis declared that here "was the kind of spirit I had to capture to bring back G.I. Joe!"[19] The challenge was not trivial, however. In the early 1980s, even children knew that the threat of total nuclear annihilation was a living reality. Enthusiasm for armed conflict between the superpowers was justifiably absent. The creative personalities at Hasbro needed to find a way to invoke patriotic pride and the raw excitement of tanks, guns, and soldiers without also triggering the fear of global conflict or the mistrust of unrestrained military action pervasive since the Vietnam War.

The breakthrough came in a moment of multimedia synergy. By 1974, the National Association of Broadcasters, under pressure from private activists, had adopted restrictions on children's programming, significantly limiting the amount of "fantasy" that could be used in advertisement (these "guidelines" employed extremely vague language, by intent). This was a strong hobble on a company that had been one of the pioneers in using television to sell toys, going back as far as Mr. Potato Head in 1951.[20] Marketer Kirk Bozigian recalls that between these codes and the FCC, TV for toys was limited.

A clever legal dodge offered a solution: the world's first television advertisements for a print comic book. These had no limitations, simply because "nobody had ever done it before."[21] The toy company made a partnership with Marvel Comics, owners of such popular properties as Spider-Man and the Incredible Hulk, to bring the toy line to life. Joe historian Darryl Depriest asserts that "this was a brand new thing, never been tried in the industry before, and it was a wild success."[22] Each media type offered certain advantages in concert with the others, forming a creative cycle. G.I. Joe's triumvirate of periodic publication, physical sculpting and retail, and television drama began rolling at the start of the 1980s, public as of the 1982 release of the first toys in the line.

These toys were designed with a careful balance of realism and science fiction. Designers conceived of "a fighting force for today, armed with the weapons of tomorrow" and not tied to the "political baggage" of international warfare. Hasbro forwarded Marvel ten black and white drawings for characters and a plan for $3 million in television support for the comic. Regarding the budget, then unmatched in the industry, Marvel's chairman said: "You're kidding."[23] Regarding the characters, Marvel writer and artist Larry Hama simply asked, "Who do these guys fight?"[24] It was a question born of the narrative idiom of comic publishing, one which the art of toy creation did not necessarily invoke. G.I. Joe of the 1960s had no specific enemies—but G.I. Joe on the printed page, like any other hero in literature, would depend on them.

Marketer Stephen Schwartz asserted who the enemies of G.I. Joe would *not* be when addressing the press following the 1982 release: "We want kids to understand that G.I. Joe is not a warmonger . . . We feel that we have a commitment to the kids of America and to their parents to properly represent the role of the military today, which is a peacekeeping force, not an aggressor."[25] This meant that the obvious go-to enemies of the 1980s Cold War climate were not to be drama's primary antagonists. Hasbro "didn't want Joe fighting Russia or China," Bozigian recalls. Hama drew on his own experience as a veteran of the Vietnam War in crafting the tone: "Soldiers don't fight for flags, ideals—they fight for each other." Facing an unusually large cast of characters that success would only increase, Hama began to organize his own notes and ideas about the characters in what he called dossiers, based on the individual 401 files he knew from the service. These were enthusiastically received by the toy company, where military enthusiast Bozigian had suggested something similar. Ultimately, versions called "Filecards" would be printed on the toys' packaging, creating a completely new literary aspect to action figures.[26] G.I. Joe of the 1960s and 1970s had been a *tabula rasa*, but the 1980s figures came with launching-off pointers equivalent to (at minimum) an improv actor's character brief.

The appeal of the team would be an extrapolation of what had been attractive in the 1960s. Depriest notes that G.I. Joe refers to "everyday heroes that kids can relate to" because of family and national connections to the military; "G.I. Joe as a concept will always be timeless."[27] Regardless of any given political situation, the perspective of children on the military is the same: not merely people in uniform, but relatives and friends in uniform. Their patriotism is apolitical, resembling the motivation for courage Hama noted about soldiers: they care about those next to them, not the flags above.

The 1982 Toy Fair lineup included Breaker, Grunt, Flash, Rock 'n Roll, Scarlett, Short Fuse, Snake-Eyes, Stalker, and Zap.[28] Stalker was African American and was one of two multilingual characters on the team. Scarlett, a counterintelligence officer, was the second female toy to hold the G.I. Joe name. Specialties in the group ranged from as basically realistic as a radio communications officer to as futuristic as a laser rifle trooper.[29] The 'action figures' (as in the 1960s, nobody dared call them dolls) were three and three-quarters inches tall, roughly the size of the competition's Star Wars figures. G.I. Joe raised the standards for quality in the 1:18 scale considerably, however. Star Wars figures had four to five points of articulation—their arms could move only at the shoulders and their legs could bend only at the hips; most could also turn their heads. The G. I. Joe figures released early in 1982 had ten, adding elbows, knees, and hips to their motion. Their accessories were interchangeable between figures—just like Barbie's outfits. Their hands were a standardized shape with a distinct opposable thumb (an advance in the evolution of military figures).

Two of the new villains were at Toy Fair alongside their opponents. From the beginning, "COBRA" was defined as an international terrorist organization. Their Filecards built up this image; "Cobra Infantry" are described as skilled with the (American) M-16 and (Russian) Dragunov alike. The "Cobra Officer" invokes the worst fears of antiterrorist campaigns through the present day: "Many are also believed to be operating as spies at defense plants, nuclear power facilities, etc."[30] These figures' faces wore the Western outlaw style of half-masks, which with their helmets gave the characters anonymous menace rather than specific national enmity.

COBRA also had a Sears-exclusive Missile Command Headquarters in 1982, suggestive as a terrorist weapon: a rocket launcher concealed within a rocky-exterior bunker.[31] The set came with the Cobra Commander, so dressed as to obscure his ethnicity and identity completely, with a mirrored mask-helmet that totally concealed his face. His Filecard notes his practice of "kidnapping scientists, businessmen, and military leaders," as well as that he "led uprisings in the Middle East, Southeast Asia and other trouble spots."[32] The baseline opponent for G.I. Joe, and by extension, the American military, is conceptualized here as a variable—an algebraic unknown. This corresponds with reality, in which the men and women of the U.S. Armed Forces face whomever they are sent up against. It especially matches an American child's perception of conflict, in which the antagonists that may confront any of their active-duty relatives are essentially distant mysteries (significantly, not stereotyped categories).

Mail order was a notable wing of the retail end of the multimedia G.I. Joe brand, using "Flag Points" on the packaging. Bozigian recalls the anger of Hasbro's postal department when they were flooded by "300 gray canvas sacks" each holding "1000 envelopes with fifty cents in each."[33] A select opportunity in 1982 introduced the fourth Cobra figure (and the first one with a visible face): Major Sebastian Bludd.[34] His Filecard comments that he received training in the Australian Special Air Service and French Foreign Legion and was "wanted for crimes in Rhodesia and Libya."[35] Bludd symbolized the developing idea of COBRA as an organization of rogue Western elements rather than enemies characterized by their alien or foreign nature.

Hama also authored Marvel's *G. I. Joe: A Real American Hero*, starting in July of 1982. Comics—the media with the longest past of marketing to children—had used G. I. Joe as subject matter in strips and magazines since as far back as 1942, well before the slang term for 'Government Issue (regular) Joes' was adopted as a brand by any toymaker. Hasbro licensed publications of titles using "G. I. Joe" as their proprietary brand from 1967 through 2009, rarely interrupted for longer than a year. The 1980s comic was written at a smart level, below the abstract adult-themed tier of the toys' faux military documentation, but above the complexity of the later television cartoon. In this way, the brand addressed a target audience across a broad range of ages and aptitudes. Hama envisions a science-fiction extreme of 1980s political realities: questionable ethics sometimes found at the summit of military command or within darkened halls of political will, pervasive antisocial corruption leading to militant terrorism, and the unimpeachable heroism of the American soldier, even to the point of martyrdom. This blend of left and right fears with straightforward patriotism made for rich plots and characters.

The first issue, *Operation: Lady Doomsday*, revolves around a character who opposes strategic aggression and military secrecy. A whistle-blowing government scientist is kidnapped by COBRA and becomes the target for rescue by G.I. Joe, even though some of the troops complain about being risked for the safety of an antimilitary activist. Hawk, their overall commander, answers their concerns bluntly: "We're soldiers. Our job is to follow orders, to do the impossible—and make it look easy."[36] The two-sided ethics presented do not take the cheap route of presenting the 'good guys' as uniform in their beliefs. Issue four depicts a paramilitary survival camp in Montana as a recruitment front for COBRA. The definite assertion is that the enemy is not "the Other," in literary analysis terms, but rather a subset of the West's own. Their leader schemes to trigger nuclear annihilation by setting off an exchange between the US and USSR. Far from being an idealized conflict of good and evil, the Cold War is presented as source of potential energy that could be exploited by the opponents of all civilization. The subterranean G.I Joe headquarters (the subterranean Pit) is described in terms of its (limited) ability to resist nuclear attack.[37] This element of chilling realism was all too familiar even to children in the early 1980s, especially those living near military facilities built for that precise purpose (such as the underground levels of the Air Force Strategic Command in Nebraska).

The top two national enemies in 1980s public awareness were communism and aggressive Islamic fundamentalism. Neither is represented in COBRA. As with the figures, rank and file COBRA troopers wear identical uniforms and masks akin to those of the iconic Western outlaw. This gives them a sense of menace while retaining their humanity. These enemy soldiers are a symbolic variable local element—by overwhelming majority they are white, English-speaking males. Their leader, Cobra Commander, wears either a blue cowl of unmistakable Ku Klux Klan appearance, or a helmet with mirrored faceplate, reflecting an onlooker's face back at them (this effect was used as the cover for issue six, placing the American G.I. Joe and Russian Red October teams as two separate sides facing the same threat). Visually, Cobra Commander incarnates evil lurking within the culture he seeks to destroy.

Kirk Bozigian and Larry Hama have noted that this way of presenting the antagonists for the series was not accidental. Bozigian describes COBRA's facelessness as indicating that they "could be anybody, which was a way to avoid targeting any ethnic group." Hama has said that a motivation in his writing was to avoid the "spectre of demonization." Knowing that real-world soldiers must face other human beings, rather than abstracted monsters, he portrayed "COBRA as people." Bozigian quips that "the most evil people in the world are tax accountants," to which Hama adds "dentists"—this humor underlies a real aspect of the local rather than the alien in terrorism.[38] A character in issue ten relates how such a chilling threat might develop, invoking fears of cultic recruitment and extreme ideology (shades of the Third Reich) rather than of other cultures:[39]

> That's the way it used to be around here...real ordinary, until the soap people came to town... It was one of those pyramid schemes. They got you to sell household cleaning products for extra money, and encouraged you to get others involved. Weekly "sales meetings" soon escalated into "leadership indoctrination," and pretty soon the ball was rolling beyond control. They were very convincing. They made it seem "un-American" not to want to get involved. Anybody who resisted was boycotted by the rest, and by that time the 'rest' was the majority. Persistent resistors simply disappeared and kids started turning in their parents!

The quality and promotion of the toy line paid off: 1982 saw $51 million in sales and "the toy was the overwhelming new boys' sensation that Christmas." Miller cites the reintroduction of G.I. Joe as "the single most critical factor" that ultimately enabled Hasbro to grow rapidly in the 1980s.[40] Depriest links the new form of the brand to the old one across the generations:[41]

> The G.I. Joe of the 1980s has a direct lineage to exactly...those principles that G.I. Joe is founded on in the 1960s, and that was to commemorate the heroes around us-- those real American heroes. So it started with a kid frame of reference with, y'know, their relatives that they knew, and it grew into a team of heroes who symbolized not just American freedom but freedom all over the world.

Instead of fundamentally similar uniforms, the individual members of the G. I. Joe team began in 1983 to be dressed in distinctly different outfits related to each character's specialties and role. This aesthetic change bridged the gap between the super-hero archetype's properties of individuality and uniqueness with the military-hero archetype's properties of teamwork and nationality. Team members lack superhuman abilities, but hold paragon-level skills within their personal portfolios. In this way, like real-world Olympic athletes or Special

Forces personnel, they are local heroes able to model goals, rather than remote heroes of divine status. Hama reinforced this concept of unity through diversity, commenting that real-world Special Forces military personnel often enjoyed a greater degree of license regarding personal uniform and equipment choices during field operations.[42] Stephen Hassenfeld described this aspect of the line in 1982: "Today's G.I. Joe is closer to tomorrow's Rapid Deployment Force."[43]

These literary and visual elements together show a reflection of the American public's transitional understanding of the armed forces. The military would no longer depend on conscription for its numbers; now, only the highly-motivated could be trusted to gain the advanced technological skill sets required. Public mistrust if the apparatus of war matured; antiwar sentiment beyond the 1980s more cleanly accrued to the highest levels of leadership than in the two decades beforehand. It is possible to see in the consumer patriotism of G.I. Joe the transition from otherness to sameness in the public view of both United States opponents and defenders.

The Leap to TV: Knowing Is Half the Battle

Pre-1980s Federal Communications Commission rules mandated mostly noncommercial content in television, as measured in hourly blocks of time. President Ronald Reagan struck down these policies by executive order, thus opening the doors to a popular (or unpopular) cultural phenomenon: the infomercial. The same stroke of the pen, however, had a more creative effect on shows for children.[44] A new class of cartoon showcasing product lines of retail toys became common during the decade, in both broadcast episodic and theatrical movie format. G.I. Joe has enjoyed the longest-running application of this technique, beginning in 1985 and continuing off-and-on through the 2009 release of a major-budget wide-release action film (*G. I. Joe: The Rise of Cobra*).

The brand's first foray into narrative television began with a five-part miniseries: *G. I. Joe: The M. A. S. S. Device*, premiering on Sept. 12, 1983. This cartoon achieved new heights of circulation, far beyond the presence at retail. Multimedia synergy occurred directly, in that the prototype animation for the series already existed in two years' worth of comic and toy commercials. The result is aesthetically impressive as a creative product. The animation is brightly colored, using the wide variety in the team members' uniforms to avoid 'crowd fatigue' in the audience. The writing follows a deliberate plan that aspires to more than selling toys (while never losing sight of that goal). Writer Ron Friedman (now a professor of screenwriting) avows that he intended to showcase "the typical American hero... somebody who is self-deprecating... intelligent in a crisis... and will always meet the challenge, particularly if it's not for his or her benefit, but it's helping someone else." He cites the fast pace of action in the show as an example of "propulsive narrative fiction," a film element explaining why "the Hollywood storytelling technique is the standard of the world." Such work can also be described as myth (larger-than-life), employing archetypical symbolism. It appeals, in Friedman's view, because the shared "transcendental, visceral kinds of stories and characters" links American audiences across her demographics: a "nation of immigrants."

Fictional media exerts influence on people; Csikszentmihalyi and Rochberg-Haltons argue that material culture does as well (G.I. Joe combining the two): "the material environment that surrounds us its rarely neutral; it either helps the forces of chaos that make life random and disorganized or it helps to give purpose and direction to one's life."[45] Friedman describes his writer's process as including the goal of "positive messages—that there *is* a higher good; that there *are* people who feel that and recognize it."[46] This illustration of heroism as a model serves one of the classic purposes of high mythology.

Affirmation of diversity in the organization is presented strongly; African American and female characters serve vital roles in the plot. This is visually reinforced by the end of each opening title sequence, in which the G.I. Joe team is shown lined up on a level plane—as equals—before the American flag. Battle images assert a patriotism theme that resonates throughout the series: defiance of international terrorism. The adversary is introduced directly in a spoken part of the theme song, performed by Jackson Beck (of radio's *The Adventures of Superman*): "G. I. Joe is the code-name for America's daring, highly-trained special missions force. Its purpose: to defend human freedom against COBRA, a ruthless terrorist organization determined to rule the world!" The very existence of this group of heroes (symbolic of the American military) is a response to the threat of an extra-national terrorist enemy. This is a transitional, 21st-century conception of the armed forces, rather than a Cold War mindset.

As with the comic and toys, the cartoon avoids the demonization of 'the other' in crafting its antagonist. COBRA appear not as ethnic aliens to America, but as English-speaking white people with a predilection for concealment. While the masking theme provides a distinct aura of menace to the enemy characters, the show does not indulge in the bloodbath treatment of dehumanized villains seen with the legions of unfortunate Storm Troopers in *Star Wars* or the faceless Russian pilots in *Top Gun*. Vehicles are destroyed in fiery explosions but their pilots always escape—the show explicitly avoids death. Arguably, combat is glorified by not being represented with realistic consequences—but the payoff for such reticence is that the show avoids absolutely the glorification of killing. Human life is held sacred—and even the villains are explicitly human.

A revealing internal flavor is that the evil of COBRA is demonstrated by characteristics associated with the darkest parts of American history. 1980s educational debate was marked by concerns of the ratio between patriotism and propaganda in covering or emphasizing unpleasant realities of past atrocities in the United States. COBRA, as a mythological abstract of American threats from within, is marked as immoral by having slaves and oppressing what appear to be a tribe of indigenous peoples, easily the two greatest American sins.

COBRA uses the *modus operandi* of terrorism mixed with the armaments of more traditional opponents. They employ tanks and fighter-aircraft but do so in attacks launched domestically and from no known territory. The fantasy is obvious—conventional armies require infrastructure for their logistics—but the symbolism is palpable. America's terrorist nightmare is a marriage of destructive extra-national organizational effort with cutting-edge technology. The plot revolves around COBRA development of a teleportation weapon; the parallel to a 'rogue nation' or terrorist network acquiring nuclear armaments is clear.

When COBRA achieves their technological objectives, they demand worldwide surrender, and attack the Eiffel Tower in an act of international terrorism. Notably, even though the plot establishes a space-based weapon for the bad guys, the targeting of that weapon is still achieved by a disguised agent on the ground placing a COBRA homing device on the objective. In this way the show subtly conveys a theme of hidden terrorists (rather than other nations armed with strategic weapons) as the enemy. The realistic fear of domestic attack was a matter of public consciousness; the bombing of the Manhattan Federal Plaza had been but months before *The M. A. S. S. Device* aired.

The second episode sends the G. I. Joe team to various exotic environments. Three elements come together in this. The traditional mythic story contains such quests. Additionally, showcasing such diverse toys as boats and snowmobiles is clever marketing. Third, however, is the public perception of the military as something that could be called upon for use in relatively small numbers (by WWII or Vietnam standards) and dispatched quickly to anywhere in the world. This transition in the operational mobility of the American armed forces is emblematic of the 1980s.

The theme of terrorism as a global danger is reinforced in the episode, along with its natural antidote. COBRA does not have limitless fuel for their weapon; the success of their plan depends on terror as motivation for everyone on Earth to give in to them. They are thwarted when "the world has refused to surrender" and find that "people are volunteering to stand and fight against us"—this last is as good a recruitment slogan as ever a volunteer military could wish. COBRA next attacks the "Red Square battalions" in Moscow. The clear message is one of terrorism as a threat indiscriminately targeting either side of the aging Cold War curtain, and in showing the enemy's ability to humiliate the great rival of the United States, America's similar vulnerability is revealed.

This theme is also reinforced by the basic limitation on the G. I. Joe team's ability to respond to COBRA effectively: locating them. The hidden Cobra Temple symbolizes the transition in opponents that occurred in the 1980s military and onward; inability to find the enemy is a War on Terrorism challenge, not a Cold War factor. COBRA strikes at "the leaders of all nations"—terrorism is depicted as the common enemy of civilization. Even Soviet-era language is co-opted against extra-national militarism, when the captured Russian commander—who relates with camaraderie to the American general Flagg—calls the COBRA leader a "monstrous imperialist" (and beats the counter as he speaks, in the manner of Khrushchev). The heroes' final victory is achieved via the crucial assistance of civilian resistance—Selena, one of COBRA's slaves, aids Duke's escape and so ultimately enables the team's triumphant assault.

Patriotism receives special attention in the last episode, when Doc places Duke in a trance in order to retrieve lost memories. Visual images of the leader's childhood show him studying, training, and defending the bullied—an ideal of sound mind in sound body alongside the virtuous use of strength. "Early on, your sense of justice and honor was tested—and you responded. It has never deserted you. It is at the heart of your idea of America—an idea despised by COBRA!" This form of patriotic beliefs is self-actualizing rather than self-suppressing; allegiance to an ideal of the common rather than solidarity with state designs.

Teamwork as a virtue is a consistent element between the comic and cartoon forms of the story. The Filecards support this construct by carefully describing each character's specialty and areas of skill, with the names of the character often reinforcing this idea of distinct roles: Snow Job the Arctic trooper, Torpedo the Navy SEAL, Mutt the dog handler. The brand as a whole modeled cooperation as a virtue even more highly than strength, as teamwork often manages to achieve G.I. Joe victory even when COBRA enjoy superior situational power. Csikszentmihalyi and Rochberg-Haltons speak of the tomorrow-oriented value of this approach to challenge: "it is possible for each individual to cultivate the goals without producing conflict within the community. This would result in an integrated group of people pursuing a common goal while contributing their own unique perspectives to that goal."[47] Marketer Sarah Baskin spoke on the intended conveying of a feeling of the child's ability to achieve the same thing as the members of the G.I. Joe team.[48] These traits of mastery and (team) loyalty are both meritorious and calculatedly likely to appeal to boys' sensibilities: "Together with courage and physical prowess, loyalty was one of the most valued qualities among boys..." and "the one that was most pervasive in boy culture was mastery."[49] Material artistic culture has effect on adults, even helping to shape them as individuals: "...men and women make order in their selves (i.e. retrieve their identity) by first creating and then interacting with the material world. The nature of that transaction will determine, to a great extent, the kind of person that emerges. Thus the things that surround us are inseparable from who we are."[50] If this is true of adults, the impact on the relative plastic of children's individual definitions must be all the greater.

The increased publicity from television had massive business impact. Toy sales nearly doubled from the already-impressive returns in 1982.[51] Considerable additional revenues drew from "outlicensing," the (multimedia) practice of renting the brand label to manufacturers of other consumer products. Hasbro cast a widespread marketer's net; over the decade, branding reached everything from breakfast cereals, clothing, and toothbrushes, to coloring kits and posters provided to elementary schools. Selling the use of the artwork and name simultaneously garnered income and spread awareness of the toys.[52] By the end of 1982, the company had made forty-five such deals, and continued expanding as the line exploded in popularity. The transition to today's style of marketing, in which companies such as Marvel and Disney depend more on outlicensing than on their core comic and movie businesses, is forecast in 1980's G.I. Joe.

The 1984 toy line included the Baroness, the first female COBRA figure. This character had already played a significant part from the first issue of the comic and the first episode of the cartoon, however, pointing to a paradox regarding female characters in the line. On the one hand, in order to create a compelling story, female characters were an essential. Hama comments simply that "it's hard to sell a comic book without any babes."[53] On the other hand, the figures consistently sold poorly. Boys seemed less interested in having female figures in their personal collections, and girls showed little interest in any of the toy line.[54] While the G.I. Nurse of 1967 had been shelved in the fashion dolls' aisle, no separation was made in the retail display of female and male figures in the 1980s line. Furthermore, while the 1960s-70s line featured such accessories as clothing and cooking implements, the new incarnation typically only involved weapons and limited gear (mostly backpacks and helmets). The change in scale had strengthened the separation between 'soldier' doll play and 'house/fashion' doll play. Girls did watch the show in considerable numbers, and read the comic book (as evidenced in the letter columns at the end of each issue)—but they typically did not buy or play with the toys. Prior to 1964, the toy industry accepted that boys did not play with dolls. After 1967, it seemed, Hasbro accepted that girls did not play with G.I. Joe.

While characters like Scarlett model the transition towards a modern egalitarian military, the focus of the brand is on masculine imagery. An open question is whether military toys have significant impact on military recruiting. Anecdotal evidence does support that such an effect is possible; designers on the 1960s G.I. Joe line recall numerous examples of hearing the brand cited as part of the influence for an armed services ambition on the part of fans.[55] At least one fan of the 1980s line felt the same: "I joined the Marine Corps because of it."[56]

Perhaps the single most famous issue of G.I. Joe, both among brand fans and the greater comic book subculture, *Silent Interlude* (March 1984) was created to deal with a deadline crisis. Narrative lettering was done outside of the Marvel studios and the mailing process alone took significant time in the pre-Internet 1980s. Hama conceived of an entire twenty-two page story that would convey an arc without use of dialogue. The issue was widely discussed in comic circles, and G.I. Joe's readership increased.[57] He freely admits that his writing was improvisational; he "never knew on page 2 what page 22 would look like."[58] This style of creation depends upon knowing the personalities of the cast and using them in an object-oriented manner. As Baskin says in appreciation, Hama always "let the character guide the story."[59] The interesting multimedia cycle here is that the writing resembles the typical play style of children using the toys to construct scenarios and meaning. As noted in child psychology, "Toys are to a kid what a hammer is to a carpenter—they enhance his ability to build things."[60] Often criticized for being a cynical method of toy salesmanship, the multimedia style of promoting G.I. Joe in the 1980s is equally laudable as an empowering way of personalizing the consumer connection to mass-produced entertainment. The style of play it encourages is similar to the sophisticated form of applied imagination employed by (adult) theatrical improvisation troupes.

Hama continued to develop his portrayal of COBRA as a threat of the self rather than the other. In issue 29, *Beached Whale,* the Cobra Commander addresses the cheering residents of Springfield in a scene with graphic visual similarity to Hitler's Nuremberg rallies:[61]

> Do not let the false rumors of our military mishaps alarm you! COBRA is winning! When the citizenry loll back on their fat haunches and hire the poor minorities to do their dirty work, we win! When love of money eclipses moral conviction, we win! When good men see the ascension of evil and do nothing, we win!... It is time for COBRA to make its next move! I present to you the Cobra Elite Trooper! A Crimson Guard! One of COBRA's best—and too good to squander on a battlefield! He is young, intelligent, good-looking, and upwardly-mobile!... Active in local politics. A concerned citizen... He will worm his way into the confidences of the mighty and work his way upward in the political machine to the Senate and, dare we hope, higher? His code name is "Smith" and he is but the first—in his footsteps will follow legions!

The enemy is presented here as an opponent in the war of ideas, expressed in War on Terrorism language. "Cuts in defense spending" are another element of the COBRA public influence campaign; again, the mixture of left wing and right wing politics is used in a way that separates the antagonist from identity with either. COBRA is composed of algebraic variables; they are defined not by ideology but by methodology. Terrorism itself is the threat definition, rather than the terrorist's motives. This corresponds with a child's understanding level of conflict involving military relatives in their real life, where the reason for the enmity is less important than the enmity itself (and the risk of personal loss it by necessity implies).

Dusty (1984 desert trooper) has a notable line on his Filecard, describing a "rapid-reaction force responsive instantaneously to explosive situations in far flung corners of the globe." On the opposite side, the Crimson Guards in COBRA "must hold a degree in either law or accounting" and their commanders "became bankers" after beginning their careers as armed mercenaries. The wedding of bureaucratic menace to paramilitary terrorism is spelled out in detail: "...their legions wear three-piece suits and fight their battles in executive board rooms. These then are the most fearsome of the COBRA adversaries. They don't fight with steel and claw, backed by muscle and honest sweat. They chase you with paper, wound you with own laws, and kill you with the money you loaned them."[62] Along with these figures, 1985 included an item famous in the industry as one of the most daring toy products ever sold: the U.S.S. *Flagg*, G.I. Joe's own aircraft carrier. The deck on this play set is nearly seven feet long; when first presented, equipped with numerous other toys, people assumed "it was a presentation table." Designer Wayne Luther recalls having to explain that the ship was the actual product. It was a fantastic hit in Christmas sales.[63] The success of the line overall is evidenced by Hasbro's willingness to even assume such a financial risk as a failure of such a large product. Safety testing was done by subjecting it to the stress of an adult man walking on top of the toy.[64]

On television, the popularity was enough to achieve an ongoing show. Producer Tom Griffin said in triumph that "we had uncorked the phenomenon that had existed in the Joe franchise from the beginning."[65] A second comic title, *G.I. Joe: Special Missions*, showed somewhat more political stories modeled after issues in the news. The introduction appeared in the *Real American Hero* title, as part of the extended-length issue number fifty, and concerned aircraft hijacking and chemical weapons. The new series begins with a story about submarine warfare and political defection (not unlike Tom Clancy's 1984 *The Hunt for Red October*; the serious tone of *Special Missions* allowed a greater degree of military fiction as an influence). The brand theme of appeal to intelligence was served by this new approach, which allowed the level of engagement of the entertainment to grow with the increasing age of the initial target audience. Discussion of history (Trotsky's assassination, Nazi war criminals, etc) was a notable story element.

With far more episodes and therefore far more presence than when it was restricted to mini-series format, the cartoon helped usher in a banner year for Hasbro. G.I. Joe achieved almost $185 million in sales in 1986.[66] This translates to "the equivalent of two G.I. Joe / Cobra series figures to every boy in the nation between the ages of 5 and 12."[67] Such market penetration implies more than simply business impact; it speaks to the range of the brand's influence on an entire generation. Henry Jenkins notes that "children's culture is shaped by adult agendas and expectations, at least on the site of production and often at the moment of reception, and these materials leave a lasting imprint on children's social and cultural development."[68]

The 1987 toy line included Gung-Ho sculpted in Marine dress blues, an interesting hark back to the authentic-look tailored dress uniforms of the twelve-inch line. The year also featured a mail-order Steel Brigade figure whose attendant Filecard and paperwork would incorporate the real-world name of the child who ordered it. This is a special example of the role-playing function of this type of interactive media. Baskin notes that the G.I. Joe team was presented as "women and men recruited from all around the world" to be the "best of the best."[69] This appeal to mastery as a virtue allows for positive self-reinforcement through modeling. In general, material goods offer this sort of process: "Late capitalism is characterized by its commodities...These serve two functions, material and cultural. The cultural function is concerned with meanings and values; all commodities can be used by the consumer to construct meanings of self, of social identity relations and social relations."[70] When the process itself is packaged as part of the good, however, the effect is surely magnified. In this way, interactive fantasy such as G.I. Joe may be an especially strong influence on the intentional and subconscious development of character, offering a constructive simulation of who a person wants to be.

The 1987 line featured another example of a mega-toy annual flagship product in the same vein as the U.S.S. *Flagg* (although in sheer scale, no other action figure product has ever matched that capital ship, even by 2010). The *Defiant* Space Vehicle Launch Complex includes armed variant versions of the American space shuttle and the NASA launch gantry that sets it up for flight, an interesting link between the 1980s form of G.I. Joe and the pride of the 1960s line: the *Friendship 7* capsule and astronaut.

Defiant also represents the last great milestone in the arc of business success for 1980s G.I. Joe. The elaborate train set that would have been the 1987 flagship toy was rejected as too expensive a risk for a line on a perceived downturn.[71] Nonetheless, by 1989 two-thirds of American boys (age five to eleven) owned at least one G.I. Joe figure, and by the end of the 1980s the brand had achieved sales of over $1.2 billion.[72] Stephen Hassenfeld died tragically in 1989, having led the company he loved in childhood to the greatest historical heights in its entire industry. In 1994, CEO Alan Hassenfeld—the second son of Merril to lead the company—pointed out in a business address that "a thousand shares of Hasbro stock purchased for less than $15,000 in 1982 would have been worth almost $1 million twelve years later." Hasbro's growth spurt placed it in the Fortune 500 well into the 1990s.[73]

Collecting the Future: In Conclusion

Based on his considerable career perspective, Bozigian believes that the collector culture of the twenty-first century has its genesis in the most popular toys of the 1980s, especially G.I. Joe.[74] The importance of object acquisitions in personal affirmation has been discussed in terms of monetary value: "To qualify as a status symbol, the object might, for instance, be rare...difficult to obtain...An object that is expensive functions in the same way. In fact rarity and expense are by and large synonymous."[75] The rarity and expense of discontinued manufactured goods, however, is of a lower magnitude than that which is possible for fine arts or luxury goods. Collecting the former is therefore a more inherently egalitarian and accessible hobby behavior than collecting the latter. Furthermore, a direct personal connection to individual examples of such items is possible for very large numbers of people. These may share the same mass media contact with it at points in their individual histories coinciding with an absolute moment (a comic or toy hitting the shelves or an episode airing on TV). Such community association with objects is rarely possible with uniquely fashioned art.

The military 'doll play' of G.I. Joe became a multimedia phenomenon in the 1980s. The astonishing popularity of this cultural artifact implies a considerable influence upon multiple generations, with the 1982-1986 range possessing the greatest impact. The internal mythology of the property forecasts the transformation of the U.S. military from a nation-to-nation Cold War footing to its contemporary War on Terrorism rapid deployment format; from a cultural studies viewpoint, it reflects the popular awareness of this change. Furthermore, the brand celebrated diversity in its content and intelligence in its design. By avoiding demonization of the other in its conflict narrative, it encouraged a form of community patriotism. G.I. Joe is a fiction that honors real American heroes: the men and women that defend the nation.

Notes

1. Mihaly Csikszentmihalyi and Eugene Rochberg-Halton, *The Meaning of Things* (Cambridge, UK: Cambridge University Press, 1981), 1.

2. Vincent Santelmo, *The Complete Encyclopedia to G.I. Joe* (Iola, WS: Krause, 2001), 14.

3. G. Wayne Miller, *Toy Wars* (New York: Random House, 1998), 69.

4. Santelmo, *G.I. Joe*, 13.

5. Miller, *Toy Wars*, 20-21.

6. Sam Petrucci and Sam Speers, "45 Years and Counting!" (presentation at the annual Hasbro International G.I. Joe Collectors' Convention, Kansas City, MO, August 2009).

7. Santelmo, *G.I. Joe*, 15, 18.

8. Miller, *Toy Wars*, 22, 25.

9. Hasbro, Inc, "G. I. Joe: America's Movable Fighting-Man." (presentation to the annual Toy Manufacturers of America Toy Fair, New York, 1964; republished on the SHOUT! G.I. Joe: A Real American Hero collection, 2009), disc 4.

10. Petrucci and Speers, "45 Years."

11. Hasbro, "G.I. Joe."

12. Miller, *Toy Wars*, 27.

13. Santelmo, *G.I. Joe*, 101, 128, 127.

14. Santelmo , *G.I. Joe*, 116, 110, 144-147, 96.

15. Santelmo, *G.I. Joe*, 135, 137-138, 167-169.

16. Miller, *Toy Wars*, 33.

17. Miller, *Toy Wars*, 31.

18. Miller, *Toy Wars*, 12, 28, 32.

19. Santelmo, *G.I. Joe*, 348.

20. Miller, *Toy Wars*, 152, 22.

21. Kirk Bozigian and Ron Rudat, "1982: In the Beginning" (presentation at the annual Hasbro International G.I. Joe Collectors' Convention, Dallas, TX, June 2008).

22. Hasbro, "Everyday Heroes."

23. Miller, *Toy Wars*, 36.

24. Kirk Bozigian and Larry Hama, "3 3/4" - The Battle Begins!" (presentation at the annual Hasbro International G.I. Joe Collectors' Convention, Kansas City, MO, August 2009).

25. Miller, *Toy Wars*, 37.

26. Bozigian and Hama, "3 3/4."

27. Hasbro, "Everyday Heroes."

28. Santelmo, *G.I. Joe*, 402.

29. Hasbro, Inc. G.I. Joe retail toy line "Filecards." Larry Hama, 1982.

30. Hasbro, "Filecards" 1982.

31. Mark Bellomo, *The Ultimate Guide to G.I. Joe, 1982-1994* (Iola, WI: Krause, 2005), 15.

32. Hasbro, "Filecards" 1982.

33. Bozigian and Rudat, "1982."

34. Bellomo, *Ultimate Guide*, 13.

35. Hasbro, "Filecards" 1982.

36. Marvel Comics, Inc. *G.I. Joe: A Real American Hero* (New York), # 1, July 1982.

37. Marvel, *G.I. Joe RAH*, # 2-3, 6-7, 1982-1983.

38. Bozigian and Hama, "3 3/4."

39. Marvel, *G.I. Joe RAH, # 10*, April 1983.

40. Miller, *Toy Wars*, 36, 15.

41. Hasbro, "Everyday Heroes."

42. Bozigian and Hama, "3 3/4."

43. Santelmo, *G.I. Joe*, 402.

44. Bozigian and Rudat, "1982."

45. Csikszentmihalyi and Rochberg-Halton, *The Meaning of Things*, 16-17.

46. Hasbro, Inc, "Looking Back with Writer Ron Friedman" (SHOUT! G.I. Joe: A Real American Hero collection, 2009), discs 1-3.

47. Csikszentmihalyi and Rochberg-Halton, *The Meaning of Things*, 11.

48. Hasbro, "Men & Women of Action."

49. E. Anthony Rotundo, "Boy Culture" in *Children's Culture Reader* (New York: New York University Press, 1998), 347.

50. Csikszentmihalyi and Rochberg-Halton, *The Meaning of Things*, 15.

51. Santelmo, *G.I. Joe*, 408.

52. Miller, *Toy Wars*, 37.

53. Bozigian and Hama, "3 3/4."

54. Bozigian and Rudat, "1982."

55. Petrucci and Speers, "45 Years."

56. Hasbro, Inc, "Greenshirts: The G.I. Joe Legacy" (SHOUT! G.I. Joe: A Real American Hero collection, 2009), disc 1.

57. Hasbro, Inc, "Declassified: A Conversation with Larry Hama" (SHOUT! G.I. Joe: A Real American Hero collection, 2009), disc 17.

58. Bozigian and Hama, "3 3/4."

59. Hasbro, "Everyday Heroes."

60. Lewis P. Lipsitt, quoted in Miller, *Toy Wars*, xiii.

61. Marvel, *G.I. Joe RAH, # 29*, Nov 1984.

62. Hasbro, "Filecards" 1985.

63. Hasbro, "Everyday Heroes."

64. Bozigian and Rudat, "1982."

65. Hasbro, "Men and Women of Action."

66. Miller, *Toy Wars*, 37.

67. Santelmo, *G.I. Joe*, 425.

68. Henry Jenkins, "Introduction" in *Children's Culture Reader* (New York: NYU Press, 1998), 26.

69. Hasbro, "Everyday Heroes."

70. John Fiske, "Understanding Popular Culture" in *Audience Studies Reader*. ed. Will Brooker and Deborah Jermyn. (London: Routledge Press, 2003), 112.

71. Greg Berndtson and Kirk Bozigian "G.I. Joe Real American Hero: Things You Have Never Seen or Heard" (presentation at the annual Hasbro International G.I. Joe Collectors' Convention, Kansas City, MO, August 2009).

72. Santelmo, *G.I. Joe*, 433, 437.

73. Miller, *Toy Wars*, 11, 5, 3.

74. Bozigian and Rudat, "1982."

75. Csikszentmihalyi and Rochberg-Halton, *The Meaning of Things*, 30.

Chapter 10

"Fixing" the Fifties:
Alex P. Keaton and Marty McFly

Michael Dwyer

Early in Robert Zemeckis's 1985 blockbuster *Back to the Future,* Marty McFly (Michael J. Fox) wanders through the main square of fictional Hill Valley, California in shock. After accidentally engaging a time machine built by his friend Dr. Emmett "Doc" Brown (Christopher Lloyd), Marty has been transported 30 years into the past to the year 1955. Struggling to orient himself, Marty stumbles on and off curbs, is nearly struck by a car, and gapes at passers-by, arousing the suspicion of a policeman on his beat. Although he has lived there his entire life, Marty's disorientation clearly registers that the town square that lays before him is not the Hill Valley he knows. Even Marty's costume, an oversized orange vest, suggests he is "lost at sea" in this new environment, a reference that is soon made into a joke at Marty's expense.

In search of a way to contact Doc Brown, Marty runs into Lou's Cafe to use a pay phone. No sooner has he walked in the door than Lou (Norman Alden) calls out, "Hey kid! Whadja do, jump ship?" When Marty's only response is a befuddled look Lou clarifies, "What's with the life preserver?" While the line might be considered as little more than a cheap gag, its structure presumes certain knowledge on the part of the film's audience. In order for the joke to work, the film's audience not only must understand the codes and conventions of fifties fashion, but also take that knowledge to be so natural and self-evident that Marty's inability to understand Lou's comment seems completely laughable. Simply put, the film relies on its audience in 1985 to be in on the joke, despite the plain fact that few members of its teenage audience had any personal memories of the 1950s to guide their response. Though Marty may struggle to grasp the reality of his time-traveling ("This has got to be a dream," he repeatedly tells himself), for the film's viewers Hill Valley 1955 appears perfectly legible. With no cinematic preparation or personal experience to guide them, *Back to the Future*'s audiences were better prepared for time travel than its protagonist.

Whether or not 1980s teenagers truly had an adequate grasp of the historical conditions of 1950s America is a question for another study. For the purposes of this essay, the salient point is that the knowledge the film presumes is not historical knowledge of the 1950s but rather knowledge of "the fifties," a cultural ideal that was understood in retrospect. In what follows, I argue that by 1985 American culture was deeply engaged in a fantasy of return to the more peaceful and prosperous fifties, a fantasy that was circulated and re-circulated in American culture throughout the Reagan Era. *Back to the Future*'s depiction of downtown Hill Valley in 1955, with its blue skies, stately town hall, bustling sidewalks and commercial prosperity is illustrative of the "fantasy fifties" I am describing. Just as the name of the town, "Hill Valley," describes a material impossibility, the vision of small town America it represents serves as an impossible yet seductive dream of "the good old days." In the scene described above, the appealing visuals of hopeful, small town America are underscored by The Four Aces' cheery rendition of "Mr. Sandman." The song both marks Marty's entrance to the square and the audience's first glimpse of 1955 Hill Valley. The "dreamlike" qualities of this 1955, referenced by Marty's dialogue ("This has got to be a dream") as well as the soundtrack ("Mr. Sandman, bring me a dream") suggest that by the time of the film's release American culture was dreaming of a return to the 1950s.

Indeed, neither the film's promotion nor its narrative were oriented toward clarifying the particular vision of the fifties *Back to the Future* would present because by 1985 the version of history it would depict had already become dominant in the cultural imaginary. The "fantasy fifties" were not only prevalent in Hollywood, but in what Lawrence Grossberg (following Gramsci) has called "the national popular." Grossberg describes the national popular as a crucial site in the construction of power relations, the realm of material cultural production that comes "to constitute the common culture of the people, and a national identity."[1] After years of intense negotiation over what "the fifties" would mean, the consistent invocation and repetition of the Hill Valley version of the fifties allowed the fantasy to become reality. The fifties that *Back to the Future* relies upon had by 1985 gained hegemonic status and became part of the collective memory and cultural identity of the United States.

Of course, critics noted 1980s Hollywood's affinity for the fifties before *Back to the Future* premiered in theaters. In the spring of 1984, *The New York Times* ran an editorial remarking upon the peculiar fascination the 1980s teen film had with fifties teen imagery, and the conspicuous absence of "the sixties" from teen films of the period. The article's author, famed critic

Michiko Kakutani, posits several potential explanations for the phenomenon—the narcissism of aging Boomer filmmakers, the cynical recycling of tried-and-true teenpic conventions pioneered by Roger Corman and American International Pictures, or the pragmatism of screenwriters looking to tell simple, "apolitical" stories. "It might be easier, in certain respects," Kakutani speculates, "to look at the unchanging primal preoccupations of youth—sex, popularity, identity—against such a neutral backdrop than against the more heightened tableau of the late 60's."[2] Regardless of the rationale behind the reproduction of fifties imagery, however, the article makes it clear that something is lost in the translation between the fifties and the eighties.

Just a few months later, Fredric Jameson's essay "Postmodernism," first appeared in *New Left Review*. While Jameson's thesis in "Postmodernism" is certainly more broad-ranging than Kakutani's, it is similarly motivated by pointing out what is obscured in the "pop nostalgia" of the 1980s. In this landmark essay Jameson identifies the characteristics of "postmodern culture" with the functions of late capitalism in terms that focus on the factors that have been lost in the transition from modernism—the author, the distinction between high art and mass culture, genuine historicity, and the connection between art and productive material processes. Jameson finds a crystallization of postmodernist characteristics—the transformation of "art" into "fashion," a "new depthlessness," and the transition of modernist style into postmodernist codes—in the explosion of fifties nostalgia in film and popular culture that "restructure[s] the whole issue of pastiche and project[s] it onto a collective and social level, where the desperate attempt to appropriate a missing past is now refracted through the iron law of fashion change and the emergent ideology of the 'generation'."[3] Although Jameson's "nostalgia films" may take any historical era for their source materials, he holds that "for Americans at least, the 1950s remained the privileged lost object of desire."[4] Jameson contends that the aesthetic discourse of "nostalgia films" emerges as a testament to contemporary society's inability to represent its current historical conditions, and its transformation of history into fashion and commodities. The end result, he argues, is a "crisis of historicity" in which "the past as 'referent' finds itself gradually bracketed, and then effaced altogether, leaving us with nothing but texts."[5] Nostalgia in postmodernist culture, he argues, reduces history to glossy, commodifiable images, and as such, is complicit with a late capitalist ideology that obscures the historical and material realities of capitalist domination.

Back to the Future could easily be understood as part of this crisis. Part of what makes the film's nostalgic look back to 1955 so appealing, from a particular point of view, is its erasure of "the sixties"—there is no trace of feminism, Civil Rights, counterculture, no student demonstrations and (until Marty's impromptu performance at a school dance) no rock n' roll. While it might be fair to say that these cultural and political movements were not fully formed by 1955, they (and the social tensions to which they responded) were certainly not completely absent, as they seem to be in Hill Valley. Beyond setting the film in a pre-sixties America, the film's nostalgic perspective simply does not allow for the possibility that the sixties might ever occur. As many scholars have pointed out, the film's logic aligns neatly with the figure that has been called "the great American synecdoche"—Ronald Reagan.[6] The film has repeatedly been referenced as a symbol of Reaganism and Reagan politics have often been described in terms of the film.[7] David Marcus had argued that Reagan embodied "in his public demeanor, professions of conservative personal values, and cultural tastes, a belief in and yearning for a nation undisturbed by the social controversies and political traumas of post-1963 America."[8] That is, one way of understanding the fifties nostalgia that is so present in both Reagan's America generally and *Back to the Future* specifically is as an effacement of a period of American history in which the social order seemed to be under the most direct assault and as such, an imaginary alternative to an unsettling present. Precisely what "the sixties" were remains a lively topic of discussion, but in Reagan's America, the sixties was for many simply a time they wished to forget.

In the spirit of the Jamesonian imperative to "always historicize"[9] as well as his urge to "think the cultural evolution of late capitalism dialectically"[10] this essay challenges the notion of nostalgia in general, and fifties nostalgia in the Reagan Era specifically, as simply a "reduction" of history—a phenomenon that is only about "loss" or "forgetting." Nostalgia is not simply the denial of history, but is also a fundamentally *productive* discursive process. Sociologist Fred Davis has argued that nostalgia is "one of the means—or, better yet, a readily accessible psychological lens—at our disposal for the never ending work of constructing, maintaining and reconstructing our identities."[11] As such, fifties nostalgia in the Reagan Era must be understood as a cultural process of construction and re-construction, not as a necessarily pernicious quality contained within bad ideological objects. Rather, as Linda Hutcheon has argued, nostalgia "is what you 'feel' when two different temporal moments, past and present, come together for you. . . .it is the element of response—of active participation, both intellectual and affective—that makes for the power."[12] Nostalgia is not inherent to a text, but rather a reading practice, a mode of encountering the text. Thus, *Back to the Future*'s nostalgia is not a defect in its understanding of history. Rather, it is a product of discourses that swirled around recreations of the 1950s in American film and popular culture throughout the 1970s and 1980s, a period coincident with the rise of Reagan and the political movement that took him as its avatar.

In the creation of this cultural fantasy, the fifties had to be doubly "fixed." First, the fifties had to be *repaired*, cleansed of the litany of anxieties and tensions which actually gripped American life in the 1950s. In order for the fifties to be considered "a simpler time," the emergence of feminism and civil rights movements, concerns over juvenile delinquency and global nuclear war, furor over the obscenity of the Beats or Elvis Presley, and sundry other cultural shocks from the Red Scare to Kinsey Reports must all be elided or forgotten. The second order of "fixing" is a process of *freezing*, or *halting*—the fantasy version of the fifties cuts the 1950s off from the years that preceded and followed them, and treats the fifties as though it existed in a historical, cultural, and political vacuum, wholly differentiated from the socio-political upheavals of the sixties. *Back to the Future* is particularly suited for an analysis of this process, for not only does it rely on the fantasy fifties to orient its viewers in history, but it also re-enacts the "doubly fixed" re-construction of the fifties within its narrative. Marty's ability to re-write history and preserve it in perpetuity not only enables his return home to 1985, but allows him to save the fate of his family entirely, and restore a "future" that they might all pursue enthusiastically. This is not just Hollywood artifice. It reflects the social, cultural, and political re-imaginings of the nation's path to progress by re-establishing the "traditional values" that were aligned with the rise of the New Right in the 1980s.

This essay's ensuing sections will follow this "double fixing" process by first consider the remaking of George's flawed masculinity to more closely align with the Reagan-Era ideal of "muscular masculinity." Second, it illustrates the development of an isolated, homogenized, and idealized "fifties" in the rhetoric of Reagan via two of his landmark speeches. Next, it demonstrates the lionization of a new "Reagan youth," as represented in the star text of Michael J. Fox, that would could galvanize and recover the strength of American families. The essay will close with an examination of how *Back to the Future* projects the family drama of "double fixing" into the civic/political sphere. Each section is meant to highlight the productive functions of fifties nostalgia, and reveal the discursive and historical origins of the fantasy fifties of the Reagan Era.

Fixing Our Fathers, Fixing Ourselves

Before Marty's interaction with Lou, he has already spent several hours in 1955. At this point, however, he can neither understand what has happened nor fathom why the people he encounters regard him with befuddlement and fear (in one scene he is mistaken for a marauding space alien and nearly killed). It is not until Marty enters the 1955 town square that he can comprehend the reality of his time travel—a moment that coincides with the first of many references to Reagan in the film. Immediately after walking into the square, Marty's gaze (here aligned with the camera) lands on a signboard advertising the feature at the downtown movie house. The film is *Cattle Queen of Montana*, an unremarkable 1954 Western starring Barbara Stanwyck and Ronald Reagan. Marty responds to the sign with a double-take, looking at the theater's marquee to confirm that, indeed, Reagan is not in Washington but in Hollywood. It is at this moment that Marty is able to orient himself in time, suggesting that the 1980s teenager is only able to locate his position in the nation's history by locating Reagan.

As I've argued, the emergence of Ronald Reagan as a mainstream political figure in the 1970s, and as President and national icon in the 1980s, was in large part made possible by his ability to embody a fantasy version of the fifties. Reagan's appearance in *Back to the Future*, then, takes on a special resonance, signaling that it is not just *any* fifties that Marty will find himself in, but *Reagan's* fifties. This realization empowers Marty to utilize his Reagan-Era knowledge and tastes to not only safely navigate history, but ultimately to master it. While it was of course clear to audiences in 1985 that *Back to the Future* is a film about a teenager traveling in time to the 1950s—it was explicitly presented in the press and promotional materials as such, and the first act of the narrative makes it no secret—what is not made explicit before the aforementioned town square sequence is precisely *which* fifties the film would depict. Such details were apparently unnecessary, if the original teaser trailer is any indication. In it, the camera seems most interested in the time travel machinery, with a series of long, slow pans in extreme close-up over the DeLorean's wheels, gull-wing doors, electronic circuitry and switches, dials and LED displays on the highly modified dashboard. This emphasis on technology is reproduced in the film's promotional poster, which depicts Marty standing astride a trail of fire, with an eerie light pouring out of the DeLorean's open gull wing door. To some degree, the emphasis on the technology of time travel can be understood as Universal's attempt to link the film to the successes of *WarGames* (1983), *Real Genius* (1985), *Weird Science* (1985) and other films that Timothy Shary classifies as "teen science" films, a subgenre characterized by its emphasis on "the newness and surprising complexity. . . of youth's involvement with science and technology."[13] In focusing exclusively on the teen and the machine, Universal promoted them as the real stars of the picture. Subsequent *Back to the Future* trailers turned their focus largely on the film's comedic elements—particularly those relating to Marty's uncomfortable romantic dealings with his mother in 1955, connecting the film to other teen sex comedies of the early to mid-1980s, such as *Meatballs* (1979), *Porky's* (1982) and *Risky Business* (1983).

The promotional materials surrounding the original theatrical release of *Back to the Future* indicate that while audiences would need preparation for (or could be enticed by) the science fiction and sex comedy aspects of the film, there was no similar preparation or appeal necessary for the film's fifties setting. Still further, the overwhelmingly positive reception from film critics in the popular press was accompanied by little to no reference to the film's historical elements. Instead, reviewers seemed enthralled with the Oedipal inversion of the film's second act, and the transmission of masculine power from the son to the father. "It ain't exactly Sophocles," said *The San Francisco Chronicle*, "it's an Oedipal trip, American style"[14] and *The New Republic* praised the "high camp Freudian comedy" of the film.[15] This "Freudian comedy" stems from Marty's accidental displacement of his father as the object of his mother's erotic desire. As a result, Marty spends much of his time in 1955 rebuffing her amorous advances, and aiding his father in winning her hand in order that he will someday be born. Marty, to save himself, must re-create his own nuclear family at its very inception in order to save the values and ideals of his own time. This is illustrated by the photograph that Marty carries of himself and his two elder siblings—as the union of his parents is endangered, the children of the 1980s disappear from the photo. In other words, it is not merely the 1980s that are at stake, but rather the future (of the McFly clan, yes, but also of the nation itself). To safeguard his family's future, Marty must intervene at the crucial site of his familial drama—as it is in Oedipus'—with the father.

Marty is immediately brought face to face with his father's shortcomings in 1955. In Lou's Café, the oafish Biff Tannen (Thomas F. Wilson) bullies George into doing his homework for him, embarrasses him mercilessly, and delights in his goons' appreciation for George's sniveling. George's inability to stand up to Biff is not only school-age submission, but a more generalized personality flaw. As Marty sees when he follows George to high school in 1955, Biff is not the only one of George's bullies. Indeed, after students passing by enthusiastically oblige the "kick me" sign on George's back, even the Vice Principal gets in on the act. When Goldie, busboy in Lou's Café, reminds George that "if you let people walk over you now, they'll be walkin' over you for the rest of your life," the film's viewers can confirm Goldie's prediction. The scene between Biff and George is an almost exact replication of a scene occurring earlier in the film, at Marty's family house in 1985. Thirty years later, Biff is still bullying George, wrecking the McFly family car and refusing to pay for insurance (instead, blaming the accident on a "blind spot"). George's inability to stand up to Biff in 1955, in the logic of the film, sets the course for the rest of his adult life.

Further, George's weakness appears to be a heritable trait, as Marty exhibits many of the same bashful tendencies as his father. Before he travels back in time, Marty is accosted by Vice Principal, who says "I noticed your band was on the roster for the dance auditions after school today. Why even bother, McFly? You don't have a chance, you're too much like your old man." By the logic of the film, Marty *is* too much like his old man. When Marty discovers that George writes science fiction stories but never lets anyone read them, George's reasoning for keeping them secret—"What if they didn't like them? What if they told me I was no good?"—is an almost exact echo of the language Marty uses to justify not sending an audition tape of his band to a record label: "What if they say I'm no good? What if they say 'Get out of here, kid, you got no future?' I just don't think I could take that kind of rejection." Hearing himself, Marty adds, "Jesus, I'm starting to sound like my old man!" Indeed, when Marty and George first meet in 1955, seated side by side in Lou's coffee shop, they strike the same pose, use the same nervous gestures, and approach one another with the same tentative distrust.

While critics have discussed Marty's role in augmenting the insufficient masculinity of his father, it is important to recognize that at the film's outset, Marty's masculinity is also positioned as insufficient. He too is unable to stand up to Biff, to face confrontation or to risk rejection. Marty's function in the fifties, then, is not only to repair the fifties masculinity of his father but also to remake himself in the process. In 1985, the vice principal menacingly tells Marty that "No McFly ever amounted to anything in the history of Hill Valley." Marty spends the rest of the film making his then-feckless riposte, "History's gonna change," a reality. This, in many ways, is not only the film's thesis, but the promise of the Reagan youth movement that will be addressed later in the essay. Marty's response to Strickland is not at all about repairing his father's legacy, for at that point in the film time-travel is not a consideration. He is speaking entirely for, and of, himself. In this way Marty embodies the Reagan Era disaffection with an America in the 1980s that was not living up to its postwar potential. The only way Marty can change history and thus change himself in the film, however, is by simultaneously remaking his father in the fifties.

In order to repair his father's masculinity and assert a place for himself in the 1980s social structure, Marty must remake his father into the hero he never was. The story of George and Lorraine's courtship—George falls out of a tree from which he was clandestinely peeping into Lorraine's windows as she undressed, is struck by Mr. Baines' car and is nursed back to health by the smitten Lorraine—is interrupted by Marty's arrival in 1955. As a result Marty supplants George as Lorraine's sexual interest, not only because Marty is hit by the car instead of George but also because Marty provides Lorraine with a more appealing model of masculinity. Where George in 1955 prefers to watch Lorraine through binoculars rather than approach her directly (because he "couldn't deal with that kind of rejection"), Marty approaches Lorraine with absolute confidence. Though Marty was never able to stand up to Biff in 1985, when Biff harasses Lorraine in 1955 Marty does not hesitate to grab the much larger Biff by his shirt collar. Marty's confidence and bravery makes quite the impression on Lorraine, who prior to Marty's intervention recalls being drawn to George because "he seemed so helpless, like a little lost puppy." After Marty's arrival, though, Lorraine has a different take on Marty's father: "George McFly? Well, he's kinda cute and all, but not. . . well, I think a man should be strong, so he can stand up for himself, and protect the woman he loves." This certainly spells trouble for George, as Marty well knows.

In response, Marty plans to force George to take a more active role in his relationship with Lorraine. Because George is too afraid of rejection to ask Lorraine out on a date Marty uses his knowledge of 1980s technology and popular culture, posing as the alien "Darth Vader from the Planet Vulcan" to trick and intimidate his father. With George properly motivated, Marty then provides him with the skills for navigating the dating process: "Tell her destiny has brought you together, tell her she is the most beautiful girl you have ever seen in the world. Girls like that stuff." But when George flubs the delivery and is interrupted by Biff, Marty arrives to save the day. Marty knocks Biff down and cunningly evades his gang. In the process Marty proves himself to be stronger than George and more clever then Biff, dramatically increasing Lorraine's desire for him.

After Marty's turn at Cyrano de Bergerac fails he resorts to outright fakery, setting out to create a scene where George can play the role of hero rescuing Lorraine from Marty's feigned sexual advances. But once again, Marty's best laid plans go awry. First, Lorraine turns the tables by becoming the sexual aggressor, taking Marty by surprise. Then, Biff and his cronies arrive and transform Marty's staged sexual assault on Lorraine into Biff's real one. When George finally arrives, he cannot simply *play the part* of the ideal fifties man (and, by extension, the ideal Reagan-era father). He must instead *become* that ideal man, by "standing up for himself, and protecting the woman he loves," as Lorraine has said. George does so, overcoming his fear and knocking out Biff with one punch. The impact on George's social standing is immediate— no longer the butt of every prank, George suddenly is transformed into the big man on campus. With this, George's future with Lorraine is secured, as if no other fate can befall the two from this point but to fall in love, be married, and have children, as they were destined to do. In the first move of what I have identified as the film's "double fixing," Marty ably performs the reparative cleansing of his father's insufficient and deviant masculinity. Once Marty has made the arrangement in 1955, it is, as if by destiny, "fixed" there for the rest of time.

As Marty promised Vice Principal Strickland, history does change, and Marty's own destiny is a new one. Upon his return to 1985, Marty discovers that his father is no longer the simpering weakling that he once knew, but is now a wealthy bestselling author and model 1980s yuppie parent. This new George plays tennis in the mornings and awaits the delivery of his next novel, while Biff waxes his car, kowtowing to him. Lorraine, noticeably thinner, no longer drinks or smokes, but basks in the sexual attention she gets from George (a radical change from the parallel scene that occurs earlier in the film, where George and Lorraine almost never occupy the same frame) and encourages Marty to call his girlfriend. Marty's two siblings—lonely and poor in the film's opening—are social and financial successes in this "new 1985," arranging office meetings and dates over brunch. Marty, of course, is not left out. In this version of 1985, Marty has the confidence to send his band's demo tape into the record company, and gets some material benefits: the new pickup truck that he's always wanted and license to spend a romantic weekend with his girlfriend at the lake. Susan Jeffords equates Marty's manipulation of history with Reagan's political mythology, arguing that his political logic of the 1980s fundamentally relied on a mobilization of fifties ideals of active, muscular masculinity: "As Marty coaches his father from a wimp to a rescuer, Reagan set out to coach America from acting the part of the 'wimp' of the Carter years . . . . From the man/country that gave his children/citizens only shame, George McFly and the America he figures is turned into a father who can give his children just what they want—a well-rounded family and material success."[16]

The difference between a successful family and a hopeless one, the film argues, lays in the strength of the 1950s father, a figure that Ronald Reagan himself embodied. But what so many of the critics who have pointed to Reagan's "Back to the Future" political strategies overlook is that simply going back in time is not sufficient, either for Marty or Reagan. Marty's time traveling transforms the past to correct for "the failures" made manifest in his own time. To improve his present, Marty, the Reagan-Era son, must transform his father into the mythic, masculine hero for which the 1980s longed. The difference between a doormat and leader of men, the film argues, can be traced to a single defining moment in the past, and it is through the mediation of the Reagan Era that history can be recreated in order to assert traditional masculine power, and ensure the prosperity of the domestic future.

The Rise of Reagan

While this chapter will not dispute Jeffords' central claim that a new muscular masculinity emerged within the films of the period, and Reagan's rise was aided by his ability to manipulate and embody those Hollywood ideals, it must also be said that Reagan's rise to power also relied on the circulation of cultural meanings and values that would direct readings of films. As we cannot simply understand "the fifties" that Reagan and *Back to the Future* present as natural or self-evident truths, we must also recognize that the "Reagan" that Jeffords references above, and the one that has regularly emerged in political debate for the last 40 years, was one that emerged as the product of shifting historical and political contexts as much if not more than from any single political vision. As Martin Anderson writes, while Reagan was able to present himself as the leader of a popular movement, neither he, nor any other of the neo-conservative acolytes (Goldwater, Nixon, et al) created the "Reagan Revolution," rather, "it was the other way around. They were part of the movement, they contributed mightily to the movement, but the movement gave them political life, not the reverse."[17]

As argued above, the rise of Ronald Reagan as a political force throughout the 1970s and 1980s owed much to Reagan's public persona as a film star in the postwar period. However, Reagan's rise was equally reliant upon an understanding of the fifties as a time of traditional family values, a healthy domestic economy and strong foreign policy. Presidential historians, biographers and film critics have all noted the ways in which Reagan's ascendancy relied on his ability to embody, in both his political rhetoric and personal manner, a nostalgia for the fifties that was popularized through "nostalgia culture" of the period. Reagan succeeded in lionizing the social order of the 1950s while simultaneously rejecting the politics of the sixties as misguided, ineffective and divisive. By no means was Reagan a singular, or even the most important, politician in the neoconservative movement. Certainly the political sphere in this period was a complex one, with many competing and overlapping interests involved. However, on the level of the national popular, Reagan served as the symbol of a constellation of socio-political attitudes and values that could be broadly defined as "the New Right." As the popular phrase "the Reagan Revolution" suggests, he also marks a new period in American history, coincident with the nation leaving behind the ashes of "the sixties" (the Vietnam conflict, the Watergate scandal, the counterculture and Great Society social reforms), and moving toward the neo-conservative age that would dominate American politics for at least thirty years.

In an attempt to understand the history of Reagan's strategic mobilization of the fifties, one must first examine the crucial turn in Reagan's early political career—where Reagan no longer defined himself solely in terms of *rejection* (of communism, of the New Deal, of Civil Rights, *of "the sixties"*) and instead began defining himself mostly in terms of *return* (to prosperity, to traditional values, to global security, *to "the fifties"*). Presidential historians have long argued that Reagan's triumph in the Presidential election was in large part due to his strategic mobilization of a narrative of national progress which identified the fifties as its high point of national strength and prosperity, "the endpoint of American historical progress, and . . . repository of the accumulated virtues and values of the past."[18]

Reagan's turn to the past for inspiration was also a turn away from an even nearer past—the political and social legacy of the New Left that came to define the sixties. Reagan's antipathy for the changes the sixties represented had its most dramatic illustration in 1969, with his decision to send 791 state and city police officers to quell demonstrations on the UC Berkeley campus, which he had denounced in his 1966 gubernatorial campaign as "a haven for communist sympathizers, protesters and sex deviants."[19] The ensuing struggle resulted in violent clashes between protesters and police, the death of bystander James Rector, and hundreds of wounded students, police officers, and community members. Despite the notoriety of this incident, Marcus argues that "Reagan's fifties-based persona helped him avoid the negative associations his involvement in sixties controversies could have engendered."[20] By the time Reagan began his national political career, this rhetorical deployment of the fifties not only enabled him to go from a fringe position on the radical right to winning forty-nine states in the landslide 1984 election, but also became the overarching political strategy for the New Right's seizure of political, social and cultural power. This rhetorical turn and its engagement with history are crucial to understanding the role of the fifties in 1980s popular culture. Reagan-Era America was presented the choice between fifties and sixties as an absolute binary, not only eliminating the continuum of historical events that connect the two periods but also flattening them both, so as to fix one homogeneous meaning to the fifties and another oppositional meaning to the sixties.

To examine this shift in Reagan's political rhetoric let us consider two pivotal speeches from Reagan's campaigning history. "A Time for Choosing," a speech given in support of Barry Goldwater's presidential campaign in 1964 reveals Reagan's anti-communist fervor at the beginning of his political career. "Time to Recapture Our Destiny," the address made to the Republican National Convention accepting the presidential nomination in July 1980, illustrates the shift in Reagan's rhetorical treatment of American history. The choice of these two public speeches, among the most famous in his pre-Presidential career, is not merely motivated by their titular focus on "time." Beyond that, a contrast between these two addresses reveals the development of Reagan's political usage of the fifties that would become dominant, celebrated, and in fact naturalized by the time *Back to the Future* became the top grossing film of 1985.

It bears remembering, after all, that Reagan's free-market conservatism was not his lifelong principle. In the 1940s Reagan was a registered Democrat who supported Roosevelt's New Deal programs, and in his (largely conciliatory) testimony to the House Un-American Activities Committee, still maintained that "I never, as a citizen want to see our country become [so] urged, by either fear or resentment of this group, that we ever compromise with any of our democratic principles."[21] Of course, Reagan's political appeal, even in his early days as president of the Screen Actors Guild, greatly relied on his acting persona— as the football hero, the good soldier, faithful cowboy and All-American "good Joe."[22] Michael Rogin goes so far as to argue that Reagan was increasingly unable to differentiate between his real life and his screen life, and as a result "merged his on- and off-screen identities."[23] Stories abound of Reagan winning over both factory workers and plant owners with his natural charm and frank demeanor while touring the nation as a spokesman for General Electric. Still, by the time Reagan rose to national notoriety politically, he was largely considered to be an affable extremist, taken much less seriously than figures on the right like William F. Buckley, Richard

Nixon, or Barry Goldwater. Reagan's status on the "radical right" was so far out of the mainstream, in fact, that in 1962 General Electric terminated his spokesman position, deeming him too extremist in his anti-communist politics.[24] His contribution to the ill-fated 1964 presidential campaign of Barry Goldwater is illustrative of Reagan's strident rhetoric in this point of his career.

"A Time for Choosing" was televised widely, first as part of the Republican National Convention in San Francisco in July 1964, then re-distributed as part of the "Rendezvous with Destiny" program in October of the same year. It is often cited as the opening salvo in the Reagan Revolution, signaling his arrival in the national political mainstream, and laying the groundwork for his successful campaign for California governor in 1966. While it was delivered in support of the Goldwater campaign against the incumbent Lyndon B. Johnson, Reagan had delivered versions of "the Speech," as it was called, for years on the GE lecture circuit. The version delivered at the RNC begins with "I have spent most of my life as a Democrat. I recently have seen fit to follow another course," both foregrounding Reagan's political history, and his image as politically independent. "The other course" that Reagan's speech references can be read as not only descriptive of Reagan's official registration as a Republican in 1962 but also the shift in course away from the Great Society social reforms that helped to define the Democratic party at the time. Though the speech relies on many of the rhetorical devices that would characterize Reagan's oratorical style as President, it is also definitively not nostalgic. A sample paragraph will illustrate:

> Those who would trade our freedom for the soup kitchen of the welfare state have told us they have a Utopian solution of peace without victory. They call their policy "accommodation." And they say if we'll only avoid any direct confrontation with the enemy, he'll forget his evil ways and learn to love us. All who oppose them are indicted as warmongers. They say we offer simple answers to complex problems. Well, perhaps there is a simple answer — not an easy answer — but simple: if you and I have the courage to tell our elected officials that we want our national policy based on what we know in our hearts is morally right.[25]

The characteristic Reagan style is in evidence in this selection—he champions "simple answers, not easy ones," recounts conversations with the "ordinary people" he encountered along the campaign trail, bases his convictions on "common sense" and shared codes of morality, and aligns himself with the "ordinary people" and against "the politicians." This speech also includes Reagan's signature invocation of sweeping historical narratives of American progress, invoking "the Founding Fathers" and the historical progress narrative. However, "A Time for Choosing" also prominently features a much different version of the "new morning for America" that his 1984 campaign would famously celebrate two decades later. This "new morning," however, was not a cause for celebration but a sign of impending catastrophe. He repeatedly insists that socialism, in the guise of the Democratic party, has caused a perversion of American ideals: "Our natural, inalienable rights are now considered to be a dispensation of government, and freedom has never been so fragile, so close to slipping from our grasp as it is at this moment." He condemns the Democrats as "taking the Party of Jefferson, Jackson, and Cleveland down the road under the banners of Marx, Lenin, and Stalin," and warns that the policies of accommodation will lead to disaster scenarios of defeat in the Cold War, "a thousand years of darkness," "the chains of slavery," and, eventually, the atom bomb. This type of "demonology" would continue throughout Reagan's career. Rogin convincingly argues that Reagan excelled at the "inflation, stigmatization, and dehumanization of political foes" that is at the center of American politics,[26] drawing stark and significant distinctions between "us" and "them."

While Reagan's "A Time for Choosing" speech was quite possibly the high point in the Goldwater campaign, this may be a case of damning with faint praise. Goldwater was slaughtered in the general election, winning only fifty-two electoral votes. Reagan's campaigning for Barry Goldwater in 1964 "mainly deepened the impression that conservatives were anti-communist paranoids who saw subversives under every rock."[27] Goldwater's landslide defeat resulted in pundits declaring "the death knell of the conservative movement" and "the demise of the radical right in America."[28] The defeat further marginalized Reagan amongst the mainstream, with journalists dismissing him "as a huffy simpleton with strong ties to the Republican right."[29] This was not at all aided by the fact that Reagan opened a Republican fundraiser with a sharp rebuke against moderates: "Good morning to all you irresponsible Republicans," he told the audience. In the same fundraiser, Reagan would claim that was "a vast conspiracy in the Eastern liberal press" to portray Goldwater as a warmonger and a savage.[30] While Reagan's oratorical skill marked him as an up-and-comer on the (bleak) Republican scene, his rhetoric, as shown here, was often seen as antagonistic, paranoid, oppositional and divisive, too caustic in its *rejection* of a particular course of action. A comparison with Reagan's rhetoric in 1980 (while still opposing an incumbent) will throw into sharp relief the way that the vision of the fifties that motivates *Back to the Future* would enable his transition from "radical fringe" to "great communicator."

Reagan's speech almost precisely twenty-four years later at the 1980 Republican National Convention in Detroit was his formal acceptance of the party's nomination. As the title indicates, "Time to Recapture Our Destiny" relies upon the power of nostalgic myth-making to define not only the recent past, but also the present and future. The rhetoric and imagery of this speech invokes grand, sweeping narratives of America's historical legacy, but strategically places the post-fifties American historical developments as *deviations from the plot,* as divergence from the pristine national narrative that began with independence from monarchy, and found its zenith in the defeat of communism. Reagan's acceptance speech gestures backward to a point at which, in the New Right's view, the nation lost its way. In the speech's opening lines, Reagan outlines his campaign's mission statement in terms of "return": "More than anything else, I want my candidacy to unify our country, to renew the American spirit and sense of purpose. I want to carry our message to every American, regardless of party affiliation, who is a member of this community of shared values."[31]

Here Reagan is able to implicitly condemn the 1960s as divisive, misguided, and damaging (hence, the need for unity), draw on his embodiment of pre-1960s stability and morality ("a member of this community of shared values"), and obscure his own participation in divisive (and indeed, violent) sixties controversy. The speech's repeated invocation of phrases like "renew the American spirit," "recapture our destiny," and "rebirth of the American tradition" gesture backwards to the fifties, the period (in the Reagan mythology) when America strongly embraced its values of "family, work, neighborhood, peace, and freedom." Furthermore, in this speech Reagan argues that the proposed move toward tradition is not merely in service of nostalgia, but intrinsically linked with the potential for future progress. "They say that the United States has had its day in the sun, that our nation has passed its zenith. . . My fellow citizens, I utterly reject that view." In short, one must go back to the past in order to move profitably forward into the future. Reagan, in the second order of "double fixing" I have identified, isolates the fifties as the zenith of American development and detaching it from what it produces—the unrest of the sixties—and *fixes* it as an unchanging time to which to return. This establishes the fantasy version of the fifties as a stable, ahistorical, and continually accessible site. As Marty must intervene in his family's life in the fifties to attain the material and social success that he desires, Reagan argues that the nation must return to its fifties traditions in order to retain its position as global superpower in the 21st century.

Dating the point of return in the fifties is implicit in Reagan's speeches, but is explicitly stated in *The Reagan Revolution,* the book published by conservative pundits Robert Novak and Rowland Evans just after the 1980 election. The text's introduction celebrates Reagan's efforts to "return the republic to an earlier day. . . that day might be fixed at 1955."[32] What is significant here is not simply the alignment of Ronald Reagan with a prior era, but the way that the alignment figures a very particular version of the fifties in relation to a national narrative, and in so doing presents a socially and politically motivated definition of the nation's history—as both a point of origin for a modern superpower, and the point to which the nation must return in order to recapture its destiny. Leading the charge of the Reagan Revolution was a new brand of politically engaged adolescents, addressing a new sort of generation gap.

Reagan Youth: Michael J., Alex P.

"Reagan's Youth Movement," a 1984 article in *The Washington Post,* announced just how effective Reagan's "back to the future" politics were for young voters. According to exit polls, 58% of voters aged 18-25 in the 1984 election cast their vote for Reagan, and 38% of young voters identified themselves as Republican, as opposed to 29% as Democrat. This represented almost a 20% gain for the Republicans since the mid 1970s, and owed much to the oldest president in American history. "He makes me feel good. He says there's opportunity out there — take it and run," says a young Texan in *The Post*'s article. Indeed, the ability of Reagan to make 1980s youth "feel good" seemed largely connected to their economic aspirations. Witness another youngster interviewed, Julia Martin, who claims she was a liberal-leaning independent until she got her first job: "It's fun to think you can save the world, but then you start working and look at that paycheck," she says, "You can switch pretty fast."[33] While polls indicated that young voters did not align themselves with conservative social positions—there was no coincident embrace of a figure like Jerry Falwell—economic pragmatism was the order for the day, even in American high schools and universities.

The star of *Back to the Future*, Michael J. Fox, had come to represent this new generation of aspiring yuppies largely due to his performance as Alex P. Keaton on the NBC sitcom *Family Ties*. The Museum of Broadcast Communications has called *Family Ties* a perfect demonstration of "the resonance between collectively-held fictional imagination and what cultural critic Raymond Williams calls 'the structure of feeling' of a historical moment."[34] The show was originally conceptualized to focus on the family life of Elyse (Meredith Baxter-Birney) a successful architect and her husband Steven (Michael Gross), a public television station manager, former hippies with three conservative children. Their only son, Alex, is a teenage supply-side economics advocate compulsively clad in business attire, carries an attaché case and the *Wall Street Journal* into homeroom, takes a date to a lecture by economist Milton Friedman, and hangs a poster of William F. Buckley over his bed. The role launched Fox's career, and propelled the show into the top ten of the Nielsen ratings for almost the entirety of its eight year run on NBC. While the show was originally written toward presenting Alex ironically, viewers responded enthusiastically to Alex and his tendency to mock his leftist parents. Alex embodied the attitudes of a new generation who were much more interested in scoring big on Wall Street than they were in supporting community television programming or designing eco-friendly homes. The first scene in the show's pilot features the family watching a slide show of the 1969 National Mobilization to End the War demonstration in Washington DC, which Steven and Elyse attended together. These slides would serve as part of the show's credit sequence for several seasons. Alex's response to the images is a mixture of contempt and ridicule, as he offers sarcastic comments like "What were you protesting, good grooming?" This dynamic is the source of the series' humor but also much of its pathos. In one early episode Steven must apologize to Alex for refusing to allow him to "be himself" by taking a date to a racially segregated country club. The series, in other words, pits Steven and Elyse's responsibilities as parents against their supposedly outdated political convictions.

In its portrayal of the tensions between Alex and his parents, sixties radicalism is positioned as the outré establishment, while conservatism is positioned as hip and rebellious. The transmission of conservative principles to the next generation was a key part of the New Right's strategies, and the popular frenzy around the figure of Alex was a testament to the appeal of Reaganism to 1980s teens, and the resonance that the character had for original viewers of *Back to the Future*. This association between Fox's television character in *Family Ties* and his *Back to the Future* screen persona lingers even today—the 2006 volume *Recycled Culture in American Art and Film* repeatedly refers to Fox's character in *Back to the Future* as "Alex."[35] Fox was so vital to Zemeckis & Gale's vision of *Back to the Future,* in fact, that he was cast for the part twice: Fox was the first choice to play Marty in *Back to the Future*, but since Baxter-Birney was on maternity leave, *Family Ties* producers would not allow for a release. The *Back to the Future* production began with Eric Stoltz as the lead, and continued for several weeks before Stoltz was relieved of his contract. An agreement with Fox and the *Family Ties* producers resulted in the entire film being shot around Fox's *Family Ties* schedule, with the bulk of shooting occurring at night or during weekends.

While it is clear that *Back to the Future* creates a fantasy vision of the fifties, it also bears mentioning that it simultaneously is carefully constructing a particular vision of the 1980s from the perspective of the Reagan-Era teen disaffected with the way that the Baby Boomers had fouled up the country and jeopardized their future. If Hill Valley in 1955 is a dream, Hill Valley in 1985 is something close to a nightmare. The initial depiction of Hill Valley's town square in 1985 is decidedly less cheery than the scene mentioned in this essay's opening. The carefully manicured lawn that stretched in front of the courthouse in 1955 has been transformed into a crowded parking lot for the town's social services buildings. The downtown movie house that ran Reagan's films has been converted into a pornographic theater. There are adult bookstores, bail bond dealers, pawn shops, seedy hotels, and several abandoned, boarded up storefronts. Both the courthouse and the high school are covered with graffiti (in Spanish, significantly), the streets are littered with trash, and all the houses in town are dingy and unkempt. Hill Valley's former mayor, Red, is a wino sleeping on park benches and the city is, as a whole, falling into disrepair. "That was always one of the major elements of the story even in its earliest incarnation," screenwriter Bob Gale says in *The Making of Back to the Future*, "was to take a place and show what happens to it over a period of thirty years. What happened to everybody's home town is obviously the same thing. They built the mall out in the boonies, and killed all the business downtown, and everything changed." The flip side of the film's fifties idealism is the notion of a city in decline in the 1980s.

If the city is in decline, the McFly family fares no better. George is a doormat working at a dead-end job, still doing all of Biff's work while receiving none of the credit. Lorraine swills gin in resignation as she makes a cake for her incarcerated brother, Joey ("We all make mistakes in life, children," she says with a loaded look in George's direction). Marty's older brother is still living at home, taking the bus to his fast-food job, and his older sister is hopelessly loveless. In fact, it seems that there isn't much hope for the future in the McFly household, or in Hill Valley at all. It seems that reveling in memories of the past is the only recourse Marty's parents have—the story of Lorraine and George's first meeting and initial courtship takes on ritual properties. As the children roll their eyes, Lorraine tells the story of how she fell in love with George after he was hit by her father's car in a freak bird-watching accident, their first date at the Enchantment Under the Sea dance, and their first kiss. "It was then," Lorraine says ruefully, "I knew I was going to spend the rest of my life with him." George, oblivious to his wife's despair, seems to take comfort only in re-runs of 1950s television series, as he gapes at episodes of *The Honeymooners*. The nostalgic past, for the McFlys, is a refuge from the failures of the increasingly bleak present. Once Marty travels back in time, however, he will discover that much of what his parents have told him about the fifties has been a lie, or at least insufficient for creating the prosperous future that Marty desires.

Much of *Back to the Future*'s entertainment stems from Marty's unmasking of the nostalgic memories of his parents for the fifties as falsehoods. The "bird-watching" that resulted in George's car accident in Lorraine's version of the story is revealed to be Peeping Tom-ism. The restrictive morality that Lorraine espouses in 1985 ("I think it's terrible, girls chasing boys. When I was your age I never chased a boy, or called a boy, or sat in a parked car with a boy") turns out to be revisionist history, as young Lorraine removes Marty's pants at their first meeting, drinks liquor, smokes cigarettes, cheats on tests (in a scene deleted from the theatrical release) and aggressively pursues a sexual relationship with Marty ("I'd love to park," she tells him before kissing him forcefully). While these revelations unsettle Marty—he has earlier expressed a belief that his mother was "born a nun"— they also provide a rationale for his mother's restrictive morality. Lorraine's fault was in being too forward with George, and the price she pays in 1985 is a life of disappointment and regret.

Though Marty is unsettled by discovering the untold secrets of his parents' past, he does take great pleasure in manipulating the circumstances of time travel to his own advantage. Using his superior 1980s knowledge and style to dominate his parents' high school society, the film suggests not only that Reagan Era teenagers understand the world of 1985 better than their parents, but that "that teenagers of the 1980s know more than anybody else who has ever lived—the past can be disregarded and conveniently changed to fit the modern adolescent's view of the way things should be."[36] It's Marty's 1980s tastes and pop culture savvy that allows him to gain the respect and admiration of the entire 1950s community. His purple designer underwear first piques Lorraine's erotic interest (she calls him "Calvin Klein" as a result). When he must convince George to go to the dance with Lorraine Marty uses a hair dryer, a Sony Walkman and a Van Halen cassette tape to position himself as an alien creature that will destroy George if he does not do his bidding. And, in yet another echo of the town square sequence that began this chapter, Marty eludes Biff and his lackeys by using his knowledge of 80s youth culture—spontaneously turning a young boy's scooter into the world's first skateboard, drawing cheers from the teenage bystanders. "He's an absolute dream," Lorraine coos, which aligns the "dreamlike" with the 1980s, and not the fifties, for the first time in the film. The ease with which Marty is able to navigate the town square on the skateboard stands in sharp contrast to Marty's initial halting, stumbling trip through Hill Valley, 1955. On his improvised skateboard he speeds over curbs, throws impressive sparks in the air while skitching behind a pickup truck and leaps over Biff's car, causing a collision between the pristine 1946 Ford convertible and a manure truck. In other words, the technology, tastes, styles, knowledge and character of the Reagan Era are able to surpass those of the fifties, if given the opportunity to thrive under the right (fifties) conditions. The ease with which Marty quickly learns to navigate and master Hill Valley, in the town square and in high school society, suggests a progress-narrative belief in the superiority each successive generation has over the past one, and a faith in the adaptability and ingenuity of American youth.

The film's most dramatic illustration of historical re-writing comes when Marty performs at the Enchantment Under the Sea dance, wowing the Hill Valley High crowd with an impromptu version of what he calls, "an oldie. . . well, it's an oldie where I come from." Marty's rollicking cover rendition of "Johnny B. Goode," inspires the bandleader to call his cousin Chuck Berry and exclaim "You know that new sound you been looking for? Well listen to *this!*" The film thus positions Marty as the real inventor of rock and roll, and the white middle class Hill Valley as its birthplace. As with the function of "Golden Oldies" on airwaves or the cover versions of soul, rock, or rhythm and blues songs that white performers churned out in the fifties, Marty's performance not only sanitizes the racial and sexual threats that early rock n' roll presented to the fifties social order, but also allows him to take all the credit and cultural capital for its invention.

Back to the Future's protagonist utilizes his technological and cultural knowledge to gain power and respect in the past. In so doing, *Back to the Future* portrays the fifties as "simpler" in both senses of the word—adults and teenagers alike in 1955's Hill Valley (with the exception of Doc Brown) are easily duped, frightened and intimidated by Marty's wrangling. But Marty's hubris never leads to his downfall. He leaves Hill Valley 1955 better off than he found it, and enthusiastically returns to a much-improved future life. In the terms of Reagan's "Recapture Our Destiny" speech, the fifties are not necessarily the best times that Hill Valley will see. That time lays in the future, if only its residents will embrace their destiny. In the world of *Back to the Future* it is the 1980s teenager that serves to spearhead that movement. In the rationale of the Reagan Era, the country would all be better off if history was simply changed to match the fantasy version of the fifties. History was changed by the circulation of stories, myths, and fantasies of the fifties as a better time, calibrated to selectively include some elements of 1950s America while screening out other elements—segregation, compulsory housework for women, and Cold War hysteria. The vision of the fifties that is present in *Back to the Future* is indicative of the allure of a carefully constructed nostalgia, a pleasant, useful falsehood that many Americans were inclined to believe.

Coda: Fixing the (Civic) Fifties

As Alex P. Keaton chafes against what he understands to be the failures of his father, so too does Marty McFly lament his father's failure. By replacing his father's credo, "I don't think I could take that kind of rejection," with Doc's mantra "If you put your mind to it, you can accomplish anything," Marty is able to reverse his family's fortune. Until Marty's intervention, the issues that face his parents in high school (George's weakness, Lorraine's vice, the inability of either to stand up for themselves against the domineering Biff) simply repeat themselves. As I have outlined, Marty's goal is to fix the broken promise of the 1950s so it better matches the fantasy version of the fifties that gained prominence through the rise of Reagan. As he "fixes" his own family's shortcomings in 1955, he simultaneously cleanses the fifties of social agitation, racial oppression and the other cultural anxieties that actually gripped the decade.

While the McFly family is the central focus of *Back to the Future*, I have tried to represent the conditions of Hill Valley, as a civic entity, as also subject to the historical transformations that allow Marty to remake his family. Consider, for a moment, the most prominent piece of the Hill Valley set—the clock tower that adorns city hall, and is the backdrop for the film's climactic scene that sends Marty back to 1985. Marty gains his knowledge of the clock in 1985, from a woman working for the Hill Valley Preservation Society. "Mayor Wilson is sponsoring an initiative to replace that clock," she tells him, "and we at the Preservation Society believe it should be preserved exactly the way it is." This suggests that the film not only needs the fifties to be changed, but also removed from history, frozen in time, for whatever events occur after 1955 will be preserved in perpetuity. The clock is the figurative site of the second order of "fixing" for which I have argued. In other words, the town clock, which we learn was struck by lightning in 1955 not only provides a power source for Marty's travel back to 1985, but also suggests that Hill Valley itself has been "frozen in time." When the lightning strikes in 1955 the clock hands are stuck at 10:04 PM, and for the next thirty years remain literally fixed to the moment of Marty's exit from his reparative visit to 1955, perpetually pointing to the moment where the town's destiny was sealed. As Marty wanders through the idyllic 1955 Hill Valley, he struggles to understand what has happened to his hometown. Simultaneously, the clock hovers behind his head onscreen, broadcasting precisely what has happened: the town is bustling and prosperous because the march of time has not yet been impeded. The chiming of the clock tower in the 1955 town square sequence coincides with Marty's realization of his travel, and the countdown until lightning strikes the tower—Marty's only chance of getting home— provides the dramatic tension for the film. The stopped clock in 1985 is a symbol of Marty's mission: for both Hill Valley and his family to be fixed, or repaired, Marty must return to the time on the clock. In other words, the film performs the process of double fixing by allowing Marty to perfect, and then freeze, his family and civic fortunes. Both of these moves are concentrated in the image of the clock tower.

As such, the fifties are given unchallenged historical significance in *Back to the Future* (and its subsequent sequels, spin-offs, and tie-ins). Neither Marty, Doc Brown, or anyone else has any ability to change the condition of their individual lives by making changes in 1985—the die is cast by that time. Further, Marty cannot change history (either the domestic history of his family, or the civic history of Hill Valley) by returning to 1968 (interestingly, the year of Marty's birth), or 1941, or any other moment in American history. It is only by returning, again and again, to 1955, that Marty's time traveling has any historical efficacy. This is the structuring logic of the film as a whole, and its treatment of history. The specific way that the film invokes the fifties as a whole (as a time when "if you put your mind to it, you can accomplish anything," as the film repeatedly asserts) as well as the specific year it references, aligns with the rhetoric that prepared the ground for the New Conservatism that had Reagan as its avatar. But Marty's success relies entirely on his Reagan-Era knowledge that allows him to repair and protect the fifties not as they actually were, but as they "should have been." In other words, the simple conceptualizations of "nostalgia" of the Reagan Era to which so many critics respond are only part of the story. The real ideological operation of nostalgia is not in what is forgotten, left out, or elided, but rather in the difference that is created and then eternalized (by Marty and Reagan) in these texts. Both *Back to the Future* and Reagan, then, suggest that the fifties represent a point of reference through which Americans' lives, as well as the condition of the world, could be understood—and solidify a cultural recognition of the fifties as such.

Notes

1. Lawrence Grossberg, *We Gotta Get Out of This Place: Popular Conservatism and Postmodern Culture*, 1st ed. (New York: Routledge, 1992), 255-6.

2. Michiko Kakutani, "What is Hollywood Saying about the Teen-Age World Today?," *New York Times*, April 22 1984, sec. Arts and Leisure, 2, 22.

3. Fredric Jameson, "Postmodernism, or The Cultural Logic of Late Capitalism," *New Left Review* I, no. 146 (August 1984): 66.

4. Jameson, "Postmodernism," 67.

5. Ibid., 65.

6. Garry Wills, *Reagan's America*. (New York: Doubleday, 1986), 371.

7. See Wills, Lou Cannon's *Reagan* (Putnam, 1985), Alan Nadel's *Flatlining on the Field of Dreams* (Camden, NJ: Rutgers University Press, 1997), among others.

8. Daniel Marcus, *Happy Days and Wonder Years: The Fifties and the Sixties in Contemporary Cultural Politics* (New Brunswick, NJ: Rutgers University Press, 2004), 62-3.

9. Fredric Jameson, *The Political Unconscious: Narrative as a Socially Symbolic Act*, 2nd ed. (New York: Routledge, 2006), 9.

10. Jameson, "Postmodernism," 86.

11. Fred Davis, "Nostalgia, Identity and the Current Nostalgia Wave," *Journal of Popular Culture* 11, no. 2 (1977): 491.

12. Linda Hutcheon, "Irony, Nostalgia, and the Postmodern," in *Methods for the Study of Literature as Cultural Memory, Studies in Comparative Literature*, ed. Raymond Vervliet and Annemarie Estor (Atlanta, GA: Rodopi, 2000), 199.

13. Timothy Shary, *Generation Multiplex: The Image of Youth in Contemporary American Cinema*, 1st ed. (Austin, TX: University of Texas Press, 2002), 181.

14. Judy Stone, "Meeting Mom in Her Past 'Back to the Future': 'Family' film with a twist," *San Francisco Chronicle*, July 3 1985, Final Edition, sec. Daily Datebook, 58.

15. Stanley Kauffmann, "Innocences." *New Republic*, (June 18, 1977), 24.

16. Susan Jeffords, *Hard Bodies: Hollywood Masculinity in the Reagan Era* (New Brunswick, NJ: Rutgers University Press, 1994), 70-1.

17. Martin Anderson, Revolution: The Reagan Legacy (Stanford, CA: Hoover Institution Press, 1990), xix.

18. Marcus, *Happy Days and Wonder Years*, 67-8.

19. Seth Rosenfeld, "The Campus Files : Reagan, Hoover and the UC Red Scare," *San*

Francisco Chronicle, June 9, 2002, Final edition, sec. News.

20. Marcus, *Happy Days and Wonder Years*, 71.

21. qtd in Eric Bentley and Frank Rich, *Thirty Years of Treason: Excerpts from Hearings Before the House Committee on Un-American Activities, 1938-1968* (New York: Nation Books, 2002), 144-7; qtd in Gordon Kahn, *Hollywood on Trial; The Story of the 10 Who Were Indicted* (Ayer Co Pub, 1948), 59.

22. J. Hoberman, *Vulgar Modernism: Writing on Movies and Other Media* (Philadelphia: Temple University Press, 1991), 57.

23. Michael Rogin, *Ronald Reagan: The Movie and Other Episodes in Political Demonology* (Berkeley: University of California Press, 1988), 3.

24. Matthew Dallek, *The Right Moment: Ronald Reagan's First Victory and the Decisive Turning Point in American Politics* (Washington, DC: Free Press, 2000), 40.

25. Ronald Reagan, "A Time for Choosing," October 27, 1964, http://wwwreaganlibrary.com/reagan/speeches/rendezvous.asp.

26. Rogin, *Ronald Reagan: The Movie*, xiii.

27. Dallek, *The Right Moment*, 64.

28. Ibid., 69.

29. Ibid., 65.

30. Ibid., 65.

31. Ronald Reagan, "Time to Recapture Our Destiny" (presented at the Republican National Convention, Detroit, MI, July 17, 1980), http://www.reaganfoundation.org/reagan/speeches/speech.asp?spid=18.

32. Rowland Evans and Robert Novak, *The Reagan Revolution* (New York: E. P. Dutton, 1981), 2.

33. Bill Peterson, "Reagan's Youth Movement; Republican Party Attracts New Generation of Americans," *Washington Post*, August 24, 1984, sec. A5, 5.

34. Michael Saenz, "Family Ties," *Museum of Broadcast Communications*, http://www.museum.tv/archives/etv/F/htmlF/familyties/familyties.htm.

35. Vera Dika, *Recycled Culture in Contemporary Art and Film: The Uses of Nostalgia* (Cambridge: Cambridge University Press, 2003).

36. Jack Kroll, "Having the Time of His Life," *Newsweek*, July 8, 1985.

PART 3:

"Take a Chill Pill, Man": Coming to Terms with the Social Ills of the 80s

Chapter 11

How Broadway Has Cared: The AIDS Epidemic and the Great White Way

Virginia. Anderson

Ask someone to name a musical depicting the AIDS crisis in America and more often than not, you are bound to hear an enthusiastic response: *"Rent!"* Jonathan Larson's adaptation of Puccini's *La Bohème* depicts life, love, loss, and hope in New York City's East Village during the peak years of the epidemic. *Rent* made its debut at a crucial moment in the history of the AIDS epidemic in the United States; the show premiered both off- and on Broadway at the New York Theatre Workshop in 1996, the year that began a period of unprecedented optimism in the treatment of HIV. The introduction of protease inhibitors to AZT combination therapy that year converted the disease's previous death sentence. This medical breakthrough gave people who were dying a new, and unforeseen, opportunity to live with the disease. In this regard, and of course in hindsight, *Rent* captures a crucial transition.[1] If *Rent*, as a Broadway musical, marks this medical and social turning point in the AIDS epidemic in the United States, let us consider how Broadway theatre, on stage and behind the scenes, documents the AIDS epidemic in America during the first decade of its crisis.[2]

First, what does one mean by "Broadway"? The Street of Dreams. The Great White Way. The test of talent, skill, and determination. Referring to theatres with five hundred or more seats and which operate with only Equity contracts, only on one level does the concept of Broadway refer to a geographic area. Within American theatre history, it functions metaphorically as an embodied idea of success and the greatest of American theatre. Above all, perhaps, Broadway theatre is concerned with economic achievement. As Brooks McNamara noted, "Broadway does not, in general, produce high art. And yet Broadway deserves closer attention."[3] Through its intrinsically commercial focus, Broadway theatre has captured shifts in popular perception of myriad social issues. The Broadway musical has received particular consideration for its capacity to document shifting attitudes and identities.[4] The commercial appeal found less than worthy of scholarly attention in the past has prompted analysis of its function as a catalyst for such changes; as Stacy Wolf notes, "pleasure motivates."[5]

The Power of Money

Before investing hundreds of thousands, if not millions, of dollars in a Broadway production, producers (and writers and directors) are compelled to gauge public perception of sensitive topics in order to predict financial viability of a production, an issue entirely separate from artistic concerns. Such analysis was particularly meaningful for Broadway productions concerning AIDS.

In his discussion of commercial theatre during the Reagan era, Alan Woods describes the relationship between popular ideology and commercial success:

> The plays and musicals which open on Broadway represent their producers' best guesses as to what the audience will accept. Successful shows presumably are profitable because large numbers of people find them worth the price of admission. *Successful productions should, therefore, either reflect concerns shared by their audiences, present views audiences find at least acceptable, or present no views at all.*[6]

Woods derives from his own argument, "commercial theatre, traditionally, reinforces the views of its paying customers, rather than challenging them."[7] While not infallible, this assertion holds credence; throughout the 1980s, productions presenting AIDS in a manner directly assaulting popular perceptions of the epidemic had considerably shorter runs than those which, in later decades, presented the disease in more familiar terms as established by the mainstream media.[8] Taking AIDS into consideration then, producers, writers, directors, and even make-up artists throughout this decade were forced to address popular perception of the disease among potential Broadway audiences in order to ensure a return upon a production's investment. It may not be surprising, then, that July 3, 1981 marked an important—and consequential—New York premiere: the seemingly innocuous yet now notorious headline, "Rare Cancer Seen in 41 Homosexuals," took the stage on page A20 of *The New York Times*. The perceived link between AIDS and homosexuals was established, planting seeds of stigma and fear that Broadway theatre would both document and attempt to undermine. Before such productions could take place however, the crisis needed to be addressed *off* stage.

The Epidemic Off-Stage: AIDS and Broadway Production

Before the stories of those living with AIDS were told on stage, many of the people who contribute to the theatrical productions—on and off the stage—fell ill. Two months before AIDS made its first appearances within the popular news, on May 11, 1981, Andrew Lloyd Webber's *Cats* opened at the New London theatre on the West End. In the time span between this opening and *Cats'* Broadway premiere on October 7, 1982 at the Winter Garden theatre, Altman's article brought public attention to the disease whose presence was already felt within New York's theatre community. Until only recently, when it was surpassed by another Lloyd Webber piece, *Cats* was the longest running musical on Broadway. But when the show closed on 25 June 2000, the run of AIDS had extended from headline to hysteria to global pandemic.

Actor David Kernan had been performing on Broadway in the late 1970s in a production of *Side by Side by Sondheim*. He describes his shock when Mike, a friend he had not seen in a while, walked into his dressing room. He asked his emaciated friend what was wrong. Mike reassured him that it was a rare form of cancer but that he was beating it. "He was dead within three months," Kernan recalled, "of a thing called 'the gay pneumonia,' and it was the start of the dreaded disease."[9]

Doug Holsclaw, now an accomplished writer and performer in San Francisco,[10] tended bar with a friend for a Broadway theatre in 1981; he recalls,

He was one of the first to go. We didn't know what AIDS was—there was no name for it, we didn't know it was contagious, we had no idea it was sexually transmitted. We didn't know it was anything. We just thought that he, alone, was ill. . . . He was twenty-six years old. And all of a sudden he just had one thing after another wrong with him.

I will never forget. He came in one day . . . he'd been to the doctor and had some of his toenails removed because of a fungus. And he had these shoes with the toes cut out and he had white bandages on and big slats sticking out of his shoes. And he weighed—I don't know—he looked like a concentration camp victim—and he was still coming to work 'cause he didn't know he had a terminal disease.

We used to . . . we used to joke about it. We used to make fun of him and tease him and say things behind his back because he was always calling in sick and he always had some ailment and this wasn't normal for a twenty six year old man. And um, we'd call him Camille and we thought oh, he was lazy and didn't want to take the trash out and we used to really complain. I did. It was something I felt very guilty about when he died.[11]

Of course, Holsclaw's friend was *not* alone, and the growing epidemic became visible in other ways. Peter Gregus, a Broadway actor who has recently appeared in the original casts of *Jersey Boys* and *Contact*, began to take dance classes in New York in 1981. Suggesting a generation of dancers that might have been, his description of his own growing awareness of the AIDS epidemic conveys the atmosphere and loss during the early years of the epidemic:

As a singer or an actor, you are kind of solitary in that you study your craft alone or in a small group with a teacher, whereas dancers, we're 40, 50 in the room taking a class. We go to auditions. We'd stand with 300 guys waiting to get in. So through that you really get to know each other. You hang out a lot. And you wait. You go in and you dance, or you wait, you talk before class or in between classes. You don't know them as best friends, but you know them in *that* community. So I started to notice [AIDS] in that when I was getting work and I'd go away in May or June and I'd come back and there'd be 3-4 guys missing from class, I'd go away for a couple of months, come back and 3-4 more guys were missing in the back row. It was like this list you would get when you'd come back. Where is so and so? After the first couple of times out on the road I'd stop asking.[12]

Gregus communicates a marked change in atmosphere and morale, the loss of performers in training suggests the epidemic's long term effects; The "evolution and maturity of talent and skill is what the AIDS epidemic has robbed from the performing arts community and the world."[13]

Practitioners were not the only observers of the subtle onset of the epidemic; the effects of the epidemic, like the absences Gregus describes, were evident to audiences, as well. Jay Parks, a former actor who now works in the archives of the Billy Rose Theatre Collection, recalls, "I think it was just that whole thing—you went to the theatre and the people you were used to seeing in shows . . . *weren't* . . . anymore . . . they were gone. . . . It was such a strange, strange time."[14]

Death, it must be stated, was not the only outcome for HIV+ Broadway theatre practitioners in the epidemic's early years. The careers of those who survived were often irrevocably altered by the epidemic. Parks explains,

The 80s were shot. You couldn't make a commitment to your career like you could today because you didn't think you had a future. . . . You thought about trying to stay alive. For me, my partner got sicker, I was trying to deal with him—I didn't have time to be an actor. After he died, I thought I was going to die and I didn't think about being an actor. There was literally a ten year period when it wasn't my life anymore. Those ten years were the period I should have been making the connections that make a career. I think for a lot of people—that's how their lives were. Where would we be right now?[15]

Those performers who continued to develop their careers faced what often proved to be insurmountable challenges. Broadway productions famously require stamina and, even with the hope offered by advancements in treatment, the requirements of performance were especially challenging for those on early medications. AZT, while offering hope, "wiped you out," Peter Gregus recalls, "You literally couldn't work. It was very powerful and very debilitating, draining energy, it would shrink your body. Adonises, I would see Adonises and they . . . That was the most shocking—when you see someone—they would walk by you, hair would be falling out, skin would be wasting, and all of that was gone. They were still alive—still, in some cases, to this day alive but surviving AZT was very difficult for a lot of people."[16] In some cases, performers who lacked the physical strength and stamina required for a life on stage moved into careers in wardrobe or other less physically demanding areas of production.[17]

Not only performers, but writers, directors, and archivists found their work affected by the growing epidemic. In 1985, playwright William Hoffman shared an experience which was no doubt shared by other writers for the theatre: "I often daydream about projects . . . The other day I pulled myself back to reality. One of the actors I was contemplating was dead of AIDS as was one of the producers. It was very sobering."[18]

Discrimination and Challenges

While homophobia and ill treatment of those with AIDS was rare in the Broadway theatre community, it undeniably occurred. In March of 1985, *Daily News* gossip columnist Liz Smith reported that *New York* magazine critic John Simon was overheard by several people following a Broadway production declaring, "Homosexuals in the theatre! My God, I can't wait until AIDS gets all of them."[19] Kevin Mahony, who served as co-head of the Manhattan Plaza AIDS Project, recalls, "When it was revealed that an actor friend of mine had AIDS— it was in a regional theater production—the lead actress refused to appear in the same scene with him."[20] Mahony subtly excuses the implicated actress by emphasizing that the incident took place within regional theatre, as if to say that such behavior would never take place on Broadway. However, fear of discrimination extended well-beyond scene-work and extended to Broadway itself; Roger, an HIV+ Broadway vocal coach chose not to disclose his diagnosis out of fear that it might prevent future employment, engendering discrimination "not necessarily by the performers, but by the producers who are concerned about possible financial loss. . . . They think we'll get sick again and won't be able to perform."[21] The legality of such decisions was questionable at best, and in January of 1990, Michael Shawn, choreographer of *Legs Diamond*, which ran 26 December 1988 through 19 February 1989 and starred Peter Allen, who himself would die of AIDS-related illnesses, won a $175,000 settlement out of court from the Nederlanders and other producers of the show following his claim that he was fired when he tested positive for AIDS.[22]

As the epidemic continued to affect individuals, it affected the maintenance of the industry as a whole. Performer unions such as Actors Equity, Screen Actors Guild, American Guild of Variety Artists, and American Federation of Television and Radio Artists feared possible depletion of their welfare funds; cautioning from 1987, "AGVA trustees have no figures on the projected number of theatrical AIDS patients who would seek assistance when treatment programs are adopted. They believe the number will be considerable and, until cures are fully developed, financial resources must be conserved."[23] Jay Parks conveys this need on a personal level:

> None of us planned for our futures. We were told we weren't having one. So now how we are, approaching retirement age with nothing because we were told we

wouldn't see 65. Maybe I'll make it to 40. Maybe I'll make it to 2000. You just assume you won't . . . I don't have a pension through Equity—I didn't work enough.[24]

Parks' experience is not unique. Whether planning for the future or living in the
moment, financial challenges continue to affect theatre practitioners with AIDS.
For example, in the epidemic's early years, individuals sometimes faced eviction, whether due to illegal discrimination or because they could not make rent
payments without the income they might have expected were they physically
able to perform. Early on, the Broadway theatre community overwhelmingly
embraced their own. Gregus recalls, "People saw the necessity and responded
instantly. Instantly. *Instantly*. . . . In the general world, people were not being
accepted into hospitals, but in the theatre community it was an immediate response."[25]

Broadway Cares/Equity Fights AIDS

The response of the Broadway theatre community reached an official capacity
through the birth of Broadway Cares, which soon merged with Equity Fights
AIDS to become the industry's largest AIDS service organization.[26] Marty Bell,
who served as Chairman of BC/EFA describes initial conversations that took
place within the wrought climate within which Broadway Cares was formed:

> The man we all called Michael, whether we knew him or not, had died not so long
> before that summer night when half a dozen friends from the Producers Group hap-
> pened to show up at the same performance of 'Dreamgirls.' Dinner after the show
> was odd—none of the usual loud after-a-blockbuster excitement, but rather the quiet
> that comes with loss. And then, walking nowhere together on Eighth Avenue after
> midnight, anger and embarrassment. Our very best and most dear were dying from
> AIDS. And as an industry we had no response. Was there still a community here?
> And if there wasn't, there had to be.[27]

Over the next few days, Bell and the others gathered over twenty theatre professionals including "actors, writers, directors, producers, designers, lawyers,
agents, union leaders, a critic. And we pledged to each other that we would pull
the theatre business together for a sprawling effort."[28] The effort of these producers led to the formation of Broadway Cares. The response from the theatre
community was overwhelming.

On 10 February 1988, more than one thousand members of the Broadway
theatre community met at the St. James theatre for the first Broadway Cares
rally "to confront the epidemic of death that is shrinking the ranks of those behind, in front of, and anywhere near, the footlights."[29] Reporting for the New
York Post, Diana Maychick observes, "This was not the Broadway that sold
more than $4 million worth of tickets last week, mostly to the three big British
imports: 'Les Miserables,' 'Phantom of the Opera,' and 'Me and My Girl.' This
was not the Broadway known as the lynchpin of the tourism industry, the

Broadway that can—given its 40,000 seats—generate $600 million a year. Or was it? This church-social Broadway, the real thing, the single piano and a belting voice kind of theater from which all theater—even the business of theater—owes its life."[30] The group of one thousand practitioners, producers, agents, and Equity representatives marched to Duffy Square carrying show window cards and signs declaring "Broadway Cares to Stamp Out AIDS." Arriving in the square, Penn and Teller climbed into a cherry picker and hung a banner announcing "Broadway Cares" over the TKTS booth. Organizers declared that the banner "will be waving in the Square until a cure for AIDS is found, symbolizing the unity of the entire theatrical community in the fight against AIDS."[31]

A few months earlier, actress Colleen Dewhurst spearheaded a nation-wide movement within Actors Equity Association. Dewhurst had been in a production of *You Can't Take It With You* with Orin Riley, who was diagnosed during its run. Dewhurst recalls, "That day I woke up. Someone I loved had AIDS. How many more would there be? How long would other well-meaning people be able to remain as numb to this as I had been?"[32] BC/EFA president Tom Viola explains that Riley, "as happened then, got sick very quickly and, frankly as happened in those days, from his realizing he was sick to his death was a number of months. She and that company sort of witnessed what he went through in that process. She and a number of people at Equity. . .said 'Something has to be done.'"[33] Equity Fights AIDS, then, was founded under the Council of the Actors' Equity Association, charged with raising money for the Actors Fund's recently launched AIDS Initiative. The organization received funds through a variety of grant-making bodies, including Broadway Cares.

The assemblage of these organizations indicates the severity of the epidemic within the entertainment industry. Tom Viola recalls,

> there was no one in the entertainment industry who hadn't witnessed firsthand the devastation that the epidemic—the epidemic was wreaking through our community and frankly all communities. . . . It was a completely different era; people were being thrown out of their apartments. You couldn't be seen by certain physicians. It was really a horrific, horrific time that people that weren't there to experience. Now twenty years later, many have no memory of [it] and thankfully don't have to experience.[34]

In the moment, however, the urgency was palpable and the combined talents of people at all levels made the success of these organizations possible. Viola explains the teamwork involved:

> Actors are extraordinarily generous. Actors are extraordinarily emotional. Actors are wonderful. Actors are not always first in line with understanding the—I don't want to say common sense—but the process of how something has to happen, especially around issues of social work. The folks who founded Equity Fights AIDS, . . . rather than raising this money and thinking 'oh, we'll do something with it. We'll take it and give it to this person, or I know this person up the street' . . . connected with the Actors Fund [and] came up with an—I don't want to say accidental, but certainly an

ingenious collaboration. We basically raised funds and then paid for the—at the time
it was reimbursement— . . . paid by the AIDS Initiative to support what was then
scores and then hundreds of clients.[35]

As the number of clients grew, so too did the demands on each organization.
Soon, neither could function efficiently on its own.

A significant change took place in May of 1992. Dewhurst, who had inspired
so many in her stewardship of Equity Fights AIDS, had died a year earlier and
many felt responsible to her legacy and determined to support the needed growth
of EFA. The two organizations merged to become Broadway Cares/Equity
Fights AIDS, adopting the missions of both organizations and acquiring 501c3,
or non-profit, charitable organization status. Nevertheless, the community and
financial resources established in the 1980s laid the foundation for what continues to be the nation's leading industry-based organization working to raise money for AIDS-related services.

AIDS on the Broadway Stage

The significance of the Broadway plays depicting AIDS during the 1980s must
be understood within the immediate context of their production. Regarding *Safe
Sex*, Harvey Fierstein wrote, "more than any other work with which I have involved myself, these plays are this moment. They could not have existed two
years ago, and probably would not be written two years hence."[36]

As Is (1985)

William M. Hoffman's *As Is* introduced the subject of AIDS to Broadway theatre.[37] Responding to and, in many ways, representing both mainstream and gay
activist perspectives, the play tells the story of Saul and Rich, two former lovers
who come together again in the face of Rich's AIDS diagnosis. In and of itself,
it is a fairly simple story of love through adversity. Through the filtered presentation of controversial issues and the careful manipulation of theatrical convention, Hoffman presents an emotional, nostalgic, and ultimately human portrayal
of the effect of AIDS on two gay men in New York City. The manner in which
this is accomplished clarifies why *As Is* emerged as the first play in this most
commercial of theatrical environments.

Let us consider the popular perceptions of AIDS by contemporary potential
and actual audience members. Initial rumors of Gay-Related Immune Deficiency
(GRID) and the early publicity of AIDS centering on the gay community find
reflection in cover stories such as "Gay America: Sex, Politics and The Impact
of AIDS" for *Newsweek*.[38] A poll included in this issue reveals that seventy-six
percent of those surveyed in 1983 did not have any homosexual friends or acquaintances. It also reveals an increase in the percentage of people who feel that
homosexuality should not be considered an accepted alternative life-style from

fifty-one percent in 1982 to fifty-eight percent in 1983.[39] Images fuelling stereotypes show leather-clad bikers clutching one another or mysterious men slipping into bathhouses, their faces away from the camera.

The same year, Larry Kramer issued his famous essay, "1,112 and Counting,"[40] published in the *New York Native*, as a call to arms for the gay men of New York City. In it, he lambastes elected officials, doctors, so-called activists, and closeted gay men in the face of a lethal epidemic, which was doubling in incidence every ten months. "If this article doesn't scare the shit out of you, we're in real trouble," Kramer writes. "If this article doesn't rouse you to anger, fury, rage, and action, gay men may have no future on this earth. Our continued existence depends on just how angry you can get."[41] Within the mainstream media, gay men facing AIDS were scapegoated and stereotyped. Within the gay media, if the disease was not ignored, gay men were being roused to anger and social warfare to secure and maintain their recently acquired freedom.

Sparked by the death of Hollywood star Rock Hudson, the cover of the July 1985 *Life* magazine declares, "Now No One is Safe From AIDS," the word AIDS filling one quarter of the page. There was a public fear and fascination with the topic as the popular media turned the crisis into a situation of "us" versus "them;" Acting Managing Editor Judith Daniels writes in her noted preface to the issue, "For a long time it seemed possible to exclude ourselves and our families from the threat, but now it is clear that as the numbers of victims grow, the problems of AIDS in American society will affect everyone."[42] Contemporary news coverage, which began to address the presence of AIDS within all demographics, commonly implied that, even though AIDS was found beyond initially determined "risk groups," people with AIDS brought the disease upon themselves, be it through prostitution, adultery, or drug use.

Given these perceptions of the illness and those affected by it, one might question how *As Is* was deemed commercially safe enough for Broadway audiences. The play made the subject palatable to a wide audience demographic for three primary reasons: first, there was already an intense curiosity about AIDS due to the illness and death of Rock Hudson.[43] Second, the AIDS body is not "ugly" in *As Is*. Third, the subject is made less threatening as a joke-cracking former nun guides the audience through its story.

In many ways, *As Is* presents a neater version of the AIDS body than that depicted by the popular media; the physical symptoms of AIDS are left generally unseen. Those who die are minor characters who do so off-stage. On a phenomenological level, Broadway audiences were, for the first time, presented with "the AIDS body" on stage. The tension between that appearance and preconceived notions lent itself to unprecedented social mediation. This tension is heightened as Saul describes the visual appearance of the epidemic in New York:

SAUL: Sometimes I'm so scared I go back on my resolutions: I drink too much, and I smoke a joint, and I find myself at the bars and clubs, where I stand around and watch. They remind me of accounts of Europe during the Black Plague: groping in

the dark, dancing till you drop. The New Wave is the corpse look. I'm very frightened and I miss you. Say something, damn it. (*Beat.*)

RICH: I have it.[44]

Rich, described only as a casually dressed man in his thirties,[45] provides no visible indications that he is ill. Perception of this apparently healthy body changes
in an instant as it acquires the connotations of death and suffering, yet tension
remains as the body nevertheless appears strong and healthy.[46]

   The physical, relatable similarities evoke a tension that provides a pathway
for empathy.[47] Throughout much of the play, Rich remains visually empathetic
to a healthy audience member; at a support group meeting, Rich explains why he
intends to stop attending: "I'm not sure I have it anymore. I feel guilty saying
this, like somehow I'm being disloyal to the group. I'm getting better, I know it.
I just have these lumps, which for some reason won't go away, and a loss of
weight, which has made me lighter than I've been for years."[48] This empathy
provides the potential for perception subversion when the experienced image of
the healthy body is transformed into the image of the sick body.

   This connection between the audience and the world of the play is reinforced
through a direct address to the audience that frames the action of the play. It
begins as "the hospice worker, a dowdy middle-aged woman walks down-stage
center and addresses the audience."[49] This woman is the antithesis of the AIDS
body portrayed in the popular media during the 1980s; she even refers to maintaining her vow of chastity. She could recall anyone's mother or grade school
teacher and as a woman she is perceived to be separated from the disease. She
provides a solid bridge between an uninfected or an un*affected* audience and
those living with the disease. Her address to the audience creates a liminal space
in which the fictional world of the play, itself set in New York, is merged with
the reality in which the audience exists.

   As Is was also subversive in the way in which it addressed, embraced, and
ultimately overturned stereotypes about gay men. *New York Times* critic Mel
Gussow called *As Is* a play "that dares to challenge the audience's apathy"[50]
Indeed, a Broadway audience had been led to believe that AIDS was not a societal concern because it only happens to "the 4Hs—Homosexuals, Heroin addicts,
Hemophiliacs, and Haitians." Homosexuals were often presented by the popular
media in dehumanizing terms and images. Hoffman incorporates and even parodies these popular notions while creating a dialectic through their opposite.

   Hoffman further parodies common assumptions about homosexuals. A photograph in an April 1983 *Newsweek* is captioned "Fears and doubts among urban
gays?" The photograph, presumably included in the article for readers who did
not think they knew any homosexuals, depicts two shirtless, bearded men in
aviator glasses and biker caps, one clutching a beer can and his partner while
standing in front of a police barrier that reads "Do Not Cross," itself a subtle
contribution to the contemporary stereotype of gay men as trouble makers. In
1983, images such as this informed popular perception of "what homosexuals

look like." Two years later, Hoffman parodies this popular image: Rich *"is back in the bar with another stranger, Clone 1, who is wearing a leather jacket and reflecting aviator glasses. . . . . Rich tries in vain to get Clone 1's attention.*

RICH: Pardon me. . . . Yo. Yoo-hoo. Hello. . . .

CLONE 1: What about you?

RICH: I'm a very interesting guy. You look like a very interesting guy. Let's talk. And if you don't want to talk, let's go back there and let's . . . (*Rich stares Clone 1 straight in the face.*) I'll do anything you want. Anything.

CLONE 1: I want you to get the fuck out of my face. Can't you see I'm cruising that dude over there? (*We notice for the first time an identically dressed man standing across the room.*)[51]

The "clones" banter back and forth, trying to determine if they had met previously at the bar on "Jockstrap Night" or for "The Slave Auction" or at the bookstore on Christopher Street, until "the clones perform a macho mating ritual of arm wrestling, punching, and ass grabbing to determine who is the 'top man.'"[52] Saul rescues Rich from this grotesque portrayal of the gay dating scene (a manifestation of popular beliefs) as if to bring him back to reality.

Hoffman prepares audiences to re-evaluate these popular stereotypes; before an audience learns much about either of their pasts, Saul is presented as a compassionate caregiver and Rich as the vulnerable patient. Once empathy has been established, characteristics are revealed that likely recall some of the earliest stereotypical images of gay men. For example, despite their demonstrated complex emotional intimacy, Saul and Rich met in a porn theatre,[53] a space in which physical intimacy is enjoyed without emotional connection, and the pair nostalgically recall carefree days of sex and drugs.[54] Although these aspects of their relationship may appear to be "sleazy" to mainstream Broadway audiences, the established loving relationship may not be ignored; one cannot bracket one set of characteristics completely in isolation from another.

As if to capitalize on the audience's empathy, Hoffman presents people from a variety of backgrounds at a support group meeting as if to say "gay men aren't the only people with AIDS." Innocence and blameful actions are similarly placed side by side, conflated through the illness and suggesting a shared isolation. A monogamous college student and a pregnant housewife find their place next to gay men and drug abusers. Their stories communicate that AIDS extends into relationships and places perceived to be "safe." The depiction of these characters contribute to a genuinely subversive idea for 1985: numerical statistics so frequently reported by the popular news media actually represent the stories of individual people, a point emphasized when Rich snarls to his doctor, "Go find another statistic for the Center for Disease Control."[55]

Finally, *As Is* conveys a crucial message of hope through Rich's ultimate decision against suicide. At its crisis point, Rich convinces Saul to procure a lethal
dose of sleeping pills for him. Rich questions, "What's so hot about living when
you're covered with lesions and you're coming down with a new infection every
day? . . . If it gets too bad, I want to be able to quietly disappear."[56] When Saul
returns from making the purchase, he shares a story of how he had intended a
double suicide but was inspired to throw the pills away when he was struck by
the vibrant colors of a neon sign outside a sex shop reflected in rippling puddle
water.[57] Ultimately, Rich chooses life. Having established instructions for his
cremation, Rich explains: "There's a café way over by Tompkins Square Park,
off of B. It holds maybe ten tables and has the skuzziest art on the walls. . . . I
want to read my work there. . . . People go there, gay, straight, with their weird
hair and their ears pierced ninety-nine different ways, they go there late in the
evening, and there's a guitarist, and they sit there politely and listen. They look
newborn, but slightly depraved. I want to read there when I get out of here. And
you'll take pictures. Okay?"[58] The ending of *As Is* offered a message of hope in
the most bleak period of the epidemic, foreshadowing Mimi's return from death
in *Rent*, but at a time when the medical advances that could plausibly save her
life were still more than a decade away.

Safe Sex (1987)

Despite its Broadway run of only one week, Harvey Fierstein's *Safe Sex*, like *As
Is*, continued to explore a redefinition of family, a concept to be explored further
the following decade.[59] While the play is not political in its tone, the advertising
for the Broadway production served a blatantly political purpose, reaching an
audience well beyond that seated before the stage. *Safe Sex* consists of three
one-act plays: *Manny and Jake, Safe Sex*, and *On Tidy Endings*. The evening
moves from abstraction to realism; Manny and Jake, two "everymen" of the gay
community mourn the intimacy afforded by promiscuity past in a blank world
filled with only a couch and dummies. In the title play, Ghee and Mead, two
more clearly defined characters weigh the effect of safe sex on the emotional
intimacy of their established relationship. Finally, *On Tidy Endings*, set in an
apartment described in detail by the author, explores the effect of AIDS on the
partner, ex-wife, and child left behind. *Safe Sex* lends the body new resonance
through the performer/playwright and the introduction of a new "AIDS body"
on Broadway: the HIV+ woman.

    Safe Sex opened on 5 April 1987 at Broadway's Lyceum Theatre—the same
space in which *As Is* had played two years earlier to great acclaim.[60] After twenty-one previews and only nine performances, *Safe Sex* closed. What had
changed? Just months earlier a workshop of these three pieces prompted the
following description by Frank Rich, quoted in length for its value as performance reconstruction:

Only a few days after seeing 'Radio Days,' I found myself at the latest of New York's proliferating plays about AIDS, surrounded by an audience as silent—and as gripped—as the mournful radio listeners in Mr. Allen's film. The place was La Mama in the East Village on an icy Sunday night, and the event was the closing workshop performance of 'Safe Sex,' a new trilogy of one-act plays in-progress by Harvey Fierstein, the author of 'Torch Song Trilogy.' Theatergoers crammed themselves into any available space in the small auditorium, seeming all but to hang from the ceiling's low rafters. The quiet at 'Safe Sex' was of another order. At the evening's exact epicenter—a monologue midway through the bill's second and titular play—the audience seemed to stop breathing.

The hush descended during a speech delivered by a homosexual man named Ghee, acted by Mr. Fierstein himself. The monologue's subject, loosely stated, was the effect of the AIDS epidemic on the relationship between the hetero- and homosexual communities. Ghee noted that homosexuals no longer belong to a 'great chic mysterious underground but are instead 'courted, polled, placated' throughout heterosexual society. 'Now they see us everywhere: hospitals, classrooms, theaters, obituaries . . . We know who we are. They know who we are. And they know that we care what they think.' Why? 'Because of a virus,' Ghee went on. 'A virus that you don't get because you're gay, just because you're human.' Mr. Fierstein took a pause, then stared directly into the auditorium and concluded: 'We *were* gay. Now we're human.'

The audience that listened to these words so intently, like most New York audiences, contained both the 'we' and 'they' of Ghee's linguistic formulation—in other words, theatergoers of both sexes and all sexual persuasions. Although any overall critical evaluation of 'Safe Sex' must wait until the production is seen in finished form on Broadway next month, there was no doubt that, in this speech and on this night, Mr. Fierstein had hit the jugular of his entire, sociologically diverse audience.[61]

Rich documents a number of crucial points about the play's role in AIDS theatre history: first, such plays were proliferating across New York. Second, audiences at La MaMa in the East Village were particularly invested in the production. In 1987, few in the East Village were untouched by AIDS.[62] Fierstein prefaces the published edition of his play, "Herein you will find my world as it exists. These are my friends and fears. These are my wants and losses. I hope they mean something to you. My only wish is that from where you now read this, in your present moment, this world of mine no longer exists."[63] Finally, Rich's reference to Fierstein himself as a performer warrants particular attention and will be discussed shortly.

If the audience was this rapt at La MaMa, what would change so much in its transfer to Broadway? Rich goes on to describe the diversity represented by audience demographics that evening; how could space make such a difference? Physical location affects perception, such that the same objects (and bodies) in one space may be perceived in a radically different way than they would be perceived in another. By the time *Safe Sex* premiered, Azidothymidine (AZT), the first antiretroviral drug, had been introduced, offering AIDS patients effective treatment for the first time.[64] While AZT was hardly a panacea, the mainstream media suggested that treatment had brought AIDS under control. In the East Village, audience members likely knew that AZT, while offering hope, was not indicative of the end of the epidemic.

More had changed than location and its effect on reception; its theatrical context affected some audience members' capacity for another play about AIDS. Fierstein notes, "In *The Normal Heart* and *As Is* gay people sat and watched gay people with AIDS. But here the audience watches gay people without AIDS. This is not a play about disease, it's a play about life."[65] Life, however, may have been too much. Jay Parks recalls that *As Is* "accurately captured that moment. . . . We hadn't seen [AIDS] on stage much." Parks explains that producing AIDS plays became a coping mechanism; "Off-Broadway, off-off-Broadway— that's all people were writing. . . . But then everybody, the AIDS community said 'enough.' I saw it, I sat there, I lived it, I cried through it because I knew people who had lived it, but how many times can I do that to myself?"[66]

The year 1987 represented the pinnacle of conservative backlash against gays. The United States Congress adopted the Helms Amendment, banning the use of federal funds for AIDS education material that was seen to "promote or encourage, directly or indirectly, homosexual activities," was often referred to as the 'no promo homo' policy.[67] The passage of this amendment may provide further explanation as to why *Safe Sex* fared better off-Broadway than on this widely commercial venue; congressional acts cannot be separated from popular opinion among home state constituents. Although Fierstein's *Torch Song Trilogy*, which offered a sympathetic portrait of gay men, still ran successfully on Broadway when *Safe Sex* premiered, it could be that a play perceived to openly "promote" the physical act of homosexual intercourse was beyond the limits of their "open" minds.

While Michael Callen and Richard Berkowitz are credited with establishing the term "safe sex" within the gay community in 1983, the wider public was still generally under-educated about AIDS prevention;[68] President Reagan's first public speech on AIDS was delivered a month after the production closed on Broadway, establishing the Presidential Commission on the Human Immunodeficiency Virus Epidemic, later renamed the Watkins Commission.[69] In June of 1988, Surgeon General C. Everett Koop supervised the first and only national mailing: a brochure entitled "Understanding AIDS."[70] Koop's preface to the brochure reveals a great deal about public attitudes toward the growing epidemic and those who carry the virus:

> This brochure has been sent to you by the Government of the United States. In preparing it, we have consulted with the top health experts in the country. I feel it is important that you have the best information now available for fighting the AIDS virus, a health problem that the President has called 'Public Enemy Number One.' Stopping AIDS is up to you, your family and your loved ones. Some of the issues involved in this brochure may not be things you are used to discussing openly. I can

easily understand that. But now you must discuss them. We all must know about AIDS. . . . I encourage you to practice responsible behavior based on understanding and strong personal values. This is what you can do to stop AIDS.[71]

The language employed for this mailing documents commonly held fear and suggests the stigma experienced by those living with HIV. While far from the blatancy of Fierstein's title a year before, the Surgeon General's gentle advocating for "responsible behavior" proved shocking enough. The *Richmond Times Dispatch* was just one of myriad newspapers to document the public reaction to the national mailing; an elderly woman with a cane in either the countryside or suburbia has fainted upon examining her mail. Her husband, clad in a plaid shirt, bowtie, and suspenders, smoking a pipe indicating their middle class, jocularly remarks, "I take it the Surgeon General's 'AIDS' pamphlet came today!. . . " The public's offense taken at the candid yet clinical discussion of condoms and physical intimacy in the mailing in 1988 indicates how upper-middle class Broadway audiences may have felt when confronted with a choice of plays for their theatre-going pleasure.

The reaction of the general public to the Surgeon General's mailing clearly suggests discomfort with the topic of "safe sex," a term which had only recently come into common parlance in the wake of the AIDS epidemic.[72] As documented in the "Understanding AIDS" brochure, "Not so very long ago, condoms (rubbers or prophylactics) were things we didn't talk about very much. Now, they're discussed on the evening news and on the front page of your newspaper, and displayed out in the open in your local drugstore, grocery, and convenience store"[73] Fierstein was aware of the temporally-based content of his play, written in the fall of 1986; he introduces the published edition of *Safe Sex*:

> So new is the world from which I address you that nothing in these plays can be assumed common knowledge. So new is the concept of safe or unsafe sex that I still can't accept its reality. I believe these plays have a great deal to say about who and what and where we are. . . . Never have I felt so of the moment, so 'time-capsulized.' Here is what I needed to say today. Here is my last phone call, the guests just leaving my home, the thought I just completed.[74]

Produced—and advertised—a full year before the Surgeon General's mailing, *Safe Sex* served a purpose of advocacy for protected sex while making a political statement in favor of the promotion of AIDS prevention materials through the implication of homosexual behavior, flying in the face of the Helms amendment.

Nearly every review of *Safe Sex* conflates playwright and performer, sometimes in admiration and sometimes in accusation (a caption beneath a photograph of Fierstein in *Safe Sex* reads "Harvey Fierstein: working the room, not his characters").[75] Frank Rich, who previously sang Fierstein's praises for *Safe Sex* when it played at La MaMa, changed his tune for the Broadway production: "While it would be absurd to suggest that a dramatic treatment of AIDS need be as grim as a clinic, the immediacy of 'Safe Sex' is often diffused by Mr. Fierstein's ugging and mugging, both as actor and playwright."[76] A phenomenological analysis of Fierstein's body in performance may account for such attention.

In the late 1980s, Harvey Fierstein represented different ideas to different audiences. In the East Village where *Safe Sex* premiered, he was well established as a gay drag performer. A popular artistic and audible voice at La MaMa,[77] his work was perceived as far more graphic in its depiction of sexual acts and the reality of AIDS than other contemporary works. On Broadway, he was likewise well established, but known for depictions of homosexual life that were comparatively asexual. One interviewer expresses surprise that "his somber demeanor had none of the inspired outrageousness that theater audiences have come to expect on stage: Harvey Fierstein the streetwise imp, Harvey Fierstein the Jewish mother from Bensonhurst, Harvey Fierstein the drag queen with a heart of gold who overcomes life's absurdities with an industrial-strength voice and a face of India rubber."[78] Just as Frank Rich documents the audience reaction to *Safe Sex* at La Mama, so too does he capture the Broadway audience response:

> In 'Safe Sex,' he appears in all but the opening segment, dominating the stage with an alacrity recalling the similarly voluminous and boisterous Zero Mostel. Like Mostel, he gets results. Dressed in a billowing nightshirt, Mr. Fierstein ignites roars of laughter by proclaiming his volatile erotic disposition—'I've got two faucets, hot and cold!'—with a self-mocking bravado worthy of Mae West. 'Safe Sex' again hopes to leave us feeling that any character played by the author is the most humorous and generous friend, lover, mother, father or child that any sensitive person could ever hope to find. If you found Mr. Fierstein adorable last time around, chances are you'll like him here, too.[79]

Fierstein had become a commercially successful drag queen, thereby distancing Broadway audiences from direct confrontation with gay sex.

Fierstein helped mainstream audiences to grow more compassionate and more comfortable with depictions of men in love but until this point, overt references to sexual acts in intimate (non-clinical settings) were kept to a minimum. The passage of the Helms amendment as discussed earlier reflects this popular discomfort. It could be that the failure of *Safe Sex* emerged from the tension between Broadway audiences' expectations based upon their previous experience with Fierstein and their perception of his performed meditation on sex—and not just gay sex, but sex between a man and a woman who knew that he had been sleeping with men. Were *Safe Sex* written and performed by any other individual, it may never have played on Broadway at all.

Conclusion: Enduring Effects

Within the Broadway theatre community, not only individual careers but those of generations of artists have been altered. Jay Parks reflects, "Who knows what would have happened. The people that would carry on the traditions. . . The business seems like this thing going, passing down, passing down, and then BAM! And now we start over and see what we come up with."[80] Many have acknowledged not only the loss wrought by AIDS, but the opportunities it has created. Parks explains this effect on what would become theatre history: "There are people in the business whose careers have soared because the people who naturally would have been the next step were gone. It's nothing against them, great for them, they've had great careers, but if you really look at it, it's because of AIDS that they have their careers."[81]

In addition to affecting the off-stage lives of those who bring productions to the Broadway stage, AIDS has heavily informed subject matter of the stories which are told. *As Is* and *Safe Sex* played an important role in the history of Broadway plays of the AIDS epidemic, both through their content and representations through their advertising. The social, medical, and political context of these plays illuminate the ways in which they both corroborated and refuted popular beliefs. The success of the former and the nearly immediate closure of the latter suggest the boundaries of public acceptance of the issues surrounding the epidemic in its earliest years.

As Is and *Safe Sex* prepared the way for Broadway plays addressing AIDS in the 1990s, including *Angels in America*, perhaps the best known play to address the crisis. *As Is* and *Safe Sex* played an important role in the history of Broadway plays of the AIDS epidemic, both through their content and representations through their advertising. The social, medical, and political context of these plays illuminate the ways in which they both corroborated popular notions of the disease and sometimes offered subtle activism. The success of *As Is* and the nearly immediate closure of *Safe Sex* on Broadway suggest the boundaries pertaining to public acceptance of the social issues that defined the epidemic in its earliest years.

With the arrival of *Angels in America* and the nearly concurrent run of the musical *Falsettos*,[82] Broadway audiences appeared prepared to tackle these issues . . . though not necessarily in their present moment. Both landmark productions kept their audiences at a safe, though critical distance from the worlds of their characters. *Angels* may have set an impossible precedent for playwrights to follow as the multi-themed plays which followed it were challenged by critics and audiences alike. Later plays may have been compared unfavorably to *Angels* no matter when they premiered, but particularly so following the 1995 introduction of protease inhibitors, which, combined with reverse transcriptase inhibitors, effectively overturned the death sentence associated with an AIDS diagnosis in the 1980s.[83] Judging by popular media portrayals, the urgency of the subject was no longer perceived within mainstream America; with this change, Broadway no longer offered space for plays directly addressing the epidemic.

As David Finkle suggested in 1985, "many of the [theatre] creators for whom AIDS has been most compelling—AIDS sufferers—have died; the surviving healthy ones, concerned though they may be, nonetheless have less at stake."[84]

Nevertheless, productions addressing the AIDS epidemic on Broadway played an activist role throughout the 1980s, not only drawing on popular perceptions of the disease, but contributing to them by increasing both education and compassion.

Notes

1. Angel's death of AIDS-related illness, coupled with the suicide of Roger's HIV+ girlfriend, April, combine to suggest how bleak one's prognosis had been through the 1980s and early 1990s. However, considered from our contemporary vantage point, the miraculous return of Mimi from death's door represents this turning point in the treatment of the disease. *Rent* thus historicizes this crucial period in the epidemic through its depiction of poverty, available treatment, and newfound optimism. By the time it closed on Broadway in 2008, *Rent* had become significantly dated, portraying a disease that had changed significantly since the musical was written. After all, Larson's final one-sentence summary of the story read, "Rent is about a community celebrating life, in the face of death and AIDS, at the turn of the century" (McDonnell, *Rent*, 37). I fear that it may have inadvertently contributed to a sense that the American AIDS crisis is a problem of the past, even in its portrayal of the contemporary New York in which it was written.

2. "AIDS" is the far more common term within popular discourse and is frequently (erroneously) used to refer to HIV. For the sake of consistency and reading ease, I will generally refer to HIV/AIDS as "AIDS" alone. Nevertheless, to clarify: HIV, Human Immunodeficiency Virus, is in fact the cause of AIDS (Acquired Immune Deficiency Syndrome), but is not exactly the same thing. If the CD4 (T-cell) count of someone HIV positive dips below 200 or if he or she develops one or more of a variety of opportunistic infections, he or she is said to have AIDS, and that diagnosis never changes, even if the CD4 count returns to a higher number or the infection goes away.

3. Brooks McNamara, "Broadway: A Theatre Historian's Perspective." *The Drama Review* 45, no. 4 (Winter 2001): 125.

4. See particularly Savran, "Historiography"; Raymond Knapp, *The American Musical and the Formation of National Identity* (Princeton: Princeton University Press, 2006); and Raymond Knapp, *The American Musical and the Formation of Personal Identity* (Princeton: Princeton University Press, 2006).

5. Stacy Ellen Wolf, "In Defense of Pleasure: Musical Theatre History in the Liberal Arts [A Manifesto]," *Theatre Topics* 17, no. 1 (March 2007): 55.

6. Alan Woods, "Consuming the Past: Commercial American Theatre in the Reagan Era," in *The American Stage: Social and Economic Issues From the Colonial Period to the Present*, ed. Ron Engle and Tice L. Miller (Cambridge: Cambridge University Press, 1993), 253. Emphasis added.

7. Ibid., 263.

8. Even the later critical and popular success of *Angels in America* presented its many arguments to the audience from a position in the past. *Millennium Approaches* begins in 1985. Harvey Fierstein's *Safe Sex* (1987) and Christopher Durang's *Sex and Longing* (1996) were set in the present and challenged media-driven perceptions of the AIDS epidemic. *Safe Sex* closed after just nine performances. Although it was set to be a limited engagement from the beginning, *Sex and Longing* was deemed by most (including Durang himself) far from a success.

9. "Flared Brightly, Died Young, BBC America" 8:12—9:03.

10. Holsclaw was also an original cast member of *The A.I.D.S. Show: Artists Involved in Death and Survival* at San Francisco's Theatre Rhinoceros, held up by many as the first theatrical production written to address the AIDS epidemic.

11. *The AIDS Show: Artists Involved With Death and Survival*, VHS, directed by Robert Epstein and Peter Adair (1986; Santa Monica, CA: Direct Cinema, 1986). This memory would inspire the imagery Holsclaw uses in his monologue, "Spice Queen," which appeared in *The AIDS Show*, the first "musical" about AIDS.

12. Peter Gregus, interview by the author, August 23, 2008, Vinyl Restaurant, New York City. Gregus' comments suggest a rationale for the decision to change the setting indicated in the *Playbill* for *A Chorus Line*. When it opened, the *Playbill* read "'An Audition, Time: Now.' Lately [ca. 1990] it's read: 'Time: 1975." Gene Brown, *Show Time: A Chronology of Broadway and the Theatre from Its Beginnings to the Present* (New York: MacMillan, 1997), 398. An audition like that depicted in *A Chorus Line* would not have existed throughout the 1980s without some indication of the presence of HIV/AIDS.

13. Rogan and Winkler, "Impact of AIDS on Archival Collections," 23.

14. Parks, interview.

15. Parks, interview.

16. Gregus, interview.

17. Ibid.

18. William Hoffman, quoted in Gerald Clarke, "Rock: A Courageous Disclosure," *Time*. August 5, 1985, 52.

19. Gene Brown notes, "Simon later says that may not be exactly what he said, but whatever he did say, he's sorry he said it." Brown, *Show Time*, 377.

20. Simi Horwitz, "The Kindness of Strangers," *TheaterWeek*. July 29, 1991, 24.

21. Ibid.

22. Brown, *Show Time*, 397.

23. Joe Cohen, "Welfare Resources Of Performer Unions Threatened By AIDS," *Variety*. May 13, 1987, 142.

24. Parks, Interview.

25. Gregus, Interview.

26. The extremely rich history of Broadway Cares/Equity Fights AIDS itself warrants more detailed attention than the limits of this study allow.

27. Marty Bell, "The Response," *Playbill* [for "The Quilt Show"], 1988. This playbill documents a performance marking the one-year anniversary of Broadway Cares. Stamped by the Theatre Collection of the NYPL on March 17 1989.

28. Ibid.

29. Diana Maychick, "Rallying Round," *New York Post*, February 11, 1988, 25.

30. Ibid.

31. Josh Ellis. Press Release: "AIDS Rally with Peter Allen, Liz Callaway, Brian Dennehy, David Dinkins, Joel Grey, Marvin Hamlisch, Jerry Herman, Judith Ivey, Lina Lain, Penn & Teller, Roy Scheider for 'Broadway Cares' Week at St. James Theater, Wed. Feb 10, Beginning at 11:30 a.m." *Broadway Cares*. February 1988.

32. Colleen Dewhurst and Tom Viola, *Colleen Dewhurst: Her Autobiography*, (New York: Simon and Schuster, 2002), 324.

33. Tom Viola and Joseph P. Benincasa, Interview by John VonSoosten and Howard Sherman, *Downstage Center*, episode 131, The American Theatre Wing, December 22,

2006,http://americantheatrewing.org/downstagecenter/detail/actors_fund_and_broadway_
cares_equity_fights-aids.

34. Ibid.

35. Ibid.

36. Harvey Fierstein. *Safe Sex* (New York: Atheneum, 1987), xi.

37. Earlier productions addressing the burgeoning epidemic include Larry Kramer's *The Normal Heart,* which opened at the Public Theater just over a week before *As Is* opened at the Lyceum. Even earlier productions include *The A.I.D.S. Show* at San Francisco's *Theatre Rhinoceros* and Robert Chesley's *Night Sweat,* which received controversial productions in both San Francisco and New York. Regarding *Night Sweat,* Hoffman wrote, "I confess my reaction was tinged with the teensiest bit of jealousy. I probably said to my lover at the time, 'How good it is to have a comrade in this struggle with a deadly epidemic that everyone wants to avoid talking about.' But underneath I was probably seething: 'How dare that fucker beat me to it?'" William M. Hoffman, "AIDS-Involved Drama Syndrome," *Poz,* February 1997, http://www.poz.com/articles/237_1688.shtml.

38. *Newsweek,* "Gay America: Sex, Politics and The Impact of AIDS," August 8, 1983, 33.

39. Ibid.

40. Larry Kramer, "1,112 and Counting," *New York Native.* Issue 59, March 14-27, 1983.

41. Ibid.

42. Judith Daniels, "Among Stories of Proms and Happy Birthdays, An Alarming Report," *Life,* July 1985, 6.

43. Hoffman, *As Is, 13.*

44. Hoffman, *As Is,* 17.

45. Ibid., 13.

46. This depiction of the healthy *looking* body versus the perceived marked body of an AIDS patient anchors the conflict in a subplot of Richard Greenberg's *Eastern Standard,* another Broadway play addressing aspects of the AIDS crisis. Compared by critics to a Lunts drawing room comedy and to a Shavian play of ideas, *Eastern Standard* addresses a variety of issues, including homelessness, urban overdevelopment, Wall Street scandals and AIDS—which is importantly never mentioned by name. The condition was nevertheless understood; consider the semiotics; Peter, who lives with HIV, is presented as a healthy-looking man, or as one reviewer described him, "a cheerful hunk with no trace of his disease." (Robert Brustein, "*Eastern Standard* (Review)," *New Republic,* 34. Clipping file. NYPL.) Only his homosexuality need be established for his words "I'm sick" to signify AIDS to reviewers (and audiences). Later descriptions of his potential for "lesions" and "skin and bones" further establish the connection. *Eastern Standard* set a similarly valuable precedent as the first Broadway "AIDS play" that was not actually *about* AIDS, though it was perceived by some to be overreaching in its scope. Theatre critic John Simon comments, "It is nice to have a playwright deal simultaneously with a heterosexual and a homosexual love affair and, though clearly more interested in the latter, be eminently fair to the former. There is concern here for many (too many) of the troubling issues of the eighties, and there is a tart intelligence at work observing them. The only thing missing is a play." John Simon, "Long Island Longueurs," (review of *Eastern Standard*) *New York.* Reprinted in *John Simon on Theater* (New York: Applause, 2005),

447. *Eastern Standard* opened on Broadway at the Golden Theater on 27 November 1988 and ran for nearly three months, a success compared to a play like Fierstein's *Safe Sex*.

47. The same visual narrative technique was applied in *An Early Frost*, the first broadcast television movie about AIDS, released earlier that year. Michael Pearson, played by contemporary heartthrob Aidan Quinn, was never seen with visible signs of his illness; neither lesion nor emaciation were apparent. However, he was presented in sharp contrast to Victor, played by John Glover, who was covered in lesions, gaunt, and losing his hair due to the chemotherapy used to treat his accompanying cancer.

48. Hoffman, *As Is*. 39.

49. Ibid., 13.

50. Mel Gussow, "Sensitive Material Presented With Compassion." *New York Times.* March 31, 1985, 3. [clippings file].

51. Hoffman, *As Is*, 23.

52. Ibid., 24.

53. Ibid., 47.

54. Ibid., 28.

55. Hoffman, *As Is*, 44.

56. Hoffman, *As Is*, 53.

57. Ibid., 54.

58. Ibid., 56.

59. In some ways, *Safe Sex*, particularly *On Tidy Endings*, set considerable precedent for the musical *Falsettos*, which also employs a child to communicate the far-reaching effect of the AIDS epidemic.

60. Similarly, *Love! Valour! Compassion!* opened in the same theatre (the Walter Kerr) as *Angels*.

61. Frank Rich, *New York Times*, Section 2, p. 5, 28. March 8, 1987. "Safe Sex" Clipping File, NYPL. Rich's generally positive review, which makes a case for the power of the theatre, stands in fairly stark contrast to his generally scathing review of the Broadway production just months later.

62. Bruce Lambert provides a district-by-district breakdown of HIV incidence in and around New York City in 1987. He quotes Dr. Ernest Drucker, "In this epidemic, geography is destiny" as he lists the highest AIDS incidence in Greenwich Village, Chelsea, Hell's Kitchen, the Lower East Side, central Harlem and Spanish Harlem. See Bruce Lambert, "New York City Maps Deadly Pattern of AIDS," *New York Times,* December 13, 1987, New York edition, Section One, page 1.

63. Fierstein, *Safe Sex*, xii.

64. AZT stopped the virus from multiplying, allowing the immune system to regenerate. Only effective for those with pneumocystis pneumonia (about half of those living with AIDS in 1996), AZT was approved by the U.S. FDA in 1987. *ABC Nightly News*, "AZT, First Drug Treating AIDS becomes Available," September 19, 1986, http://abcnews.go.com/Video/playerIndex?id=2031693.

65. Glenn Collins, "In 'Safe Sex,' Harvey Fierstein Turns Serious," *New York Times*, April 5, 1987,http://query.nytimes.com/gst/fullpage.html?res=9B0DE6DA153CF936A3 5757C0A961948260&sec=&spon=&pagewanted=all

66. Jay Parks, interview by the author, August 23, 2008. New York Public Library for the Performing Arts. New York City.

67. Kaiser Family Foundation, *Global HIV/AIDS Timeline*.

68. See Richard Berkowitz, *Stayin' Alive: The Invention of Safe Sex* (Cambridge: Basic Books, 2003). Included in the appendix of Berkowitz's fascinating social history is a reprint of the forty-page booklet he published with Michael Callen in 1983, *How to Have Sex in an Epidemic*, the first published guidelines for safe sex, remarkable in part for its frank language and documentation of the hysteria and discrimination surrounding the outbreak of the epidemic within the gay community. Initially distributed in San Francisco, two years later the booklet was expanded in New York City to address the popularity of poppers through a safe-sex campaign entitled "Safe Sex is Healthy Sex" (180). They captured the attention of the gay community in New York City early in the epidemic with their article, "We Know Who We Are: Two Gay Men Declare War on Promiscuity," published in the *New York Native* in 1982, reprinted in Mark Blasius and Shane Phelan, *We Are Everywhere: A Historical Sourcebook of Gay and Lesbian Politics* (New York: Routledge, 1997).

69. See Craig A. Rimmerman, "Presidency, U.S.," *The Body: The Complete HIV/AIDS Resource,* http://www.thebody.com/content/art14034.html.

70. The significance of this mailing, which began on 26 May 1988, cannot be overstated. Between its distribution and the sensational coverage of the illness and death of Rock Hudson, AIDS had firmly entered mainstream consciousness, further evidenced by the introduction of World AIDS Day on 1 December, 1988.

71. C. Everett Koop, *Understanding AIDS*, (Rockville, MD: U.S. Department of Health and Human Services, Public Health Service, Centers for Disease Control, 1988).

72. Joel Moskowitz provides a concise history of the term's usage:

The earliest reference to "safe sex" in the professional literature was in a November 1984 paper discussing the psychological impact of HIV/AIDS on homosexual men and the need to educate them about sexual practices (Morin, Charles & Malyon, 1984). The term first appeared in the *New York Times* the following year in an article which noted that some doctors counseled their AIDS patients about the practice of safe sex (Whitmore, 1985). The concept included limiting the number of sexual partners, using limiting the number of sexual partners, using prophylactics, avoiding bodily fluid exchange, and resisting use of drugs that reduced inhibitions for high-risk sexual behavior (Collins, 1985). In 1986 "an 88-page book entitled, Safe Sex in the Age of AIDS, was published that discussed a 'positive approach' to safe sex labeling abstinence and monogamy a 'negative approach'" (Institute for the Advanced Study of Human Sexuality, 1986). Sexual behaviors were classified as either 'safe,' 'possibly safe,' or 'unsafe.' Safe sex included dry kissing, hugging, massage, body-to-body rubbing, mutual masturbation, exhibitionism and voyeurism, telephone sex, sado-masochism without bruising or bleeding, and use of separate sex toys. At that time, latex condoms were considered 'possibly safe' due to concerns that the virus which causes AIDS might traverse latex.

Joel M. Moskowitz, et al., "How Do Californians Define Safe Sex?," *Californian Journal of Health Promotion*, 4 no. 1 (2006): 109.

73. Koop, "Understanding AIDS," 4.

74. Harvey Fierstein, "Preface," *Safe Sex*, xi.

75. Howard Kissel, "Hiding Behind One-Liners," *Daily News*, April 6, 1987. Extra. 3. Clipping File, NYPL.

76. Frank Rich, "Stage: Harvey Fierstein's 'Safe Sex'" *New York Times*. 6 April 1987. C13.

77. Fierstein began his career as a female impersonator at a gay club in the East Village when he was sixteen years old. His discovery directly led to a long relationship with La MaMa, beginning with Andy Warhol's play, *Pork*, in 1971 and continuing through regular performances there inclusive of *Safe Sex* in 1987.

78. Collins. "In 'Safe Sex.'"

79. Rich, "'Safe Sex.'"

80. Parks, Interview.

81. Ibid.

82. *Angels* opened on May 4, 1993, *Falsettos* ran April 29, 1992 through June 27, 1993.

83. For a comprehensive overview of this change in treatment, see "Attacking AIDS With a 'Cocktail' Therapy. *FDA Consumer*. 33.4 July-August 1999. http://www.fda.gov /FDAC/features/1999/499_aids.html

84. David Finkle, "The Post-AIDS-Play Play," *The Village Voice*, August 29, 1985, 78.

Chapter 12

Counterpublic Art and Social Practice

Philip Glahn

Public art in the 1980s was a site of struggle. Art activists and collectives occupied the battlegrounds of urban space and gallery walls, communities and billboards, memories and histories. Public art constituted a fight over where and how images and identities are made and seen, in terms of both channels of communication and the very possibilities of expression and discourse—at once implementing and questioning methods of resistance and of participation in the making of culture, knowledge, and meaning. In an era of renewed conservative politics and an ever-expanding commodification and privatization of culture, artists in the U.S. devised strategies to broaden art's constituencies and audiences, to integrate excluded experiences and histories into the apparatus of cultural production that declares what is important and relevant to society as a whole. The practices that for all their diversity are now commonly referred to as "New Genre Public Art," "Art in the Public Interest," or "Community Art"— practices of making and pasting posters onto bus shelters and lampposts, of creating alternative spaces to make and show art, of projecting images onto memorials and producing television programs, of working with the homeless, students, and AIDS activists, to name but a few examples—were ultimately a struggle over both the ideal and the use-value of the public sphere itself.[1] This public art achieved its most profound success when it took the form of "counterpublic art," when rather than transgressing the boundary between public and private, and between dominant and marginal culture, it engaged in a critical analysis and rearticulation of the relationship of public and private as a fundamental element of modern capitalist culture.

The following remarks are an attempt to trace this critical analysis within its specific historical context of U.S. politics and culture in the 1980s. The conservative cultural climate, which memorably led to struggles over public space and federal arts funding, forcefully gave visibility to a development that philosopher and sociologist Jürgen Habermas had observed in the advent of Nineteenth and

Twentieth century capitalist democracies—the erosion of the so-called bourgeois public sphere, a site of critical exchange among citizens, autonomous by
definition, situated between the state and the private sphere, to "mediate between a society of private property owners and the state."[2] Originally conceived
as an arena of productive dissent, the bourgeois public sphere revolved around
culture (the visual arts, literary criticism, and talk shows) as the primary tool of
critical exchange. The matters to be discussed within a given culture were supposed to be universal, to address the needs and interests of society as a whole.
But as the channels of critical exchange became more overtly commodified,
with the state ostensibly acting on behalf of the general population, as a guaran-
tor of public welfare in a system of free-market capitalism, the bourgeois public
sphere turned into a "facade of legitimization," veiling the production of social
hegemony while offering up ideals of the greater good in place of those of discord and debate. In a backlash against the diversification of American culture
since the Civil Rights movement, during the 1980s the public sphere became a
site where social norms and values were affirmed and cemented rather than
opened to negotiation. In response, art activists and social advocates began to
challenge the idea of the public sphere as a site of harmony and homogeneity,
demanding the inclusion of a plurality of experiences rather than the prescription
of universal moral standards. This call for inclusivity presents a powerful critique of the normative capacity of the bourgeois public sphere as described (and
ultimately advocated) by Habermas. For rather than simply assimilating a plurality of histories and imaginations under a general will, 80s activist public artists
sought to create what Oskar Negt and Alexander Kluge have called a "proletarian" or "counterpublic" sphere.[3] Rather than seeking to complement or complicate the existing public sphere, counterpublic art questions the very dynamic of
"public" and "private" and aims to articulate what Negt and Kluge call the "relationality" between the spheres where experiences are produced and circulated,
and to posit such relationality as an experience in and of itself. As Miriam Hansen points out, this counterpublic sphere of experience presents a radically new
definition of what it means to participate in a social structure: "While Habermas'
notion of public life is predicated on formal conditions of communications (free
association, equal participation, deliberation, polite argument), Negt and Kluge
emphasize questions of constituency, concrete needs, interests, conflicts, protest,
and power."[4] The counterpublic sphere is based on a pragmatic notion of commonality that redistributes the tools of cultural production according to temporary alliances formed around problems and experiences, including the experience of exclusion and the mechanisms that separate the officially public from
the presumably private.

    Published in Germany four years after the height of the Student Movement,
Negt and Kluge's 1972 book *The Public Sphere and Experience: Toward an
Analysis of the Bourgeois and Proletarian Public Sphere* captures a historical
climate as much as it tries to transform it. Translated in part into English and
published in American journals over the next decade, the text provides a theoret-

ical lens for the work of several American visual artists in the 1980s, and in some cases directly inspired them.[5] The book was first and foremost an attempt to come to terms with the 1968 attempt at a social and cultural revolution (almost immediately deemed a failure), and to provide a model for continued critical and political engagement—a redefined commitment to the ongoing or resuscitated project of enlightenment and radical change. Today, as "social practice" in the arts has attained a new popularity, it is particularly illuminating, and increasingly urgent, to revisit Negt and Kluge's groundbreaking concept of the counterpublic sphere. For while the trend has sparked a slew of exhibitions, writings, and even art school degree programs (such as the California College of the Arts' concentration in "Social Practice" and the School of Visual Arts' new MFA in "Social Documentary Film"), a number of social-practice theorists and historians of public art have returned to a traditional, if not outright conservative model of political artistic engagement that once again begs to be superseded. As the last part of this text will argue, counterpublic art continues to provide a viable basis for productive aesthetic engagement today.

Conservative Action and the Limits of the Public Sphere

During the 1980s, the consolidation of conservative political power and the increasing commercialization of visual culture worked in tandem to irredeemably compromise the public sphere as an ideal arena of autonomous public discourse and opinion. The landslide election of Ronald Reagan in 1980 and the ensuing stranglehold of the "moral majority" comprised a devastating attack on the politics of participation and cultural diversity ushered in by the counter-culture, women's, and Civil Rights movements. After what many people experienced as an era of both civic freedom and ideological uncertainty, American culture was emphatically reined in by old-fashioned ideals of unity and conformity.[6] Crises such as the AIDS epidemic and a spike in homelessness were downplayed or outright ignored, designated by neo-liberalists as matters of private choice and individual lifestyle rather than of public interest and responsibility.

A range of phenomena, from conservative attacks on federal funding for the arts to art's complicity in the gentrification of New York City neighborhoods, made it painfully clear that there was much more at stake with public art than just the beautification of civic space. Non-site-specific outdoor art—"plunk" or "parachute art," as Lucy Lippard once called it—merely extends the institutional sphere of the art museum or gallery into urban space, and especially when it comes in the form of modernist, abstract objects, functions as a symptom as well as a perpetuating enforcement of the myth of the bourgeois public sphere's inclusivity, autonomy, and participation.[7] The absence of a particular motive or narrative and the sculpture's literal, physical accessibility come to embody social ideals, or as Rosalyn Deutsche put it, to "bolster illusions of stability, universal values, and gentility."[8] One of the most infamous art controversies to jeopardize such illusions began with the installation of Richard Serra's *Tilted Arc*, a site-specific rolled-steel sculpture commissioned by the General Services Administration in 1979 for Foley Square in New York. Installed in 1981, Serra's enormous contribution to a heavily trafficked public space outside a federal office building aggressively cut through the open site, complementing the existing fountain with a metal wall 120 feet long and 12 feet high. As a form of outdoor sculpture that demanded to be reckoned with, commanding the plaza rather than lending it aesthetic grace, *Titled Arc* was met with great hostility by those who had to walk around it in order to get to work or eat lunch in its giant shadow. It was considered a security threat compromising surveillance and a screen sheltering illegal activities such as loitering and drug abuse. It was felt to be an attack on the common man by an artistic elite and a misappropriation of public funding. The well-documented debate and trial that followed ultimately led to the sculpture's removal in 1989.[9] Most crucial to the topic at hand are Serra's attempt to "confront the premises of public sculpture" and the insights that the ensuing debate provides regarding the assumptions that were underlying the concept of public space and, by extension, the public sphere.[10]

The persistent notion of public art as civic outdoor sculpture and mural painting is a symptom of what Habermas famously called the "structural transformation of the public sphere" from a relatively autonomous arena of critical discourse into its own symbolic abbreviation, systematically undermined by private interests and the state as the protective agent of popular rights and needs. According to Habermas, public space was traditionally determined by the places where people gathered as private persons to discuss civic matters, such as the market, "salons, and coffeehouses."[11] Once these sites are established, they become defined as discursive spaces a priori, and "plunk" art plays a key role of conferring an aura of autonomy and universality on public space and discouraging any direct critical engagement with socio-political reality. The debate that ensued around *Tilted Arc* could be considered a return to public discourse, a discussion about the socio-political role of art and public space. But, as art historian Robert Storr has pointed out, by pitting "experts" from the art community who came to defend Serra's sculpture in court against the "philistines" who wanted it removed, the exchange missed the opportunity to function as public discourse in the Habermasian sense, which, after all, by definition, would have to have been a debate conducted among equals, leading to a productive, progressive shaping of social common sense.[12]

But outdoor sculpture as "bourgeois public art" not only discourages dissent, as illustrated by the *Tilted Arc* controversy; by maintaining an active, mythical function, it effectively veils the very real intrusion of private interest into the public sphere, creating what Negt and Kluge call a "pseudo-public sphere."[13] The function of bourgeois public art as "aesthetic disguise for the brutal realities of 'revitalization'" has been most prominently analyzed by Rosalyn Deutsche.[14] Discussing the urban "redevelopment" of Union Square and Battery Park City in New York during the 1980s, Deutsche shows how outdoor sculpture and memorials, as demarcations of a functioning bourgeois public sphere, through their projection of unity and universality, conceal the private dimension of urban planning and revitalization, as urban space is restructured to maximize the presence of and exchange among a certain socio-economic stratus. The struggle over urban space as a social and economic structure is repressed by repossessing and marking such space as "public," evicting from its premises those who appear to threaten public life such as drug users and dealers, prostitutes and the homeless: "an ideology of 'the public' justifies particular exclusions as natural."[15] Under the guise of access and inclusion, the "pseudo-public sphere," comprising the dysfunctional bourgeois public sphere and private, economic interest, functions as a mechanism of exclusion and homogenization.

The decade's conservative backlash against cultural and social diversity culminated in the National Endowment for the Arts controversies toward the end of the '1980s, which continue to resonate today. The case against the exhibition of Robert Mapplethorpe's photographs is the preeminent example of the era's battle over what constitutes, as one Republican representative called it, "public standards of taste and decency."[16] The crusade led by Republican senators and congressmen against the publicly funded display of Mapplethorpe's work focused on "obscene" images of male nudes and homosexual and at times sadomasochistic subject matter found among the still lifes and portraits.[17] The 150-work traveling retrospective "Robert Mapplethorpe: The Perfect Moment" was organized by the Institute of Contemporary Art in Philadelphia and supported by a $30,000 grant from the NEA, and had been well received in its original venue and in Chicago, where it was on view at the Museum of Contemporary Art. Scheduled to open at the Corcoran Gallery of Art in Washington DC in 1989, the show attracted the attention of legislators and administrators who threatened not only to close the exhibition but also to strip the NEA of its budget on the grounds that it was showing "morally reprehensible trash."[18] Senator Jesse Helms's attempt to introduce a Senate amendment that would forbid the public funding of "indecent" art underscores the fundamentalist desire for the public sphere to be an arena of consensus rather than dissent. In fulminating against the federal funding of Mapplethorpe's project based on his opinion of its quality, Helms unwittingly illuminates the point of public funding for the arts in general, which aims to ensure a rich cacophony of voices whose work may not be recognized by the market and may be critical of the status quo—a cacophony expressly protected in this country by the First Amendment. (While the grounds for determining eligibility for public funding remain hotly debated, the NEA has survived the many assaults on its program mostly intact, and has even found grudging champions among conservatives, who are obliged to acknowledge that its wide-ranging support of the arts—artist communities, arts education, dancers, folk and traditional artists, writers and translators, local arts agencies, musicians, directors, actors, and singers—serves a crucial public purpose: improving quality of life, fostering economic growth, and engendering an aware and educated citizenry.[19]) The correlate of the NEA controversy is the Reagan Administration's strategic refusal throughout the 1980s to acknowledge the political and social dimension of AIDS and homosexuality, homelessness and prostitution, women's rights and ethnic diversity.[20] And worse, as Carol Vance has observed, when the work of Mapplethorpe is decried as deeply anti-American, the attack on the artist and his subject matter results in a "rhetoric disavowal of citizenship."[21] At stake is thus the individual right and requirement to participate in the discursive construction of what Negt and Kluge call the "social horizon of experience in which everything that is actually or ostensibly relevant for all members of society is integrated."[22] In the decade's struggle over images and sites, the ideal of the bourgeois public sphere and its humanist veil serves to separate what is deemed worthy of public consideration from what is not, according to criteria based on a nostalgic vision of social harmony through categorical similarity rather than continuous negotiation, effectively denying some the ability to participate in the processes of identity formation as part of a greater social community. As such, the public sphere is compromised, exclusive, and de facto the arena where a few determine what is relevant for the many.

"Crawling Under the Fence": Participation and Inclusion in Cultural Practice

The call for traditional forms of culture to separate what is pertinent to the "greater good" from the publicly irrelevant was sounded not only by reactionary politicians and televangelists but also by art professionals and intellectuals. While some critics and writers welcomed the so-called postmodern challenges to the modernist conventions of cultural and historical classification, to the binaries of high and low culture, art and politics, center and margin, others, like the founding editor of *The New Criterion*, Hilton Kramer, and the philosopher Allan Bloom, voiced nostalgic longings for "a tidier and more fastidious intellectual universe."[23] In 1982, Kramer left his position as art critic for the *New York Times* to pursue a form of publishing that would help the "values of high art ... to survive and prosper" in light of the "fateful collapse in critical standards and in the very idea of critical disinterestedness."[24] True to Habermas's description of the original bourgeois public sphere, Kramer demands of art and art discourse autonomy and authenticity. The time had come to apply a "criterion of truth" to judging what should hang in museums and be taught in classrooms, even though, Kramer acknowledges, "due to the nature of democracy, with its multiplicity of interests and tastes," the task would be "difficult."[25] Bloom, author of the infamous book *The Closing of the American Mind* (1987), struck a similar note in his attempt to save truth and morality from pluralism, "cultural relativism," and "the tendency toward indiscriminateness."[26] It is ironic that, for Bloom, the critical analysis of notions long taken for granted, of the "great questions" such as "God, freedom, and immortality," had led to a "loss of immediacy in all experience."[27] Like Kramer, Bloom blames the "radicalism" of the 1960s for turning what was once natural (being, identity, common sense, historical consciousness) into artifice. But it was precisely the artificial and actively depoliticized nature of the narratives and artifacts that constituted the American dream that the movements for civil rights and liberties questioned, demanding that the very palpable, everyday experiences excluded from it would be made visible and accounted for.

At the end of the 1960s, for example, the Art Workers' Coalition had held an Open Hearing in order to deliver statements forcefully and eloquently calling for greater artistic control over various modes of cultural production and distribution, including the presence of artists on the boards of cultural institutions and rental fees for works exhibited where admission is charged.[28] The AWC's members also demanded greater representation of women and "artists of color" in museum collections and exhibitions, as well as of the range of contemporary artistic practices in place of the enshrinement of a few personalities according to the standards of modernist art history. Pitting the private interests of art institutions against their public mission, the Art Workers questioned art's social purpose and audience, effectively denouncing the museums' function as "pseudo-public spheres." Gene Swenson talked about the "wider community" that the art institutions had failed, and about the responsibility of bringing "moral accuracy to the projections of our society." Hollis Frampton, Ken Jacobs, and Michael Snow spoke of art's "public responsibilities... for the whole people, to teach, to move, to delight them." And Dan Graham, referring to "Marx, Zola, and Brecht's time," argued that "we must go back to the old notion of socially good works..., i.e.: art to go public."[29] Here, the limits of the public sphere were challenged, and a more inclusive, heterogeneous arena was called for that would allow for the representation and articulation of multiple and at times seemingly incompatible experiences.[30]

More than a decade later, 1980s activist and public artists found that the efforts made by the Art Workers' Coalition and the many other like-minded groups of the 1960s and 1970s—such as the Ad Hoc Women's Artists' Committee and the Artists Meeting for Cultural Change—were in danger of being compromised by renewed calls for cultural hegemony. Accordingly, they sought new strategies to further expand the social horizon of experience—strategies to take into account and articulate the plurality of actual, heterogeneous experiences in the face of recent attempts to define the public sphere as an arena of homogeneity and "harmony."[31] In 1981, Tim Rollins, a painter working at a Bronx high school as part of New York City's "Learning to Read through the Arts" program targeting dyslexic and emotionally challenged Hispanic and black youth, founded the Art and Knowledge Workshop, later known as K.O.S. (Kids of Survival). In this ongoing program, the students read classical literature together, including Franz Kafka's *Amerika* and Herman Melville's *Moby Dick*, and then express their responses in collaborative drawings and paintings. The students are able to articulate their own everyday experiences and dreams in relation to the canonical narratives of Western culture and develop a form of visual literacy beyond standardized reading and math tests. Here, art is a form of access, as relating the stories to their own daily lives enables the students not only to better understand the texts they read but to work with and express their experiences from outside the educational environment. Furthermore, the ability to initiate a dialogue with what Bloom calls "the great books" transcends the classroom; works by K.O.S. have been exhibited in galleries and museums, included in biennials and art fairs, bought by private collectors, and acquired for the finest public collections, including the Museum of Modern Art, the Philadelphia Museum of Art, and the Dia Foundation.[32] Hanging in proximity to old and new masters of modern art, the stories told by K.O.S. are made visible among the narratives of high culture.

Critical of such attempts at aesthetic integration and the attendant dangers of cooptation, other artists sought to establish spaces of cultural production beyond the reach of the commercial art system. Finding the official channels of public production too stifling, a number of collectives established venues that would compete with rather than complement the sites where and ways in which art was made and seen. New York's Lower East Side, for example, became the home for ventures such as Group Material (founded in 1979), ABC No Rio (1980), Political Art Documentation/Distribution (1980), Paper Tiger Television (1981), and Bullet Space (1985), all collective endeavors invested in what Alexander Kluge in a 1979 interview called "crawling under the fence."[33] Kluge insists that a public sphere is actively produced, not simply given, and that alternative modes of knowledge and fantasy are possible despite the increasing appropriation of the public sphere by private interest: "[The] fence erected by corporations, by censorship, by authority, does not reach all the way to the base but stops short— because the base is so complex—so that one can crawl under the fence any time."[34] In their book *The Public Sphere and Experience*, Negt and Kluge discuss the possibility of a "proletarian public sphere" precisely along the lines of finding ways to repossess the tools used to create experience.[35] It is important to understand the term "proletarian" in a sense that does not merely reproduce antiquated, nostalgic notions of working-class struggle. The public sphere, defined by Negt and Kluge as "what enables experience or, on the other hand, what limits and cripples it," is a matter of access to the production and distribution of experience: to history books and newspapers, to music and radio stations, to education, memory, art, television, and film.[36] The proletarian is defined by Negt and Kluge in the most general sense as "separated from the means of production," not just industrial production but "all similarly restricted productive capacities," such as the production of experience, values, identities, etc.[37] The challenge to such separation lies at the heart of an alternative public sphere.

Formed as a consequence of *The Real Estate Show*, an exhibition organized in 1980 by a group of artists around the theme of property and housing, ABC No Rio became an arts and community center driven by the conviction that culture was only truly public when it was created and used by those whose life it reflected and affected. Its community includes "nomads, squatters, fringe dwellers, and those among society's disenfranchised who find at ABC No Rio a place to be heard and valued."[38] The space features a print shop, a darkroom, and a 'zine library, resources with which artists, activists, and members of the community at large can express and communicate their ideas. Though primarily reflecting the collective's struggle over issues of real estate, the following excerpt from its 1998 brochure "Founders Era" makes a powerful statement regarding the public sphere as a place where identities and experiences are formed: "'Space' should be defined by those who directly use it in the business of living rather than by those who would manipulate these blocks of space in the interests of profit at the expense of communities."[39]

Similarly, to intervene in and produce the spaces where history and memory are constructed was the founding mission of the artists' collective Political Art Documentation/Distribution (PAD/D). A forum for exchange among artists and non-artist activists, the group also made art and staged a number of events and interventions.[40] One of these so-called public actions, "Death and Taxes" (1981), was initiated through an open invitation to "produce public works protesting the use of federal taxes for military instead of social programs," and included Micki McGee's altered and recirculated tax forms informing the taxpayer that "53¢ of every tax dollar goes to military and defense budgets" and outlining payment choices to public transportation and "the arts and humanities" instead of aircraft carriers and "war debts" (Fig 12.1)—as well as the projection of Alain Resnais' film *Hiroshima Mon Amour* onto the facade of the 26th street Armory building in Manhattan.[41] In 1983 and 1984, members of PAD/D formed a subgroup titled Not For Sale, a project that yielded several events including exhibitions at various venues, guerilla stencil and poster campaigns, and video and cabaret presentations in an effort to address the increasing gentrification of the Lower East Side. This kind of attempt to address and actively shape the making of a place and a community through cultural production might be PAD/D's most valuable contribution to the formation of alternative public spheres in the 1980s. After all, to shape identities and knowledge through artistic expression is to directly engage in the imagining of a collective memory. PAD/D's original mission to establish an archive of politically committed art and to distribute the knowledge, methods, and strategies collected therein through print and action led the group to write and actively reappropriate the use-value of history, to repossess, as Negt and Kluge had called for, the tools for building a social—a public—consciousness.

To art groups like Group Material, forming a collective meant structuring the making of art as a participatory, collaborative process in order to reclaim the sphere of cultural production as constituted by a truly public practice and not, as in the bourgeois public sphere, by the empty promise of participation. To art groups, "collective social form," according to Blake Stimson and Gregory Sholette, "assumed that the ideal of collectivism was to realize itself not in the social model or plan but in the to-and-fro of cultural exchange."[42] Group Material was founded by twelve young artists (including Tim Rollins) who wanted to organize, exhibit, and promote an art innovative in form and social engagement. Based in a storefront gallery in a mostly Hispanic, working-class neighborhood, the collective provided a site of cultural exchange and social interaction between artists and non-artists, organized around specific social issues. Group Material made a conscious attempt to broaden the public sphere beyond its official sites and institutions to include, for example, the concerns and dreams of their neighbors. Aiming to make work that was "accessible and informal without sacrificing complexity and rigor," the collective organized exhibitions and events around issues such as "gender, the 'aesthetics' of consumption and advertising, alienation, political art by children ... cooking as working class art, and many more."[43] The 1981 exhibition "The People's Choice" (Fig 12.2) consisted of images and objects contributed by the group's neighbors following an invitation to donate "things that might not usually find their way into an art gallery: the things that you personally find beautiful, the objects that you keep for your own pleasure, the objects that have meaning for you, your family, and your friends.... Choose something that you feel will communicate to others."[44] "The People's Choice" was a great success, and included a vast array of objects and images such as family photographs and handicrafts, personal mementos and folk art, dolls and religious artifacts, sports memorabilia and reproductions of works of art.

From the collective's inception in 1979, the members of Group Material were aware of the limitations and problems of creating an "alternative space," a place where experiences that lay outside the social horizon of experience could be articulated. Like many other artists and collectives, Group Material felt the necessity to rethink the very structure of the public sphere, since the activist attempt to include the excluded remained mired within the existing structure, merely reproducing it with a different population. If the traditional model of the public sphere was inadequate, why aim to be part of it? Moving out of their storefront gallery in 1981, Group Material declared the following: "We hated the association with 'alternative spaces' because it was clear to us that most prominent alternative spaces are, in appearance, policy and social function, the children of the dominant commercial galleries in New York."[45] Moving into what they called "that most vital of alternative spaces—that wall-less expanse that bars artists and their work from the crucial social concerns of the American working class," Group Material sought to address the concept of the public sphere itself: an ideological structure based on binary oppositions such as inside and outside, inclusion and exclusion, art and politics, and, most importantly, public and non-public.[46] A truly alternative public art needed to articulate the *relationship* between the public sphere as the arena where, as Negt and Kluge define it, "everything that is actually or ostensibly relevant for all members of society is integrated," the experiences excluded from that arena, *and* the experience of such exclusion, hence, the struggle over the spaces and tools used to produce knowledge and meaning, imagination and identity. A proletarian public sphere could transcend its own structural limitations when not only those lives and dreams kept from public consideration were made visible, but the mechanisms of separation were offered up for scrutiny and change.

Relationality and Struggle:
Proletarian Experience in Counterpublic Art

Abandoning the storefront gallery in 1981 and moving into "headquarters" instead, Group Material launched a series of interventions into the "wall-less expanse" of visual culture. Member Julie Ault recalls the collective's motivation in planning the poster project *DaZiBaos* (Fig 12.3): "We were thinking at that time, in 1982, about ways in which public opinion is instrumentalized and wielded by the media in the United States and how opinions and views are reduced to a yes or no, with no complexity or gray area in between, replicating cycles of reductive thinking."[47] *DaZiBaos* or *Democracy Wall* consisted of large red-and-yellow posters illegally pasted on the exterior of the old S. Klein department store building in New York's Union Square. Printed on the posters were twelve interrelated statements concerning current issues—six by organizations working on social and political problems (including Planned Parenthood, the Prison Reform Board, and the Committee in Solidarity with the People of El Salvador), and six by individuals approached randomly on the street and interviewed about those problems (including a receptionist and a homeless person). The first statement on the wall was by Group Material: "Even though it's easy and fun, we're sick of being the audience. We want to do something, we want to create our culture instead of just buying it." This statement was juxtaposed with an observation by a housewife: "Government funding of the arts should depend on the actual purpose, what they are giving it for. If it was being based on as far as to help other people or something like that I could see it." Another pair of posters addressed the issue of labor unions. One featured a comment by an office worker: "Unions benefit society, but not in my office." The other statement by the Home Health Care Workers Union read: "These are rough times to stand alone. Even though people are now paid for working, the attitude of masters towards servants remains the same." *DaZiBaos* charted the dialectic of public and private by juxtaposing spheres that in their complexity do not fall into such neatly defined categories: the format of propaganda and advertising used to communicate a range of opinions rather than assert a truth; Union Square as a public space determined by private, monetary interest (advertising, shopping) rather than an autonomous arena; and organizations working with individual points of view on issues either neglected by the "public" media or safely relegated to the realm of the private (drug abuse, homelessness).

Other Group Material interventions that revealed the public sphere as a contested arena and at the same time engaged in such contesting included the projects *M-5* (1981) and *Subculture* (1983), which placed artworks in the advertising-card slots on buses and subways. Appropriating the space and language of mass-media imagery, the projects engaged commuters in social and political issues that otherwise received very limited everyday attention, such as alienation from labor and urban life, the problems of public education, independence for Puerto Rico, and the "new face of Uncle Sam."[48]

What makes this alternative form of public art a counterpublic practice is the notion of relationality. As private individuals and organizations increasingly hold a monopoly over that production, the ideal of the inclusive, enabling bourgeois public sphere clashes with the proletariat's (in Negt and Kluge's sense of the term) experience of exclusion. The counterpublic sphere then "assumes the active function of mediating between social being and consciousness."[49] This mediation takes place through the establishment of a "block of real life" consisting of "a complex of contradictory tendencies in the internal organization of human psychic experience."[50] The counterpublic sphere is the organization of proletarian experience into this block of real life, which, unsubsumed by "profit-maximizing," private interests, holds the potential for social and political change.[51]

In 1989, Gran Fury, a self-described "band of individuals united in anger and dedicated to exploit the power of art to end the AIDS crisis," created the poster *Kissing Doesn't Kill* (Fig 12.4), which shows three interracial couples kissing, two of them of the same sex.[52] Appropriating the format and look of print advertising, *Kissing Doesn't Kill* competed with commercial images on New York and San Francisco buses, Chicago train platforms, in mainstream and alternative presses, and many other venues. As art historian Richard Meyer has pointed out, this "activism classic" does more than direct visual attention to the AIDS crisis—"it affirms the power of queer desire in the face of an ongoing epidemic, insisting that lesbians and gay men fight the efforts of the larger culture to render their sexuality—their desiring bodies—invisible."[53] The poster's text in its entirety reads: "Kissing Doesn't Kill: Greed and Indifference Do. Corporate Greed, Government Inaction, and Public Indifference Make AIDS a Political Crisis." Gran Fury thus exposes the structure of knowledge production by pointing to what is absent from the social horizon of experience, not just by exclusion, but through the spread of misinformation regarding who can be infected and how. While the bourgeois public sphere (according to Habermas, and as advocated by conservatives like Kramer and Bloom) by definition excludes the apparently banal, manipulated and commodified experiences mediated through the "culture industry," Gran Fury appropriates the techniques of graphic design and advertising to articulate the complex relation between the image of AIDS, the commercial surfaces of mass transportation, and sex education. *Kissing Doesn't Kill* addresses what Negt and Kluge call *Berührungsstellen*, or points of contact, of contiguity between different forms and arenas of experience—

between the realities of the disease as experienced by those who live with and die from it, those who study and fight it, who confront it, do their best to ignore it, or demonize it, and its distorted public image, or lack thereof.[54]

Similarly, in his *Homeless Projection*, Krzysztof Wodiczko articulates the relationships among public monuments, gentrification, and homelessness. This unrealized project, conceived in 1986 as what Rosalyn Deutsche called a "counter-image of redevelopment," produces points of contact between ways in which New York's Union Square has been perceived as a public, urban space.[55] In order to make the real estate surrounding the square and its park attractive to investors and a young, professional clientele willing to repopulate the American metropolis, the city's Planning Department, with the aid of a number of consulting architects, urban planners, and developers, launched a public-relations campaign that cast the site as one of "unification," of communal attempts to improve the quality of urban life. The history and future of Union Square was presented as one of reconciliation: commissioned reports emphasized patriotic events like Civil War–era gatherings where rousing speeches bound citizens through the patriotism of anti-Southern sentiment while four statues slated for refurbishment featuring Washington, Lafayette, Lincoln, and a bronze group of a mother and children embodied social ideals and civic values. Other narratives and experiences remained conveniently absent from such memorialization, including histories of Union Square as a place of unrest, of May Day celebrations and labor protests, political rallies and demonstrations by the unemployed and homeless, and the contemporary presence of drug users and a dispossessed population inhabiting the park during the 1980s.[56] Against this traditional, bourgeois, and at times outright hostile enforcement of the public sphere as site of visual and ideological harmony, Wodizcko proposed the juxtapositions of ideas, ideals, and experiences that would neither retain nor replace the prevailing tales of public, urban life in Union Square but produce an understanding of the site's competing realities. *Homeless Projection* literally projects images onto the statues, transforming them into platforms of negotiation between past and present, ideal and real. Washington's neoclassical, heroic pose, for example, is augmented by a Windex bottle and a rag, transforming his outstretched, commanding arm into a gesture stopping cars in traffic to squeegee a windshield and ask for some spare change (Fig 12.5). Lincoln, through the addition of a crutch and beggar's cup, becomes a down-and-out commander in chief, while the projection of a facade of an emptied building onto the presidential body asks the viewer to make the connection between the memorials and the redevelopment of urban space. Employing montage to challenge the use-value and ownership of Union Square, *Homeless Projection* questions the physical and symbolic stability of public sculpture and space and the notions of permanence and harmony enforced through them.

Historians and critics including Hal Foster, Grant Kester, and Miwon Kwon rightly observe and record some of the problems and pitfalls that certain examples of public art as social practice have encountered over the last decades, such as "ghettoization" and "balkanization"—the inverted "otherness" of a marginalized community as a site for experiential "authenticity," the reproduction of existing power relations through the artist's role as enabler and liberator, or the proliferation of cultural separatism by mythologizing cultural differentiation as a democratic antidote to the homogenizing effects of mass mediated spectacle.[57] (Urban community-based revitalization initiatives such as Tyree Guyton's Heidelberg Project in Detroit and Edgar Arceneaux's Watts House Project in Los Angeles are particularly vulnerable to such criticism, which highlights the often stark contrast between theoretical musings and an artwork's practical effect.) Yet such critique can be unproductive in cases where its parameters are based on rigid dichotomies of public and private, while the work under scrutiny set out to challenge this structure. It is important to understand the concept of the counterpublic sphere and the legacy of 1980s counterpublic art as reflecting on and transcending rather than relying on and reinscribing this binary, which is ultimately the very foundation of the bourgeois public sphere. Kwon's recent call for a return to a Habermasian form of the public sphere reiterates an undialectical positioning of particular versus common interest: "As many have said before, the public sphere is always necessarily an ideal, an idealized construction (fantasy), insofar as it imagines a possibility and potential of overcoming social differences to debate issues of common concern."[58] Though Kwon's reconsideration of Habermas's vision of the bourgeois public sphere emphasizes that this "collective identification, a different form of intimacy, [is] not for affirmation, consensus, or unification (not a self-same identification)," the idea of the public sphere advocated here is, again, based on a notion of democratic access rather than on the very struggle for such access.[59] After all, as Habermas as well as Negt and Kluge have pointed out, democracy remains an ideal when the concept obfuscates the limits of its enactment.

In his contribution to Martha Rosler's 1989 project *If You Lived Here: The City in Art, Theory, and Social Activism*, Kluge argued for the struggle over the use-value of the public sphere, to acknowledge that the public sphere is not given but produced.[60] A collaboration among artists and academics as well as public-interest coalitions, art activist groups, and members of the general public, *If You Lived Here* aimed to rise to the challenge and create various approaches to how we know and see urban life, thus creating a counterpublic sphere along points of contiguity connecting numerous urban experiences. The project included three exhibitions (including artists such as Wodizcko and the Downtown Community Video Center, ACT UP and Allan Sekula, Susan Day and Andrew Castrucci, Third Street Men's Shelter and Dan Graham) and four discussion forums addressing issues such as homelessness, gentrification, and AIDS—problems highly visible in postmodern America but far from being considered of public significance. The city as a historical entity—mediated through poetry and government data, film and advertising, painting and crime reports, taking the subway, walking though parks, and sitting on stoops—was opened up as a site of communication, rearticulating the possibilities of navigating urban life between myth and encounter, memory and fantasy. "Fantasy" in this case differs from Kwon's notion of fantasy: it is not what Kwon describes as a necessarily abstract exercise in imaging a democratic public sphere but an already existing pool of overlapping urban experiences and its potential for collaborative actions. Fantasy designates the temporarily unassimilable surplus-consciousness of experience produced by the counterpublic sphere as it not only imagines but practices different, competitive methods of action and intervention based on a pragmatic notion of commonality that redistributes the tools of cultural production according to temporary alliances formed around problems and experiences.[61] Negt and Kluge define fantasy as "the organizer of mediation."[62] In that sense, *If You Lived Here* as a whole, as well as in the individual projects therein, "offer forms that are grounded in a collective experience of marginalization and expropriation, but these forms are inevitably experienced as mediated, no longer rooted in face-to-face relations, and subject to discursive conflict and negotiation."[63] This does not mean, however, that these forms of solidarity and reciprocity are inconclusive or relativist. Quite the contrary—they are strategic and very pragmatic ways of rethinking the idea of the public and public art as a dialectics of agency that is the advanced struggle over the physical and psycho-social organization of everyday experience.

It is as this "advanced struggle" that the concept of the counterpublic and its development in 1980s public art and discourse retains its importance for an artistic practice today. During the '90s, activist groups like REPOHistory took it upon themselves to continue a counterpublic art practice deeply invested in the dialectics of agency, constructing artistic resistance as a critical negotiation between the social universality of common sense and the specificity of experiences challenging its ideological homogeneity. Working primarily in urban sites ranging from Houston to Atlanta to New York, REPOHistory opened up already charted territories for visual and intellectual renegotiation by installing street signs that presented forgotten, buried, or displaced stories. These narratives remapped areas naturalized and depoliticized by the absence of past experiences and, in many cases, their replacement with hegemonic histories mediated by tourist guides and historical markers, history books and media coverage. These projects did not so much add a more valid truth to the sites as they returned to the sites the quality of contestation.[64]

Central to this work as well as to the more recent phenomena that have become known as Tactical Media and Interventionism is the understanding of the public sphere as a plurality of experiential manifestations. Rather than seek to replace one experience with another, these projects produce an awareness of the interconnectedness between ideas and fantasies, actions and agencies, mainstream and alternatives. At the heart of counterpublic art remains the notion of cultural production as labor, as making something whose value is negotiated in relation to other forms of production. As such, counterpublic art is dependent on alliances with and proximities to its audience, other media, different practices, known expectations, and unknown possibilities. Its use-value thus resides in its active participation in a vast network of cultural production and in the possibilities it opens up for its audience to give meaning, project experiences, lend knowledge, and make sense.

Today, artists and intellectuals again find themselves forced to redefine notions of community and participation, democracy and collaboration, accessibility and audience. After 1989, the limits of the "victory over capitalism" soon became apparent, and the ensuing economic crises only re-entrenched the division between those with access and ownership and those without. Meanwhile, increasingly global networks of information and finance distribution have further consolidated the power to avail and participate in knowledge and experience, identity and history.[65] We continue to live in a culture of binary thinking, and the critical engagement with this cognitive system is an ongoing necessity. In the end, counterpublic art remains a model for art that is dialectically situated within its environment—that articulates the ways in which we are imagining and imaging the world that we live in. This dialectical ability to situate the self historically in a process of reference and self-reference, of reflection and self-reflection, and to create from that historical positioning a basis for analysis and judgment, is a productive continuation of an enlightening project.

Notes

1. See Suzanne Lacy, ed., *Mapping the Terrain: New Genre Public Art* (Seattle: Bay Press, 1995); Arlene Raven, ed., *Art in the Public Interest* (Ann Arbor and London: UMI Research Press, 1989); and Grant Kester, "Aesthetic Evangelists: Conversion and Empowerment in Contemporary Community Art," *Afterimage* (January 1995): 5–11.

2. Peter Hohendahl, "Jürgen Habermas: 'The Public Sphere' (1964)," *New German Critique* (Autumn, 1974): 47. Habermas's study *The Structural Transformation of the Public Sphere: An Inquiry into a Category of Bourgeois Society* was originally published in German in 1962. It first appeared in translation in the U.S. in its entirety in 1991 (Cambridge, Mass.: MIT Press). Excerpts and shortened versions were available to an American audience at least as early as 1974, when the *New German Critique* published Habermas's "The Public Sphere: An Encyclopedia Article (1964)," (Autumn 1974): 49–55.

3. Oskar Negt and Alexander Kluge, *The Public Sphere and Experience: Toward an Analysis of the Bourgeois and Proletarian Public Sphere* (Minneapolis and London: University of Minnesota Press, 1993).

4. Miriam Hansen, "Foreword," in ibid., xxx.

5. A number of artists were very much aware of Negt and Kluge's work. For example, Martha Rosler included a previously published text by Kluge in her 1989 multi-exhibition

project *If You Lived Here. The City in Art, Theory, and Cultural Activism* (Alexander Kluge, "The Public Sphere," in *If You Lived Here. The City in Art, Theory, and Cultural Activism. A Project by Martha Rosler*, ed. Brian Wallis [Seattle: Bay Press, 1991], 67–70). Yvonne Rainer, for her part, interviewed Kluge for *The Independent* in 1989 (Yvonne Rainer and Ernest Larsen, "'We Are Demolition Artists': An Interview with Alexander Kluge," *The Independent* [June 1989]: 18–25).

6. For a selection of primary sources documenting this development, see Gilbert T. Sewall, ed., *The Eighties: A Reader* (Reading, Mass.: Perseus Books, 1997).

7. Lucy Lippard, "Looking Around," in Lacy (ed.), *Mapping the Terrain*, 114–130.

8. Rosalyn Deutsche, "Krzystof Wodiczko's *Homeless Projection* and the Site of Urban 'Revitalization,'" *October* (Autumn 1986): 79.

9. See, for example, Clara Weyergraf-Serra and Martha Buskirk, eds., *The Destruction of* Tilted Arc*: Documents* (Cambridge, Mass. and London: MIT Press, 1991) and Harriet F. Senie, *The* Tilted Arc *Controversy: Dangerous Precedent?* (Minneapolis and London: University of Minnesota Press, 2002).

10. Robert Storr, "*Tilted Arc*: Enemy of the People?" *Art in America* (September 1985): 96.

11. For a detailed history of such public spaces and places, the "institutions of the public sphere," see Habermas, *The Structural Transformation of the Public Sphere*, 31–43.

12. Storr, "*Tilted Arc*: Enemy of the People?": 93–95.

13. For a discussion of the function of the "decaying postbourgeois forms of the public sphere" in relation to the commercial, privately owned "new public spheres of production," see "Chapter 1: The Public Sphere as the Organization of Collective Experience" in Negt and Kluge, *The Public Sphere and Experience*, 1–53.

14. See Deutsche, "Uneven Development: Public Art in New York City," *October* (Winter 1988): 3–52.

15. Ibid., 11.

16. Representative Dick Armey (R-Tex), quoted in Carol S. Vance, "The War on Culture," in *Theory in Contemporary Art since 1985*, ed. Zoya Kocur and Simon Leung (Malden, Mass. and Oxford: Blackwell, 2005), 124.

17. For an insightful discussion of the charges of obscenity, their art world defense, and the democratic potential of the discussion of Mapplethorpe's work in the context of identity politics, see Dustin Kidd, "Sexual Politics in the Defense of Art: Culture Wars, Mapplethorpe, and the Road from Formalism to Identity Politics," *Politics of Change: Sexuality, Gender and Aging. Research in Political Sociology*, Vol. 13 (2004): 79–112.

18. Armey, quoted in Vance, "The War on Culture," 124.

19. See The Ninety-Second American Assembly, *The Arts and the Public Purpose*, Columbia University, NY, 1997. Cited in Michael Rushton, "Public Funding of Controversial Art," *Journal of Cultural Economics* (November 2000): 267.

20. For examples of the ways in which issues of AIDS and homosexuality were treated (or ignored) by the Reagan Administration as well as by prominent religious and cultural figures, see Douglas Crimp, "AIDS: Cultural Analysis/Cultural Activism," *October* (Winter 1987): 3–16, and Richard Meyer, "This Is to Enrage You: Gran Fury and the Graphics of AIDS Activism," in *But Is It Art? The Spirit of Art as Activism*, ed. Nina Felshin (Seattle: Bay Press, 1995), 51–83.

21. Vance, "The War on Culture," 126.

22. Negt and Kluge, *The Public Sphere and Experience*, 2.

23. Hilton Kramer and Samuel Lipman, "A Note on *The New Criterion*," *The New Criterion* (September 1982): 1. An adequate discussion of the debate surrounding the "postmodern" and "postmodernity" lies, unfortunately, beyond the scope of this article. For an analysis of the "postmodern condition," see David Harvey, *The Condition of Postmodernity: An Enquiry into the Origins of Cultural Change* (Oxford and New York: Blackwell, 1989), and Fredric Jameson, *Postmodernism, or, The Cultural Logic of Late Capitalism* (Durham: Duke University Press, 1991). For a discussion of art and postmodernity in particular, see Hal Foster, ed., *The Anti-Aesthetic: Essays on Postmodern Culture* (Seattle: Bay Press, 1983), and Brian Wallis, ed., *Art after Modernism: Rethinking Representation* (New York: New Museum of Contemporary Art and Boston: Godine Publishers, 1984).

24. Kramer and Lipman, "A Note on *The New Criterion*," 1, 5.

25. Ibid., 4–5.

26. Allan Bloom, "Our Listless Universities" (1982), reprinted in Sewall (ed.), *The Eighties: A Reader*, 233, 231.

27. Ibid., 230, 232.

28. The documents of the Art Workers' Coalition Open Hearing have recently been made available in the form of a photocopied booklet on the occasion of the exhibition "That Was Then... This Is Now" at P.S.1 Contemporary Art Center, New York, June 22–October 5, 2008. The text is also available online at www.primaryinformation.org.

29. Art Workers' Coalition, *Open Hearing* (photocopied, bound version of original documents), 13, 24–26, 93–94.

30. For a history of the AWC, see Lucy Lippard, "The Art Workers' Coalition: Not a History," in *Get the Message? A Decade of Art for Social Change* (New York: E. P. Dutton, 1984), 10–19.

31. For a selective history of such initiatives, see Julie Ault, ed., *Alternative Art New York, 1965–1985* (Minneapolis and London: University of Minnesota Press, 2002).

32. Bloom, "Our Listless Universities," 242.

33. Alexander Kluge, interview by Klaus Eder (1979), in Alexander Kluge, "On Film and the Public Sphere," *New German Critique—Special Double Issue on New German Cinema* 24/25 (Fall 1981–Winter 1982): 214. The interview is reprinted as Alexander Kluge, "The Public Sphere," in Wallis (ed.), *If You Lived Here*, 67–70.

34. Ibid.

35. See especially "Chapter 2: On the Dialectic Between the Bourgeois and the Proletarian Public Sphere," Negt and Kluge, *The Public Sphere and Experience*, 54–95.

36. Fredric Jameson, "On Negt and Kluge," *October* 46 (Fall 1988): 157.

37. Oskar Negt and Alexander Kluge, *Geschichte und Eigensinn* (Frankfurt: Zweitausendeins, 1981), 445.

38. See the group's website at http://www.abcnorio.org/about/about.html.

39. Cited in Julie Ault, "A Chronology of Selected Alternative Structures, Spaces, Artists' Groups, and Organizations in New York City, 1965–85," in Ault (ed.), *Alternative Art New York*, 59.

40. PAD/D could be considered a kind of umbrella group for 1980s art activism, as its members' affiliations span numerous organizations and collectives (past, present, and future), including the AWC, Artists Meeting for Cultural Change, Red Herring, Group Material, World War 3 Illustrated, Colab, and Carnival Knowledge. See Gregory Sholette, "A Collectography of PAD/D," unpublished manuscript available at www.gregorysholette.com. Sholette was one of the founding members of PAD/D. An

overview of the holdings in the PAD/D archive, now housed at the Museum of Modern Art, New York, can be found at www.moma.org/research/library/library_faq.html#padd.

41. Sholette, "A Collectography of PAD/D," 8.

42. Blake Stimson and Gregory Sholette, "Introduction: Periodizing Collectivism," in *Collectivism after Modernism: The Art of Social Imagination after 1945*, ed. Stimson and Sholette (Minneapolis and London: University of Minnesota Press, 2007), 10.

43. Group Material, "Calendar of Events" (1980), reprinted in Jan Avgikos, "Group Material Timeline: Activism as a Work of Art," in Felshin (ed.), *But Is It Art?*, 92.

44. Reprinted in ibid, 95.

45. Group Material, "Caution: Alternative Space" (handout, Sept. 1981).

46. Ibid.

47. Julie Ault, untitled lecture, as part of the 1996/97 series on "Public Art/Gates 2: La Generazione Delle Immagini," organized by *UnDo.Net Network for Contemporary Art*, http://www.undo.net/cgi-bin/openframe.pl?x=/Pinto/Eng/fault.htm.

48. Avgikos, "Group Material Timeline," 105.

49. Eberhard Knodler-Bunte, et al., "The Proletarian Public Sphere and Political Organization: An Analysis of Oskar Negt and Alexander Kluge's *The Public Sphere and Experience*," *New German Critique* (Winter 1975): 56.

50. Negt and Kluge, *The Public Sphere and Experience*, 107; Knodler-Bunte, et al., "The Proletarian Public Sphere and Political Organization," 65, respectively.

51. Negt and Kluge, *The Public Sphere and Experience*, 107.

52. From an unpublished Gran Fury fact sheet and exhibition history, cited in Richard Meyer, "This Is to Enrage You," 51.

53. Ibid., 52.

54. Negt and Kluge, *Geschichte und Eigensinn*, 484.

55. Deutsche, "Krzystof Wodiczko's *Homeless Projection* and the Site of Urban 'Revitalization,'" 87.

56. See ibid.

57. See, for example, Hal Foster, "The Artist as Ethnographer," in *The Return of the Real* (Cambridge, MA and London: MIT Press, 1996), 171–203; Kester, "Aesthetic Evangelists: Conversion and Empowerment in Contemporary Community Art"; Miwon Kwon, "Public Art as Publicity," in *In Place of the Public Sphere: On the Establishment of Publics and Counterpublics*, ed. Simon Sheikh (Berlin: b_books, 2005), 22–33.

58. Kwon, "Public Art as Publicity," 32.

59. Ibid.

60. Kluge, "The Public Sphere," 67-70.

61. See "The Workings of Fantasy as a Form of Production of Authentic Experience" in Negt and Kluge, *Public Sphere and Experience*, 32–38.

62. Negt and Kluge, *Public Sphere and Experience*, 37.

63. Hansen, "Foreword," xxxvi.

64. For a discussion of REPOhistory's work, see Gregory Sholette, "Authenticity Squared: REPOhistory CIRCULATION: Anatomy of an Activist, Urban Art Project," *The New Art Examiner* (December 1999): 20–23, 70–71.

65. As concepts of the "nation state," "the people," and "class" are being replaced by notions of "empire," "multitude," and "cultural paradigm," the categories of "public" and "private" appear to be ineffective and outdated analytic and strategic tools. In their latest publication, *Commonwealth*, for example, Michael Hardt and Antonio Negri seek to institute the "common" as a political project that replaces the "false alternatives" of public and private. Michael Hardt and Antonio Negri, *Commonwealth* (Cambridge, MA:

The Belknap Press of Harvard University Press, 2009), ix. Yet a proposal such as the "common" likewise must arise from a counterpublic practice—a practice that acknowledges the dangers of the ideal as a palpable, political reality to be opened up as a site of struggle in order to be overcome.

Form **1040** Department of the Treasury—Internal Revenue Service **1980** U.S. Individual Income Tax Return

For Privacy Act Notice, see Instructions | For the year January 1–December 31, 1980, or other tax year beginning _____ 1980, ending ____ 19

Use IRS label. Otherwise, please print or type.

Your first name and initial (if joint return, also give spouse's name and initial) | Last name | Your social security number

Present home address (Number and street, including apartment number, or rural route) | Spouse's social security no.

City, town or post office, State and ZIP code | Your occupation ▶ | Spouse's occupation ▶

Form 1040 (1980)

. . . over half your tax dollar . . .

Page 2

Tax Computation
(See Instructions on page 11)

32 Amount from line 31 (adjusted gross income) **32**

33 If you do not itemize deductions, enter zero . . . . } **33**
If you itemize, complete Schedule A (Form 1040) and enter the amount from Schedule A, line 41 . . . }
Caution: If you have unearned income and can be claimed as a dependent on your parent's return, check here ▶ ☐ and see page 11 of the Instructions. Also see page 11 of the Instructions if:
  • You are married filing a separate return and your spouse itemizes deductions, OR
  • You file Form 4563, OR
  • You are a dual-status alien

34 Subtract line 33 from line 32. Use the amount on line 34 to find your tax from the Tax Tables, or to figure your tax on Schedule TC, Part I **34**
Use Schedule TC, Part I, and the Tax Rate Schedules ONLY if:
  • Line 34 is more than $20,000 ($40,000 if you checked Filing Status Box 2 or 5), OR
  • You have more exemptions than are shown in the Tax Table for your filing status, OR
  • You use Schedule G or Form 4726 to figure your tax.
Otherwise, you MUST use the Tax Tables to find your tax.

35 Tax. Enter tax here and check if from ☐ Tax Tables or ☐ Schedule TC **35**

36 Additional taxes. (See page 12 of Instructions.) Enter here and check if from ☐ Form 4970, } **36**
☐ Form 4972, ☐ Form 5544, or ☐ Section 72(m)(5) penalty tax . . . }

37 Total. Add lines 35 and 36 . . . . ▶ **37**

Credits
(See Instructions on page 12)

38 Credit for contributions to candidates for public office . . . | 38
39 Credit for the elderly (attach Schedules R&RP) . . . . . | 39
40 Credit for child and dependent care expenses (attach Form 2441) . | 40
41 Investment credit (attach Form 3468) . . . . | 41
42 Foreign tax credit (attach Form 1116) . . . . | 42
43 Work incentive (WIN) credit (attach Form 4874) . . . . . | 43
44 Jobs credit (attach Form 5884) . . . . | 44
45 Residential energy credits (attach Form 5695) . . . . . | 45
46 Total credits. Add lines 38 through 45 . . . . **46**
47 Balance. Subtract line 46 from line 37 and enter difference (but not less than zero) . . ▶ **47**

Other Taxes
(Including Advance EIC Payments)

48 Self-employment tax (attach Schedule SE) **48**
49a Minimum tax. Attach Form 4625 and check here ▶ ☐ **49a**
49b Alternative minimum tax. Attach Form 6251 and check here ▶ ☐ **49b**
50 Tax from recomputing prior-year investment credit (attach Form 4255) **50**
51a Social security (FICA) tax on tip income not reported to employer (attach Form 4137) . . **51a**
51b Uncollected employee FICA and RRTA tax on tips (from Form W–2) **51b**
52 Tax on an IRA (attach Form 5329) **52**
53 Advance earned income credit (EIC) payments received (from Form W–2) **53**
54 Balance. Add lines 47 through 53 . . . . ▶ **54**

Payments
Attach Forms W–2, W–2G, and W–2P to front.

55 Total Federal income tax withheld . . . . | 55
56 1980 estimated tax payments and amount applied from 1979 return . . | 56
57 Earned income credit. If line 32 is under $10,000, see pages 13 and 14 of Instructions . . . . | 57
58 Amount paid with Form 4868 . . . . | 58
59 Excess FICA and RRTA tax withheld (two or more employers) | 59
60 Credit for Federal tax on special fuels and oils (attach Form 4136 or 4136–T) . . . . | 60
61 Regulated Investment Company credit (attach Form 2439) | 61
62 Total. Add lines 55 through 61 . . . . ▶ **62**

Refund or Balance Due

63 If line 62 is larger than line 54, enter amount OVERPAID . . . . ▶ **63**
64 Amount of line 63 to be REFUNDED TO YOU . . . . ▶ **64**
65 Amount of line 63 to be applied to your 1981 estimated tax . . ▶ | 65
66 If line 54 is larger than line 62, enter BALANCE DUE. Attach check or money order for full amount payable to "Internal Revenue Service." Write your social security number on check or money order . ▶ **66**
(Check ▶ ☐ if Form 2210 (2210F) is attached. See page 15 of Instructions.) ▶ $

Please Sign Here

Under penalties of perjury, I declare that I have examined this return, including accompanying schedules and statements, and to the best of my knowledge and belief, it is true, correct, and complete. Declaration of preparer (other than taxpayer) is based on all information of which preparer has any knowledge.

▶ Your signature | Date | ▶ Spouse's signature (if filing jointly, BOTH must sign even if only one had income)

Paid Preparer's Use Only

Preparer's signature and date ▶ | Check if self-employed ▶ ☐ | Preparer's social security no.
Firm's name (or yours, if self-employed) and address ▶ | E.I. No. ▶
| ZIP code ▶

Can you afford another war?

Photo 12.1. Micki McGee's individual taxpayer form intervention for PAD/D's Death and Taxes project (1981).

Source: Images courtesy of Micki McGee and Political Art Documentation/Distribution.

Photo 12.2.   Group Material, The People's Choice, Group Material Headquarters, New York, 1981
Source: Courtesy of Group Material

Photo 12.3.   Group Material, DA ZI BAOS, Union Square, New York, 1982.
Source: Courtesy of Group Material

Photo 12.4.   Kissing Doesn't Kill (1989).
Source: Courtesy of Gran Fury.

Photo 12.5. *The Homeless Projection: A Proposal for Union Square, 1986.* Installation
view: 49th parallel, Centre for Contemporary Canadian Art, New York
Source: © Krzysztof Wodiczko, courtesy Galerie Lelong, New York

Chapter 13

Date Rape and Sexual Politics

Caryn E. Neumann

The 1980s are the decade of Ronald Reagan, the Moral Majority, and AIDS. It is not a decade that appears on the surface to be particularly progressive with respect to women and sexuality. Yet date, or acquaintance, rape appeared on the public agenda for the first time in the 1980s and the decade witnessed numerous reforms that reflected a sea change in public attitudes toward rape. The criminalization of date rape shows that the conservative politics of the 1980s could not suppress a feminist movement that had become a powerful force in American society. Yet although the decade is a pivotal one, the pivot did not turn all the way around. Stereotypes about appropriate sexual behavior for men and for women remained strong and hampered efforts to convince the general public that date rape was real rape.

It is ironic that date rape would become an issue in the Reagan years. The 1980s were marked by an anti-feminist backlash in nearly every arena, especially popular culture and politics. However, by the 1980s, women had arrived on the public stage. Recent scholarship has indicated that feminism reworked the shape and mission of many mainstream organizations by the start of the decade.[1] The notorious backlash to women's rights in the 1980s may have reflected the omnipresence of women in public life, as Sara Evans has argued.[2] Women had become entrenched enough in positions of power to frighten those who feared equality between the sexes.

The backlash to feminism did succeed in creating a lasting portrayal of feminists as anti-male and anti-family but it did not prevent public mobilization on all feminist issues. Rape became a feminist issue in the 1970s.[3] In the 1980s, it became a subject of considerable attention as the public came to realize that the boy next door and the dangerous rapist could be the same individual. The recognition of date rape in the 1980s is a triumph for feminism.

History of Anti-Rape Activism

The battle against date rape began when feminists successfully challenged popular notions about rape. Activism against sexual assault grew out of the feminist mobilization of the 1960s that challenged sexism and discrimination against women in all aspects of society. The anti-rape movement of the 1970s focused on eliminating incorrect perceptions about rape victims to reduce the trauma of victims and to help prosecute rapists. This first wave of reform took aim at difficulties in proving the crime.

Rape, as the feminists of the 1970s stressed, was not a crime of sexuality and passion but one of violence and control. Susan Brownmiller, who wrote the history of rape in the landmark *Against Our Will* (1975), emphasized that rape has always been about men's control of women. Activists like Brownmiller lobbied to enact such reforms as the rape shield law, which limited the evidence of a victim's sexual past that could be admitted at trial and shifted responsibility for the assault away from the victim to the attacker. Brownmiller is also the first to coin the term, "date rape." In *Against Our Will,* she wrote, "Date rapes and rapes by men who have had prior relationships with their victims also contain elements of coercive authority that militates against decisive resistance."[4]

The feminist movement also sought to remove the marital exemption for rape, to develop a degree structure for rape, and to remove evidentiary roadblocks to prosecution such as corroboration requirements. (Corroboration requirements grew out of the advice offered by Lord Matthew Hale, a noted British judge of the seventeenth century, who warned that women tended to charge rape out of spite or embarrassment. Such requirements assumed that women could not be trusted and forced women to prove that they were not liars.) All of these anti-rape initiatives were an attempt to create victim-friendly rape laws that would force the legal system to take sexual assault and women seriously.

The flurry of activity led to a few legal successes for anti-rape activists in the 1970s but rape reform clearly remained in its infancy. In 1976, Nebraska became the first state to prohibit the rape of wives by husbands but most Americans only learned about marital rape in 1978. In that year, an Oregon jury acquitted John Rideout of raping his wife, Greta, after a heavily-publicized trial. In 1977, the U.S. Supreme Court banned the death penalty for rape cases on grounds that such a penalty is unconstitutional in *Coker v. Georgia.* The decision has been credited with increasing both the reporting of rapes and the successful prosecutions of rapists. Congress stepped in to address rape reform in 1978 by passing the federal Privacy Protection for Rape Victims Act, which prohibits the sexual history of a rape victim from being brought out in court. Many rape victims had refused to prosecute for fear of being cross-examined over their sexual history.[5]

By the end of the 1970s, the public had gained increasing knowledge about rape from the victim's point-of-view. In the next decade, rape reform would reach its pinnacle. The second wave of rape reform moved beyond issues of proof to questioning the very understanding of rape itself. Many of the anti-rape reforms of the 1980s would center upon the type of sexual assault termed "date rape" and would focus on the general public instead of Congress and state legislatures.

Recognizing Date Rape

The phrase "date rape" only entered the public consciousness in the 1980s. Date rape is a form of acquaintance rape in which a romantic relationship leads to a sexual attack. The prevalence of date rape is impossible to determine. Rape is considered by legal authorities to be the most underreported of felonies and accurate figures are notoriously difficult to compile.

In the 1980s, rape researchers estimated that only 10 to 50 percent of rapes were ever reported to authorities. In 1987, 609 rapes and 73 attempted rapes were reported to the Portland [Oregon] Women's Crisis Line. Seventy-five percent of these victims did not report the attacks to police. The Federal Bureau of Investigation (FBI) in the 1980s disputed the claim that rape victims were not reporting rapes. Harper Wilson, chief of the FBI's Uniform Crime Reporting Program stated in 1987, "If we're talking about common sense, you could come up with a lot of reasons for not reporting rape, but there are no figures that say that's actually happening. It's educated speculation [to think rapes are much higher than reported] but pure speculation."[6] The FBI compiled its crime statistics from data supplied by police, not rape crisis centers. The vast majority of reported rapes historically have been acquaintance rapes, thereby presumably making date rape into a fairly common type of sexual assault.

Date rape began to become a public concern chiefly because of research into the prevalence of rape. Psychologist Mary P. Koss is widely credited as the primary impetus for the recognition of the widespread nature of date rape.[7] When Koss began her research career in 1976, she sought to study "hidden rape" because the expression "date rape" had not yet entered the common lexicon. Koss recalled that no convincing evidence existed in the 1970s that "normal" men engaged in rape or exceptionally sexually aggressive behavior. P. B. Bart, one of the more prominent researchers into rape, indicated that 71 percent of the victims that she studied in 1980 had been raped by complete strangers. In another prominent study of the early 1980s, 57 percent of victims were attacked by complete strangers while only two percent were raped by dates.[8] At the same time, many legal authorities suspected that rapes, especially those involving acquaintances, were the most underreported of major crimes. Koss obtained federal funding in 1978 to conduct a survey of sexual aggression and victimization among 4,000 students at Kent State University in Ohio. The project, completed in 1982, formed the basis of the first national magazine article to address date rape when *Ms.* published it.[9]

With the survey, Koss became the first researcher to examine the attitudes held by women who had been raped. Many police officers and rape crisis counselors had adhered to a hypothesis that rape victims possessed a rape-supportive belief system or characteristics that rendered them uniquely vulnerable to being raped. These characteristics could include passivity, over-submissiveness, or insensitivity to social nuances. Other citizens followed the situational blame model in which sexual assault is made more likely by certain circumstances surrounding the assault, such as the response of the victim. Koss realized that choosing victims from police or crisis center files, as Bart and the other researchers had done, would miss the 50 to 90 percent of rape victims who had never reported being attacked. She looked for women who had experienced a sexual assault that would legally qualify as rape but who did not view themselves as rape victims. They were asked if they had experienced "forced sexual intercourse."[10]

As she had expected, Koss uncovered widespread date rape. She tried as much as possible to avoid overstating the problem. As she explained, "We did not ask women, 'Have you been raped?' We used legal definitions to write questions that specified the behaviors we were interested in." One of Koss's typical questions is: "Have you had sexual intercourse when you didn't want to because a man threatened or used some degree of physical force (twisting your arm, holding you down, etc.) to make you?" The survey did not include situations in which a man used only psychological tactics. The results confirmed Koss's belief that the FBI statistics on rape did not represent anywhere near the real number of rapes.[11]

A victim could be any woman. Among the college-age Ohio women who were surveyed in the study, 38 percent reported sexual victimization that met the legal definition of rape. Yet only four percent of these women had reported their sexual assault to the police. Of the women who reported forced sexual intercourse, 59 percent of women who reported the crime knew their attacker. Among the women who did not acknowledge being raped but who fit the definition of a rape victim, 100 percent knew their attacker. Koss found that 31 percent of acknowledged rape victims and 76 percent of unacknowledged rape victims were romantically involved with their attacker.[12]

Koss realized that, while a state-wide study had undeniable merit, only a nation-wide study would fully illuminate the magnitude of date rape. Koss, working with the *Ms.* Magazine Campus Project on Sexual Assault with funding by the Center for Antisocial and Violent Behavior of the National Institute of Mental Health, completed her national rape survey in 1985. She interviewed 6,159 college students at 32 schools across the country. Classes were chosen at random from course catalogues and the poll had a 98.5 participation rate. Koss famously found that one in four college women reported having been the subject of an attempted or completed rape. The subsequent report in a national magazine, *Ms.*, brought widespread notice of the date rape problem.[13]

Koss then decided to focus on the differences between stranger and acquaintance rape. She found that both types of rape have the same effect on the victim but only stranger rapes are commonly reported. This study, conducted in the

1985-1986 school year, queried 3,187 female college students that had been randomly selected at 32 colleges and universities. In general, date rapes were rated as less violent than stranger rapes. No differences were found in the levels of psychological symptoms between victims of stranger rape and victims of date rape. Only 27 percent of the women deemed to have been the victims of rape or attempted rape considered themselves to be crime victims. The study found that 84 percent of the rape victims knew their assailants, but only 5 percent told police that they had been attacked. Koss and other experts concluded that victims of sexual assaults did not report the attacks because of a "rape culture" that held women primarily responsible for the outcome of relationships with men, even when they are overpowered. [14]

The Bureau of Justice Statistics, a separate department from the FBI but also under the jurisdiction of the U.S. Department of Justice, provided numbers in the early 1980s that showed for every rape victim who knew her assailant, more than two did not. Koss effectively challenged these numbers. [15]

The Koss study raises the question of why date rape became a public issue in the 1980s if over 70 percent of date rape victims did not identify themselves as victims. In the 1970s, feminist activists sought to persuade the public to see women who had been raped as traumatized and innocent victims of a crime instead of sinners with a case of regret. Susan Brownmiller's *Against Our Will* played a pivotal role in this effort. By the 1980s, the focus of anti-rape activists had shifted to empowering women. With acquaintance rape as the most common type of rape, this form of sexual assault naturally received the most attention.

It is doubtful that the number of date rapes suddenly skyrocketed in the 1980s. If such attacks could be linked to a more sexually-promiscuous era, date rapes should have jumped with the sexual revolution of the 1960s. It is quite possible that such attacks did increase in the 1960s and 1970s but the reporting of such crimes lagged. The climate of the 1980s permitted activists to make date rape into a public issue, thereby increasing awareness of sexual victimization and demonstrating the need for increased rape prevention.

Date Rape *is* Real Rape

It is not just women who had trouble identifying forced sexual intercourse as rape. In the mid-1980s, three Texas A & M researchers asked male college students whether date rape could be justifiable. These young men rated rape as significantly more justifiable if the couple went to the man's apartment, if the woman asked the man out, and if the man paid all the dating expenses rather than splitting them with the woman. To these men, women were indicating that they wanted sex by failing to conform to traditional expectations of how women should behave. Women who traditionally allowed men to pay were interpreted as trading for sexual favors. None of the men would fit the stranger rapist role but all would match the description of a date rapist. Yet they did not see themselves as rapists but rather as men who had every right to take sex. [16]

American society socializes boys and girls to have different expectations. Males have been socialized to be aggressive, to be leaders, and make the decisions. Females have traditionally been taught to be yielding, passive, and submissive. These learned behaviors contribute to date rape.

Like Mary Koss, Susan Estrich aimed at both an academic and a popular audience. Estrich, an attorney, had personal experience with rape. During her senior year at Wellesley in 1974, she had been raped by an unknown assailant. She was attacked in an alley behind her apartment building in Boston as she was struggling out of a car while carrying two bags of groceries. The man held an ice pick to her throat and threatened to kill her. It took Estrich a long time to recover. In 1986, she wrote about the attack in the *Yale Law Journal*, using it as an introduction to an article that called for reform of the criminal justice system's casual handling of rape, particularly date rape. The article was the final piece in her bid for tenure at Harvard, and it was considered a risky choice because no one discussed rape. Larceny and assault received attention in law schools but rape simply did not seem important enough to merit any time. Estrich subsequently expanded the article into the best-selling 1987 book, *Real Rape.*[17]

As Estrich noted in *Real Rape,* many men believed that they could force women to have sex against their will without committing a rape. Date rapes were not always taken seriously because they did not fit the classic rape scenario of a stranger leaping out from the bushes. Both the public and the criminal justice system tended to minimize rapes that were not aggravated assaults and that "only" involved a man forcing a woman to have sex.[18]

For her efforts to combat date rape, Estrich faced the charge of being "unromantic." The allegation reflected the difficulty that many people experienced in seeing date rape as real rape. Estrich replied to the charge, "If a man is in doubt, he ought to ask. I don't think that's unromantic. And if the answer is no, he ought to stop. If that means we have a little less sex, so be it. We'll also have a lot less forced sex."[19]

Estrich urged victims and society to view rape as no different from something like a car theft. She explained, "If you leave your keys in the car and someone steals it . . . it's still car theft. It would be no defense in court that it was easy to steal the car. No one would say to the thief, 'Oh, in that case, you had a right to drive the car away.' It's as if, unlike every other crime, we were enforcing with rape some notion of contributory fault. Inviting a man up for a drink doesn't mean you consented to sex. And it doesn't mean he had a right to demand it."[20]

Estrich also challenged the long tradition in the law of fear that women will abuse the weapon of a rape charge. She pointed out that there are false reports of all crimes. In a 1987 interview, she said, "What we do with [false reports] is afford police and prosecutors substantial discretion to screen them out. And no one has ever proved that false complaints of rape are any more likely to be made than false complaints of any other crime. Given the humiliation involved, there's every reason to believe they will be fewer."[21]

At the tail end of the 1980s, legal philosopher Lois Pineau contributed to the project of rethinking rape. She defined date rape as nonconsensual sex that does not involve substantial physical injury or the threat of physical injury. With this definition, she addressed the type of assault for which there was least agreement about the appropriateness of criminalization. Pineau argued that both the first and second wave of legal reforms had not gone far enough to purge the law of deeply gendered injustice toward women. The reforms still required proof that the victim did not consent. They focused on what the man actually thought or what he reasonably could have thought. Pineau sought to aim the legal spotlight on the woman, to determine whether she had actually consented to the sexual encounter. She developed a model of "communicative sexuality" that included a requirement to respect the wishes of the other. Each partner should be trying to understand the aims of the other and to further those ends. Coerced sex is not respectful, therefore it is criminal.[22]

Pineau's work, acclaimed with an award by the American Philosophical Association in 1992, had limited influence in the 1980s and 1990s possibly because she left academia and the U.S. in 1992. Antioch College, a small residential liberal arts college in Yellow Springs, Ohio with a long history of progressive activism, used Pineau's theory to develop a sexual offense policy in 1992.[23] The policy, widely mocked by the media, sought to educate students that sex must be consensual. Students generally liked the policy, reporting that they found the resulting discussions on dates to be quite erotic.

Clearly, both men and women needed to be educated about date rape. Victims of such assaults suffered as much as victims of stranger rapes. Once the problem of date rape had been identified by researchers, anti-rape activists began to publicize its prevalence and to explore its effects.

Publicizing Date Rape

In the 1980s, reports of rape jumped substantially on college campuses. Rape quickly surpassed theft as the principal security concern at schools around the country. As attorney Michael Smith, author of *Coping with Crime on Campus*, explained to a reporter in 1989, "Rape is, of course, the single growing problem on campus. What has been so surprising is the failure to recognize the offense."[24]

Reports of rape increased because more women were identifying date rape as real rape. The mass media helped women to identify as victims of a sexual assault. Phil Donahue, host of one of the more popular daytime television talk shows, offered a fairly early discussion of date rape. In 1984, his show, *Donahue,* invited two date rape victims as well as the director of the Rape Treatment Center in Santa Monica, California and Chicago psychiatrist Helen Morrison to discuss the growing date rape problem. The speakers focused on the psychological trauma resulting from date rape as well as the social and legal difficulties that the crime presented. It is possible that *Donahue* informed many women for the first time that date rape was real rape. Women, particularly housewives, made up the vast bulk of *Donahue*'s audience. Four years after the episode aired, it became available for purchase by schools.[25]

Viewers who missed *Donahue* could learn about date rape through other shows. In 1988, the CBS production *Cagney and Lacey* regularly made the top ten list of the most popular shows on television. Part of the cop buddy genre, *Cagney and Lacey* broke from precedent with two female leads. Tyne Daly played Mary Beth Lacey, the married and stable New York City detective. Sharon Gless portrayed her partner, Christine Cagney, single and struggling with alcoholism.

In the episode that aired at 10 p.m. on January 5, 1988, the tough Cagney became the victim of a date rape. She went on a date with Brad Potter, a businessman who was smooth and elegant enough to impress Lacey. The evening shown to viewers seems like an ideal date. Potter brings Cagney to her door and, as a perfect gentlemen, respects her wish not to invite him in for a drink. He departs and then Lacey receives a phone call from Cagney. Potter has raped her. He returned to her apartment, claiming that his car battery had died and that he needed to telephone for assistance. (Cell phones were not commonplace in the 1980s.) Once inside the door, Potter attacked Cagney and threatened to kill her if she did not submit. Cagney then has to deal with the aftermath of the assault. She undergoes a sexual assault examination and has to cope with a fellow police officer who is openly skeptical about her story. As Cagney, who is clearly set up to be a model for every woman dealing with date rape, argues, "Damn it, it's my body. He had no right." The episode ended with Cagney returning to the bottle.[26]

Cagney behaved in a way that enabled women to relate to her. She was not attacked by a stranger leaping out of the proverbial bushes. She chose to go on a date with a man who seemed perfect. She did not behave in a promiscuous manner. She acted in a socially correct way yet she still became a traumatized victim of a rape. Television dramas can have as much ability to educate as documentaries. This drama clearly educated women and men that real rape could be date rape.

Cagney and Lacey had addressed rape prior to covering it in the "Don't I Know You?" episode. Previous stories focused on an acquaintance rape and a stranger rape of a police officer. Both attacks were shown through the eyes of a third person. In this episode, suggested by Gless and based on interviews with a rape treatment center director, *Cagney and Lacey* showed the rape through the eyes of a main character to give the issue more impact.[27]

A few months earlier, television producers had offered a drama for teenagers about date rape. The episode of "New Image Teens" that aired nationally on PBS in 1987 used members of a teenage theatrical troupe in San Diego to dramatize issues of importance to other youths. According to publicity materials sent to reporters, the episode titled "Date Rape: 'No' Isn't Always Enough," focused on "honest communication" but also happened to explicitly center upon sexual assault. In San Diego, a 30-minute televised discussion of date rape between the coordinator of the local rape crisis center, a psychiatric social worker, and a detective from the San Diego Police Department sex crimes unit followed the showing of the program.[28]

The show addressed different perceptions of rape. It opened with a young man, played by Peter Smith, who is regaling his buddies in a locker room about his Saturday night exploits. Then, the program shifts to a young woman, played by Amy Bamberger, who states that she started screaming when the same young man ripped her blouse. The young man boasts and brags while the young woman mourns, "I will never be the person I was before – never, ever." She concludes with, "He didn't even think of me as a person. I was just a thing." Another segment in the program shows Elizabeth Petteway portraying an anguished teenage girl who tells her mother that she has been raped by her boyfriend. The character later tries to tell a friend about the trauma of the attack.[29]

"New Image Teens" sought to promote discussion and it undoubtedly did so with this episode. The difference in how the evening went according to the young man and the young woman is striking, as it was meant to be. The episode underlines the point that anti-rape activists were focusing heavily on public education and that young adults were particularly at risk for date rape.

The Challenges of Date Rape Education

Date rapes are a particular problem where there are large dating pools, such as high schools and college campuses. Women who re-entered the dating population in middle age after a divorce were also quite vulnerable. Most of the educational efforts, however, focused on teenagers and young adults. In 1984, the National Center for Prevention and Control of Rape reported that date rape victims were mostly women between the ages of 15 and 24.[30]

By 1985, date rapes had been reported at small schools like Carlow College in Pittsburgh as well as larger, elite schools such as Yale, Stanford, Cornell, and Columbia. A 1984 survey at Brown University in Rhode Island found that among 500 students, 16 percent of the women had been forced to have sexual intercourse by men whom they either knew or were dating. Eleven percent of Brown men said that they had forced a woman to have intercourse. Officials at the Rape Treatment Center at the Santa Monica [California] Hospital Medical Center noticed a dramatic increase in the number of women reporting assaults on campus. In 1987, the center saw 65 more rape victims than it had served in 1986 with 16 of those women reporting attacks in a six-week period. To college administrators, rape had suddenly become a growing problem. As psychologist Mary P. Koss explained, however, "In the past, these cases would not have come to light. But today, more women are willing to recognize that the problem exists."[31]

The furor sparked by the sudden recognition of date rape prompted colleges and universities to hold discussions on the topic to teach young women to be clear about their intentions and young men to seek explicit consent for sexual activities. The discussions expanded into various programs and helped make common the phrase, "No means no." Mary Virga, head of the University of California at San Diego's Rape Prevention Education Program pointed out that date rape is more common than people realize and, as a result, "Universities throughout the country are realizing this and are setting up prevention programs."[32]

Part of the problem in reducing date rapes involved removing the standard image of a rapist from the minds of students. A Carlow College junior had been attacked by a "sweet, but not macho" boy that she met at a fraternity party. As Anne Sadler, a legal advocate at the Pittsburgh Action Against Rape crisis center explained in 1985, "Women are hesitant to think that someone they met in an English class or at a fraternity party might assault them. We tend to visualize rapists as wearing stocking masks and jumping out at women from dark alleys." Some date rapes came at the hands of boyfriends that women had known for months or even years.[33]

In a case at the University of Florida, a student brought his girlfriend to the campus psychologist to be "fixed." He explained that she was "frigid" and did not enjoy sex. When Claire Walsh, the psychologist involved and also the director of the campus Sexual Assault Recovery Service, spoke with the woman, she discovered that the boyfriend had been raping her on a daily basis. The boyfriend did not categorize the incidents as rape. Walsh elaborated, "He was not at all interested in her sexual response or emotional well-being, or in interacting with this young woman on an intimate level. What he was interested in was fulfilling his male destiny to score and be sexually sophisticated." The young woman was shocked when Walsh suggested that she had been raped since "of course, nice girls don't get raped" and she was a "nice girl." However, the woman had said "no." She did not want to have sex with her boyfriend. She also never returned to Walsh's office. Walsh speculated that she might have graduated into marriage and become a battered spouse.[34]

Women had trouble identifying themselves as possible victims of a sexual attack because of the perception that only bad girls got themselves into such situations. Crimes did not happen to good girls. "People have this vision of [a date rape] only happening to a sexy, nubile 16-year-old in hot pants, but it's more likely to be a good child out on a date with someone she knows and her family knows," said Pam McDonnell in 1985. McDonnel co-directed New York City's Safety and Fitness Exchange (SAFE), which specialized in crime prevention and self-defense.[35]

Women also tended to blame themselves for date rape attack since it was not a stranger rape. The Carlow College student wondered whether her blouse was too low-cut or whether she had said or done something to provoke the rape. Other women believed that they were partly responsible for the attack because they had exercised poor judgment by getting into a car or leaving a party with a man. Darleen C., a 35-marine biologist suffered a rape in the early 1980s and blamed herself. "I never thought about reporting," she explained in 1988, "because I was sure it was my fault... I was stupid. I trusted him and he raped me."[36]

Laurie Ford handled many date rape cases as director of San Diego's Rape Crisis Center in the 1980s. She observed that victims tended to blame themselves for not being more assertive or not realizing that a date would lead to rape. "The victim is very embarrassed and the whole situation is so horrible that she just wants to forget it," Ford said in 1985. She added, "At first a man seems real nice to a woman until he gets her alone and isolated someplace. And then his personality radically changes."[37] Ford's comments highlight the trauma suffered by the victim and the planning of the attacker. In essence, she portrays date rape as a real crime.

Date rape victims who do not acknowledge that they have been raped are often perplexed when they suffer rape trauma syndrome. A psychological and physical illness suffered by many rape victims for up to four years after a rape, the symptoms of rape trauma included nausea, paranoia, sleeplessness, nightmares, and a wide variety of other abnormal behavior. "The bottom line is that you don't act like that – having nightmares, trauma – unless something is wrong. That doesn't happen with consenting sex," declared Ford.[38]

The inability of women to recognize a date rape as a crime hindered prosecution. In 1981, Carol, a 26-year-old attorney, presumably had some familiarity with the laws about sexual assault. Nevertheless, when raped by a date, she hesitated for five days before going to the police. The man had spent 10 hours alternating between raping Carol and strangling her. Carol had such a strong fear of being killed that she did not fight back. Yet, she did not go to the police. She later related, "All I wanted was to either pretend it hadn't happened or that I was concerned about getting him help. I was in shock. I later realized I was feeling a lot of guilt – as though I had caused it." Carol's delay in contacting the authorities plus the character references provided by the accused prompted the U.S. attorney to decline to prosecute.[39]

The Trouble with Men

Many men had trouble seeing themselves as rapists when they had forced a woman to have sex. They simply believed that they had been the dominant aggressor in a date. Dr. Mark Stevens, a clinical psychologist at The Ohio State University, explained in 1988 that "Some men have the capacity to fool themselves into thinking that date rape is normal behavior. They believe the myth that when she says no, she really means yes." Mary Otto, a crime prevention representative with the Multnomah County district attorney's office in Oregon echoed Stevens' statement later that same year. She stated, "[Men] don't think it's rape. They're acting out the role society has given him."[40]

Popular culture reinforced the belief that a man should not take "no" for an answer. For decades, the media had perpetuated the idea that a woman, despite her initial protests, will ultimately succumb to a man's advances. The classic example is Scarlett O'Hara in "Gone With the Wind" who kicks and screams when a drunken Rhett Butler carries her up the stairs to the bedroom but then is shown awakening the next morning with a contented sigh.

"Motley's Crew," a popular nationally-syndicated comic strip, appeared in newspapers throughout the 1980s. The comic, drawn by Ben Templeton and Tom Forman, focused on the blue-collar family of Mike and Mabel Motley. The comic strip published on September 12, 1988 featured a man who was rewarded for not accepting "no" from a pretty woman. The joke, oft-repeated before and after it appeared in the comic strip, perpetrated the myth that women want to be raped and that it is acceptable to refuse to believe what a woman says to a man.[41]

Date rape accounts include numerous examples of men who would not take "no" for an answer. In a heavily publicized case, Michael P. McCoy, age 22, was charged in December 1987 with the date rape of a female student on the University of California at Berkeley campus. The instance became the first reported date rape at UC Berkeley. McCoy had met the woman at a fraternity house gathering during a drinking party. According to the woman, McCoy walked her to her dormitory and they kissed. The woman told police that McCoy wanted more than a kiss and, when she refused his advances, he raped her. Mary, a freshman at the University of California at San Diego, had a similar story about being raped on a date by a senior on the football team in the early 1980s. She agreed to go back to his dorm room and necking soon led to the football player lifting Mary on to his bed. She realized that he intended to have sex with her regardless of her resistance. Mary related, "He was like, 'Great! I'm gonna get one more trophy.' "[42]

Such men reflected the notion put forth by the media that women were nothing more than pieces of meat. A woman had no value other than her body. Neil Malamuth, chair of Communications at the University of California at Los Angeles in 1985, explained that the date rapist "usually sees himself as more masculine than other men and part of that masculinity involves forced sexual experiences."[43] These rapists did not see themselves as rapists but as simply manly men.

Laura X, director of the National Clearinghouse on Marital and Date Rape, offered a slightly different explanation for the prevalence of date rape. She saw a monetary explanation for rape rather than just a refusal to accept a woman's decision. In 1989, she explained that, "What happens is that a guy pays for dinner, the movies, and he thinks you get what you get in marriage. They see [a date] as a mini, quasi-marriage.[44] Laura X's explanation reflected her uneasiness with the place of women in American society as well as her focus on ending the legal exemption for marital rape. While many states criminalized rape within marriage in the 1980s, the last state to do so only enacted legislation in 1994.[45]

The long-existing marital rape exemption emphasized that men deserved sex from women. Cultural habits underlined the power differential between the genders. The dynamics of a traditional date in which the man asks the woman, decides where to go, pays for the entertainment, and provides the transportation places power in the hands of the man. Jennifer Weiss, crime prevention representative for the Portland [Oregon] Police Bureau's sexual assault prevention program spoke to a reporter in 1988 about the sudden spike in reported sexual assaults in Multnomah County. In 1987, there were 697 reported rapes – 20 percent more than in 1986. The majority of attacks were acquaintance rapes, with 73 percent of the victims knowing their attackers. Weiss blamed the attacks on the power differential in a date in which the man held the "power chips". She elaborated, "He can say, 'I spent all this money on you. You're in my car. You agreed to go out with me. What did you think was going to happen?' "[46]

Children are a good indicator of the values and attitudes held by adults. From February to December 1987, the Rhode Island Rape Center surveyed 1,700 sixth through ninth graders regarding their attitudes toward rape and the abuse of women. The results of the survey indicated that children believed that rape could be acceptable, that women owed sex to men regardless of their own feelings, and that it is the woman's fault if rape and/or sexual abuse occur. Twenty-four percent of the boys and 16 percent of the girls said that a man had the right to force a woman to have sex with him if he has spent money on her. Sixty-five percent of the boys and 47 percent of the girls agreed that a man had the right to force a woman to have sex if they had been dating for more than six months. Thirty-one percent of the boys and 32 percent of the girls said that it would not be improper for a man to rape a woman who has had previous sexual experiences. The author of the survey, Jacqueline Jackson Kikuchi, concluded that such attitudes could lead to date rapes.[47]

The more relaxed sexual mores of the 1980s also undoubtedly led to rapes. Many men came to expect sex as a normal part of a date. In the 1950s, good girls always said "no." After the sexual revolution, many good girls said "yes." Laurie Ford, head of the San Diego Rape Crisis Center, blamed the frequency of date rapes on societal changes. In 1985, she told a reporter from the *San Diego Union-Tribune* that the line between consenting sex and acquaintance rape is a fine one because "society has no rules."[48]

Men struggled with what society expected from them. Ford noted that, "There are a lot of men who feel that sex [at the end of a date] is expected of them, or he's a wimp or a homosexual."[49] Lack of communication between men and women when setting the ground rules for a date undoubtedly contributed to date rapes, a point made by philosopher Lois Pineau.

Some men believed that they deserved sex, especially if they had become sexually aroused by kissing and caressing. A somewhat informal survey among 179 male and female students at the University of South Florida in the mid-1980s revealed that 16 percent of respondents agreed that there were occasions when it was acceptable for a man to force a woman to have sex. (The survey did not distinguish between male and female respondents.) A 22-year-old woman who wrote to newspaper advice columnist Ann Landers in 1985 asked, "What has happened to good old-fashioned necking? . . .I'm the kind of girl who will go to first, second, or third base. And then I like to say 'good night' and go home." Landers responded that she "didn't know any men in their early 20s who are satisfied with first, second, or third base." [50] The response reinforced stereotypes about male sexual aggression but also indicated that the parameters of acceptable sexual behavior had shifted to the point that sexual intercourse had become a socially acceptable part of casual dating..

Many men also did not understand the seriousness of a rape and, by extension, why a woman would not get enjoyment from sex. Lieutenant Bob Staehle of the University of South Florida Police Department found it difficult to educate men about date rape in the late 1980s. After leading seminars for women, Staehle realized that no one spoke to men about being part of the solution. He devised a seminar in late 1986 to educate men about rape but discovered that few men's groups wanted to hear his message. In 18 months, he delivered the seminar to only five groups of men. He spoke to an average of one group of women per week. In 1987, the University of South Florida served 24,000 students. Staehle explained at the time that his biggest problem was in getting men to realize how devastating a rape is to a woman. He said, "It's so hard for a man to understand how intercourse can be anything but pleasurable."[51]

At the University of Iowa, the coordinator of the Rape and Victim Advocacy Program in 1987 had also heard the argument that a woman sent positive signals throughout a date and therefore the sex that resulted could not be rape. Karla Miller replied, "Fair or not, she has a right to say "no." It is never the victim's fault and there are no exceptions to that. None. I don't care if someone is alone in a Laundromat, drunk, at 2 a.m., in a miniskirt. You may be asking for approval, you may be asking for attention, but you're not asking someone to have sex with you against your will."[52]

Despite the reforms, ambivalence remained about the definition of a victim. In the 1980s, women were seen as victims of rape and men as the perpetrators. Few people acknowledged that men could be victims and that women could be perpetrators or that men could sexually assault other men. The Federal Bureau of Investigation's Crime Statistics identified rape as a crime against a woman. State laws generally did so as well. Oregon's state law is typical. While men could not be raped under Oregon's legal definition of the crime, an assailant could be charged with felony-level sodomy and sexual abuse.[53]

There is some evidence that men were also the victims of date rape but this particular aspect of sexual assault received practically no attention from researchers or the public. In 1987, a poll of 623 male students at the University of South Dakota indicated that 16 percent of the men had been forced to have sex on dates with women who locked them in cars or "blackmailed" them until they submitted. A follow-up study clarified that half of these South Dakota men said that their dates used psychological pressure to seduce them while another 26 percent cited physical tactics too. The researcher, Professor of Psychology Cindy Struckman-Johnson, cautioned that date rape is more widespread and traumatic for women but men could be victims too even if they cannot be coerced by physical force alone to have sex with a woman. The South Dakota study earned a mention in the June 1987 edition of *Glamour*, a magazine that aimed at young adult women with a mix of fashion advice and serious journalism, but apparently went no farther.[54]

Date Rape Education

Could education change attitudes toward rape? Jacqueline Jackson Kikuchi, who had interviewed children about their attitudes toward rape in her capacity as a staff member of the Rhode Island Rape Crisis Center, found that rape education did have a dramatic impact. Kikuchi conducted rape education seminars in 1987 with sixth to ninth graders, a substantial number of whom had initially believed that rape could be justified. After participating in the workshops, less than 25 percent of the children thought that rape or forced kissing was appropriate in any situation.[55]

Students at every level became the focus of date rape education in the 1980s. Unlike other potential crime victims, students formed an easy-to-locate population that could be forced to sit still and listen. In 1988, district attorneys in Washington County, Oregon began visiting middle and high schools to educate students about date rape. They recognized that confusion surrounds sexual conduct and hoped to make young people aware of the date rape issue before it was too late. Each attorney would present a scenario in which a couple has been dating for six months. The young man pesters the young woman about engaging in sexual intercourse. The woman says no but does not forcefully resist the man when he insists on completing the act. A crime has been committed. "Once a female says no, a curtain comes down," stated Rick Knapp, one of the deputy district attorneys.[56]

Colleges and universities responded to the date rape epidemic by focusing on education. At the University of Wisconsin, a student group called Men Stopping Rape held a series of workshops across campus in 1988 to allow men and women to act out the frustrations that they experienced while on a date. Many of the frustrations involved the difficulties of figuring out what the other person was thinking. Ohio State taught women how to recognize a potential date rapist and how to fend off an attack.

The Ford Foundation, one of the organizations that developed a feminist agenda in the 1970s, financed a guide on date rape that was produced by the Association of American Colleges (AAC) in 1987. The first copies of "Friends Raping Friends: Could It Happen to You?" went to college presidents and deans. As Bernice R. Sandler, co-author of the guide and executive director of the AAC's Project on the Status and Education of Women explained, "Date rape is one of the most controversial issues on campus today. It occurs on virtually all campuses, small or large, private or public, rural or urban. Studies have indicated that one in eight college women has been raped by someone she knew. The sooner date rape is recognized as a serious problem, the sooner people can do something about it."[57]

The AAC guide addressed common views about women that were likely to lead to date rape. It warned women to watch out for men who did not listen to women since, "Such men generally have little respect for women and would be more likely to hear 'no' as meaning 'convince me.'" It urged women to avoid men who ignored personal space boundaries, acted in an excessively possessive manner, and accused women who resisted their sexual overtures of being up-tight. It advised that men who have wrong or unrealistic ideas about women, such as "women are meant to serve men," would be more likely not to take a woman's objections to sex seriously.[58]

The guide concluded with tips for women about avoiding situations that might lead to date rape. The suggestions are notable because they are clearly influenced by the feminist movement. Women were advised to take control of their bodies and take charge of their lives. The suggestions show how embedded feminist thought had become in mainstream society by the 1980s.

In these tips, the AAC told women to examine their feelings about sex. The guide warned that, "Many women have been socialized to believe that sex means that they will be swept away with the emotion of the moment or that they can 'make out' and then decide whether to say 'yes' or 'no' to sex later. The problem with this kind of thinking is that it gives too much control to the other person." Feminism is about empowering women.[59]

Women were told to abandon subordination to men. The guide included these lines: "Be independent and aware on your dates. Do not be totally passive. Do have opinions on where to go. Do think about appropriate places to meet (not necessarily at your room or his) and, if possible, pay your own way or suggest activities that do not cost any money." Feminism is not about surrendering to men.[60]

Lastly, the guide reminded women to set sexual limits. The authors wrote, "It is your body and no one has the right to force you to do anything you do not want to do. If you do not want someone to touch you or kiss you, for example, you can say, 'Take your hands off me,' or 'Don't touch me,' or 'If you don't respect my wishes right now, I'm leaving.'" Feminism is about respect for women.[61]

The programs sponsored by colleges typically only touched on pieces of the date rape program. A videotape produced by the Auburn University Rape Awareness Committee that received wide national distribution is representative. In the 25-minute video, a psychologist interviews a student who has been the victim of a date rape. Many schools likely used the Auburn video as the center-piece of their date rape educational efforts. The University of Maryland Baltimore County showed a 20-minute videotape, "Not a Sanctuary" to every freshman via the university's cable television circuit. Stanford University's Rape Education Project and Towson State University in Towson, Maryland both distributed pamphlets to students that listed safety tips and telephone numbers for university police.[62]

No college or university had a comprehensive program, as officials at the Rape Treatment Center at the Santa Monica [California] Hospital Medical Center realized when they surveyed schools. The Center distributed a booklet that recommended that colleges modify living arrangements if the victim and the accused live in the same dormitory; that schools develop a statement of policy condemning rape, including that date rape will not be tolerated, and that colleges teach rape prevention strategies at freshman orientation.[63] It is not known how many schools adopted the recommendations.

In an echo of the 1970s, Dorothy Siegel of Towson State explained that her university was engaged in "consciousness-raising."[64] The phrase referred to the process by which a woman recognized that she had been a victim of sexism and that sexism was endemic in the United States. In the 1980s, with the women's movement having reached a mature state, women were quick to recognize sexism. The anti-rape movement of the era helped alert many women to the fact that they had been the victims of a real crime and that real rape was endemic in the United States.

Challenges with Combatting Date Rape

Such programs may have reinforced a blame-the-victim mentality by educating women about rape rather than stopping men from raping. Colleges, with a few notable exceptions such as Florida State University and the University of South Florida, tended to aim date rape prevention programs at women. Such an emphasis fit a sexually conservative viewpoint that good girls do not put themselves into situations that can lead to date rape. This viewpoint also assumes that normal men will "take advantage" of a date when she is too drunk to resist or consent. Such programs put the burden of preventing acquaintance rape on women, thereby making the victims responsible for the crimes committed against them.

By shifting the blame for rape from the attacker to the victim, such programs may have had the unintended effect of reducing the reporting of date rapes. At the National Conference on Campus Violence, held in 1989 at the University of Maryland, Laura X advised that many college women raped by their dates did not report the attacks because they blamed themselves for losing control.[65]

Remaining Challenges

By the end of the 1980s, rape activists still struggled to persuade prosecutors and juries to regard date rapes as serious crimes. The criminal courts continued to be biased against rape victims who knew their attackers, especially when the accused attacker looked respectable and middle class rather than like the mythological lunatic stalker that women had long been taught to fear and that society felt comfortable in punishing. The thoroughness of a police investigation, the choice of whether or not to prosecute a charge, the likelihood that the defendant would be convicted, and the likelihood of incarceration have all been shown to vary significantly along acquaintance rape/stranger rape lines. As a result, a number of rape crisis counselors in the 1980s did not encourage date rape victims to press charges.[66] They feared that the women would be traumatized by the legal experience after already being traumatized by their attackers.

As a result of the difficulties of proving date rape, such attacks were rarely reported to the authorities. If a victim did report an assault, rape would most likely be charged and tried only when the following conditions were met: a prompt report to the police, the existence of witnesses who could testify to similar crimes committed by the suspect, physical injury to the survivor, and corroboration of the individual's story. To increase prosecution of date rape, North Dakota became the first state to pass a date rape law in 1987. Prior to the passage of this legislation, a North Dakota man who raped a female acquaintance could escape being charged with a felony if the victim was a "voluntary companion" or if the couple had a previous sexual relationship.

Some women also began taking their cases to civil court instead of criminal court. In civil court, the burden of proof is somewhat less onerous and, unlike in criminal court, defendants can be forced to testify. A victim can win with less than a unanimous jury. The men involved were not the only ones being sued. Third party lawsuits were increasing as businesses, universities, and fraternities were held responsible for rapes that occurred on their premises or during events that they had sponsored. Fear of litigation prompted some of these institutions, especially colleges and universities, to offer educational programs about date rape.

Despite putting the burden of preventing date rape upon women, most of the educational programs reflect a progressive view of women. Although education efforts do not always link date rape awareness programs to the feminist movement, each program is explicitly about empowering women. The clear implication is that women have the right to control their own bodies. The feminism is not explicit but it is certainly implicit and such subtlety reflects how deeply feminism had become entrenched in the 1980s.

Lastly, there is the question of whether the fear of AIDS influenced the attitudes of various authorities towards date rape. AIDS, which became a widespread public health concern in the 1980s, does not appear in news accounts of rapes in this decade. It is probable that most people still viewed AIDS as the "gay disease" and that heterosexual transmission of the virus simply did not register as a likelihood. People recognized that sexually transmitted diseases could be spread through rape but such a disease was presumably spread only by that stranger rapist who jumped out of the shadows to attack a woman walking down a dark alley. The boy next door did not have disease.

Conclusion

The efforts to educate the public about rape and to improve the security of female students continued into the 1990s. One of the most significant pieces of legislation pertaining to rape arose from a 1986 attack by a stranger upon Jeanne Ann Clery at Lehigh University in Bethlehem, Pennsylvania in 1986. A fellow student, Joseph Henry, who was unknown to Clery, entered her dormitory through a series of doors propped open by pizza boxes. He entered Clery's room, then raped and beat her before strangling her to death to prevent Clery from identifying him later. Clery's parents sued Lehigh and raised the legal issue of the university's responsibility and obligation for student safety. Although Lehigh denied responsibility, it settled out of court. Clery's family used the money to establish Security on Campus, which focuses on increasing campus security and victim assistance. They also lobbied for federal laws, including the 1990 Crime Awareness and Campus Security Act, also known as the Clery Act after Jeanne Clery.

At the time the Clery Act passed, only about a fifth of college and university campuses reported rape statistics. The legislation forced schools receiving federal funds to maintain a daily log of all reported and alleged crimes, to give timely notification of crimes that threaten campus safety, to publish a consolidated security report, and notify all students of the existence of that report. The report must include procedures for victims of sexual offenses. The legislation gave universities who needed to attract students a clear financial interest in reducing all types of crime, including sexual ones. However, organizations such as the National Organization for Women have faulted campus administrators for counseling students against reporting rapes to civil authorities and then addressing such crimes as an administrative matter within the university.

The movement of the debate from whether date rape is a problem to how to best protect women from such sexual crimes indicates the success of the 1980s anti-rape activists. They had advanced rape education. Rape had become part of the public agenda. Rapists were no longer strangers lurking in shadows but could also be fellow students sitting in an English class. The change in public thinking reflects a major change in attitudes toward rape. Date rapists were no longer simply decent young men with strong sex drives. They had become public embarrassments, who shamed universities in crime reports and constituted a public menace.

The recognition of date rape as real rape reflected the power of women. It reflected the power of the women's movement. In 1985, a psychology professor at the University of California at Los Angeles made the point to a reporter that the women's movement had contributed to the increased attention given to date rape. Jacqueline Goodchild said that more people were willing to speak openly about female sexuality. She added, "Now people are talking about this, as well as marital rape. Women are coming forward and that's due to the notion of equal power and egalitarianism."[67]

Yet the concerns of some women about sexual coercion continued to be dismissed, as they had been in the past. Society as a whole still had trouble recognizing that a woman had the right to control her body and the right to be heard when she said "no." The anti-rape movement shows the breadth and depth of feminism within American society in the decade of the 1980s. It also shows that much work remained to be done in the 1990s and beyond.

Notes

Angela Yesh, Marianne Cotugno, John Heyda, and Margo Lambert generously read and commented on a draft of this chapter.

1. Susan M. Hartmann, *The Other Feminists: Activists in the Liberal Establishment.* (New Haven, CT: Yale University Press, 1998), Susan Levine, *Degrees of Equality: The American Association of University Women and the Challenge of Twentieth Century Feminism* (Philadelphia: Temple University Press, 1995), Caryn E. Neumann, "Status Seekers: Long-Established Women's Organizations and the Women's Movement, 1945 to the 1970s" (Ph.D. diss., The Ohio State University, 2006).

2. Sara M. Evans, "Feminism in the 1980s: Surviving the Backlash." In Gil Troy and Vincent J. Cannato, eds. *Living in the Eighties* (New York: Oxford University Press, 2009), 86-88.

3. Maria Bevacqua, *Rape on the Public Agenda: Feminism and the Politics of Sexual Assault.* (Boston: Northeastern University Press, 2000), Susan Brownmiller, *Against Our Will: Men, Women, and Rape.* (New York: Simon and Schuster, 1975), Judith Ezekiel, *Feminism in the Heartland.* (Columbus: The Ohio State University Press, 2002).

4. Brownmiller, 257. The first mention of date rape in the popular media is apparently a 1978 *New York Times* article. See Leslie Maitland, "Conviction Reversed in 'Date' Rape Case," *New York Times,* May 14, 1978, sec. A, 30.

5. Leigh Bienen, "National Developments in Rape Reform Legislation," *Women's Rights Law Reporter* 6 (1980): 170-213.

6. Mary P. Koss, "The Scope of Rape: Implications for the Clinical Treatment of Victims," *Clinical Psychologist* 36 (1983): 88-91; Bobbie Hasselbring, "Most Rape Victims Locally and Nationally Assaulted by Friends, Acquaintances; Old Sex Roles Partly Blamed," *The Oregonian,* September 12, 1988, sec. B, 1; David Streitfeld, " 'Date Rape': The Damage Rises," *Washington Post,* February 24, 1987, sec. C, 5.

7. David G. Curtis, "Perspectives on Acquaintance Rape," *American Academy of Experts in Traumatic Stress,* 1997 http://www.aaets.org/article13.htm (Accessed November 2, 2009).

8. P.B. Bart, "A Study of Women Who Both Were Raped and Avoided Rape," *Journal of Social Issues* vol. 34, no. 4 (1981): 123-137; Resick, P.A., Calhoun, K.S., Atkeson, B.M., and Ellis, E.M, "Social Adjustment in Victims of Sexual Assault," *Journal of Consulting and Clinical Psychology* 49 (1981): 705-712.

9. Robin Warshaw, *I Never Called It Rape: The Ms. Report on Recognizing, Fighting and Surviving Date and Acquaintance Rape.* (New York: Harper & Row, 1988), 189.

10. Mary P. Koss, "The Hidden Rape Victim: Personality, Attitudinal, and Situational Characteristics," *Psychology of Women Quarterly* 9 (1985): 193-212.

11. David Streitfeld, " 'Date Rape': The Damage Rises," *Washington Post,* February 24, 1987, sec. C, 5.

12. Koss, "The Hidden Rape Victim," 197, 206.

13. Mary P. Koss, "Date Rape: The Story of an Epidemic and Those Who Deny It," *Ms. Magazine,* October 1985, 10-14.

14. Mary P. Koss, "Hidden Rape: Sexual Aggression and Victimization in a National Sample of Students in Higher Education." In A.W. Burgess, ed. *Rape and Sexual Assault* (New York: Garland Publishing: 1988), 3-25; Mary P. Koss, "Stranger and Acquaintance Rape: Are There Differences in the Victim's Experience?" *Psychology of Women Quarterly* 12 (1988): 1-24.

15. David Streitfeld, " 'Date Rape': The Damage Rises," *Washington Post,* February 24, 1987, sec. C, 5.

16. Charlene L. Muehlenhard, Debra E. Friedman, and Celeste M. Thomas, "Is Date Rape Justifiable?: The Effects of Dating Activity, Who Initiated, Who Paid, and Men's Attitudes Toward Women," *Psychology of Women Quarterly* vol. 9, no. 3 (1985): 297-310.

17. Caryn E. Neumann, *Sexual Crime* (Santa Barbara, CA: ABC-CLIO, 2010), 170; Susan Estrich, *Real Rape: How the Legal System Victimizes Women Who Say No.* Cambridge, MA: Harvard University Press, 1987.

18. Estrich, *Real Rape.*

19. Estrich is quoted in this article. David Streitfeld, " 'Date Rape': The Damage Rises," *Washington Post,* February 24, 1987, sec. C, 5.

20. David Streitfeld, " 'Date Rape': The Damage Rises," *Washington Post,* February 24, 1987, sec. C, 5.

21. David Streitfeld, "'Date Rape': The Damage Rises"

22. Francis, 1-26.

23. Francis, 134-137.

24. Deirdre Carmody, "Increasing Rapes on Campus Spur Colleges to Fight Back," *New York Times,* January 1, 1989, sec. 1, 1.

25. Phil Donahue, *Donahue,* FFH 1599 (Princeton, NJ: Films for the Humanities and Sciences, 1988).

26. "Cagney and Lacey," episode 112, "Don't I Know You?," originally aired on January 5, 1988; John J. O'Connor, "TV Review: Date Rape on "Cagney and Lacey," *New York Times,* January 5, 1988, sec. C, 18.

27. Joan Hanauer, "Chris Cagney and Date Rape," United Press International, January 1, 1988, BC cycle.

28. John Corry, "TV Reviews: 'New Image Teens' Offers Vignettes on Youth Issues," September 30, 1987, sec. C, 26; Robert P. Laurence, "Teen Theater Drama Examines 'Date Rape,'" *San Diego Union Tribune,* June 10, 1987, sec. D, 9.

29. John Corry, "TV Reviews: "New Image Teens" Offers Vignettes on Youth Issues, September 30, 1987, sec. C, p. 26; Robert P. Laurence, "Teen Theater Drama Examines 'Date Rape'" *San Diego Union Tribune,* June 10, 1987, sec. D, p. 9.

30. Colman McCarthy, "Date Rape," *Washington Post,* December 12, 1987, A23.

31. Deirdre Carmody, "Increasing Rapes on Campus Spur Colleges to Fight Back," *New York Times,* January 1, 1989, sec. 1, 1; Beth Sherman, "A New Recognition of the Realities of Date Rape," *New York Times,* October 23, 1985, sec. C, 1.

32. Suzanne Choney, "He Is Often Someone the Victim Knew – Or Thought She Did," *San Diego Union Tribune,* November 27, 1985, sec. C, 3.

33. Beth Sherman, "A New Recognition of the Realities of Date Rape," *New York Times,* October 23, 1985, sec. C, 1.

34. David Streitfeld, " 'Date Rape': The Damage Rises," *Washington Post,* February 24, 1987, sec. C, 5.

35. Iris Krasnow, "Acquaintance Rape: When a Date Becomes a Crime," United Press International, May 25, 1985, BC cycle.

36. Beth Sherman, "A New Recognition of the Realities of Date Rape," *New York Times,* October 23, 1985, sec. C, 1; Bobbie Hasselbring, "Most Rape Victims Locally and Nationally Assaulted by Friends, Acquaintances; Old Sex Roles Partly Blamed," *The Oregonian,* September 12, 1988, sec. B, 1.

37. Suzanne Choney, "He is Often Someone the Victim Knew – Or Thought She Did," *San Diego Union-Tribune,* November 27, 1985, sec. C, 3.

38. Suzanne Choney, "He is Often Someone the Victim Knew – Or Thought She Did"

39. David Streitfeld, " 'Date Rape': The Damage Rises," *Washington Post,* February 24, 1987, sec. C, 5.

40. Bobbie Hasselbring, "Most Rape Victims Locally and Nationally Assaulted by Friends, Acquaintances; Old Sex Roles Partly Blamed," *The Oregonian,* September 12, 1988, sec. B, 1.

41. Marie Franzosa Corvallis, "Letter to the Editor: No Means No," *The Oregonian,* September 17,1988, sec. D, 6.

42. No author, "First 'Date Rape' Case in Berkeley," United Press International, December 14, 1987, PM cycle; Rachel Reynolds and David Jefferson, "The Crime Few Victims Will Report; Rapes Committed By Acquaintances Called Epidemic," *San Diego Union-Tribune,* August 26, 1985, sec. A, 1.

43. Rachel Reynolds and David Jefferson, "The Crime Few Victims Will Report; Rapes Committed By Acquaintances Called Epidemic," *San Diego Union-Tribune,* August 26, 1985, sec. A, 1.

44. Beth Sherman, "A New Recognition of the Realities of Date Rape," *New York Times,* October 23, 1985, sec. C, 1; John Roll, "Many Rape Victims Blame Themselves, Fail to Report Attacks," *New York Times,* January 12, 1989, AM cycle.

45. Caryn E. Neumann, *Sexual Crime* (Santa Barbara, CA: ABC-CLIO, 2010), 176.

46. Bobbie Hasselbring, "Most Rape Victims Locally and Nationally Assaulted by Friends, Acquaintances; Old Sex Roles Partly Blamed," *The Oregonian,* September 12, 1988, sec. B, 1.

47. Eileen A. Steinbugler, "Kids' Rape Views Not Surprising," *Post-Standard* [Syracuse, New York], May 18, 1988, sec. A, 14; No author, "School Students Find Rape Acceptable in Some Instances," Associated Press, May 2, 1988, AM cycle.

48. Rachel Reynolds and David Jefferson, "The Crime Few Victims Will Report; Rape Committed by Acquaintances Called Epidemic," *San Diego Union-Tribune,* August 26, 1985, sec. A, 1.

49. Rachel Reynolds and David Jefferson, "The Crime Few Victims Will Report."

50. Charlotte Sutton, "USF's 'Men Only' Date-Rape Seminar is an Eye Opener," *St. Petersburg Times* [Florida], June 30, 1988, 8; Rachel Reynolds and David Jefferson, "The Crime Few Victims Will Report; Rapes Committed by Acquaintances Called Epidemic," *San Diego Union-Tribune,* August 26, 1985, sec. A, 1.

51. Charlotte Sutton, "USF's 'Men Only' Date-Rape Seminar is an Eye Opener," *St. Petersburg Times* [Florida], June 30, 1988, 8; Colman McCarthy, "Date Rape," *Washington Post,* December 12, 1987, A23.

52. Colman McCarthy, "Date Rape," *Washington Post,* December 12, 1987, A23.

53. Janet Christ, "Sexual Crimes: Deputy DA Sets Students Straight," *The Oregonian*, December 15, 1988, 1.

54. No author, "South Dakota Males Victims of 'Date Rape'," United Press International, May 11, 1987, PM cycle.

55. No author, "School Students Find Rape Acceptable in Some Instances," Associated Press, May 2, 1988, AM cycle.

56. Janet Christ, "Sexual Crimes: Deputy DA Sets Students Straight," *The Oregonian*, December 15, 1988, 1.

57. Patricia McCormack, "New Guide Aims to Curb 'Date Rape' On College Campuses," United Press International, June 7, 1987, BC cycle.

58. Ibid.

59. Ibid.

60. Ibid.

61. Ibid.

62. Auburn University Rape Awareness Committee, *It Still Hurts* (Goshen, KY: Campus Crime Prevention Programs, 1985), VHS cassette; Deirdre Carmody, "Increasing Rapes on Campus Spur Colleges to Fight Back," *New York Times,* January 1, 1989, sec. 1, 1.

63. Deirdre Carmody, "Increasing Rapes on Campus Spur Colleges to Fight Back," *New York Times,* January 1, 1989, sec. 1, 1.

64. Deirdre Carmody, "Increasing Rapes on Campus Spur Colleges to Fight Back."

65. John Roll, "Many Rape Victims Blame Themselves, Fail to Report Attacks," *The Associated Press,* January 12, 1989, AM cycle.

66. Robin Warshaw, "Take Acquaintance Rape to Civil Courts," *New York Times*, February 24, 1989, sec. 4, 24.

67. Iris Krasnow, "Acquaintance Rape: When a Date Becomes a Crime," United Press International, May 25, 1985, BC cycle.

Chapter 14

A Culture in Panic: Day Care Abuse Scandals and the Vulnerability of Chilren

N'Jai-An Patters

With a final cost to the government of fifteen million dollars, the McMartin Preschool trial was the most expensive and longest running criminal case in US history at its conclusion in 1990, seven years after the first accusation of child molestation was leveled against Ray Buckey. Four hundred children were questioned over the course of two trials in which the defendants were charged with more than three hundred counts of child abuse. The accusations included claims of sexual assault, animal sacrifice, and ritualistic satanic abuse. Both print and television news media covered the case, presenting the allegations of children and parents largely unchallenged. Ultimately, no convictions were obtained against Buckey and six other employees of the McMartin Preschool (including Buckey's mother, grandmother, and sister). The acquittals and mistrials further polarized the community of Manhattan Beach, California, and they offered little remedy to the defendants whose careers, finances, and reputations were irreversibly damaged by what most observers now admit was a modern day witch-hunt.

Despite its high profile, the McMartin case was one of several that gripped American communities in the 1980s. From 1982-1984 several residents of Bakersfield, California were arrested and convicted for participating in a series of child sexual abuse rings.[1] Away from the West Coast, allegations of the ritualistic satanic sexual abuse of children circulated in Jordan, Minnesota in 1983, and against day care workers in Edenton, North Carolina in 1989. The existence of ritualistic satanic abuse has since been discredited, and the child abuse panics of the 1980s are now seen as cautionary tales about the dangers that public hysteria poses to the innocent. Nevertheless, what are now acknowledged as the moral or sexual "panics" of the 1980s represent both a response to the sexual politics of the 1960s and '70s as well as a foundation for the "war on pedophiles" of the 1990s and 2000s.[2]

The abuse panics took place on the heels of highly publicized child murders in Atlanta, Georgia and Oakland County, Michigan.[3] As these cases unfolded, parents and teachers renewed their efforts to inform children about "stranger danger." Fears about child safety were reflected in the prevalence of public service announcement enquiring about the whereabouts of children. At the same time, however, information about the likelihood of abuse at the hands of a person known to the child (rather than a stranger) was beginning to reach wider audiences. The panics of the 1980s arose as a kind of culmination of the fears and dangers that already surrounded children. In affected communities, every child was perceived as vulnerable and every adult was a potential perpetrator.

These cases and others like them mark American cultural politics in the 1980s and speak to a profound and persistent preoccupation with children's sexuality. In the first half of the essay, I situate the abuse panics in this broader context. Children's sexuality captured popular imagination and shaped political discourse beginning in the 1960s when several states adopted lower age of consent laws and continuing through the much-publicized sexual abuse trials of the 1980s.[4] The controversy and publicity that surrounded the three cases discussed in this essay—the McMartin pre-school trial on the West Coast, allegations of ritualistic satanic sexual abuse in Jordan, Minnesota and the prosecution of a husband and wife for pedophilia in North Carolina—suggests that cities and towns across the United States were equally subject to the hysteria of child sex scandals.[5]

While the first half of this essay examines the ways the child abuse panics endemic to the 1980s fit into broader public and political preoccupation with children's sexuality, the second half argues that attention to the sexuality of children produced a cultural consensus about children as victims. That is, despite their rhetorical differences, various forms of media, as well as politicians and groups from all along the political spectrum, ultimately endorsed the same vision of children's (lack of) sexual subjectivity. In the 1970s attention to consent was the focus of debates about children's and youth sexuality, but the 1980s ushered in the era of the child-victim, a figure that was presumed to be (sexually) innocent but whose vulnerability left it open to manipulation both by sexual predators and by the agents charged with apprehending them. Even as media coverage became more skeptical of new child abuse panics, the figure of the child was nonetheless marked by the panics of the 1980s. The latter part of this essay explores the ways that these panics successfully foreclosed cultural discussions of children's sexuality outside of the limits of innocence and victimhood.

That the 1970s and 80s represented a time of political transformation for the American left as well as the broader political society has long been accepted. The years between the 1960s and the 1990s witnessed profound sexual reorganization in the U.S. that has not yet been adequately examined for the ways that its attention to children reshaped sexual discourse. Sociologist Joel Best noted, "Most historians agree that modernization has increased adults' concern for children's well-being...However, during the 1970s and 1980s, child-victims began receiving a larger share of public attention."[6] The close of the sexual rev-olution, the ascendancy of its conservative backlash, and academic and political culture wars all centrally positioned sexuality. Indeed, the social and political upheaval that characterized the period may account for the increased focus on sexuality within popular discourse. As feminist scholar Gayle Rubin noted, "Disputes over sexual behavior often become the vehicles for displacing social anxieties, and discharging their attendant emotional intensity."[7] The panics of the 1980s reveal that the anxieties surrounding children and child-care would be inextricably linked to charges of sexual misconduct.

To say that the figure of the child was a rhetorical tool in the late twentieth century is not to ignore the realities of (sexual) exploitation and erasure that faced American children. Rather, it is to acknowledge the ways that political discourses of children's sexuality participated in and indeed sometimes pro-duced that exploitation and erasure. For example, foregrounding children's sex-ual victimization established a paradigm in which children's sexual subjectivity was virtually unthinkable just as fighting against children's sexual repression endorsed ideas of sexual precocity that made allegations of abuse less credible.[8] Through an investigation of journalistic representations of these positions, this chapter exposes the ways that debates about child sexuality were used to shape American cultural politics in the 1980s.

The Cases

Reports of sexual abuse of children, even of infants, in day-care institutions have shocked the nation, provoking demands for harsh penalties and instant re-forms...The crisis is evident.[9]

The crisis elaborated upon in the *Times* article, which cites cases in the Bronx, Manhattan Beach, California, Chicago, Reno, and Alabama as sites of multiple day care abuse allegations, was one that hit small towns and big cities across the country. Even those communities that were spared the costly trials were visited by an increase in day care and preschool closures, and media outlets from news-papers and magazines to television documentaries and feature films covered the crisis as it spread throughout the decade and into the one that followed. Indeed, the first and last of the big 1980s day care abuse cases both ended in the 1990s.

After seven years and two trials, the McMartin Preschool case finally ended in 1990 with no convictions against any of the seven accused. More than four hun-dred children were questioned by police, therapists, and prosecutors to generate the hundreds of charges that were filed against Virginia McMartin, owner of the preschool; her daughter, Peggy McMartin Buckey; and Peggy's children, Ray and Peggy Ann Buckey; along with preschool teachers, Mary Ann Jackson, Bette Raidor, and Babette Spitler. The McMartin case distinguished itself as the most widely publicized, most expensive, and longest running criminal trial with an interwoven cast of characters and escalating series of events worthy of a soap opera. Over the course of the investigation, the McMartin school was vandalized and set on fire, the original complainant died after being hospitalized following a psychotic break induced by paranoid schizophrenia, the investigative journalist who first broke the story had a live-in affair with the social worker who "uncovered" the abuse, and one of the prosecuting attorneys resigned rather than continue working a trial in which he believed in the innocence of the defendants.

The McMartin family was close-knit and headed by matriarch, Virginia McMartin. Touted by some in her neighborhood as "St. Virginia," she had devoted her adult life to working with and on behalf of children and had been repeatedly honored for that work.[10] After working for several years as a school bus driver, Virginia McMartin had saved enough money to open the McMartin Preschool in the Los Angeles suburb of Manhattan Beach, California. The school was a family affair from the beginning, with Virginia's daughter Peggy Buckey working as an administrator. By the time the case erupted, the school had been open for more than twenty-five years, and McMartin's daughter and grandchildren had all worked there. The remainder of the teachers and staff had attended church with the McMartin family for several years, and the atmosphere at the school encouraged closeness between employees. At the time of her indictment in March 1984, seventy-six-year-old Virginia McMartin was taken into custody in a wheelchair wearing dark glasses to shield her eyes after cataract surgery. Peggy was fifty-seven, and teachers Mary Ann Jackson and Bette Raidor were both in their sixties.

The events that were eventually described as "scarr[ing] a whole generation of children" began with a single accusation.[11] In August 1983, prompted by her son's painful bowel movements, Judy Johnson reported to the police that the two-and-a-half-year-old had been sodomized by McMartin school aide, Ray Buckey. Buckey, the grandson of school's founder, Virginia McMartin, and the son of Peggy McMartin Buckey, an administrator at the preschool, denied all wrongdoing. Over the next two months Johnson continued to levy increasingly bizarre accusations against Buckey and other employees at the McMartin preschool alleging that, among other things, her son was "buried alive...[and] sodomized by a lion."[12] Johnson would also accuse her husband of abusing their son, but police and prosecutors, who had already begun mounting a case against Buckey, were reluctant to pursue another investigation that could undermine the McMartin case.

After Buckey's September arrest, he was released for lack of evidence. It was at this time that police chief Harry Kuhlmeyer sent a letter to the parents of 200 current and former McMartin Preschool students. The letter informed parents of the ongoing investigation against Buckey and instructed them to question their children to see if they had been abused or witnessed abuse while at the preschool. The letter asked parents to gather "any information from your child regarding having ever observed Ray Buckey to leave a classroom alone with a child during any nap period, or if they have ever observed Ray Buckey tie up a child."[13] After the letter was distributed, the number of victims and charges quickly multiplied. Within five months, Virginia McMartin and her daughter were forced to close the school permanently.

Overwhelmed by the growing number of children involved in the case, the police department asked Kee MacFarlane, a social worker with Children's Institute International (CII), to interview the children and make a determination regarding alleged abuse. Though she was not licensed in any state, MacFarlane had worked with abused children for more than a decade. She taped all of her interviews and used anatomically correct dolls to allow the children to identify body parts and actions and hand puppets to put the children at ease and allow them to gain distance from disclosures of abuse. As the case generated more publicity, MacFarlane became a kind of spokesperson for abused children, and she was portrayed and accepted as an expert, eventually testifying before Congress about "an organized operation of child predators designed to prevent detection." Prompted by circumstantial evidence, MacFarlane claimed that within such networks preschools "serve as a ruse for larger unthinkable crimes against children."[14]

The McMartin case was picked up by the national news media after Wayne Satz aired a series of exclusive investigative reports on the case for local Los Angeles station, KABC. Satz's two year long coverage of the McMartin case won him two Golden Mikes awards, and is frequently credited with catapulting the case into the national spotlight. In fact, one reporter working the case has gone on record saying that "the D.A. might never have filed charges in the McMartin case had it not been for Channel 7's stories and the public attention they generated."[15] Both the District Attorney and Satz himself deny that his reports had this level of influence. However, after his initial reports aired, charges of abuse at McMartin and other area preschools and day care centers increased dramatically, forcing several to close. Satz underwent further criticism for pursuing a romantic relationship with Kee MacFarlane, a primary prosecution witness, though Satz defended his behavior and insisted that there was no conflict of interest. By the time indictments were handed down against the seven defendants, KCBS reporter Ross Becker claimed that, "the story took on a life of its own."[16]

After the grand jury handed down indictments against McMartin, the Buckeys, Jackson, Raidor, and Spitler in March 1984, the seven were quickly arrested. At their bail hearings, prosecutor Lael Rubin argued against bail for the defendants, claiming that they had committed 397 crimes in addition to the 115 on which they had been indicted, and that the nature of the crimes combined with the threats made against the victims made remand necessary in this case. Bail was denied for Ray Buckey, and bail for Peggy Buckey was set at $1 million. Unable to make bail, all defendants except for Virginia McMartin were imprisoned awaiting trial. Over the course of the pretrial proceedings, which lasted nearly eighteen months, Peggy Ann was released on bond. And in 1986, the newly elected district attorney, Ira Reiner, dismissed charges against all defendants except Peggy and Ray Buckey, both of whom had remained incarcerated, citing "incredibly weak evidence."[17] The prosecution proceeded to trial against Ray and Peggy Buckey on 65 counts of child abuse.

The trial against Ray and Peggy Buckey was unprecedented not only because of it duration and cost, but also because of the scope and sensitivity of the issues involved. Before it was over "63,000 pages of testimony, 917 exhibits and 124 witnesses" were generated.[18] Over the course of the 33-month trial, the defense strategy seemed to be to highlight the errors made by the police, the staff at CII and the district attorney's office. In the end, many jurors were convinced that something had happened to the children, but they were unable to return a guilty verdict. Their reluctance to convict stemmed from the misconduct on the part of police who released Buckey's name to parents before charges were filed, what they perceived as coercive therapeutic techniques, and inconsistent testimony from prosecution witnesses. On January 18, 1990, more than six years after Judy Johnson made the first complaint, the jury found the Buckeys not guilty on 52 counts, and deadlocked on 13 others. Echoing statements made in juror interviews, Ray Buckey's attorney, Daniel Davis, told reporters after the conclusion of the trial, "I did not win this case by pluck or brilliance...The prosecution was never ready. They never conducted an organized, methodical investigation of the case before going to trial. This case was exceedingly easy to defend."[19] A mere two weeks later, the district attorney's office announced its intention to retry Ray Buckey on eight of the thirteen counts for which no verdict had been reached. The second trial, though quicker, also ended in a hung jury.

If, as Gail Rubin asserts, disputes over sexual behavior mask broader social anxieties, then the day care abuse crisis ignited by the McMartin case can be read as evidence of Americans' ambivalence about the care of their children.[20] In the 1970s, feminists identified the home as a potentially dangerous place when they publicized the realities of incest in the face of class- and race-based fears of stranger danger.[21] At the same time, steady increases in women's work force participation saw greater numbers of American children in day care facilities in the 1980s. As the child-abuse panics of the later decade spread, the media framed the issue as one of oversight, with some in the public demanding greater regulation and higher standards for day care facilities and others pointing to women's absence from the home as the root cause of children's increased vulnerability.[22] With both the home and the school identified as sites of danger to children, Americans' fears about their children's well-being were on the rise.

The sphere in which children were perceived to be at risk was not the only shift from the 1970s to the 1980s. Debates about children and youth sexuality also underwent significant transformation. The earlier decade witnessed the rise of public debates about young people's ability to possess sexual desire and consent to sexual activity.[23] The 1980s elevation of the child-victim shifted public discourse from a focus on consent to one on vulnerability. Even the nature of the scandals that received media attention reveal this shift, highlighted by the 1970s media focus on adolescent prostitution and the 1980s attention to day care abuse.[24]

What McMartin and other subsequent cases revealed, however, was that the discourse of children's vulnerability was complex, and that it often identified multiple actors as dangerous to children. That is, perpetrators of sexual violence were not the only threats to children when "overzealous prosecutor[s]...and a 'cottage industry' of child-abuse psychologists" were also capable of manipulating children into believing that abuse had occurred.[25] That children were in peril seemed not to be in doubt; it was the source of children's danger that was unclear. As children and their parents lamented the failures of the justice system with the same intensity displayed by the defendants and their attorneys, it was clear that this trial ushered in a new set of concerns for the child-victim and those accused of child abuse.

After the first McMartin jury returned not guilty verdicts on more than fifty counts, some jurors conceded that they believed that children had been abused, but held that the prosecution had not convinced them that the abuse had taken place at the McMartin preschool or at the hands of Peggy or Ray Buckey: "I believe that the children believed what they were saying was true in the courtroom...At CII I could not tell from watching the tape that the children were telling what actually happened to them or if they were repeating what they were told by their parents or other people."[26] For others on the jury, however, the credibility of the children was at issue: "I tried to believe the children, but I had a hard time picking fact from fiction."[27] Indeed, the McMartin case would begin a debate in both judicial and psychological circles about the ability of children—especially very young children—to provide credible testimony. This question would be raised throughout subsequent abuse trials in the '80s, and would persist in the face of suspect therapeutic techniques and children recanting.[28]

Members of both the prosecution and the defense, along with police officials, social workers and legislators all agreed that the McMartin case provided useful lessons and hoped that its legacy would be to see those lessons borne out. After the verdict, social worker and key prosecution witness, Kee MacFarlane said, "I hope that people will see [the verdict] as the anomaly that it is, that parents won't be afraid to bring their children forth, that prosecutors won't be afraid to prosecute."[29] Judicial analysis turned to the length of the trial and to the special needs of child witnesses.[30] In a statement made after the verdict, district attorney Reiner said, "The very idea that a case in trial for two and one half years can lead to a rational result is preposterous."[31] Because of the case's seven-year duration, however, these observations came too late to halt similar panics from cropping up. After the case first came to public attention in 1984, however, a rash of similar cases emerged throughout the country. The extent of the accusations and the frequency of day care closures prompted a national debate about the need for regulation in nursery- and preschools, and for new guidelines for questioning children. Still, for those involved, the resolution of the case provided no comfort.

Similar charges were filed in Jordan, Minnesota in 1983. Within a year, 25 adults and one juvenile were arrested, dozens of children were removed from their parents' custody, the FBI and state police launched an investigation into alleged child pornography and infanticide, the state attorney general decried the handling of the case as "a tragedy," and the only trial based on the charges resulted in acquittal. Like other child abuse cases in the period, the charges in Jordan quickly multiplied, and stories of ritualistic satanic abuse surfaced. Unlike the McMartin case, however, one suspect pleaded guilty, and key witnesses admitted to fabricating charges by the end of 1984.

The arrest of more than two-dozen people for participating in a "sex ring" rocked the small town of Jordan, Minnesota. Thirty-five miles outside of Minneapolis, Jordan was founded in the mid-nineteenth century. Despite its proximity to the Twin Cities, it was described as "rural, a safe haven from the crime and social upheaval of urban America."[32] Heavily wooded, with homes nestled on bluffs or waterfronts, the town celebrated its "rural" feeling by setting aside forested land in a series of state and federal parks. The community of 2,700 was transformed by the allegations: "There's more paranoia in the town of Jordan and in Scott County than I've seen anywhere. Everybody is afraid to bathe their children, hug their children, go to a fair in the country."[33]

The case began in September 1983 when a resident reported that her nine-year-old daughter had been sexually assaulted by trash collector, James Rud, a man twice convicted of child molestation who was then under probation. In a 113-page statement made in August 1983, Rud implicated others in Jordan, including a deputy sheriff, a police officer, mechanics, and waitresses.[34] By the time the first case proceeded to trial, more than forty children, ranging in age from toddlers to teenagers, were identified as victims of twenty-five adults. The accused were said to have abused their own and each other's children in an elaborate sex ring in which parents exchanged children with each other for the purposes of sexual exploitation. Once three boys came forward claiming to have witnessed the sacrifice of babies, the Minnesota Bureau of Criminal Apprehension (BCA) and the FBI were called in to investigate. In addition to the sexual abuse and murder charges, authorities began looking for evidence of a child pornography syndicate based in the town.

Ultimately, no evidence of murder or pornography was found, and the case, from its initial investigation to its ultimate prosecution, was described by state attorney general, Hubert H. Humphrey III, as having "clearly [gone] awry."[35] Though attorneys from Humphrey to Supreme Court Justice Antonin Scalia acknowledge that abuse occurred in Jordan, James Rud was the only one of the accused to be convicted as a result of a guilty plea.[36] Rud agreed to testify against other Jordan defendants, and in exchange, Scott County attorney, R. Kathleen Morris, agreed to drop 98 of the 100 charges pending against him. Ultimately, this plea undermined the credibility of the prosecution's case and contributed to the not guilty verdict in the only case that went to trial. The acquittal combined with CBA and FBI findings, with witnesses recanting, and with Rud's own admissions that he had made false statement to obtain leniency, left prosecutors with little choice but to drop the remaining charges.[37]

The only case to go to trial was that of Robert and Lois Brentz, a husband and wife who were charged with molesting their six-year-old son and four other Jordan children. The couple was acquitted after a four-week long trial and two days of jury deliberation. As in the McMartin case, children's vulnerability to manipulation focused attention both on those accused of sexual abuse and on the leading tactics of the prosecution and its witnesses. In response to the verdict, county prosecutor R. Kathleen Morris proclaimed, "This doesn't mean they're innocent. It means that I didn't prove they were guilty. *This means that we live in a society that does not believe children.*"[38] In a case that "rested almost exclusively on the credibility of the children," an acquittal suggested that even if community hysteria contributed to child abuse panics, skepticism still prevailed in the jury room.[39]

As the 1980s drew to a close, the small town of Edenton, North Carolina made national news when the owners of its most prominent day care, Little Rascals, were arrested for the sexual abuse of children in their care. Unlike the cases in Minnesota and California, the Little Rascals case was set apart because jury convictions were obtained against some of the accused, and because the media coverage ranged from uncritical to skeptical. The quiet calm of small town life was disrupted when the first allegations surfaced in January 1989. By the time the final Little Rascals charge was dismissed in 1997, more than four hundred counts of abuse were levied against seven people, including Bob and Betsy Kelly, the daughter and son-in-law of a local business owner and politician, and Scott Privott, son of a judge, successful business owner, and country club president. In fact, coverage of the scandal and subsequent trials revealed a community equally as shocked by the nature of the crimes as it was by the status of the people who were accused.

Bob and Betsy Kelly, owners of the Little Rascals Day Care Center, were at the heart of the case. The couple married in 1979 and opened Little Rascals in 1986. Two years later the couple moved the day care into a converted bottle factory owned by Betsy's father. The new location allowed them to care for more children and to hire additional staff. Located just one block east of Edenton's main street, Little Rascals became the town's "most prestigious day care."[40] This distinction carried weight in a town like Edenton, whose population in the mid-1980s was about six thousand. The small town atmosphere was based on more than the number of residents, however. The rural community on the edge of the Albemarle Sound boasts a number of historical markers as a testament to its eighteenth century founding and long-ago stint as unofficial state capital. Within its borders, many residents live in colonial homes and are part of families whose members have known one another for generations.

The closeness of Edenton residents became evident as the Little Rascals scandal unfolded. Three days after the new location opened, Bob slapped Joel Mabrey, the four-year-old son of Betsy's friend Jane. The circumstances surrounding the incident remain unclear; however, the Kellys refusal to apologize to Jane Mabrey, though they eventually claimed that the slap was an accident, are well documented.[41] According to interviews conducted as part of the first of three *Frontline* documentaries covering the allegations and subsequent trials, Jane was "devastated" by the incident. After her son told her that he had been slapped, she "knew that life would never be the same again...If I couldn't trust a day care owned by my best friend for my child to be safe in, then I knew that I probably wouldn't be able to trust much of anything else."[42] Upset that no one seemed to take the slapping seriously, Jane confronted the Kellys: "And we had a very bad scene. I was crying and weeping and saying, 'How could this happen?' at the time still thinking it was an accident, but knowing I could never bring Joel back down there unless he understood that adults could make mistakes and they can rectify them. And that was never done."[43] No apology from the Kellys was forthcoming. Jane's dissatisfaction with the resolution of the event was still evident two months after the incident that prompted her to remove Joel from Little Rascals. She approached the Kellys again: "I was hoping that both Bob and Betsy would realize that losing Joel was a loss, mainly because he was my son and Betsy and I were friends."[44] Bob and Betsy's continued refusal to acknowledge the wrong that had been done to her son compelled Jane to act.

Betsy Kelly's sister, Nancy Smith, believed that Jane instigated the panic that consumed Little Rascals less than four months after Jane removed her son from the day care. According to Nancy, "She knew that, legally, physical abuse, which is what she thought was justified in charging, wasn't going to close the day care. One incident wasn't going to do it."[45] Indeed, Jane's own words indicate that she uncovered what would become the first allegation of abuse after she began speaking with parents whose children attended Little Rascals: "my understanding is this one particular mother [Audrey Stever] I talked to was concerned—in our talking it raised some more red flags and she pursued it and found that it wasn't a physical abuse that was taking place, but that it was sexual abuse. And that's what precipitated the investigation by the social services."[46]

After her conversation with Jane, Stever approached police officer, Brenda Toppin. Stever and Toppin were friends, and Toppin, who had recently attended a seminar on child sexual abuse, told Stever how to question three-year-old Kyle. During this next round of questioning, Kyle told his mother that Mr. Bob played doctor with him and other boys at the day care. According to Kyle, "playing doctor" meant "sticking things in your butt." As a result of this conversation, a complaint was filed with social services, and eventually, a full scale investigation was launched.

The social service complaint alleging abuse was filed January 19, 1989. By February two more children disclosed abuse at Little Rascals, and each passing month saw the number of allegations grow. Though several parents initially rallied around Bob, the tide of public support shifted as the list of allegations grew. Bob Kelly was arrested in mid-April, and by the end of the month the day care was forced to close. Unable to pay a bond that eventually reached 1.5 million dollars, Bob remained in prison awaiting trial. At his first pre-trial hearing in April, members of the prosecution approached Kelly's lawyer, Chris Bean, to tell him that his son had been named by other children as a victim of abuse at the hands of Bob Kelly. Just after the grand jury handed down the first set of indictments against Kelly, Bean withdrew from the case. Bean's refusal to represent Kelly was seen by Jane Mabrey and other Edenton residents as confirmation of Kelly's guilt.

Toppin and other police officials encouraged parents whose children had ever attended Little Rascals to have them evaluated by trained therapists. As the case grew, the state set aside monies to pay for these evaluations, and in some cases, to pay for treatment as well. Four therapists were recommended by the police, and the prosecution based the bulk of its case on their findings. Parents who refused to have their children evaluated were made to feel neglectful, while those who wanted independent evaluations from professionals removed from Edenton and Little Rascals had to pay for the services themselves. More than ninety percent of the allegations were based on statements made to Toppin or one of these four therapists, but the defense was not able to question them or review their notes.

By September, more than ninety children were involved in the case. In fact, the case had grown so much that Bill Hart was appointed as special prosecutor. The police and prosecution looked beyond Bob Kelly, and charges were filed against other Little Rascals employees. Betsy Kelly was the first to be arrested, charged with several counts of sexual abuse and even more counts of conspiracy. Scott Privott was arrested the same day as Betsy, his bail set at $1 million. Privott maintained throughout his questioning and imprisonment that he had never even been inside Little Rascals. After Betsy's and Privott's September arrest, the others followed in rapid succession. By the end of the month Dawn Wilson, the cook at Little Rascals, and Shelly Stone, who worked with older children were also arrested. Bail was set at $880 and $375 thousand respectively. In January, the last two arrests were made when Robin Byrum and Darlene Harris were taken into custody.

Though seven arrests were made in connection with alleged abuse at Little Rascals, only two defendants ever made it to trial: Bob Kelly and Dawn Wilson. Kelly's trial was first. It lasted eight months, was covered extensively in the print media, and was the topic of the second *Frontline* documentary on the Little Rascals scandal. The therapists never took the stand, and their reports were never made available to the defense team. Twelve children testified, all between the ages of three and five when the alleged abuse took place. The jury deliberated for two weeks before finding Kelly guilty on 99 of 100 charges. The next day, on April 23, 1992, he was sentenced to twelve consecutive life sentences.[47] The Little Rascals case had frequently been compared to McMartin because of its scope and cost, but the conviction became the biggest difference between the two cases. This resolution was hailed as a victory by the prosecution and by Edenton parents. According to a juror interviewed just after the trial, "the children were convincing."[48]

In November of 1992 the prosecution mounted its case against Dawn Wilson. Wilson, the single mother of a young daughter, was offered a plea bargain just before her case proceeded to trial. In exchange for pleading guilty on some of the charges, the prosecution offered her a drastically reduced sentence of 1-2 years, and they would count the seventeen months Wilson had already spent in prison as part of her time served. Rather than facing multiple life sentences, Wilson could conceivably serve no additional jail time. She refused the offer. Only four children testified against Dawn, but this time the prosecution introduced the therapy reports into evidence just before the jury began its deliberations. After just under three months, Wilson was convicted on all counts and sentenced to life in prison.

A few months after Dawn Wilson returned to prison, Scott Privott's bond was reduced from $1 million to $50,000. Unable to make bond before this reduction, Privott had been in jail awaiting trial for three years. He and the remaining four defendants waited to see who would be brought to trial next. More than three years had passed since the initial allegations were made, and each of the five had been offered several increasingly good deals by the prosecution. All had stated their unwillingness to confess to crimes that they did not commit. Moved by the convictions of Bob Kelly and Dawn Wilson, and haunted by her own years of imprisonment, Betsy Kelly pleaded no contest on January 28, 1994. She served ten months. Scott Privott, after being promised that he would have to serve no additional jail time, also pleaded no contest in June 1994.

Defense teams for Bob Kelly and Dawn Wilson filed several appeals, alleging, among other things, jury misconduct. In January 1995, they argued their cases in front of the state court of appeals. On May 2nd, the Appellate Court overturned the convictions of Bob Kelly and Dawn Wilson, and in September the state supreme court upheld the appellate court decision. Dawn Wilson had been released and placed under house arrest pending her appeal, while Bob Kelly had spent the time in prison. With these decisions, both were free on bond pending new trials. In 1996, more than seven years after the initial allegations were made, charges were dropped against Robin Byrum, Shelly Stone, and Darlene Harris after their lawyers argued that the prosecution had violated their sixth amendment right to a speedy trial. The next year, all remaining Little Rascals charges were dropped against Bob Kelly and Dawn Wilson.

Unlike the doomed McMartin and Jordan cases, the initial prosecution wins against Little Rascals defendants were heralded as victories for the children. Just as in the first two cases, the verdict "hinge[d] on testimony by a dozen children."[49] Jurors in this case, however, believed the children. After delivering the verdict, jury foreperson, Katherine Harris, reported: "As far as the children, for them to get up there and say something like that, it certainly made me believe them."[50] Though the defense tried to paint a town that had been swept away by hysteria and allegations that were the product of fanatical therapists, and though the second Frontline documentary revealed a fractured jury, the unanimous verdict in both trials was vindication for the children and their parents as well as for the therapists involved in the case.

The credibility of the children was also at issue in the successful appeals that ultimately overturned the verdicts and ordered new trials in both cases. Defense lawyers argued that misconduct on the part of the prosecution, especially their exclusive reliance on child testimony and therapy reports in the absence of corroborating evidence or point of contact documentation, had compromised the proceedings and resulted in a miscarriage of justice. The appellate decision can be read as a vote of no confidence in the handling of very young children in these cases up to and including their testimony. The mixed messages of the Little Rascals trials were centered on children's (lack of) credibility stemming from their particular vulnerabilities.

Conclusion

The so-called molestation of the young is the start of politics.[51]

With this statement, Mitzel ended his polemic about activism surrounding a late 1970s pedophile panic and attempted to create a space for advancing children's sexual subjectivity.[52] Unlike Mitzel, this piece has not attempted to re-imagine the dynamics of intergenerational relationships ("so-called molestation"). Instead, I use this quote to demonstrate the ways that "so-called molestation" came to drive politics and culture at both the community and the national levels and to highlight the peculiar landscape of sexual politics in the 1980s. On the heels of calls for more expansive sexual politics from boy-lovers in Boston to best-sellers like *Our Bodies, Ourselves* that celebrated sexuality as a healthy part of life from infancy to old age, the sexual revolution of 1970s gave way to the sexual panics of the 1980s. Indeed, these panics may be read as a response to the *laissez-faire* approach advocated by Mitzel and the sensual awakening promoted by the authors of *Our Bodies, Ourselves*.

With the implementation of new standards for child testimony and new approaches to child therapy, the legacies of these panics remain with us twenty years later. And though day-care panics remain, for now, a thing of the past, the media frenzy generated by the (white) child in peril is still very much felt. If anything, cultural anxieties about the sexual dangers facing American children remain high.

The specter of the pedophile continues to loom large as the United States considers registration and civil commitment of sex offenders, the dangers posed by "on-line predators," and the international sale of children into sexual servitude. At the same time, persistent debates about sexual education, the availability of contraceptive devices to youth, and parental notification for reproductive services reveal the ways that consensual sexual contact between young people is also controversial. In recent decades these debates and others within the culture wars have arguably defined American politics on both the right and the left.[53] Concerns about "sexting" and increased internet access have sparked debates about the sexual misadventures young people get into without aid or pressure from adult predators, while technologies like cell phones and GPS tracking systems are marketed to parents as tools to protect their children, allowing adults to maintain a watchful eye even when children are not in their presence.

This surveillance is a legacy of the abuse panics of the 1980s. Both children and their extra-familial caretakers are subjected to ever-increasing methods of tracking from fingerprinting and ID badges for children to nanny cameras, background checks and psych profiles for caretakers. In addition to this surveillance, we are arriving at a cultural consensus to restrict children's mobility and limit them from being outdoors without supervision, whether for play or transportation. Together this increased surveillance and restricted mobility amount to the virtual imprisonment of youth in the name of protection and safeguarding.

The 1980s left us with a child that is at once imperiled and perilous. Despite the exoneration of defendants and the condemnation of therapeutic and investigative tactics, the child-victim remains a powerful paradigm. The pedophiles and predators on display on talk shows and television dramas continually (re)present the child-as-victim while stirring fears of omnipresent danger and conspiracies of abuse. Even the attention given to the sexual exploits of youth reify ideas of childhood innocence and victimization. Young people engaged in sexual activity are often presented as victims of sex-saturated culture who have "grown up too fast." In this framework, sexual activity remains understood as the province of adults, and youth who engage in sex are still framed as victims.

In as much as the 1980s revealed fissures in children's credibility, the child also became dangerous. The abuse panics exposed how easily manipulated children could be both by those seeking to harm and those seeking to protect them. As such, children's vulnerability became a danger to the innocent, to the justice system, and to communities that too easily got swept away in a hysteria of allegations and prosecutions.

Historically complex and contentious, public debate about children's sexuality presents varied readings of both sexual subjectivity and political identity. With echoes of sixties counterculture and the emergence of new movements for women's liberation and gay rights, and steeped in 1970s amorphous calls for "sexual revolution," the 1980s provide an ideal time to examine the ways that debates about age and sexuality shaped cultural debates about the vulnerability and credibility of children and of the American justice system. These cases highlight the ways that the 1980s, though distinctive, laid the foundation for current sexual politics.

Notes

1. Many of the Bakersfield convicted have since been exonerated, released from prison after serving decades, and, in some cases, awarded settlements by the state.

2. In my discussion of moral panics, I am relying on the frameworks first outlined by Stuart Hall and Stanley Cohen. See especially, Stuart Hall, *Policing the Crisis*, (New York: Holmes & Meier, 1978); and Stanley Cohen, *Folk-Devils and Moral Panics*, (London: Routledge, 2002). On October 4, 2005, Oprah Winfrey declared war on pedophilia and began offering rewards for information leading to the arrest of persons on her child predator watch list.

3. Twenty-eight children and two adults were murdered in Atlanta between 1979 and 1981 in what investigators believed to be a related string of attacks, and at least four children were murdered in southwestern Michigan between 1976 and 1977 by an unidentified assailant referred to as "the Babysitter."

4. As early as the 1960s, six states (New York, Hawaii, Illinois, Wisconsin, Pennsylvania and South Dakota) began to recognize children's sexual behavior through the implementation of lower age of consent laws. By the 1970s, these laws were joined by new federal and state statutes designed to protect children from physical and sexual misuse— i.e. Child Abuse Prevention and Treatment Act of 1974 and the Kildee Murphy (Child Pornography) Bill of 1977. The development of these two sets of laws parallels increasingly public intellectual and political debates about children's sexuality. At the same time, child abuse scandals like the McMartin Preschool Trial, the controversy with the Minneapolis Children's Theater, and others reveal the cultural tension associated with expanding young people's sexual freedom.

5. Phillip Jenkins, *Moral Panic: Changing Concepts of the Child Molester in Modern America* (New Haven, CT: Yale University Press, 1998); and Joel Best, *Threatened Children* (Chicago: University of Chicago Press, 1990).

6. Joel Best, *Threatened Children: Rhetoric and Concern about Child-Victims*, (Chicago: University of Chicago Press, 1990), 5-6.

7. Gayle Rubin, "Thinking Sex: Notes for a Radical Theory of the Politics of Sexuality" in Carole S. Vance, ed., *Pleasure and Danger: Exploring Sexuality* (1984) reprinted in Henry Abelove, Michèle Aina Barale, David M. Halperin eds., *The Lesbian and Gay Studies Reader* (New York: Routledge, 1993), 4.

8. Steven Angelides, "Feminism, Child Sexual Abuse, and the Erasure of Child Sexuality," in *GLQ* 2 (2004), 141-177.

9. Fred M. Hechinger, "Abuse at Centers: Underlying Flaws" *New York Times* August 28, 1984, pg. C6.

10. Virginia McMartin received four public citations for community service, including the Rose and Scroll Award, the city's highest honor. See Virginia McMartin, "Virginia McMartin Preschool," unpublished autobiography, 1982 or early 1983; *Huntington Beach News,* August 14, 1987.

11. "Details of Sexual Abuse Case at School Described," *New York Times* Apr 7, 1984, pg. 8.

12. Quoted in Dr. Roland C. Summit, "The Dark Tunnels of McMartin," in *Journal of Psychohistory* 21 (4) Spring 1994.

13. "Letter to McMartin Preschool Parents from Police Chief Kuhlmeyer Jr." September 8, 1983.

14. Nadine Brozan, "Witness Says She Fears 'Child Predator' Network" *New York Times* September 18, 1984 pg.A21.

15. David Shaw, "Reporter's Early Exclusive Triggered a Media Frenzy" *Los Angeles Times* January 20, 1990.

16. Quoted in David Shaw, "Reporter's Early Exclusive Triggered a Media Frenzy" *Los Angeles Times* January 20, 1990.

17. Susan Schindehette, "The McMartin Nightmare" *People* February 5, 1990. Vol. 33 No. 5

18. Ibid.

19. Ibid.

20. Rubin, "Thinking Sex: Notes for a Radical Theory of the Politics of Sexuality."

21. The Boston Women's Health Collective's *Our Bodies, Ourselves* devoted considerable space to detailing the physical and emotional traumas associated with rape and incest and was among the first widely distributed texts that both highlighted the likelihood that victims would know their assailants and framed prominent stranger danger myths as being inspired by racism and class bias. See: The Boston Women's Health Collective, *Our Bodies, Ourselves: A Book By and For Women, Revised and Expanded* (New York: Simon and Schuster), 1976. See also: Vikki Bell, *Interrogating Incest: Feminism, Foucault, and the Law,* (New York: Routledge), 1993; and *Gender Violence: Interdisciplinary Perspectives,* Laura O'Toole, Jessica Schiffman, and Margie Kiter Edwards, eds., (New York: NYU Press, 2007), 297-364.

22. Fred M. Hechinger, "Abuse at Centers: Underlying Flaws," *New York Times* August 28, 1984, pg. C6; Robert Lindsey, "Increased Demand for Day Care Prompts a Debate on Regulation," *New York Times* September 2, 1984, pp. 1, 52.

23. See especially, *The Age Taboo*, Daniel Tsang, ed., (Boston: Alyson Publications), 1981; Mitzel, *The Boston Sex Scandal,* (Boston: Glad Day Books), 1980.

24. Two prominent child prostitution cases were heavily publicized in 1970s Boston, the Sunshine Girls case in which a group of under-aged girls was alleged to have been prostituted to prominent business men and the pedophile panic in which gay teens were reported to have been at the root of the arrest of gay men in the Boston public library.

25. Robert Reinhold, "2 Acquitted of Child Molestation in Nation's Longest Criminal Trial," *New York Times* January 19, 1990 pg. A18.

26. Juror, Brenda Williams quoted in Robert Reinhold, "2 Acquitted of Child Molestation in the Nation's Longest Criminal Trial," *New York Times* January 19, 1990, pg. A18.

27. Juror Daryl Hutchins quoted in Seth Mydans, "For Jurors, Facts Could Not Be Sifted From Fantasies," *New York Times* January 19, 1990, pg. A18.

28. Children in McMartin and subsequent cases would recant allegations, sometimes before trial proceedings concluded, sometimes years later. See: Roger Wortington, "Abuse testimony a story, boy says," *Chicago Tribune* January 25, 1985, pg. 1.

29. Kee MacFarland quoted in Robert Reinhold, "2 Acquitted of Child Molestation in the Nation's Longest Criminal Trial," *New York Times* January 19, 1990, pg. A18.

30. "Child Abuse—and Trial Abuse," *New York Times* January 20, 1990, pg. A24; Robert Reinhold, "Long Child Molestation Trial Viewed as System Run Amok," *New York Times* July 27, 1989, pg. A1; E.R. Shipp, "The Jeopardy of Children on the Stand," *New York Times*, September 23, 1984, pg. E8.

31. Reiner quoted in Robert Reinhold, "2 Acquitted of Child Molestation in the Nation's Longest Criminal Trial," *New York Times* January 19, 1990, pg. A18.

32. Peter Carlson, "Divided by Multiple Charges of Child Abuse, a Minnesota Town Seethes with Anger," *People* October 22, 1984, Vol. 22, No. 17.

33. Marck G. Kruzman quoted in E.R. Shipp, "Rumors of Murder Haunt Town Since Dropping of Sex Charges," *New York Times* October 25, 1984, pg. A18.

34. "Admitted Child Molester Sentenced to 40 Years" *San Diego Union-Tribune* January 19, 1985 pg. A2; and E.R. Shipp, "Two in Abuse Case Found Not Guilty," *New York Times* September 20, 1984, pg. A21.

35. Hubert H. Humphrey, III, "Review of the Scott County Investigation" February 12, 1985.

36. Humphrey, "Review of the Scott County Case"; J. Scalia dissenting opinion in *Maryland v. Craig* 497 US 836.

37. E.R. Shipp, "Boys Recant Stories of Child Murders," *New York Times* November 21, 1984, pg. A12; "Molester Admits False Testimony" *Washington Post* November 29, 1984 pg. A12.

38. Quoted in E.R. Shipp "Two in Abuse Case Found Not Guilty," *New York Times,* September 20, 1984, pg. A21, emphasis mine.

39. Humphrey, "Review of the Scott County Case."

40. *Innocence Lost,* Frontline original air date May 7, 1991.

41. *Innocence Lost: the Verdict,* Frontline, original air date July 20-21, 1993. (The entire incident is covered in both the first and second installment of the series, but in the second one the narrator refers to the slap as an accident.)

42. Frontline, *Innocence Lost.*

43. Ibid.

44. Ibid.

45. Ibid.

46. Ibid.

47. Ronald Smothers, "Child-Abuse Case Is Ordeal for a Town," *New York Times* Aug 19, 1991, pg.A13; "Day Care Owner is Convicted of Child Molesting," *New York Times,* Apr 23, 1992, pg. A16.

48. "Day-Care Owner is Convicted of Child Molesting" *New York Times* Apr 23, 1992, pg A16.

49. Ronald Smothers, "Big Molestation Trial Nears Its Close," *New York Times* Mar 23, 1992, pg. A18.

50. Quoted in "Sex Abuser Gets 12 Life Terms in Day-Care Case," *New York Times* Apr 2, 1992, pg. A14.

51. John Mitzel, *The Boston Sex Scandal,* (Boston: 1980), 137.

52. *The Boston Sex Scandal* outlined the origins of the North American Man/Boy Love Association (NAMBLA) from its beginnings as The Boston/Boise Committee and situated it in relation to broader liberation struggles, cultural change and institutional power. Mitzel's heroic tale of resistance represented a dramatic revision of legal, political, and medical authority.

53. See especially: John McMillian and Paul Buhle, eds., *The New Left Revisited* (Philadelphia, 2003); Thomas Frank, *The Conquest of Cool: Business Culture, Counterculture and the Rise of Hip Consumerism,* (Chicago, 1997); Lisa Duggan and Nan Hunter, *Sex Wars: Sexual Dissent and Political Culture,* (New York, 1995).

Chapter 15

What's Class Got to Do with It?: Facets of Tracy Chapman through Song

Heather E. Harris

Introduction

It was the decade that I graduated high school to the sounds of Madonna; watched the first show of the syndicated Entertainment Tonight; drooled over Marvin Gaye's rendition of the American National Anthem at the NBA All Star Game while watching cable at my cousins' home; peered in awe at Whitney Houston's first album cover through a music store window in a wealthy section of the city; and watched the wedding of Prince Charles to Lady Diana Spencer. It was the 1980s, and I was coming of age in the city of Montreal. My family had no cable, or high tech stereo system. We had a record player and a 25-inch color television set with about three English channels and perhaps as many French. I do not know for sure because I never checked. I could not afford the material symbols of the times, the jeans, shoes, or even the albums. For me, participation in this era of opulence was not dependent on the material possessions but on the experiences, the images, and the music. It was a time when I simultaneously wanted to dance with someone, and talk revolution, and it was all in the midst of the trickle down economics spearheaded by United States President Ronald Reagan and British Prime Minister Margaret Thatcher.

In the 80s, the music broadcast on the airwaves seemed to reflect an unprecedented mix of genres as well as artists' collaborations. Seemingly, for one decade in time, musical enclaves gave way to a musical eclecticism that was both heady and connecting. On television, programs provided fantastical and voyeuristic views of the lifestyles of the wealthy on Southfork, and in California's wine country as well as on new celebrity-centric shows. However, the reality of the decade was less gloss and more grind for many Canadians and others around the world. Beneath the patina of the 80s extravagance existed an often obscured and sobering reality. For example, in spite of having a standard of living second only to the United States, Canada's unemployment rate hovered at 10 percent, according to Scott McDonald.[1] The country also faced the potential secession of one of its provinces—namely Quebec, as the Francophone population's quest for respect and sovereignty strengthened. Additionally, Carl Mollins recalled the fortunes lost on the Toronto Stock exchange as a result of the Black Monday Crash of October 19, 1987.[2] The open secret was there was little depth to the shine of the 80s. As a result, it is perhaps the seemingly stark contrast of the October Crash to the opulence of the 80s that created a space for this unspoken truth to be voiced in the form of singer/songwriter Tracy Chapman. As Heather Nunn and Anita Biressi stated, "like ghosts from an earlier era—the "socially marginalised inconveniently haunt the present, chipping away at notions of the classless progressive society, making social divisions manifest and impossible to ignore."[3]

Tracy Chapman's eponymously titled album was released in 1988, one year after the crashes (Canada and the United States). J.R. Reynolds and Thom Duffy recalled how her album went to number one on the charts and spent a total of 61 weeks on the Billboard 2000.[4] Dubbed the Anti-Material girl in an article by Ian Aldrich, the writer added that her acoustic fare diverged from the popular synthesized music of the decade.[5] The singer who grew up with a sibling and a single mother in Cleveland, Ohio claimed the rawness of her music was fed by anger, according to Christopher Farley.[6] The *Nation's* Gene Santoro described the music of Chapman as follows: "Her songs are tales of power and menace—love, racism and sexism are the structural components of her world." [7]

This chapter thematically explores the messages of Chapman's debut album in order to determine how class is manifested, particularly in the United States, since this is the country about which Chapman sings. The major themes of Radical Change, Elusive Dreams, and Twisted Love emerge from her lyrics and are laced with the subthemes of despair and escape. A cultural studies lens serves as the framework. According to Douglas Kellner, this lens enables one to gain insights, from the 80s in this case, by examining how the media (Chapman's music) impacted the ideology of the period. [8] Lawrence Grossberg posits that "Cultural studies, while it has no pretensions to totality or universality, does seek to get a better understanding of where 'we' are so that we can get somewhere else, hopefully somewhere better, leaving open the question of what is better and how one decides, as well as the question of who 'we' are."[9] He further stresses that cultural studies is fundamentally about context.[10] Therefore, the context of the analysis of Chapman's music is within the aforementioned economic and musical conditions of the 80s. In accordance with Grossberg, the insights from the analysis are not intended to be definitive but rather what I understood and understand them to be.

Anthony DeCurtis claimed that musical success in the 80s required more than stellar musicianship; in the new era following Michael Jackson's Thriller, and the omnipresence of MTV, pop stars were likely to be more favored if they had acting skills and pretty faces.[11] Chapman possessed neither the acting skills nor the "pretty" face as prescribed by the media. Rather, her natural, thick hair and clean-faced image offered a prelude of her sobering music, and the need for us to cast our gaze and our consciousness, if only for the duration of a song, or the entire album, from the glitz to the gloom that simultaneously existed during that period. In the following three themes, Chapman sings about the types of change desired by those who have been economically marginalized in Radical Change. She then explores cash and consumerism as the cure for pain and poverty in Elusive Dreams. Finally, in Twisted Love, love is most often sick in search of a remedy. Yet she sings of the hope that once true love is found, all will be well.

Radical Change

With an image as bare as the messages in her music, Chapman exhibited none of the trappings of the 1980s pop stars. There were no pointy bras, big hair, or quasi-military garb in her performances. She countered with a simplicity that included a makeup-free face, dreadlocked hair, and an acoustic guitar. The minimal image rather than detract from her music may have made it louder considering the cultural hangover that was being experienced after the stock market crashed. Her debut album contained 11 songs written between 1982 and 1987. It was as if she knew the bubble would burst, simply because it always does. For instance, in the first single *Talkin' Bout A Revolution,* she sings about those experiencing economic hardship, and the need for a radical shift in positions among the haves and the have-nots in order for the haves to grasp the depth of the economic pain experienced by poor and/or disadvantaged men, women and children. This song and others such as *Across The Lines, Behind The Wall, She's Got Her Ticket, and Why* shift our attention to the travails of women and men in search of something more and better for themselves. She sings about the futility of welfare, unemployment and charity lines. For instance, in one song, there is a nameless woman being unmercifully and repeatedly brutalized by her partner while others listen through the thin walls of an apartment building. The police say it is okay because it is just a family squabble. In another song, children are maimed and killed for crossing racial lines represented by a town's railroad tracks. She literally asks why, and she liltingly warns us that a shift has begun.

Elusive Dreams

Langston Hughes asked, "What happens to a dream deferred?"[12] Chapman ponders the question and its consequences in *Fast Car* and *Mountains O' Things.* Her desire for the songs' characters to participate in the promise of the "dream" is palpable. Yet, the dreams are birthed out of despair, and a desire to escape rather than of hope. In *Fast Car* she sings of driving away to a better life. Yet she shows how a better life requires more than a change of physical environment, it also requires a reorientation of an individual's mental and emotional spaces. In *Mountains O' Things* the mode of escape is to go inside of her head. She fantasizes about a luxurious lifestyle where she sarcastically intimates that those who are living it have as their only worry being born with too much. She envisions herself "making it" and being surrounded by the televised version of wealth—good jobs, nice homes, furs, maids, caviar, champagne, and good relationships. All desired, yet all elusive except for the few who she describes simply as "you:" those people who exploit others on their way up the proverbial ladder of success, and/or in order to remain at the top.

Twisted Love

Tina Turner asked about it. Huey Lewis and the News encouraged us to feel its power; and Chapman wanted us to consider how we live it. In *Fast Car; Baby Can I Hold You; For My Lover; If Not Now...;* and *For You*, she professes her desire for love, if not relationship. Unfortunately, the love for which she yearns is plagued with resignation, abandonment, and rejection. For example, she implores someone in the song *If Not Now...* to recognize the temporal nature of love and the fact that it is one of the aspects of our lives that is usually free.[13] Yet the price the individuals in these songs pay for love is in many cases more costly that cash. The price is often their physical and emotional vulnerability, their self-esteem, and their freedom. *Fast Car* depicts the love that we sometimes practice due to internalizing and modeling the dysfunctional habits of those closest to us. The song's protagonist escapes with her partner to create a new life hopefully centered on love and security. She, however, creates a mirror of what she left—a drinking, jobless partner, while she becomes his downtrodden working mate.[14] In *For My Lover* she gladly spends time in jail as a sacrifice for the affection of her lover; and states boldly that their love is incomprehensible to others outside of the coupling. [15] Her partner in *Baby Can I Hold You* is unable to say the word love far less any other words that may serve as a balm in which love might settle and bloom.[16] Finally, in *For You* she extols characteristics of her all consuming and angst-producing love—she is out of control.[17] Throughout there is a profound desperation for something she believes exists outside of herself, something she seems deprived of, that can only be fulfilled by her lovers. She seeks them to be her shield from her diminished reality—a reality void of self-love.

Analysis

Intentionally or not, Chapman's aforementioned themes address issues of class that are described by Stephen Resnick and Richard Wolff as the costs of capitalism.[18] Although not unique to the United States, the authors posit that the type of capitalism that exists in countries varies only in matters of the degree.

U.S capitalism also shows another face, the other side of its coupling high exploitation with high levels of individual consumption...Endless statistical series document
these interrelated costs: legal and illegal drug abuse; work exhaustion; psychological
depression; environmental degradation; spousal, child, and sexual abuse; divorce;
interpersonal violence; gun fetishisation; rejection of civic participation (as in voting, parental involvement in schools, widespread disinterest in world affairs or any
public political debate); road rage, and the lonely isolation of daily life. The result is
a very fragile US working class.[19]

Chapman's themes touch on many of costs of capitalism and its inherent class
structure without mentioning either capitalism or class. For example, under Radical Change there is an unquenchable thirst for change—change from the nebul-
ous mechanisms that perpetuate the poverty, unemployment, self and other
abuse, sexism, and racism. Those in her songs aspire to rise up. They want those
(unnamed) who are unaffected by the dismal life circumstances to run; but to
where and from whom is not stated. Elusive Dreams confuses consumption for
class ascension. The hope is that once the list is checked off—the houses, maids,
fur coats, champagne and caviar—the accumulation of things will lead to fanta-
sy-based healthy relationships. The consumption will also result in the unnamed
(those who understand the value of money) recognizing the consumer as one of
their own. Ironically, those who understand the value of money may also view
those with little of it as unnamed. Since things tend to only exist when named,
the namelessness on both sides creates a space of invisibility where life happens
in certain ways but no one really knows why or how. In Twisted Love, her characters have seem to internalize the oppression and confusion that is fostered by
the unnamed force or forces; and they display these characteristics in unhealthy
love relationships whether with themselves or with others. There is little respite
from the cycle of yearning, spurning, and misplaced affection. At first reading, it
would be easy to blame the victim for the poor decisions and the disastrous out-
comes, but that is exactly the reading the feeds the cycle. Such a reading ignores
our interconnectedness as human beings in societies as well as the ripple effect
produced when the capitalist rocks are thrown into the sea of class. Those who
throw the rocks are ever present. They are able to hide in plain sight because of
our lack of awareness of the systems that we so eagerly participate in. Hence,
the daily miseries, deferred dreams, and unhealthy love relationships become
unsolvable due to the inability of those affected by the unnamed forces to identify and target the source of their unyielding grief.
    The success of Chapman's debut album speaks to its ability to avert our atten-
tion momentarily. We listened but we did not act. We continued our quest for
the cultivated panacea known as consumption, and what Chapman describes as
Mountains O' Things. We allowed, and continue to allow, ourselves to be seduced into craving the luxurious lifestyle and its accompanying commodities. It
seemed everything could be had, for a price, by anyone. Yet, did we really get
what we paid for? According to Resnick and Wolff, the answer is yes, because
they state that consumption serves as a coping mechanism for the majority of

people in a capitalist and class based society.[20] It is a position shared by George Lipsitz, as cited by Pepi Leistyna, who asserts that "Advertisers worked diligently to redefine the meaning of the American Dream from the search for a better life, to the pursuit of a consumer lifestyle...They effectively perpetuated the myth that buying products would bring about class mobility." [21] We bought the goods, but neither they nor the ability to cope with the realities of the capitalism last for long. Furthermore, class mobility remains a vague and ever-moving target for most.

While consumption was excessive in the 80s, it was not new. Resnick and Wolff affirm that consumption has been central to the US capitalist and class system since the Civil War.[22] Additionally, Andy Merrifield describes the wages of the working classes as decreasing between 1979 and 1999. He also notes that during the 80s, the decrease in wages was especially acute for those in the lower income brackets. As a result, many workers were forced to increase their hours with a second or third job. Hence, as their hours increased, so did their personal stress.[23] In the midst of the opulence remained the oppression and oppressive forces. Both the oppression and the oppressors were merely reconfigured but never truly identified, according to Michael Yates, who says that economic marginalization is less about a digital divide or which political party is holding office.[24] "What is never said, because it cannot be said, is that inequality is a normal feature of capitalist economies, and growing inequality is a natural consequence of capitalism when there is a quiescent working class, as in the case of the United States and much of the world."[25]

The dominant ideology of the need for rigid class-based societies remained beneath revamped packaging of apparent classlessness based upon the ability to buy or to commodify oneself. The ability to commodify oneself also appeared to solidify a new class category, that of the celebrity class. Amid the under, working, middle, and upper classes emerged a class that had individuals from many of the lower classes. These individuals were able to "transcend" their class of origin due to their particular, if not extraordinary, talents. Programs like *Entertainment Tonight* profited from and enabled the lifestyles of this new class consisting of the pop stars, movie stars, the curious, and the notorious. The creation and existence of the celebrity class reinforced the point argued by Nunn and Biressi that during what they refer to as Thatcherism, class was made invisible by promoting the idea that class mobility was linked to consumerism.[26] In other words, the deception was that upward class mobility could be attained through purchasing power or the selling of self. Additionally, if we were not able to make it into the celebrity class, we could literally self-brand with designer labels as a means of making ourselves appear worthy in a time of excess.

I conceptualize and define this class/classlessness shifting and invisibility as the "chameleonization of class." Its characteristics include: the absence of a lens or language to recognize or articulate class as a phenomenon that impacts our daily lives; the camouflage of low wages and rigid class categories through consumerism; and the creation and perpetuation of pseudo classes (such as the celebrity class) as a means of maintaining the dominant capitalist and class quo. Furthermore, it can be viewed the way Stuart Hall conceptualizes ethnicity as historically framed. How ethnicity is interpreted and/or experienced is dependent upon the historical context.[27] I believe the same is true for class. Grossberg echoes Hall when he espouses the essential need for context in our understanding of experiences.[28] Hence, how the "chameleonization of class" is manifested depends the ethos of a period: what class boundaries have been established, and what the general populace has been indoctrinated to believe about those boundaries. While in the moment the shifting may be difficult to discern, hindsight provides a vantage point. As a result, for example, it may be said that the creation of the celebrity class was a major legacy of the period. One of the most fluid classes due to its high out of favor rate, it provided, and continues to provide, a meta class space of hope for seekers of the good life.

In the 80s, class was obscured but it had not disappeared. Its presence, although somewhat veiled, is what made the stock market crashes important. Many people were losing money and jobs before the crashes; however, the "you" that Chapman advises to run in *Talkin' Bout A Revolution,* and the exploiters at the top in *Mountains O' Things*, these were the ones now experiencing financial pain due to the crashes. The commodity producing classes had received damage to their protective shields—their stocks. If they did lose their modes of production and could not produce, members of the working and middle classes could not spend. Class dynamics dictate that workers' needs come after, and often at the expense of, the financial security of the wealthy. The crashes could have brought class to the foreground—its chameleon nature stripped away. It should have been distinguishable from the glitz that cloaked it during the early part of the decade. In recognizing and addressing the losses of the wealthy, some attention could have been cast upon the sustained and intense hardships of the lower classes that Nunn and Biressi describe as being perceived by many in the upper classes as the undeserving poor. Many of these poor people, according to the authors, are those who exist beneath the working class. They are a group considered disorganized in their poverty and consisting mostly of females, including single mothers.[29] I argue that these and members of the working class are some of the people that Chapman sang about not because she perceived them as undeserving, but as a child of a single mother herself, she was perhaps able to recognize the condition of those affected by the trickle down economics of the age. Unfortunately, the crashes did not provide deeper insights into the often difficult life circumstances of the majority of people living in class-based societies. It was not a teachable moment, because lessons learned may have led to structural change.

Although Chapman is a woman, and Nunn and Biressi describe the undeserving poor as being primarily women, I contend that Chapman's intention was to share some of the realities of those who were being economically marginalized. Race and gender are mentioned more as descriptors while class, though unnamed, is the core thread in her interpretation of disenfranchisement. Furthermore, the author posits that while initially it may appear that Chapman presents counter hegemonic messages to the opulence ideology of the time, her messages actually served as a safe and soothing balm for both consumers and capitalists of the time. Her music and messages may have seemed to cast clouds in the skies of abundance with a reality check, but the author's perception is that they were used by the sustainers of the dominant ideology as a tool to quell what could have been a real threat to status quo after the 1987 stock market crashes. Through her music, the ire and frustration of the various populations could be calmed by way of lyrics and rhythms rather than expressed in the society itself in the form of protests and demands for fundamental change to structures of various societies that maintain the "class quo." The true power in her messages was contained while the purveyors of the opulence ideology steeled themselves momentarily in order to rise and/or change again. For example, it seems hardly coincidence that according to Chuck Arnold none of Chapman's subsequent albums attained the success of her debut.[30] Hers was not a social movement for radical change. No dent was made in the dominant class ideology of the 80s because of her music as James Lull deems necessary for an alternative ideology to take root.[31] Chapman would have required more voices, more listeners, and naming class and those who construct it in order to be considered even slightly counter-hegemonic. Nevertheless, her contribution is important because she raised timeless questions about the inequalities being experienced in an 80s world. Because of this, the momentary shift in gaze, if not consciousness, that she asked of us through her music served a purpose because it got us thinking about how many of us live in misery in the midst of plenty.

Conclusion

Chapman's message in her first album is as relevant in the Twenty-First century as it was a generation ago for she sang not of an 80s condition but of human conditions. She provides a snapshot of where we were. Furthermore, the afore-mentioned themes of Radical Change, Elusive Dreams, and Twisted Love all speak to the psychic, emotional, and physical violence class based societies can and often do produce upon the unaware and the uninitiated. Race, ethnicity, and gender appeared to serve more as subcategories along the spectrum in the class prism. In a decade that provided the illusion of equality for all, we were able to avail ourselves of an unprecedented variety of music, musicians, and entertain-ment. We were able to purchase much of what we were led to desire. Our posi-tion on the class ladder seemed to be a non-issue, and purchasing power equaled success, if not a shift in status. Yet, have we arrived someplace better because of where we were in the 1980s? I believe the answer is no. When many of us recall the 1980s, we remember the glitz as opposed to the gloom. Furthermore, we continued to participate in the "chameleonization of class" in the form of dot coms and bubble housing markets in subsequent decades. These enticements as avenues to the good life superficially teased rather than structurally transformed our nameless class dynamics. Unfortunately, this type of behavior also constitutes the human condition, and it keeps us in a space of surface class shifts instead of one where the foundational deconstruction of the class monolith is our priority. We missed the revolution that Chapman sang about because we did not recognize that revolution was, and still is, necessary.

Notes

1. Scott McDonald, "The Wealth of a Nation," *Vital Speeches of the Day*, 49 no.1 (October 1982): 7-10.

2. Carl Mollins, "The Excessive 80s," *Canadian Business*, 76, no.17 (September 2003): 71-74.

3. Heather Nunn and Anita Biressi, "The Undeserving Poor," *Soundings*, 41, (Spring 2009): 108.

4. J.R. Reynold and Thom Duffy, "New Wave of Black Artists Breaking into Folk-Pop Genre," *Billboard*, 106, no. 2 (August 1994):1-2.

5. Ian Aldrich, "Anti-Material Girl," *Yankee*, 65, no.6 (July/August 2001):93.

6. Christopher Farley, "Telling Her Stories," *Time*, 155, no.8 (February 2000):92.

7. Gene Santoro, "Music," *Nation*, 247, no.3 (July/August 1998):107-108.

8. Douglas Kellner, "Toward a Critical Media/Cultural Studies," in *Media/Cultural Studies: Critical Approaches*, ed. Rhonda Hammer and Douglas Kellner (New York, NY: Peter Lang, 2009), 5-24.

9. Lawrence Grossberg, "*Cultural Studies:What's In A Name?(One More Time)*," in *Media/Cultural Studies: Critical Approaches*, ed. Rhonda Hammer and Douglas Kellner (New York, NY: Peter Lang, 2009), 32.

10. Grossberg, *Cultural Studies*, 25.

11. Anthony DeCurtis, "80s. (cover story)," *Rolling Stone* 591 (November 1990):59-64.

12. Langston Hughes, "Montage of a Dream Deferred" http://matthewsalomon.wordpress.com/2008/02/12/langston-hughes-from-montage-of-a-dream-deferred/ (accessed December 15, 2009)

13. Tracy Chapman, "*If Not Now,*" Tracy Chapman, 1988, Elektra/Asylum Records.

14. Chapman, *Fast Car.*

15. Tracy Chapman, "*For My Lover,*" Tracy Chapman, 1988, Elektra/Asylum Records.

16. Tracy Chapman, "*Baby Can I Hold You,*" Tracy Chapman, 1988, Elektra/Asylum Records.

17. Tracy Chapman, " *For You,*" Tracy Chapman, 1988, Elektra/Asylum Records.

18. Stephen Resnick and Richard Wolff, " Exploitation, Consumption, and the Uniqueness of U.S. Capitalism" *Historical Materialism*, 11 no.4 (2003):209-226.

19. Resnick and Wolff, "Exploitation, Consumption," 218.

20. Resnick and Wolff, "Exploitation, Consumption," 217.

21. Pepi Leistyna, "Social Class and Entertainment Television," in *Media/Cultural Studies*, eds. Rhonda Hammer and Douglas Kellner, 339 (New York: Peter Lang, 2009).

22. Resnick and Wolff, "Exploitation, Consumption," 216.

23. Andy Merrifield, "Class Formation, Capital Accumulation, and the Downsizing of America" *An Independent Socialist Magazine*, 51 no. 5 (October 1999): 32-43.

24. Michael D. Yates, "More Unequal: Aspects of Class in the United States" *An Independent Socialist Magazine*, 59, no.6 (November 2007): 1-6.

25. Yates, *More Unequal*, 2.

26. Nunn and Biressi, *The Undeserving,* 107.

27. Stuart Hall, *"New Ethnicities,"* in *Black British Cultural Studies: A Reader*, ed. Houston A. Baker, Jr., Manthia Diawara and Ruth H. Lindeborg (Chicago, IL: University of Chicago Press, 1996) 163-172.

28. Grossberg, *Cultural Studies*, 25.

29. Nunn and Biressi, *The Undeserving,* 107.

30. Chuck Arnold, "Tracy Chapman," *People,* 64, no.12 (September 2005): 56.

31. James Lull, "Hegemony," in *Gender, Race, and Class in Media: A Text-Reader,* ed. Gail Dines and Jean M. Humez (London, U.K.: SAGE Publications, 2003) 61-66.

PART 4:

"We are the World": Understanding the 80s Beyond America's Borders

Chapter 16

Reading MTV: Proliferation of United States Culture in the Age of Globalization

Suzuko Morikawa

When a global commercial media system with new satellite and digital technologies opened its door in the 1980s, the multi-layered cultures of the United States quickly traveled across the oceans. At the dawn of the end of the Cold War, the globalization of the 1980s-era United States has mainly been demonstrated as represented by, on the one hand imperialistic capitalist icons such as McDonald's, Disney, Nike, and Levi's, and on the other hand as the breakthrough of media that tailored a new method of disseminating a particular image of the United States through such cable television networks as CNN, ESPN, QVC, and MTV. Through such a new medium of television, the United States "exported" a carefully crafted image of America to the world.

Music Television (MTV) represented not only the major spectrum of 1980s music, but also a mass market capitalist economy that had an enormous capacity to co-opt innovative ventures into a new product by fragmenting into various television and magazine markets. The emergence of music videos via MTV also played a significant role in internationalizing United States culture, including new conservative Reaganomics, diverse Catholic and Protestant religious morals, and the emerging queer, multicultural immigrant, and newly expressed post-Civil Rights era African American cultures. In this essay, I argue that this manufactured cultural identity of the United States derived from apprehension over the economic tragedy in the 1970s, as well as in response to competition from Europe, particularly England, about which the United States has always felt a cultural inferiority complex, and from Asia, particularly Japan, which advanced within the financial world based on advanced electronic and computer devices in the 1980s.

See it even in current election, how women supposed to look, etc

Video Killed the Radio Star: Innovations of Influential American Cultural Products

At the decline of the disco music scene, MTV debuted with its innovative scope of televised combinations of music and image, on August 1, 1981. Music Television, popularly known from the beginning as MTV, was a by-product of credit-card corporations, via American Express' expansion into the communications field, by purchasing fifty percent of the Warner Cable Corporation (WCC).[1] In 1983, when Viacom formed a joint venture with the WCC, MTV became a joint operation of MTV.[2] Although MTV struggled to make a profit in its early years, partly due to a relatively shallow penetration of cable television in urban areas, such as New York City and Los Angeles,[3] the channel became a money-making breakthrough with their domestic and international expansion, especially after the creation of MTV Network (MTVN) in 1984 and the official purchase of MTV by Viacom in 1985. Within ten years of its debut, MTV was spread across 201 million households in 77 countries in Europe, Oceania, Asia, and the Americas, including 48 million homes in the United States.[4]

In the 1980s, the International Monetary Fund (IMF), World Bank, and United States government deregulated and privatized media and communication systems due to new satellite and digital technologies,[5] which made it possible for a giant firm like Viacom to further pursue their business interests through MTV. This development coincided with a new method of television system, i.e. the cable network; this digital revolution at the dawn of the internet and dotcom boom in the 1990s occurred with a new theory of communication and control, i.e. communication through the cyber domain.[6] The technoculture of the 1980s derived from the early cyber domain system, which was based on increasingly widespread networking between computers, which in turn was based on the advancement of powerful computers from Apple, Commodore, and IBM, as well as the innovation of computer game technology in arcade games such as *Space Invaders* and *Pac-Man* and later the Nintendo and Sega home systems.

The expansion of cable television was also complemented by the invention of the videocassette recorder (VCR) and the remote control,[7] which gave viewers easy access to television programs by being able to skip the commercials and record the programs, as well as switching the channels much faster and easier. Furthermore, MTV's new concept of a "channel without programs" attracted teenagers and young adults, as seen in all-news for CNN, all-sports for ESPN, and all-weather for the Weather Channel. Music videos were broadcasted around the clock and introduced by "vee jays," the network's replacement for "DJ." MTV successfully captured the baby boom generation, the roughly 76 million Americans born from the late 1940s to early 1960s who were exposed to popular culture in the 1980s.

MTV introduced a different way of promoting songs and albums, which made the record companies and artists create imaginative, technically innovative, and costly music videos for consumers. Although MTV first started off with the

Buggles' innocuous video, "Video Killed the Radio Star," this concept consequently stimulated the entire music industry, including radio, by promoting more
record sales; the record companies and artists were given the commercial opportunities through music videos via MTV, which was totally innovative in the music scene. Many influential artists with distinctive visual looks, such as Boy
George, Stray Cats, and Men At Work, took great advantage of promoting their
albums via music videos, as did older artists, such as the Rolling Stones, ZZ Top,
and the Go-Go's, who were able to recreate their image to invigorate their
record sales.[8]

Two initiators of 1980s music on MTV, the popular music stars Michael Jackson and Madonna, greatly benefitted from their exposure on MTV, advertising
not only their music, but also dance and fashion. Michael Jackson's *Thriller*,
released in 1983, became the best selling album of all time worldwide, due
mostly to the release of the legendary music video of the song "Thriller." While
many traditional rock and roll artists did not experience as significant a bump
from their popularity in prior decades, Bruce Springsteen, U2, and other soft
rock artists, such as Huey Lewis and the News, Lionel Richie, and Air Supply
received heavy airplay. Heavy metal, however, experienced a legendary decade,
with groups like Guns N' Roses, Van Halen, Queensryche, and Metallica regularly appearing in music videos on MTV. Rap music rose to major prominence
in the music scene in the 1980s, though airtime devoted to rap artists' music
videos was limited.[9] Run D.M.C., L.L. Cool J., Public Enemy, Ice Cube,
N.W.A., M.C. Hammer, and other rap artists appeared more after 1986, partly
due to the development of samplers that could electronically record, modify,
save, and mix in at the touch of a few buttons.[10]

The emergence and success of MTV in the 1980s was a product of rapid capital development based on the Republican-led laissez-faire government and conservative economic system, as exemplified by global media giants such as Viacom which owned MTV, as well as changes in consumer culture. The targeted
young baby boom audience purchased CDs, taped songs on cassette tapes, and
listened to their mix tapes on Sony's innovative Walkman, which drew consumers further into the music scene. In addition, as a response to and critique of the
"American way of homogenizing, nationalizing, and rationalizing tendencies
against diversity and freedom,"[11] MTV served a crucial role in demonstrating a
radical transformation in United States and world culture by openly projecting
images of sex and violence. For this reason, MTV can be also considered to
have spawned a new social awareness through media, including different ethnic,
gender, and national groups. Advocates of diversity, post-modern social consciousness, or ambivalence toward the future will be associated with the image
of MTV, though such image was carefully crafted with the coverage of artists.

When I wasn't allowed to watch it b/c of words / sexualization

Frankie Goes To Hollywood: **British Domination of the Popular Music Scene**

Subsequent to the "British Invasion" of the American music scene in the 1960s, MTV set the stage for a unique form of British musical influence, known as the "Second British Invasion" in the 1980s. Beginning with the Beatles in 1964, the original term "British Invasion" was obviously created by American music critics, in an admission that rock and roll and other popular music forms were not exclusively American products any longer.[12] The Rolling Stones, The Who, the Dave Clark Five, and others utilized electric guitars and stimulated the American music scene by dominating the United States music charts.[13] Furthermore, ironically the British musicians introduced American MTV audiences to so-called "black music" that had been banned in white American music stores and radio stations, but which was available to adolescents in England and Ireland. They were very heavily influenced by blues and by R&B by singers such as Chuck Berry, Sam Phillips, Bo Diddley, and others. Many early British Invasion records (including those from The Beatles and The Stones) were covers of this "black music," which previously could not secure airtime at white-owned radio stations.[14] The "invasion" thus signifies not only their continuous success in controlling the hit chart or making great profit from selling the records, but also the influence of the British artists' life-style, fashion, image, and personality on American youth culture.

The MTV era brought a second distinctive music revolution with music videos in the post-British punk/rock wave. It was due partly to the international exchange of music occurring via global satellite and communication systems in the 1980s. The international influence on the American music scene via MTV was not limited to the artists from Great Britain as represented by Bananarama, Depeche Mode, Wham!, Duran Duran, Tears for Fears, and numerous others, but included Australian groups such as Men At Work and Toto, A-Ha! from Norway, U2 from Ireland, Billy Ocean from Trinidad, Nena from Germany, Europe from Sweden, and Loverboy and Bryan Adams from Canada, while American rock and roll, heavy metal, rhythm and blues, and popular music artists also thrived on the music scene in the 1980s. However, American competition with Great Britain in the music industry transcended the music itself, as Great Britain's supremacy in the area of broadcasting and print media as seen in the satellite TV via British Sky Broadcasting (BSkyB) and cable growth in the late 1980s had repercussions on both sides of the ocean.[15] Although MTV adopted the example of music video promotion from England in the beginning, MTV slowly established its innovative advertising and network series that is unique in the United States and the world.[16]

According to Graham Thompson in his *American Culture in the 1980s*, there are two major reasons for the growing popularity of British music among Americans in the 1980s. One reason is due to the intense rivalries in regional levels in Great Britain, such as London, Manchester, Liverpool, and Birmingham; in addition, the post-punk and new wave movements emerged based on a new electronic sound, especially the fusion of soul with electronic synthesizers.[17] The popularity of Duran Duran, David Bowie, Spandau Ballet, the Eurythmics, the Human League, and Depeche Mode derives not only from their distinctive new sound, but also from their looks, attitudes, and style, which appealed to the United States audience. Thompson argues that the music climate of the United States in the 1980s, specifically the eclipse of American pop scene, is another reason that the popularity of British artists, or the "second British invasion" was possible.[18] With the exception of certain distinctive artists such as Barbra Streisand and Hall and Oates, the United States music scene was experiencing less ground-breaking innovation until the appearance of Madonna, Michael Jackson, and Prince in the mid-1980s.

Joe Stuessy discusses in his *Rock and Roll: Its History and Stylistic Development*, the United States' vulnerability to European, and especially British, culture and arts. He argues that the United States tends to compete against, and at the same time, seek affirmation from Europe in regards to music.[19] Jazz and rock and roll are uniquely American and in fact, they are the most significant American musical contribution to world culture; however, Americans have historically viewed these music genres as not worthy of being taken seriously, until Europe pays attention and "legitimizes" the music.[20]

Since the Beatles hit the American rock and roll scene, British artists dominated the American music hit chart for more than a decade. This cultural inferiority complex, particularly in the mid-1960s after John F. Kennedy's assassination, has permeated American youth and adolescence, which made the United States vulnerable to this "British invasion" of the music scene.[21] Although the 1980s experienced the "Second British invasion," MTV's timely "launch" of a uniquely American network television aptly chose as its first image a montage of the Apollo 13 moon landing. MTV answered this question of "Americanness" in the music scene and overcame cultural inferiority to Europe, which ultimately made it an American cultural icon in the 1980s.

As a result of MTV's influence, a more bidirectional cultural and musical exchange occurred in the 1980s, unlike the original "British invasion" period in the 1960s. With the decline of British punk/rock, British rock artists sought their new sound from hip hop, rap, and soft rock in the United States, as exemplified by groups such as the Eurythmics, Wham!, and Culture Club. There was also collaborative work represented in duet songs between British and American artists in the 1980s, such as Paul McCartney and Michael Jackson, Phil Collins and Philip Bailey, and Sheena Easton and Prince. Furthermore, several British artists recorded songs about United States politics, such as U2's praise of Martin Luther King Jr. in *Pride (In the Name of Love)* and Genesis' chastisement of Ronald Reagan in *Land of Confusion*. Such popularity of British music among the American audience and vice versa made satellite devices more ubiquitous, which facilitated communication worldwide at the end of the 1980s.

As MTV spread throughout the world in the late 1980s, which led to the creation of MTV Europe, MTV Networks, MTV France, MTV Japan, and other
channels, including 16 MTV related channels in the U.K. alone, American culture became more internationalized. While MTV initially experienced British
domination, American artists who carried an inimitably distinctive appearance
and fashion sense, such as Madonna, Cyndi Lauper, and Michael Jackson, impacted European audiences. For Europeans, the United States had served as a
negative pole to define "European-ness" by providing an image of "who Europeans are not"; yet in the 1980s, the United States was paramount in television
production and trade. With this cultural power of domination through media,
along with American products and iconography, such as jeans, rock records,
Hollywood films and advertising images, European cultural sovereignty with old
values was tested in the 1980s, and such United States' influence was considered "American invasion."

Domo Arigato Mr. Roboto: The Economic Reins of Multina-
tional Capitalism

The new media order, often described as "global media," prevailed decisively in
the 1980s as a consequence of the multifaceted interplay of technological, economic, and regulatory changes. The underlying idea of this new media order,
coinciding with the emerging global economy and politics, was to "remove the
barriers" for trading, and MTV became one of the "products" of a wholesale
distributor, along with CBS and HBO, based on "universal principles of international consumer culture."[22] This global economy in the 1980s, championed by
Reaganomics capitalism, was justified as a means to acquire United States mul-
tinationals, which resulted in Japan's take over of United States landmark businesses and real estate. In the 1980s, Japanese computer, audio and digital products started to arrive on a mass scale, including popular game items, such as
Atari including *Galaxian* and *Pac-Man,* by Namco. Japanese financial domination, especially of the music industry, was represented by Japanese conglomerate Sony's purchase of Columbia Pictures Industry, a deal which included Coca-Cola and TriStar Pictures, a joint venture with HBO and CBS, followed by
Matsushita's purchase of MCA-Universal as well as a $600 million investment
in the Walt Disney Corporation.[23] These deals, along with Japanese real estate
interests in Manhattan's Rockefeller Center and Radio City, caused Japan to be
severely criticized by the United States for an "economic invasion," sometimes
referred to as "Japan Panic," or "techno-Orientalism"; Americans feared that
Japanese companies would move beyond buying Hollywood and New York
landmarks and "steal America's soul."[24]

As the United States established a "New World Order" with economic and
military control over developing countries through the International Monetary
Fund (IMF) / World Bank and the World Trade Organization (WTO) as witnessed by Ronald Reagan's declaration on Nicaragua affairs in 1986, the Reagan

administration believed that "America's basic freedoms and economic self-interest require that the United States be and act as a first-rate power."[25] On the one hand, Ronald Reagan enabled corporate merger frenzy by rewriting the anti-trust law and protecting American business interests abroad,[26] but on the other hand, a new Orientalism rose based on anti-Japanese racism, which has also been known as the "Japan problem."[27]

The United States' inferiority complex, therefore, continued beyond cultural thrust and media devices as seen in the competition among the countries across the Atlantic Ocean, and reached across the Pacific Ocean. The United States developed a fear of being economically controlled by Japan and other Asian countries after witnessing Japan's outperformance of the United States in the arenas of global economy and technology. With Sony Walkmans, Toshiba television sets, and Nintendo home video games, the advancement of the Japanese economy into American capitalism bewildered American businesses and society, which led American cultural imperialism to fear rather than to chauvinism or superiority. While American consumers embraced Japanese technology, as in the Styx song, "Mr. Roboto" (Mr. Robot) in 1983, questions for the American capitalist economy and culture during Cold War arose derived from the inferiority complex to England and Japan. This uncertainty created a backlash that engendered the concept of cultural homogenization and the determination that American popular culture would dominate the world, which often used terms such as "McDonaldization" or "Disneyzation."[28]

When such American popular culture with business, fashion, and food industry names entered in Japan in the 1980s, Japan was in a so-called "subculture boom." Known as "sabu-karuchā" in Japanese, the concept of "subculture" was imported from the United States and quickly permeated not only the academic disciplines of anthropology, sociology, and ethno-history, but also everyday Japanese culture, society, and politics. Although Japanese "subcultures" developed based on the concept and theory of Cultural and Ethnic Studies from the United States after the Civil Rights and Anti-War Movements, i.e. distinctive values of different social, ethnic, religious, and cultural subgroups, Japanese subcultures had their unique and independent significance, which prompted a new understanding of Japanese society and culture that debunked the existing social structure, philosophy, and tradition by focusing on newly emerging cultures in different social and economic groups, driven mainly by youth and adolescents in Japan.[29]

In the midst of this "subculture boom" in 1980s Japan, in combination with the concurrent permeation of American icons, such as McDonald's, which reached the top foreign food industry in Japan in 1982,[30] and Disneyland, which opened its first theme park outside the United States in Tokyo in 1983, MTV launched smoothly into Japanese youth culture and successfully introduced the American popular music scene. Although MTV Japan was not established until 1992,[31] several Japanese television stations had contracted directly with MTV to both rebroadcast music videos and create their own programming since MTV's

inception in 1981.[32] Such Japanese music programs employed attractive Japanese American vee jays who introduced music videos in fluent American English and then presented original programming in Japanese, which appealed to
Japanese youth's desire for exposure to both the English language and to American and more broadly Western culture. The idea of "home-grown" music videos
was introduced to Japanese popular music groups in the mid-1980s due to influence from MTV, and led to Japanese singers' expansion into music video; yet
MTV remained a strong source of American cultural influence, which became
one "subculture" in Japanese society in the 1980s.

Born in the U.S.A.: Diversity of American Subcultures

Under the conservative governments of Reagan, Thatcher, and Nakasone in the
1980s, the United States, England, and Japan's suppression of neo-liberal economic policies and political views created rapid growth of reactive diverse subcultures in each society. Having a paternalistic view of the "vulgar" United
States' culture in contrast to "traditional British values," the idea of English or
European "high culture" was challenged by the British working class, which
supported Americanization, in which America symbolizes the allure of the "tra-
dition-less."[33] In Japan's case, a counter culture of mainstream or high culture
led to the rise of Japanese "popular culture," such as anime, video games, street
fashion, and disco music, which also extended to the interests in American
popular culture that was brought by MTV. MTV quickly became a clearinghouse for American fashion, hairstyle, dress, products, and music, especially
through Madonna, Michael Jackson, Cyndi Lauper, and Prince. Therefore, the
Americanization of the West and East in the 1980s was successful via the music
videos which themselves became an advertisement of American culture through
MTV.

With these cultural and economic exchanges across both sides of the oceans,
the United States circulated their culture through MTV wisely. MTV vividly
depicted American mainstream and subcultures through the lyrics of the songs
and the images from the music videos. For example, while Madonna's *Material
Girl* expressed 1980s mainstream economic culture with luxurious dress as well
as the connotation of equal economic power as men, songs such as *Allentown* by

Billy Joel, *Living on a Prayer* by Bon Jovi, and *Born in the U.S.A.* by Bruce
Springsteen depicted poverty and protested Reaganomics capitalism in their
lyrics. Beyond themes related to the United States society, MTV aired songs,
including *Everybody Wants to Rule the World* by Tears for Fears, *Toy Soldier* by
Martika, and *Final Countdown* by Europe, which instilled in the young audience
keen international awareness, especially of the Cold War.

Though the lyrics of political songs had a significant effect on their corres-
ponding music videos, sophisticated choreography, cinematography, and other
visual aspects also contributed to introduce United States subcultures of the
1980s. Elaborated music videos reflect tremendous economic and technological

advancement in the 1980s Hollywood film industry and throughout the 1980s, at many times, record sales depended on the quality of music videos that aired on MTV. The most notable music video in the 1980s is typically deemed to be Michael Jackson's *Thriller* that was first aired in December 1983.[34] Directed by a popular film director, John Landis, this 14 minute music video of the title track completely shocked the audience with its extensiveness and technical virtuosity, which led to the biggest global selling album of all time.[35] Michael Jackson's brilliant music videography generated an artist, Al Yankovic, who made great success in music video parodies, such as *Eat It* and *Fat* (music video parodies of Michael Jackson's *Beat It* and *Bad*). Furthermore, well-regarded videos, such as *Take on Me* by A-Ha, *Money for Nothing* by Dire Straits, and *True Face* by New Order offered a memorable visual impression than more stripped-down videos that focused primarily on the music, an impression that translated into record sales; in addition groups such as Duran Duran who did not have strong musical chops were still able to become an iconic success in the music industry due to their outstanding video production on songs such as *Hungry Like the Wolf, Girls on Film* and *Rio.*

The visual nature of music videos also greatly influenced the global fashion industry. Madonna, Cyndi Lauper, Michael Jackson, and Prince quickly became fashion icons among their teenage audiences throughout the world. Particular clothing, accessories, cosmetics, and hairstyles, such as long bright color shirts with a big belt, fashion gloves and hats, big hoop earrings and bracelets, blue eye-shadow, and big hair bands represent the 1980s. The leather jacket and sparkly glove of Michael Jackson, the flamboyant dress shirts of Prince, and the casual beach style clothing of Huey Lewis and the News also became iconic men's fashion, followed by African American hip hop and rap artists who introduced "bling" in the form of big necklaces and established sportswear such as Adidas and Pro-Keds.

The fashion of the 1980s also includes the connotation of sex and sexuality, championed by Madonna with her heavy make-up, tight-fitting short skirts, and lace gloves that were fetishized and sexualized. Sex and sexuality were mostly expressed in lyrics, such as Human League's *Don't You Want Me,* Cars' *Hot Hot Hot,* and Duran Duran's *Hungry Like the Wolf* in the 1980s songs on MTV, yet highly sexual acts in the video for and lyrics of *Like a Virgin* by Madonna caused a sensation for the public for its explicit and provocative images of sexuality. The issues of sexuality also extended to queer culture, which surfaced with distinctive style and fashion mostly by British artists, such as Boy George of Culture Club, some members of Frankie Goes to Hollywood, Freddie Mercury of Queen, and the Pet Shop Boys. Their songs not only became popular in the gay club scene, but also addressed many social issues, such as targeting male homosexual communities amid the rise of the AIDS epidemic and the section 28 bill passed by the British government in the 1980s.

As a reaction to such open expressions of sex and sexuality during the 1980s, the New Christian Right also demonstrated their political and religious views through music videos of openly conservative Christian singers such as Amy Grant and Steve Taylor. Although their ideological roots can be traced back to the mid-1940s, the New Christian Right emerged as a coalition of conservative organizations and activists who reacted militantly against the Equal Rights Amendment and Affirmative Action, as well as liberalism and secular human-ism, as were demonstrated by African Americans and new immigrant groups and gay and lesbian communities.[36] As "video killed the radio star," television preaching, televangelism, replaced the radio communication formerly practiced by Catholic priest Charles Coughlin in the 1930s and Protestant evangelical preacher, Billy James Hargis in the 1950s. Television as a method of spreading religious messages changed the culture of the Christian Right significantly in the 1980s.[37] The development of cable and satellite not only skyrocketed MTV onto the music scene, but also helped the Christian Broadcasting Network (CBN) syndicate their programs.[38] With the rapid growth of such "electronic churches," which served approximately 7 to 14 million viewers in the mid-1980s,[39] there was inevitably spillover into other broadcast media. By incorporating artists like Amy Grant, the mainstream popular music scene on MTV attracted Christian youth; in this way, as in so many others, MTV was reflecting society in the 1980s.

The American culture exported through MTV was, however, comprised of carefully selected images, which consequently reflected a controlled representa-tion of American culture to be transmitted abroad, especially these two rival countries, England and Japan. For example, MTV was infamous for blocking African American musicians. In 1984, 83% of the videos featured a white male singer or frontman, 11% featured white females and only 5% featured non-white musicians of either sex on MTV.[40] Although so-called "crossover artists," such as Michael Jackson, Prince, and Whitney Houston, made their debut on MTV, MTV was reluctant to air "black music," an attitude similar to *Rolling Stone Magazine*'s long-time reluctance to put African American stars on the cover.[41] Rap artists, such as Run-DMC, Public Enemy, and De La Soul, emerged after such "crossover" artists "broke the color barrier" on MTV and later black style was accepted as in the program, "Yo! MTV Raps," in 1990.

We Are the World: How America Leads in Globalization

The 1980s witnessed a full recurrence of the Monroe Doctrine under the Reagan administration. During the Twentieth century, the United States claimed interest in Latin America, the Caribbean, and Asia, leading to military confrontations in Nicaragua, Haiti, El Salvador, Korea, Vietnam, and the Philippines, in addition to the invasions of Grenada and Panama, the Iran-Contra Affair, and the bomb-ing of Libya in the 1980s, though such economic and political intervention in these countries was against United States' Law. As the United States flexed its muscles by returning to the imperialism of the early Twentieth century under the pretext of the Monroe Doctrine, American artists united to release the album *We*

Are the World to save children from famine in Africa in 1985. Harry Belafonte and Quincy Jones undertook the project *We Are the World,* for which they recruited a large group of artists under the name USA for Africa, immediately after having recognized the importance of *Do They Know It's Christmas?* by Band Aid, a British charity collaboration among singers. Band Aid, organized by an Irish punk rock artist, Bob Geldof, sold almost 10 million dollars worth of records and received extensive MTV rotation despite the criticisms of their controversial lyrics which, amid reminders to reach out to people affected by the famine, exhort listeners to express their appreciation to God that Africans were suffering from hunger instead of citizens of the developed world.[42] In spite of critiques that the song was "more moral than musical" by the *Los Angeles Herald Denominator* and that it represented "the service of toothless one-worlder do-goodism" by *Village Voice, We Are the World* became a huge success along with *Do They Know It's Christmas* promoting the campaign against hunger around the world.[43]

MTV aggressively promoted and supported this charity campaign by donating a significant amount of money and airtime playing these songs. Among subsequent charity events such as Farm Aid and the Amnesty International human tours, Live Aid became the biggest event, simultaneously broadcast in three cities, London, Philadelphia, and Sydney, and electronically connecting 1.5 billion people in one hundred countries on July 13, 1985.[44] The technology of the 1980s made this massive event a huge success with satellite-link technology across the Atlantic and Pacific Oceans. MTV became the most important media outlet to broadcast the event, since it was difficult for the commercial, non-cable-based networks to replace their traditional line-ups of Saturday sports events for rock music; the *New York Times* even dubbed the telecast of the event as "relentless self-promotion" of MTV.[45]

These mega-events of fund raising efforts by famous artists in the 1980s were the reflection of Woodstock or the Monterey Pop Festival in the 1960s and the 1970s. This time, the events promoted awareness of the poverty, hunger, and homelessness by redirecting youth's focus from sex, drugs, and violence, thus emphasizing the social responsibility of music.[46] However, the idea of charity in the 1980s has been viewed as unrecognized irony on the part of the western nations, since the dramatic images of poverty in Africa due to the food shortages were the result of inequitable distribution of wealth that can be traced back to American and more broadly Western capitalist-imperialist policies. Furthermore, under the Reagan administration, the gap between rich and poor within the United States drastically widened because of the systematic undermining of social programs, shortages of services, shortages in both hi-tech positions in skilled industries and low-paying positions in unskilled service industries, and a decline in the creation of traditional blue-collar jobs;[47] in other words, the American underclass was suffering in poverty while helping the impoverished people in Africa.

[margin handwriting: MTV was like News]

Bob Pittman, the founder and CEO of MTV in the 1980s, was "proud to be using MTV's exposure to help....for a purely humanitarian purpose,"[48] though this "humanitarian effort" was still manufactured by mainstream society and promoted by media industries of the United States. While spending enormous amounts of money on invading other small countries and further enforcing un-equal distribution of the wealth of their citizens, the United States tried to com-modify the image of American culture by using MTV as a supplier. As Bob Geldof commented, Americans and the British "in the music business have made drugs fashionable; [they] have made wild hair style fashionable; [they] have made unusual clothes fashionable;" therefore, they can make "conscious-ness rising about world hunger" fashionable.[49] The USA for Africa campaign, including MTV's enthusiastic promotion, was the ultimate propaganda to per-suade the world that the United States will save the world based on American economic, political, and cultural hegemony. That now-famous title phrase exhi-bits the imperialistic implication that, within the context of the song, "we" does not mean "all the people in the world," but rather "the United States."

Conclusion

Almost 30 years after its establishment, the MTV franchise broadcasts in 35 countries serving a global viewing population of about one billion people through 22 customized feeds in 18 different languages.[50] In the United States alone, MTV is available to 77 million households. Even with its massive expan-sion, MTV still maintains its original character as a youth-driven, sexually charged, fun-filled purveyor of televised music. MTV has long since abandoned the "no-programming" model and now airs more original programs than music videos. MTV remains a unique media voice in capitalist entertainment in 21st century United States society and still broadcasts the image of America through its sister stations throughout the world.

Even in the age of the internet, cable television, and advanced worldwide news media, MTV's global influence remains strong, with an impact on youth culture throughout the world, particularly in relation to fashion and other visible cultural exports. American culture, as commodified on MTV, travels around the world via commercialization of American brands, such as Nike, Gap, and Ralph Lauren that are infamous for labor exploitation in developing countries, which leads to a further imposition of cultural and economic hegemony. Furthermore, MTV also contributes to "selling" images of alcohol use, drug use, sex, and vi-olence that have subsequently begun spreading among high school and college students among non-western cultures. While MTV has participated in more re-cent humanitarian efforts, including the Live 8 concerts to benefit the ONE Foundation, fundraising for those displaced by Hurricane Katrina in 2005, and a new incarnation of USA for Africa's "We Are The World" to benefit those af-fected by the devastating earthquake in Haiti in 2010, the network has not demonstrated the same level of involvement as in the 1980s. As such, MTV still is and will be the *face*, but not the *reality*, of American culture.

Notes

1. R. Serge Denisoff, *Inside MTV* (New Brunswick, NJ: Transaction Publisher, 2002), 7.

2. http://www.viacom.com/aboutviacom/Pages/history.aspx (Accessed December 10, 2009).

3. Paul Friedlander, *Rock and Roll: A Social History* (Boulder, CO: Westview Press, 1996), 263.

4. Lane Crothers, *Globalization and American Popular Culture* (Lanham, MD: Rowman & Littlefield Publishers, 2006), 60-61. Marjorie Williams, "MTV's Short Takes Define a New Style," *Washington Post*, December 13, 1989.

5. Robert McChesney, "The Global Media Giants," *Extra!* November/December, 1997.

6. Graham Thompson, *American Culture in the 1980s*, (Edinburgh, U.K.: Edinburgh University Press, 2007), 25-30.

7. Crothers, *Globalization and American Popular Culture*, 47-49.

8. Ted Cox, "Talkin' about a Revolution: MTV Turns 20 and Goes from Radical to Institution," *Daily Herald*, July 27, 2001.

9. Joe Stuessy, *Rock and Roll: Its History and Stylistic Development*, (Englewood Cliffs, NJ: Prentice Hall, 1994), 386. Thompson, *American Culture in the 1980s*, 141-146.

10. Stuessy, *Rock and Roll: Its History and Stylistic Development*, 288.

11. Richard King, "The Eighties," *Introduction to American Studies* (London: Longman, 1998), 313.

12. Stuessy, *Rock and Roll: Its History and Stylistic Development*, 154-155.

13. Ibid.

14. *History of Rock 'N Roll*, DVD. Directed by Andrew Solt, Bud Friedgen, Obie Benz, and Ted Haimes. (Des Moines, IA: Time-Life Video) 2004.

15. Edward Herman and Robert McChesney, *The Global Media: the New Missionaries of Corporate Capitalism* (London: Cassell, 1997), 166-170.

16. Richard Harrington, "Rock's Video Generation: How the Small Screen Changed the Sound of Music," *the Washington Post*, December 31, 1989.

17. Thompson, *American Culture in the 1980s*, 164-165.

18. Ibid.

19. Stuessy, *Rock and Roll: Its History and Stylistic Development*, 104-106.

20. Ibid.

21. Ibid.

22. David Morley and Kevin Robins, *Spaces of Identity: Global Media, Electronic Landscapes and Cultural Boundaries* (London: Routledge, 1995), 11.

23. Ibid, 149-150.

24. Ibid.

25. Jack Nelson-Pallmeyer, *War Against the Poor: Low-Intensity Conflict and Christian Faith* (Maryknoll, New York: Orbis Books, 1989), 8.

26. Bruce Kuhre, "United States Foreign Policy in the 1980s: Business Almost As Usual?" *Constructing the Eighties: Visions of an American Decade* (Germany: Gunter Narr Verlag Tubingen, 1992), 67-81.

27. Morley and Robins, *Spaces of Identity*, 167.

28. Crothers, *Globalization and American Popular Culture*, 24-25.

29. Toshiya Ueno and Yoshitaka Mori, *The Introduction to Cultural Studies Karuchuuraru Stadeizu Nyumon*, (Tokyo: Chikuma Shinsho, 2000).

30. McDonald's Japan, "Corporate History -- Enkaku " *Corporate Information – Kigyojoho*, http://www.mcdonalds.co.jp/company/outline/enkaku.html (accessed January 30, 2010)

31 MTV Japan, *Corporate Information – Kigyojoho*, http://www.mtvjapan.com/global/about.html (accessed January 30, 2010)

32. Tatsuya Yasukawa, "Play Back to the 80s – MTV Generations" *Sony Music*, http://www.sonymusic.co.jp/Music/International/Special/80slover/playback/index.html (accessed in February 5, 2010)

33. Morley and Robins, *Spaces of Identity*, 50-57.

34. Thompson, *American Culture in the 1980s*, 127.

35. Ibid, 127-128.

36. Bruce Kuhre, "The 'Politicization' of the 'Christian Rights' and Its Union with the 'New Right'," *Constructing the Eighties: Versions of an American Decade,* ed. Walter Grünzweig, Roberta Maierhofer, and Adi Wimmer. (Tübingen: Gunter Narr Verlag Tübingen, 1992). 51-66.

37. Thompson, *American Culture in the 1980s*, 16-17.

38. Ibid.

39. Sean Wilentz, "The Trials of Televangelism," *Culture in an Age of Money: The Legacy of the 1980s in America,* ed. Nicolaus Mills. (Chicago: Ivan R. Dee, 1990), 142-155.

40. http://themediamademecrazy.com/papers-projects/mit-cms/mit-cms-mtvhistory/ (Accessed on February 20, 2010)

41. Marjorie Williams, "MTV's Short Takes Define a New Style; Rock Videos Transform the Language of Marketing Series: The Eighties: The Fragmenting of Culture Series Number:4/5." *The Washington Post*. Washington Post Newsweek Interactive Co. 1989.

42. R. Serge Denisoff, *Inside MTV*, 269.

43. Ibid, 271.

44. "Fact Sheet: Live Aid: The Day the Music Changed the World" http://www.aptonline.org/catalog.nsf/0ae3941e1535ac9f85256db10052d22d/6517cbf416 9a345f85256f9b006a9d02/$FILE/LIVEAID.pdf (Accessed on February 20, 2010)

45. R. Serge Denisoff, *Inside MTV*, 274-278.

46. Paul Friedlander, *Rock and Roll: A Social History*, 265-267.

47. Richard King, "The Eighties," *Introduction to American Studies,* ed. Malcolm Bradbury and Howard Temperley. (London: Longman, 1998), 308-309.

48. R. Serge Denisoff, *Inside MTV*, 272.

49. Ibid. 271.

50. Paul Friedlander, *Rock and Roll: A Social History*, 265-267.

Chapter 17

The United States and Apartheid

Paul M. Pressley

The decade of the 1980s was a time of uncertainty and revolution for most southern Africans. Rhodesia became Zimbabwe, South Africa experienced a decade of civil strife, Botswana realized it needed an army to defend itself and Mozambique and most of the other frontline states were involved in the apartheid system through supporting freedom fighters or quelling assaults from the South African government. The Republic of South Africa was in the middle of an epic battle that stretched across the continent with its effects reaching as far as North America and Europe. Events in southern Africa in the 1980s did, if only for a moment, dominate conversations at the water cooler. Africa was making front page news and was no longer being ignored.

A main reason for a renewed interest in Africa had to do with the foreign policies of United States (U.S.) President Ronald Reagan. The Détente Era of the 1970s was considered a failure by Reagan and so many others primarily due to Carter's final year in office. Reagan set out to show the world that the US was a strong and powerful country. He was determined to return a strong America to the forefront. One of his biggest challenges was the apartheid state of South Africa.

Apartheid was explained by an Afrikaner, the former Minister of Native Affairs and South African Prime Minister Dr. Hendrik Frensch Verwoerd, as he stated in a speech to Black Africans of Soweto in 1950. "Must the future development of the Bantu and white societies take place together, or separated at far as possible? . . . If the answer is together, then it should be clearly realized that rivalry and clashes will take place everywhere. . . In such clashes, the whites will come off as best at least for a long time, and the non-white will come off second best in every sphere."[1]

Based on this discourse, an Afrikaner's definition of apartheid kindly boils down to *separateness* and *separate development*. Verwoerd and his followers expressed that Whites and Blacks needed to be separated so that both cultures could develop and reach their maximum potential. Underlying these words was the fact that NP leaders felt that Blacks were heathens who were unable to be civilized, educated, and Christianized. A Black man, as they believed, was not worthy of the life of a White man and should not be taught to appreciate the White man's world. The Afrikaners maintained and perpetuated their skewed ideas based on their history, the religion of the Dutch Reform Church (DRC) and their racist beliefs.

South Africa would dominate international news in June 1976 when thousands of students in Soweto began an early morning protest against the Afrikaans language policy which the government was going to implement through the Bantu education system. Afrikaans is the language of the White descendants of the Dutch. It is a mixture of Dutch, Portuguese and indigenous African languages, spoken primarily by the Afrikaners and those with whom they associate.

"English," the Afrikaners thought, ". . . represented unity in the national struggle"[2] as it was spoken by most South Africans and united people from various ethnic groups. English was the lingua franca of the region and allowed people from all African ethnic groups, Indians, Coloureds, Asians and other anti-apartheid protesters to communicate in a common language. Most important, Afrikaans was the *language of the oppressor* as the students chanted during the protest. It was a psychological and economical move by the Afrikaner dominated government to further strangle the development of the Black South African.

Given all the facts surrounding the Afrikaans language policy, the Soweto Uprising was much more than a demonstration against the language. It was a manifestation of a repressed society living in draconian conditions and being subjected to the most inhuman conditions of life. It was the thoughts of Black Consciousness placed into action. It was the actions of a new generation which hated the ways in which its parents lived. It was a reaction to the oppression in which Black Africans lived every day of their lives. The Soweto Uprising was the unheard voices of the oppressed telling the apartheid government it was unhappy with its current situation and expected a change in future endeavors.

After the Soweto Uprising of 1976, the South African government lowered its heavy hand on the Blacks, ultimately squashing almost all opposition through the use of force and every legal means of oppression. They banned almost every significant individual, group or element of opposition to the government. Copies of Rev. Dr. Martin Luther King's "I Have a Dream" speech and lectures of Malcolm X were passed from student to student and intensely studied by ANC underground members and other supporters of the struggle, yet, if one was caught possessing or reciting them they were subject to the harsh discipline of the apartheid regime. King's speech and most of his works and the writings of Malcolm X were also banned. Almost anything that promoted Black awareness or that stood in opposition to the apartheid regime was banned.

Children from the townships abandoned South Africa and joined the ANC in Exile, as it was the most organized entity in exile and able to accept the large number of youth fleeing the country. It was also the most capable organization that was able to give military training. Those who stayed in South Africa were subjected to constant harassment and ongoing abuse by government authorities. Various trials ended with numerous youths going to prison for years at a time. The inadequate system of Bantu Education grew worse, later reaching a point where education was nearly non-existent. Entering the decade of the 1980s seemed like there was very little hope for Blacks in South Africa. With the exception of the State of Emergency in 1960, the beginning of the 1980s was a quiet and bleak time for many South Africans.

Reagan's 1980 Presidential victory saw the Executive Branch and part of the Legislative Branch fall under control of the Republican Party, a party not in total favor of divesting from and boycotting South Africa. Reagan was determined to do business with South Africa and would use the rhetoric of communism to justify his positions. Chester Crocker, Assistant Secretary of State for African Affairs, acknowledged that the previous administration's policies towards southern Africa were fairly good, but he wrote,

> the years 1975-1981 represented an effective and fairly rapid assertion of US leadership in a previously neglected region. (Yet he continued), U.S. engagement in regional problems contained risks and potential downsides, but no guarantees of success. Carter's hyperactive African diplomacy—with its visceral tilt towards black African perspective and its schizophrenia towards Soviet-Cuban adventurism—was also divisive and controversial at home.[3]

Crocker's statement set the stage for his future policies on South Africa. In one of Reagan's first televised speeches as the President, he called South Africa "A friendly country, a wartime ally and a country of strategic importance to the free world."[4] *A friendly country* demonstrated how naïve and inexperienced Reagan was and gave plenty of propaganda for the South African government to use for promotion. One of the biggest differences in the Reagan's and Carter's policies was the associated perceptions held by others, but a real and very important difference was Reagan's Strategy of *Constructive Engagement*.

Constructive engagement was a policy which called for the US government to fully engage South Africa with the purpose of appealing to and providing incentives to the government so that it would change its policies of apartheid. It was the brainchild of Crocker who viewed Carter's harsh rhetoric as destructive. He felt the constant degradation and flagellation provided no reason for South Africa to change it policies. Crocker explained constructive engagement:

> Unvarying hostile rhetoric levelled at the apartheid regime in South Africa only served to increase Pretoria's mistrust and dislike of Washington. . . this approach merely hardened Pretoria's intransigence and made the South African government more hostile toward the idea of a gradual dismantling of the apartheid regime. . .
> Constructive engagement would involve an open dialogue with Pretoria, together with a reduction of counterproductive punitive measures such as certain export restrictions. In this way, Washington could maintain a friendly relationship with the

South African government—which was important for an American geostrategic and economic/trading interests—while gaining the confidence of Pretoria and thus enabling Washington to influence South Africa towards a gradual change away from apartheid.[5]

Where Carter openly criticized South Africa's apartheid policies, Reagan decided it was best not to dwell on how they governed. He wanted dialogue with his counterparts, even at the expense of the Black man. While Carter was instrumental in initiating the peace talks in Rhodesia, Reagan saw no need to pressure South Africa to change it policies. He did not like the apartheid system, but put the interests of the US before those of the Black South African.

As the Reagan era began, South Africa was in a quiet state of reevaluation. The country's security forces virtually shut down all overt opposition within the country. Black leadership was effectively quieted, but still not defeated. The harsh and brutal reaction against protestors and opposition took its toll. Black groups in and outside of South Africa had to rethink their strategy in trying to defeat apartheid. Although the situation seemed dispirited, the ANC was not inactive, but instead just being very secret.

The ANC underground and the ANC in exile, were planning and executing various actions to continue its struggle. The ANC Underground continued its missions of retaliation against the government. They made clear the objects of destruction were not people, but the infrastructure which supported apartheid. Their goal was to strike fear in the government and its supporters. The armed and destructive campaign waged by the ANC, no matter how humane it intended to be, did not sit well with the Reagan Administration. Initially Crocker wanted ANC officials to meet with him and South African representatives, but the South African government refused to meet with them until they renounced violence. Both Reagan and Crocker also maintained this position until 1986.

In the US, a growing number of events presented opportunities for those who opposed apartheid. In response to the new conservative government, anti-apartheid groups in the US decided they must act collectively if they wanted to push their fight against the South African government. Franklin Thomas was the first African American President of the country's largest foundation, the Ford Foundation. Franklin headed the Rockefeller Commission which studied US policies on issues involving southern Africa, but the primary focus was on South Africa. In 1981, it published the report, *South Africa: Time is Running Out*. The commission concluded:

> We cannot ignore South Africa. What happens in that country affects the United States. . . There is another reason for the United States to seek to advance the cause of representative government in South Africa. That is the issue of race . . . The United States has a long history of conflict, experiment and accommodations in racial and ethnic matters. . . Sustained racial violence in South Africa would initiate a bitter domestic debate over the appropriate U.S. response, a debate that could erode the consensus favoring progress on race relations here. . . Both whites and blacks in South Africa tend to look to the United States with hope. . . More specifically, some

black leaders have borrowed ideas from the civil rights and black power movements in the United States.[6]

Thomas urged businesses to abide by the Sullivan Principles and advocated for banks to forgo loaning money to South Africa. Randall Robinson, Executive Director of TransAfrica, a private advocacy group designed to bring awareness to and lobby for the needs of Africans and people of the Caribbean, began pushing Black legislatures to act on the situation in South Africa. Colleges and universities also started reviewing how they invested their endowments, looking to end any financial relationships they had with South Africa. There was a growing awareness in corporate, educational, and major industrial circles that South Africa was a country which should not be a part of their agendas.

In September 1981 the Interfaith Center on Corporate Responsibility brought together more than 50 American organizations to discuss the situation of South Africa. Over the next four years, many public and private organizations based their collective relationships with South Africa based on their investment portfolios with regard to the apartheid country.

Meanwhile, Crocker was in South Africa meeting with top officials explaining the new policy of the United States in southern Africa. For the U.S. to abandon South Africa's commitment to change would, in his mind, abandon the people of South Africa, both Black and White, and the foreign policies of the U.S. The situation was not helped when Robinson challenged Crocker's strategy. Crocker responded, "In South Africa, it is not our task to choose between black and white. 'In this rich land of talented and diverse people, important Western economic, strategic, moral, and political interests are at stake."[7]

At the end of 1982, Congressman William Gray, III (D-PA) challenged the Reagan Administration in their efforts to loan money to South Africa. Gray was a leading member of the Congressional Black Caucus (CBC), held a seat on the prestigious Appropriations Committee and was named the first African American Chairman of the Budget Committee. Through a *secret* government document obtained by TransAfrica, Gray learned that the apartheid government was to be a recipient of more than a $1 billion loan from the International Monetary Fund (IMF), but was told it should delay its request until after the IMF's annual meeting (September 1982). This infuriated Gray. He understood financing and capital and how it affects nations. He understood that if the loan was to be made, in essence, it would allow South Africa to operate as normal.

Gray was not the only one who opposed the loan. United Nations (UN) members were nearly unanimous against loaning the money to South Africa, as were at least 35 other members of Congress who strongly voiced their opposition. Still, Gray had resistance. Senator Nancy Kassebaum (R-KS), Chairperson of the Senate subcommittee on Africa and a host of others wanted to give constructive engagement a chance to succeed. In their opinion, Gray's position would be detrimental to the situation of apartheid. Denying the loan would not only hurt South Africans, but also place an unnecessary strain on the relationship which Reagan was trying to establish.

In South Africa, community groups or civics as they were called, were very popular and effective in organizing people to fight together. Civics were designed to fight against the effects of the Group Areas Act and the Black Local Authorities[8] since these two pieces of legislation had the most detrimental effects on Black South Africans in urban areas. Civics, if only for a short period of time unified various groups towards a common goal which proved to be very effective and left government officials puzzled as to how they could stop such large protests. It was quite apparent that the many more organizations (in South Africa) of all colors and backgrounds were very much in favor of overturning their draconian government, but without the unity and cooperation of all the smaller groups working as one, it was a near impossible task to do.

In 1977 Prime Minister John Vorster called on then Minister of Defence, P. W. Botha, to develop a new constitution that would reduce some of the threats the Afrikaner government faced. Years later, as the Prime Minister, Botha would introduce the Tricameral Parliament. The Afrikaner led government was trying to maintain its superiority throughout South Africa. Since 1976, their position of strength had grown weaker. The *swart gevaar* or Black Threat could only be defeated by creating a larger Afrikaner supported base of citizens. The Tricameral Parliament was enacted by the 1983 Constitution Act. As the Blacks saw a need to consolidate its resources in the struggle against apartheid, the government also saw a need to consolidate and strengthen its dwindling support in order to maintain its stranglehold over the nation.

In 1982, many of the student leaders who were arrested in the 1970s were now being released. Hundreds of them went to prison as children but were returning home as adults. Michael Zweniyazuza Xego was one of those men who was released from Robben Island in 1982 and returned home to Port Elizabeth. While imprisoned, Xego went through an extremely intensive educational process conducted by many of the ANC's older prisoners. They learned about the US and the Soviet Union. They read Adam Smith's *Wealth of Nations*, Karl Marx's *Das Kapital* and *Principles of Economics* and John Maynard Keynes' *General Theory of Employment, Interest and Money*. Xego still owns one of the books he was required to read in prison, *History of the USA*.[9] Because he was a follower of the Black Consciousness Movement (BCM), he was already exposed to teachings of W.E.B. DuBois, M. L. King, Jr. and Malcolm X. By reading and understanding King, he was able to understand how South Africans could conduct its struggles as African Americans did during the Civil Rights Era.

Upon his release from Robben Island, Xego was considered a *university graduate*,[10] as he was now charged to lead the fight against apartheid. Xego would become a regional player in the United Democratic Front (UDF) after its creation in August 1983. The UDF was created in opposition to the new Tricameral Parliament. The national entity grew to officially include more than 600 organizations and more than 3 millions individual members of all races, religions and socioeconomic backgrounds. Although the UDF did not make policy, it did formally admonish the US and Britain for its *imperialism*.

In November 1983, the white voters of South Africa approved the new constitution while Botha gloated in triumph. The victory would eventually make Botha the President, giving him supreme power over all government affairs. Many organizations believed the election was a sign of a changing country. The US Department of State saw the elections as a positive event and viewed it as forward progress for South Africa. South African officials celebrated the event as a successful point of progression towards separate development, and Botha continued stating that he could not envision Black Africans voting in a South African election or occupying seats of government.

Despite all of the official rhetoric, the new constitution was a bust. On September 3, 1984, the date on which the new voters, Coloureds, Indians and Asians, could exercise their civil rights, Blacks were also allowed to vote, but only for their African led township Mayors, Deputy Mayors, councillors and other administrators. Not surprisingly, only 14% of the Blacks in Sharpeville voted. Many lives ended that day as violence left dozens of people dead in township after township, city after city.

In South Africa, simmering tensions from the early 1980s boiled into deadly conflict as the chess match between the apartheid government and the anti-apartheid activists continued. In the US, divestment and embargoes were the centers of conversations about South Africa. Leon Sullivan pushed corporate America and the US government to act morally, ethically and be responsible with regards to South Africa. Ever since he authored the Sullivan Principles in 1976, he continually sought corporations (within the US and abroad) to abide by his principles of desegregation in the work environment. The Sullivan Principles are:

Principle I: Nonsegregation of the races in all eating, comfort, and work facilities.
Principle II: Equal and fair employment practices for all employees.
Principle III: Equal pay for all employees doing equal or comparable work for the same period of time.
Principle IV: Initiation of all development of training programs that will prepare, in substantial numbers, blacks and other nonwhites for supervisory, administrative, clerical, and technical jobs.
Principle V: Increasing the number of blacks and other nonwhites in management and supervisory positions.
Principle VI: Improving the quality of employees' lives outside the work environment in such areas as housing, transportation, schooling, recreation, and health facilities.[11]

At the end of 1984, the Code was expanded to include:
• Companies to influence other companies to follow equal rights path;
• Companies must support the rights of black workers to seek jobs wherever they exist;
• Companies must support the rights of black businesses to operate in urban areas;
• Companies must support the rescinding of all apartheid laws.[12]

The Sullivan Principles are a set of voluntary guidelines used to help organizations achieve success to its fullest while simultaneously developing and being respectful to its workforce and the community it serves. The key point of the principles is that they are voluntary, not to be forced upon an organization. One which does not abide by the principles is an organization that is destined to fail. In South Africa, companies tried to walk a fine line between caring for their employees and maximizing profits. In most cases, the results were ambiguous.

The cynic reminded Sullivan that there was a war torn atmosphere in the townships and that education was suffering. Many South African children were not going to school making the fourth and sixth principles irrelevant. Others enlisted in the program for fear that without doing so, the organization would run afoul with the local communities. It was seen as a strategic move to state that a company abided by the Sullivan Principles. Still other companies, no matter how hard they tried, could not afford to comply with all of the principles but managed to do the best they could stay in business.

In the early 1980s, many in the United States patiently waited to see if constructive engagement would work. Sullivan himself initially saw a drop in interest as he continued to push for corporations to abide by his principles. By 1983, Sullivan reported that a bit more than half of all US companies with entities in South Africa were employing the Sullivan Principles. Another report stated the majority of US firms operating in South Africa were using the Sullivan Principles. There were successes too. The US Chamber of Commerce, with the assistance of IBM and a few other US companies, created the Project for the Advancement of Community Education or PACE Community College, a state of the art high school in Soweto which educated up to 600 students.

Michael Samuels, Visiting Vice President of the US Chamber of Commerce used the school to advocate businesses staying in South Africa. Following the Reagan Administration, he believed sanctions would do more harm than good to the Blacks. Sullivan used the school to demonstrate how his principles, particularly Principles IV and VI, improved the living conditions of people and communities. Sullivan also pointed out that all Sullivan signatory organizations had more than 500 Black South Africans in various training programs.

A bigger measure of commitment to the South African cause were the issues of divestment and sanctions. They were extremely important in the ideological battle of actions taken or not taken against South Africa. It was crucial for the Reagan Administration and Crocker's constructive engagement policy to avoid divestment and sanctions on South Africa at all costs. "The most significant practical manifestation of his (Crocker's) policy was an improved political relationship with Pretoria, and one of the clearest results of this would be an improved and open trading relationship,"[13] stated J. E. Davies. Although Crocker himself did not view sanctions and divestment as the antithesis of constructive engagement, he did understand that the two actions, as well as the implementation of the Sullivan Principles were greatly undermining his strategy.

Following Reagan's second presidential victory, support for divestment and sanctions gained real momentum. Initial supporters of the policy saw no real progress in Reagan's first term. Robinson respected Carter's position on Rhodesia. He gave the benefit of the doubt to Reagan in his first term, but going into his second term, was primed for change. It was quite clear that many US officials felt that engaging South Africa in normal relations was not at all helping to improve the lives of the majority of oppressed Blacks. Instead, it allowed the White minority to maintain power over the Black majority. Constructive engagement did not help the Black South African in 1980, nor had it helped them in 1984. On November 21, just weeks after the election, members of the Free South Africa Movement (FSAM) protested outside the Embassy of South Africa in Washington, DC. FSAM was created to promote issues of South Africa through various staged protests in media covered arenas providing maximum exposure to the audiences. The event made history. Robinson handcuffed himself to the embassy gates, was arrested and taken from the scene by police. A Republican US Senator was also arrested for civil disobedience giving more credence to the fight against apartheid and the constructive engagement policy exercised by the Republican president. Robinson's simple act of defiance was broadcasted on national television, leading to a surge in awareness and anti-apartheid activities in the US. Robinson stated, "Many historians believe that this bold action provided a spark that set off a series of protests on college campuses across the United States."[14] Three days later, Rev. Joseph E. Lowery, President of the Southern Christian Leadership Conference was also arrested at the embassy. CBC members Robert V. Dellums (D-CA) and John Conyers (D-MI) and members of the D.C. City Council found their way onto the rap sheets of the police. The protest was so successful that it was continued for a few more weeks, limiting the arrests per day to three so it could continue to be an irritant to those in the South African Embassy. Anti-apartheid rallies, demonstrations and protests were commonplace after Robinson's actions. College students, professors, government officials, union members, churchgoers, mayors, actors, singers, clergy were all instrumental in protesting at South African Consulates throughout the US. By this time, the idea of constructive engagement was reduced solely to an unworkable theory. Its merits, if there were any left to salvage, were overshadowed by the events seen by the entire world.

Following a Reagan presidential victory, one would have expected a great deal of joy in being the victor, but events continued to put the American public at odds with constructive engagement. Showing their disdain for the policy, 35 Republican Congressmen released the details of a letter they wrote to South African Ambassador, Brand Fourie. Representatives Vin Weber (R-MN), Bob Walker (R-PA) and Newt Gingrich (R-GA) led the group of dissenters as they urged the Ambassador to immediately end the violence and demonstrate concrete measures to end apartheid. The same group threatened the Ambassador with support for economic sanctions if these measures were not implemented. Crocker believed it was the accumulation of these events that began the battle of

US policy towards South Africa.[15] If one was to view divestment and economic sanctions as the converse to constructive engagement, they may say this short epoch was the beginning of the end of constructive engagement.

Looking back on the events of late 1983-1984, Crocker stated, "If one stopped to think about it, the situation was bizarre."[16] He referred to the rapidly escalating violence being filmed by an international media and shown to an international audience, the awarding of the Nobel Peace Prize to South African Anglican Bishop, Desmond Tutu, and the FSAM demonstration outside the South African Embassy in Washington, DC, beamed throughout the US and the world. "A tactical alliance mushroomed before our eyes. Each partner made the other into a larger-than-life threat to the local status quo."[17]

On April 4, 1985, thousands of college and university students across the nation joined together in a massive protest against apartheid. Participating schools included Columbia University, where some 300 students took over the academic building and staged a hunger strike, Howard University and Michigan State University, two institutions that had already completely divested their South African associated investments, Harvard University, where students were encouraged to donate to alternative school funds and not the general fund which still had investment ties to South Africa, and the University of California, Berkeley. Protesting students sent a message that was not only directed at their institution's leadership, but also at the local and state officials who had investments in South African associated companies. There was probably no direct divestment action taken due to these protests, but like the previous media covered events, this too further enlightened the public to the issues of South Africa.[18]

In 1985, Gray co-authored a bill that essentially banned new investments and new loans to South Africa. It also directed all American companies that conduct business in the country and have more than 25 employees to abide by the Sullivan Principles. With the complete support of the CBC, the Democratic controlled House passed the measure by a 295 to 127 margin. Fifty-six Republicans voted for the House Bill. Soon after, the Republican controlled Senate was drafting its own bill on South Africa. Senator Richard Lugar (R-IN), Chairman of the Senate Foreign Relations Committee authored a similar but weaker bill which also passed in the Senate by an 80-12 vote. By then, even Kassebaum, who gave constructive engagement a chance to succeed, wanted the President to act decisively against the Afrikaner government. Party politics were set aside leaving Reagan, Crocker and constructive engagement in a corner by itself. Major US corporations had already begun to pull out of South Africa. Coca-Cola, IBM, Ford Motor Company, General Motors, AT&T, and Johnson & Johnson were among the many that left the country.

Fighting to gain an upper hand in the apartheid debate, Reagan issued Executive Order 12532 calling South Africa an unusual threat to the economy of the US. The order prevented the US from exporting nuclear related equipment and *encouraged* organizations doing business in South Africa to implement the Sullivan Principles. More importantly, the Executive Act did not ban nuclear transactions (under international control) intended for humanitarian purposes and did not ban the import of uranium from South Africa. This was followed by the National Security Decision Directive 187 (NSDD). NSDD called for the Executive Branch to implement a public relations campaign to stop Congress from passing legislation contrary to the President's initiatives, design a program for the US Embassy in South Africa to better relate to the blacks in the country, and develop a long term plan with support from American and South African citizens to establish and execute programs designe to reform the embattled nation. In December, the Department of State announced they created an advisory committee on South Africa. The committee was supposed to devise methods which the US could use to convince South Africa to abandon apartheid. In essence, the Executive Act, the NSDD and the advisory committee tried to give the public the impression that the administration was acting forcefully against apartheid.

On October 2, 1986 the US Congress passed the Anti-Apartheid Act (CAAA) of 1986 after it was vetoed by Reagan (12% of Reagan's vetoes were overturned, not a high number compared to his last few predecessors). The hard fought victory by Gray, Robinson, Thomas, Sullivan, the CBC and many other anti-apartheid activists was a referendum ending constructive engagement. The Reagan/Crocker construct was no longer. The CAAA ordered a ban on all economic relations with South Africa and told the President to persuade other developed nations to follow the lead of the US. It called for the US to pursue avenues of communications with the ANC and to determine what countries violated the international arms embargo.

As companies, corporations, universities and other major organizations divested from and pulled their business interests out of South Africa, others called for a cultural ban of everything South African. Protests dominated college campuses and speakers from the BCM, ANC, End Conscription Campaign and a host of other anti-apartheid groups toured the US speaking against the South African government. The cast and crew (many of them were children) from the musical *Sarafina!* were banned from returning to South Africa after performing in London and the US. Mark Mathabane toured the US promoting his worldwide bestseller, *Kaffir Boy*. American musician Steven Van Zandt formed the group Artists United Against Apartheid and released the album *Sun City* in protest of the South African government. He was joined by other American artists such as Grandmaster Melle Mel, Bob Dylan, Herbie Hancock, Run DMC, David Ruffin, Eddie Kendricks, Afrika Bambaataa, Kurtis Blow, Jackson Browne, George Clinton, Bobby Womack, Darryl Hannah, Bonnie Raitt, Hall & Oates, Gil-Scott Heron, Nona Hendryx and Pat Benatar. From its top selling single, the lyrics read, "Our government tells us we are doing all we can, constructive engagement is Ronald Reagan's plan. Meanwhile people are dying and giving up hope, well this quiet diplomacy ain't nothing but a joke."[19]

In South Africa, 1985 was an explosive year that would only get worse. The violence from the UDF protests were only the beginning of the firestorm coming. In Port Elizabeth, violence was being carried out by security forces in order to quiet dissidents. On the 25th Anniversary of the Sharpeville Massacre, police fired on a group of people in Langa Township (Uitenhage) killing 29 as they were marching to a funeral. Of the 47 people who were shot, reports showed 35 of them were shot in the back, indicating they were fleeing from the police. The next day riots broke out in cities throughout the country. Later that summer, the murders of the Cradock Four (Matthew Goniwe, Fort Calata, Sparrow Mkhonto, and Sicelo Mhlawuli) caused a major uproar and would lead to the first State of Emergency (Martial Law) since 1960. Black leaders by the hundreds were arrested and jailed indefinitely as the violence from both sides escalated to an unseeingly impossible level.

Anti-apartheid activist Mkhuseli Jack was tired of the violence. A very bright and dynamic man, Jack rallied people toward peace and away from violence, even as he lived in one of the most violent areas in the country. Jack wondered why all that was bad happened in the Black townships. He felt the struggle should be taken out of the townships and placed at the foot of the Whites. In the summer of 1985, Jack announced a nationwide Consumer Boycott of all White owned establishments. All consumer products would be purchased only in approved Black owned stores. The boycott was envisioned to be on par with the Montgomery Bus Boycott of 1955, a nonviolent and peaceful protest by African Americans. On the first day of the boycott, shops on the North End (the shopping area frequented by Blacks in the Port Elizabeth area) were empty save the Whites that worked there. Within five days, Pretoria (the Administrative Capital of South Africa) ordered a State of Emergency in Port Elizabeth and other magistrates that were deeply affected by the activism. Jack had to go into hiding. He was wanted by the police. After his arrest on August 2, Crocker publicly called for his immediate release. Even South African newspapers carried this story on their front pages.

Jack employed a weapon to which the government had no answer. He showed the world the fiscal force of the Black Community, made the White establishment seek him, a Black man, to talk about concession to end the boycott, made the White Community feel the effects of apartheid and united practically the entire Black community in a common and achievable goal. He also ensured that the White business owners pressured the government to meet demands he set before the boycott was lifted. In retrospect, the Consumer Boycotts were ironic twists on the situation faced by US lawmakers. Robinson, Gray, the CBC and a host of others were successful in preventing the US from selling its goods in South Africa, while the Black South Africans were also successful in preventing their communities from buying White goods. During the boycotts, the always charismatic Jack stated, "Our buying power, our buying power is going to decide the future that is going to decide our destiny in this country."[20]

As bleak as it was in South Africa, 1986 was bright for the anti-apartheid activists in the US. The Reagan administration made its first contact with ANC officials. In July, US Ambassador to Zambia, Paul Hare, met with three top ANC officials in Lusaka. In September, Crocker met with ANC President Oliver

Tambo in London. The most controversial meeting came in January 1987, after the passage of the CAAA and after the Consumer Boycotts and the arrests and chaos which followed. Apartheid was no longer viewed as an institution that may or may not last. It would only be a matter of time before apartheid was dead. This made the next US/ANC meeting crucial, if not controversial. Secretary of State George Schultz hosted Tambo in Washington, DC. With both parties having distrust for each other, anything tangible was not expected. Tambo expressed his regrets that he could not meet with the President but appreciated the encounter. Surprisingly, the State Department characterized the ANC as having *a voice concerning South Africa*, yet Schultz would also reiterate his dislike for the ANC's communist connections and its inability to renounce violence. Some viewed the verbal scolding as an appeasement to the right wingers who disapproved of any contact with the ANC. Others viewed the entire series of meetings as a shift in policy for the Reagan administration. The reality is somewhere in between the two.

In August 1986, Botha announced another State of Emergency, this time for the entire country. Jack and the rest of the organizers of the Consumer Boycotts were arrested. Tens of thousands of other people were also arrested. Entire communities lived without the majority of their leaders. The Amabutho—a loosely knit group of youths who thrived on chaos and violence—ran the townships through fear and intimidation. Violence was as much a part of the townships as the dirt roads and shanty homes. Dead bodies were left scattered on the roads on a daily basis. Schools were virtually nonexistent. The sense of community that once prevailed in all Black townships was virtually gone.

Between 1987 and 1988 South Africa was hell. Workers began mass protests and stay-a-ways (day long strikes from their place of employment) as the violence continued. A delegation of 60 prominent White South African business and community leaders departed for Senegal where they met and talked with Tambo. In 1987, union mine workers numbering more than 200,000 staged a three week strike, causing severe damage to the industry. In June 1988, an estimated 3,000,000 Black laborers went on strike against the government for what they called anti-labor legislation. Violence in KwaZulu and the Natal increased as Inkatha and UDF supporters continued their deadly clashes.

In mid 1988, the US successfully mediated talks between South Africa, Angola and Cuba over issues concerning peace in southern Africa. South West Africa (Namibia) would receive its independence and Cuban troops would withdraw from Angola. Simultaneously, the ANC agreed to forgo all military bases in South West Africa. In November 1989, free elections were held and on 21 March 1990, South Africa finally removed its flag from Namibia granting them full independence.

The world saw the Changing of the Guard 1989. In Washington, George H.W. Bush became President and in South Africa F W de Klerk was elected the new Chairman of the National Party. With the new leaders came a new outlook of governing. Both men met with their opposition. Bush met with Tutu, Reverend

Allan Boesak, President of the World Alliance of Reformed Churches, and Reverend Beyers Naudé, Afrikaner Clergyman who for decades denounced apartheid, in May 1989 and followed that meeting by hosting Albertina Sisulu and other prominent UDF leaders. In July, Botha (he was still President) went to Cape Town (Pollsmoor Prison) to meet Mandela. A month later he would resign as President, passing the reins to de Klerk. Change was sweeping South Africa. Even though the violence continued, a dying apartheid system was fading fast. On February 11, 1990, the man who would become the First Black President of South Africa, Nelson Mandela, walked out of prison a free man, symbolizing a freedom for all South Africans.

Scholars question whether or not Reagan's foreign policies in southern Africa assisted in the Africans receiving their freedoms. Some would say that his policies were detrimental to their advancement. Crocker would tell you that the debate cannot be made since constructive engagement was not seen for what it was, but instead viewed as the opposite of sanctions. Since constructive engagement was supposed to provide incentives to encourage South Africa to eliminate apartheid, it could not be measured. Again, the latter statement is debatable since many anti-apartheid activists gave Reagan time to demonstrate he had an effective policy. It was after his reelection to the Presidency when the pressure to divest and apply sanctions became most prominent. Crocker did state, "We are not against sanctions. We just want to get sanctions right."[21] He continued to say that he thought eliminating loans to South Africa was a good thing to do.

In almost any form, constructive engagement should be viewed as a failure. Looking at Reagan's first term, one cannot point to a single incentive or any progress towards changing the apartheid policy. If anything, the South African government grew more repressive against Blacks. One could argue that the new constitution in 1984 was progress, but that argument is moot since the constitution was approved not by the majority of South Africans, but *by the majority of South African voters*, most all of whom were White. The new constitution still prevented Blacks from fully participating in government and continued to deny their civil rights.

Where the Reagan policies were supposed to provide incentives for change, Reagan officials never included the Black South Africans who were to benefit from these changes. Crocker and the Reagan Administration refused to meet with the ANC (until placed under severe pressure to do so), the group with the majority of support from Black Africans. How, one wonders, can a policy effect change when those who will benefit from the change have not been consulted. "The fact remains that the Reagan Administration operated an anti-*apartheid* strategy for eight years without any real positive results" wrote lecturer Alex Thomson after reviewing much that was written on constructive engagement soon after 1990.[22]

Gray, on the other hand, is always happy to talk about his successes. When asked if the Sullivan Principles had a role in eliminating apartheid, Gray replied,

"I think it had a very important role. . . later I was able to write the Anti-Apartheid Act that became law and put real sanctions on it. But Leon had to do the Sullivan Principles to show a first step. And it was a big step, it was important and it was revolutionary at the time."[23] There is no doubt that the Sullivan Principles and the CAAA was a monumental victory for the anti-apartheid movement in the US. It was a victory for those who fought hard against the Reagan policies. But was the CAAA as effective in eliminating apartheid as Gray stated? If so, why then did Dellums call for harsher sanctions in 1988 with a bill that made it through the House with only Democratic support? It is very hard to measure the actual affects of the CAAA, but its positive psychological effects in the US cannot be disputed. The CAAA was responsible for killing constructive engagement and it gave a huge boost to the anti-apartheid forces. It also united the US with much of the other world in the moral battle against the South African regime. Many governments talked loudly against apartheid, but acted in another manner. The CAAA did not allow this from the US. It made the Reagan administration enforce real sanctions against a dying government and act in other ways which it would not have done. It also demonstrated to the apartheid regime that the checks and balances of the US government (overriding the Presidential veto) was not going to allow its President to abandon the desires of the majority of the population and deal with an unethical and immoral government. The CAAA proved to be damning to the South African government as Gray later stated,

What sanctions did was devalue the currency of South Africa. It closed down all credit to South Africa and to South African government. And without capital, it meant that the economy began to shrink. Who does that have the greatest impact on? Not the poor, but those who are living in those beautiful houses with black servants who were the ruling class they were the first to feel it and they were the ones first to say, hey, we have got to change.

And I think F. W. deKlerk did the right thing because he understood that the west was serious when the largest democracy, the U.S. stepped forward and said: Enough is enough. Racist totalitarian regimes must be opposed. We can oppose them economically, and that was when deKlerk said we have to change.

And he did the right thing and I have to commend him for having the foresight to understand that. . .[24]

Between constructive engagement and CAAA, is the argument for success lacking the role of the Black South African? Going back to 1652 with the arrival of Jan van Riebeeck, Black South Africans resisted the invading oppressors whenever possible. One can write about the slave revolts, Frontier Wars, Anglo-Zulu Wars, South African War, creation of the South African Native National Congress (the precursor of the ANC), Defiance Campaign of 1952, Nobel Peace Prize to Albert Luthuli (1960) and all of the other previously mentioned activities. In the debate as to whose policies best helped to defeat apartheid, no one should ever forget the Black South African who bore the brunt of brutality for so many generations. As Carter called for tighter economic sanctions, teenagers by the thousands had already fled their families, friends and country so they could take arms against their government while those who stayed rioted on their streets. When Reagan was entering office, thousands of Black youths were being thrown in prisons. As Congress passed the CAAA, tens of thousands of Blacks were jailed, or worse, killed. Violence turned the townships into war zones, and children chanted *liberation before education!* But, it did end, with much thanks to so many entities, including a strong US Congress that faced their leader head on.

South Africa would become the last country on the continent to receive its freedom from its colonial rulers. In April 1994, all citizens of the *Rainbow Nation* voted Mandela to become their first Black President. Achieving this milestone took hundreds of years of Black resistance. It is almost irrelevant whether or not constructive engagement or the Sullivan Principles and the CAAA had the most impact on the nation's freedom. What is most relevant are the ties maintained between the Blacks in South Africa and the Blacks in the US who supported their fight for freedom. That does not mean that Whites and other people did not play a role in the struggle. They did, but ties to the Diaspora rarely equates to non-Blacks. Sullivan, Gray, Dellums, Conyers and a host of other African Americans understood how the Black South Africans lived under apartheid. It was not so long ago that these men lived through much of what the Black South African experienced. An important message of this struggle was the fact that African Americans were able to enact legislation to influence events on the continent from where they originally came. A group of brave and intelligent souls who recently overcame years of legal discrimination, lynching and Jim Crow laws were now helping to overthrow a similar structure in a faraway land, a land that still provided a strong kinship with living there. An African connection was forged once again.

Notes

1. Robert Kinloch Massie, *Loosing the Bond: The United States and South Africa in the Apartheid Years* (New York: Doubleday, 1997), 27.

2. Mark Sanders, *Complicities: The Intellectual and Apartheid* (Durham, NC: Duke University Press, 2002), 150.

3. Chester A. Crocker, *High Noon in Southern Africa: Making Peace in a Rough Neighborhood* (New York: W.W. Norton & Company, 1992), 38-39.

4. J. E. Davis, *Constructive Engagement? Chester Crocker & American Foreign Policy in South Africa*, Namibia & Angola (Oxford: James Currey, 2007), p. 28.

5. J. E. Davis, Introduction to *Constructive Engagement?*, 1.

6. Introduction to *South Africa: Time Running Out: The Report of the Study on the U.S. Policy Toward Southern Africa*," Foreign Policy Study Foundation, Inc. (Berkeley and Los Angeles, CA: University of California Press, 1981), xvii – xxi.

7. Massie, *Loosing the Bonds*, 492.

8. Paul M Pressley, "Protest and Resistance in Port Elizabeth, South Africa, 1976-1990" (PhD diss,. Howard University, 2006), 151-152.

9. Pressley, *"Protest and Resistance*," 112.

10. Anthony W. Marx, *Lessons of the Struggle: South African Internal Opposition, 1960-1990* (New York: Oxford University Press, 1992), 97.

Ravan Press, 1987), 129.

11. *South Africa: Time Running Out*, 462–464.

12. J. E. Davies, *Constructive Engagement?*, p. 43.

13. J. E. Davies, *Constructive Engagement?*, p. 41.

14. The JBHE Foundation, "Randall Robinson: He Drove the First U.S. Stake into South African Apartheid," in *The Journal of Blacks in Higher Education*, http://www.Jstor.org/stable/2999073 (accessed October 28, 2009).

15. Crocker, *High Noon*, 257-260.

16. Crocker, *High Noon*, 259.

17. Crocker, *High Noon*, 259.

18. David Dent, "Students vs. Apartheid," *Black Enterprise*, July 1985, 21.

19. lyrics.time, "Artists United Against Apartheid Lyrics, 'Sun City'," http://www.lyricstime.com/artists-united-against-apartheid-sun-city-lyrics.html. (accessed 28 October 2009).

20. Steve York, *A Force More Powerful, Episode 3*, Produced and directed by Steve York, Film for the Humanities and Sciences, FFH11071, York Zimmerman, Inc., Washington, DC, 1999. DVD.

21. J. E. Davies, *Constructive Engagement?*, 50.

22. Alex Thomson, "Incomplete Engagement: Reagan's South Africa Policy Revisited," *The Journal of Modern African Studies*, http://www.jstor.org/stable/161547 (accessed July 21, 2009).

23. "Interview with William H. Gray, III, October 1999, Washington, DC," http://muweb.marshall.edu/revleonsullivan/pdf%20files/gray.pdfInternview. (accessed 28 October 2009).

24. "Interview with William H. Gray, III, October 1999, Washington, DC," http://muweb.marshall.edu/revleonsullivan/pdf%20files/gray.pdfInternview. (accessed 28 October 2009).

Chapter 18

The Opening of China and the Evolution of China-U.S. Cross-Cultural Understanding

James Schnell

The 1980's was a time of significant change for China, both within China and regarding Chinese relations with foreign powers such as the U.S. The beginning of the decade witnessed incremental opening to the outside world that flourished via significant increased relations with the U.S. and ended with a crushing reminder, during the 1989 Tiananmen Square crackdown that China had not changed as much as some thought.

The study of communication phenomena in China, by a foreigner, poses unique challenges. It requires not only understanding the particular phenomenon under analysis but also the cultural backdrop within which the phenomenon exists. In *Chinese Perspectives in Rhetoric and Communication*, Ray Heisey stresses how the integration of Eastern and Western perspectives on communication will benefit from understanding the cultures within which these communicative practices exist.[1] It is in that spirit I have proceeded with this analysis.

I have chosen to focus on meanings conveyed in 1987 that were related to the government campaign against bourgeois liberalization in China. This requires Western appreciation of bourgeois liberalization within the Chinese cultural context and the year 1987 as a particular point in post-Mao China. Mao Tse Tung was a key Chinese leader, who died in 1976, that led China at the time the current government took control of the country in 1949. This campaign is significant as a representative transitional period in China as it portrays China addressing a primary issue regarding how to import U.S. technology and expertise while concurrently rejecting other fundamental facets of U.S. culture.

When China was closed to the outside world it could resolutely reject all things foreign. However the opening of China forced it to, in many ways, embrace the very phenomena it had condemned for so long. The campaign against bourgeois liberalization exemplified such a love-hate relationship. It was a love-hate relationship in that by seeking to learn from the U.S. China was acknowledging the superiority of the U.S. At the same time the U.S. was consistently described as a decadent culture that was to be despised. Thus, China "loved" the U.S. for its technology but "hated" the United States because of its culture.

A brief orientation will provide helpful context regarding cultural and chronological developments. After being closed to the outside world for thirty years, the People's Republic of China reversed its policy of isolation in the late 1970's by initiating a variety of economic, political, cultural, and educational reforms. The primary objective behind these reforms has been to modernize China and help it compete in the world market. The modernization of such a large country has involved a variety of obstacles. The 2008 Olympics in Beijing evidenced a significant achievement regarding Chinese modernization.

One such obstacle has been how to import western technologies without importing western lifestyles. Increased interaction with the U.S. best exemplifies this situation. The People's Republic of China is a socialist society, governed by a communist party, and the U.S. is a capitalist society governed as a democracy. Thus, the Chinese government can benefit greatly from foreign interaction but stands to have its cultural values affected in major ways if this interaction is left unchecked.

The opening of China is a complex situation. China is comprised of a variety of cultures that date back thousands of years. An ironic contradiction to the Chinese way of life is the existence of Hong Kong in the south. Hong Kong, which was governed by England until 1997, is connected geographically but is miles apart ideologically. Hong Kong is very developed as a capitalist power in the world market. In 1997, China recovered jurisdiction of Hong Kong, and it recovered Macao (a similar type of capitalist area previously governed by Portugal) in 1999 and has been faced with the question of what to do with its control of two former capitalist protectorates.

The current plan is for China to allow Hong Kong to keep its capitalist system for at least 50 years. This approach, referred to as "one country, two systems," has provided a testing ground for the acquisition of Macao and the intended acquisition of Taiwan. The recovering of Hong Kong is vaguely described by the Chinese government. "To keep Hong Kong's system unchanged, it is imperative to maintain socialism with Chinese characteristics under the leadership of the Communist Party."[2]

The Chinese government has a sensitive task to deal with: how to praise (and adopt the developments practiced by) countries that have political perspectives which are contradictory to those of China. This presents a political tightrope where the Chinese government must praise and condemn at the same time. It is obvious, even to the casual observer visiting China, that American values have found their way onto the Chinese landscape. American music, western clothing, and the widespread use of the English language attest to such developments in the popular culture. As the Chinese people embrace American technology they also seem to be embracing the American way of life. The Chinese government earlier labeled this negative practice as "bourgeois liberalization."

One will frequently hear this expression, or see it in the press, but rarely find a definition of it. Otherwise articulate individuals become somewhat puzzled and confused when asked to define it. It is recognized as important but not easily defined.

For the reader who has never visited China much of this may be confusing because China is typically understood to be a traditional culture. While such historic practices are very much at the foundation of Chinese culture the period since 1980 has been marked by bold significant changes in a relatively short amount of time. In contrast, the U.S. is an ever changing culture but such change has occurred throughout the course of U.S. history. It has not occurred so much in short periods of time.

This report will analyze the term "bourgeois liberalization" and describe how it has been used by the Chinese government as a label for unwanted American influences. I will focus primarily on 1987 as this period set the stage for the nationwide protests in 1989. This discussion will be based on a review of literature produced by and about the Chinese government and a written survey of student opinions at Northern Jiaotong University in Beijing. This subject is significant for speech communication scholars, as the term "bourgeois liberalization" represents language that is created to be purposely vague. The term draws part of its meaning from this intentional vagueness. The expression was created by the Chinese government to describe unwanted ideas and values which have been readily identified as American or Western.

When terms such as this are created, meanings are communicated through high context interaction processes. That is, the meanings are implied through vague hints. This requires message receivers to interpret intended meanings. Low context interaction processes, such as we have in the U.S., tend to stress more precise meanings through direct language.

In September 1986, the Chinese government issued a document entitled *Resolution of the Central Committee of the CPC on the Guiding Principles for Building a Socialist Society with an Advanced Culture and Ideology*. This official document defines bourgeois liberalization as "negating the socialist system in favor of capitalism" and goes on to say it "is in total contradiction of the people's interests and to the historical trend, and it is therefore firmly opposed by the masses."[3]

The Chinese media consistently emphasized that the modernization of China must be done in accordance with the "four cardinal principles." The principles are "keeping to the socialist road, upholding the people's democratic dictatorship, upholding the leadership of the Communist party, and upholding Marxism-Leninism and Mao Zedong thought."[4] The frequent emphasis on these principles by the Chinese government cannot be overemphasized.

China is eager to open to the outside world, but only on its own terms. The following paragraph provides a description of these terms:

Closing one's country to external contact results only in stagnation and backwardness. We resolutely reject the capitalist ideological and social systems that defend oppression and exploitation, and we reject all the ugly and decadent aspects of capitalism. Nevertheless, we should do our utmost to learn from all countries . . . . Otherwise, we shall remain ignorant and be unable to modernize our own country.[5]

This proposed objective is referred to as socialism with Chinese characteristics.

China's embracing of American technology exemplifies a love-hate relationship with the American culture. Zhao Ziyang, former Premier of the State Council, underscores this situation in his *Report on the Work of the Government*. "Opening to the outside world is a basic policy of our state. . . . In 1987 we shall open wider to the outside world and explore new possibilities for the effective use of foreign funds, the import of advanced technology and the earning of foreign exchange through export."[6] Deng Xiaoping, shortly before stepping down as the leader of China, stated a similar view. "The nation should emerge from its long-term seclusion and open itself to the outside world, because its development needs overseas capital, advanced technology and management expertise."[7]

While praising interaction with the west on the one hand, Chinese leadership sharply warns of the dangers of adopting western values on the other hand. "We must not unthinkingly praise these western things, still less regard the decadent capitalist values and outlook on life as new ideas and disseminate them as such. Otherwise, they will contaminate and corrupt people's minds."[8] Examples of negative western influences are frequently cited in the Chinese press. Some of these examples point to the corruption of youth, increased crime, the trashing of literature, and misunderstandings in the universities.

Interaction with the West has been interpreted as both a problem and an opportunity for the youth of China. *China Daily* reported that "the motive for most crimes was money or sex oriented and that youth and juvenile delinquents were responsible for most of the cases."[9] The report continues, "Bourgeois lifestyles and publicity given to violence and crimes through films, television, pictorials and magazines stimulate teenagers to go astray."[10]

An interesting contrast in viewing western influences is provided in an article entitled "A New Way to Teach." This article describes how interaction with the west is changing the teaching of children.

In the past we tried to mold children into ones who were not used to using their minds. But we cannot afford to do it to today's children, because they will enter a world full of competition. They have to be prepared to use their own questioning minds.[11]

This unusual occurrence illustrates an area where western approaches are preferred over traditional Chinese approaches. Generally, only western scientific technologies have been formally adopted.

Zhen Tianxiang, president of the Supreme People's Court, emphasizes the need to combat western influences to curb crime. He suggests "intensifying publicity about various laws and education in morality, ideals, discipline, and general knowledge, along with the efforts to resist all decadent and ugly aspects of capitalism."[12] Bourgeois liberalization has been blamed for literary problems such as rejecting the leadership of the Communist Party, divorcing art from politics and the encouragement of "sex literature." *China Daily* reports that "many talented young writers have been going astray and producing bad books due to the influence of bourgeois liberalization."[13]

A warning to writers was noted in April 1987. Zhang Xianliang, a leader of the National Committee of the Chinese People's Political Consultative Conference, stated that the "struggle against bourgeois liberalization will make Chinese writers politically more mature, better able to understand life and more perceptive to reality."[14] Six weeks later, in an article entitled "Guidelines For Literature," misguided writers were taken to task for their "incorrect ways." "Some writers, however, have forgotten their social responsibilities . . . spreading corrupt ideas, blindly worshipping foreign cultures and copying foreign things mechanically. This has been resented and criticized by the masses."[15]

Zhao Ziyang's *Report on the Work of the Government* stresses the necessary struggle against bourgeois liberalization. "If bourgeois liberalization were allowed to spread unchecked, it would adversely affect even more people (especially a part of the young people) who would lose their bearings, and it would plunge our country into turmoil. . . "[16] He concludes, "We must take a firm, clear-cut stand in relation to this struggle and never hesitate or waver."[17]

The most widely publicized aspect of the campaign against bourgeois liberalization during this period resulted after student demonstrations that occurred in December 1986. Key leaders of the movement were criticized for their actions and the protests were dismissed as misguided youthful exuberance. Yet the opening of China continued to pose problems on the campuses.

Robert L. Jacobsen, a writer for the *Chronicle of Higher Education*, wrote a series of reports on higher education in China. Regarding the opening of China, and its effects on campuses, Jacobsen quotes a group interview he conducted.

"Once you open your society," says one of China's more progressive university leaders, "you cannot close it again." But on hearing that, another official at the same institution retorts, "I've always believed that when you come to a turn in the road, you have to slow down."[18]

Chinese leaders do not underestimate the influence of student protesters since many of them were once student protesters.

In April 1987 the opinions of a class of graduate students were surveyed at Northern Jiaotong University in Beijing. The survey dealt with the development and meaning of bourgeois liberalization. All fourteen students in the class voluntarily participated in the survey. Their participation was not rewarded and the results were not shared. Their ages ranged from 24 to 26, and the survey was done anonymously.

The survey provided an uncommon opportunity to solicit student views on a sensitive subject. Opportunities to collect such information are far less common in China, compared to the United States, due to the social and political climate. This consideration is discussed later in this chapter.

The survey indicates an increased usage of the term bourgeois liberalization in the six-month period prior to the survey, as 93% indicated the term had not been common until recently (question three). Bourgeois liberalization is far more evident in literature (question seven) than in other forms of expression such as clothing, dancing, and music (questions four, five and six).

Fifty-seven percent felt bourgeois liberalization ideals are becoming more common because of increased trade with the U.S. (29% were neutral) but only seven percent felt the best way to eradicate bourgeois liberalization is to cease trade/interaction with the U.S. (seven percent were neutral). These areas are covered in questions eight and nine. Seventy-two percent agree (14% were neutral) that if left unchecked bourgeois liberalization can become a serious problem in the People's Republic of China (question ten).

Interpretation of the survey responses must be done in light of the fact that an American was collecting the information. Although their names were not connected with their responses, they did know a foreigner would be interpreting their responses. Aside from their possible reticence to share their thoughts with a foreigner they may have modified their views so they would not be offensive.

The media and students were readily aware of bourgeois liberalization and its possible effects in China but nobody seemed to want any major crackdown similar to that experienced during the cultural revolution. The lessons of those years (1966-1976) seem to be too painfully recent to risk a similar situation. Perhaps this explains why only seven percent of students surveyed supported the ceasing of trade/interaction with the United States as a means of eradicating bourgeois liberalization.

The fears of any reaction against bourgeois liberalization which might resemble the cultural revolution period were found in the press. *Newsweek* quotes a confidential party directive as saying "the party leadership urged communists not to allow their campaign against bourgeois liberalization— meaning western influences—to degenerate into personal vendettas against other party members."[19] Chinese leader Zhao Ziyang, in his *Report on the Work of the Government*, stated, "No attempt will be made to ferret out exponents of bourgeois liberalization at various levels, to implicate people at higher or lower levels or to have everybody make self-criticisms."[20] He has emphasized that "no cultural revolution type political campaigns would be launched."[21]

A new phrase evolved in August 1987 which was an interesting follow-up to bourgeois liberalization. *Newsweek* reported "editorials that recently attacked bourgeois liberalization now denounce ossified thinking—a code phrase for positions that undercut Deng" (Deng Xiaoping's reforms).[22] Ironically, the term bourgeois liberalization was coined to oppose reform, and "ossified thinking" was coined to promote reform. Governmental usage of such vague terms must surely be confusing for one who is trying to follow the party line. As indicated earlier, analysis of the term bourgeois liberalization is relevant to the speech communication scholar, as the term represents language that is created to be purposely vague.

Devito states that language is "a social institution designed, modified, and extended (some purists might even say distorted) to meet the ever changing needs of the culture or subculture."[23] In this case, the term bourgeois liberalization was introduced because there was a need to vaguely describe ideas and values which were to be discouraged but could not be accurately defined according to the communication context of the Chinese language. The element of context is important in this understanding. "As we grow up in the world, our experience is formed by the language in which it is presented and talked about, and this language becomes so much a part of the mind as to seem a part of nature."[24] Ochs emphasizes this degree of context more strongly in saying that "language is the major vehicle for accomplishing communication, language functions both *in* context and *as* context, simultaneously constructing and being constructed by the social occasion."[25]

Chinese people, and the Chinese language which reflects the culture, are less likely to communicate ideas in a direct manner in comparison to people in the United States. "Within Chinese conversational style is a tendency to respond in terms of expectations, goals, even models rather than mundane facts."[26] The important role of context cannot be overstated when the aforementioned is paralleled with the system of government in China. "China's governance involves both the overt system of public institutions with whose members we interact rather easily and the more shadowy system of political and security organs whose work is not open . . . "[27] Thus, analysis of the term bourgeois liberalization indicates that the Chinese government communicates meaning on this subject in a manner which parallels the way meanings are communicated in day-to-day interactions in China. This process is defined as high-context communication. It is purposely an indirect form of communication.

Hall states that high-context cultures must provide a context and setting and let the point evolve. Low-context cultures are much more direct and to the point.[28] Andersen explains that "languages are some of the most explicit communication systems but the Chinese language is an implicit high context system."[29] He goes on to explain that "explicit forms of communication such as verbal codes are more prevalent in low context cultures such as the United States and Northern Europe."[30]

The term bourgeois liberalization, and to a lesser degree "ossified thinking," represent words which can be best understood in the high-context communication system which exists in China. The terms were created to be intentionally vague by the Chinese government to promote desired changes in China's political climate. While this system might be confusing to most Americans (who are used to low-context interactions) this approach is more accepted in the Chinese culture (a high-context culture).

The opening of China provides a variety of opportunities for China to develop economically, technologically, educationally, and culturally. Similarly it offers western countries, such as the U.S., opportunities to expand in the same types of areas. Such development and expansion can be beneficial, but there is bound to be integration which creates conflict. Study of government emphasis on bourgeois liberalization during 1987 provides an opportunity to better understand how one culture chose to deal with such a conflict.

Chinese government concern with bourgeois liberalization and related issues has continued since the period under study (1987). Similarly, our understanding of variables linked to bourgeois liberalization has grown. The 1989 student-led protests, and subsequent government crackdown, brought worldwide attention on China and the challenges it faces as it modernizes. These challenges consistently evidence an emphasis on bourgeois liberalization.

On June 9, 1989, less than a week after the Chinese military opened fire on Chinese citizens in and around Tiananmen Square, Deng Xiaoping delivered his "June Ninth Speech to Martial Law Units." He stated "The nature of the current incident is basically the confrontation between the four cardinal principles [described earlier in this article] and bourgeois liberalization."[31]

On the third anniversary of the 1989 government crackdown, the U.S. Public Broadcasting System broadcast an episode of Frontline titled "China After Tiananmen." The role of bourgeois liberalization was stressed throughout the documentary. The following quotes exemplify this emphasis.

> Any word or deed that seemed threatening to the Party's leadership or authority became bourgeois liberalization. . . . Bourgeois liberalization? We often heard that word but, really, what does it mean? When we open the window of reform, some flies and mosquitoes may come in. . . . We'll just kill the flies and mosquitoes, so we can resist the invasion of decadent influences like bourgeois ideas and lifestyles.[32]

This evidences how bourgeois liberalization evades clear definition even under media scrutiny.

It is fitting that the 1980's ended with the Tiananmen Square crackdown and intense mass media reporting of the event in that it serves as a closing comment on the decade regarding firm Communist control of the country. It is easy for foreigners to mistakenly see Chinese modernization as a total overhaul of the Chinese way of life. However, in that regard, the Tiananmen Square crackdown clearly underscored that when the Chinese Communist Party feels threatened it will act with firm resolve to crush any opposition, real or imagined. The two decades since then have continued to recognize this reality.

The Chinese government will typically seek to initially address such challenges via high context cues so as to caution the Chinese population about the sensitivity of some issues, as exemplified with bourgeois liberalization, but such measures will usually serve as pretext for extreme tactics if needed. The Tiananmen Square crackdown clearly evidences this and remains in the public mind, domestic and international, as a vivid reminder of the Mao Tse Tung dictum that "power grows out of a barrel of a gun" and that there should be no mistake that the guns are loaded. Again though, focus on bourgeois liberalization measures allow for understanding on a variety of levels.

An explanation for social problems related to bourgeois liberalization was conveyed by Goh Keng Swee, a former deputy premier from Singapore who became an economic adviser to China. He indicates the Chinese political structure is not compatible with a market economy. "The problems stem from Beijing's attempts at grafting a market economy on a political system designed for a command economy."[33]

Eradication efforts by the government against bourgeois liberalization continued during the 1990's and beyond. "China started off 1997 with a strong media assault against immoral literature and dance. . . . The government's ongoing 'spiritual civilization' campaign follows a call from Chinese President Jiang Zemin to toe the party line at all costs."[34] "The leadership in Beijing is planning a campaign to crack down on 'pro-West' intellectuals. . . . President Jiang Zemin has warned against these intellectuals in internal speeches, and is reportedly ready to launch an ideological purge of the party's 'bourgeois liberal' elements."[35]

Understanding bourgeois liberalization and its implications is a challenge for Chinese citizens and even more so for non-Chinese. It is a purposely vague concept and is constantly subject to modified interpretation. In hindsight, perhaps the most basic description of bourgeois liberalization in 1987 and beyond can be found in the explanation conveyed by Jack Linchuan Qiu. "The crucial difference between the 'political reform' and 'bourgeois liberalization' is that the former is within the party-state institution, while the latter is without. Political changes for the destruction of Communist ideology are offensive, whereas those for improvement inside the socialist framework are tolerable."[36]

The reader should interpret dynamics presented in this chapter within the reality that much of modern day China has been dominated by foreign powers. This resulted in the closing of China in 1949 during the founding of The People's Republic of China. Chinese society is very sensitive to this foreign domination and contemporary China must be understood in light of this challenging past.

Awareness of language norms, in this case focusing on the 1980's, portrays the 1980's as a relevant transitional period in the evolution of Chinese culture. The 1980's was a unique decade in China in that it was very transitional regarding the opening and modernization of China. At the start of the decade China was very much still closed to the outside world but, by the end of the decade, it had opened and modernized considerably. Many aspects of Chinese life evolved during this progression and language practices, as described in this chapter, highlight such realities.

Notes

1. D. Ray Heisey, *Chinese Perspectives in Rhetoric and Communication* (Stamford, Connecticut: Ablex Publishing Corporation, 2000), xix.

2. "No Change in Hong Kong Policy," *Beijing Review*, April 27, 1987, 5(N).

3. *Resolution of the Central Committee of the CPC on the Guiding Principles for Building a Socialist Society with an Advanced Culture and Ideology.* (Beijing, China: Foreign Language Press, 1986), 13.

4. *Resolution of the Central Committee*, 1986, 4.

5. *Resolution of the Central Committee,* 1986, 6.

6. Zhao Ziyang, *Report on the Work of the Government* (Delivered at the Fifth Session of the Sixth National People's Congress on March 25, 1987), 25.

7. "Deng's Book Draws Lessons from History," *China Daily,* May 11, 1987, 4(N).

8. Zhao, *Report on the Work*, 34.

9. Ma Lixin. "Meeting Over Youth Crimes," *China Daily,* April 21, 1987, 1(N)

10. Ma, "Meeting Over," 1(N).

11. Li Xing. "A New Way to Teach," *China Daily,* April 7, 1987, 5(N).

12. Guo, Zhongshi. "Chief Points to Obvious Drop in Violent Crimes," *China Daily,* April 7, 1987, 1(N).

13. "In Literary Circles," *China Daily,* April 17, 1987, 4(N).

14. "Struggle Makes Writers More Realistic," *China Daily,* April 8, 1987, 1(N).

15. Chen Danchen. "Guidelines for Literature," *Beijing Review,* May 25, 1987, 4(N).

16. Zhao, *Report on the Work*, 28.

17. Zhao, *Report on the Work*, 28.

18. Robert L. Jacobsen, "Expectations Rise for Higher Education in China as Reform Temper Begins to Take Hold," *The Chronicle of Higher Education,* October 28, 1987, 42(N).

19. "The Long Shadow of Mao," *Newsweek* (March 16, 1987): 40.

20. Zhao, *Report on the Work*, 30.

21. "On Student Unrest and the Question of Bourgeois Liberalization," *China Reconstructs* (May, 1987): 24-27.

22. "Deng's Balancing Act," *Newsweek* (August 17, 1987): 3.

23. Joseph A. Devito, *The Interpersonal Communication Book* (New York: Harper and Row, 1986), 148.

24. James B. White, *When Words Lose Their Meaning: Constitution and Reconstitutions of Language, Character, and Community* (Chicago: University of Chicago Press, 1984), 276.

25. Edward Ochs, "Introduction: What Child Language Can Contribute to Pragmatics," in *Developmental Pragmatics,* eds. Edward Ochs and Benjamin Schiefflen (New York: Academic Press, 1979), 206.

26. Donald P. Murray, "Face-to-Face: American and Chinese Interactions," in *Communicating with China*, ed. Robert A. Kapp (Chicago: Intercultural Press, 1983), 13.

27. Murray, "Face-to-Face," 10.

28. Edward G. Hall, *The Dance of Life: The Other Dimension of Time.* (Garden City, New York: Anchor Press, 1984), 37.

29. Peter Andersen, "Explaining Intercultural Differences in Nonverbal Communication" (paper presented at the annual meeting of the Speech Communication Association, Boston, Massachusetts, November, 1987) 23.

30. Andersen, "Explaining Intercultural Differences," 24.

31. Xiaoping Deng, "June Ninth Speech to Martial Law Commanders," Beijing Domestic Television Service (June 27, 1989).

32. "Frontline: China After Tiananmen," Episode #1020, Public Broadcasting Service (June 2, 1992).

33. Goh, Keng Swee, "Problems Could Hurt China's Dramatic Economic Growth," *China News Digest/Global News*, http://www.cnd.org (accessed January 6, 1997).

34. Haosheng Zhou and Jia Daluo, "China Started Off 1997 With a 'Spiritual Civilization' Campaign," *China News Digest/Global Edition*, http://www.cnd.org (accessed January 6, 1997).

35. Ouhong Wang and Yiyi Wu. "Crackdown of Pro-West Intellectuals," *China News Digest/Global Edition*, http://www.cnd.org (accessed April 6, 2000).

36. Jack Linchuan Qiu, "Interpreting the Dengist Rhetoric of Building Socialism With Chinese Characteristics," in *Chinese Perspectives in Rhetoric and Communication*, ed. Ray D. Heisey, (Stamford, Connecticut: Ablex Publishing Corporation, 2000). 57.

Chapter 19

U.S. Foreign Policy in Latin America on Film: The Case of *Salvador*

Kristin Sorensen

One approach to investigating the significance of the 1980s is to consider the decade as it was experienced by Latin Americans. The 1980s was a grim period for many Latin Americans as many countries in the Southern Cone of South America were still under dictatorships imposed with U.S. support in the 1960s and 1970s, and in Central America, people experienced more violence than during any previous decade as militaries working under Reagan Administration-supported dictatorships and, as labeled by scholars Edward S. Herman and James Petras, "death-squad democracies," committed massive violations of human rights against peasants, political dissenters, and indigenous populations. According to political scientist Kathryn Sikkink,

> In the 1970s and 1980s, many countries in Latin America suffered a wave of intense repression, including widespread executions, disappearances, political imprisonment, and frequent use of torture. In almost all cases, military governments committed these human rights violations either directly through security forces and police or through paramilitary groups closely linked to the government... This was a time of intense fear and insecurity for many citizens in Latin America.[1]

Latin Americans who fled northward as refugees encountered pockets of support from Americans volunteering through oftentimes clandestine solidarity networks. However, the vast majority of Americans were ignorant of the hardships that these people had suffered, due in large part to U.S. foreign policy, and some Americans treated these refugees, who they perceived as illegal "aliens," with hostility.

As Ana del Sarto explains in "The 1980s: Foundations of Latin American Cultural Studies,"

With regard to Latin America, the dominant powers erected diverse obstacles to limit the continual widening of democracy and social justice; different means were used to disarticulate hope, replacing it with the glitter of globalization: deregulation of markets and flexibilization of capital and labor, privatization of the public sphere, ideology of the obsolescence of the state, expansion of the culture industry and its most valued offshoot, mass culture. A genealogical arch could be traced by uniting six dissimilar but equally forceful historical instances that triggered and summarize in only two decades all the aforementioned side effects: from the elimination of the gold exchange standard, which freed the U.S. dollar in 1971, to the coordinated inception of authoritarian regimes throughout Latin America in the early 1970s to counteract the spread of national-socialist movements, the end of the Central American conflicts (Esquipulas II[2]) and the Latin American debt crisis of the 1980s, the fall of the Berlin Wall in 1989, and the Gulf War in 1990. When seen in perspective, these not-so-distant events, ultimately, provide a dual, not at all redemptive, illumination: on the one hand, it sheds light back on the roots of what has been called the "lost decade" within Latin America; on the other hand, it elucidates onward the new "nature" of the global hegemonic system at the end of the millennium.[3]

Some of these ironies, tragedies, and contradictions of the 1980s are represented poignantly in films which were produced during that decade, both by Latin Americans and Americans. This chapter will investigate one of these films: *Salvador* (1986) by controversial American director Oliver Stone, who created a narrative film based on the real experiences of American photojournalist Richard Boyle while working in El Salvador.

At the beginning of the 1980s, most countries in the Southern Cone of South America (Chile, Argentina, Uruguay, Paraguay, Bolivia, and Brazil) were still ruled by U.S.-backed, right-wing dictatorships, under which tens of thousands of people were killed or disappeared, and many more were tortured and exiled. With help from the C.I.A., these military governments had highly sophisticated intelligence networks which allowed the militaries and secret police agencies to track the movement of individuals within and across these countries. This project was called Operation Condor and began with the hosting of a meeting by Chilean General Pinochet's right-hand man, head of the secret police and C.I.A.-paid operative, General Manuel Contreras, which was held in Santiago in November 1975. The governments' agents of torture, murder, and disappearances sometimes worked together in their efforts, including the transportation of prisoners and bodies across national borders.[4] As journalist and author John Dinges explains, "Under the leadership of Henry Kissinger, first as Richard Nixon's national security adviser and later as secretary of state, the United States sent an unequivocal signal to the most extreme rightist forces that democracy could be sacrificed in the cause of ideological warfare. Criminal operational tactics, including assassination, were not only acceptable but supported with weapons and money."[5]

As the countries in South America slowly transitioned to democracies throughout the 1980s, U.S. government and covert operations attention shifted to and increased in Central America, in which the U.S. consistently supported right-wing authoritarian governments again, and where hundreds of thousands of people were killed or disappeared in Guatemala, El Salvador, Honduras, Panama, and Nicaragua, and many more were displaced and became refugees. Writing at the time of these events in the 1980s, Herman and Petras explain,

> Under the two Duarte regimes and the in-between openly military governments, 50,000 Salvadoran civilians were murdered, and a large fraction of dissident trade union, university, professional, and other groups were physically eliminated. The situation in Guatemala is little different: elections are held there for a terrorized, atomized population, herded into strategic hamlets and killed by the army and death squads at rates that have averaged several thousand per year over the past decade.[6]

It is now known that in the case of Guatemala, between 100,000 and 150,000 people were killed during this period.[7] As James Petras and Morris Morley explain,

> Since 1981, an additional factor has reinforced the growing U.S. military presence in the region: the need of the Reagan administration to achieve a military victory in order to justify the vast armaments program that is the core of the new Cold War. El Salvador, in particular, has become the theater in which Reagan hopes to demonstrate that force, not negotiation, works – thus intertwining regional with global politics. Central America as a whole has become an arena for recouping America's worldwide supremacy through military confrontation and military victory... Between 1981 and 1984, El Salvador received over $950 million in U.S. security assistance, of which approximately $400 million was in the form of congressionally authorized military aid. In the process, at least 15,000 Salvadoran soldiers and officers benefitted from Pentagon training expertise.[8]

Oliver Stone's feature film *Salvador*, based on the real life experiences of an American photojournalist in El Salvador during the conflict between civilians, guerillas, and the military, offers a striking counterpoint to the manner in which these conflicts were represented in the mainstream U.S. media of the time, which, on the rare occasions when it did pay attention to Central America, did so according to the agenda set by the Reagan Administration (i.e., Nicaragua, where the C.I.A.-backed "Contras", short for counter-revolutionaries, who were represented as the good guys, were fighting against the Sandinistas who had overthrown the Somoza dictatorship in 1979 and then were democratically elected to power in 1984. That same year, the U.S. Congress passed the final portions of the Boland Amendment, which made direct funding of the Contras illegal; from that point forward, all U.S. support needed to be covert, which contributed to the causes for the Iran-Contra scandal, in which the U.S. sold weapons to Iran, with whom there was a weapons embargo, using Israel as a middleman, for which the profits were sent to the Contras. Fourteen U.S. officials were charged with crimes; eleven were convicted; all were pardoned at the end of the George H.W. Bush presidency).

The 1980s were also a turning point in the U.S. media industry. "Since the early 1980s – a period routinely referred to in the trades as 'the corporate era' in Hollywood – increasing deregulation and a dramatic reinterpretation of antitrust guidelines, the introduction of junk-bond financing and its use in leveraged mergers and acquisitions, and the growing consolidation of assets and power by large corporations within the deeply incestuous and collusive industry subculture have dramatically altered the way business is conducted in Hollywood".[9] Within this environment, which had altered so dramatically since Stone had been hailed as a brilliant original filmmaker in the 1970s when more artistic, political films ruled the day, Stone created *Salvador*. The film received mixed reviews when it was released, which is not surprising, given the social and political climate in the mid-1980s. "Clearly, Stone is a left-of-center thinker, working in a culture when anything left of center is cause for ridicule by the right."[10] As Stone explains in his comments on the DVD, "It died quickly and was removed from theaters." However, after Stone's *Platoon* was released that same year to a much more positive response, new fans of his work found *Salvador* on video, where it achieved more success. It was nominated for and won several awards[11]. In hindsight, the film perhaps is one of the most politically and historically relevant to come out of Hollywood during that decade.

The opening credits of the film appear over real black and white footage of a massacre outside of a church in San Salvador. Text informs viewers that the time period is 1980 to 1981. Black and white footage switches to color images, which we soon discover are coming from the television broadcasting to the sleeping protagonist Richard Boyle (James Woods) in his San Francisco apartment. He wakes to the sound of his landlord banging on the door, giving him, his wife, and baby an eviction notice. Boyle is an unlikely film protagonist; he is first depicted as a selfish man without any moral integrity, willing to do whatever it takes to earn a quick buck. He is not one of the economic winners at the dawn of 1980s America. He gets pulled over for speeding and is thrown in jail after the officer reminds him of his many unpaid speeding tickets. His buddy "Doc" (Jim Belushi) bails him out; Boyle thanks him by ranting about the "goddamn yuppies." Things do not go well for either one of them as Doc learns that his dog Bagel, who was apprehended by the pound, has been put to sleep (Doc's angry tirade towards the sweet woman at the pound who expresses sympathy for his loss, in which he asks if the workers at the pound have any sense of humanity, could be interpreted as a foreshadowing of events to come in Central America, where people there seem to be treated worse than pets in the United States), and Boyle discovers that his wife has left him and taken the baby.

Boyle, with Doc in the passenger seat, starts driving south and convinces Doc that it is also in his own best interest to join him so that they can escape the yuppies; he tells Doc that they are going to Guatemala, for easy sun, sex, drugs, alcohol, and no yuppies – the reverse of what they experience and abhor in the U.S. Actually, much to the chagrin of Doc, they drive all the way to El Salvador, where Boyle has freelanced before; Boyle thinks that he can get some more work there now that the conflict is increasing, especially since he once had an article published in a right-wing newspaper there. It does not take long for either of them to realize that they have just entered a very dangerous environment when they nearly get killed by soldiers within miles of the national border.

Despite the dangers, we see that Boyle feels right at home, reconnecting with María, one of his many global girlfriends, whose infant daughter was fathered by a man who is "disappeared." As Robert Kolker describes it, Stone's cinematic representations are "bigger and bolder images, filled with the excess of a foreign culture as they might be seen from a diminished foreign perspective."[12] This characterization seems to ring true especially strongly when Boyle and Doc enter El Salvador, where the people they encounter verge on the ludicrous; the bad guys have greasy hair, dark sunglasses, and permanent sneers on their faces, while the good guys are quiet and noble, simple people trying to mind their own business. Nonetheless, the stark contrasts between the rich and poor, good and bad, should have been fairly obvious to any observer who found oneself in El Salvador at that time. The vast majority of Salvadorans were suffering:

> From 1972 to 1981 farm workers' salaries dropped between 20 and 70 percent, depending on the crop and the area. In 1981 El Salvador boasted the most unequal distribution of land and wealth in Latin America. In the countryside 90 percent of the people were illiterate. There was one doctor for every thirty-five hundred Salvadorans, the lowest ratio in Central America. Life expectancy in rural El Salvador was thirty-five years. In 1981 only a third of all Salvadorans had safe water; 39 percent had electricity; 41 percent earned less than $10 a month.[13]

In the director's commentary available on the *Salvador* DVD, Stone observes the hyperbole of his good and bad characters and laughs, but explains that at that time, he felt the need to make the representations so explicit because the situation was so dire, and Americans were usually viewing opposite representations on TV. He says that he was trying to borrow the "agit-prop" style of early Soviet filmmakers, but if he had the chance to do this over, he would be more subtle.

With time, even Doc starts to enjoy his time, and his blundering, comedic character is often the cause of several near-misses with the Salvadoran military and its associates. We learn that the "guerillas" are actually simple peasants – men, women, and children – with rudimentary weapons, hiding out in mountains, and that the military and associated death squads are committing genocide against their own people. No scene shows this more explicitly than one in which Boyle and a photographer colleague, John Cassady, trip over bodies, which have been dumped by the military on a hillside, as they take photos of the dead while carrying on a fairly normal conversation (these professionals have hardened as a consequence of their constantly working in conflict zones across the globe; at one point, Boyle references his recent time in Chile, Vietnam, and Cambodia; he is teased by U.S. officials in El Salvador for getting it wrong, along with his "lefty" colleagues, in Cambodia – not being able to predict the atrocities of the communist Khmer Rouge regime).

We learn that most American journalists hardly ever bother to leave the U.S. Embassy in San Salvador and simply parrot explanations of the conflict which have been handed to them by government officials. Before we are introduced to the journalists at the embassy, we see television footage of then Presidential candidate Ronald Reagan explaining what he believes should be policy towards El Salvador. His rhetoric reinforces the typical Western "domino effect" theory to explain why the "communists" must be stopped. The American journalist who represents the complacent behavior most explicitly is Pauline Axelrod, a blond, Barbie Doll-looking woman who bungles her first story which we hear from the lush grounds of the U.S. Embassy, where U.S. presidential election results have just been announced (Reagan beat Carter) because Doc, upset that she had insulted him, slipped drugs into her drink.

We later observe her criticize Boyle for asking a tough question to the ruthless leader of the military who is running for office. Earlier in the film, we watched television ads for this candidate, running for the "Mano Blanca" ("White Hand") party, one with his family, all dressed in white and roaming through green pastures, another with him explaining how communists are like watermelons, green on the outside, and (after he violently slashes a watermelon open) red on the inside. Stone explains in his comments on the DVD that almost all representations in his film are based on real events; he merely conflated them so that they were more interconnected and touched the lives of his main characters.

When U.S. soldiers arrive at the San Salvador airport in order to back the Salvadoran military in their fight against guerillas, she greets them by giggling and chit chatting about sports when the soldiers tell her that they are not allowed to speak with reporters. Stone scathingly critiques the approach taken by most American journalists working for the mainstream networks, blinded by the U.S. State Department, to cover the contemporary violence experienced by Central Americans who find that their repressors are financed and militarily supported by U.S. government administrations.

"Stone looks for moments of transcendence, for his characters, their culture, and even the viewer."[14] In *Salvador*, we witness the first moment of transcendence when Boyle happens to go to church, to ask for forgiveness for his sins so that he can marry María, just before Archbishop Oscar Romero is about to be assassinated. Prior to visiting the church, he tells María that he knows that he is a flawed man, but he thinks that he can change for the sake of her and her children. Inside the church we see the faithful congregants and a few men, with their evil stares through dark sunglasses, who are clearly there for the wrong reasons. Stone acknowledges on the DVD that "the imagery is a little on the simplistic side, but powerfully clean." Before being assassinated by the military, Archbishop Romero speaks to his congregation, offering a moment of transcendence for film viewers. He proclaims that Americans do not understand what is actually taking place in his country.

I have called upon the United States repeatedly to stop military aid to this Army until it satisfactorily resolves the problems of the Disappeared... and submits itself to civilian control. When a dictatorship seriously violates human rights and attacks the common good of the nation... when it becomes unbearable and closes all channels of dialogue... when this happens, the Church speaks for the rights of the victims of the violence! We are poor. They in Washington are so rich. (Incidentally, the English subtitles to this monologue in Spanish read, "You in Washington are so rich.") And they are so blind. (The English subtitles read, "Why are you so blind?") My children... you must look to yourselves to protect yourselves in this sad time for El Salvador. I wish to close with an appeal to the men of the Army and in particular the National Guard. Brothers, you are part of our people. Yet you kill your own peasant brothers and sisters. But before a man may kill, the law of God must prevail. And that law says, 'Thou shalt not kill.' No soldier is obliged to obey an order against the law of God. Violence on all sides is wrong. Violence breeds violence. Refuse violence in the name of God and in the name of these suffering people whose laments rise to Heaven each day more tumultuous. I beg you... I ask you... I order you in the name of God: Stop the repression!

Many significant discourses are circulating in this lecture, and the nuances related to assumed listeners are important. Archbishop Romero is explaining and justifying the stance of clergy members who believe in liberation theology – the ideology which argues that it is morally just for the Church to align its political sentiments with leftist ideas which support the rights of the poor and underprivileged. This justification is aimed at several potential audiences, including Catholic film viewers who do not agree with liberation theology. Another crucial element which needs attention is the switching in the subtitles to a direct address towards American viewers. While the Archbishop speaks to his congregation of Americans in the third person, the English subtitles take on a voice of their own, and viewers who do not understand Spanish would not notice that the Archbishop had said something else. Clearly, Stone is trying to be as direct as possible in his call for Americans to take action, become critical thinkers, and challenge the messages that they are fed from their own government and mainstream media sources. In the following scene, Romero is shot and killed as he administers communion to his congregation, which further reinforces the urgency of his lecture. In his DVD comments, Stone claims that the speech is "mostly accurate".

As Kathryn Sikkink has explained, regarding the 1980 murder of Romero,

Many Salvadorans concluded that if killers could execute the Archbishop of San Salvador in broad daylight with impunity, no one was safe. Their conclusions would prove correct. Although it would intensify in the 1980s, intense repression in El Salvador started during the Carter administration.[15]

Nonetheless, despite the fact that violence in El Salvador was highest during the final year of the Carter administration, when many Americans were disenchanted with U.S. foreign policy and the administration was trying to make concessions to the conservatives during an election year, there is plenty of evidence to suggest that military leaders from across Latin America interpreted the rhetoric coming from the Reagan campaign and later administration to assume that they would be free to continue and increase violent repression measures in the years to come. Sikkink notes that

> the Reagan administration's authoritarian allies took its public disregard for human rights seriously... there was a notable upsurge in human rights violations in Latin America in the early period of the Reagan administration. Michele Montas, expelled from Haiti in December 1980, explained that Haitian authorities "thought the international climate was favorable to this sort of thing. They thought human rights was over." The Salvadoran military may have had similar thoughts. On November 27, 1980, killers associated with the Salvadoran government abducted, tortured, and executed six top leaders of the main political opposition group in El Salvador. Less than a week later, Salvadoran National Guard officers abducted, raped, and murdered four U.S. churchwomen who worked in El Salvador. A month after that, a couple of Salvadoran National Guard agents killed two U.S. advisors and the Salvadoran head of the Institute for Agrarian Reform.[16]

Salvador depicts the rape and murder of the four churchwomen. In the film, one of the four women is a friend of Boyle, whom we have already had a chance to get to know in earlier scenes of the film – a young, idealistic, upbeat, endearing character. After the four women are raped and killed by men associated with the military, Axelrod tells Boyle, as they are peering over the mutilated bodies, that she heard a rumor that the nuns drove past a roadblock and exchanged gunfire. Stone explains on the DVD that this allegation came from actual Secretary of State during the Reagan Administration, Alexander Haig, who suggested that the nuns had been gun-runners; Jeanne Kirkpatrick, who was Reagan's foreign policy advisor during his 1980 campaign, then a member of his Cabinet, and later the first female U.S. Ambassador to the United Nations, suggested the same.

Boyle is desperate to get María and her two children out of the country; her brother has been killed, and because she has no *cedula*, her national ID card, she can be killed too. He offers U.S. officials photos he took of the peasant guerillas living and training in the mountains in exchange for a *cedula*. They ask him to give specific information, to serve as a spy, for the U.S. and its allies, the Salvadoran military. Boyle refuses and gives them a speech about U.S. foreign policy. According to Robert Kolker, Stone's approach is a "fearless plunge into recent history and a clear statement of what he thinks it means."[17] Through Boyle's impassioned speech, we find out exactly what Stone thinks this situation means.

> What are the death squads but the brainchild of the C.I.A.? But you'll run with them because they're anti-Moscow. You let them close down the universities. You let them wipe out the best minds in the country. You let them kill whomever they want. You let them wipe out the Catholic Church, and you let them do it all because they aren't commies. And that, colonel, is bullshit. You've created a major Frankenstein... You pour 120 million bucks into this place so you can turn it into a military zone, so you can have chopper parades in the sky. All you're doing is bringing mi-

sery to these people. I don't want to see another Vietnam. I don't want to see America get another bad rap... I believe in America. I believe that we stand for something. For a Constitution. For human rights. Not just for a few people, but for everybody on this planet. You gotta think of the people first. In the name of human decency, something we Americans are supposed to believe in. You gotta at least try to make something of a just society here.

Stone explains here on the DVD, "This speech gave me the chance to vent my true feelings."

By this point in the narrative, Boyle seems to have redeemed himself. He has a purpose, to save the lives of the people he cares about, and he knows what he believes in – human rights. While he already knew about the hypocrisies of U.S. foreign policy, he is no longer willing to use that to serve his own ends. He has become a man with integrity. According to Tina Rosenberg,

Tutela Legal, the human rights office of the Catholic archdiocese, documented more than 9,000 killings by the military or paramilitary death squads in 1980 alone. The following year the death squads killed 13,353 people, proportionately analogous to a half million people in the United States. Anyone with a vague connection to those suspected of wanting change – nuns, labor leaders, students, mothers of students, neighbors of mothers of students, cousins of neighbors of mothers of students – was considered subversive. Bodies piled up on roadsides and in the fields and hills around the city. In 1982, as the Reagan State Department certified that the regime had made a "concerted and significant effort" to respect human rights, 13,794 people were killed in death squad violence.[18]

In the closing scene, Boyle, María, and her two children have just crossed into the United States, "after spending the day in Nogales to do some shopping," they tell the guard at the border checkpoint. They are on a Greyhound bus heading north and are finally beginning to relax, as Boyle tells María that he feels hopeful that everything will work out and that the U.S. is a great place to live, if you have enough money. Suddenly the bus is pulled over by two Border Patrol officers. They take one look at María and start giving her the third degree. Anxious, María claims that cannot understand their questions. Boyle tries to speak for her and keep her on the bus. Finally, María agrees to get off the bus with her children. "It's okay," she tells Boyle in English. "We'll go back."

Boyle screams,

If you send her back, they will kill her! They will rape her, and they will mutilate her if you send her back there! If you send the kids back, they will kill them too! You don't know what it's like in El Salvador! You have no idea what it's like there!

As María and her children are placed in one car while Boyle is forced to go into another one, we hear an officer talking to someone on the radio: "Checkpoint: Two illegals. One female Latino and two children. Bringing them in." The final shot is of Boyle with a look of desperation on his face, staring out the back window of the car in the direction of María in the other car. During the closing credits, we learn that "To date... the same military leaders continue in power. Salvador continues to be one of the largest recipients of U.S. military aid in the world." According to Rosenberg, "From 1980 to 1990 the United States gave Salvador $1 billion in military aid and at least an equal amount that indirectly supported the war effort."[19]

In short, the 1980s were a grim decade for many Latin Americans – an era which violently and irrevocably changed many lives for the worse. What makes the pain of those who suffered more severe is their knowledge that many "North Americans" have minimal knowledge of what happened during this dark decade, including the role that the U.S. government and its various military and intelligence institutions played in the violence. On a hopeful note, by the end of the 1980s and with the official end to the Cold War with the collapse of the Soviet Union, democracy began to regain its footing in many Latin American countries. However, the legacy of this dark era continues. To this date, very little "truth and justice" has been achieved for those who suffered human rights violations under these U.S.-backed regimes, and those who supported these violent regimes still wield much power in many of these countries. And many Latin Americans observe current U.S. involvement in Latin America with a watchful eye, i.e. suspected CIA support of a failed coup attempt in Venezuela in 2002 and massive military alliances with the Colombian government.

As we reflect on the legacy of U.S. foreign policy in Central America during the 1980s, we must wonder what opportunities may have been missed for less violence and more peace and understanding. Perhaps we must conclude that the more things change, the more they stay the same. On June 28, 2009, democratically-elected President of Honduras, Manuel Zelaya was forced out of his position in a military coup and has been living in exile since then; he currently resides in the Brazilian embassy in Tegucigalpa. While the Obama Administration has expressed concern for the situation, they have continued diplomatic relations with the interim unelected Honduran administration of Roberto Micheletti, President of the Congress who was named as Zelaya's replacement, enforced by the Honduran military. Now, new elections have just been held, and the declared winner was Porfirio Lobo, who is scheduled to take office in January. When asked by reporters if Zelaya should be allowed to finish his term, he dismisses that notion. At the same time, many Central Americans continue to flee north to escape extreme poverty and sometimes violence in their home countries. In the United States, where Hondurans, Salvadorans, and Guatemalans are oftentimes labeled as "Mexicans" if not merely "illegals", they struggle to lead lives of dignity in the shadows of a superpower which they have learned to fear and embrace. The global economic recession has impacted these immigrants' abilities to earn wages in the United States, and as a consequence remittances to Honduras have declined dramatically. The situation in Central America looks dire again.

Notes

1. Kathryn Sikkink, *Mixed Signals: U.S. Human Rights Policy and Latin America* (Ithaca: Cornell University Press, 2004), 90.

2. Esquipulas II refers to a peace agreement signed by five Central American presidents in Guatemala City on August 7, 1987, which declared a ceasefire within ninety days and a general amnesty. The agreement gets its name from the Guatemalan town where the first meetings took place.

3. Ana del Sarto, "The 1980s: Foundations of Latin American Cultural Studies," in *The Latin American Cultural Studies Reader*, ed. Ana del Sarto, Alicia Ríos, and Abril Trigo (Durham: Duke University Press, 2002), 156.

4. See J. Patrice McSherry, *Predatory States: Operation Condor and Covert War in Latin America* (New York: Rowman & Littlefield Publishers, 2005) and Peter Kornbluh, *The Pinochet File: A Declassified Dossier on Atrocity and Accountability* (NewYork: The New Press, 2004), 331-363.

5. John Dinges, *The Condor Years* (New York: The New Press, 2005), 19.

6. James F. Petras with Howard Brill, Dennis Engbarth, Edward S. Herman, and Morris H. Morley, *Latin America: Bankers, Generals, and the Struggle for Social Justice* (Totowa, NJ: Rowman & Littlefield, 1986), 91.

7.See Victoria Sanford, *Buried Secrets* (New York: Palgrave Macmillan, 2003), 14.

8. *Latin America: Bankers, Generals, and the Struggle for Social Justice*, 109.

9. Jon Lewis, "Money Matters: Hollywood in the Corporate Era," in *The New American Cinema*, ed. Jon Lewis (Durham: Duke University Press, 1998), 87.

10 . Robert Kolker, *A Cinema of Loneliness*. 3rd Edition (New York: Oxford University Press, 2000), 79.

11 . In 1987, the film was nominated for two Oscars (best actor in leading role, best writing of a screenplay written directly for the screen), was nominated for several and won one Independent Spirit Award (nominated for best cinematography, best director, best feature, best female lead, best screenplay; won best male lead – James Woods), won two Kansas City Film Critics Circle Awards for best director (Stone tied with himself for *Platoon* [1986]) and best film (tied with *The Mission* [1986]), and was nominated by the Writers Guild of America for best screenplay written directly for the screen (http://www.imdb.com/title/tt0091886/awards). (Accessed Sept 23, 2009).

12. Kolker, *A Cinema of Loneliness*, 62.

13. Tina Rosenberg, *Children of Cain: Violence and the Violent in Latin America* (New York: Penguin Books, 1991), 243.

14. Kolker, *A Cinema of Loneliness*, 62.

15. Sikkink, *Mixed Signals*, 141-42.

16 .Sikkink, *Mixed Signals*, 150-51.

17. Kolker, *A Cinema of Loneliness*, 63.

18. Rosenberg, *Children of Cain*, 247.

19. Rosenberg, *Children of Cain*, 250-251.

Chapter 20

Cold War Crucible: The Berlin Wall and American Exceptionalism

Kirk Tyvela

Introduction: American Exceptionalism

U.S. foreign policy during the 1980s—every bit as much as that decade's popular culture, technological developments, and socio-economic trends—constitutes a vital and significant aspect of that history. For Americans living in the 1980s, the Cold War had supplied a four decades-old narrative of their nation's role in the wider world. According to this comforting trope, the animating spirit of American foreign policy was essentially that of guiding humanity towards the universal path of liberal democratic capitalism, of which the United States was the sole exemplar. Of course, this path to progress was closed to millions of people around the world from Eastern Europe to Latin America to Southeast Asia who suffered under despots and dictators who resisted this particular model of modernity. In this way, the purpose of American power was to help these unfortunate others consummate this universal aspiration. As historian Godfrey Hodgson observes, "It seems from all evidence to have been a profound assumption in the United States since the Revolution, sometimes expressed, sometimes not directly spoken, that people all over the world would be happier if they could get rid of their current governments and be ruled by the American Constitution."[1]

At the core of this Cold War narrative was the concept of American exceptionalism. Defined briefly, it is the belief that the United States is an extraordinary nation with a special mission to play in human history—a nation not only unique, but superior to all others. Exceptionalism is a core element of American nationalism and is furthermore an integral part of the cultural and political framework in which American foreign policy is made: it provides political leaders with the official language and metaphors by which they communicate to the public a normative vision of a complex world in which American power naturally inspires and serves humanity.[2]

This deeply ingrained belief in the exceptional nature of American purpose extends to John Winthrop, governor of the Massachusetts Bay Colony. En route to found that Puritan colony in 1630, Winthrop sermonized to his fellow believers onboard the *Arbella*: "We must consider that we shall be as a City upon a Hill, the eyes of all people are upon us." In Winthrop's own time, that message took on an inward-looking dimension that emphasized an ethic of work necessary to build and refine that model for the sake of the Puritan community. Over time, the uniquely Puritan roots of this belief have formed a kind of genetic blueprint for American national identity. Assertions of the nation's "manifest destiny" to fulfill this particular mission—often inscribed in such rhetoric as liberty, freedom, and democracy—were a prominent feature of American westward expansion across the North American continent throughout the 1800s. Into the 20th century, confidence in the ability of the United States to fulfill this divine plan informed grand and lofty presidential rhetoric. Woodrow Wilson's desire to "make the world safe for democracy," Franklin Roosevelt's efforts at building an "arsenal of democracy," and John F. Kennedy's exhortation to "bear any burden, pay any price"—all flowed from the nation's deep-seated sense of its own exceptionalism. The end of World War II provided American policymakers with propitious conditions in which to seek a preponderance of power in order to shape global conditions toward these ends.[3] In this way, American national security during the Cold War was redefined as global security without borders, a seemingly natural outgrowth of Winthrop's model of exceptionalism.

By the 1980s, this centuries-long effort had attained mythological status in American public culture. It was in the divided city of Berlin that President Ronald Reagan (1981-1989) found a compelling symbol of America's renewed commitment to this mission. Thus the 1980s were a critical decade, wherein Berlin was recast as an extension of that hoary Puritan project. In this effort, the president found a receptive audience in the reinvigorated anticommunist popular culture that spawned *Red Dawn* (1984) and especially Sylvester Stallone's *Rambo—First Blood II* (1985). Although Reagan's foreign policy contributed only marginally to the actual collapse of the Berlin Wall, that signal event in 1989 became inextricably linked to American exceptionalism in the minds of many. To better understand why is the purpose of this essay.

Berlin: Forging the Cold War Crucible

The construction of Berlin as a Cold War crucible began in earnest in 1948. The crisis that erupted in the divided city of Berlin that year stemmed from decisions during World War II by the Allied Powers (U.S., Great Britain, and USSR) about the fate of postwar Germany. A formal decision to create four occupation zones (including one for France) had been made at the Potsdam Conference in August 1945. Nevertheless, imprecision concerning Western access to Berlin (located one hundred miles inside the Soviet zone) as well as fundamental disagreements between the Soviets and Americans over the political-economic future of divided Germany erupted in crisis. At a decisive Foreign Ministers conference in London in January 1948, the Americans, British, and French agreed to unify their respective occupation zones (Bizonia) and moved toward the formal creation of a separate West German state fully integrated into the American-orbit. The centerpiece of this effort was the introduction of a common currency for the proposed united Western zone occupation. The Soviets retaliated that same day (June 18) by shutting off access to the city from the west. Three days later, all traffic, electricity, coal, food and supplies intended for West Berlin were shut off by the Soviets. In response to this provocation, the Western allies began airlifting these vital supplies to the besieged Western zone on June 23. This intensive effort lasted 324 days and succeeded in delivering some 2 million tons of supplies. Code named Operation Vittles, this American-led effort served an important ideological function well beyond the immediate physical relief such supplies provided West Germans.[4] President Truman framed these actions in terms that American public opinion could easily understand and support. In October 1948, just months after the start of the airlift, Truman addressed an audience in Boston in which he explained: "In Germany, we have taken the frank and firm position that communism must not spread its tentacles into the Western Zone. We shall not retreat from that position. We shall feed the people of Berlin and the people of Germany will be given their chance to work out a decent life under a democratic government."[5]

When the airlift came to a peaceful end in May 1949, the successful outcome encouraged the conviction of many Americans that their nation's resolve in the face of Soviet perfidy had justly prevailed. The forging of Berlin as an American Cold War crucible was best expressed by a fawning *Time* magazine cover story. "The incessant roar of the planes," the article emphasized, "throbbed in the weary ears of Berlin's people who were bitter, afraid, but far from broken; it echoed in the intently listening ear of history. The sound meant one thing: the West was standing its ground and fighting back."[6] Subsequent events further strengthened the connection between Berlin and the burgeoning narrative of American exceptionalism in the Cold War fight against communism.

The forging of that crucible was manifested in literal terms during the presidency of John F. Kennedy (1961-1963). The construction of the Berlin Wall was intended to prevent the "brain drain" of some 2.5 million East Germans who had fled west since 1945, the vast majority of whom were young, educated professionals and skilled workers.[7] This mass exodus was widely interpreted as confirmation that the American-inspired model of liberal democratic capitalism was far more alluring than the Soviet authoritarian system. On the morning of August 13, 1961—known as "Barbed-Wire Sunday"— Soviet premier Nikita Khrushchev ordered barbed wire and barriers around the perimeter of the city in order to restrict access into the Western sectors. A larger set-up of concrete walls—some 12 feet high and 100 miles long—was soon erected. The wall was but one piece of a massive, interlocking system that completely encircled West Berlin and contained numerous check points, bunkers, watch towers, trenches and land mines. The results stood as a stark symbol of Soviet repression and effectively formed the pivotal Cold War fault line between the United States, the Soviet Union, and their respective allies in Europe.

In the face of this provocation, Kennedy and his advisers essentially accepted this *fait accompli.* "A wall is a hell of a lot better than a war," Kennedy remarked to aides in private.[8] Recognizing that there was no real military solution to this crisis, Kennedy instead sought to provide symbolic reassurance to West Berliners by dispatching troops there as a show of American support. As the president himself informed Willy Brandt, then governing mayor of Berlin and later the first Social Democratic Party Chancellor of West Germany: "the best immediate response is a significant reinforcement of the Western garrisons. The importance of this reinforcement is symbolic—but not symbolic only. We know that the Soviet Union continues to emphasize its demand for the removal of Allied protection from West Berlin. We believe that even a modest reinforcement will underline our rejection of this concept."[9]

Kennedy further sought to reassure Brandt that acceptance of the wall did not signal American abandonment of the people of Berlin. "We must not be shaken by Soviet actions which in themselves are a confession of weakness," he wrote to Brandt. "West Berlin today is more important than ever,"

and its mission to stand for freedom has never been so important as now. The link of West Berlin to the Free World is not a matter of rhetoric. Important as the ties to the East have been, painful as is their violation, the life of the city, as I understand it, runs primarily to the West—its economic life, its moral basis, and its military security. You may wish to consider and to suggest concrete ways in which these ties might be expanded in a fashion that would make the citizens of West Berlin more actively conscious of their role, not merely as an outpost of freedom, but as a vital part of the Free World and all its enterprises. In this double mission we are partners, and it is my own confidence that we can continue to rely upon each other as firmly in the future as we have in the past.[10]

This rhetorical construction by Kennedy of West Berlin as a crucial and constitutive element of the American-led free world provided an essential foundation for Ronald Reagan's later efforts at linking the destruction of the wall to American power and resolve.

In a final gesture meant to underscore his previous promise to Brandt, Kennedy traveled to Berlin to deliver a speech on June 26, 1963. Standing on a platform in front of Schöneberg City Hall, Kennedy exclaimed: "Two thousand years ago the proudest boast was 'civis Romanus sum.' Today, in the world of freedom, the proudest boast is 'Ich bin ein Berliner'. . . .There are many people in the world who really don't understand, or say they don't, what is the great issue between the free world and the Communist world. Let them come to Berlin. There are some who say that communism is the wave of the future. Let them come to Berlin. And there are some who say in Europe and elsewhere we can work with the Communists. Let them come to Berlin." In closing the speech, Kennedy reiterated publically what he had told Brandt privately two years earlier. "Freedom is indivisible," the president declared, "and when one man is enslaved, all are not free. When all are free, then we can look forward to that day when this city will be joined as one and this country and this great Continent of Europe in a peaceful and hopeful globe. When that day finally comes, as it will, the people of West Berlin can take sober satisfaction in the fact that they were in the front lines for almost two decades."[11]

The creation of Berlin as a Cold War symbol thus became inseparable from the narrative of American exceptionalism that Ronald Reagan revived in the 1980s. As Andreas Daum argues, Kennedy's speech transformed Berlin into America's city. "West Berlin's role as the Cold War frontline city—as an island in a communist sea and an outpost of freedom, as two popular metaphors put it—made it an attractive example to those who wanted to cast U.S. history as the story of America's successful mission to spread freedom around the world," he writes.[12] As we will see, the twinning of Berlin with the rhetoric American exceptionalism resulted in a widely shared belief that such rhetoric *caused* the collapse of the wall in November 1989.

Morning in America? Ronald Reagan and American Exceptionalism

In the aptly chosen words of biographer Lou Cannon, the office of the president was for Reagan the "role of a lifetime."[13] This purposeful allusion to Reagan's background as a Hollywood movie star underscores his seemingly preternatural gift for stagecraft. Here a July 1986 *Time* magazine cover story ("Ronald Reagan: Yankee Doodle Magic") provides a kind of conventional wisdom bellwether of the appeal of Reagan throughout the 1980s. "His life is a sort of fairy tale of American power," the article suggested. "Ronald Reagan is a sort of masterpiece of American magic—apparently one of the simplest, most uncomplicated creatures alive, and yet a character of rich meanings, of complexities that connect him with the myths and powers of his country in an unprecedented way."[14]

As a prominent spokesperson for General Electric in the 1950s and then as governor of California (1967-1975), Reagan adhered to a form of social conservatism that increasingly gained purchase in national politics following the domestic tumult of the 1960s and early 1970s. After failing to secure the Republican Party's nomination in the 1976 presidential campaign, Reagan reprised his most famous role as "the Gipper" (*Knute Rockne*, 1940) to present himself to an audience yearning for an all-American hero.

During the 1980 presidential campaign Reagan fully embraced the language of American exceptionalism, cast in confrontationist terms. On foreign policy matters he aggressively attacked the incumbent, Jimmy Carter, for his administration's perceived weakness on national security. Long a staple of the Republican Party's electoral success—dating to the charge that the Democrats had "lost" China to communism in 1949—this tactic painted Carter's promotion of human rights in sinister terms. On the campaign trail Reagan exclaimed: "We have been unrealistic in our approach to the Soviets all these years. They have one course and one course only. They are dedicated to the belief that they are going to take over the world." Astonishingly, just two week before the election Reagan even told a reporter that President Truman had erred in deciding to air-lift supplies in Berlin, suggesting that if he were president at the time he would have sent trucks overland and "called the Soviets' bluff."[15] On other occasion Reagan warned that "the Soviet Union underlies all the unrest that is going on," depicting Carter as "totally oblivious to the Soviet drive for world domination." Echoing the so-called "lesson of Munich," he further declared that Carter's foreign policy "border[ed] on appeasement."[16] Despite the bluster of such rhetoric, Reagan clearly appealed to voters who had grown disenchanted with Carter's manifest failure to manage pressing problems both foreign and domestic: the Iran hostage crisis and an economy mired in stagflation.

In the face of these conditions, Reagan was an appealing figure who exuded warmth and confidence. Nothing epitomized the appeal of Reagan and his effort to resuscitate the nation's exceptionalist narrative more than his 1984 reelection campaign. Featuring the slogan "morning in America," an extensive television ad campaign depicted Reagan as having restored Americans' sense of purpose and optimism. "It's morning again in America," a soothing voice intoned over images depicting hard working Americans in idyllic city and rural landscapes. "And under the leadership of President Reagan, our country is stronger, and prouder, and better. Why would we ever want to return to where we were less than four short years ago?"[17]

Two speeches, one in Britain in 1982 and another in Florida in 1983 are emblematic of Reagan's appropriation of American exceptionalism and the Cold War crucible of Berlin. In early June 1982, Reagan undertook an extensive European trip in order to "renew our bond," as he explained it, with America's allies. Here Reagan's address to the British Parliament on June 8 stands out for its invocation of Berlin and of American exceptionalism. "Berlin, where there stands a grim symbol of power untamed," Reagan admonished. "The Berlin Wall, that dreadful gray gash across the city, is in its third decade. It is the fitting signature of the regime that built it." After reaffirming the historic "special relationship" between the United States and Great Britain, Reagan pleaded for both nations to renew their efforts at spreading freedom in a world witnessing "the decay of the Soviet experiment." As he promised, this effort to promote democracy would soon "leave Marxism-Leninism on the ash heap of history," a provocative and intentional allusion to Leon Trotsky's warning to opponents of the Bolshevik Revolution in 1917. In startling language that he would soon reprise in another speech, the president asked: "Must freedom wither in a quiet, deadening accommodation with totalitarian evil?" As Reagan concluded, "We must be staunch in our conviction that freedom is not the sole prerogative of a lucky few, but the inalienable and universal right of all human beings."[18]

Closer to home, Reagan addressed the National Association of Evangelicals annual conference in Orlando, Florida on March 8, 1983. The speech was aimed at nourishing his party's newly emergent political base—the "New Right" that dominated Republican Party politics in the 1980s. After assuring the faithful in attendance that "there is a great spiritual awakening" and a "renewal of [America's] traditional values," Reagan identified the Soviet Union as the primary threat to this religious-based morality that had long served American "goodness and greatness." As Reagan put it: "Let us pray for the salvation of all of those who live in that totalitarian darkness—pray they will discover the joy of knowing God. But until they do, let us be aware that while they preach the supremacy of the state, declare its omnipotence over individual man, and predict its eventual domination of all peoples on the Earth, they are the focus of evil in the modern world." In the speech's most famous construction, Reagan implored his audience never "to ignore the facts of history and the aggressive impulses of an evil empire" that threatened the American "experiment in liberty, this last, best hope of man."[19] Behind the scenes this rhetoric was reinforced by a rapid militarization of policy. Reagan officials planned on spending some $2.7 trillion during the 1980s on one hundred MX intercontinental ballistic missiles, fifteen Trident submarines, new B-1 bombers and development of the B-2 stealth bomber, among scores of other military hardware, training, and preparedness programs. "We're going to be far more successful," Reagan believed, "if the adversary knows that the alternative is a buildup" in defense spending that the Soviets could not match.[20]

What observers failed to detect at the time, however, was a significant shift in Reagan's own thinking about the Soviet Union. According to Reagan himself, he grasped the need to engage the Soviets in diplomatic negotiations. "Somewhere in the Kremlin, I thought," according to his memoirs, "there had to be people who realized that the pair of us standing there like two cowboys with guns pointed at each other's heads posed a lethal risk to the survival of the Communist world as well as the free world. Someone in the Kremlin had to realize that in arming themselves to the teeth, they were aggravating the desperate economic problems in the Soviet Union, which were the greatest evidence of the failure of Communism."[21] Publicly, Reagan advanced this more accommodationist view of the Soviets in a January 1984 White House address. Eschewing the Manichean rhetoric just one year earlier of an "evil empire," Reagan instead called for "peaceful cooperation" between both superpowers because "we all cherish our children's future." After highlighting his administration's efforts at rebuilding America's deterrent power, the president explained that "Neither we nor the Soviet Union can wish away the differences between our two societies and our philosophies, but we should remember that we do have common interests and the foremost among them is to avoid war..."[22]

In Mikhail Gorbachev, Reagan would soon discover a willing partner in the effort. By all accounts he personally admired and liked his Russian counterpart, the youthful and vigorous reformer of the bloated Soviet state who implemented vast structural changes to the economy (*perestroika*) and a more general policy of openness (*glasnost*) that permitted greater tolerance of internal dissent. Crucially, Gorbachev recognized that these domestic reforms were inextricably linked to Soviet relations with the United States. "World war is an absolute evil," Gorbachev declared in a speech before the Soviet Ministry of Foreign Affairs. In his first official communication with Reagan in March 1985, Gorbachev wrote: "Our countries are different by their social systems, by the ideologies dominant in them. But we believe that this should not be a reason for animosity."[23]

With this backdrop in place, Reagan's famous speech in the shadow of the Berlin Wall while standing before the Brandenburg Gate on June 12, 1987 merits close analysis. The oft-repeated quote from that speech—"Mr. Gorbachev, tear down this wall!"—belies a significant policy shift away from that kind of confrontational rhetoric. At surface level the speech appears to be of a piece with Reagan's earlier addresses, particularly the "evil empire" locution, in that Reagan strongly implied the use of force to create such conditions. Reagan thus declared that "there is only one Berlin" and that "every man is a Berliner." The Berlin Wall could not, the president implied, separate humanity from itself in perpetuity. "As long as this gate is closed," Reagan exhorted, "as long as this scar of a wall is permitted to stand, it is not the German question alone that remains open, but the question of freedom for all mankind." At the rhetorical heart of the speech, Reagan challenged the Soviets to permit freedom to take its natural course:

> We hear much from Moscow about a new policy of reform and openness. Some political prisoners have been released. Certain foreign news broadcasts are no longer being jammed. Some economic enterprises have been permitted to operate with greater freedom from state control. Are these the beginnings of profound changes in the Soviet state? Or are they token gestures, intended to raise false hopes in the West, or to strengthen the Soviet system without changing it? We welcome change and openness; for we believe that freedom and security go together, that the advance of human liberty can only strengthen the cause of world peace. There is one sign the Soviets can make that would be unmistakable, that would advance dramatically the cause of freedom and peace. General Secretary Gorbachev, if you seek peace, if you seek prosperity for the Soviet Union and Eastern Europe, if you seek liberalization: Come here to this gate! Mr. Gorbachev, open this gate! Mr. Gorbachev, tear down this wall![24]

This bellicose rhetoric suggested intent to force the Soviet leader to do precisely that. However, this toughness obscured a more conciliatory private diplomacy that Reagan had been pursuing with Gorbachev. This public-private interplay was a critical factor in allowing both leaders the necessary public political cover to facilitate a new kind of normalization. As James Mann argues, the tough anticommunist rhetoric of the speech "demonstrated to the American public that, even as he proceeded to do business with Gorbachev, Reagan had not been beguiled by the charismatic Soviet leader and had not altered his beliefs about the nature of the Soviet system." In this manner, the Berlin speech was "the political prerequisite for the president's subsequent efforts to work with Gorbachev in easing the tensions of the Cold War."[25]

Further evidence of this more cooperative approach to dealing with the Soviets came during Reagan's state visit to Moscow in May 1988. Reagan and Gorbachev conducted several one-on-one meetings. During the final visit, the leaders exchanged gifts: a denim jacket for Gorbachev and a scale-model of the Kremlin for Reagan. Immediately following this exchange the two leaders took a walk outside in the Red Square. Reagan was queried by ABC News correspondent Sam Donaldson whether the "evil empire" epithet from Reagan's 1983 speech still applied to the Soviet Union. The president replied: "No, I was talking about another time and another era." Indeed, just one day later Reagan expanded on this change in terminology at a press conference prior to departing Moscow. "I think that a great deal of [this change] is due to the General Secretary, who I have found different than previous Soviet leaders....A large part of it is Mr. Gorbachev as leader," Reagan stated, further emphasizing that the previous differences between both countries "continue to recede."[26]

Several months later, Reagan prepared to exit stage left from the White House, confident in having restored America's mission in the world. Fittingly, he departed the presidency as he entered it—by highlighting the exceptional nature of American power and purpose. In January 1989, during his final radio address as president, Reagan spoke of the enduring influence of Winthrop and his fellow Puritans as a source of inspiration and guidance for Americans entering a new decade. "The story of these last eight years and this Presidency," he said,

> goes far beyond any personal concerns. It is a continuation really of a far larger story, a story of a people and a cause—a cause that from our earliest beginnings has defined us as a nation and given purpose to our national existence. The hope of human freedom—the quest for it, the achievement of it—is the American saga. And I've often recalled one group of early settlers making a treacherous crossing of the Atlantic on a small ship when their leader, a minister, noted that perhaps their venture would fail and they would become a byword, a footnote to history. But perhaps, too, with God's help, they might also found a new world, a city upon a hill, a light unto the nations. Those words and that destiny beckon to us still. Whether we seek it or not, whether we like it or not, we Americans are keepers of the miracles. We are asked to be guardians of a place to come to, a place to start again, a place to live in the dignity God meant for his children. May it ever be so.[27]

Within less than one year's time, Reagan's invocation of Winthrop framed the dramatic denouement of America's mission in Berlin. Just months after Reagan's final radio address, his successor, George H.W. Bush, sought to claim that mission as his own. Speaking in Mainz, West Germany in late May 1989, Bush revived the language and imagery of Reagan's 1987 speech at the Brandenburg Gate. "Nowhere is the division between East and West seen more clearly than in Berlin," Bush stated. "There, a brutal wall cuts neighbor from neighbor and brother from brother. That wall stands as a monument to the failure of communism. It must come down!"[28]

Collapse: The End of the Cold War Crucible in Berlin

Just six months after Bush's exhortation, events in Berlin accelerated toward that very end. A voluminous amount of recent scholarship has painstakingly detailed and analyzed the complex forces that led to that epochal moment. Deteriorating economic conditions, popular protest movements, and internal revolt within the ruling Communist elite—all figure as prominent factors that went into the making of history in 1989.[29] Here it is instructive to emphasize one seemingly small but significant detail in order to demonstrate the contingency of events that eventually led to the end of the Cold War. Few at the time would have believed that a minor bureaucratic bungle was sufficient to hasten the collapse of communism in Europe. This was precisely, however, the starring role of Günter Schabowski, who was the public spokesperson for the East German Communist Party Politburo. On the evening of November 9, he detailed for reporters new travel and visa regulations that would allow for greater access into West Berlin from the East. Significantly, the East German government had previously rescinded a ban on travel to Czechoslovakia, whereby some 20,000 East Germans used the opportunity to cross over into Austria. Attempting to better manage this growing crisis, the Politburo decided to permit citizens in possession of the appropriate visas and passports to use any border crossing if they wished to leave East Germany. All of this was intended to take place "in an orderly manner."

As Schabowski informed the press of this new policy, however, he neglected to mention that this new regulation was not supposed to go into effect until the following day, November 10. When questioned by reporters concerning the appropriate time frame, however, Schabowski shuffled through his papers and announced that these changes were to go into effect "immediately, without delay." His ambiguous and flustered response to a reporter when queried "what is going to happen to the Berlin Wall now?" was that "several other factors [would have to be] taken into consideration."[30] Just minutes later, after the news conference had ended, several news organizations reported that the GDR was suddenly opening its borders. Within hours, thousands of East Germans began pouring through the checkpoints heading into West Berlin. Events quickly cascaded beyond the control of East German border guards, who simply opened the gates. Soon tens of thousands of Berliners from both sides converged that night at the wall and ushered in the end of communism.[31]

Reaction to these fast-paced developments in the United States was best expressed by the *New York Times*. Just two days after Schabowski's announcement, an editorial exclaimed: "Crowds of young Germans danced on top of the hated Berlin wall Thursday night. They danced for joy, they danced for history. They danced because the tragic cycle of catastrophes that first convulsed Europe 75 years ago...seems at long last to be nearing an end."[32] Public opinion polls in the United States showed that Americans found these events "exciting and encouraging," prompting President George H.W. Bush to tell his aides that "if the Soviets are going to let the Communists fall in East Germany, they've got to be really serious—more serious than I realized."[33] In this way, the destruction of the Berlin Wall—what Reagan had early labeled a "scar" on humanity—was transformed into an American-led effort.

A final and highly unorthodox explanation for the collapse of the Berlin Wall features the exploits of 1980s pop culture icon David Hasselhoff. Best known in the United States as the star of the popular television shows "Knight Rider" (1982-1986) and "Baywatch" (1989-1999), Hasselhoff was even more celebrated as a pop singer in divided Germany. In mid-1989, his anthemic "Looking for Freedom" was a runaway hit; just one month prior to the wall's transformation from Cold War crucible to memorabilia object, that song was the single most popular on West German radio. Hasselhoff then reprised his hit song while standing athwart the rubble of the wall in front of Brandenburg Gate on New Year's Eve 1989. As he later lamented—without hint of irony—in a 2004 interview with Germany's TV Spielfilm magazine, "I find it a bit sad that there is no photo of me hanging on the walls in the Berlin Museum at Checkpoint Charlie."[34]

The correlation between Reagan's Brandenburg Gate speech in 1987 and the sudden collapse of the Berlin War two years later was quickly seized upon by Republican Party officials and conservative pundits as evidence of causation. In this rendering, the president's rhetoric—not Gorbachev's leadership nor the "people power" that bravely confronted the sclerotic communist system throughout Central and Eastern Europe—was the prime mover of these events. According to Robert McFarlane, who served as the president's national security advisor (1983-1985), the defeat of communism provided "a vindication of [Reagan's] seven-year strategy."[35] Peter Schweizer, a prominent proponent of this Reagan "victory school" interpretation, argues for the primacy of the president in ending—and winning—the Cold War. In attempting to prove a causal relationship between Reagan's rhetoric and the collapse of the Berlin Wall, Schweizer applauds the "bold" and "radical break" from previous policy that merely sought to contain Soviet communism. Reagan, he avers, "was determined to transform the superpower relationship. And it was because of these policies that Reagan succeeded in toppling the Soviet Union."[36] Although he cautions that "no one factor can be singled out as the cause of the Soviet demise," Schweizer nevertheless gives Reagan's "radical (and highly controversial) policies" pride of place in causing that demise.[37] However, as Beth Fischer points out, none of the core claims in support of this "victory school" argument, particularly that the Reagan administration sought to defeat, not merely normalize relations with, the Soviets are borne out in the archival evidence. "It is clear," she argues, "that the administration sought to improve superpower relations, not to destroy the Soviet Union…key officials in the Reagan White House themselves reject the notion that the administration forced the collapse of the USSR or that they even intended such a feat."[38]

Although the overwhelming bulk of historical scholarship denies—or at least heavily qualifies—the centrality of Reagan in ending the Cold War, this "victory school" remains extremely durable and popular outside of academe.[39] The most egregious manifestation of this trend features Ann Coulter, the ubiquitous conservative cultural warrior and Fox News commentator. "Reagan" she writes in a 2003 book equating liberalism with treason, "said the Soviet Union was an evil empire and we would prevail. He called the ball, the shot, and the pocket, and he won the game. But now we're supposed to believe he was lucky. Liberals lie about Reagan's victory because when Reagan won the Cold War, he proved them wrong on everything they had done and said throughout the Cold War. It is their last defense to fifty years of treason."[40]

Despite efforts by more sober scholars, the causal connection between Ronald Reagan's narrative of exceptionalism and the collapse of both the Berlin Wall and Soviet communism appears to be firmly entrenched. Tellingly, most of the surviving remnants of the wall itself are displayed as memorials not within Germany but the United States.[41] According to Gallup Poll data, Reagan left office with a final presidential job approval rating (63% favorable) second only in the post-World War II period to Bill Clinton (66%).[42] In the decades since Reagan left office his presidential reputation has grown apace. A February 2009 USA Today/Gallup Poll asked respondents: "If you had to choose, which one of these U.S. presidents would you regard as the greatest: George Washington, Abraham Lincoln, Franklin Roosevelt, John Kennedy, or Ronald Reagan?" Astonishingly, Reagan received the highest marks (24%), with George Washington garnering last place among the five at a paltry 9%.[43]

The End of History? The Search for a New Crucible

Watching these astonishing events unfold in 1989 was a then obscure State Department official and RAND Corporation analyst named Francis Fukuyama. Writing just months before the collapse of the Berlin Wall in *The National Interest*, a neoconservative foreign policy and international affairs journal, he advanced the startling proposition that the increasingly self-evident failures of communism represented a total eclipse of challenges to free-market capitalism and liberal democracy. Borrowing from the German philosopher Georg Wilhelm Friedrich Hegel the concept of history as a dialectical process advancing toward a singular, universal destination, Fukuyama argued thus "What we may be witnessing is not just the end of the Cold War, or the passing of a particular period of postwar history, but the end of history as such: that is, the end point of mankind's ideological evolution and the universalization of Western liberal democracy as the final form of human government."[44]

kind's ideological evolution and the universalization of Western liberal democracy as the final form of human government."[44]

For Fukuyama, however, the terminus of the Soviet challenge to this Western model of modernity oddly represented a kind of gloomy resignation to a monochrome world devoid of great power competition. "The end of history will be a very sad time," he wrote. "The struggle for recognition, the willingness to risk one's life for a purely abstract goal, the worldwide ideological struggle that called forth daring, courage, imagination and idealism, will be replaced by economic calculation, the endless solving of technical problems, environmental concerns, and the satisfaction of sophisticated consumer demands. In the post-historical period there will be neither art nor philosophy, just the perpetual caretaking of the museum of human history."[45] Three years later, coinciding with the collapse this time of the Soviet Union itself, Fukuyama published an expanded version of the essay as *The End of History and the Last Man* (1992), the titular "last man" referring to a Western liberal democratic capitalist.[46]

Re-reading Fukuyama's essay itself as history allows us to further define the 1980s as both a critical and transitional decade. As a kind of relic from that epochal transformation of the international system, we can see that Fukuyama's thesis was consonant with the widely shared optimism that greeted the end of the Cold War. Although Fukuyama expressed this transformation in less than sanguine terms, his many interlocutors shared no such resignation. For them, the end of this competition was cause for unequivocal celebration of the United States' Cold War triumph over communism. "We faced the most puissant enemy we or anyone had ever known," boasted a prominent neoconservative scholar in 1992, "and we brought it down without having to fight a big war."[47]

We can plainly see just how tenuous, even illusory, that triumphalism was twenty years on, however. Now a very different kind of intellectual current informs Americans' thinking about their capacity to export that Puritan "city upon a hill" model, or even whether that model still pertains at home. Representative of this view is Andrew Bacevich, an historian and bestselling author who self-identifies as a Catholic conservative. In *The Limits of Power* (2008), this Vietnam veteran echoes many radical historians and scholars of that generation who similarly scrutinized and deplored the nation's growing embrace of militarism as the primary means of demonstrating America's exceptionalism. "The impulses that have landed us in a war of no exits and no deadlines," as Bacevich frames the ongoing wars in Iraq and Afghanistan,

come from within. Foreign policy has, for decades, provided an outward manifestation of American domestic ambitions, urges, and fears. In our own time, it has increasingly become an expression of domestic dysfunction—an attempt to manage or defer coming to terms with contradictions besetting the American way of life. Those contradictions have found their ultimate expression in the perpetual state of war afflicting the United States today. Gauging their implications requires that we acknowledge their source: They reflect the accumulated detritus of freedom, the by-products of our frantic pursuit of life, liberty, and happiness.[48]

In this sense, the destruction of the Berlin Wall in 1989 signaled not an end but instead the prelude to a new, more troubling era.[49] The sudden collapse of the wall and the end of the Cold War prompted a search by Americans for a new crucible in which to forge a more stable international order reflective of their sense of exceptionalism. The results of that effort in Iraq and Afghanistan—indeed the larger "global war on terror"—are even more uncertain and unsettling. In this regard, Mikhail Gorbachev's plaintive remark to Colin Powell remains as prescient as ever. During his state visit to Moscow as Reagan's national security adviser in April 1988, Powell was queried by Gorbachev: "What are you going to do now that you've lost your best enemy?"[50]

Notes

1. Godfrey Hodgson, *The Myth of American Exceptionalism* (New Haven: Yale University Press, 2009), 165-166.

2. On the relationship between exceptionalism and American foreign relations, see especially H.W. Brands, *What America Owes the World: The Struggle for the Soul of Foreign Policy* (New York: Cambridge University Press, 1998); Anders Stephanson, *Manifest Destiny: American Expansion and the Empire of Right* (New York: Hill and Wang, 1995); and William O. Walker III, *National Security and Core Values in American History* (New York: Cambridge University Press, 2009).

3. Melvyn P. Leffler, *A Preponderance of Power: National Security, the Truman Administration, and the Cold War* (Stanford, CA: Stanford University Press, 1992).

4. Andrei Cherny, *The Candy Bombers: The Untold Story of the Berlin Airlift and America's Finest Hour* (New York: Putnam, 2008).

5. Harry S. Truman, "Address at Mechanics Hall in Boston," 27 October 1948, *Public Papers of the President of the United States: Harry S. Truman, 1945-1953*, www.presidency.ucsb.edu/ws/?pid=13073 (accessed January 10, 2010).

6. "The Siege," *Time*, 12 July 1948.

7. Frederick Taylor, *The Berlin Wall: A World Divided, 1961-1989* (New York: Harper, 2007), xviii.

8. Kennedy quoted in George C. Herring, *From Colony to Superpower: U.S. Foreign Relations Since 1776* (New York: Oxford University Press, 2008), 710.

9. Letter, Kennedy to Brandt, 18 August 1961, *Foreign Relations of the United States, 1961-1963*, vol. XIV: *Berlin Crisis, 1961-1962*, www.state.gov/r/pa/ho/frus/kennedyjf /x iv/15862.htm (accessed November 1, 2009).

10. Letter, Kennedy to Brandt, ibid.

11. John F. Kennedy, "Remarks in the Rudolph Wilde Platz, Berlin," 26 June 1963, *Public Papers of the President of the United States: John F. Kennedy, 1961-1963*, www.presidency.ucsb.edu/ws/?pid=9307 (accessed February 5, 2010).

12. Andreas W. Daum, *Kennedy in Berlin* (New York: Cambridge University Press, 2008), 220-221.

13. Lou Cannon, *President Reagan: The Role of a Lifetime* (New York: Public Affairs, 2000). For an excellent interpretive history of the 1980s, focusing on the fusion of politics and celebrity which Reagan both shaped and was shaped by, see Gil Troy, *Morning*

in America: How Ronald Reagan Invented the 1980s (Princeton, NJ: Princeton University Press, 2005).

14. "Ronald Reagan: Yankee Doodle Magic," *Time*, 7 July 1986.

15. "Meet the Real Ronald Reagan," *Time*, 20 October 1980. Recent archival evidence demonstrates Reagan's own contribution to developing these issues. As one historian emphasizes, "Reagan wrote most the script he brought to the White." See Chester J. Pach, Jr., "Sticking to His Guns: Reagan and National Security," in W. Elliot Brownlee and Hugh Davis Graham, eds., *The Reagan Presidency: Pragmatic Conservatism and Its Legacies* (Lawrence: University Press of Kansas, 2003), 85.

16. Reagan quoted in Campbell Craig and Fredrik Logevall, *America's Cold War: The Politics of Insecurity* (Cambridge, MA: Harvard University Press, 2009), 312; William M. LeoGrande, *Our Own Backyard: The United States in Central America, 1977-1992* (Chapel Hill: University of North Carolina Press, 1998), 52; and David F. Schmitz, *The United States and Right-Wing Dictatorships* (Cambridge, MA: Cambridge University Press, 2006), 200. For an excellent contemporaneous assessment of the link between Reagan's foreign policy and American exceptionalism, see Tami R. Davis and Sean M. Lynn-Jones, "'City Upon a Hill,'" *Foreign Policy* no. 66 (Spring 1987): 20-38.

17. Quoted in Cannon, *President Reagan*, 451. For the actual television advertisement, see "1984: Reagan v. Mondale," *The Living Room Candidate: Presidential Campaign Commercials, 1952-2008*, www.livingroomcandidate.org/commercials/1984/prouder-stronger-better (accessed March 4, 2010).

18. Ronald Reagan, "Address to Members of the British Parliament," 8 June 1982, *Public Papers of the President of the United States: Ronald Reagan, 1981-1989*, www.reagan.utexas.edu/archives/speeches/1982/60882a.htm (accessed March 1, 2010).

19. Ronald Reagan, "Remarks at the Annual Convention of the National Association of Evangelicals," 8 March 1983, *Public Papers of the President of the United States: Ronald Reagan, 1981-1989*, www.reagan.utexas.edu/archives/speeches/1983/30883b.htm (accessed February 5, 2010).

20. Reagan quoted in Melvyn P. Leffler, *For the Soul of Mankind: The United States, the Soviet Union, and the Cold War* (New York: Hill and Wang, 2007), 346.

21. Ronald Reagan, *An American Life* (New York: Simon and Schuster, 1990), 268. For an extremely useful compilation of Reagan's own voluminous hand-written correspondence and pre-presidential radio addresses, see Kiron Skinner, Annelise Anderson, and Martin Anderson, eds., *Reagan, In His Own Hand: The Writings of Ronald Reagan That Reveal His Revolutionary Vision for America* (New York: Free Press, 2001), and Kiron Skinner, Annelise Anderson, and Martin Anderson, eds., *Reagan: A Life in Letters* (New York: Free Press, 2004).

22. Ronald Reagan, "Address to the Nation and Other Countries on United States-Soviet Relations," 16 January 1984, *Public Papers of the President of the United States: Ronald Reagan, 1981-1989*, www.reagan.utexas.edu/archives/speeches/1984/11684a.htm (accessed February 1, 2010).

23. Gorbachev quoted in Leffler, *For the Soul of Mankind*, 375, 377.

24. Ronald Reagan, "Remarks on East-West Relations at the Brandenburg Gate in West Berlin," 12 June 1987, *Public Papers of the President of the United States: Ronald Reagan, 1981-1989*, www.reagan.utexas.edu/archives/speeches/1987/061287d.htm (accessed February 1, 2010).

25. James Mann, *The Rebellion of Ronald Reagan: A History of the End of the Cold War* (New York: Viking, 2009), 120.

26. Reagan quoted in James Mann, *The Rebellion of Ronald* Reagan, 304-305.

27. Ronald Reagan, "Final Radio Address to the Nation," 14 January 1989, *Public Papers of the President of the United States: Ronald Reagan, 1981-1989,* www.reagan.utexas.edu/archives/speeches/1989/011489a.htm (accessed January 5, 2010). Supreme Court justice Sandra Day O'Connor read Winthrop's speech to honor the memory of Reagan at the president's funeral in June 2004. James T. Patterson, *Restless Giant: The United States from Watergate to Bush v. Gore* (New York: Oxford, 2005), fn 2, 152.

28. Bush quoted in Mann, *The Rebellion of Ronald Reagan*, 326.

29. See especially Jeffrey A. Engel ed., *The Fall of the Berlin Wall: The Revolutionary Legacy of 1989* (New York: Oxford University Press, 2009), Mary Elise Sarotte, *1989: The Struggle to Create Post-Cold War Europe* (Princeton: Princeton University Press, 2009), Stephen Kotkin, *Uncivil Society: 1989 and the Implosion of the Communist Establishment* (New York: Modern Library, 2009), Constantine Pleshakov, *There is No Freedom Without Bread! 1989 and the Civil War That Brought Down Communism* (New York: Farrar, Straus and Giroux, 2009), Archie Brown, *The Rise and Fall of Communism* (New York: Ecco, 2009), and Vladislav Zubok, *A Failed Empire: The Soviet Union in the Cold War from Stalin to Gorbachev* (Chapel Hill: University of North Carolina Press, 2008).

30. Press Conference—GDR International Press Center, 9 November 1989. The full transcript is available in the *Cold War International History Project Bulletin* Issue 12/13 (Fall/Winter 2001): 157-158.

31. Taylor, *The Berlin Wall*, 420-428.

32. "The End of the War to End Wars," *New York Times*, 11 November 1989.

33. Michael Beschloss and Strobe Talbot, *At the Highest Levels: The Inside Story of the End of the Cold War* (Boston: Little, Brown, 1993), 132; Don Oberdorfer, *The Turn: From the Cold War to a New Era* (New York: Poseidon Press, 1991), 365.

34. BBC News, "Did David Hasselhoff Really Help End the Cold War?" 6 February 2004, news.bbc.co.uk/2/hi/3465301.stm (accessed November 2, 2009).

35. McFarlane quoted in Michael Schaller, "Reagan and the Cold War," in Kyle Longley, Jeremy D. Mayer, Michael Schaller, and John W. Sloan, *Deconstructing Reagan: Conservative Mythology and America's Fortieth President* (New York: M.E. Sharpe, 2007), 3.

36. Peter Schweizer, "Did Ronald Reagan Make the Berlin Wall Fall Down?," in Gil Troy and Vincent J. Cannato, eds., *Living in the Eighties* (New York: Oxford University Press, 2009), 141. For a fuller exposition, see Schweizer's *Victory: The Reagan Administration's Secret Strategy That Hastened the Collapse of the Soviet Union* (New York: Atlantic Monthly Press, 1994) and *Reagan's War: The Epic Story of His Forty Year Struggle and Final Triumph Over Communism* (New York: Doubleday, 2002).

37. Schweizer, "Did Ronald Reagan Make the Berlin Wall Fall?" 149. For representative views from conservative pundits and authors who promote the "victory" school, inevitably tending towards hagiography of Reagan himself, see Martin Anderson, *Revolution: The Reagan Legacy* (Stanford: Hoover Institution Press, 1990), Peggy Noonan, *What I Saw at the Revolution: A Political Life in the Reagan Era* (New York: Random House, 1990), Jay Winik, *On the Brink: The Dramatic Behind-the-Scenes Saga of the Reagan Era and the Men and Women Who Won the Cold War* (New York: Simon and Schuster, 1996), Dinesh D'Souza, *Ronald Reagan: How an Ordinary Man Became an*

Extraordinary Leader (New York: Free Press, 1997), and Peter Robinson, *How Reagan Changed My Life* (New York: Regan Books, 2003).

38. Beth A. Fischer, "Reagan and the Soviets: Winning the Cold War?" in W. Elliot Brownlee and Hugh Davis Graham, eds., *The Reagan Presidency: Pragmatic Conservatism and Its Legacies* (Lawrence: University Press of Kansas, 2003), 129.

39. For valuable synthetic overviews of this vast and growing scholarly literature, see Michael Cox, "Another Transatlantic Split? American and European Narratives and the End of the Cold War," *Cold War History* vol. 7, no. 1 (February 2007): 121-146; Jeremi Suri, "Explaining the End of the Cold War: A New Historical Consensus?," *Journal of Cold War Studies* vol. 4, no. 4 (Fall 2002): 60-92; and Vladislav M. Zubok, "Why Did the Cold War End in 1989? Explanations of 'The Turn,'" in Odd Arne Westad, ed., *Reviewing the Cold War: Approaches, Interpretations, Theory* (London: Frank Cass, 2000), 343-367.

40. Ann H. Coulter, *Treason: Liberal Treachery from the Cold War to the War on Terrorism* (New York: Crown, 2003), 190.

41. Daum, *Kennedy in Berlin*, 221.

42. Gerhard Peters, "Final Presidential Job Approval Ratings," *The American Presidency Project*, www.presidency.ucsb.edu/data/final_approval.php (accessed February 5, 2010).

43. USA Today/Gallup Poll, February 6-7, 2009, www.pollingreport.com/wh-hstry.htm (accessed March 8, 2010).

44. Francis Fukuyama, "The End of History?" *The National Interest* vol. 16 (Summer 1989), 3, 18.

45. Francis Fukuyama, "The End of History?"

46. Fukuyama, *The End of History and the Last Man* (New York: Free Press, 1992). For a withering assessment of Fukuyama and other American intellectuals who framed the end of the Cold War as a triumphal "celebration of ourselves," see Bruce Cumings, "Time of Illusion: Post-Cold War Visions of the World," in Ellen Schrecker, ed., *Cold War Triumphalism: The Misuse of History After the Fall of Communism* (New York: New Press, 2004), 71-99.

47. Joshua Muravchik, "Losing the Peace," *Commentary* vol. 94, no. 1 (July 1992): 39.

48. Andrew Bacevich, *The Limits of Power: The End of American Exceptionalism* (New York: Metropolitan Books, 2008), 5. See also *The New American Militarism: How Americans Are Seduced by War* (New York: Oxford University Press, 2005), in which Bacevich offers a more detailed analysis of how the nation's military power has increasingly defined American national identity.

49. For an early argument to this effect, see John J. Mearsheimer, "Why We Will Soon Miss the Cold War," *The Atlantic Monthly*, vol. 266, no. 2 (August 1990): 35-50.

50. Colin L. Powell and Joseph E. Perisco, *My American Journey* (New York: Random House, 1995), 375.

PART 5:

"Totally Awesome 80s": A Decade of Arts and Entertainment

Chapter 21

Fear of a Black Planet: Michael Jackson, Michael Jordan, and Eddie Murphy and the Globalization of Black Masculinity

Reynaldo Anderson, Jason Thompson, and Nikita Harris

Black Masculinity was an important component in the global spread and influence of American Sports and Entertainment in the 1980s. Representing the first generation of the post civil rights generation; contemporary Black athletes and entertainers showcased their athletic prowess, musical tastes, styles, idioms, and culture all over the world on the vast array of American multi national media networks, corporations and channels. This chapter seeks to specifically examine the influence of African American Male entertainers in relation to Black Masculinity and Globalization during the Reagan Era of the 1980s. According to Coleman, contemporary African American ethnicity and "Blackness" are products of corporate media and influenced by the ideologies, histories, and politics of race in the United States.[1] The purpose of this study is threefold: (a) to illuminate how Black Male performers interpret Black Masculinity in relation to media, (b) to understand how African American males construct social identities, and (c) to illustrate how corporate media marketed and commodified Black Male cultural identity in a globalized context.

In the following we present a review of literature on the historical formation of African American entertainers, Black Masculinity, stigma and the corporate appropriation of Black culture in the 1980s for use in the global diffusion of cultural commodities. Subsequent to the review of relevant literature, we explain the research methods employed during the research. Finally, the case study findings are presented in order to highlight the implications for the social construction of Black Masculinity in relation to commodification, and globalization and we also present new research opportunities.

Background

During the 1970s, an example of communication technologies that would impact African American society and its ability to mobilize around communication was the explosion in mass media control. African Americans had been able to mobilize during the civil rights era with the aid of Black radio disc jockeys and independent Black newspapers. Two derogatory images that were vehemently opposed by members of the Black community were the White created images of Sambo and Mammy.[2] Gillens explains, "More importantly, perhaps, the desire to maintain the slave system created material incentives for Whites to view Blacks in particular derogatory ways. Negative stereotypes of Blacks were used in arguing that slavery was necessary to keep Blacks in check, or even that slavery was in the Black's own interest."[3] Due to the success of fierce protest by Civil Rights trailblazers of the early seventies, many of these images had successfully been eliminated. However, with the appearance of Melvin Van Peebles *Sweet Sweetback's Badasss Song* in 1971 Hollywood became aware of the market potential in the Black urban community and the era of Blaxploitation was born.[4] Whereas *Sweet Sweetback's* had visually shown the radical potential to entertain, politically educate Black audiences, and generate revenue independently, what came to be known as the Blaxploitation genre undermined the ethos of the Civil Rights/Black Power phenomenon. "These films were released during the height of the Civil Rights/Black Liberation movement, yet their subject matter of sex, violence and super cool individualism was the antithesis of what contemporary Black political organizations, like SNCC, the NAACP, or SCLC supported for Black people; hence the name *Blaxploitation*, a term coined by *Variety* magazine [was created]."[5] Therefore, instead of the heroic and political character of Sweet Sweetback, Black audiences were influenced by apolitical movies represented by characters like *Shaft* and *Superfly*. Having knowledge of this background is important because the era of Blaxploitation did not cease at the end of the 1970s decade. Instead, the practice of 1970s blaxploitation simply laid the foundation for things to come. This practice bled into the 1980s decade, gaining strength and becoming increasingly pervasive with the advent of sophisticated global multimedia and technology tools. Further, blaxploitation did not solely involve film but it also metastasized to sports and movie entertainment. We argue that this type of activity gave birth to a slightly different, yet similar period, neo-blaxploitation, which was glaringly apparent during Reagan era 1980s.

The political ascendance of Ronald Wilson Reagan to the American presidency following the defeat of Jimmy Carter in 1980 signaled the rise to power of the conservative movement in American politics. Following his election Reagan moved to dismantle federal programs that focused on anti-poverty, job training, and affirmative action programs and appointed conservative officials to agencies charged with protecting the interests of citizens, reducing their impact of complaints against business interests.[6] At the same time there was an exodus of

Black middle class professionals from inner city communities, increasing the social isolation of inner city communities, black unemployment rose to 13.2 percent by 1985 and the number of incarcerated African Americans increased from 58,000 in 1980 to 87,000 by 1985.[7] Also, Reagan, along with his British counterpart, Margaret Thatcher, articulated a brand of reactionary politics that asserted social problems were primarily due to deficiencies in character and were ultimately the problems of people, not the State.[8] However, the Black middle class was symbolically and politically threatened by the efforts of the American conservative movement to sharply curtail civil rights, dismantle affirmative action policies and anoint their own conservative Black leadership spokespersons.[9]

Finally, at the same time the political interests of the Black middle class were under political attack by the conservative movement, the Black underclass was impacted by unemployment, incarceration and drugs. The U.S. drug culture exploded in the late seventies and early eighties largely because of the influx of new ethnic criminal elements, joblessness, government reduction of public assistance and the need for the U.S. government to raise money for covert operations.[10] Jamaican drug organizations were largely composed of elements fleeing the political upheavals in Jamaica that was influenced by CIA operatives hostile to the Manley administration because of its support for Fidel Castro in Cuba.[11] Establishing bases in east coast cities from Miami to New York, Jamaican drug gangs took advantage of the popularity of a new drug called crack and developed a nationwide distribution network.[12] Latino migrants fleeing Nicaragua after the 1979 revolution helped initiate and establish the West coast crack trade raising funds for the CIA, under the leadership of Oliver North, to gain weapons for the CIA's covert Contra army in Central America.[13] The rising culture of violence by urban youth interacting with poverty converged to frighten many White suburban voters into supporting harsher sentencing rather than tackling root issues of poverty. The result of the drug war would lead huge numbers of poor inner city African American males to be swept into the criminal justice system and in many cases losing the right to vote upon serving their sentence.[14]

However, in spite of the policies of the Reagan administration a contemporary Black Masculinity via the mass mediated cultural vehicle of Hip-Hop culture flourished. The culture in its early stages had some limited commercial success as primarily an east coast phenomenon from the New York City area, but by the end of the decade of the 80s, Hip-Hop had established itself as the vanguard element of American popular culture. Emblematic of the 80s era with its urban joblessness, drug war, and reactionary conservatism, Rap performers like Afrika Bambaataa, and Grandmaster Flash and the Furious Five in 1982 put out hits, "Planet Rock" and "The Message," that were prophetic critiques of the urban crisis and the broader American society.[15]

However, at this time in entertainment and sports certain types of African American performers (e.g., Bill Cosby) were promoted in a way that resonated with the new conservative environment. The ascendancy of Michael Jackson,

Michael Jordan, and Eddie Murphy represented an image of Black Masculinity that did not threaten the system of inequality and sought to downplay the existence of Black and White friction. Further, their ascendance instantly caught the attention of power-players in the entertainment industry (i.e., White male Producers and Directors), providing these power-players with an opportunity to manufacture innovative ways to exploit these entertainers' talent for personal gain.

In this study, we examine the social representations and appropriation of the Black Masculine identity of Michael Jackson, Michael Jordan, and Eddie Murphy and their global influence in the 1980s. Each of the aforementioned individuals left an indelible mark on the music, professional basketball, and comedy/movie industries, respectively. Also, each of their careers showcased the new of era of blaxploitation as their likenesses and images were placed on videotapes, audiotapes, posters, the World Wide Web, and CDs to be bought and sold by those in the public domain. Jackson, the self-proclaimed King of Pop, dazzled the music industry from a very young age, creating a global image that was universally adored.[16] During the 1980s he was arguably the most popular figure in the industry, single-handedly galvanizing the movement of a new generation with a palpably different genre of music.[17] Similarly, Jordan was the most admired basketball player of the late 1980s, particularly. His signature long, hanging shorts, bald head, and dangling tongue were mimicked by youth, both Black and White, in the United States and around the world. His global economic impact has him considered by many not just a basketball player, but also a universal figure.[18] Murphy, adept at both stand-up comedy and movie making, was at the forefront of the comedy industry during the entire period of the 1980s. His overwhelming talent was recognized by Hollywood producers, and consequently every effort was made to include him in many box office hits as his presence spurred enormous ticket sales. Taken together, we have three different individuals and three different contexts. Yet, at the same time, there is one similar thread that stretches across each individual and context: the deliberate commodification of their talents in an effort to enrich those in power (neo-blaxploitation).

Black Culture and Commodification

Modern African American masculinity emerged in the Eighteenth century in the formation of Masonic lodges and following the civil war with the formation of organizations like the Freedmen's Bureau.[19] These institutions encouraged Black males to transform their labor into training and profit for themselves or in the case of the Freedmen's Bureau, influenced by racism and white agricultural interests, discouraged black men to participate in self-made masculinity.[20] By the 1960s Black Masculinity was undergoing a transformation influenced by the civil rights movement and the Black Power movement. In the case of the Black Panther Party for Self-Defense there was a particular emphasis in addressing the masculine question in the form of survival programs that encouraged a nurturing form of masculinity although a more violent form was also promulgated within the organization. Also, a seminal work in relation to Black Masculinity, sport and labor appeared in the 1970 book, "The Revolt of the Black Athlete" by Harry Edwards that argued the relationship between sport and capitalism represented a form of alienated labor and because Black labor in America emerged out of the plantation system was doubly alienated and undervalued. Conversely, by the early 1970s a more aggressive apolitical type of Black masculinity was generated in popular entertainment with figures represented in the movies *Shaft* and *Superfly* representing the Hollywood establishment's effort to make money off the Black urban market.[21]

The construction of modern African American masculinity is also influenced by the way Black athletes have been stereotyped in the sports arena.[22] For example, Black athletes are typically recognized for their physical ability in sports, as opposed to their intellectual ability.[23] In fact, it has been suggested that white athletes know how to "think the game" and that Black athletes, on the other hand, rely more on their advanced physical attributes. Previous research specifically calls attention to this disparity as the study explains how Blacks and Whites are perceived in the sport of basketball; noting: "[Blacks] tend to be more aggressive, better jumpers and rebounders, better at playing close to the basket, better at individual moves, and more flamboyant. Whites, on the other hand, tend to be better outside shooters and free throwers, more disciplined, and better grounded in the fundamentals."[24] In this passage, the difference in language used to describe Black basketball players and White basketball players is clearly evident. The implication is that Black players are not as smart as White players. This further implies that Black players solely rely on their physical gifts in order to thrive in the game of basketball. White athletes are "more grounded in the fundamentals" which means that they know how to think through the intricacies of the game. Conversely, Black athletes do not think but instead they react.

African Americans in Film, Sports and Entertainment

Blackface minstrelsy was first performed in the 1830s and was popular through the remainder of the nineteenth century.[25] The first Blackface minstrels were portrayed by Irish immigrants with the most famous character referred to as "Jim Crow."[26] The globalization of the Black face minstrel was transported by the Wild West Show of Bill Cody that performed all across courts of Europe in the late nineteenth century.[27] It was 1914, the year the first White-produced and directed film *Uncle Tom's Cabin* that included an African American was created and distributed.[28] However, the portrayal of Blacks in entertainment had its origins following the American Civil war with White actors using burnt cork to start the *Blackface* tradition in cinema tradition.[29] For most of the twentieth century African American actors were excluded from media performances or were required to portray *sidekick* roles with White actors.[30] However, during the Cold War in the 1950s African American Jazz performers and dancers like Martha Graham were frequently representatives of the U.S. State Department and traveled to Africa, Europe, Asia, were prominently featured on Voice of America radio programs and were regarded as some of the most effective propaganda agents for American foreign policy of the time.[31] The image of the happy negro "Sambo" was also portrayed by the Harlem Globetrotters, a black basketball team founded in 1927.[32] The Globetrotters perpetuated some of the worst southern stereotypes about Black males and their performances often portrayed Black men as loud, lazy, shiftless, and laughing. [33] However, along with their music and entertainment counterparts the Globetrotters were utilized as ambassadors during the Cold War to help the country downplay its domestic problems with race and civil rights.[34] The past and current film and entertainment business is characterized by system-supportive themes and messages to reinforce the American status quo by justifying inequality or focusing on individuals and ignoring social structures.[35] For example, an entertainment product can characterize Blacks as inferior and justify White privilege or deny inequality exists and portray the idea that if Blacks and Whites can get along prejudice will disappear.[36]

The Global Media

Through the media, popular culture is a field upon which the dominant classes or groups attempt to gain and organize consent to their control.[37] Culture is symbolic, and interconnecting. Culture can be pleasurable and revolting, political and non-political. A culture has two aspects, the known meanings and directions that it gives the people and the new observations and meanings that the members of the culture are offered and tested.[38] Also, a culture that people are a part of needs to be interpreted in relation to the underlying structures of production; that the cultures we participate in, clearly are affected by economic forces.[39] Thus, it is the goal of cultural studies to examine how these "cultural" positions are constructed, whose interests are served, and for what purpose? For example, an international network was already in place following the formal end of colonialism in the English speaking countries around the globe from India, Africa, the Caribbean, and Asia that had long standing ties to the British Commonwealth that American cultural industry could tap into to sell and market products.[40] Therefore it was in the interest of American cultural industries, entertainment, sports, etc. to maintain a doctrine of a "Free Flow" of information as an integral part of U.S. foreign policy.[41]

Media cultural imperialism is derived from the socio-political and economic system of imperialism.[42] Media cultural imperialism is a component of an advanced economic system that operates symbiotically with the goals of existing financial, industrial, and political paradigms.[43] However, within the advanced western economies these media entities exist to serve the interest of consumer society. This relationship "is an extension and creation of consumer society."

Therefore, *culture* can be said to operate within the context of political economy, thus serving the interest of existing socio-political economic realities.[44]

Previously within a global context, it could be asserted that the world existed largely within three spheres of influence: (a) First world or Democratic-finance capital societies, (b) Second world or socialist countries and, (c) Third world or underdeveloped countries.[45] However, within the last couple of decades this political reality has been altered. The second world with few exceptions has now largely disappeared, and those former countries, particularly the eastern European states are now in varying modes of finance capital integration with the western consumer societies. With the collapse of the opposition of the former second world countries many of the underdeveloped countries are helpless before the overwhelming influence of western consumer society and a world market economy.

> The corporate media cultures have expanded in recent decades and now occupy most of the global space. The cultural submersion now includes the English language itself, public malls, the telephone system . . . Cultural domination means also adopting broadcasting systems that depend on advertising and accepting deregulatory practices that transform the centers . . . that is better understood as transnational corporate cultural domination.[46]

Finally, because of the dearth of existing capital in most of the underdeveloped societies, the ruling class has no alternative but to cooperate with western capital.[47] Previously, the analysis of cultural imperialism has been investigated from two distinct research approaches. The approach of the political economist is grounded in neo-Marxist theory, while the second tradition is that of the social scientist who seeks a media effects approach.[48] However, both approaches contain flaws that make each approach ultimately problematic, but the primary problem is "what is the proper locus of investigation, the motives of the senders . . . or the effects of the receivers."[49]

Cultural Studies Framework

For the purposes of this study, the utilization of a Cultural Studies approach would be most appropriate for two reasons: (1) to analyze the continued economic domination of western transnational corporations upon globalization, and (2) to understand the potential ramifications of commodification of Black Masculinity in a global context. Cultural studies focuses upon the cultural struggle for *meaning* by analyzing the various cultural practices that construct, reinforce, constrain, and discredit meaning through popular culture texts. Often, these cultural practices are influenced by cultural structures that construct meaning and perpetuate ideologies. According to Corcoran, one of the cultural structures that maintain the status quo is the media. The print media as a cultural structure are commonly perceived as apolitical, however, cultural studies explains how the print media perpetuates ideologies that serve certain group interests.[50] The media, either knowingly or unknowingly, indoctrinates members of the society who consume and give credence to their message. Cultural studies are interested in how the mass media define social relations and political problems while seeming to function as a transparent bearer of meanings in society. Members of a free society shape and are shaped by meanings communicated by the media.[51]

Second, meaning is determined by the cultural context.[52] A key aspect of rhetorical criticism is explaining the meaning of a rhetorical text. Cultural studies directly analyze the construction of meaning of rhetorical texts through a cultural perspective. Inhabitants of the culture are influenced differently by messages propagated in the culture. For that reason, cultural studies argue that meaning comes from the culture and culture is comprised of competing ideologies and competing discourses.[53] However, the actions of these media texts can be interpreted as the result of the influence of transnational global corporations that impact how meaning is perceived by potential consumers of the corporations' "product." The implication is that a product can be communicated to the public in such a manner that disguises the social significance of the product in relation to existing capitalist social paradigms.[54] An example of this is the attitude of African Americans towards the purchasing of certain clothing lines from companies that may be covertly racist, but this bias is not present in the advertisement which may be targeted at an African American audience. Thus the "real and full meaning of production" of the item, to economically exploit African Americans, is "hidden beneath the empty appearance in exchange," the item advertised with an African American actor.[55]

However, with regard to Black masculinity and globalization it is important to think of the relationship between entertainment, sport and the nation. Black Masculinity, sport, entertainment, and cultural studies should utilize a diasporic analytic framework.[56] Building upon the idea of a Black Atlantic or broader diasporic cultural formation of people of African descent will allow for an analysis that crosses national boundaries and can incorporate a critique of performance, and movement within the world-system.[57] Concerning texts, previous scholarship notes that text or discourse is defined by the area of social experience that is able to make sense of the social location from which that particular sense is made, for example the way media will report differences between management and labor; management "offers" and labor "demands."[58] This textual analysis makes explicit that media frequently operates in the interest of the more powerful group, in this case, management. This position is further supported by the idea that with respect to text, one of the primary foci is on literary production with the goal of using criticism to make explicit what is implicit in a cultural text. From this perspective the cultural critique would be interested in exploring texts for the sake of clarity to illuminate how Black Male performers interpret Black Masculinity in relation to media, to understand how African American males construct social identities, and to illustrate how corporate media marketed and commodified Black Male cultural identity in a globalized context.

The King of Pop

A review of textual data presents fluid ideas of what it means for Michael Jackson to portray himself as being beyond "race." During the Reagan administration, following his exodus from the music group, Jackson Five, Michael Jackson sought to re-brand himself for a broader audience. Although Jackson was part of a rich musical legacy of black male performers like Bill Bojangles Robinson, Jackie Wilson, Chuck Berry and James Brown, by the end of the decade he had transformed his facial appearance into a whitened caricature of his former self. However, Michael Jackson was a product of the eighties selling over 110 million records and becoming a one man culture industry commanding millions of viewers when he released a music video. Yet, Michael Jackson, similar to other African American artists, went to extraordinary lengths to cultivate an image of Black Masculinity that Whites could embrace and went as far to have cosmetic surgery to close the aesthetic social distance between himself and his Caucasian public.[59] However, Jackson was careful to cultivate a Black aesthetic that initially helped him build his initial fan base in the Black community. For example, in the 1970s when he was a member of the Jackson Five, Michael wore a stylish afro that resonated the cultural influence of the Black Power movement, although his management team took great pains to distance him from any association with that aspect of Black political culture.[60]

During the "Victory" tour of 1984 Jackson launched his solo career with the release of the solo "Thriller" and accompanying music video.[61] Conversely, the rap group Run DMC was following the successful release of their 1983 release "Its Like That" with 1984's "Rock Box" heralding the emergence of the first Rap super group of the decade. The emergence of Run DMC with their tough hip urban look and support from an emerging generation X contrasted the more effeminate appearance and cosmetically enhanced Jackson and the Baby Boomer generation. Jackson's changing appearance seemingly represented an attempt on his part to symbolically distance himself from the notion of a "nigger" entertainer and represented the idea of a changing cultural landscape where Whites could embrace the success of talented Blacks achieving the "American Dream."[62] Ironically, Jackson's success contributed to the commercial rise of Rap music and other Black artists due to the breaking of the color barrier on the music channel MTV in January 1983 with the video release of the song "Billy Jean." Although, Jackson would follow his "Thriller" album with his first solo "Bad" tour of 1987 to 1989, he would not approach the commercial success of his earlier release. However, the "Bad" tour was a marketing success; with five number one hits off the "Bad" album, Jackson, backed by multinational corporation PepsiCo, had the most financially successful and largest crowd music tour in world history. PepsiCo with its global reach in soft drinks, fast foods chains, and other distribution networks, helped to propel Jackson into an international marketing juggernaut in the music business. By the late 1980s, roughly twenty years after de-colonization in Africa, Asia, and Latin America, following the

U.S. civil rights movement, at the height of the Cold War, through the American military base clubs network around the world, Michael Jackson had become the face of Black masculinity.

In websites, texts, and social commentary, Michael Jackson is portrayed as a complex person that arose from the limited circumstances of a working class Black family, under the mentorship of Berry Gordy. He broke media barriers culminating in the best selling album "Thriller" and yet frayed cultural and community relationships later in his career due to his improper relations with young boys and the seemingly racial distancing act of using cosmetic enhancements to "Whiten" his features. The career of Michael Jackson during the 1980s and Cold War era occurred in a social milieu of changing cultural practices that attempted to reify, constrain, and reinterpret American popular culture consumption for a broader global audience and promote multinational business interests.

Air Rising

In many ways Michael Jordan represented a clean break from the more militant Black athletes who preceded him. Since the release of Jordan's shoe line by Nike in 1985 the athletic shoe business has never been the same. Prior to Jordan, athletes such as Jim Brown and Muhammad Ali did not hesitate to reveal their disdain for the racist society that oppressed them. Also, Ali had no problem calling attention to his religious ideology. These types of behaviors did not sit well with many in the public domain, nor did these behaviors sit well with the commissioners in either league. Both would have preferred these athletes to go along to get along rather than rock the boat by revealing things that stood in contrast to the norms of society. Thus, it was no surprise why Ali and Brown's images were not greatly marketed and advertised by cereal, beverage, and clothing/shoe apparel companies, among others. Companies stayed away from them because their images would likely cause customers to refrain from purchasing certain products. They represented an economic liability. For example, Brown, Ali, or Curt Flood, an African American athlete responsible for changes in free agency in professional baseball, represented a challenge to the corporate structure of athletics and portrayed a form of uncompromising Black Masculinity in the face of the broader White society.

Jordan, on the other had, blazed an entirely different path. For example, similar to Michael Jackson's aesthetic embrace of the Afro to build his initial fan base, Jordan, breaking with tradition adopts the colors red and black for his tennis shoes, *two of the three colors of the Black Power movement*, instead of colored in conventional white. Jordan refused to make public any comments about political beliefs. Jordan also deliberately stayed away from social issues that caused him to take a side. This type of behavior made it easy for companies to both market and advertise their products which were emblazoned with his image. For example, it was well known during the 1980s period that Reebok supported apartheid in South Africa. Reebok sneakers were worn by some professional basketball players, as well as athletes from other sports. By 1984 Nike had surpassed Adidas as the number one sports shoe and they consistently marketed an image of Jordan that was "humble" to a fault and catered to young kids and older adults, building international sales up to $3 billion by the end of the 80s.[63]

Although Jordan only donned Nike shoes, he never made any mention of his feelings concerning Reebok's questionable social discriminatory practices. Instead, he protected his image, maintaining neutrality that belied the militant, social reformist ways of some of the athletes who preceded him. Another example is the sweat shops that exist in many third world countries as they manufacture Nike products (i.e., shoes & apparel). It was known that some countries took advantage of cheap labor to create the Nike products. At no point did Jordan ever communicate his feelings about Nike's unfair labor practices. Instead, again, he kept quiet in an effort to protect his own interests. These interests included maintaining his lucrative deals with his various sponsors. If Jordan became a militant social activist then he would have destroyed his neutral, choir boy image that was meticulously crafted and maintained for his entire professional basketball career. Jordan's behavior made it easy for him to be commodified. Ironically, in a move that belies the figure of an assimilated token black, Jordan helped quietly bankroll the production of the movie "Malcolm X" directed by Spike Lee. Yet, Jordan personifies the emergence of the athlete entrepreneur; individuals who can utilize their personal brands to develop several lucrative enterprises. Athletes such as Tiger Woods, building on Jordan's success, have practiced much of the same behavior. Woods has maintained his neutrality on some of the more sensitive topics regarding social injustice (among others). This makes it simple for his sponsors to maintain their relationship with him, while at the same time keeping satisfied the many fans (particularly White) who adore him.

Heir to King Richard

Eddie Murphy is one of the most successful actors in entertainment history. Billing himself as a disciple of the style made famous by the greatest Black comic of the 1970s, Richard Pryor, Murphy emerged from obscurity during the 1980-81 season as a regular of the popular late night comedy show *Saturday Night Live* Murphy's rise to superstardom in movie and television parallels the emergence of Michael Jordan and Michael Jackson in the 1980s. However, it was not only Murphy's comedic gifts and impersonations of famous African Americans like Bill Cosby and James Brown that drew attention, but his satirical characterizations of African American stereotypes and homophobic routines that routinely caused criticism.

Initially Murphy embraced a stereotype of Black Masculinity based upon his comedy routines that were observed as hypersexual, homophobic, and raunchy. Murphy's hit comedy skit *Delirious* in 1983 followed by *Raw* in 1987 were successful and were emblematic of a more aggressive Black Masculinity that was interspersed with stock and trade stereotypes about Black characters, Black relationships, Black families, homosexuals, and sex. Yet it was the release of the movies *48 hours* in 1982 and *Trading Places* in 1983, distributed by Paramount Pictures that shot Murphy into a trajectory of international stardom, becoming the first actor to command 1 million dollars per film by the mid 1980s. Blaxploitation films had disappeared by the 1980s due to pressure from the civil rights community and lack of interest from major studios. However, combined with the success Michael Jackson had breaking the color barrier on the MTV network, and due to the fact in the 1980s that many movie studios generated a fraction of their sales outside the Unites States, the need to attract more customers made Murphy a hot commodity, a young Black male whose buffoonery on *Saturday Night Live* made him acceptable to the larger White population. Following the release of *Beverly Hills Cop* 1 and 2 in the late 1980s Murphy reached his peak with the 1988 film "Coming to America," a spoof about an African prince coming to the United States to find a bride. However, unlike Michael Jordan or Michael Jackson, Murphy's career did not flourish as well into the next decade. The Berlin wall was dismantled in 1989, there were lousy scripts, and new markets were opening up to Hollywood cultural products and Murphy's *Schtick* did not sell as well domestically although box office sales continued to do well overseas.

However, Murphy has been roundly criticized by director Spike Lee for not helping other African Americans in the movie business and has been under suspicion in relation to his sexual orientation following his arrest for picking up a transsexual prostitute. Yet, despite claims from several other transsexuals, Murphy has been able to settle libel cases in relation to his sexual orientation out of court. Finally, Murphy, along with Jordan and Jackson, represented the commodification of a particular type of Black Masculinity that catered to traditional Black stereotypes that served not only the cultural comfort zone of the White community, but the commercial interests of multinational corporations.

Ideological Implications

Previous scholars define ideology as structure that constitutes members of society to live their relations in and through conditions of production.[64] Within this context, the historical mode of production that explicitly transforms raw materials into products, transforms social relations, and delineates an ideological practice that is implicitly present in the everyday reality of the individual's social construction.[65] Because of the previous inability of these structures of discourse to critique aspects of human reality that simple economic determinism can conceal, it is necessary to slightly extend certain aspects of analysis. Previous commentary notes that from the point of view of the oppressed, the economic substructure also operates as a superstructure.[66] Furthermore, "The cause is the consequence; you are rich because you are white, you are white because you are rich . . . The governing race is first and foremost those who come from else-where, those who are unlike the original inhabitants, "the others."[67] This racial aspect has psychological ramifications with respect to the colonized peoples attempting to forge a national identity. The resulting pathologies may result in violent aggression against other oppressed people, false sense of sexual prowess, and an overzealous sense of attributing one's fate to the "Devil" or "God" rather than systematic discrimination.[68] Many of these pathologies and contradictions can be observed in the texts of rap lyrics which consistently refer to negative stereotypes of women and minorities and never address underlying structures of the society which create and exploit the people who create the music.

Conclusion

The contemporary negative portrayal of Black Masculinity is in direct propor-tion to the global hegemony of Western communication media imperialism un-der the leadership of the United States.[69] The conclusion one can draw from this analysis is that some nations, particularly underdeveloped nations, are increas-ingly developing into information colonies as the world enters the Information Age. The internet and other modern communications technologies have influ-enced the pace of communication.[70] Previous commentary on the pace of infor-mation and its influence on social awareness notes:

> Today, after more than a century of electric technology, we have extended our cen-tral nervous system itself in a global embrace, abolishing both space and time as far as our planet is concerned. Rapidly, we approach the final phase of man—the tech-nological simulation of consciousness, when the creative process of knowing will be collectively and corporately extended to the whole of human society, much as we have already extended our senses and our nerves by the various media.[71]

However, the internet and modern communications are disproportionately controlled and managed by multi-national corporations. Internationally, the cur-rent situation in mass communication and modern communication technology has asymmetrically created a situation of *electronic colonialism.*[72] The implica-tion is that the Black Atlantic Diasporic community and others are in a predica-ment whereby information controlled by other entities can impact the culture of the community. Finally, race still persists as a problem in relation to cultural and corporate domination, and dissemination of a version of Black Masculinity, and Black Culture that relies on a portrayal of a certain level of aggressiveness, ste-reotypes, and accommodation to corporate interests. [73]

Notes

1. R.R. Means Coleman, Introduction. In R.R Means Coleman (Ed.), *Say it Loud! African Americans, Media, and Identity* (New York: Routledge, 2002).

2. Martin Gillens, *Why America Hates Welfare: Race, Media and the Politics of Anti-Poverty Policy.* (Chicago: University of Chicago Press, 1999).

3. Gillens, *Why America Hates Welfare: Race, Media and the Politics of Anti-Poverty Policy.*

4. Jesse Algeron Rhines, *Black Film, White Money.* (New Brunswick, NJ: Rutgers University Press, 1996).

5. Rhines, *Black Film, White Money.*

6. James B. Stewart, Message in the Music: Political Commentary in Black Popular Music from Rhythm and Blues to Early Hip Hop *The Journal of African American History* 90, No. 3; The History of Hip Hop (Summer 2005): 196-225.

7. Stewart, Message in the Music.

8. Ellis Cashmore, *The Black Culture Industry.* (New York: Routledge, 1997).

9. Robert Smith, *We Have No Leaders: African Americans in The post Civil Rights Era.* (New York: State University of New York Press, 1996).

10. Gary Webb, *The CIA, The Contras, and The Crack Cocaine Explosion.* (New York: Seven Stories Press, 1998).

11. Webb, *The CIA, The Contras, and The Crack Cocaine Explosion.*

12. Ibid.

13. Ibid.

14. Ibid.

15. Charise Cheney, *Brothers gonna work it out: Sexual Politics in the Golden Age of Rap.* (New York: New York University Press, 2005).

16. Lisa D. Campbell, *Michael Jackson: The King of Pop* (Boston: Branden Publishing Company, 1993).

17. Margo Jefferson, *On Michael Jackson.* (New York: Random House, 2007).

18. David L. Andrews, *Michael Jordan, Inc: Corporate Sport, Media Culture, and Late Modern America* (New York: SUNY Press, 2001).

19. Judith Newton, *From Panthers to Promise Keepers: Rethinking The Men's Movement.* (Lanham, MD: Rowman & Littlefield, 2005).

20. Newton, *From Panthers to Promise Keepers: Rethinking The Men's Movement.*

21. Ibid.

22. Susan Tyler Eastman and Andrew C. Billings, Biased Voices of Sports: Racial and Gender Stereotyping in College Basketball Announcing. *Howard Journal of Communications* 12 (2001): 183-201.

23. Richard E. Lapchick, *Five Minutes to Midnight: Race and Sports in the 1990s.* (New York: Madison Books, 1991).

24. D. Stanley Eitzen and George H. Sage, *Sociology of American Sport* (Boston: McGraw Hill, 2003) (7th ed.).

25. John G. Blair, First Steps toward Globalization: Nineteenth-Century Exports of American Entertainment Forms. In R. Wagnleitner & E. May (Ed.), *Here, There and Everywhere: The Foreign Politics of American Popular Culture.* (Hanover, NH: University Press of New England, 2000).

26. Blair, First Steps toward Globalization.

27. Ibid.

28. Stephanie Greco Larson, *Media and Minorities: The Politics of Race in News and Entertainment*. (Lanham, MD: Rowman & Littlefield, 2006).

29. Larson, *Media and Minorities: The Politics of Race in News and Entertainment*.

30. Ibid.

31. Penny Von Eschen, Satchmo Blows Up the World: Jazz Race and Empire During the Cold War. In R. Wagleitner and E. May (Ed.), *Here, There and Everywhere: The Foreign Politics of American Popular Culture*. (Hanover, NH: University Press of New England, 2000).

32. David K. Wiggins, Great Speed but Little Stamina: The Historical Debate of Black Athletic Superiority. *Journal of Sports History* 16, no. 2 (Summer 1989).

33. Wiggins, Great Speed but Little Stamina.

34. Mary L. Dudziak, *Cold War Civil Rights: Race and the Image of American Democracy*. (Princeton University Press, 2000).

35. Larson, *Media and Minorities: The Politics of Race in News and Entertainment*.

36. Ibid.

37. Aniko Bodroghkozy, We're the Young Generation and We've Got Something to Say: A Gramscian Analysis of Entertainment Television and the Youth Rebellion of the 1960's, *Critical Studies in Media Communication* 8, no. 2 (June 1991): 217-30.

38. Raymond Williams, *Culture and Society 1780-1950*. (London: Chatto and Windus; Harmondsworth: Penguin Books, 1958).

39. Williams, *Culture and Society 1780-1950*.

40. Mark Alleyne, *International Communication and International Power*. (London: St. Martins Press, 1995).

41. Alleyne, *International Communication and International Power*.

42. Hebert I. Schiller, Not Yet the Post-Imperialist Era. *Critical Studies in Mass Communication* 8, (1991): 13-28.

43. Schiller, Not Yet the Post-Imperialist Era.

44. Ibid.

45. Ibid.

46. Ibid.

47. Ibid.

48. Ibid.

49. Michael B. Salwen, Cultural Imperialism: A Media Effects Approach. *Critical Studies in Mass Communication* 8, (1991): 29-38.

50. Salwen, Cultural Imperialism: A Media Effects Approach.

51. Ibid.

52. Ibid.

53. Farrel Corcoran, Cultural studies: From Old World to New World. *Communication Yearbook* 12, (1989): 602.

54. Corcoran, Cultural studies: From Old World to New World.

55. Sut Jhally, *The Codes of Advertising: Fetishism and the Political Economy of Meaning in Consumer Society*. (New York: Routledge, 1990).

56. Gamel Abdel Shahid: *Who da man?: Black Masculinities and Sporting Cultures*. (Toronto: Canadian Scholars Press Inc. 2005).

57. Shahid, *Who da man? Black Masculinities and Sporting Cultures*.

58. Cashmore, *The Black Culture Industry*.

59. Ibid.

60. Ibid.

61. Ibid.

62. Ibid.

63. Donald Katz, Triumph of the Swoosh. *Sports Illustrated.* 16 August, 1993: 53-73.

64. John Storey, *An Introductory Guide to Cultural Theory and Popular Culture.* (Athens, GA: University of Georgia Press, 1993).

65. Storey, *An Introductory Guide to Cultural Theory and Popular Culture.*

66. Ibid.

67. Ibid.

68. Frantz Fanon, *The Wretched of the Earth.* (New York: Grove Press, 1963).

69. Manthia Diawara, Black studies: Performative Acts. In J. Storey (ed.), *What is Cultural Studies? A Reader.* (New York: St. Martin's Press Inc, 1996), 300-07.

70. Storey, *An Introductory Guide to Cultural Theory and Popular Culture.*

71. Thomas L. McPhail, *Electronic Colonialism: The Future of International Broadcasting and Communication.* (Beverly Hills, CA: Sage, 1987) (2nd ed.).

72. Emmanuel Ngwainbi, Black Connections and Disconnections in the Global Information Supermarket. In John Barber and Alice Tait (Eds.) *The Information Society and the Black Community* (Westport: Praeger, 2001), 237-258.

73. Patricia Hill Collins, The Meaning of Motherhood in Black Culture and Black Mother-Daughter Relationships. In M. Zinn, P. Hendagon-Setelo, M. Messner (Eds.), *Gender Through the Prism of Difference.* (New York: Prentice-Hall, 2005).

Chapter 22

Matter and Mammon:
Fiction in the Age of Reagan

Alan Bilton

This chapter explores the oft-cited materialism of the eighties in terms of a dialogue between matter and immateriality in American fiction of the period, a critical interplay between "there" and "not there," absence and presence. On the one hand, a great deal of writing from the period stresses the sheer physicality of *things* – whether the junk and detritus of Paul Auster's trash-strewn New York, the unyielding desert spaces of Cormac McCarthy, or the stress on commodity culture and shiny consumerism in the work of Bret Easton Ellis and Tom Wolfe. However, alongside this imaginative stress on *things* – their weight, scale, color and form – one may also posit an antithetical stress on disappearance, intangibility and emptiness; after all, Ellis's *Less Than Zero* (1985) opens with the famous injunction "Disappear Here," whilst Auster's novels are full of missing people, disembodied voices and eerie caesura. Nothingness, the void, and a kind of unbearable lightness haunt both McCarthy's bone and flesh stick-figures and Tom Wolfe's angst-ridden yuppies; the chapter explores American fiction of the period in relation to both a cultural obsession with waste and trash and, crucially, as a literary engagement with the intangible economics of the futures market. Time and time again in eighties fiction, unearthly realms of information technology seem to float above dense, compacted pockets of matter: the chapter argues that this recurrent motif is linked to the economic realities (and fantasies) of the period – or more specifically the strange, shadowy realm of Platonic Capital itself.

Indeed, the two major American works of cultural criticism published in the decade – which is to say, Marshall Berman's *All That Is Solid Melts Into Air* (1982) and Fredric Jameson's "Postmodernism, Or, The Cultural Logic of Late Capitalism," originally published in the *New Left Review* in 1984 – both frame their readings of the American scene in terms of the mercurial, unstable and constantly changing nature of global capital itself. Berman's brilliant, ambivalent exposition of Modernism (he regards so-called "Post" Modernism as merely another stage in Modernism's endless reinvention) argues that "its energies, insights and anxieties spring from the drives and strains of modern economic life," the radical shifts in time, space and perception orchestrated by *avant-garde* art merely the pale reflection of even more destabilizing and unsettling forces at work in the marketplace.[1] Capitalism requires ceaseless change, conflict and flux, Berman argues. Fierce competition necessitates constantly revolutionizing the means of production, inventing new products, testing new technology, maximizing efficiency. This constant upheaval in turn spills over into the very fabric of social life; workers must be flexible, fluid, able to adapt to a constantly changing environment. Whatever stands still is swiftly obsolete (complacency and sloth are the cardinal sins of the marketplace); what remains is a sense of struggle, agitation and disturbance, the defining characteristics of the Modern age (and its art). The end result of limitless competition isn't progress but change for change's sake, Berman argues, likening the law of capital to an enormous snake devouring its own tail. How does the market maximize its profits? By constructing buildings only to tear them down, selling new products before old ones have worn out, carving new market space by destroying everything that came before. Capitalism, in Berman's imagining, is a kind of demonic perpetual motion device, unable to stop itself (or even slow down) as it demolishes the past in order to hawk the new. Subject to the white heat of market forces, nothing is safe: cherished traditions, much-loved institutions, even shared social values. Nothing is less conservative than those who argue for the primacy of the marketplace, Berman's book argues. The old, the uncommercial, and the slow: all are obliterated by the immutable law of what's hot and what's not. Hence the radical instability of the Modern Age: nothing lasts (or is built to last), no sphere of social or cultural life is untouchable. There is no hiding place from the market, Berman argues, no safe bolthole; what's here today is sold tomorrow. Hence the title of Berman's book, derived, of course, from Marx;

> All fixed, fast-frozen relations, with their train of ancient and venerable prejudices and opinions, are swept away, all new-formed ones become antiquated before they can ossify. All that is solid melts into air, all that is holy is profaned...[2]

"All that is solid melts into air" ... on the one hand, Berman stresses the *material* consequences of capitalism – urbanization, industrialization, pollution, the concreting (or mall-ing) of our world – but at the same time he stresses its constant disintegration and *dematerialization,* the ticking time-bomb built into all of its manifestations. Land is cleared, buildings dynamited, companies broken up: instability is built into the system. There is no solid ground under capitalism, Berman argues, no safe haven or rock to cling to; dizziness and disorientation define its chief mode of perception, its manifestations constantly on the verge of exploding, melting, and decomposing. Capitalism is all about *things,* it's true, but these things (goods, systems, raw materials, and people) continually fracture and explode. The destructive waste of capitalism (rather than say, the inequitable distribution of its resources) is the real enemy for Berman, the way in which companies blindly saw away at the very branch they're clinging to. Both Berman and Marx are drawn toward a kind of apocalyptic lyricism when describing the market; edifices crumble, fashions are shredded, machines pulverized, books burn. "The pathos of all bourgeois monuments is that their material strength and solidity actually count for nothing and carry no weight at all," Berman writes, "... they are blown away like frail reeds by the very forces of capitalist development they celebrate."[3] This is a world precariously poised at the point of deliquescence, flickering, disappearing. For Berman, the aesthetic nature of Modernism is an attempt to capture precisely this fitful transience, the breakdown (whether in cubism, expressionism or surrealism) of all stable forms. Like investment bankers leaping from their windows at the onset of the Great Crash, the market, for Berman, always seems poised at the precipice of a great void; the blur is the rush as we all plummet over.

Is there anything then that might slow down the relentless bulldozer of Berman's imagining? One could perhaps argue that environmental concerns or fears of diminishing natural resources might temper the market's reckless profligacy, its instinctive urge to throw away and start again, but Berman isn't so sure. Less raw materials and a decline in production might only exacerbate the process, he argues: with less to go round, you had better grab what you can. But is this the whole story? Paradoxically, salvation (of a sort) seems to come from a very unlikely quarter: not Marxist revolution but capitalist self-interest itself. A completely "free" market (one without legal, institutional or state restraint) is in reality as rare as hen's teeth; those in positions of power will do all they can to remain there, including stifling competition, lobbying governments, and doing their best to construct self-serving monopolies. Corporate muscle always aims for total market saturation and therefore economic dominance. After all, who wants upstart competitors snapping at one's heels? No, better to drown them at birth (or buy out their intellectual copyright if necessary). In this sense, corporate interests paradoxically serve to restrain the infinite conflict of Berman's model. In the place of social revolution we find a revolution in marketing, the same companies pumping out the same products but rebranded and repackaged for the new season. In this model we still live in an accelerated culture, but any sense of "future-shock" is now gone, change now merely a function of merchandising, promotion and consumer-spin. This then is the world of Fredric Jameson's Postmodernism: not the free flowing of capital but the interlocking of vast corporate and bureaucratic networks, the construction of a global "system" which resembles a vast prison (or shopping mall) rather than the anarchic battleground of Berman's economic fantasy.

All That Is Solid offers us a vision of a material world perpetually falling apart, dismembering itself; Jameson shifts his focus to the "post-industrial." where "things" are displaced by intangible data, stocks, shares, the incorporeal mysteries of the futures market. Factories, mines, heavy industry; all these are increasingly outsourced to the developing world; in the information age,

Jameson argues, the real "means of production" (in Marxist terms) are the control and dissemination of information, images, and spectacle[4]. Whilst the violence of Berman's world is *physical* (crushing, rending, devouring), Jameson suggests an eerie disembodiment, a loss of depth and meaning. Signs (such as one's NASDAQ rating) replace things, floating free from their original referent to pursue their own semiotic destiny (not so much how efficient one's company is, as the degree of confidence expressed in it by the stock market). If Berman's Modernism creates experimental art as artists struggle to orientate themselves in the new vortex of experience, Post Modernism, aligned to "late capitalism" creates a sense of aesthetic exhaustion. "We seem increasingly incapable of fashioning representations of our own current experience," Jameson writes, "art" merely another commodity whose "value" is entirely dependent upon the marketplace[5]. If Modernism captures the moment when all solid ground seems to crumble, the Postmodernism floats in the void left in its wake.

"I Think We've Hit the Jackpot" – Ronald Reagan[6]

In retrospect, these theoretical notions can also be seen as very much a product of their (economic) times. The Seventies shuddered to a close under the burden of crippling "stagflation," a lethal combination of spiralling inflation and economic decline. Attempts by Carter's administration to stimulate the system by pumping in millions of federal dollars, only served to ratchet up prices whilst simultaneously creating an upward pressure on wages and costs. The sluggish US economy could no longer compete with leaner, "hungrier" manufacturers in low-cost developing nations, whilst the high price of oil simultaneously crippled America's heavy industry. Unemployment, mounting debt and a declining tax base augured economic doom. Berman's profoundly pessimistic work, influenced by both the economic decline of New York and, more personally, by the death of his son, offers a vision of America as things began to disintegrate, a nightmare vision of capitalism as a tightening noose. What then was the solution?

For those on the right, the answer was "supply-side" economics, later nicknamed Reaganomics or "Voodoo economics" (originally a snipe by George Bush senior, of course). If government interference in the market had failed, then the cure, fiscal libertarians believed, was radical deregulation. Such a position also possessed an ideological bent of course: "socialized" intervention was an affront to "fundamental freedoms," Reagan argued, an Un-American attempt to stifle national creativity[7]. More mediation (such as trade barriers, for example) was therefore anathema; instead of concentrating on supply and demand, it was the area of investment and capital that needed freeing from Carter's faltering hand. Reagan therefore cut taxes (especially corporate taxes), deregulated the financial industry, and allowed the market free rein to follow the great white whale of economics, 'Capital'.

Although Reagan's first act upon coming into power was to place all banks ostensibly under the control of the federal reserve, this move in practice opened up the financial system to unlimited mergers, take-overs and virtually unrestrained competition – the result as violent and merciless a battleground as anything in Berman's apocalyptic theorizing. Virtually overnight the tranquil waters of a fusty banking industry were ravaged by a seemingly endless round of aggressive mergers and acquisitions (famously misheard as "murders and executions" in Bret Easton Ellis' *American Psycho* (1991)[8]. Although in theory antitrust legislation survived, in practice Reagan's cronies were loath to enforce it. For a time, anything went: economic historians calculate that there were some 25,000 mergers or buy-outs between 1980 and 1988, with a total value of some $2 trillion.[9] Asset-strippers bought out companies, devoured profitable sectors and cut free the rest. Junk-bond dealers deliberately bought out high-risk companies at very low prices, buffed up their images (after all, if such sharp traders were buying then they had to be worth something) and sold them on as shamelessly shoddy goods – a kind of toxic, globalized game of Old Maid. The worth of shares thus became wholly dependent upon their market image (how much other people are willing to pay for them) rather than any kind of accurate representation of a company's business prospects. Financed by massive borrowing, investors snapped up stocks that looked likely to be subject to a further take-over bid, a self-fulfilling prophecy which served to inflate the market to near-elephantine levels. The "real" economy no longer mattered; the rustbelt of the Mid-West was in terminal decline and production was shifting overseas. New technology – namely the facilitation of global, computerized trading – created an emergent virtual market, stocks and shares sold globally (and instantaneously) in a new kind of simultaneous time/space continuum. This nascent electronic "frontier" (a phrase used again and again in writing from this period) opened up a different kind of market, no longer rooted in *national* production as such, but rather a nascent form of *global exchange*. Whilst it might seem that corporate interests now trumped national ones (much of American industry went into deep recession during the early eighties), Reagan argued that the vast profits gleaned from this sector would eventually (via consumerism) trickle-down into the wider economy—albeit unequally, and with these consumer goods now being made over-seas. Under Reagan, the "real" world of seventies deprivation and poverty was thus fading from the screen. Although enormous vanity projects such as the Trump Tower were still being constructed, the most important empires were now built on electronically intangible foundations. And if concerns about "insider trading" (the illegal selling of information about future share deals) periodically rocked the system – Ivan Boesky's indictment in 1987 for example – it also made it clear that information was the true commodity in this new marketplace. In Postmodern terms, the sign replaces the signified. The once-solid economy was now truly as light as air.

Down in the Hole

The most obvious consequence of Reagan's policies was massive social inequality, a widening of the gap between rich and poor. In terms of fiction, the decline of traditional industry and the hard-times of its blue-collar workforce inspired a range of realist, stripped-down narratives of economic recession, including Bobbie Ann Mason's *In Country* (1985), Jayne Ann Phillip's *Machine Dreams* (1984) and the minimalist miserablism of Raymond Carver, pared-down prose for lean times. The other side of the equation however – the rise of the yuppie and an extreme flaunting of wealth and consumerism – simultaneously produced a drive to hyperbolic excess whose clearest manifestation is Tom Wolfe's *The Bonfire of the Vanities* (1987).

Wolfe's great subject (and also the source of the book's near-perfect merger of form and content) is materialism: objects, commodities, acquisitions, from interior design to designer clothing to an almost tangible dirt and squalor. Although Wolfe saw himself as an American heir of Tolstoy, his stress on the tangible and the physical actually seems closer to one of the Modernist themes: the reduction of people to *things*. Consider the cop, "like a great slab of meat with clothes on," rich socialites, skinny as "x-rays," or the guard examining prisoners' mouths "like someone inspecting a crawl space in a cellar."[10] And even when characters aren't being treated as objects, they are still defined by them: one need only think of Gene Lopowitz's log-fireplace, displaced from an English gentleman's club and transplanted to the offices of bond-traders Pierce & Pierce, whose "hardwood logs, sculpturally perfect, perfectly clean, utterly antiseptic" are "buggered with enough insecticide to empty a banana grove of everything that moves ... permanently installed, never to be lit."[11] This one object sums up everything we need to know about Lopowitz – his ineffectuality, his simulation of authority, even his old-school conservatism, so completely at odds with the rapacious activities of his company. Character isn't action in Wolfe, but décor. Indeed the astonishingly excessive attention to descriptive detail – pursued to an extent that would make even Wolfe's Nineteenth Century idols, paid by the word, blush – is the novel's central philosophy. From light fittings to soft furnishings to granite worktops, Wolfe's novel reads like an interior-design magazine (for which the wife of the novel's protagonist, Sherman McCoy significantly works) by way of *The Age of Innocence* (1920) on steroids. Display is everything: self-definition is achieved only via one's possessions. However this intense materialism also possesses a negative capacity too; after his arrest, McCoy finds that he "now noticed the smallest things ... the egg-and-dart molding around the cornice on the main-floor ... the old bronze shades on the lamps on the check-writing desks in the middle of the lobby ... the spiral fluting on the posts supporting the railing between the lobby and the section where the officers sat," a microscopic obsession with detail and texture he can neither control nor switch off[12]. Moreover, as McCoy begins his descent down the social scale, he also discovers an ugliness and pungency of physical detail that shocks him with the force of a philosophical discovery. Crouching by a sluice-drain in a holding cell in the Bronx, bent-over amongst the urine and the vomit and the crud, McCoy discovers that the physical is "where mankind sought its own level, and the meat spigot was on."[13] This notion of man as meat in turn links Wolfe's book to John Dos Passos' *Manhattan Transfer* (1920), written some seventy years earlier; for both Wolfe and Dos Passos, all is matter and matter decays – a motif underlined by Arthur Ruskin's death amongst the fine dining of an ultra-smart Manhattan eatery, a *memento mori* reminding those present of "the grim remains of the joys of the flesh."[14]

If the shiny surfaces and lovingly detailed finishings of McCoy's apartment represent one pole of the novel's materialism, then the ravaged wasteland of the Bronx represents its other, the "dark matter" expunged from Manhattan style-guides and cover-page photo-shoots.[15] In the *purgatorum* below the Atlantic Avenue Overpass lie the rusted shells of carjacked autos, great mounds of trash and waste, the abandoned and the derelict.

> All at once there was no more ramp, no more clean, cordoned expressway. He was at ground level. It was as if he had fallen into a junkyard. He seemed to be under the expressway. In the blackness he could make out a cyclone fence over on the left ... something caught in it ... A woman's head! ... No, it was a chair with three legs and a burnt seat with the charred stuffing hanging out in great wads, rammed halfway through a cyclone fence ... Who on earth would jam a chair into the mesh of a cyclone fence. And why?[16]

Down amongst the detritus, Wolfe's unfailing eye for the physical latches onto a different kind of palpability – broken, jagged, filthy. Apart from the occasional liquor store or Chinese Take-Out, there is merely ruinous, decrepit *stuff* – mountains of cans, bottles, razor-wire – or even more terrifyingly, the absence of stuff – "entire blocks of the city without a building left standing," a nothingness that seems to presage some kind of terrible void, "utterly empty, a vast open terrain," blackness as nullity, nothingness, a philosophical black hole.[17] There is, of course, an overt racial aspect to all of this (McCoy registers "all the dark faces" and interprets the underpass as an "uncivilized jungle"), but for the purposes of this essay, it is Wolfe's stress on decomposition and waste that is most striking.[18] It is as if matter has decayed to the point of vanishing, great black spaces appearing like melanoma spots upon the city surface. "Under the expressway's black underbelly" is an elephant's graveyard of trash, where matter comes to die.[19] Paradoxically it suggests both the antithesis of the electronic screen that McCoy stares into all day ("the world ... the little green symbols that slid across the black screen"), and a strange mirror image of its "non-space," as Jameson would put it.[20] Material density fuses with immaterial absence: just like the society it displays, the heavy material weight of Wolfe's book is constantly on the verge of imploding, floating free from the conventions of nineteenth century realism to suggest something stranger, less certain.

Welcome to the *Merzbau*

The most complex working out of this relation between waste and nothingness is to be found in the work of Paul Auster, both in his most famous work, *The New York Trilogy* (1987) and even more explicitly in his subsequent novel, *In The Country of Last Things* (1987). The accent throughout both works is on the broken and the derelict, "the city... a junk heap" as Auster writes, "an inexhaustible storehouse of broken things."[21] Indeed, Auster's New York resembles a vast municipal dump, "a mountain of rubbish," scraps, fragments, litter.[22] If T. S. Eliot's *The Wasteland* (1922) can be described as a library on fire, with snatches of disparate texts saved from the conflagration, Auster's book is a giant land-fill, everything torn, squashed, distorted, Andy Warhol's soup cans flattened to the point of abstraction. In terms of art, the most obvious link is to Cubism – not just in terms of the way the work meditates upon its own mode of representation, the way in which the text both constructs and negates its own internal meanings–but also in terms of its mangled subject matter, crushed bottles, furniture, junk, randomly compacted and combined until they begin to take on strange new forms and meanings. When we look at early Cubist paintings by Picasso and Braque today, they seem, for "modern" art, incredibly *old*–faded, dingy, brown, conjuring up a vanished world of smoky zinc bars, dirty chessboards, and crumpled newsprint. Likewise Auster's apparent abstraction seems rooted in the specifics of New York in the eighties, which is to say the decay and brokenness of great parts of the city. "I have come to New York because it is the most forlorn of places, the most abject," notes Stillman Senior in *The New York Trilogy*. "The brokenness is everywhere, the disarray is universal. You only have to open your eyes."[23]

Whilst great swathes of New York profited from a massive property boom, fuelled by tax breaks and sweeping changes in zoning regulations, by the end of the decade New York's homeless tally had risen to 90,000, with over a third HIV positive and one in seven New Yorkers infected with TB[24]. The return of large-scale corporate investment to New York after the infamous "white-flight" (and loss of tax base) of the seventies thus brought mixed fortunes. On the one hand white-collar jobs in finance, technology and communications brought enormous affluence to specific neighborhoods; Selma Berrol, for example, quotes the case of a grocery store on Columbus Avenue paying $400 a month in rent in 1977, but then becoming a designer boutique paying $4000 per month only a decade later[25]. At the same time however, 22% of the city's inhabitants were dependent upon government handouts (a welfare system progressively dismantled by Reagan's administration) and the infrastructure of great chunks of the city appeared pockmarked, dilapidated and near ruin[26]. Interviewed by Larry McCaffery and Sinda Gregory in 1989, Auster argued that his early work was as much influenced by the view outside his window as the Modernist nightmares of Beckett or Kafka[27]. In this sense, the surrealism of his early work was also rooted in the local, New York, as Auster put it, "rapidly turning into a third world city before our eyes."[28]

To capture the decomposition of the city, Auster drew inspiration from both the work of the great dada artist Kurt Schwitters, the Gaudi of the gutter, and Robert Rauschenberg's "trash-art." Schwitters didn't produce paintings of junk, but rather collected the thing itself – tattered, stained, rusty, bent, and torn. He would then squirrel away this material inside his house in Hanover, the so-called *Merzbau*, inside of which he built a veritable city of crap, filling several stories and his cellar, the cast-off items molded and wielded into fantastical new shapes, weird catacombs of encrusted walls, screens and props, the rooms awarded outlandish titles like "The Cathedral of Erotic Misery," Murderer's Cave, or the Sex Crime Den. Sadly the house was blown to pieces by an allied bomb in 1943, but the idea of it influences a great deal of Auster's work, particularly the notion that the work of art itself might become a kind of trap, eventually caving in and entombing the artist. Before the bombers did their house cleaning, Schwitters feared being buried alive in his own creation, the walls advancing in on him, his living area getting more and more cramped every day, and this idea appears again and again in Auster, the artist's garret also a kind of prison cell cutting one off from the outside world. One of the central parables in "The Locked Room" concerns the survivor of an avalanche, pinned within his shelter, watching his every breath add to the ice that will kill him[29]. Marooned both within their own apartment and their own minds, Auster's heroes experience the city as a kind of solitary confinement, sequestered in box-like cells staring out at the midden-pit. Indeed, the fear of venturing outside is central to much of his eighties fiction. "In his dream ... he found himself in the town dump of his childhood," writes Auster, "sifting through a mountain of rubbish."[30]

In American terms, the undisputed king of the rag and bone artists was Robert Rauschenberg, who collected cardboard cartons, stuffed animals, smashed clocks, storefront dummy and broken umbrellas, and then sprayed them with thick, grimy paint, collected from yard-sales or factories. His most famous work, Monogram (1955-59), was constructed using a stuffed angora goat – spotted in the window of a Manhattan typewriter store – rudely inserted through a huge deflated tyre. Many of Rauschenberg's aesthetic methods are explicitly captured in the character of Peter Stillman in Auster's *City of Glass*. In an interview, Rauschenberg noted "I had a kind of house rule ... If I walked completely around the block and didn't find enough to work with, I could take another block and walk around it – but that was it."[31] Similarly in Auster's novel, the crazed Stillman takes oddly structured tours around his neighbourhood, seeking out broken, discarded or worthless objects, his itinerary spelling out words when transcribed onto the city grid. In the same interview, Rauschenberg notes, "I tended to work with things that were either so abstract that nobody knew what the object might be, or so mangled that you couldn't recognize it any more, or so obvious that you didn't think about it at all."[32] Likewise, Auster's novel asks

What happens when a thing no longer performs its function? Is it still the thing, or has it become something else? When you rip the cloth off an umbrella, is the umbrella still an umbrella? You open the spokes, put them over your head, walk out in the rain, and you get drenched. Is it possible to go on calling this object an umbrella? ... It might resemble an umbrella, it might have once been an umbrella, but now it has changed into something else. The word however, has stayed the same. Therefore it can no longer express the thing. It is imprecise; it is false; it hides the thing that it is supposed to reveal."[33]

This gap between words and things – the idea that language is as broken as the various objects Stillman retrieves from the gutters and junk heaps–is of course central to the trilogy. His is a broken city, where the flotsam and jetsam of the streets has reached such a point of decomposition that the original names no longer seem to apply.

In Auster's *In the Country of Last Things* (1987) the unnamed city in the book – part New York, part Leningrad under siege, part Warsaw ghetto – likewise constantly shifts and changes, its inhabitants leaving their homes, never knowing if they will be able to find their way home again. The novel's heroine, Anna, walks down a side street only to find no way back: buildings, shops, landmarks all appear and disappear at will, replaced by rubble, giant holes, or new monolithic structures. The result is akin to the history of a city filmed using time-lapse photography, but also a portrait of a city in terminal decay. Paint peels and blisters, wood rots, concrete erodes, plants shrivel, bodies putrefy. Nothing new enters the city – no babies are born, nothing is built, grown or created – so its inhabitants most scavenge from what is left, recycling the things that remain. Everything in the city is broken, tattered, splintered, until, like Stillman's umbrella in *City of Glass*, nothing is itself any more, everything spare-parts, bits or scraps, haphazardly fused together. Things lose shape, color and form – everything seems to be decaying into a kind of base-matter – a kind of '*it*' ness, just stuff, "some particle or agglomeration of matter that cannot be identified" – and, as in *The New York Trilogy*, this seems to apply to the city's citizens as well.[34]

For language too is disappearing from this metropolis of last things. Words vanish from inside characters' minds; signifiers such as "aeroplane" remain but nobody knows anymore what they refer to[35]. Strange gaps or shadows open up within the dictionary, letters fade, and with this loss of communication, both memories and a sense of self begin to fall apart too. Words themselves are precious commodities in the book, a scarce resource, constantly on the verge of running out; when the narrator has no more pages in her note-book, and no more words to describe her surroundings, the novel must inevitably come to an end.

City of Glass also ends with a kind of extinction of language and reversion to base matter. The detective, Quinn, has by now lost track of all the principal characters in the strange case he is trying to crack, and not knowing what else to do, he stations himself outside the window of the apartment of the mysterious Mrs. Stillman and elects to wait. This "surveillance" (if one can dignify it with such a term) goes on for months. He sleeps rough, uses a dustbin as a bathroom, and slowly, mysteriously starts to turn into discarded matter himself[36]. As he does so he also starts to think not in words but in things, "part of the world at large, as real and specific as a stone, or a lake, or a flower," the perfect merger of sign and signified that the novel is obsessed with.[37] No longer able to be described in language, he literally disappears from the page, now belonging wholly to the realm of things. Auster leaves it open as to how we are to interpret this conclusion: is Quinn's ultimate fate terrifying or transcendent? Are we intended to see this reversion to base matter as a sign of decay or as a strange form of redemption – even the return of the real? Certainly this ontological immersion in real things isn't entirely dissimilar to Romantic dreams of being at one with nature: except of course that the base matter here is filth, slime, shit.

White Noise, Waste Products

In many ways images of junk and waste seem as central to American culture in the 80's as the effluvia and litter of the modern city were to turn of the century Cubism. One might think of the bizarre sculptures of Nancy Graves, who took soft, perishable, rotting items such as fruit or leaves or food stuffs, and then cast them in bronze and welded them to machine parts or tin-cans to create strange new creatures, or the poetry of Charles Simic, with his two-dimensional city streets, as flimsy as film-sets, full of storefront dummies, broken toys, soapbox derelicts and crazed preachers with sandwich boards. And of course when it comes to images of recycling, one immediately thinks of the most iconic (or at least the most discussed) film of the decade, Ridley Scott's *Blade Runner* (1982), with its retrofitted vision of the future composed from the detritus (old detective movies, pulp sci-fi, crumbling architecture) of the past.

As suggested earlier, this stress on matter can be seen a response to the Postmodern sphere of the image, matter what is left behind after the rapture of the simulacrum. This image seems central to the work of Don DeLillo (who indeed would go on to write the Great American novel of waste-disposal, *Underworld*, in 1997), calling to mind some of the stranger characteristics of his best known work, *White Noise* (1984). *White Noise* is set in Blacksmith, a day-glo version of small-town America, that appears as two parts sitcom to one part soup commercial, a theme-park simulation of American suburbia. Here the sky is picture book blue, the grass astro-turf green, and the novel's central family, the Gladneys, live on a leafy drive indistinguishable from a film-set or merchandising campaign. However, as the novel progresses, something begins to interfere with the community's reception, and this generic picture begins to intangibly flicker. The residents experience an eerie sense of foreboding, nervously contemplating what other particles, apart from cathode rays, may be floating in the air – invisible fumes from the local chemical plant, radiation emanating from household appliances, trace elements somehow finding their way into the water supply[38]. Anxiously recording his son's receding hairline, Gladney asks

Did his mother consume some kind of gene-piercing substance when she was pregnant? Am I somehow at fault? Have I raised him, unwittingly, in the vicinity of a chemical dumpsite, in the path of air-currents that carry industrial wastes capable of scalp degeneration, glorious sunsets? (People say the sunsets around here were not nearly so glorious thirty or forty years ago)[39].

The ever more lurid sunsets (one might think of Fredric Jameson's definition of Postmodernism as "what you have when the modernization process is complete and nature is gone for good") presage the collapse of the Gladney's artificial world into an infinitely less recognizable (and more alienating) abstraction, as if the channel on the town's remote has been changed one time too many, the local station now picking up only static (the "white noise" of the novel's title)[40]. DeLillo develops this sense of the alien and the abstract impinging upon the everyday through the Gladneys' trips to the local hypermarket, the shopping mall marking the frontier between suburbia and a dazzlingly unfamiliar, technological realm. Initially, these shopping expeditions are joyous and sustaining, the packaging and advertising blanketing each product reinforcing the life-style connotations that bestow identity and belonging. By the end of the novel, however, these familiar commodities have been replaced by unknown blank goods, family-friendly packaging erased by "smeared print and ghost images."[41] Unlike the happy shoppers of yore, the final patrons in the novel stagger lost and confused amongst the ever-shifting aisles which reconstitute themselves like liquid circuitry, following signs they cannot understand, scared by the bagging staff, deafened by the "ambient roar."[42] DeLillo frames the mall as the site of a radical dematerialization, a fractal space outside of time or space, where shoppers wander dazed amongst a hallucinogenic flow of vivid but insubstantial images, their features distorted and refracted across endless banks of video monitors, mirrored corridors and merchandising displays, no longer certain where they end and the spectral projections begin. With a disarming lack of irony, Gladney's fellow lecturer at "The College on the Hill," describes the mall as an ancient Tibetan lamasery, a "portal" to another world (earlier in the novel a vanished elderly couple turn up dazed and confused inside its walls); it is as if shoppers have followed their credit card details into the grid, or stumbled from the TV screen into the web of circuitry behind it. But if this strange new world inspires awe, it also manufactures compliance. Befuddled shoppers line up quietly, waiting for the contents of their baskets to be verified. "At the end it doesn't matter what they see or think they see," DeLillo writes. "The terminals are equipped with holographic scanners, which decode the binary secrets of every item, infallibly. This is the language of waves and radiation, or how the dead speak to the living."[43]

In this virtual environment, where the sky is indistinguishable from a screen-saver, and sunsets are filled with artificial colorants just like one's food, can anything be said to be real or authentic? Ironically, only waste products, bodily effluvia and household trash, still possess any degree of organic tangibility in the novel.

I walked across the kitchen, opened the compactor drawer and looked inside the trash bag. An oozing cube of semi-mangled cans, clothes hangers, animal bones and other refuse. The bottles were broken, the cartons flat. Product colours were undiminished in brightness and intensity. Fats, juices and heavy sludges seeped through layers of pressed vegetable matter ... Was this the dark underside of consumer consciousness? I came across a horrible clotted mass of hair, soap, ear-swabs, crushed roaches, flip-top rings, sterile pads smeared with pus and bacon fat, strands of frayed dental floss, fragments of ballpoint refills, toothpicks still displaying bits of impaled food[44]

Such trash acts as the antithesis of the mall's extra-territorial abstraction; here products once again attain the status of Auster's base-matter. But is this intended to be seen as positive in the novel, junk as the corporeal antithesis of the electronic terminals, the "waves and radiation" invisibly present elsewhere? DeLillo expands upon this notion in *Underworld,* configuring waste as a kind of dark matter, the sublimation of all of our most authentic impulses – appetites, bodily functions, habits, needs – everything that the air-brushed image seeks to conceal. In this sense, waste functions as a kind of material unconscious, a physical reality that carries in it suggestions of both excretion, and (that ultimate decomposition), death. *White Noise* likewise toys with the notion that death is the one physical truth that cannot be easily assimilated within the consumerist matrix, but the novel also mocks its own hero's pretentiousness (all that cod-Keatsian talk of Gladney as "a walker in the mists of death") and connects this veneration of the deathly to Nazism; nevertheless the return of this theme in *Underworld* suggests that at some level DeLillo takes the binary opposition between the material and electronic abstraction deadly seriously[45]. One might argue that base matter is at least "real" or tangible, and in this sense suggests something of what Nature (with a capital N) provided for previous artistic movements: something palpable to measure ourselves against, an escape from the artificial, the illusory, and the simulated. Might (in a kind of aesthetic alchemy) the sheer weight of waste matter save us from the unbearable lightness exhibited elsewhere?

The Vanishing Point

This strange fall into lightness appears throughout eighties fiction, from the plunge into cyberspace in William Gibson's astonishingly prescient *Neuromancer* (1984), whose exploration of "the consensual hallucination that was the matrix" predates Keanu Reeves' Neo by a good decade and a half, to the "placelessness" of writers such as Douglas Coupland and Lynne Tillmann, whose texts likewise seem to exist in an artificial media-scape devoid of tangible referents[46].

In a famous passage from Jean Baudrillard's *America* (1988), Baudrillard compares American reality to a special effect, a trick of the light, a "hologram" rather than a country.

The hologram is akin to the world of phantasy. It is a three-dimensional dream, and you can enter it as you would a dream. Everything depends on the existence of the ray of light bearing on the objects. If it is interrupted, all the effects are dispersed, and reality along with it. You do indeed get the impression that America is made up of a fantastic switching between similar elements, and that everything is only held together by a thread of light, a laser beam, scanning the American reality before our eyes. In America the spectral does not refer to phantoms or to dancing ghosts, but to the spectrum into which light disappears."[47]

Travelling across America by plane or air-conditioned auto, peering into TV screens and video monitors, Baudrillard experiences not the size or scale of the continent but rather a sense of emptiness, disappearance and absence. Los Angeles in particular seems to exist close to a kind of a kind of existential vanishing point, the glare of the sun making things lighter, transparent, invisible. "Things seem to be made of a more unreal substance," notes Baudrillard; "they seem to turn and move in a void by a special lighting effect."[48] The novel closest in spirit to Baudrillard's soporific heat-haze is Bret Easton Ellis' *Less Than Zero* (1985), with its flat, stunned quality and narrative enervation; this is a novel on heavy medication, anesthetized to the point of absolute indifference. Every character is blonde, tanned and young, each day is hot, sunny and perfect, but this endless reproduction (like that of the sunset in *White Noise*) drains the world of meaning: one can imagine Dali's melting clocks here, time dripping like glue, the nothingness of a permanent vacation where it's simply too hot to move (or care). Exhaustion, indifference and ennui are the constituent elements of Ellis's universe, the book's narrative progressing through short, disconnected fragments lacking in any sense of continuity or progression. People never meet up, appointments are never kept, nobody answers the phone; time is too liquid, or rather too viscous for any kind of resolution. Yet another party, drug deal, sexual conquest: nothing registers, nothing matters. For all the mindless hedonism of its setting, this is where desire peters out, physical bodies made translucent by the sun.[49]

Like Baudrillard, Ellis defines Los Angeles in terms of nothingness, the "nowhere" of an achieved utopia. The ocean, the desert, and the city grid are all equally featureless, flat planes of nothingness reproduced and reproduced. There is no *here* here, merely infinite detachment ("Disappear here" reads the billboard that haunts the novel's narrator, Clay), watching rather than *being*.

We park and walk through the empty, bright Beverly Centre. All the stores are closed and as we walk up to the top floor, where the movies are playing, the whiteness of the floors and the ceilings and the walls is overpowering and we walk quickly through the empty mall and don't see another person until we get to the theatres. There are a couple of people milling around the ticket booth. We buy our tickets and walk down the hall to theatre 13 and Trent and I are the only persons in it and we share a joint inside the small, hollow room.[50]

Interestingly, the movie doesn't even rate a mention; the novel's attention span isn't up to it anyway. Everything blurs, evaporates, erases. Characters are indistinguishable, dialogue lobotomized, description limited to brand names. As one party blurs into another, night turns into day and the novel's present-tense narration scrolls on listlessly, it seems as if there's no more terra firma to be had.

Or is there? Clay – his name suggestive of both malleability as well as a faint echo of something real – is obsessed with the desert space that lies outside the city limits, the arid plains beyond the mall and freeway. There, infernal winds howl in from the hinterlands, uprooting palm trees and cutting power lines, flash-fires erupt without warning, sudden earth tremors prophecy an almost Biblical end. Occasionally fleeting glimpses of the real – poor folk, crashed cars, a dying coyote – disrupt the hologram of endless leisure and ceaseless pleasure that is Clay's lot[51]. For Clay, the desert appears in the guise of an Old Testament deity, the vengeful father so different from his own indulgent, neglectful parents, the return of a repressed judgement he both fears and paradoxically desires. And the heart of the "real" for Clay? Not nature but another junkyard, the valley of wrecked cars intentionally evoking the valley of ashes of Fitzgerald's *The Great Gatsby* (1925). Here, his friend Rip informs him that "on some quiet nights, late, you can hear the screeching of tires and then a long silence; a whoosh and then, barely audible, an impact. And sometimes, if one listens very carefully, there are screams in the night that don't last too long."[52] As with DeLillo, for a second, death penetrates the simulacrum. "And standing there on the hill, overlooking the smog-soaked, baking Valley and feeling the hot winds returning and the dust swirling at my feet and the sun, gigantic, a ball of fire, rising over it, I believed him" Clay notes, the only moment of belief in the entire novel.[53] Just for a moment, it seems, something might possess weight.

In this mechanical graveyard, at the very end of America's westward push, Berman's vision of febrile, feverish, yearning Modernism seems to come to an end. Berman conceptualizes capitalism in terms of a manic acquisitiveness, a perpetual desire for "the new" and the original. In Ellis' work however, all appetites are sated, restrictions annulled, longings evaporated: instantaneous gratification takes the place of the wish and in so doing inaugurates a blessed-out, lackadaisical "post-orgy" world.[54] For Ellis' characters, there is no more virgin territory to yearn for, no remaining taboo to be broken, and no new experience to be had. Instead everything has been seen and done a million times – movies, songs, permissive rebellion – and all that remain are boredom and lassitude. Gatsby's materialism in Fitzgerald's novel is redeemed by its link to a romantic idealism that sees in "things" an echo of a larger, expanded life, a possibility evoked by the green light of Daisy's mansion across the bay; in a sense it is his capacity for longing (that most American of traits) that makes Gatsby great. But there is nothing left to long for in Ellis–his spoilt rich-kids have already bought it all. Instead his characters stare into the headlights like stunned rabbits, a light that blurs and refracts until it seems to melt the entire world.

Terra damnata

I would like to conclude this exploration of weight and lightness in eighties fiction with a consideration of one of its greatest achievements, a novel which, though set in a very different era (the American West of the 1840's) nonetheless encapsulates many of the central themes outlined in this essay: Cormac McCarthy's *Blood Meridian* (1985).

In many ways, of course, it seems wholly appropriate that one of the great novels produced during Reagan's presidency should be a western; after all this was a president who believed "having a horse between my knees makes it easier to sort out a problem," and who couched the rejuvenation of America in terms of the rugged individualism and practical virtues of the old West[55]. McCarthy's text self-consciously deconstructs such myths (the cowboy's chivalric code, America's manifest destiny, the noble taming of the wilderness) offering in its place a vision of endless, meaningless butchery, "a baroque of thieving, raping, shooting, slashing, hanging, scalping, burning, bashing, hacking, stabbing" as Peter Josyph puts it.[56] One's abiding memory of the book is that of ragged stick-figures endlessly slaughtering each other on a vast and empty plain, crudely animated cadavers acting out a slapstick ritual of chopping and cutting, a kind of "death hilarious" or terrifyingly violent St. Vitus Dance.[57] Caked in dust or mud, McCarthy's figures seem barely human, closer to "mud effigies" or "voodoo dolls", mud, clay, meat and excrement constantly changing form, a kind of intercine warfare taking place within matter itself.[58,59]

One could certainly come up with a political interpretation of all this. Under the guise of progress, patriotism and civilization, the novel posits a world governed by aggression in its most naked form, imperial ambition concealed beneath the triumphal rhetoric of nation building and the imposition of (economic) law. In the context of the eighties, this both echoes the atrocities of Vietnam and shadows America's dubious activities in Central America, an image of American power as irredeemably violent, expansionist and rapacious. Although the novel may resemble an abstract inferno, its atrocities are also grounded in the grubby economic realities of historical fact: namely the payment of dollars for scalps to stem Comanche raids on the northern Mexican state of Chihuahua. The savagery of the novel is always linked to commodity *exchange,* albeit one where the currency (scalps) shifts and mutates so that ultimately Mexican skin will do just as well as Indian. The violence in the novel is both frenzied (the west an abattoir devouring the weak) and yet strangely shorn of significance (massacre follows massacre follows massacre), the sheer scale of the landscape (the *"terra damnata"*) draining the bloodletting of meaning. In the context of the mineral reality of the desert, the organic seems only provisional, fleeting, crude lumps of flesh that will soon decay.[60] Indeed, as in the other texts we have looked at, McCarthy's "changeling land" is both heavy and light at the same time, both visceral and vacant, at once a bone yard and an empty lot.[61]

"Flat and true as a spirit level," the desert space seems composed from varying degrees of nothingness, the sky a "hole" in the heavens, the ground a "void" or "caesura," the earthly manifestation of the emptiness above. Perspective is annihilated here, as is any notion of depth or scale.[62] Instead all seems made from the constituent elements of dust and bone, which is to say, the deathly. "Death seemed the most prevalent feature of the landscape," notes McCarthy, the wilderness a cast ossuary, the only signs in the emptiness the bodies, bones and tracks of the departed.[63] From the tree of pierced infants to the caves of prehistoric relics and mummified remains, the sole signposts in the novel are corpses, the only markers the dead. In this sense, as with DeLillo, the novel's single absolute reality is death, the pastoral transformed into the terminal, the "awful real" of McCarthy's universe. As with the junkyards discussed elsewhere, *Blood Meridian* posits a poisoned wilderness where matter runs wild, mutating, decaying, metamorphosizing into ever stranger and more deathly forms. This focus on the material certainly seems rooted in various social factors (increased ecological awareness, environmental disaster, the twin threats of nuclear destruction and nuclear waste) but also links to the strange mixture of mass and immateriality that can be traced throughout the fiction of this period.

McCarthy's desert, like the cities of Wolfe and Ellis, the junkyards of Auster or the disembodied mystery of DeLillo's mall, is both there and not there, poised between brute matter and its disappearance. Heavy and obdurate though its rock and mud may be, it is also a land perpetually at the point of vanishing: into darkness, dust, the "holocaust" and "distant pandemonium" of the blinding sun.[64] In place of the American narrative of historical progress, McCarthy tracks an incessant circle, "some maelstrom out there in the void, some vortex in that waste apposite to which man's transit and his reckonings alike lay abrogate."[65] Such language in a sense provides a link between Berman's Modernism and Jameson's Postmodernism, whilst simultaneously suggesting contradictory forces within capitalism itself. The void and the mass, the glare and the glut: these are central to a decade whose constituent elements – material consumption and immaterial transactions – continue to define the economic reality of today.

Notes

1. Marshall Berman, *All That Is Solid Melts Into Air* (London: Verso, 1983), 121.
2. Berman, *All That Is Solid,* 21.
3. Ibid., 99.
4. Fredric Jameson, *Postmodernism* (London: Verso, 1993), 4.
5. Jameson, *Postmodernism,* 21.
6. Ronald Reagan, in a speech announcing the deregulation of the Savings & Loans sector in 1982. Quoted by Michael Schiller, *Reckoning with Reagan: America and Its President in the 1980's* (New York: Oxford University Press, 1992), 109.
7. Schiller, *Reckoning with Reagan,* 99.
8. Bret Easton Ellis, *American Psycho* (London: Picador, 1991), 202.

9. Graham Thompson, *American Culture in the 1980's* (Edinburgh: Edinburgh University Press, 2007), 10.

10. Tom Wolfe, *The Bonfire of the Vanities* (London: Picador, 1989), 352, 20, 516.

11. Wolfe, *Bonfire*, 466.

12. Ibid., 475.

13. Ibid., 518.

14. Ibid., 611.

15. Ibid., 89.

16. Ibid., 93.

17. Ibid., 96.

18. Ibid., 88, 99.

19. Ibid., 100.

20. Ibid., 153.

21. Paul Auster, *The New York Trilogy* (London: Faber, 1987), 78.

22. Auster, *New York*, 72.

23. Ibid., 78.

24. Peter Brooker, *New York Fictions* (London: Longman, 1996), 129.

25. Selma Berol, *The Empire City: New York and its People* (Westport CT: Praeger, 2000), 171.

26. George L Lankevich, *American Metropolis* (New York: New York University Press, 1998), 231.

27. Paul Auster, *The Red Notebook* (London: Faber, 1995), 148.

28. Auster, *Red Notebook*, 149.

29. Auster, *New York*, 255.

30. Ibid., 72.

31. Robert Hughes, *The Shock of the New* (London: Thames & Hudson, 1991), 334.

32. Hughes, *Shock of the New*, 334-5.

33. Auster, *New York*, 77.

34. Paul Auster, *In the Country of Last Things* (London: Faber, 1989), 35.

35. Auster, *In the Country*, 87.

36. Auster, *New York*, 130.

37. Auster, *New York*, 130.

38. Bilton, *An Introduction to Contemporary American Fiction* (Edinburgh: Edinburgh University Press, 2002), 24.

39. Don DeLillo, *White Noise* (London: Picador, 1986), 23.

40. Jameson, *Postmodernism*, ix.

41. DeLillo, *White Noise*, 326.

42. Ibid., 326.

43. Ibid., 325-6.

44. Ibid., 258-9.

45. Ibid., 104. In *Symbolic Exchange and Death* (1994), Jean Baudrillard likewise frames death as an "unrepeatable, unrepresentable act" and therefore "the only means of escape from the code, and its incessant play of signification and equivalence". 64.

46. Thompson, *American Culture*, 58.

47. Jean Baudrillard, *America* (London: Verso,1988), 30.

48. Baudrillard, *America*, 29.

49. Bilton, *Contemporary American Fiction*, 199-200.

50. Bret Easton Ellis, *Less Than Zero* (London: Picador, 1986), 100.

51. Ellis, *Zero,* 142.

52. Ibid., 195.

53. Ibid., 195.

54. Baudrillard, *America,* 46.

55. Schiller, *Reagan,* viii.

56. Barcley Owens, *Cormac McCarthy's Western Novels* (Tucson: University of Arizona, 2000), 8.

57. Cormac McCarthy, *Blood Meridian* (London: Picador, 1985), 53.

58. McCarthy, *Blood,* 13, 8.

59. Bilton, *Contemporary American Fiction,* 102.

60. McCarthy, *Blood,* 66.

61. Ibid., 47.

62. Ibid., 42, 66.

63. Ibid., 48.

64. Ibid., 105, 185.

65. Ibid., 96.

Chapter 23

Alternative for Alternative's Sake: Progressive College Radio's Programming Struggles

David Uskovich

In 1992, alternative rock band Nirvana, on the heels of their hit single "Smells Like Teen Spirit" and its accompanying album *Nevermind*, made the cover of *Rolling Stone*. In the photograph, singer and guitarist Kurt Cobain wears a hand-made t-shirt that reads, "Corporate Magazines Still Suck." The phrase was an allusion to a structure of feeling within United States independent music scenes made famous by punk record label SST, whose slogan, "Corporate Rock Still Sucks," critiqued the major labels' discovery in the early 1990s of under-ground—or alternative—rock music. Cobain's t-shirt showed solidarity with the subculture from which Nirvana had emerged. Nonetheless, numerous progressive college radio stations, which were part of that same subculture, refused to add *Nevermind*, the band's major label debut, even though those same radio stations had supported them throughout the late 1980s. By making this programming decision, these progressive college radio stations demonstrated their commitment to and support of independent music, clearing the three minutes of airtime that would have otherwise been occupied by "Smells Like Teen Spirit" to make space for an artist on an independent label. The idea that corporate rock sucked was not only part of Nirvana's but also alternative culture's ethos. However, this conflict within the American rock underground over artistic autonomy and capitulation to capitalism began in the early days of the Reagan years and played out, among other places, within progressive college radio.

We think of the 1980s as a rupture, as a decisive break with the 1960s both in terms of the decade's conservative ascendancy, its celebration of affluence, and its postmodern focus on images and surface. Indeed, Ronald Reagan's presidency announced an antagonism towards the 1960s. As Craig Watkins writes, the "chief demon of the Reaganite imagination was not a person, a political party, or even a special interest group but rather the turbulent decade of the 1960s."[1] In the symbolic realm, Reagan the image stood for the erasure of the United States' radical past, embodying the family values of the idealized small town, according to James Combs, so that "[i]t was as if the 1960s and 1970s . . . had not, or should not, have happened."[2]

If the 1980s were marked by a return to small town family values, they were also marked by images of excess, and an excess of images, both of which appeared to leave little room for counterhegemonic critique. Jane Feuer suggests that the "fantasies of unlimited wealth and unlimited visual pleasure that came into office with [Reagan] were, somehow, the realities of the era."[3] She argues that between *Dynasty*'s palatial sets and extravagant *couture,* which celebrated the affluent excesses of "the supply-side aristocracy"[4] embodied by the Reagans and MTV's emphasis on the pleasure of the image for image's sake, the postmodern media of the era "[deconstructed] the very oppositions between commodity and art, complicity and critique."[5]

It was at this moment that hardcore punk emerged in the United States, which would influence the wider, less-stylistically specific U.S. music scene that, at different times, was called new wave, new music, alternative, indpendent, and underground. Fueled by the energy of the anti-authoritarianism, anti-corporatism, and cultural insurgency of the first iterations of U.S. and British punk from the mid-1970s, hardcore's do-it-yourself ethos became the operating discourse for alternative rock in the 1980s, which like hardcore, was politicized by Reagan's victory in 1980. This new youth subculture sustained its sense of community through zines, unsigned bands, performance art and independent record labels and film and video production companies, all committed to creating a culture outside of the gaze and hearing of the "mainstream" entertainment industries. As an important distribution mechanism for punk rock and independent music, progressive college radio was part of this cultural matrix. I use the term "progressive" to emphasize the fact that the college radio under study here privileged a progressive format, meaning it placed an emphasis on unsigned artists, artists on independent labels, and artists that did not receive airplay on commercial radio. Furthermore, progressive college radio followed the example set by the community radio movement in the 1960s and 1970s through its commitment to underserved communities and progressive politics.

That Reagan's conservatism was emergent at the same moment as independent music and college radio makes for a strange historical coincidence, one which points to the importance of studying an obscure topic like progressive college radio in the 1980s. I say "strange" because one event symbolized a political and cultural shift to the right, and the other represents a vestige of mid-twentieth century progressive politics. If media historians characterize the 1980s as postmodern, as an era of surfaces and affluence, of an image president in an age of images, then progressive college radio opened up the airwaves to discordant music. It provided a counter-narrative by countering excess with a preferred aesthetic of noisy, raw, ugly sounds. If postmodern media and politics collapse distinctions between art and commerce, complicity and critique, containment and resistance, progressive college radio's relentless—if contested—anti-commercialism maintains those distinctions.

This chapter examines progressive college radio at a moment of transition, when the corporate entertainment industry began noticing that college radio stations were playing something called "new music," which was an industry catchall for a variety of musical styles that had emerged in the wake of 1970s British and American punk rock. However, even as progressive college radio became a testing ground for the major labels and thus became part of the music industry, its practitioners were divided over what its role in relation to the corporate music industry should be and debated the meaning of "alternative." In short, progressive college radio DJs in the 1980s argued over to what extent corporate rock sucked. This medium's history in the 1980s asks us to rethink the ways we characterize the decade and reminds us that eras overlap. Therefore, this chapter argues that at a time when radical politics were being erased from the national narrative, progressive college radio served as a site of a counternarrative, although, as I shall demonstrate, one that was contested by its practitioners.

A Brief History of U.S. College Radio

College radio did not suddenly appear in the 1980s; it is as old as the medium. While a comprehensive history of U.S. college radio is beyond the scope of this chapter, a brief overview demonstrates that it has always offered an alternative to corporate broadcasting and was always part of a cultural vanguard. In 1916, 9XM at the University of Wisconsin was the first college station on the air.[6] During the broadcast boom of the 1920s, 128 university stations were not the only amateur operators crowding the ether; non-profit groups like labor unions and churches, and businesses such as auto dealers, newspapers, and department stores were licensed operators, who used radio to speak to constituencies and attract customers.[7]

University radio stations had been broadcasting educational programming for over a decade when, by the late 1920s and early 1930s, they joined a reform movement that struggled to establish an alternative to the developing system of commercial broadcasting. However, as media historian Robert McChesney demonstrates, in the period from 1927 to 1934, the federal government naturalized the advertising-based broadcasting system we know today and slowly squeezed out educational broadcasting. Corporations like RCA, who had, by the end of the 1920s, realized that broadcasting could turn a profit through the sale of advertising time, lobbied the government to limit licensing, arguing that fewer stations with more power and better technology than the low-powered amateurs could better serve the needs of the entire country. In response, the government established the Federal Radio Commission (FRC) with the passage of the Radio Act of 1927, which declared services like college or church radio specialty or "propaganda" stations. By contrast, the FRC declared the commercial stations "general public service" broadcasters, even though the advertisers who supported these stations had a special interest, namely, the selling of audience's ears to advertisers.[8]

With their licenses revoked and frequencies reallocated to commercial broadcasters, the number of college radio stations continued to decline—less than thirty were on the air by the end of the 1930s—and educational broadcasting did not recover until the end of the 1940s, when the FCC allocated 88-92 MHz on the FM band for educational and noncommercial stations. As an incentive to get more FM operators on the air, the FCC lowered the minimum wattage for licensing from 250 to ten watts, making it possible for universities to start stations on a shoestring budget.[9] Once again, college radio broke new technological ground and found itself on the cutting edge of an alternative to commercial AM radio; as the 10 watt stations proliferated, they introduced an ever increasing audience to FM's sonic superiority over AM.[10]

College radio in the 1950s was not associated with any particular kind of music in the same way it would be associated with alternative music in the 1980s. College stations in the 1950s broadcast adult education, recorded theatrical productions, national and local news and public affairs, college sports, classical music, folk, jazz, and show tunes.[11]

From the available evidence, rock music would not show up on college radio playlists until the late 1960s, perhaps influenced by or influencing the underground and independent FM stations of the time. A program director writing a history of WNUR in approximately 1973 marks the moment college radio does become associated with music: "We would take our music very seriously. We would intelligently program music in whatever form . . . rock, jazz, classical, country, bluegrass, show. Our announcers would be chosen FIRST for their taste and secondly for their 'dynamic radio voice.'"[12]

Sometime in the late 1970s, punk joined the playlists on progressive college radio and cemented the relationship between progressive college radio and music. The post-psychedelic music of the Grateful Dead and Pink Floyd dominated playlists up to the mid-1970s when punk's anti-corporate stance found a home on college radio's non-commercial, left-of-the-dial frequencies.[13] Operating on shoestring budgets granted to them by their universities and supplemented by annual fundraisers and some underwriting by local businesses, not only were they not beholden to sponsors, but also they could not afford Arbitron subscriptions, and therefore were free from ratings concerns.[14] They could, however, afford to be experimental and play music no commercial stations would touch. Punk and new wave crept into the college stations via late night specialty shows like the *S&M Show*, which went on the air in 1978 at KTRU at Rice University in Houston.[15] Furthermore, the arrival in 1978 of trade publication *College Music Journal*, or *CMJ*, "was the first national acknowledgement of a relationship between college radio and music."[16] *CMJ* also helped to establish the connection between progressive college radio and alternative music by demonstrating to the outside world that it was playing music that no one else would play.

College Radio as Genre

However, even as college radio gradually made the commitment to rock programming, punk or otherwise, the mainstream media of the 1970s took little notice of that fact. It was not until the early 1980s, then, that major publications, major labels, and commercial radio had noticed progressive college radio. Articles in major publications commented on college radio's unusual formats, which privileged music that commercial radio eschewed, as well as the fact that progressive college radio, like free form, underground FM of the 1960s, was the only radio left where the DJs played music they liked rather what demographic statistics demanded. Addressing their readers as potentially shocked, mildly amused adults befuddled by the vagaries of youth cultures, journalists in the 1980s foregrounded the shocking names and discordant sounds of bands on college radio playlists: Alien Sex Fiend, Butthole Surfers, Gun Club, Flesheaters, Subhumans, Agent Orange, Beastie Boys, Slaughter and the Dogs, Malfunction. Many were befuddled that stations at Catholic universities played songs like "Locust Abortion Technician" and "The Catholics Are Attacking" and that the playlists included not only these raw, noisy sounds but were mixed with artists such as blues legend Howlin' Wolf and Nigerian musician King Sunny Ade.[17]

Moreover, journalists and industry executives framed college radio not only within institutional policies but also within the demands of the music industry. Generally viewing college radio as a rather untenable medium for selling records to begin with, the broadcasting industry had ignored it altogether, while the major labels' support had waxed and waned.[18] During the industry slump of the late 1970s, the major labels began charging college stations for records, withdrawing what had formerly been a free service.[19] By the early 1980s, however, commercial radio and major labels realized that among the Alien Sex Fiends, Sex Gang Childrens, and Flesheaters, progressive college radio also programmed the eccentric but less aggressive sounds of the Police, the Go-Go's, and Duran Duran. Some within the music industry noted that it was less the stations' power to sell than it was the fact that progressive DJs and their audience were trendsetters who could influence the tastes of others.[20] As one industry insider noted, "In a way college radio has become another consultant for commercial radio—but a consultant who listens with *ears*, not demographic information."[21]

The industry, therefore, saw progressive college radio as an indicator of and springboard for an artist's eventual commercial success,[22] but for many a PCR DJ, a preference for the cultural margins made them poor trendspotters for future hitmakers. Indeed, in an interview with *Flipside* zine, Mike Watt, bassist for LA art-punk band The Minutemen, noted that the staff at KXLU, the radio station at Loyola-Marymount University in Los Angeles, were not in fact representative of the student body, but were an assortment of misfits who brought their love of extreme music with them to college.[23]

For example, Marilyn Mock, co-host of KTRU's *Shawn and Marilyn*—or *S&M—Show* at Rice University in Houston, TX, says, before she was a DJ that her tastes ran towards

> Anything cutting edge and rebellious - from *Zap* magazine to the book and movie *A Clockwork Orange*. Was already into Velvet Underground, MC5, Joy Division and the New York Dolls which led me to The Ramones, Devo, Iggy Pop, Buzzcocks, Television, Richard Hell and the Voidoids, Sex Pistols, The Clash, Siouxsie and The Banshees, The Slits and X-Ray Spex.[24]

The problem for Mock was that, in the late 1970s and early 1980s, "None of these bands were played on any local radio station in Houston." Therefore, "I was always on the lookout for a radio station that played music that was not just the standard, boring, Top 40, middle-of-the-road, and college and independent radio provided that alternative." [25]

Mock makes an interesting point in that, while we might think of radio, and specifically progressive college radio of the 1980s, as having mostly to do with music, a broad interest in non-mainstream culture created a specific context that shaped the musical tastes of PCR DJs. The youthful Mock saw connections between underground comix, art cinema, and punk. For her, it was all of a piece.

Like Mock, Ted Carroll, program director for KXLU, had a youthful interest in the cultural margins. Counting John Fante, the Beats, and Ken Kesey among his favorite writers, he also saw in punk and other kinds of non-mainstream music of the 1980s a connection with outsider literary movements:

> Music and books were the primary influence in my world at that time. I was exposed mostly to the "Top 40" of the underground/punk/alternative market. The San Fernando Valley had no real adventurous radio stations, most of my introduction to music was through browsing record stores, listening to KPFK and KROQ and [reading] magazines. I was more exposed to alternative literature, which seemed easier to gain access to and, at the time, easier to connect the dots from the influence of one writer upon another.[26]

Here, Carroll counts Southern California's San Fernando Valley—just over the Santa Monica mountains from the Hollywood sign—as a cultural desert, positioning it much like Mock positions Houston.

Pam Moore, also a DJ at KXLU in the 1980s, notes that the West Side of Los Angeles brought some "new wave" music, but she and her friends felt that it was too conservative:

> I grew up in Los Angeles and was into early L.A. punk bands – When I started listening to KXLU, I don't think the term "college radio" had been coined yet. It was just a station that played the music I was listening to. There was a commercial sta-

tion, KROQ, that was playing new wave music, and we did listen to specialty shows on that like Rodney Bingenheimer's show, but for the most part we thought that station was too commercial and wimpy. And there were certain shows that I would listen to on KCRW, though neither of those stations were consistently reliable with their programming... or I should say KROQ was reliably too tame.[27]

In high school in the early 1980s, Kim Fix, a program director for KXLU, thought that commercial new wave station KROQ was as fringe as radio stations got: "I listened mostly to KROQ as that was, at least I thought, the only station out there playing new/alternative music. Rodney on the ROQ was popular. I went to clubs as much as I could although a lot of them were 21 and over. I like the whole Mod deal early in high school but that didn't last long and then it was more punk."[28]

In addition to my own contacts with PCR DJs of the 1980s, contemporary writers confirmed the DJs' participation in marginal cultures. Ralph Rugoff notes that merely four years before his article about KXLU, the station was a tiny student organization playing 1970s style hard and progressive rock, "when a different breed of students," steeped in punk rock, "began flocking to the offices."[29] Indeed, as one staff member put it: "I loved punk rock, wanted to be a part of the 'movement' in one-way or another, and this seemed the most accessible venue for me."[30]

Throughout the decade, DJs at PCR stations were reaching out to these audiences on the cultural margins. In the late 1980s, after eight years of progressive programming, WNUR's rock program director Octavia Kincaid wanted to reach "people like high school kids who have just heard the Sex Pistols and Dead Kennedy's [sic]. I'd like to provide a place where they can expand their musical taste." [31]

Clearly, PCR did reach high school students interested in alternative music and culture. In some cases, future staff members enrolled at a particular university *because* of its radio station. Carroll and Moore both entered Loyola Marymount University in the mid-1980s, shortly after KXLU had established itself as a PCR station and had received attention from the press. Carroll comments, "College Radio is probably the single most important factor in my going to college. I had read about KXLU in *Rolling Stone* and was the preeminent factor in my attendance of LMU."[32] Moore concurs: "I heard about our college radio station KXLU through word of mouth... then I applied to go to school there primarily so I could be a DJ."[33]

The Struggle over the Meaning of "Alternative"

It was this commitment to fringe culture that made PCR DJs receptive to new music, and what prompted them to play bands that eventually broke into commercial success, but it was this same commitment that caused them often to be unsupportive of a record, especially if the act had gone commercial. By the early 1980s, a split had begun to emerge among progressive and even not-so-progressive radio stations. Being "consultants" for commercial radio creates a tension: "Do [college radio stations] keep on playing the same music and risk duplicating commercial radio, or do they move toward more drastic programming?"[34] This debate dragged on throughout the decade. In internal documents within radio stations, in articles about the stations, and especially in the pages of *CMJ*, DJs, record company representatives, and station directors struggled over the meaning of "alternative."

Indeed, even industry insiders could be split on the exact role college radio should play. Whereas some felt that PCR should stay "a little more progressive than [commercial radio] and find *newer* talent," a sentiment echoed by independent labels (emphasis original), others took a different angle: "It's kind of scary to us. College radio tends to shy away from what's played on commercial radio, and we're worried that now they'll get more extreme."[35]

Despite this reputation for the extreme, in the "Dialogues" pages of *CMJ*, a forum where the industry and college radio corresponded with each other in monthly reports, many station directors actively pursued service from record labels. Mark Richardson, co-music director of WYCC at Miami University in Oxford, OH, announced to his label reps: "Attention all labels, majors and indie's [sic]: WYCC is back for the college year and ready to play your music. We had a good summer but are looking forward to a great year on the air . . . . After the summer layoff we have no new music."[36] Another music director apologized for not keeping up with her correspondences: "Hello everybody! I just wanted to let you know that we're still alive up here in northern Maine. I also wanted to apologize to all of you college music reps who haven't heard from me in a while. But now I'm back and will continue to be until I graduate in May of '87."[37]

As trendspotters for the music industry, then, many PCR staff felt it was important to *not* take a stance against the majors in favor of the independents, but to program music from both types of labels. A DJ for WUOG at the University of Georgia said in 1982: "It doesn't bother me at all to play the same songs that AOR plays. The role of non-commercial radio is simply to expose the best new music coming out."[38] Mark Richardson, in the same "Dialogues" correspondence quoted above, echoes Smith, dismissing the debate over whether or not to privilege indie over major: "I'd like to add my two cents to the petty argument taking place in the Dialogue. We're here to play the BEST music—who cares what label the stuff is on."[39] Furthermore, whereas in the comments above, many DJs listened for fringe music and realized their audiences did too, just as many felt that the audience did not feel comfortable with the cultural margins. According to Daryll Ohrt of Western Connecticut State University's WXCI, "If we play completely obscure music, we'll just alienate our audience. . . But if we play [Men Without Hats' Top 40 hit] 'Safety Dance' back to back with something they haven't heard, the listeners will feel safe and also hear new music."[40]

Nonetheless, for all the DJs who welcomed major labels, there were many who did not. "Many college radio stations, though, studiously avoid AOR acts, dropping former college radio mainstays like Joan Jett, U2 and even Simple Minds when AOR picks them up."[41] Rugoff notes "that if a song is picked up by the commercial rock stations, it's never heard again on KXLU. It just wouldn't be alternative anymore." [42]Though some of the DJs quoted above argued that what was important was that college radio play the "best" new music no matter the mode of production, "best" remained a contested term, with some DJs arguing that independent music, or at least what some might call more "extreme" music, was "best."

While their peers often accused DJs who supported dropping major label acts from PCR playlists of elitism, as I will demonstrate below, at least part of the reason for this policy had to do with its proponents' understanding of the role of college radio. Once PCR broke artists to the mainstream, they had the full power of the transnational entertainment industry behind them, which meant, at the very least, airplay on numerous radio stations, as well as heavy retail promotion, licensing of merchandise, touring, and, since this was the 1980s, getting airplay on MTV.

Though success was never guaranteed, PCR staff felt that these artists no longer needed their services. In fact, the word "need" crops up frequently in interviews with PCR staff that believed in dropping artists once they went to the majors. For example, in 1983 WNUR music director Mike Metz explained his station's dropping of a Eurythmics' album—which the station broke—to a representative from the band's label, RCA, by saying, "It's number two in the country. What does *he* need us for? We're more interested in the new Bongos record."[43]

Señor Amor, who has been a DJ at KXLU FM at Loyola Marymount University since 1987 explains a similar attitude among staff at KXLU in the 1980s that cast a shadow into the 1990s. The station had supported Beck from the end of the decade up until his major label debut on Geffen in 1994. "Once Beck is being played on KROQ and all those stations he's the same as the Beatles. So it's like we need those three minutes however many times a day to play somebody else. I think there's that belief...It's like, 'Well, he doesn't *need* us. He's moved on.'"[44]

However, there is another way that the idea of need plays out, and it stems from a particular conception of PCR's connection to its community. In 1983, John Loscalzo of New York University's WNYU told journalist Steve Pond that the major labels' discovery of college radio's value to new music is a "'gray area. I guess we're searching for the *next* big thing.'" [Pond writes], "He pauses, then adds the kind of comment you hear a lot in college radio: 'I think we have an *obligation* to be alternative.'"[45] Loscalzo doesn't explain the meaning of this obligation, but obligation implies responsibility *to* something, and he is not the only one who feels it. In the late 1980s, one WNUR director made a comment that echoes this sense of obligation: "We can't say we won't play REM at all [who were on a major label by this point], but assuming there are other artists of equal validity, we'd be neglecting a lot of other bands."[46] In other words, the important point is not that major label artists no longer need PCR but that independent artists *do*.

Calvin Johnson, former DJ at KAOS, Evergreen State's station in Olympia, WA, and founder of Beat Happening and K Records, elaborates on this point. By the time he began DJing at KAOS at the end of the 1970s, it had established itself as a community radio station, "responding to the needs of the community and the disenfranchised groups [in the] community in your particular area. [Working at KAOS] really profoundly affected me. I felt all college radio stations should behave as though they're community radio stations. . . Your moment on the air implied some responsibility." Specifically, KAOS's staff had decided to "extend the community radio idea to music—not just to programming but to music programming as well, so the disenfranchised groups are independent labels or artists on independent labels or [artists] without labels. So. . .KAOS came up with [this idea] of extending this community concept into music programming and prioritizing local performers and independent labels."[47]

In a demonstration of prioritizing local performers, Mark Hejnar, the host of WNUR's *Fast 'n' Loud* show decided to help Chicago bands who were already doing it for themselves, further demonstrating PCR's conception of artists as a disenfranchised group and emphasizing its commitment to its community. Hejnar produced the hardore punk compilation *Middle of America*, which featured well-known bands like Articles of Faith, the Effigies, and Naked Raygun, as well as Nadsat Rebel, a band from Evanston Township High School. Just as the *Fast 'n' Loud* show gave voice to local Chicago punk bands, so the hosts of the show "wanted the album to benefit the Chicago musicians and keep the early punk message alive." Hejnar stresses the possibilities for democratic communication when he describes the way punk bands are non-professionals seizing the means of production: "It's about a 16-your-old kid saying, 'I want to be a rock star' so he forms a band. . . . It's a do-it-yourself medium and that's what the album is about."[48]

Like Johnson and Hejnar, most DJs who advocated not playing major label music did so out of support for local bands, even when those bands were not really local. For example, Bob Weston, co-owner of Chicago Mastering Company, bassist for Shellac and formerly of Volcano Suns, recalls that when he began working at WJUL in Lowell, MA, in the early1980s, the staff referred to any band not on a major or without a large national following as "local." Likewise, Senor Amor explains both the excitement and sense of responsibility engendered when KXLU would receive records that had been produced by the bands themselves. He describes how, in the 1980s, before digital technology streamlined the recording process, musicians invested a fair amount of labor in rehearsing, finding a studio, finding an engineer or recording themselves, pressing a record, distributing it, and marketing it.

[It was] a much more labor intensive process and with that time and with that labor comes more emotion, so that when we got a record from Peoria, Illinois, and it had that postmark on it, we treated it with some weight and appreciated . . . where it came from and how it came to us and why and they hoped that we'd play their record so they could come to L.A. and do a show here.[49]

However well-intentioned it might have been, for many, dumping popular bands from a playlist to make room for little-known bands "made the programming seem snobby, elitist—the playlist often seemingly guided by the credo: 'The more obscure, the better.'"[50] Signing on to "Dialogues" in a 1986 issue of *CMJ* as "More Alternative Than You," the music director of WNMC in Traverse City, MI, writes:

Backlash! R&R magazine says that certain 'College Radio Bands' are getting, of all things, mass recognition. Well, I guess it's time to drop those bands. They suck anyway. Atta boy! Those bands don't need our support. We'll show our audiences just how hip we are! Let's. . . publish charts of uncool bands. I'd put Sonic Youth at the top of my list![51]

As the debate over this policy took place in the pages of *CMJ* and in the pages of the newspapers interviewing the DJs, it also was taking place within radio stations and the communities to which they belonged. In a series of composition books and spiral notebooks known as *Groans and Gripes*, KTRU's staff vented their disagreements over programming and the purpose of their station, struggling over its direction as it added the new music to its playlist of jazz, classical, folk, country, blues, and especially, 1960s and 1970s rock. Elitism and the idea that "the more obscure the better" are the strongest underlying themes in the *Groans and Gripes* notebooks. As the music directors at KTRU began introducing alternative music, other staff members complained about a growing clique at the station.

For example, in a *Groans and Gripes* from September 25, 1981, one DJ left the following anonymous message:

At last, my chance....How could anyone possibly trade away some of the best new music being put out today and put trash like Siouxsie and the Banshees, Alt. T.V., Magazine, Human Sexual Response, the Scars and the Subhumans on playlist? What kind of criteria do you use to make these mysterious decisions? Anyhow, my opinion is that the above listed bands are terrible. I can find very few even partially decent songs and most of the cuts are grating, unmusical and boring in their harsh, over-stated ugliness. Why can't you at least provide the albums of the established, demanded bands in the stacks to the dj's whose taste is not quite as extreme as yours can get to them? Your playlist does not reflect the results of last year's survey and I feel that the station should serve the University before the punk population of Houston.[52]

Below this commentary, music director Michael Zakes, replies:

Admittedly, the Subhumans, Scars, and Human Sexual Response are not terribly good, but they are coming up with some fresh ideas. . . . Magazine, Siousxsie and ATV are all fairly solid bands with good development of new musical ideas. Had you mentioned any bands in particular, I could give you reasons why they're not on the playlist. Our playlist does not serve on the Punk population of Houston, it serves to acquaint all of our listeners with music not available on commercial radio. . . . We strive to put forward the best possible new music. Were we to change to serve the majority of Rice's interest, we would wind up sounding like a cross between [Houston's commercial stations], ignoring people willing to take a chance and try new music. I personally am glad to have been exposed to some of the bands on playlist.[53]

These correspondences stand as physical evidence of PCR's tendency to get more "extreme" in order to stay ahead of the commercial music industry. The transition from what would soon be called classic rock, to synth-pop, to harder-edged punk and post-punk happens literally right before the eyes. Furthermore, they reveal just how contested the definition of "the best new music" was. In the following exchange, one DJ deals with these issues by ascribing the changes in programming to the whims of a clique. In an entry dated February 2nd, 1982, Jack Tanner wrote: "Gang of 4's 'History's Bunk' is the shittiest piece of music I've heard in years. . . . is awfully high for noise and screaming." One Donald B. responded, "Obviously jack we prefer the Gang's screaming over yours." "Donald—I've often accused certain members of the station of being 'cliqueish' [sic]. . . .only to be told time and again I'm wrong and paranoid. . . .Who the fuck are you to say 'we'?...[Near] as I can tell you are a 'DJ' speaking only for yourself."[54]

Music Director Ray Shea seems to have been a controversial figure, earning the ire of numerous staff members. In an undated *Groans and Gripes*, Shea responds to requests for records by Missing Persons and INXS by calling their music "swill" and saying: "You want a straight answer? No, seriously, I think it's time KTRU moved away from the synth-pop/disco/new wave/commercial/MTV/swill-type stuff. Not that they're <u>awful</u>, but they're just not KTRU music. I also sort of regret Depeche Mode, AFOS, etc. I <u>still</u> like Prince, though."[55] Decisions like this earned Shea comments like this:

Okay Ray—this sucks and I' pissed—it's five fucking fifty AM and I've been wanting to play the goddamn new Madonna song since my shift began—I've even been thinking of what it sounds like all week---The album even legitimately came up on our playlist! Look, <u>HITLER</u>—I'm sorry you feel like you had to go to such extremes [illegible] it up THAT SUCKS!!!!! Sincerely pissed and Tired of the Crap.[56]

In addition to accusing Shea and others of belonging to a clique that dictated tastes at KTRU, one DJ criticized the direction of the station as difference for its own sake:

Must we always be so different all the time just for the sake of being obnoxiously different. [sic] Example: why do we file under 'Crème and Godley' what everyone else including the album covers call 'Godley and Crème.'. [sic] . . . . Did the KTRU click [sic] think this was cute and would make them cooler people just because its annoying and different. Also I'm fucking sick of little brats calling up wanting to hear DOA, Fear, etc.[57]

Shea responds, doing his best to dispel the myth of the clique, but also asserting the direction of KTRU.

First of all, the people who originally filed the albums under 'Crème and Godley' probably graduated while you were still in high school. So which 'click,' [sic] are you referring to, the present one or the one from five years ago? . . . . I like requests for DOA, Fear, etc., but I'm sick of little brats calling up wanting to hear Depeche Mode, Heaven 17, Visage, Blancmange, etc., etc., ad infinitum.[58]

These struggles over format, the purpose of the station, and even the meaning of "alternative" extended even to a debate about classical music programming at KTRU. In addition to the *Groans and Gripes* notebooks, staff posted large sheets of sprocketed computer paper around the walls of the station, on which they could leave anonymous comments. Appropriately titled "Graffito," one sheet shows this debate in numerous dense, hand-written comments. For example, one writer posts, in regards to classical music,

There are other stations that play quiet boring [sic] music on Saturday. WHY SHOULD WE?" to which another writer responds: "BECAUSE WE'RE NOT ALL KNEE-JERK 'ALTERNATIVISTS.'" This encouraged an all-caps rejoinder: "REMEMBER...BEING ALTERNATIVE DOESN'T MEAN BEING EVERY POSSIBLE ALTERNATIVE. WE'RE ALTERNATIVE IN THE WAYS WE CHOOSE, AT THE TIMES WE CHOOSE, TO THE DEGREES WE CHOOSE.[59]

Another set of DJs argue this point as, once again, different for the sake of being different, or alternative for alternative's sake:

And why have a show to play music that someone ELSE ALREADY PLAYS 24 hours a day 6 days a week just because they change for a few hours? Should we play KLOL'S PL every time they go to news?" "Then don't do it in the name of being 'alternative!' Do it because/if it needs to be done![60]

A similar debate occurred at WNUR in 1985, in which a student accused college radio of being different for differents' sake. Writing for "TGIF," the entertainment section of the *Daily Northwestern*, Jon Cummings criticizes the way WNUR, and most PCR stations at the time, dropped artists once they made it onto the commercial charts. To him, WNUR appears to be deliberately playing unpopular, unsuccessful, and unlistenable bands. He argues that what WNUR was playing at the time was not what Northwestern—or any—students were listening to. By refusing to play what Cummings guesses they consider "pop losers," WNUR's programming decisions seemed like deliberate hostility and snobbery directed at Northwestern's students. Appealing to populism, he laments the loss of new wave band Simple Minds[61] from college radio, scheduled to appear in concert on campus around this time. Presumably a student favorite, Cummings cannot understand why WNUR would ignore them. "By the time *Rolling Stone* listed [the band] at the top of its college charts in March, campus stations already were pulling it off the air because they knew that it would be a different chart by the beginning of June. With the pop charts and stations opening up to new music, the days may be numbered for campus radio stations and college critics who self-righteously deify bands that no one will ever hear."[62]

In response, fourteen members of WNUR's staff wrote a letter to Northwestern's newspaper criticizing Cummings for his "misconceptions" about college radio. They find especially problematic the fact that Cummings never interviewed any of them or asked any staff member about WNUR's programming policies. Laying out the reasons behind these policies, the writers of the letter invoke all of the tenets that proponents of PCR used throughout the decade. They called on the fact that WNUR's non-commercial status gave it an unusual opportunity to provide alternatives to the AOR and Top 40 stations that dominate the Chicago market, and noted that there is an audience for fringe programming not "satisfied with repetitive playlists on Top 40 stations." They note their legal obligation to serve Chicago, since the FCC granted them a license for 7200 watts, and that in Chicago, "there is a definite need for the alternative music we play." Finally, echoing mainstream journalists, the WNUR group emphasizes the station's unique ability as a non-commercial entity to give DJs a chance to play music they like.[63]

Another student declared on the same letters page: "College is a chance to experiment with individuality and to learn about expanding fields, including the field of rock and roll. College radio stations and music critics *should* experiment with developing rock and roll, not review the established sound. Let the establishment and high scholars do that."[64]

In another letter responding to Cummings, another WNUR staff member, J. Little, explains the stations' reason for playing "unpopular" music, using the idea of need as outlined above: "Because Simple Minds gained popularity, they no longer need the exposure college rock stations can offer. There are a million new groups out there needing airplay." Admitting that WNUR is "self-righteous," Little explains that in the interests of programming new music, the old must be swept aside or risk "denying new bands *their* chance to be heard."[65]

Conclusion

The debates between progressive college radio DJs over the meanings of alternative center on aesthetic choices, cultural capital, and different conceptions of the audience. There is one other sense of "alternative," however, which these debates leave untouched, and it is necessary to understand this other sense in order to understand progressive college radio's role in the transitional and critical decade of the 1980s. Prior to its close association with the music played on college radio, the word encompassed a range of community radio programming practices. Since progressive college radio is a type of community radio, it shared these practices. For example, program guides and internal memos from the 1970s demonstrate that PCR stations considered localism, diversity, exposing the audience to obscure cultural artifacts, ideas or minority views, and a passion for the practice of radio as part of what constitutes alternative broadcasting.[66] Certainly, as student-run university stations, education was a priority, but community radio generally trades in the idea that bringing a variety of underrepresented content to its audience results in a more informed and cosmopolitan citizenry. Moreover, using these criteria to make programming decisions presents an alternative to commercial programming criteria: "Public radio is a monastery of liberal humanism in the dark age of mercantilism. It is often the only broadcast source of the liberal tradition and its intellectual and cultural manifestations."[67]

Like other liberal humanist manifestations that promised social change, however, community radio in the 1980s found itself challenged by what William Barlow calls a "conservative counterinsurgency."[68] Just as Ronald Reagan broke the air traffic controllers' strike in a blow to labor and rolled back the Great Society reforms in a blow to civil rights legislation, so his administration cut funding to community radio, causing many stations to shut down.[69] Reagan's head of the FCC, Mark Fowler, famously said that television is a "toaster with pictures," suggesting that telecommunications technologies, including radio, are not public resources in need of government protection, but appliances whose usefulness should be determined by market forces.[70] At the level of the so-called culture wars, conservatives went after liberal "bias" in the media; public television and community radio came under intense scrutiny and even government investigation.[71]

Given this historical backdrop, to understand the resistance of PCR DJs to the music industry only as a group of young music fans' fear of "selling out" is to isolate PCR from its cultural context. Since they received university funding, and since their low wattage allowed them to fly under the radar of conservative media watch dogs, PCR stations were generally immune from federal budget cuts and investigations. This meant that in an environment hostile to community radio, PCR could provide a site for counterhegemonic media practice in relative safety.

However, while the DJs themselves did not articulate it, the way PCR fell under the scrutiny of the music industry is symptomatic of the way most radical media and social movements of the mid-twentieth century butted up against the market-oriented "mercantilism" of the conservative 1980s. The transition which saw progressive college radio become an arm of the music industry and "alternative" music become a genre unto itself effaced the other radio practices and meanings associated with the word. By the early 1990s, alternative as a mode of radio production had now become yet another aesthetic category to be weighed according to commercial viability, its new meaning the exact opposite of what it had been during the middle years of the twentieth century.

Nonetheless, even as it struggled to stay one step ahead of the rest of the music industry, and even as its DJs argued about being alternative for alternative's sake, progressive college radio in the 1980s continued to privilege unique and diverse programming, to support its local community, and to program content that its DJs actually liked. Even as conservative ascendancy marked a new era of acquisitive consumption, deregulation, and political quietism, progressive college radio offered possibilities for forms of communication not structured by relations of exchange, and thus offered an alternative to the dominant narrative of the Reagan years.

Notes

1. Craig Watkins, *Representing: Hip hop Culture and the Production of Black Cinema* (Chicago: University of Chicago Press, 1998), 33.

2. James Combs, *The Reagan Range: The Nostalgic Myth in American Politics* (Bowling Green, OH : Bowling Green State University Popular Press, 1993), 64-65.

3. Jane Feuer, *Seeing Through the Eighties: Television and Reaganism* (Durham: Duke University Press, 1995),1.

4. Feuer, *Seeing Through the Eighties,* 1.

5. Ibid., 10.

6. Peter Fornatale and Joshua E. Mills, *Radio in the Television Age* (Woodstock, NY: The Overlook Press, 1980), 168.

7. Robert McChesney, *Telecommunications, Mass Media, and Democracy* (New York: Oxford University Press: 1993), 14.

8. McChesney, *Telecommunications, Mass Media, and Democracy,* 27-28, 66-67.

9. Fornatale and Mills, *Radio in the Television Age,* 170-173; and Lawrence Soley, *Free Radio: Electronic Civil Disobedience,* (Boulder, CO: Westview Press, 1999), 38-43.

10. Fornatale and Mills, *Radio in the Television Age,* 124-125, 170-173; Soley, *Free Radio,* 38-40.

11. WNUR Spring Schedule '57," Records of WNUR, 1953-1994, University Archives, Northwestern University.

12. "Portrait of a Young Man as An Artist (Indeed—the Magic's in the Music and the Music's at 89.3," Records of WNUR, 1953-1994, University Archives, Northwestern University, n.d., n.p.

13. See Gina Arnold, *Route 666: On the Road to Nirvana,* (New York: St. Martin's Press, 1993), 23; and Ira Robbins, "Waving Goodbye to 1978," in *CMJ 10: The First Decade,* ed. Diane Turofsky et al. (New York, College Media Inc.: 1989), 147.

14. See Holly Kruse, *Site and Sound: Understanding Independent Music Scenes* (New York: Peter Lang, 2003), 65; Steve Pond, "College Radio's Brave New Wave," *Rolling*

Stone, New York, September 29, 1983. 85-86; Tom Popson, "A Different School of Broadcasting," *Chicago Tribune,* Chicago: April 18-24, 1986, 5-6; Ralph Rugoff. "Making Waves: Just what are those ungodly sounds these good Catholic kids are broadcasting?" *Los Angeles Herald,* May 5, 1985, 4-7. Steve Weinstein, "Jesuits Run Radical Rock Station at LMU," *Los Angeles Times,* June 24, 1987, 1-7.

15. Kim Ogg, "Radio Station KTRU Brings Nu-Wave Music Free," *Inner View,* Houston, TX, April 1983, 1-2.

16. Elizabeth Ann Hansen, "Becoming College Radio: WNUR's Movement Toward Free-Form Independent Music Programming" (Master's report; University of Texas 2008), 22.

17. See Pond, "Brave," 85; Popson, "Different," 5; Rugoff, "Making Waves," 5; and Weinstein, "Jesuits," 7.

18. See Kruse, *Site,* 72; and Pond, "Brave," 86.

19. Pond, "Brave," 86.

20. See Pond, "Brave," 85; and Popson, "Different," 6.

21. Quoted in Pond, "Brave," 86.

22. See Pond, "Brave," 86; and Popson, "Different," 6.

23. Jon Matsumoto, "Flipside Interviews the Minutemen," *Flipside* 46 (n.d.): n.p., http://www.operationphoenixrecords.com/flipsideminutemen.html

24. Marilyn Mock, e-mail message to author, July 1, 2009.

25. Marilyn Mock, e-mail message to author, July 1, 2009.

26. Ted Carroll, e-mail message to author, May 25, 2009.

27. Pam Moore, e-mail message to author, June 11, 2009.

28. Kim Fix, e-mail message to author, June 9, 2009.

29. Rugoff, "Making Waves," 4.

30. Ted Carroll, e-mail message to author, May 25, 2009.

31. Amy Reinholds, "Who's Listening? WNUR's alternative playlist appeals to 'invisible' off-campus audience," N.p., n.d., n.p, Records of WNUR 1953-1994, University Archives, Northwestern University.

32. Ted Carroll, e-mail message to author, May 25, 2009.

33. Pam Moore, e-mail message to author, June 11, 2009.

34. Pond, "Brave," 86.

35. Rick Carroll and Barry Levine, respectively, quoted in Pond, "Brave," 86.

36. Mark Richardson, "Dialogues," *CMJ,* November 7, 1986, 32.

37. Sharon Stevens, "Dialogues," *CMJ,* November 7, 1986, 32.

38. Chris Smith, quoted in Pond, "Brave," 86.

39. Richardson, "Dialogues," 32.

40. Quoted in Pond, "Brave," 86.

41. Pond, "Brave," 86.

42. Rugoff, "Making Waves," 4.

43. Quoted in Pond, "Brave," 86.

44. Señor Amor, personal interview with author, 25 August 2007.

45. Quoted in Pond, "Brave," 86.

46. Amy Reinholds, "WNUR."

47. Calvin Johnson, personal interview with author, July 7, 2008.

48. Marisa Fox, "Fast 'n' Loud 'n' Cheap in Middle America," *The Daily Northwestern,* October 12, 1984, 5-7.

49. Señor Amor, personal interview with author, 25 August 2007.

50. Reinholds, "Invisible," n.p.

51. Pat Whalen, "Dialogues," *CMJ*, November 7, 1986, 31.

52. "Groans and Gripes," September 25, 1981, KTRU box 26 folder 11, Rice University.

53. "Groans and Gripes," September 25, 1981.

54. "Groans and Gripes," February 2, 1982.

55. "Groans and Gripes," n.d.

56. "Groans and Gripes," Fall, 1984, KTRU, box 26 folder 11, Rice University.

57. "Groans and Gripes, Fall, 1984.

58. "Groans and Gripes," Fall, 1984.

59. "Grafitto," 1980s, KTRU box 26, folder 1. Rice University.

60. "Grafitto," 1980s.

61. Simple Minds made a name for themselves when John Hughes used their single, "Don't You Forget About Me" in his film, *The Breakfast Club*.

62. Jon Cummings, "College Radio ignores successful pop sound, choosing music most students won't enjoy," *Daily Northwestern*. October 11, 1985, 7.

63. "Radio Column Misses Boat," *Daily Northwestern*, October 19, 1985, 9.

64. Carolyn Metcalf, "New music on College radio," *Daily Northwestern*. October 18, 1985. 9.

65. J. Little, "College Radio Staffers," *Daily Northwestern*, n.d., n.d.

66. "Portrait;" KXLU Program Guide, December 1980, Records of KXLU, University Archives, Loyola-Marymount University; KSPC Program Guide, 1978, Records of KSPC, University Archives, the Claremont Colleges.

67. Larry Josephson, "Why Radio?" *Public Telecommunications Review* (March/April 1979),6-18, quoted in Fornatale and Mills, 185.

68. William Barlow, "Community Radio in the U.S.: the struggle for a democratic medium," *Media Culture and Society* no. 10 (1988): 96.

69. Barlow 97.

70. Allison Joyce Perlman, "Reforming the Wasteland: television, reform, and social movements" (PhD diss., University of Texas, 2007), 112.

71. Barlow 99-100.

Chapter 24

"Life in Marvelous Times:"[1] Commemorative Narratives of the Golden Era in Hip Hop Culture

James Braxton Peterson

"This is Bed-Stuy '82 /9ᵗʰ floor, three tiny rooms, one view"
—Mos Def, "Life in Marvelous Times"

From its humble origins in the South and West Bronx, to its initial splash on mainstream radio in 1979, rap music and Hip Hop culture struck many music critics and cultural bystanders as a passing fad amongst troubled inner city youth. In the last 30 years Hip Hop culture has developed from a relatively unknown and largely ignored inner city culture into a global phenomenon.[2] The foundational elements of Hip Hop Culture (DJ-ing, MC-ing, Breakdance, and Graffiti/Graf) are manifest in youth culture across the globe, including Japan, France, Germany, South Africa, Cuba, and the UK. Considering its humble beginnings in the South and West Bronx, the global development of Hip Hop is an amazing cultural feat. The 1980s were both a critical and transitional time period for the development of Hip Hop Culture. In addition to and maybe in spite of the implementation of various urban/social policies dictated via "Reaganomics," the music and culture began to flourish. One signal transition in the 1980s was the shift from the immediacy of the live Hip Hop performance to the mass disseminated/distributed records, films, or music videos of Hip Hop performance. With the advent of MTV, the internet, and the tentative acceptance of Hip Hop culture as American popular culture, what was once considered a fad was fast becoming central to the American mainstream's public sphere. Hip Hop entered the 1980s as an obscure, regional artistic blip and exited the 1980s as the flagship of American popular culture. This chapter briefly explores, documents, and dissects several of the commemorative highlights of Hip Hop's developments in the 1980s.

My analysis engages several texts through narrative analyses that reflect back on the 1980s era of Hip Hop culture in multifaceted ways across genres. These texts include: Jay-Z's "Blue Magic," Nicholas James' "Hip Hop's Magical Year," Danny Simmons' *'85*, Colson Whitehead's *Sag Harbor* and Mos Def's "Life in Marvelous Times." James' essay, "Hip Hop's Magical Year," delineates a "Top Ten" list of the "people, moments, politics and catalysts" that made 1988 the magical year of Hip Hop culture. According to James, "Not only did the rap music industry swell in '88, but the collective culture forced its way into the social, political, economic and popular ethos across American soil."[3] Danny Simmons' *'85* is a dark noir-styled graphic novel featuring 'appearances' by Run DMC, Russell Simmons, Jean Michel Basquiat, and Andy Warhol. Simmons' graphic narrative is drenched in nostalgia for an 80s (under)world of sex, drugs and violence; where black art is exploited and subsequently disregarded. *Sag Harbor* is Colson Whitehead's semi-autobiographical novel that chronicles the seasonal coming of age experiences of a group of young Black men, several of whom are cultural constituents of Hip Hop. Whitehead brilliantly captures the aesthetic feel of 80s Hip Hop culture via his characters' vernacular speech, dress codes, and various attempts at performing the lyrics of their favorite rappers.

Each of these narratives views Hip Hop culture in the 1980s and each is thematically consistent with rapper, Mos Def's poignant single, "Life in Marvelous Times." According to one reviewer: "On 'Life in Marvelous Times,' . . . Mos Def flips back and forth between memories of his youth and the present day." Each of these "bright moments" describes the stark realities of urban life, pointing out the gap between the rich and poor ("They green grass is green, our green grass is brown"); ultimately, the message and song's overall tone is triumphant, shown by the song's title, as well as the final verse:

> And we are alive in amazing times
> Delicate hearts, diabolical minds
> Revelations, hatred, love, and war
> And more and more and more and more
> And more of less than ever before
> It's just too much "more" for your mind to absorb
> It's scary like hell but there's no doubt
> We can't be alive in no time but NOW

In compelling ways, each of the aforementioned narratives lives in the "now" of the 1980s and in particularly powerful ways each narrative commemorates Hip Hop culture during its most fluid transitional period from underground subcultural eruption toward popular mainstream ubiquity. This chapter attempts to chronicle this emergence through these various commemorative texts and perspectives on the most enduring cultural product of the 1980s.

A narrative can engender commemorative functionality in a number of ways. Commemorate means either to call to mind or recall to mind; it can also denote memorial recollections or celebrations and/or a celebratory recollection of a particular event or life (e.g. a commemorative stamp).[4]   Memory and the study of the cognitive processes associated with memory have been integral components of the body of scholarship dedicated to narrative studies. "Much of the research on memory relevant to narrative has focused on the role schematic information plays in the understanding and recall of narratives."[5] The narratives of Hip Hop culture employ various schema in order to poetically and critically commemorate a relatively immediate history. In this discussion these narratives include song lyrics, critical writing, literary and graphic novel/comic narratives. Within these commemorative narratives, schema can be defined as lyrical/linguistic items that: "encode generalizations across individuals' experiences with categories of people, places, events, and so on. When people understand narratives, schemas help structure their understanding."[6] Schema then are the lyrical, visual or literary hinges by which listeners, readers, and other constituents of Hip Hop culture might fully understand narratives that commemorate the culture during the 1980s, maybe Hip Hop's most dynamic decade.

For his tenth studio recording, rapper and business mogul, Jay-Z released an album entitled *American Gangster*, named after the 2007 film that chronicles the life of Frank Lucas, a 1970s gangster and drug lord who made hundreds of millions of dollars from dealing heroin. Although Jay-Z's *American Gangster* is inspired by a 2007 film based on a 1970s gangster, many of his song lyrics feature narrative schema that point to Jay-Z's own exploits as a drug dealer and hustler in Brooklyn, New York during the 1980s. In "Blue Magic," a song named after the brand moniker attached to Frank Lucas' ultra-potent form of heroin (for which he became (in)famous), Jay-Z suggests that "niggas" want to return to the 1980s. Jay-Z is fine with that return to the 80s since that is where he emerged as a bona fide hustler.[7] Here two schematic generalizations develop abiding narratives whereby listeners might (via narrative insertion) understand and appreciate Jay-Z's sentiments. "Niggas" is the first schema that both taps into the sociolinguistic dynamics of the ultra-racially charged N-word and generalizes the subjectivity of those who desire to recall the 80s.[8] Several figures or entities might fall into this category. Certain sartorial trends have been (and continue to be) recalled by rappers and entertainers, ranging from Kanye West to the average constituent of Hip Hop who might wear "dookie" (i.e. large and ostentatious) gold chains or "phat" shoelaces in 80s-style Pumas or Adidas sneakers. 80s-style rap music has also been embraced by up and coming "underground" groups like the Cool Kids; while films such as *Juice*, *New Jack City* and others chronicle the socio-cultural backdrop of 1980s urban America. Bringing back the 80s has been a consistent stylistic maneuver within Hip Hop culture for well over a decade. Jay-Z's schematic generalization resources all of these artistic narratives and annunciates his particular place in the decade's materialistic emergence/explosion. The "they" in the second line is likewise situated within this particular commemorative narrative.

The "making" of Jay-Z is a more nuanced schema. Within the context of the song's lyrics, Jay-Z is made in the complex cauldron of a materialistic America in the throes of Reaganomics. In *Morning in America*, an extensive study of the impact and far-reaching influence of Ronald Reagan's presidency, Gil Troy devotes the "1985" chapter of the text to "Brooklyn, New York: Bill Cosby's Multicultural America Meets Ronald Reagan's Celebrity Presidency." Herein he details the confrontation between Cosby's sanitized Brooklyn and *The Cosby Show's* idyllic black nuclear family with the environment out of which individuals like Jay-Z emerged: broken family, dilapidated Marcy Housing Project, rampant drug dealing, abuse, and the violence that these phenomena often entailed. President Reagan's celebrated celebrity in the American public sphere belied the ugly, socially debilitating undertow of socioeconomic neglect in America's inner cities. According to Troy: "[t]hinking about Reagan as the Celebrity President suggests his unique synthesis between Burbank and the Beltway. Frequently, both benign neglect and symbolic embraces took on lives of their own, often disconnected from what actually occurred in the wide corridors of the federal bureaucracy or on the streets of Brooklyn and the rest of the country. But a society that was increasingly addicted to so many media forms, a media environment increasingly providing 'infotainment', a culture increasingly enthralled by all kinds of celebrities, from presidents to pop singers, blurred the line between the symbolic and the substantive, between tone-setting and governing."[9] This is the cultural context of Jay-Z's "making." Growing up in abject poverty with limited and/or truncated opportunity the young Shawn Corey Carter turned to hustling crack cocaine. At least according to the narratives in his lyrical corpus, he became exceedingly successful. On another track from *American Gangster* entitled "Dope Boys," Jay employs the double entendre of the slang word for drugs in order to celebrate the material freedom afforded to him through the illegal drug trade. As a result of the selective but widespread economic empowerment garnered through dealing various drugs, most especially crack cocaine, the term "dope" also engendered various positive and superlative meanings. Thus, "dope" in the 1980s referred to drugs as well as all things cool and aspirational.[10]

Jay-Z riffs on this particular schema later in "Blue Magic" when he suggests that President Reagan made him a (drug dealing) monster and that he distributed contraband that "they" (i.e. Reagan and Oliver North) sponsored. In *Book of Rhymes*, a brilliant exegesis on the poetics of rap music, Adam Bradley glosses these lyrics in order to uncover the ways in which Hip Hop artists utilize homonyms and homophones in advanced poetic wordplay. "It testifies to Jay-Z's lyrical ingenuity that even though we fully experience these poetic lines by ear rather than by eye, looking at them on the page calls attention to their individual effects, not just their cumulative impact. Equally as impressive as the homonym – Iran Contra and I ran contraband -- is that he delivers it while making a fairly complicated point, all while rhyming four lines together."[11] The "fairly complicated point" hinges on several schemas in conjunction with Jay-Z's astute wordplay. Celebrity President Reagan is to blame for Jay's descent into the underground economy of the drug trade. This is a fairly general accusation of the policies that exacerbated the post-industrial effects on America's inner cities, especially the under-funding of public schools and the political emphasis on individual capital accumulation. Note well here that Jay-Z acknowledges the fact that dealing crack is a monstrous endeavor with respect to his own impoverished community. By placing the blame on Ronald Reagan, he invokes a narrative that emphasizes the structural and environmental factors (over the individualistic and behavioral ones) that contribute to the challenges faced by American inner city communities throughout the 1980s. Fingering Oliver North's role in the Iran-Contra scandal diverts attention away from Jay's drug dealing exploits toward the political and military leadership of the United States. The suggestion here is that one of the models for the 80s, the decade in which Jay-Z was "made," is the complex corruptive attitude that the ends justify the means. In this particular case, the Reagan administration sold arms to Iran under the auspices of liberating American hostages. "Iran received 2,008 antitank missiles and tons of spare parts, and two hostages were released . . . Meanwhile, [Oliver North] began diverting profits from the Iranian arms sales to fund the Contras."[12] North's "rogue" efforts to fund the Contras reflected the Reagan administration's ideological policy to confront and eradicate communism in Central America. This territorial offshoot of the Cold War ignored the convoluted complexities of Nicaraguan and El Salvadorian sovereignty. Jay-Z's lyrical suggestion that he "ran" (i.e. hustled) drugs that "they" sponsored alludes to a contested narrative regarding the C.I.A.'s alleged role in facilitating the distribution of crack cocaine in America's inner city neighborhoods. According to this narrative, some shadowy figures connected to the Iran-Contra scandal sold large amounts of cocaine (attained from Central American Contras) and military-grade weaponry to gang members and drug dealers in the United States in order to continue secreted American support of the Contra's political and military efforts. This influx of weapons and cocaine allegedly generated the crack explosion of the late 1980s.[13] Jay-Z then suggests that before he began his rap career he was, via his drug dealing exploits, "in concert"' with the government's scandalous Iran-Contra policies; a suggestion that is simultaneously indicative of his current lyrically critical stance.

Of course Jay-Z is not the original narrator of the 1980s – Ronald Reagan rap connection. Jeff Chang titled his "1982" chapter of *Can't Stop Won't Stop A History of the Hip Hop Generation*: "Rapture in Reagan's America." *Can't Stop Won't Stop* is a groundbreaking comprehensive history of Hip Hop culture. The "Hip Hop Generation" to which the subtitle refers, was coined by Bikari Kitwana in 2002.[14] Chang's work thoroughly chronicles the 1980s through the lenses of Hip Hop culture. Throughout "Rapture in Reagan's America," he details a plethora of rap singles, important nightclubs, and insights from Hip Hop culture's pioneers and in turn depicts a portrait of Hip Hop in the 80s. Several of these points/details are critical to this discussion even though they cannot necessarily be considered commemorative narratives. "In April of 1982, Afrika Bam-baataa unleashed a grand statement for what he was now calling the hip-hop movement. It was called 'Planet Rock.'"[15] Bambaataa, one of the founding DJs of Hip Hop culture is a storied figure who many Hip Hop historians and journal-ists credit with transforming the Black Spades, one of New York City's largest and most notorious street gangs of the late 70s, into the Universal Zulu Nation, Hip Hop's oldest, most enduring (and endearing) community arts organization. "'Planet Rock' was hip-hop's universal invitation, a hypnotic vision of one world under a groove, beyond race, poverty, sociology and geography."[16] "Pla-net Rock" established an afro-futuristic vision for Hip Hop culture. It was a cor-nerstone in the culture's development during the early portion of the decade. It also set the stage for the stark socio-economic contrast that the political machi-nations of the 80s deviously cultivated. "Outside the floating world of the Roxy [a popular disco-turned-Hip Hop night spot], Reagan's recession had bloated unemployment levels to the highest levels since the Great Depression – 30 mil-lion searching for work. The official Black unemployment rate hit 22 percent. Poverty rates were soaring too. Black poverty hit a twenty-five-year peak in 1983."[17] Chang presages Jay-Z's narrative-blame directed at President Reagan. And the stark contrast between the utopian vision of a "Planet Rock" soundtrack to the Roxy's Dionysian interior and the raw poverty of inner city New York's eroding exterior would be clarified in yet another signal rap single released in the early 1980s: "The Message."

In *Brothers Gonna Work It Out*, Charise Cheney claims that: "Grandmaster Flash and the Furious Five's 1982 rap classic 'The Message' – overwhelmingly referred to by artists and academics alike as one of the most important songs in hip-hop history – is a lyrical picture of the urban crisis that produced hip-hop culture."[18] "The Message" poignantly narrates the urban blight so readily asso-ciated with the post-industrial landscape of urban America in the 1980s. Melle Mel of The Furious Five lyrically depicts bleak ghetto environs littered with broken glass, and overrun by foul smells, loud noises, rats and roaches. These now classic rap lyrics narrate the urban alienation and socioeconomic claustro-phobia that was the corollary to the policies associated with Reaganomics. The refrain, "it's like a jungle sometimes it makes me wonder how I keep from going under," emphatically underscores Cheney's assertion that rap music poetically expressed the urban crises of the 1980s. However, Cheney's argument that these urban crises produced Hip Hop culture over-reaches and relegates the emer-gence of Hip Hop to a common deficiency model proffered by some sociologists and cultural critics.[19] A more accurate picture emerges betwixt both "Planet Rock" and "The Message," through the aspirational narrative vision of the for-mer and the bleak narration of inner city angst chronicled in the latter.

Cheney also argues that "The Message" is a precursor to the "golden age of rap nationalism" formulated in 1988 with Public Enemy's *It Takes a Nation of Millions to Hold Us Back* and culminating in 1993 with the release of Ice Cube's *Lethal Injection*.[20] Public Enemy front man, Chuck D (and various journalists and scholars) agree with Professor Cheney on this point. Chuck D cites Melle Mel (of The Furious Five) as one of his seminal influences and explains the genesis of Public Enemy thusly: "[t]he sociopolitical meaning of Public Enemy came *after* we decided the group would be called that, because the meanings and the connections of what were about fit right in. The Black man and woman was considered three-fifths of a human being in the Constitution of the United States. Since the government and the general public follow the Constitution, then we must be the enemy."[21] This glimpse of the group's emergence in 1986 is surely suggestive for Cheney's incisive discussion of the "golden age of rap nationalism." However this 'golden age' is (only) a significant portion of the golden era referenced in this chapter. The golden *era* roughly extends from the early-mid 1980s into the early 1990s and it includes rap music and aspects of Hip Hop culture that do not necessarily espouse a Black Nationalist ethos. Furthermore for all of the value and historical import of Chang's exhaustive work, Cheney's astute analyses, and/or the brilliant artistry of "Planet Rock" and "The Message," these critical and artistic touchstones are not (exactly) commemorative narratives of 1980s Hip Hop culture.

Hip Hop scholar, teacher and cultural critic, Nicholas James, argues that 1988 is one of the most important years in the history of Hip Hop culture. In "Hip Hop's Magical Year" James effectively makes his case through commemorative narration and a Top Ten list. I will reproduce the list here (in abbreviated form) for ready reference. At number ten, James lists Nelson George, author of Hip Hop America, for his uncanny ability to make journalistic interventions on behalf of Hip Hop culture in several important mainstream musical arenas. Number nine cites the death of Jean-Michel Basquiat as both a powerful memorial signifier for the first Hip Hop generation and as a symbol of the mortally fast-paced exploitation of Hip Hop's arts. The eighth entry points to the 1988 release of Dennis Hopper's *Colors* as an early primer on the now legendary Bloods vs. Crips conflict in Los Angeles. James notes that the film is not considered a "Hip Hop" film and that the soundtrack garnered some critical success even though the film did not. At number seven, James lists the emergence of Dapper Dan's Fashion Boutique. Dapper Dan was responsible for designing the outfits of Hip Hop folk including various rappers and athletes, and as James notes, the outfits sported by Eric B. and Rakim on the cover of *Follow the Leader*. Number six is the introduction of the Nike Air Jordan III, the first in the series to sport the "jumpman" logo – nuff said. Number five references the creation of *The Source* at Harvard University by David Mays and John Schecter. Although *The Source's* reputation has diminished recently, between 1988 and 1998, it was regularly referred to as the "bible" of Hip Hop culture. Number four mentions Jesse Jackson's second presidential campaign as one of the most important political touchstones for the Hip Hop generation. Three cites the birth of "New Jack Swing" courtesy of Teddy Riley as a starting point for Hip Hop and R&B hybrids. Number two is the Stop the Violence Movement, which was an early attempt on the part of Hip Hoppers to address unchecked violence in inner city America. And number one is the premier of *Yo! MTV Raps*.[22]

As a part of James' commemoration of "Hip Hop's Magical Year" he engaged in an online discussion with readers who questioned his choices and debated the list. One schema of this essay was the general invitation to join the discourse; an invitation made formally via *The Root*, but one that also emerges naturally from the running superlative narratives of Hip Hop culture. *The Source* magazine and *Yo! MTV Raps* are not controversial entries on this list. That each media product was launched in 1988 lends undeniable credibility to James' commemoration of this year as a "magical" one in the development of Hip Hop culture. *The Source* eventually established "serious" and sustained journalistic approaches to Hip Hop culture. *Yo! MTV Raps* ushered Hip Hop music and culture through a paradigmatic shift into what would become an image-centered visual music culture. Each of these media "properties" (for Hip Hop culture) contributed greatly to Troy's sense that during the 80s, America became "increasingly addicted to so many media forms, a media environment increasingly providing "infotainment," a culture increasingly enthralled by all kinds of celebrities." Other entries on the list (e.g. Dapper Dan's or the death of Jean Michel Basquiat) resonate with the discursively invitational schema and satisfy Hip Hop communal desires to seek and attain further knowledge about the culture.

Another important schema or narrative framework in the "Magical Year" essay is the "Top Ten List" format itself. Popularized by David Letterman's NBC show, *Late Night* in 1985, the Top Ten List was originally designed as an ironic critique of similar lists entrenched in celebrity culture and regularly published in *People Magazine* and other print media of popular ilk. The original Letterman list, "The Top Ten Things That Almost Rhyme With Peas" was a comedic hit with Letterman's audience and he continued using the format even after he moved his program to CBS, renamed *The Late Show with David Letterman*. In *Story Logic*, an incisive work on narrative "as a discourse genre and a cognitive style," David Herman analyzes and quantifies schemas and other frame-like structures of narrative. "[R]esearch suggests that the mind draws on a large but not infinite number of 'experiential repertoires', of both static (schematic or frame-like) and dynamic (or script-like) types. Stored in the memory, previous experiences form structured repertoires of expectations about current and emergent experiences."[23] The "Top Ten List" has, over time, become a dynamic schema formulating various repertoires of expectations. For David Letterman's audiences these expectations include a count down or reverse ordering, irony, sarcasm, and increasingly, delivery by special guest celebrities.[24] For the constituents of Hip Hop culture, the intended audience for "Hip Hop's Magical Year," the comedic expectations are displaced by an abiding willingness to engage in superlative and/or evaluative discourses in and about Hip Hop culture. Often these narratives are shaped by schema such as "who is the best/greatest MC" or "what is the most famous beef (i.e. conflict between artists) in Hip Hop." The "Top Ten List" schema for "Hip Hop's Magical Year" accesses these repertoires and by navigating established narrative discourses on Hip Hop, James commemorates 1988's signal time slot in the development of the culture.

Commemorative narratives of the 1980s in Hip Hop culture do not necessarily recall Hip Hop's foundational or developmental attributes. In Danny Simmons' and Floyd Hughes' graphic novel, *'85*, the seedier underbelly of Hip Hop's cultural and artistic development is visually exposed and juxtaposed with the socioeconomic contexts alluded to in classic rap singles like "The Message." Crow, *'85*'s protagonist (or antihero), is a cocaine – not crack – junky who pilfers several paintings from his friend Danny. He intends to sell the paintings so that he might be able to pay for his next fix and his rent. When Crow attempts to fence the paintings he is assumed to be the artist by a potential buyer and subsequently thrust into the exclusive booming downtown New York art scene of the 80s. Seminal and enigmatic figures such as Andy Warhol and Jean Michel Basquiat have already become eagerly sought after artists and instant celebrities in a world overrun by drugs, posturing, and rampant materialism. Some clues to Simmons' commemorative perspective include scenes/panels of gratuitous sex and drug use and his conspicuous insertion of himself as a character – Danny is surely Danny Simmons, brother of both Russell Simmons, founder of Def Jam Records and Run from Run DMC. Simmons then is the artist who is robbed of his paintings and who never enjoys the fruits of his artistic labor. This particular narrative of artist exploitation resonates with the Hip Hop generation. By the mid-1980s many rappers, DJs, graffiti artists, and break "dancers" are being exploited, misrepresented and generally overexposed by a culture industry with little or no respect for Hip Hop. In *'85*, Simmons' character's artwork is doubly exploited since he receives no credit or remuneration for his work and the fleeting fame to which Crow gains access is totally closed off to him. This narrative commemorates the experiences of Jean Michel Basquiat, Lady Pink, and Grandmaster Caz, all artisans of Hip Hop culture who were notoriously denied access to the economic fruits of their own labor and/or deliberately overexposed and exploited as was the tragic case of the life of Basquiat. Another dynamic schema of *'85* is the classic confrontation between and deconstruction of "high" art and "low" art. Like most artisans of 1980s Hip Hop culture, Simmons (and of course, Crow) have no formal training yet their class and ethnic identities become another fetish for the fickle "high" art world.

The dark, black, and white visuals of the graphic novel struggle to realize Simmon's recollection of artistic exploitation in the 1980s. Hughes' style is asymmetrical and angular which conveys an unpolished look that suggests the "low" art styling of the novel's characters. Still certain panels or scenes convey powerful schema for the Hip Hop generation and those narratives that commemorate New York City life in the 80s. When Crow rides the subway, he is paranoid and edgy because he is in need of his next fix. But as he rides and surveys the interior of the subway car he articulates several recollective insights. From his perspective: "the subway had humanity frozen in *frames* . . . fear in the aged, alienated, rebellious kids cutting school, the weighted, stooped shoulders of the

lonely, and predators pacing their cages, sizing up their next victim. [my empha-
sis]"[25] This perspective of the subway as a dangerous and dark space was crys-
tallized in the 1985 case involving Bernhard Goetz who was targeted as a victim
by four black teenagers but quickly turned the tables on his would-be muggers,
shooting all four of them – some in the back as they ran away. Goetz was a heroic figure to some, but the story reflects the schema inherent in Simmons's and
Hughes depiction of the New York subway system as a dangerous place where
people's humanity is frozen in frames. "[E]ven as New York revived in the
1980s, even as the Metropolitan Transit Authority would buy new cars . . . as
part of a huge renewal program, the noisy, filthy, gritty, tardy, and crime-
plagued subway system still symbolized New York's breakdown during the
1970s."[26] Although Simmons' vision in '85 does not transcend his own nostalgic look at the 1980s and/or possibly his own artistic frustration, scenes such as
those depicted in the aforementioned "subway" panels deftly capture the ways in
which dangerous subway realities can be commemorated by the Hip Hop generation.

The 1985 of Colson Whitehead's *Sag Harbor* is depicted in stark contrast to
the dark underworld imagery rendered in Simmons' and Hughes' graphic novel.
Sag Harbor's protagonist, Benji Cooper, is a student at an elite preparatory
school in Manhattan, but he and his family spend their summers in Sag Harbor,
an exclusive community in the Hamptons, frequented by mostly middle to upper
middle class African Americans. Benji is an awkward first-year high school
student who begins to come of age during the summer of 1985 in Sag Harbor.
Hip Hop culture is present but somewhat tangential to Benji's narrative since his
brother has a more pointed affinity for the sartorial styles and musical aesthetics
of the culture. But since he tends to define himself over and against his younger
brother, Reggie, some of their experiences are inextricably linked. "There was
something in the human DNA that compelled people to say 'Benji 'n' Reggie,
Benji 'n' Reggie' in a singsong way as if we were cartoon characters or mascots
of some twenty-five-cent candy."[27] Benji both admires and despises his brother
as he continuously attempts to distinguish himself from him amongst their small
crew of black teenaged males. They are the exact opposite of the teens who had
designs on mugging Bernard Goetz, and Whitehead poignantly situates their
comical exploits within the picturesque backdrop of Sag Harbor so that readers
cannot confuse or profile one group as the other. Benji and company are not
trolling the subways of New York City looking for victims. They are chillin' in
beach houses coming up with new and inventive ways to insult each other. "The
trend that summer, insult-wise, was toward grammatical acrobatics, the unlikely
collage. One smashed a colorful and evocative noun or proper noun into a pejor-
ative, gluing them together with an –in' verb."[28]

Whitehead's sheer hilarity belies the systemic and ritualistic nature of these
sets of insults. The grammatically acrobatic insult is an innovative form of playing the dozens, a time-honored ritualistic practice that has been traced back to
the origins of the African American experience. Playing the dozens is seamless-

ly interwoven in the fabric of rap music as well as the everyday practices of members of the Hip Hop generation. Thus by commemorating (his own) childhood experiences, Whitehead simultaneously taps into the sociolinguistic roots of Hip Hop culture. This instance is only one of several in which Benji's encounters with aspects of Hip Hop serve to commemorate Whitehead's experiences with the culture in New York City (and Sag Harbor) during the 80s. Others include his experiences with graffiti; a chapter entitled "Breathing Tips of Great American Beatboxers," where he and his friends endure a host of poorly plotted shenanigans in order to get into a U.T.F.O. concert; and one of the novels most insightful reflections where Benji compares 1980s Run DMC lyrics (from "Here We Go") to 1990s Ice Cube lyrics (from "Now I Gotta Wet'cha"). "Something happened that changed the terms and we went from fighting (I'll knock that grin off your face) to annihilation (I will wipe you from this Earth). How we got from here to there are the key passages in the history of young black men that no one cares to write about. We live it instead."[29] For Whitehead, Run DMC's lyrical repertoire represents narratives of innocent poetic musings when juxtaposed with the gangsta" violence of Ice Cube's oeuvre. He commemorates Run DMC through this semi-autobiographical narrative and reflects on the struggles he and his cohort faced en route to adult black masculinity. As middle class, private-school-attending black boys, Benji and his friends were subject to ridicule and ritual assaults on their manhood. Thus Ice Cube's posture, symbolized potently in the violent themes of "Now I Gotta Wet'cha," which essentially means now I have to shoot you until your shirt/clothes become soaked in your own blood, suggested a subjectivity preferable and more authentic than their own. Upon further reflection, Benji/Whitehead concludes: "[w]e got guns. We got guns for a few days one summer and then got rid of them. Later some of us got real guns."[30] Acquiring guns somehow became the "key passages" for young black men in the 1980s regardless of class background. And while Whitehead refrains from draping the blame of gun violence amongst young black men upon the scaffolding of Hip Hop culture he does ask the tough question here with respect to the imagery proffered by authentic gangster figurations within the culture. To this there are no simple answers, but the commemorative narrative here conflates the dynamic, script-like schema (i.e. get guns if you are young and black in 1985) with a static rejection of that repertoire by reflecting on the abrupt paradigmatic content-shift in the music and the overall inescapability of the violent narrative's suggestive force.

Returning briefly (and by way of conclusion) to the epigraph that quotes Mos Def's "Life in Marvelous Times," the demographic pendulum swings back to Brooklyn New York, Manhattan's neighboring borough, but in many ways many miles away from Benji's upper middle class existence. For Mos Def, who "grew up" in the 1980s, a life in "Marvelous Times" engenders a certain sad irony. Like many rappers (and poets) before and after him, Mos Def lyrically deciphers the contradictions and ironies inherent in inner city living during the post-industrial "Reaganomics" moment. That from these challenging circumstances, Hip Hop culture continued to emerge and eventually thrive is a memorable narrative worth commemorating. While the term marvelous often refers to some thing, person, place, or event as being extraordinarily good or great, it also connotes wonder and astonishment. For Mos Def's narrator in "Life in Marvelous Times," all of these meanings maintain as his lyrics vacillate between positive and negative designations. This lyrical oscillation captures several themes and examples discussed in this chapter. Mos Def raps: "This is Bed-Stuy '82 / 9th floor, three tiny rooms, one view." The singular view from the interior of a cramped high-rise apartment building obscures the bifurcated themes of Mos Def's entry amongst the Hip Hop, circa 1980s, commemorative narratives. The commemorative pendulum swings throughout his verses. "Delicate hearts, diabolical minds/Revelations, hatred, love, and war/And more and more and more and more/And more of less than ever before."[31] Through this dynamic schema, Mos Def captures the range and in-depth complexities of the commemorative narratives of Hip Hop culture in the 1980s. Within this dynamic, the diverse future of Afrika Bambaataa's "Planet Rock" coexists integrally with Grandmaster Flash and the Furious Five's "The Message;" the making of Jay-Z the crack dealer is situated within the evolving context of Shawn Carter's success as an entrepreneur and his incisive critique (in "Blue Magic") of Ronald Reagan's domestic and foreign policies. The dark imagery of Simmons' and Hughes' *'85* finds both resonance and balance in the deceptively light-hearted veneer of Colson Whitehead's *Sag Harbor*. Only through these broad ranging static and dynamic schemas is the fully fleshed out significance of the 1980s writ accurately upon the scrolls of Hip Hop history.

Notes

1. "Life in Marvelous Times" Written by Dante Smith and Gilles Bousquet. Copyright © 2009 by Downtown DMP Songs (BMI), Medina Sounds Music (BMI) and Blue Mountain Music Ltd. All Rights Reserved. Used By Permission.

2. From these origins, Hip-hop's development can appropriately be broken down into several eras:

(1) **The Old School Era:** From 1975 to 1983 Hip Hop culture cultivated itself in and through all of its elements, usually remaining authentic to its counter cultural roots in the post-industrial challenges manifested in the urban landscape of the late Twentieth century. Artists associated with this era included Grandmaster Flash and the Furious Five, The Sugarhill Gang, Lady B, Big Daddy Kane, Run DMC, Kurtis Blow and others.

(2) **The Golden Age Era:** From 1984-1993 rap and rappers begin to take center stage as the culture splashes onto the mainstream platform of American popular culture. The extraordinary musical production and lyrical content of rap songs artistically eclipse most of the other primary elements of the culture (breakdancing, graf art, and DJ-ing). Eventually the recording industry contemplates rap music as a potential billion dollar opportunity. Mass mediated rap music and Hip-Hop videos displace the intimate, insulated urban development of the culture. Artists associated with this era include: Run

DMC, Boogie Down Productions, Eric B and Rakim, Salt N Pepa, Queen Latifah, De La Soul, A Tribe Called Quest, Public Enemy, NWA, and many others.

(3) **The Platinum Present:** From 1994-the present Hip Hop culture has enjoyed the best and worst of what mass mediated popularity and cultural commodification has had to offer. The meteoric rise to popular fame of gangsta rap in the early 90s set the stage for a marked content shift in the lyrical discourse of rap music toward more and more violent depictions of inner city realities. Millions of magazines and records were sold, but two of Hip-Hop's most promising artists, Biggie Smalls and Tupac Shakur were literally gunned down in the crossfire of a media fueled battle between the so-called East and West Coast constituents of Hip Hop culture. With the blueprint of popular success for rappers laid bare, several exceptional artists stepped into the gaping space left in the wake of Biggie and Tupac. This influx of new talent included Nas, Jay-Z, Master P, DMX, Big Pun, Snoop Doggie Dogg, Eminem, and Outkast.

3. Nicholas James, "Hip Hop's Magical Year," *The Root* 2008, http://www.theroot.com/views/hip-hops-magical-year (accessed December 20, 2009).

4. Definition paraphrased from The Merriam Webster Dictionary, p.144, (2004).

5. David Herman, Manfred Jahn, and Marie-Laure Ryan, eds., *Routledge Encyclopedia of Narrative Theory* (New York: Routledge, 2005), 299.

6. Herman, Jahn, and Ryan, *Narrative Theory*, 299.

7. Jay-Z, "Blue Magic," *American Gangster*. New York: Def Jam Records, 2007.

8. Many scholars (Randall Kennedy, Cornel West, Jabari Asim, and Michael Eric Dyson, to name just a few) have engaged in the public debate about the use, meaning, and racist/racial implications of the term. Many of these debates center on the multi-layered meaning of the term, the various sociolinguistic incarnations of it (nigga vs. nigger, niggaz, nigguhs, etc.), and the ability, or lack thereof, of changing the semantics of the term by shifting its contexts chronologically, racially, and discursively. My argument is simple. There must be a public / private split with respect to how we attempt to regulate the word or not. That is, in the public it is extremely difficult to divorce the word from its historical origins. Thus whenever a member of the Ku Klux Klan or the Aryan nation scrawls the word in a public place or uses the word in public to refer to people of African descent then the term engenders the "hate speech" designation so problematically protected by the First Amendment. This public / private distinction also applies to any rapper who uses the term in public or records the term on a record that will be publicly released. I do not suggest that we censor these uses, only that we recognize that the deconstructive readings or hearings of the word cannot be guaranteed in the public sphere. That being said, censoring the term will not in and of itself root out the history and awful legacy of racism in America.

9. Gil Troy, *Morning in America: How Ronald Reagan Invented the 1980s* (Princeton, NJ: Princeton University Press, 2005), 177.

10. Consider Boogie Down Production's (BDP) 1986/7 classic, "Dope Beat" on the *Criminal Minded* album. The refrain is "I got a dope beat!"

12. Adam Bradley, *Book of Rhymes: The Poetics of Hip Hop* (New York: Basic Civitas, 2009), 111.

13. Troy, *Morning in America*, 245.

13. The late *San Jose Mercury* reporter, Gary Webb published a hotly contested (and some say debunked) series of exposes claiming that the CIA was involved with a "Dark Alliance" with Central American contras. He later (1998) published a book entitled *Dark Alliance: The CIA, the Contras and the Crack Cocaine Explosion.*

14. In *The Hip Hop Generation*, (Basic Civitas 2002), Bikari Kitwana defines this generation as those born between 1964 and 1985 who subscribe to Hip Hop culture as a central frame or schema through which they experience life. For these Hip Hop generational constituents certain events and historical developments formulate the zeitgeist of their lives. Some of these include: living in a post-civil rights, post-racial segregation America, the rise of the Prison Industrial Complex, The War on Drugs, the emergence and spread of HIV/AIDS and the unsolved murders of Tupac Shakur and The Notorious B.I.G.

15. Jeff Chang, *Can't Stop Won't Stop: A History of the Hip Hop Generation*, (New York: St. Martin's Press, 2005), 170.

16. Chang, *Can't Stop Won't Stop*, 172.

17. Chang, *Can't Stop Won't Stop*, 177.

18. Charise L. Cheney, *Brothers Gonna Work It Out: Sexual Politics in the Age of Rap Nationalism*, (New York: New York University Press, 2005), 8.

19. In *Prophets from the Hood* (Duke University 2004), Imani Perry formally challenges this common, deficiency-oriented explanation of the origins of Hip Hop culture and instead proffers a discussion that does not ignore the socioeconomic contexts of Hip Hop's emergence, but focuses more on the ingenuity and creativity that actually led to the development of Hip Hop's core artistic elements.

20. Charise Cheney, "In Search of the Revolutionary Generation: (En)Gendering the Golden Age of Rap Nationalism," *The Journal of African American History* 90, no. 3 (Summer 2005): 278-298.

21. Chuck D and Yusuf Rah, *Fight the Power: Rap, Race and Reality*, (New York: Dell Publishing, 1997), 86.

22. Here is a less abbreviated version of the list from The Root.com:

> 10. *Nelson George*. Having written articles in the *Village Voice* and serving as black music editor of *Billboard* magazine, Nelson George used his journalistic savoir-faire to force literary and critical media to review rap as black popular music.

> 9. *The Death of Jean-Michel Basquiat*. Jean-Michel Basquiat, also known as SAMO by way of his early graffiti endeavors, joined, captivated and unequivocally changed the art world. With the assistance of pop-art luminary Andy Warhol, Basquiat made a healthy living as a painter and was en route to iconic status before dying of a heroin overdose in the summer of '88. His cultural influence can most readily be found in the lyrics (and hallways) of hip-hop artisans from Fab Five Freddy to Jay-Z.

> 8. *Dennis Hopper's Colors*. Rarely regarded as hip-hop cinema, this '88 film was the first to offer an insightful perspective into the vicious world of gang violence in South Central Los Angeles between the infamous Bloods and Crips. Unfortunately, the film was not received well by critics, and in spite of the success of the soundtrack's title song by Ice T, *Colors* failed to soften the resounding blow of what was on the horizon in the form of West Coast Hip-Hop; otherwise referred to as "Gangsta Rap."

> 7. *Dapper Dan's Fashion Boutique*. This clothing store sat on 125th Street in Manhattan, and its storekeeper, Dapper Dan himself, designed many an outfit for many rappers in '88. To quote Dapper Dan, "the rappers wanted to look like the gangsters," and proof of this rests on the cover of the classic '88 album: Eric B. and Rakim's *Follow the Leader*. The cover art portrays the duo fully clad

in ghetto-altered Gucci sweatsuits (a Dapper Dan signature) with their names weaved into their backs. Dapper Dan's gained more notoriety in '88 when Mike Tyson broke his hand after getting into an altercation with fellow heavyweight Mitch "Blood" Green outside the boutique. The champ was going in to purchase his custom-made jacket with the title of the '88 P.E. cut "Don't Believe the Hype" articulately sewn onto the back of it.

6. *The Nike Air Jordan III.* Nike and Tinker Hatfield designed and marketed the Air Jordan III in '88 by creating the Jumpman logo (a staple in Hip-Hop fashion) to signify Michael Jordan's NBA Slam Dunk Contest victory. The sneaker company laid a pop-culture foundation for the Air Jordan brand as well as the groundwork for a bourgeoning Hip-Hop consumerism.

5. *The SOURCE.* What would ultimately become the powerful voice for Hip-Hop began as a newsletter in '88. While students at Harvard University, David Mays and John Schecter began critically analyzing rap music with *The SOURCE* pamphlet and gained a growing group of admirers anxious for such scrutiny in Hip-Hop culture.

4. *Jesse Jackson's Michigan primary victory.* The possibility of Jesse Jackson becoming the first black president helped to expand the conversation between rappers and listeners into the political realm. Jesse did not win the Democratic nomination in '88, but this conversation has clearly been resurrected 20 years later, as Barack Obama and a significant cadre of emcees speak openly and honestly about the future of our country.

3. *New Jack Swing.* The production of this hybridized musical composition of Hip-Hop and R&B was attributed to a young artist named Teddy Riley. In '88, Riley molded an edgy sound that mixed between and mingled with various black musical genres (think Bobby Brown) and changed the face of black popular music forever.

2. *Stop the Violence Movement.* [This] collective included KRS-One, Public Enemy, Stetsasonic, MC Lyte and a host of others, and was called the Stop the Violence Movement. The movement would go on to record a vital cut in Hip-Hop (and popular music) history, "Self-Destruction," and donate all proceeds from the 12" single to the National Urban League.

1. *Yo! MTV Raps.* Thanks to the courage of the late director/producer Ted Demme and the cultural sense of Fab Five Freddy, hip-hop culture would be broadcast nationally for the first time on cable television's biggest music outlet, MTV. Many critics rightly consider "Yo!" the most revolutionary cultural moment in television history, as the Saturday afternoon, hour-long program brought Hip-Hop culture to living rooms worldwide, suburban and otherwise and truly changed the game, for better or worse, forever.

23. David Herman, *Story Logic: Problems and Possibilities of Narrative*, (Lincoln, NE: University of Nebraska Press, 2002), 89.

24. Many celebrities have taken their turns at doing Letterman's "Top Ten List" segment including: Britney Spears, John McCain, Cindy Crawford, John Malkovich, Rudolph Giuliani and even some animated characters such as Homer Simpson and Optimus Prime of the *Transformers* animated series.

25. Danny Simmons and Floyd Hughes, '*85*, (New York: Atria Books, 2008), 2.

26. Troy, *Morning in America*, 180.

27. Colson Whitehead, *Sag Harbor*, (New York: Doubleday, 2009), 3.

28. Whitehead, *Sag Harbor*, 41.

29. Whitehead, *Sag Harbor*, 146.

30. Whitehead, *Sag Harbor*, 147.

31. Mos Def, "Life in Marvelous Times," *The Ecstatic*, (New York: Downtown Records, 2009).

Chapter 25

"Do We Get to Win This Time?" Movies, Mythology, and Political Culture in Reagan Country

Stephen McVeigh

Rambo: First Blood Part II (1985) and *Back to the Future* (1985) may, on the surface, have very little in common. Both are produced in the 1980s, both are significant box office successes, but they belong to very different genres and are aimed at different sectors of the theatre going audience. However, in thinking about how American film production in the 1980s is linked to the political culture of the period, their roles as exemplars of wider trends are apparent. Each film delineates a strategy for dealing with the trauma of recent history. The strategy employed by *Rambo: First Blood Part II* is to replay an aspect of that history to achieve the victory that was denied to America the first time around. This is not a film remembered for the quality of its writing. Its dialogue is pared down to a minimum and action is privileged. And yet the screenplay delivers perhaps the most precise and insightful articulation of the tendencies in political culture and popular cinema in the 1980s. The simple question, "do we get to win this time?" in narrative terms motivates Rambo's decision to return to Vietnam and rescue American service men listed as MIA. In a wider sense it provides the opportunity to re-fight the war to a happier conclusion. These same sentiments underpin a decade of revision, of reconfiguration and the subsequent rehabilitation of American history, mythology and identity by reversing the damage caused by the defeat Rambo references. *Back to the Future*, another phrase which has rich parallels with the character of the 1980s, engages a different strategy to achieve the same end. Rather than replaying history or re-fighting its battles and thereby securing the present, the film uses the time travel motif to literally cut the 1960s and 1970s from the continuum of American history altogether. The dysfunctional McFly family at the beginning of the film is representative of the extent to which traditional American values have been traumatized by recent history. The film celebrates the 1950s as a time before trauma, as a period of innocence. Marty's adventures in 1955, the modifications he makes to events in his and his family's past quite literally "fix" the present. When he returns to 1985, his family is the picture of the American nuclear unit.

These two reverberative narrative patterns are not exclusive to these movies. They were replayed and reworked throughout the decade in a number of key 80s genres and a study of these provides a fascinating insight into the efforts undertaken to reconstitute American mythology after its central tenets were so badly damaged in the wake of the 60s and 70s. The tone, texture and intent of the films produced in the 1980s are significantly altered from those of the preceding decades. Movie production in the 1980s was an integral feature of the wider political and cultural effort to rebuild American self-confidence and self-concept in the aftermath of 20 or so traumatic years. While acknowledging that film had always to some degree provided a commentary upon American politics and society, it can be argued that movies and political culture had never been so consistently in step as they were in America in the 1980s. This synergy is broadly apparent in terms of their pronounced celebrations of American characteristics and virtues, but it is very specifically demonstrated in the performance of President Ronald Reagan. There had been other presidents adept at manipulating the media. Consider for example Franklin Roosevelt's fireside chats, delivered by radio, or John F. Kennedy's understanding of television as evidenced in the debates of 1960. However, in Reagan, Hollywood and politics intermingled as never before. Movies were central to his biography, they were a recurrent inspiration in his rhetoric and they established his approach to the delivery of the role of Commander-in-Chief. Portraits of President Reagan as an actor in a role are manifest. Lou Cannon described the presidency as "the role of a lifetime".[1] Dick Wirthlin, a member of Reagan's marketing team stated that polling in the run up to the 1984 election endorsed "a strong, can-do approach to leadership... The role was written for a leading man like Reagan – a serene, self-confident hail fellow unburdened by doubt or morbid introspection". Alan Nadel quotes a White House Chief of Operations with a similar take on Reagan: "He was an actor working from a script... If you gave him a script he would do it."[2]

Reagan's mission was in part that of a healer, tending and mending the wounds of recent history. Cannon suggests that, "because of his ability to reflect and give voice to the aspirations of his fellow citizens, Reagan succeeded in reviving national confidence at a time when there was a great need for inspiration."[3] To this end, he can also be described as a revisionist, taking recent history and reconfiguring it, making it safe. This he did by turning history into a movie, at least narratively. He reworked a troubled history of violence, pain and suffering into stories of sympathetic heroes, identifiable villains and happy endings. As Nadel points out, "Like *Back to the Future*, [Reagan] proved that tampering with the space-time continuum was not dangerous but beneficial."[4] Significantly, these endings offered lessons to be learnt, the warning that history must not be allowed to repeat itself. Such retellings suggested that these tragic events were aberrations and that the fault lay, not with the ordinary American, but with flawed bureaucrats. Throughout, Reagan inferred the values of the 1940s and 50s, values which had been badly damaged by the 1960s and 1970s. This transmission of values and ideals from a perceived better age is a recurring motif in 1980s American cinema. These are clearly important factors in accounting for Hollywood's special tone in the 1980s, but underpinning all of these things was the rehabilitation of American mythic structures, structures that had been thoroughly subverted for much of the previous decade and a half. It is in this combination of politics, myth and popular culture that Hollywood would produce a body of work that was simultaneously new and traditional, that was concerned with reality and mythology, and that celebrated contemporanity and nostalgia.

The Care and Repair of American Myth

In the seminal *Foreign Affairs* article, "The Care and Repair of the Public Myth," William McNeill in 1982 commented that "discrepancies between old myths and current realities are great enough to be troubling." He went on,

> a people without a full quiver of relevant, agreed upon statements, accepted in advance through education or less formalized acculturation, soon finds itself in deep trouble, for, in the absence of believable myths, coherent public action becomes very difficult to improvise or sustain.[5]

The article was a response to the diminution of American power since 1945. The impact of the defeat in Vietnam and the further loss of American prestige it signaled, although not specifically named, provided an occasion for McNeill's observations. American mythology had indeed been compromised by the events of the 1960s and 1970s, as well as by the trend towards historical revisionism. The problem as McNeill articulates it is that revisionists dismantle myths without offering suitable alternatives and thereby erode the possibilities of a unified national identity and coherent public action. The integrity of mythic structures relating to America's frontier past, to its archetypes of heroism, to issues surrounding American exceptionalism had been thrown into doubt. The sense of doubt, of introspection is a tangible element in 1970s America. John Hellman describes American society as "moving incoherently into the future from a past they no longer found intelligible."[6] The United States' self concept reeled from the events of two troubled decades. American identity, its fundamental beliefs and values, its core institutions, were badly shaken. The unraveling of the Nixon White House as a consequence of the Watergate break-in, the disgrace of resignation, compounded the sense that the very idea of America had been corrupted. It is no surprise then to find that the films of this period were subversive, challenging the establishment, questioning national institutions and wary of perceived American virtues and characteristics. Such questioning pervaded Hollywood's output in these years. Consider for example the apocalyptic trends in science fiction in movies like *Soylent Green* (1973), *Logan's Run* (1976), *Invasion of the Bodysnatchers* (1978), *The Omega Man* (1971), *The Exorcist* (1973) or *THX 1138* (1971). The political ramifications can be observed in the cycle of paranoid conspiracy thrillers made in the wake of Watergate such as *All the President's Men* (1976), *The Parallax View* (1974), *The Conversation* (1974), or *The Three Days of the Condor* (1975). In each case, the American traditions of heroism and happy endings are visible casualties.

Although some Hollywood legends continue to direct films into the 1970s, for the most part, the movies that are most strongly associated with the decade were being made by a new generation of film-makers. Directors and writers such as Francis Ford Coppola, Steven Spielberg, George Lucas, Martin Scorsese, Brian DePalma, and John Milius, a generation of "movie brats" according to the title of a book by Michael Pye and Linda Myles, produced a body of sometimes challenging, often personal work that ranks among the best Hollywood has ever produced. These were young men, not brought up in the Hollywood establishment but rather they were graduates of film school, technically proficient and connoisseurs of cinema. These films lay bare the social context that underpin McNeill's article. Pye and Myles offer this sketch of the new generation:

> They inherited the power of the moguls to make film for a mass audience. And they know the past of cinema like scholars…Knowledge and power and spectacular success all make them the true children of old Hollywood. They…have made films more successful than any others in history. They knew the history of Hollywood from the late night television movies and the corner theaters; and because they chose to learn it at film school; and because they have sought out, analyzed, and enjoyed film of every kind.[7]

Although working within the Hollywood system, they did not feel obliged to conform to its trappings. As Pye and Myles state, they "share a distaste for the superficial social round of Beverly Hills and the old Hollywood… They know that Hollywood is an invention, a firework display designed by press agents and promoters."[8] As a consequence, they were able to bring to their films a darkness and a critical incisiveness that was unusual in Hollywood product. Much of their output can be described as a cinema of social comment, or as George Lucas would suggest, of "isn't-it-terrible-what's-happening-to-mankind" movies. And yet, out of this darker, more subversive approach, would paradoxically emerge the building blocks for the rehabilitation of American mythology that marks 1980s Hollywood.

Steven Spielberg and George Lucas are generally credited with establishing the tone of 1980s Hollywood. To some extent with *Jaws* in 1975 and certainly with *Close Encounters of the Third Kind* in 1977, Spielberg can be held responsible for establishing many of the conventions of the special effects blockbuster, the movie as amusement park ride, or in more economic terms, the tall revenue feature. Spielberg's gifts for combining traditional storytelling with cutting edge technology became his signature style and, so successful was it, that the industry has attempted to mimic it ever since. In the pursuit of commercial success, many argue that creativity more often than not took a back seat, and considering the emphasis on sequels and franchises such critics may have a point. Relying on demographic research and testing, Hollywood has sought out that one massive event film that would attract audiences, domestic and international. Special effects, A-list stars, soundtracks and enormous publicity budgets are all marshaled in the effort to create this kind of success, with the logic that one such hit could support a studio and its less successful or more prestigious productions.

The phenomenal success of George Lucas' *Star Wars* (1977) was similarly influential, but it also inaugurated another significant development that Hollywood would pursue in the 1980s and after. In commercial terms, *Star Wars* was the film that established the practice of merchandising, of tying film into many and various products from food and clothing to books and toys. In an industry that was having its profits pinched, this kind of diversification was seized upon.[9] In cultural terms, it was the first film to consciously make use of Joseph Campbell's thesis in *The Hero with a Thousand Faces*, to explicitly follow narrative patterns that have endured for thousands of years and thereby create stories that were timeless and universal. In so doing, Lucas' *Star Wars* set the pattern for the coming decade, artistically as well as economically. It is crucial to note the self-consciousness of these attempts to get away from the contemporary cinematic style of the 1970s, to return to traditional mythic structures. It is telling that Lucas made *Star Wars* because he could not bring himself to direct *Apocalypse Now*.

McNeill argues in his 1982 article that "In a time such as ours, when inherited myth systems are in disrepair and no great political leader has yet emerged, historians, political scientists and other academics that are paid to educate the young and think about matters of public importance ought to feel special responsibility for proposing alternatives to accepted ideas."[10]

Considering that Hollywood and President Reagan are so clearly engaged in this very project, it seems that McNeill is looking in the wrong direction and to the wrong people for alternatives. Spielberg's and Lucas' return to tradition, to comforting fairy tales and mythic patterns represented a deliberate and popular strategy, a return to safer narrative terrain. Reviewing *Star Wars* for the *New Yorker,* Pauline Kael wrote, "the excitement of those who call it the film of the year goes way past nostalgia to the feeling that now is the time to return to childhood."[11] Hollywood was emphatically involved in this process to repair the damaged American psyche.

In 1985, Christopher Vogler, a production executive at Disney, captured this tendency in a 7-page memo intended for screenwriters. Entitled "A Practical Guide to Joseph Campbell's *The Hero with a Thousand Faces*", the memo was an attempt to distill Campbell's seminal work, his structural analysis of the form and function of mythology, and re-package it as the foundations of cinematic storytelling. The memo detailed the 12 stages of the "Hero's Journey," a narrative structure which Vogler suggests is "infinitely flexible, capable of endless variation without sacrificing any of its magic, and it will outlive us all." As a document, the memo is simultaneously *timeless* (describing and codifying narrative patterns that reach back to civilizations' earliest stories) and *of its time* (the very concept of a memo as a means of disseminating artistic values, of divining a formula for guaranteed success (narrative and commercial) fit well with the materialistic dimension of the decade). The urge to standardizing and codifying narrative form and structure and the privileging of the mythological all resonate perfectly with cinematic production in and the economic climate of the 1980s. Considering the self consciousness with which politics and culture went about the business of repairing its broken myths, it is little surprise that the dominant genres of the 1980s made important contributions to this effort. An exploration of the Vietnam War film and the cop/action thriller illuminate this process of mythic restoration.

Going Back–The Vietnam War Film in the 1980s

Toward the end of the 1970s, films employing the Vietnam War as a narrative context became increasingly common. Films like *The Deer Hunter* (1978), *Taxi Driver* (1976), *Apocalypse Now* (1979), *Coming Home* (1978), *Go Tell the Spartans* (1978), depicted the trauma of the war for Americans "in country" and at home. However, these films are not attempts to realistically portray the conflict in Southeast Asia. In each instance they deal with the effects of the war rather than the war itself. So in *Apocalypse Now* the war is constructed as a psychedelic trip, a journey in the minds of Captain Willard (Martin Sheen) and Colonel Kurtz (Marlon Brando), a surreal series of images suggesting the Vietnam War was such an onslaught on the senses that it could not be understood in any conventional way. In *Taxi Driver*, the experience of war transforms Travis Bickle (Robert De Niro) into a vigilante, seeking beauty amidst the corruption on the streets of New York. *The Deer Hunter* spends most of its running time, not in Vietnam, but in Clairton, the Pennsylvania steel town from which the protagonists hail. It also foregoes historical authenticity in the Russian roulette sequences. There were no recorded incidences of American captives being forced to play the game. Rather it is simply a gripping dramatic device. The ending of *The Deer Hunter* offers a sense of the ambivalence of the era toward the war. After Mike's (Robert De Niro) attempts to bring Nicky (Christopher Walken) back to America end in the latter's death, the surviving members of the community, all of whom have been touched by the war in some way, are seated around a table, celebrating Thanksgiving. One of their number begins to sing "God Bless America" and in time the others join in, ultimately presenting a heartfelt rendition of the anthem. Crucially, the meaning of the sequence is left up to the audience, and it poses a series of questions. Do they mean it? Are they endorsing America and American action? Or is it an ironic comment? Is the film an attack upon the blind faith that led the nation into the war? Regardless, this ambiguity was not to last. In the Reagan era, Hollywood, echoing the President's revisionist approach, was instrumental in helping Americans to come to terms with the Vietnam War and its aftermath.

At the dedication ceremony of the Vietnam Memorial in Washington D.C. in 1982, President Reagan made a speech that articulated the shift perceptions of the war in the 1980s:

> We remember those who were called upon to give all a person can give, and we remember those who were prepared to make that sacrifice if it were demanded of them in the line of duty, though it never was. Most of all, we remember the devotion and gallantry with which all of them ennobled their nation as they became champions of a noble cause. I'm not speaking provocatively here. Unlike the other wars of this century, of course, there were deep divisions about the wisdom and rightness of the Vietnam War. Both sides spoke with honesty and fervor. And what more can we ask in our democracy? And yet after more than a decade of desperate boat people, after the killing fields of Cambodia, after all that has happened in that unhappy part of the world, who can doubt that the cause for which our men fought was just? It was, after all, however imperfectly pursued, the cause of freedom; and they showed uncommon courage in its service. Perhaps at this late date we can all agree that we've learned one lesson: that young Americans must never again be sent to fight and die unless we are prepared to let them win.

This recasting of the war as a "noble cause" and the defeat as an internal problem lies at the heart of Reagan's revisionism. In cinematic terms it opened the way to rehabilitate the war and the mythology it damaged through its most notable casualty: the Vietnam veteran. The veteran had been the focus of the nation's outrage, their needs dismissed or ignored in the effort to drive the war from memory. In film from 1975 to 1982, the moment Reagan delivered his speech at the Vietnam Memorial, veterans were generally represented as misfits and psychopaths, as dysfunctional and volatile individuals who represented a threat to the society to which they had been returned but into which they could not re-integrate.

To be sure, the figure of the traumatized veteran had some basis in fact, but this character soon became merely a workable stereotype. Travis Bickle is perhaps the best example. Marginalized by a society that would rather forget about him and his experiences, he is eventually provoked into violent retaliation. At the end of *Taxi Driver*, his head shaven into a Mohican, he enacts a bloody rampage in an effort to cleanse the dirty streets of the city. The implication is that the Vietnam veteran is a traumatized casualty of war who sees around him a corrupt society that has betrayed him. As in *The Deer Hunter*, questions are raised, but answers are not necessarily forthcoming. Who is to blame for the war? Who is guilty? Is the veteran responsible for the defeat or America itself? This angst is described by Robert Jay Lifton when he noted that, "Americans who [had] not seen Vietnam [felt] something of a national descent into existential evil, a sense that the killing and dying done in their name [could not] be placed within a meaningful system of symbols."[12] One of the central tenets of Reagan's revision of the Vietnam War, and consequently a feature in American popular culture, is the transformation of the veteran from dangerous outsider to American hero. In a conversation with Bobby Muller, the founder of the Vietnam Veterans of America Foundation, Reagan said, "Bob, the trouble with Vietnam was that we never let you guys fight the war you could have done, so we denied you the victory all the other veterans enjoyed. It won't happen like that again, Bob."[13]   A version of the sentiments in his 1982 speech, veterans were no longer scapegoats for all that had gone wrong in the aftermath of the war. Vietnam veterans were repositioned now as victims of the nation's error, and this was an interpretation which Hollywood vividly portrayed.

First Blood (1982) and *Rambo First Blood Part II* enact the process of the veteran's rehabilitation, from outcast to superhero. In *First Blood*, Rambo (Sylvester Stallone) is the veteran as perceived menace. From the moment he walks into town (and the film is set entirely in America), he is provoked by figures of authority, most notably Teasle, the town's sheriff (Brian Dennehy). He tries to ignore the provocation, but he is forced to strike back. It is important to note that his capacity for carnage is not directed toward people but property. In a striking allusion to Vietnam War imagery, Rambo burns the town, inviting parallels with the torching of hamlets.   The intervention of Rambo's former Green Beret commander, Trautmann (Richard Crenna), persuades him to stop fighting. In an exchange between the two, the legacy of the war is made clear: "I did as you asked. I did what I had to but you wouldn't let me win."

However, when Rambo returns in *First Blood Part II* the moral ambiguities of the war have been re-evaluated, and the veteran is now a potential source of national redemption: going back to Vietnam to win the victory that should have been America's the first time around. The transformation of the veteran is symbolized by its star, Sylvester Stallone, presented as a muscle-bound superhero. As significant as the question that prefigures the action of the movie ("Do we get to win this time?"), those at the end are equally important: "We want for our country to love us the way we love it." Between these sentiments, the Vietnam War is re-fought to a very different conclusion than that experienced by America in reality. Using Reagan's revisionism as a guide, Hollywood achieves what America couldn't: victory.

Once the Vietnam War had been "made safe," Hollywood proceeded to explore the war in more direct terms. A sequence of films in the late 80s that were, at least on the surface, more realistic portrayals of the war received great critical and commercial acclaim. *Hamburger Hill* (1987) and *Full Metal Jacket* (1987) are interesting attempts to authentically reproduce the war on screen. However, it was *Platoon* (1986) which became the accepted rendition of America's war in Vietnam. Great claims were made for the film's authenticity but closer analysis reveals yet another example of Hollywood mirroring the rhetoric of Reagan's revisionism.

The film is in essence a rite of passage, detailing Chris Taylor's (Charlie Sheen) struggles with Sergeants Elias (Willem Defoe) and Barnes (Tom Berenger). In a traditionally mythic pattern, the former is good, the latter bad, and the two are "fighting for possession of [Taylor's] soul."   It is this narrative structure that resonates with Reagan's rhetoric. The war, the film suggests, was actually an internal conflict wherein a few Americans lost their way. The voiceover at the film's end makes the point vividly:

> I think now, looking back, we did not fight the enemy, we fought ourselves, and the enemy was in us. The war is over for me now, but it will always be there, the rest of my days. As I am sure Elias will be, fighting with Barnes for possession of my soul. There are times since I have felt like the child born of those two fathers. But be that as it may, those of us who did make it have an obligation to build again, to teach to others what we know and to try with what's left of our lives to find a goodness and meaning to this life.

Platoon's take on the war had appeal across the political spectrum. Liberals thought the film suggested the war was morally dubious, and America's involvement had been wrong, while conservatives saw it as a celebration of the courage with which the ordinary soldier had fought the war in the face of mismanagement at higher levels. *Platoon* dramatizes, then, Reagan's narrative that America's defeat was America's fault, encapsulated in Taylor's observation that "we fought ourselves."

Lethal Westerns: The Cop Movie in the 1980s

Any account of the state of American mythology in the 1980s needs to consider the influence of the western. As long as there had been film production in America, there had been westerns. The genre functioned as the embodiment of symbols of national identity, of models of heroism, morality, and American character. That said, the genre was responsive to the times and had warped and changed over the course of the 20th century. By the 1960s, the western and its depiction of American values were being interrogated, in films like *The Man Who Shot Liberty Valance* (1962) (which contains the memorable and insightful line, "When the legend becomes fact, print the legend") and *Ride the High Country* (1962) (U.S. title, *Guns in the Afternoon*). Even though its structures were being used for increasingly subversive ends, it remained a viable genre. During the 1970s this capacity to be reworked was exploited by film-makers who wished to discuss the Vietnam War but who were prevented from doing so. In films such as *Soldier Blue* (1970) and *Little Big Man* (1970) the western was employed as a stand-in for Vietnam, cavalry massacres of the Indians oblique representations of American infantry massacres on Vietnamese villages. Through the Spaghetti Westerns of Sergio Leone and vividly violent films of Sam Peckinpah, the demonic persona of Clint Eastwood and the death of John Wayne, the Western arrived at the beginning of the 1980s much changed from its golden age form. And it is an interesting paradox that in a decade so concerned with mythology, the western "dies."

The direct cause of death was the production of *Heaven's Gate* (1980). Michael Cimino, fresh from his Oscar success with *The Deer Hunter*, delivered to

United Artists a sprawling, muddled epic western which portrayed Wyoming's Johnson County Range Wars. The film came in at almost six times its original budget (from $7.5 million to a staggering $44 million). The first cut stood at a monumental 5 hours and 25 minutes, but was cut drastically to 219 minutes for its premier in November 1980. The critical and commercial response was poor and the film was immediately pulled from screens. It was re-edited and re-released five months later, in a cut shortened by a further 70 minutes. The critics were no kinder second time around and audiences failed to materialize. Cimino was of the same generation as the movie brats, and *Heaven's Gate* was clearly intended to replicate the kind of critical and commercial success of Coppolas' *The Godfather*, the blockbuster hit of 1972. In reality, *Heaven's Gate* became the biggest flop in film history up to that time. With a domestic box-office take of around $1.5 million, the film lost somewhere in the region of $40 million. So massive was this loss that United Artists' parent company, Transamerica, was forced to sell the studio to MGM for a relatively small figure of $350 million. What *Heaven's Gate* seemed to demonstrate was that the audience for the western had gone and that a studio should think carefully before investing in the genre in the future. There were other westerns in the 1980s though. In 1985, Clint Eastwood directed and starred in *Pale Rider*, an explicit reconfiguration of *Shane* (1953) and in the same year, Lawrence Kasdan directed *Silverado*. Although they were both interesting and well made films, neither stimulated a resurgence of interest in the genre. The western in its most traditional form looked to have had its day, but the mythological underpinnings of the genre were still very much in demand. As noted, the films of the 1980s were primarily concerned with Americanness and mythology, with nostalgia for a United States that had been lost. If the western was no longer fit for purpose, then its mythological structures would have to be reshaped, modified to fit into more contemporary patterns. And even if the western was dead as a cinematic structure at the beginning of the 80s, as a political reality, in the figure of Ronald Reagan, it was very much alive. In presidential campaign materials Reagan would be depicted as the Sheriff, adorned in a cowboy hat, wearing a badge with "President" emblazoned upon it, and set against a frontier backdrop labeled Reagan's Country. It would be a key genre of 1980s movies, the action/cop thriller, that would maintain the myth for the contemporary audience.

The cop film was by no means an 80s innovation. In the late 60s and 70s, there were several examples such as *Dirty Harry* (1971) and *Serpico* (1973), films very much in the vein of the era. These were narratives concerned with the excesses of the counter-culture or institutional corruption rather than the repackaging old myths.

The 1980s cop film was clearly an element of the mission to repair American myth. Films like *Witness* (1985), *Beverly Hills Cop* (1984) and *Black Rain* (1989) updated the western story of the outsider who enters a community and "cleans it up." However, two movies in particular illuminate the genre's contribution to the care and repair of American myth post-Vietnam: *Lethal Weapon*

(1987) and *Die Hard* (1988). Both films were deliberately contemporary. They were urban, foul mouthed, knowing and replete with advanced weaponry, spectacular stunts and pyrotechnic special effects. Both films set the box office alight and both films spawned incredibly successful franchises as well as many imitations. As such it is easy to dismiss them as trivial and populist. However, a closer inspection reveals that both movies, quite consciously, hark back to the traditions of the old-fashioned western.

Richard Donner, the director of *Lethal Weapon* (and its subsequent sequels), is explicit in terms of his inspiration and intentions for the film:

> I tried to make it more like an old-fashioned western. Sure there were a lot of deaths, but they died like they died in westerns. They were shot with bullets, they weren't dismembered. I like action and a strong story line. I like to turn my head away in suspense, not in disgust.[14]

The film centers on the relationship between Riggs (Mel Gibson) and Murtaugh (Danny Glover), a mismatched pair of detectives. The former is an ex-marine, recently widowed and on the verge of suicide at the beginning of the film. Murtaugh, while also a veteran, is by contrast a stable family man with a long record of police service and, as he is introduced, celebrating his fiftieth birthday. Reluctantly partnered, they slowly come to trust each other as they become increasingly embroiled in the film's violent plot. The models of heroism represented by the two are immediately familiar. Indeed there is, in Riggs' articulation as a dangerous outsider with a past and Murtaugh's representation of a family man capable of action, an element of that most mythological of westerns, *Shane*. More generally though, they are depicted as having the natural skills of the frontiersman/cowboy: both men have excellent sharp-shooting abilities, they are resilient (both men are brutally tortured in the film), and both operate on a simple moral division of "good guys" and "bad guys" (the film has a high body count, but there is no moral angst about the violence because the majority of those who fall are "bad men"). Elsewhere, the film employs other western tropes. Linguistically, the characters use evocative references to the western, such as Riggs' observations about Murtaugh when they first meet that he is an "old timer" because he carries "a six-shooter". Other such references lie behind the use of the Indian name, "Cochise" as a term of endearment.

Lethal Weapon also offers a version of the urge to re-fight an historical defeat to a successful conclusion. The Vietnam War haunts the plot of the film. Both Riggs and Murtaugh are Vietnam veterans. Murtaugh has adjusted back to civilian life, while Riggs is still suffering some measure of PTSD. Riggs' story arc is partly a familiar transformation from troubled psychopath to family saviour. Further, the villains in the story are also veterans, American officers employed by the CIA and involved in the agency's Air America program. These corrupt figures are using the drug connections made during the war to ship heroin into the U.S. This resonates with Reagan's concept that the war was lost as a consequence of a few corrupt individuals who perverted the aims of the war. Once again, Hollywood provides a victory. Toward the end of the movie, as things look bad for Murtaugh and his daughter, the leader of the villains, the Colonel, taunts him that there are no more heroes left in the world, an articulation of the American mythological landscape after Vietnam. However, the film's mythological function is made abundantly clear when, moments later, Riggs bursts through a door, guns blazing, proving the Colonel's statement gloriously false. As Riggs and Murtaugh satisfyingly dispatch the villains, they simultaneously establish that heroism has returned and help expunge the corruption from American memory.

Die Hard is another high concept, big budget star vehicle and another excellent example of how the western myth retained its relevance. John McClane is a New York detective flying to Los Angeles to spend Christmas with his estranged wife and children. His wife works for a Japanese corporation and he is to meet her at the company building for a Christmas party. Within moments of arriving however, German terrorists take control of the building and lock it down. Although they make demands to release terrorist comrades in prisons around the world, they are actually common thieves, intending to steal the billions of dollars of bearer bonds in the company's safe. The institutional law enforcement that quickly surrounds the building are portrayed as broadly ineffective, and even incompetent, leaving McClane to remedy the situation alone. An element of the film's mythological function can be seen in the choice of locale and villain. The Nakatomi Building, representative of Japanese economic dominance and the German terrorists position McClane in relation to two of America's recent enemies and are evocative of a conflict that was free from moral ambiguity.

In John McClane, popular cinema created a very American type of hero. While he embodies the traditional abilities of the frontier hero (adept with guns and fists, resilient, morally assured) he is imbued with a contemporary knowingness. Much of the film's energy comes from his exchanges with Gruber (Alan Rickman), the terrorist leader. Their dialogue frames the centrality of western mythology to the film:

GRUBER: But you have me at a loss. You know my name, but who are you? Just another American who saw too many movies as a child? Another orphan of a bankrupt culture who thinks he's John Wayne? Rambo? Marshal Dillon?

MCCLANE: Actually, I was always partial to Roy Rogers. I really dug those sequined shirts.

GRUBER: Do you really think you have a chance against us, Mr. Cowboy?

MCCLANE: Yippee-ki-yay motherfucker.

Before this exchange, McClane has already given Powell (Reginald Veljohnson), the beat cop who discovers the terrorist take over, the name Roy as an alias. In doing so, his actions can be read as those not only of a contemporary action hero, but also as a traditional frontier hero. As the Colonel dismisses the possibility of heroism in *Lethal Weapon*, so Gruber tries to do the same in *Die Hard*. And like Riggs, McClane demonstrates that he is entirely wrong.

Taking America Back to the Future

In his Farewell Address, Reagan offered an interesting reflection on his eight years in the White House:

> They called it the "Reagan Revolution." Well, I'll accept that, but for me it always seemed more like the great rediscovery, a rediscovery of our values and our common sense...And as I walk off into the city streets, a final word to the men and women of the Reagan Revolution, the men and women across America who for 8 years did the work that brought America back. My friends: We did it. We weren't just marking time. We made a difference. We made the city stronger; we made the city freer; and we left her in good hands. All in all, not bad–not bad at all.

At the core of his rhetoric is the idea of going back, recovering, rediscovering, as he puts it, lost and damaged values and re-integrating them in the ongoing project of America. Much of American cinema in the 80s can be seen to reflect or comment upon such rescue of older values, but it is *Back to the Future* that most accurately connects with the idea of rediscovering American myth. Produced by Spielberg, this was a trademark event movie, globally successful, visually spectacular and high concept: the perfect Hollywood product. The premise is a simple one: an 80s teen is transported by an eccentric scientist's time machine back to 1955. The complications occur when he encounters his parents, prevents the event that brought them together and consequently puts his very existence in peril. For much of the movie, Marty (Michael J. Fox) is creating his own history, manipulating events to guarantee that his parents meet, fall in love and produce the family of which he will be a part. However, his influence on events in 1955 dramatically alters the timeline and ultimately demonstrates the benefits of tinkering with the past. The innocence, energy and character his parents display in 1955, and which has been destroyed by the passage of history in the original 1985, is brought forward to the reconfigured 1985. In this way, the movie is a precise and incredibly self-conscious projection of Reagan's revisionist mission. It is no mere detail then that Reagan "appears" in the movie but is rather an indication of its connection to the historical moment. When Marty arrives in 1955, the cinema that in 1985 is showing adult movies, is advertising a western, *Cattle Queen of Montana* (1954), starring none other than Ronald Reagan. Later in the movie, as he tries to convince an incredulous Doc Brown that he is indeed from the future, Doc quizzes Marty:

Doc: So tell me, future boy, who's president of the United States in 1985?

Marty: Ronald Reagan.

Doc: Ronald Reagan? The actor? Then who's vice president? Jerry Lewis? I suppose Jane Wyman is the first lady... And Jack Benny is secretary of the Treasury.

Reagan's "presence" in the 1950s and the 1980s serves to authenticate his revisionist rhetoric by establishing his credentials as a repository of the values of the 50s and as a channel for their transmission into a future America. Reagan's belief in the power of the movies meant that the business of politics and the film industry were inextricably woven into the fabric of American society in the 1980s. President Reagan and Hollywood worked to reintroduce Americans to the stories and values upon which the nation was founded. In his farewell address, Reagan is unequivocal about the importance of the maintenance of American mythology now that he will not be around to guarantee it:

> there is a great tradition of warnings in presidential farewells, and I've got one that's been on my mind for some time. But oddly enough it starts with one of the things I'm proudest of in the past eight years: the resurgence of national pride that I called the new patriotism. This national feeling is good, but it won't count for much, and it won't last unless it's grounded in thoughtfulness and knowledge...An informed patriotism is what we want. And are we doing a good enough job teaching our children what America is and what she represents in the long history of the world? Younger parents aren't sure that an unambivalent appreciation of America is the right thing to teach modern children. And as for those who create the popular culture, well-grounded patriotism is no longer the style. Our spirit is back, but we haven't reinstitutionalized it.

His concerns were prophetic as the broad cultural consensus of the 1980s turned into the fractured multiculturalism of the postmodern 1990s. Situated between two political and cinematic eras which sought to challenge established patterns and institutions, the 1980s is unique in the evolution of American film. This uniqueness rests in Hollywood's provision of the imaginative space that was integral to Reagan's revisionist mission, the landscape upon which America would, mythologically at least, get to win this time.

Notes

1. Lou Cannon, *President Reagan: The Role of a Lifetime* (New York: Simon and Schuster, 1991), 837.

2. Alan Nadel, *Flatlining on The Field Of Dreams* (New Brunswick: Rutgers University Press, 1997), 16.

3. Cannon, *President Reagan: The Role of a Lifetime*, 837.

4. Nadel, *Flatlining on The Field Of Dreams*, 21.

5. William H. McNeill, "The Care and Repair of the Public Myth," *Foreign Affairs* vol. 61, no. 1 (Fall 1982): 5, 1.

6. John Hellman, *American Myth and the Legacy of Vietnam* (New York: Columbia University Press, 1986), 205.

7. Michael Pye and Linda Myles, *The Movie Brats: How The Film Generation Took Over Hollywood* (London: Faber, 1979), 7

8. Pye and Myles, *The Movie Brats,* 11.

9. It is worth noting that the 1980s was for Hollywood a period of pronounced transition in business terms. The central feature of this change was the focus on synergy. Film production costs had risen significantly in the period leading up to the 80s which increasingly impacted upon the profitability of theatrical features. As a consequence, a pattern of 'conglomerization', which had begun in the 1960s, intensified. Mergers and acquisitions such as United Artists and MGM in 1981 and the subsequent sale of the companies film library to Ted Turner in 1986; the takeover of 20th Century Fox by oil tycoon Marvin Davis in 1981 and then the shared ownership deal with publisher Rupert Murdoch in 1985; the purchase of Columbia Pictures by the Coca-Cola Company in 1982 who subsequently sold it to the Sony Corporation of America; the merger of Warner Communications and Time Inc. in 1989. The logic was simple: it "provided...a safety net for a large investment – losses in theatrical film divisions could be offset by the profitability of other areas." Steven Neale, *Genre and Contemporary Hollywood* (London: BFI, 2002), 20.

10. McNeill, "The Care and Repair of the Public Myth," 6

11. *New Yorker*, September 26th, 1977.

12. Robert Jay Lifton, *Home from the War* (New York: Basic Books, 1985), 67.

13. John Pilger, *Heroes* (London: Pan Books, 1989), 118.

14. *New York Times*, 3rd April, 1987.

Bibliography

Anderson, Martin. *Revolution: The Reagan Legacy*. Stanford: Hoover Institution Press, 1990.

Andrews, David L. *Michael Jordan, Inc: Corporate Sport, Media Culture, and Late Modern America*. New York: SUNY Press, 2001.

Baer, Kenneth S. *Reinventing Democrats: The Politics of Liberalism from Reagan to Clinton*. Lawrence: University of Press of Kansas, 2000.

Beschloss, Michael and Strobe Talbot. *At the Highest Levels: The Inside Story of the End of the Cold War*. Boston: Little, Brown, 1993.

Berkowitz, Richard. *Stayin' Alive: The Invention of Safe Sex*. Cambridge, MA: Basic Books, 2003.

Berlet, Chip and Matthew N. Lyons. *Right-Wing Populism in America: Too Close for Comfort*. New York: Guilford Press, 2000.

Berman, Marshall. *All That Is Solid Melts Into Air*. London: Verso, 1983.

Brandt, Karl Gerald. *Ronald Reagan and the House Democrats: Gridlock, Partisanship, and the Fiscal Crisis*. Columbia, MO: University of Missouri Press, 2009.

Brest, Joel. *Threatened Children: Rhetoric and Concern about Child-Victims*. Chicago: University of Chicago Press, 1990.

Campbell, John. *Margaret Thatcher*. London: Jonathan Cape, 2000.

Cannon, Lou. *President Reagan: The Role of a Lifetime*. New York: Public Affairs, 1991.

Carpenter, Joel. *Revive Us Again: The Reawakening of American Fundamentalism*. New York: Oxford University Press, 1997.

Chang, Jeff. *Can't Stop Won't Stop: A History of the Hip Hop Generation*. New York: St. Martin's Press, 2005.

Cohen, Stanley. *Folk-Devils and Moral Panics*. London: Routledge, 2002.

Combs, James. *The Reagan Range: The Nostalgic Myth in American Politics*. Bowling Green, OH: Bowling Green State University Popular Press, 1993.

Crothers, Lane. *Globalization and American Popular Culture*. Lanham, MD: Rowman and Littlefield Publishers, 2006.

Cumings, Bruce. "Time of Illusion: Post-Cold War Visions of the World." *Cold War Triumphalism: The Misuse of History after the Fall of Communism*, ed. Ellen Schrecker, 71-99. New York: New Press, 2004.

D, Chuck and Yusuf Rah. *Fight the Power: Rap, Race and Reality*. New York: Dell Publishing, 1997.

Dallek, Matthew. *The Right Moment: Ronald Reagan's First Victory and the Decisive Turning Point in American Politics*. New York: Free Press, 2000.

D'Antonio, Michael. *Fall From Grace: The Failed Crusade of the Christian Right*. New Brunswick, NJ: Rutgers University Press, 1992.

Decker, John F. *Revolution to the Right: Criminal Procedure Jurisprudence during the Burger-Rehnquist Court Era*. New York: Garland, 1992.

Dempsey, Paul Stephen and Andrew R. Goetz. *Airline Deregulation and Laissez-Faire Mythology*. Westport, CT: Quorum Books, 1992.

Denisoff, R. Serge. *Inside MTV*. New Brunswick, NJ: Transaction Publisher, 2002.

Derthick, Martha and Paul J. Quirk, *The Politics of Deregulation*. Washington DC: The Brookings Institution, 1985.

Engel, Jeffrey A., ed. *The Fall of the Berlin Wall: The Revolutionary Legacy of 1989*. New York: Oxford University Press, 2009.

Erickson, Paul D. *Reagan Speaks: The Making of an American Myth*. New York: New York University Press, 1985.

Estrich, Susan. *Real Rape: How the Legal System Victimizes Women Who Say No*. Cambridge, MA: Harvard University Press, 1987.

Faludi, Susan. *Backlash: The Undeclared War against American Women*. New York: Crown, 1991.

Feuer, Jane. *Seeing Through the Eighties: Television and Reaganism*. Durham: Duke University Press, 1995.

Frank, Thomas. *The Conquest of Cool: Business Culture, Counterculture and the Rise of Hip Consumerism*. Chicago: University of Chicago Press, 1997.

Fukuyama, Francis. *The End of History and the Last Man*. New York: Free Press, 1992.

Gaddis, John Lewis. *The Cold War: A New History*. New York: The Penguin Press, 2005.

Gelbspan, Ross. *Break-ins, Death Threats and the FBI: The Covert War against the Central America Movement*. Boston: South End Press, 1991.

Gillens, Martin. *Why America Hates Welfare: Race, Media and the Politics of Anti-Poverty Policy*. Chicago: University of Chicago Press, 1999.

Goldman, Peter and Tom Matthews. *The Quest for the Presidency 1988*. New York: Simon and Schuster, 1989.

Gordon, Diana R. *Return of the Dangerous Classes: Drug Prohibition and Policy Politics*. New York: W.W. Norton, 1994.

Grossberg, Lawrence. *We Gotta Get Out of This Place: Popular Conservatism and Postmodern Culture*. London: Routledge, 1992.

Grünzweig, Walter, Roberta Maierhofer, and Adi Wimmer eds. *Constructing the Eighties: Versions of an American Decade*. Tübingen: Gunter Narr Verlag, 1992.

Harvey, David. *The Condition of Postmodernity: An Enquiry into the Origins of Cultural Change*. Oxford and New York: Blackwell, 1989.

Hertzke, Allen D. *Echoes of Discontent: Jesse Jackson, Pat Robertson, and the Resurgence of Populism*. Washington, DC: Congressional Quarterly Press, 1993.

Irwin, John and James Austin. *It's About Time: America's Imprisonment Binge*. Belmont, CA: Wadsworth, 1996.

Jameson, Fredric. *Postmodernism, or, The Cultural Logic of Late Capitalism*. Durham: Duke University Press, 1991.

Jefferson, Margo. *On Michael Jackson*. New York: Random House, 2007.

Jeffords, Susan. *Hard Bodies: Hollywood Masculinity in the Reagan Era*. New Brunswick, NJ: Rutgers University Press, 1994.

Keck, Thomas M. *The Most Activist Supreme Court in History: The Road to Modern Judicial Conservatism*. Chicago: University of Chicago Press, 2004.

Lea, John and Jock Young. *What Is To Be Done About Law and Order — Crisis in the Eighties*. Harmondsworth: Penguin, 1984.

Leffler, Melvyn P. *For the Soul of Mankind: The United States, the Soviet Union, and the Cold War*. New York: Hill and Wang, 2007.

Lofland, John. *Polite Protestors: The American Peace Movement of the 1980s*. Syracuse: Syracuse University Press, 1993.

Mann, James. *The Rebellion of Ronald Reagan: A History of the End of the Cold War*. New York: Viking, 2009.

Marcus, Daniel. *Happy Days and Wonder Years: The Fifties and the Sixties in Contemporary Cultural Politics*. New Brunswick, NJ: Rutgers University Press, 2004.

Massie, Robert Kinloch. *Loosing the Bond: The United States and South Africa in the Apartheid Years*. New York: Doubleday, 1997.

Meyer, Richard. "This Is to Enrage You: Gran Fury and the Graphics of AIDS Activism." *But Is It Art? The Spirit of Art as Activism*, ed. Nina Felshin, 51–83. Seattle: Bay Press, 1995.

McGirr, Lisa. *Suburban Warriors: the Origins of the New American Right*. Princeton: Princeton University Press, 2001.

Mollins, Carl. "The Excessive 80s." *Canadian Business* 76, no.17 (2003): 71-74.

Moody, Kim. *An Injury to All: The Decline of American Unionism*. New York: Verso, 1988.

Morales, Walrtraud Queiser. "The war on drugs: a new US national security doctrine." *Third World Quarterly* 11, no. 3 (1989): 147-169.

Olsen, Frances. "The Supreme Court, 1988 Term: Comment: Unraveling Compromise." *Harvard Law Review* 103 (1989): 105-135.

O'Sullivan, John. *The President, the Pope and the Prime Minister: Three Who Changed the World*. Washington, D.C.: Regnery, 2006.

Palmer, William. *Films of the Eighties: A Social History*. Carbondale: Southern Illinois University Press, 1993.

Pleshakov, Constantine. *There is No Freedom Without Bread! 1989 and the Civil War That Brought Down Communism*. New York: Farrar, Straus and Giroux, 2009.

Reed, Adolph L. *The Jesse Jackson Phenomenon*. New Haven: Yale University Press, 1986.

Roberts, Paul. *The Supply-Side Revolution*. Cambridge MA: Harvard University Press, 1984.

Rogin, Michael. *Ronald Reagan: The Movie and Other Episodes in Political Demonology*. Berkeley: University of California Press, 1987.

Roy, Subroto and John Clarke, eds. *Margaret Thatcher's Revolution: How it Happened and What it Meant*. London: Continuum, 2006.

Schmitz, David F. *The United States and Right-Wing Dictatorships*. Cambridge, MA: Cambridge University Press, 2006.

Sewall, Gilbert T., ed. *The Eighties: A Reader*. Reading, MA.: Perseus Books, 1997.

Shostak Arthur B. and David Skocik, eds. *The Air Controllers' Controversy: Lessons from the PATCO Strike*. New York: Human Sciences Press, 1986.

Shilts, Randy. *And the Band Played On: Politics, People, and the AIDS Epidemic*. New York: St. Martin's Press, 1987.

Sikkink, Kathryn. *Mixed Signals: U.S. Human Rights Policy and Latin America*. Ithaca: Cornell University Press, 2004.

Smith, Christian. *Resisting Reagan: The U.S. Central America Peace Movement.* Chicago: University of Chicago Press, 1996.

Thompson, Graham. *American Culture in the 1980s.* Edinburgh: Edinburgh University Press, 2007.

Torr, J.D. ed. *The 1980s: America's Decade.* Farmington Hills, MI: Greenhaven Press, 2000.

Totenberg, Nina. "Essays on the Supreme Court Appointment Process: The Confirmation Process and The Public: To Know or Not to Know," *Harvard Law Review*, 101 (1988): 1213-1229.

Troy, Gil and Vincent J. Cannato, eds. *Living in the Eighties.* New York: Oxford University Press, 2009.

Troy, Gil. *Morning in America: How Ronald Reagan Invented the 1980s.* Princeton, NJ: Princeton University Press, 2005.

Wallis, Brian, ed. *Art after Modernism: Rethinking Representation.* New York: New Museum of Contemporary Art and Boston: Godine Publishers, 1984.

Wapshott, Nicholas. *Ronald Reagan and Margaret Thatcher: A Political Marriage.* New York: Sentinel, 2008.

Watkins, Craig. *Representing: Hip Hop Culture and the Production of Black Cinema.* Chicago: University of Chicago Press, 1998.

Webb, Gary. *The CIA, The Contras, and The Crack Cocaine Explosion.* New York: Seven Stories Press, 1998.

Wilcox, Clyde and Carin Larsen. Onward Christian Soldiers? *The Christian Right in American Politics.* Boulder: Westview Press, 2006.

Wilentz, Sean. *The Age of Reagan: A History, 1974-2008.* New York; Harper Perennial, 2009.

Wills, Garry. *Reagan's America.* New York: Doubleday, 1986.

Woodward, Bob. *Veil: The Secret Wars of the CIA 1981-1987.* New York: Simon and Schuster, 1987.

Index

About the Contributors

Reynaldo Anderson is an assistant professor of Arts and Sciences at Harris-Stowe State University. Dr. Anderson currently serves as a member of the Board of Directors for Imagine Career Charter Schools, the Executive Board of the Missouri Arts Council, and the Saint Louis Prison and Performing Arts Council. Reynaldo's research interests are in African American Studies, Literary Criticism, Rhetoric, and Cultural Criticism.

Virginia Anderson is an assistant professor of Theatre at Cal Poly, San Luis Obispo. She received her Ph.D. from Tufts University with her dissertation, "Beyond Angels: The AIDS Epidemic and the Broadway Theatre." Her research has taken her to England, China, and Cuba, and her advocacy work has been recognized by the National Center for HIV, STD, & TB Prevention, Centers for Disease Control and Prevention (CDC) and AIDS Action Committee of Massachusetts.

Alan Bilton is Lecturer in literature and film at Swansea University, Wales. He is the author of *An Introduction to Contemporary American Fiction* (Edinburgh/New York University Press, 2002) and co-editor of the three-volume *America in the 1920's* (Helm 2004). He has also published articles and book chapters on subjects as diverse as Buster Keaton, Saul Bellow, F. Scott Fitzgerald, Don DeLillo and F. W. Murnau. His first novel, *The Sleepwalkers' Ball*, described by one critic as "Mary Poppins meets Kafka," was published by Alcemi in 2009. He is currently at work on a monograph on American silent film comedy, *Constantly Moving: Happiness Machines*, as well as a second novel.

Duncan A. Campbell teaches American Studies at the University of Maryland Baltimore County and holds a Ph.D. from Cambridge University. He has long been fascinated by comparative history and has published extensively in the areas of Anglo-American political, cultural, economic, and diplomatic relations in the late nineteenth and early twentieth centuries. His most recent book, *Unlikely Allies: Britain, America and the Victorian Origins of the "Special Relationship,"* was published by Continuum in 2007. He is currently working on a study on the origins of the idea of the "Anglosphere", a comparative cultural and political examination of late nineteenth-century/early twentieth-century Britain, the United States, Canada, Australia, New Zealand, southern Africa and the Caribbean.

Jeffery B. Cook is a professor of history at North Greenville University. Professor Cook is a contributor to several encyclopedias and he has written several scholarly articles and reviews for academic publications. His first book, *The Presidency of Harry S Truman* is part of the NOVA Science Presidential Series will be published in 2010. His wife Laura is a Kentucky native, and they have three daughters Margaret Anne (Maggie), Sara Elizabeth, and Samantha Joy.

Michael D. Dwyer is Assistant Professor of English and Communications at Arcadia University, specializing in film, media studies, and cultural studies. His research centers on the function of nostalgia in popular culture, evolving practices of allusion and quotation, and their relationships with history and cultural memory. He has also published work on Reaganism in popular culture, riot grrrl, Sadie Benning, the aesthetics of street protests, online fan communities, and cultural geography in Hitchcock's films.

Philip Glahn is Assistant Professor of Critical Studies and Aesthetics at Tyler School of Art, Temple University. He was a Critical Studies Fellow at the Whitney Independent Study Program and received his Ph.D. from the Graduate Center/CUNY. His writings have appeared in *Art Journal, Afterimage* and *BOMB,* and he is currently working on a book about the influence of the work of German playwright Bertolt Brecht on 1960s and '70s US art and contemporary activist practice.

Ivan Greenberg received a Ph.D. in history from the CUNY Graduate Center. His book, *The Dangers of Dissent: The FBI and Civil Liberties since 1965*, was recently published by Rowman and Littlefield/Lexington books. He also has written on immigrant working-class issues in educational history.

Heather E. Harris is Associate Professor of Business Communication at Stevenson University and holds a Ph.D. from Howard University. Dr. Harris' research focuses on cultural studies, representations of Africana women in media, and women in romantic relationships. She is the co-editor, and contributor, of *The Obama Effect: Multidisciplinary Renderings of the 2008 Presidential Election*.

Nikita Y. Harris is Assistant Professor of Communication at Columbus State University. In 2009, she received Educator of the Year, the university's highest teaching award. She holds a doctorate in organizational communication from Howard University and a master's in communication from Auburn University.

Her research interests concern communication, culture, and organizational socialization. She is a writer, researcher and consults widely with groups in the public, nonprofit and private sectors.

Jana K. Lipman is Assistant Professor of History at Tulane University where she holds the Andrew W. Mellon Young Professorship in the Humanities. She is the author of *Guantánamo: A Working-Class History between Empire and Revolution* (2009), which was the co-winner of the Taft Prize in labor history. Her current research investigates the relationship between US military bases and refugee operations.

Stephen McVeigh is Director of the War and Society program at Swansea University. His teaching and research explores American political culture and military history in literature and film. He is the author of *The American Western* (2007) and his essays have appeared in the *Journal of War and Culture Studies* (2009), Engel's *Clint Eastwood: Actor and Director* (2007), Kapell and Lawrence's *Finding the Force of the Star Wars Franchise* (2006) and Kapell's *Star Trek as Myth* (2010). He is currently writing a book on the impact of 9/11 on American culture and he is co-editing a collection of essays on the movies of James Cameron.

Scott A. Merriman is a lecturer of history at Troy University, having earned his Ph.D. from the University of Kentucky. He is currently researching the Espionage and Sedition Acts in the Midwest during World War I. Dr. Merriman has written or edited several books, including *Religion and the Law in America: An Encyclopedia of Law and Public Policy*, *The History Highway: A 21st Century Guide to Internet Resources*, and *History.edu: Essays on Teaching with Technology*.

Kimberly R. Moffitt is an assistant professor in the Department of American Studies and affiliate assistant professor in the Department of Africana Studies at University of Maryland Baltimore County and holds a Ph.D. from Howard University. Her teaching and research interests focus on mediated representations of marginalized groups as well as sports icons. Moffitt is the co-editor of *Blackberries and Redbones: Critical Articulations of Black Hair and Body Politics in Africana Communities* (Hampton Press, 2010) and *The Obama Effect: Multidisciplinary Renderings of the 2008 Campaign* (SUNY Press, 2010). Her latest projects include audience reception studies of Disney's *The Princess and the Frog* and *The Wire*.

Suzuko Morikawa is currently an associate professor of history at Chicago State University. Her area of research centers on comparative historical studies between African Americans and Asian Americans in 20th century United States, as well as the history of the slavery in the Americas, and Africans in the diaspora. Her works have been published in *The Journal of Black Studies*, *Asian American History and Culture: an Encyclopedia,* and *Emerging Voices: The Experiences of Underrepresented Asian Americans.*

Andrew R. Murphy is an associate professor of political science at Rutgers University, New Brunswick. His research focuses on the interconnections between religious and political thought and practice, most particularly in the Anglo-American tradition. He is the author of *Conscience and Community: Revisiting Toleration and Religious Dissent in Early Modern England and America* (2001) and *Prodigal Nation: Moral Decline and Divine Punishment from New England to 9/11* (2009); he is editor or co-editor of *The Political Writings of William Penn* (2002), *Religion, Politics, and American Identity: New Directions, New Controversies* (2006); and *Literature, Culture, Tolerance* (2009).

Caryn E. Neumann is Visiting Assistant Professor of History at Miami University. She is the author of *Accidental Feminists: Women's Organizations in Mid-Twentieth Century America* (2010) and is currently working on a book about the impact of the feminist movement. She earned a Ph.D. from The Ohio State University.

N'Jai-An Patters received her Ph.D. from the University of Minnesota. Her research interests include histories of sexuality, gender, and politics in the United States.

James Braxton Peterson is an assistant professor of English at Bucknell University. Peterson's academic work focuses on Africana Studies, narrative, graphic novels and hip hop culture. He is the founder of Hip Hop Scholars, LLC, an association of Hip Hop generational scholars dedicated to researching and developing the cultural and educational potential of Hip Hop, urban, and youth cultures. Peterson has appeared on CNN, MSNBC, ESPN, and various national/local television networks as an expert on Hip Hop culture, popular culture, urban youth, race and politics.

Paul M. Pressley is Director of Mentoring and Professional Development at Howard University's Graduate School. He received his Ph.D. in African Studies and Research from Howard University. As the Director or External Affairs at Rutgers University, School of Business-Camden, he taught International Marketing focusing on business in southern Africa. Dr. Pressley served in the United States Army as a Psychological Operations Officer with an expertise in sub-Sahara Africa.

Demian Ryder holds associate degrees in Literature and in Theatre Technology. He lives in Omaha, Nebraska, where he acts, directs, games, and writes. For their individual and treasured contributions, he thanks Kirk Bozigian, Lauren Carlson, Ora McWilliams, and Lynette Ryder.

Thomas F. Schaller is Professor of Political Science at the University of Maryland Baltimore County. He is author of *Whistling Past Dixie: How Democrats Can Win Without the South*, and co-author of *Devolution and Black State Legislators: Challenges and Choices in the Twenty-First Century*. A political columnist for the *Baltimore Sun* and blogger for fivethirtyeight.com, his book about the Republican Party after Ronald Reagan's presidency is forthcoming from Yale University Press.

Jim Schnell is Professor in the Social & Behavioral Sciences Division at Ohio Dominican University. He holds a Ph.D. from Ohio University. He retired, at the rank of Colonel, from the U.S. Air Force Reserve in 2007 after serving as an Air Force Attache to China between 1993-2007. He has traveled to China over 20 times and served as visiting professor at Beijing Jiaotong University. He was a Fulbright Scholar to Cambodia in 2005-2006 and has held three Visiting Fellowships at the East-West Center in Honolulu. He has authored two books on China: *Perspectives on Communication in The People's Republic of China* and *Mortar Between the Bricks: A U.S. Military Attache Working in China.*

Kristin Sorensen is an assistant professor of global studies at Bentley University. She teaches cross cultural understanding, global commerce and human rights in Chile, human rights in global media, and Latin American cinema. Her research investigates the manner in which historical memories and their associated traumas circulate through the media and public culture in contemporary Latin America. Her book, *Media, Memory, and Human Rights in Chile*, was published by Palgrave Macmillan in 2009.

Jessie Swigger is an assistant professor in the History Department at Western Carolina University. Her research interests include public history, urban and suburban history, and popular culture. She received her Ph.D. in American Studies from the University of Texas at Austin and her current research project is titled "History is Bunk": Assembling the Past at Henry Ford's Greenfield Village.

Jason Thompson is Assistant Professor of Communication Studies at Brooklyn College – City University of New York and holds a Ph.D. from University of Nebraska-Lincoln. He specializes in interpersonal and family communication. His research has explored communication that is supportive, manages private disclosures, motivates, and gains compliance within families and other personal relationships. His research has also explored prevailing stereotypes of Black athletes and how the media both manufactures and perpetuates these stereotypes.

Kirk Tyvela is an assistant professor of history at the University of Wisconsin—Washington County, where he teaches courses on American foreign policy and politics. He received his Ph.D. in history from Ohio University and is currently completing a book manuscript on U.S. diplomatic relations with the Alfredo Stroessner regime in Paraguay during the Cold War.

David Uskovich is a Ph.D. candidate in the Department of Radio-Television-Film at the University of Texas at Austin. His research interests include popular music, alternative media, youth cultures, sound, technology, media and cultural history, and the mediated representation of race, class, gender, and sexuality. He has been part of the international underground noise/punk music community for over two decades, where, as a musician and college radio DJ, he has wedded media theory to media practice.

Robert P. Weiss is a professor of sociology at SUNY Plattsburgh. In addition to serving for many years on the editorial board of *Social Justice*, for which he also guest-edited several special issues, Dr. Weiss has edited two books, published fourteen chapters and numerous journal articles on criminal justice privatization, penal labor history, and comparative imprisonment. He spent much of the 80s teaching radical criminology to crime war casualties at various maximum-security prison college programs.